THE INTERNATIONAL CRIMINAL COURT IN ONGOING INTRASTATE CONFLICTS

In recent decades, international courts have increasingly started investigating armed conflicts. However, the impact of this remains under-researched. Patrick Wegner closes this gap via a comprehensive analysis of the impact of the International Criminal Court in the Darfur and Lord's Resistance Army conflicts. He offers a fresh approach to peace and conflict studies, while avoiding the current quantitative focus of the literature and polarisation between critics and supporters of applying justice in conflicts. This is the first time that the impact of an international criminal court has been analysed in all its facets in two conflicts. The consequences of these investigations are much more complex and difficult to predict than most of the existing literature suggests. Recurrent claims, such as the deterrent effect of trials and the danger of blocking negotiations by the issuing of arrest warrants, are put to the test here with some surprising results.

PATRICK S. WEGNER works for the German Federal Foreign Office. He researched this book while completing a PhD at the University of Tübingen, Germany.

THE INTERNATIONAL CRIMINAL COURT IN ONGOING INTRASTATE CONFLICTS

Navigating the Peace-Justice Divide

PATRICK S. WEGNER

CAMBRIDGE
UNIVERSITY PRESS

CAMBRIDGE
UNIVERSITY PRESS

University Printing House, Cambridge CB2 8BS, United Kingdom

Cambridge University Press is part of the University of Cambridge.

It furthers the University's mission by disseminating knowledge in the pursuit of education, learning and research at the highest international levels of excellence.

www.cambridge.org
Information on this title: www.cambridge.org/9781107069473

First published 2015

A catalogue record for this publication is available from the British Library

Library of Congress Cataloguing in Publication data
Wegner, Patrick Sebastian, 1984– author.
The international criminal court in ongoing intrastate conflicts : navigating the peace-justice divide / Patrick Sebastian Wegner.
pages cm
Based on author's thesis (doctoral)– International Max Planck Research School on Dispute Resolution and the University of Tübingen, 2013.
Includes bibliographical references and index.
ISBN 978-1-107-06947-3 (Hardback)
1. International Criminal Court. 2. Civil war. 3. International criminal law. I. Title.
KZ7312.W44 2015
345′.01–dc23 2015010544

ISBN 978-1-107-06947-3 Hardback

CONTENTS

FIGURES

TABLES

ACKNOWLEDGEMENTS

Sitting in sunny Addis Ababa in November 2014, and looking back at the time I first started working on the International Criminal Court, it strikes me as almost absurd that it all started with serendipity. In early 2010, I was looking for PhD scholarship opportunities and started writing proposals to a number of different research schools working on my areas of interest. A call for proposals of the International Max Planck Research School on Dispute Resolution inspired me to start thinking about the role of international courts and tribunals in conflicts. Weeks later I found myself with my proposal in front of a committee at the Max Planck Institute for International Law and Comparative Public Law in Heidelberg, as the only political scientist among a number of excellent legal scholars. I doubt that I would recognise much of my initial proposal in this book today, but it was my first encounter with a research topic that soon became a fascination and even somewhat of a hobby.

The path from the first proposal to this book was long and winding, and I would never have arrived at its end without the support of many people. I would like to thank the Max Planck Institute for International Law and Comparative Public Law for the funding of my research and particularly its former director, Professor Wolfrum, for seeing the potential in my proposal and supporting my field work. Thanks also go to several staff members at the Institute who were willing to share their expertise on the topic. Also, I would like to thank Professor Andreas Hasenclever of the University of Tübingen for accepting to supervise my PhD thesis at a time at which most German universities were swamped by a wave of PhD students. I am also deeply indebted to Prof. Hasenclever for pointing me towards the suitable theoretical framework to conduct my research. Prof. Thomas Diez of the University of Tübingen was kind enough to accept to review my dissertation on short notice and opened my eyes to the contribution of critical human rights literature to transitional justice research, for which I am grateful. I would also like to thank my fellow PhD students at the Max Planck Institute and the

University of Tübingen for their support and thoughtful criticism where appropriate.

Literature and media sources were systematically included in this book until January 2012. Probably my biggest regret is that I was not able to cover some of the more recent and interesting political events surrounding the ICC, including the motion of the Kenyan Parliament to cease being a Member State to the Rome Statute. Time constraints did not allow for a comprehensive update of the book.

This book benefited hugely from the comments and writings of brilliant scholars and would not have been written but for the readiness of nearly fifty interviewees, some of them anonymous, who were kindly willing to share their insights and knowledge. I thank all of them. While this book is in many ways the result of a collective effort, its failings and shortcomings are entirely my own. The views and opinions expressed here are also my own and made in a private capacity as a scholar.

My field research in Uganda would not have been possible without the kind support of the German Academic Exchange Service (DAAD) and benefited hugely from the help of Berna Ataitom, Dr Chris Dolan, Lyandro Komakech, Moses Chrispus Okello and Stephen Oola of the Refugee Law Project, as well as Mathias Kamp and Yusuf Kiranda of the Konrad Adenauer Foundation in Kampala.

Mark Kersten of the London School of Economics was something of a brother-in-arms during most of my work on this book. I profited hugely from our evening chats over beer in Kampala and am still looking back fondly to our cooperation in the scope of the Justice in Conflict blog.

Last but not least I would like to thank my friends, old and new. You accompanied me during the process of writing this book and helped me to remember that there was a life beyond books and journals, be it in Frankfurt, Kampala, Tegel (Berlin) or Addis Ababa. Most importantly, I would like to thank my family and my wonderful fiancé for their ongoing love and support.

ABBREVIATIONS

ACP	African, Caribbean and Pacific states that cooperate with the EU
AI	Amnesty International
AL	Arab League
ARLPI	Acholi Religious Leader Peace Initiative
ASP	Assembly of the States Parties (ICC organ)
AU	African Union
AUPD	African Union High-Level Panel on Darfur
CAR	Central African Republic
CoH	Cessation of hostilities
CPA	Comprehensive Peace Agreement signed between the Government of Sudan and the Sudan People's Liberation Army in January 2005
CSCE	Conference for Security and Cooperation in Europe
DPA	Darfur Peace Agreement signed in May 2006 in Abuja
DPP	Department of Public Prosecutions of the Republic of Uganda
DRC	Democratic Republic of Congo
DUP	Democratic Unionist Party, Sudanese opposition party from the north
EDF	Equatoria Defence Force, a militia group in Sudan, initially made up of ex-UNLA cadres
FARDC	Forces Armées de la République Démocratique du Congo, the army of the DRC
FIDH	Federation for Human Rights
GCC	Gulf Cooperation Council
GoS	Government of Sudan
GoSS	Government of Southern Sudan, Government of South Sudan if used post July 2011
GoU	Government of Uganda
HRC	Human Rights Center of the University of Berkeley (NGO)
HRW	Human Rights Watch
HSM	Holy Spirit Movement, spiritual rebel movement in Uganda during the late 1980s
ICC	International Criminal Court
ICD	International Crimes Division of the Ugandan High Court

ICG	International Crisis Group
ICID	International Commission of Inquiry on Darfur, Commission created by the UNSC to investigate war crimes and crimes against humanity in Darfur
ICRC	International Committee of the Red Cross
ICTJ	International Center for Transitional Justice (INGO)
ICTR	International Criminal Tribunal for Rwanda
ICTY	International Criminal Tribunal for the former Yugoslavia
IRIN	Integrated Regional Information Network, a UN news agency
JEM	Justice and Equality Movement, Darfurian rebel movement
JLOS	Justice Law and Order Sector of the Government of Uganda comprising, e.g. the Ministry of Justice, the Department of Public Prosecutions and the different courts
LJM	Liberation and Justice Movement, Darfurian rebel group, JEM splinter
LRA	Lord's Resistance Army (Northern Ugandan rebel group)
MSF	Médicins Sans Frontières
NAM	Non-Aligned Movement
NCHR	National Commission for Human Rights in Sudan
NDA	National Democratic Alliance, Sudanese opposition umbrella group from east
NISS	National Intelligence and Security Service, Sudanese internal intelligence agency
NRA/M	National Resistance Army/Movement, former rebel group and now government party in Uganda
NRF	National Resistance Front, alliance of JEM, SLA factions and SFDA created after Abuja signature of SLA-MM
NRM	The political wing of the NRA
NSF	National Salvation Front, Darfur rebel splinter group
OHCHR	Office of the High Commissioner for Human Rights
OIC	Organisation of Islamic Conference, multilateral organisation
OTP	Office of the Prosecutor (ICC Organ)
PFA	Popular Forces Army, Darfur rebel group of Arab tribes
PTC	Pre-Trial Chamber of the ICC
RDC	Resident District Commissioner, representative of the President in Uganda's districts
RLP	Refugee Law Project of the Makerere University School of Law
RPF	Rwandan Patriotic Front (the party in government in Rwanda)
SAF	Sudanese Armed Forces
SCCED	Special Criminal Court for Events in Darfur
SCSL	Special Court for Sierra Leone, hybrid court created by UN and Sierra Leone

SFDA	Sudanese Federal Democratic Alliance, former Darfur governor Ahmed Diraige's party
SLA	Sudanese Liberation Army (Darfurian rebel group)
SLA-AW	SLA splinter around Mohamed Abdel Wahid
SLA-MM	SLA splinter around Minnie Arka Minawi
SLA-Unity	SLA splinter
SPLA	Sudanese People's Liberation Army
SPLM	Sudanese People's Liberation Movement
SPLM-N	Sudanese People's Liberation Movement – North SPLM forces in regions that remained with Sudan after Southern Sudan's independence
SRF	Sudan Revolutionary Front, umbrella group of northern Sudanese rebels including Beja Congress, JEM, SLM-AW, SLM-MM and SPLM-N, founded November 2011
TDRA	Transitional Darfur Regional Authority, an institution created after the signing of the Darfur Peace Agreement to implement the provisions of the Agreement
TFV	ICC Trust Fund for Victims paying for rehabilitation projects in areas affected by the crimes of ICC indictees
TJ	Transitional justice
UFLD	United Front for Liberation and Development
UHRC	Uganda Human Rights Council
UN	United Nations
UNHCHR	United Nations High Commissioner for Human Rights
UNHCR	United Nations High Commissioner for Refugees
UNHRC	United Nations Human Rights Council in Geneva
UNLA	Uganda National Liberation Army, the army of the Obote II regime
UNMIS	United Nations Mission in Sudan
UNOCHA	United Nations Office for the Coordination of Humanitarian Affairs
UNSC	United Nations Security Council
UNSG	United Nations Secretary-General
UPDA	Uganda People's Democratic Army, northern Ugandan rebel movement
UPDF	Ugandan People's Defence Forces, Ugandan Army
VRWG	Victims' Rights Working Group
WHO	World Health Organisation

1

Introduction

> *A new era of international law has dawned in which national leaders can no longer be sure that they can get away with mass murder. It is about time. The long dark age when war lords and dictators could commit atrocities with impunity is coming to an end.*
>
> (Greg Stanton in de Waal and Stanton 2009, p. 339)

> *Why should anyone imagine that bewigged judges in The Hague will succeed where cold steel has failed? Holding out the prospect of ICC deterrence to the weak and vulnerable amounts to a cruel joke.*
>
> (John Bolton, former US Ambassador to the UN, cited in IRIN 2006)

When armed conflicts break out anywhere in the world today and cost the lives of innocent civilians, calls to stop the violence and hold perpetrators to account are raised faster than ever (albeit often still too late). As a consequence, human rights bodies as well as international criminal tribunals and courts start to investigate these crimes in ever shorter periods after they have been committed. The International Criminal Court (ICC) is at the vanguard of this development and is nowadays even investigating crimes in conflicts that are still ongoing. Yet, little is known about the effects that international investigations have on conflicts. No one has systematically examined the effects of these interventions. Opinions and general observations on the performance of courts and tribunals in conflicts abound, while in-depth empirical research is lacking (also Hannum 2006, p. 586, Meernik et al. 2010a, p. 103, van der Merwe et al. 2009, p. 4). This book will take a first step towards closing this gap by focusing on the ICC investigations in Darfur and Uganda.

The hope that delivering justice could play a role in preventing crimes in future conflicts was born sixty-five years ago, in Nuremberg, Germany, when the Allied Forces brought some of the worst perpetrators of crimes committed by the Nazi Regime and its followers to trial. This hope was abandoned for several decades as Cold War disagreements rendered the establishment of further international criminal tribunals all but impossible. Today, the work of institutions like the International Criminal Tribunal for the former Yugoslavia (ICTY) and the ICC has reinvigorated this approach. While ensuring accountability for these crimes is the principal mandate of these bodies, many scholars and practitioners do believe that tribunals and courts can help to further peace in conflict-ridden areas and prevent future conflicts. This ongoing discussion about whether it is possible to further peace or to prevent conflict escalation by implementing retributive justice through international criminal trials is the overall context of this book. In many ways, this discussion is still led along a peace-justice divide. While some authors claim that trials pose additional dangers to conflict resolution efforts, others claim there can be no lasting peace without justice through trials. The book aims to transcend this divide in the academic debate and look at the grey zones, the difficult compromises that need to be struck between peace and justice when an international court investigates in a conflict situation. There is no better institution than the ICC to serve as an 'object of study' for this purpose.

The Court, established in 2003, recently celebrated its tenth anniversary. But while the ICC started its operations amongst great expectations, it has witnessed tumultuous times. It has opened investigations in eight countries at the time of writing, namely, the Central African Republic (CAR), the Democratic Republic of Congo (DRC), Uganda, Kenya, Côte d'Ivoire, Libya, Sudan and Mali. It has been drawn into highly politicised internal conflicts in Sudan, Libya and Côte d'Ivoire. Its investigations have sparked national controversies in Kenya and Uganda. The ICC's first Chief Prosecutor, Luis Moreno Ocampo, has been heavily criticised by African politicians and diplomats as well as by NGOs and aid workers. His tenure, which ended in June 2012, was marred with controversy, and leaves behind a Court that is conducting active investigations in a host of complicated conflict settings. While the scope of the ICC's activities is a success in itself – few would have thought such an active role possible when the Rome Statute was passed in 1998 – the Court has also been drawn into an ongoing political controversy with many African governments and the African Union at large. Some of the African Member States, which were important pillars of support for the ICC in its founding phase, have become its fiercest critics. This development culminated in the declaration of Ethiopian Prime Minister Hailemariam Desalegn, Chairman of the African Union, during the meeting on the fiftieth anniversary of the AU, that the ICC system is flawed and biased against 'Africans' (Lough and Maasho 2013).

This clearly shows how the debate surrounding the ICC has become emotionalised. For some it is the story of a Court that has defied its critics by becoming fully operational in a remarkably short time-frame and by becoming a factor to be reckoned with in international politics. For others it is the story of a Court that has only managed to finish one trial in its first ten years of existence, delivering a controversial sentence that ended a trial stricken by delays and a feud between the Office of the Prosecutor and the Trial Chamber. In any case the debate revolves around a Court that has started operating in ongoing conflicts with results that are hard to predict. And this novel role for a Court, to become a player in ongoing conflicts, is posing a host of unanswered questions to politicians, diplomats, aid workers, and academics alike. The following sections will throw some light on these questions that will be subject to intense scrutiny for the rest of the book. Since the discussions surrounding the ICC are already emotionalised, it is important to point out that it is not the objective of the book to judge the work of the ICC from a normative standpoint. It is rather a neutral assessment of the impact of its investigations on ongoing conflicts.

1.1 The ICC in ongoing conflicts

How did a Court whose main mandate is to ensure accountability for international crimes become a player in ongoing conflicts? The development of the ICC in its first ten years of existence is not a self-evident result of its establishment in 2003. The aim of the ICC is first and foremost to counter impunity for crimes that go beyond the scope of domestic legal systems. The institutional requirements for punishing these crimes are either not in place at the domestic level, or the perpetrators are (former) wielders of power who can ensure their impunity through their influence on the national legal system. In some cases the state in question is also simply unwilling to tackle the issue of crimes committed in the past.

But latest when these perpetrators – with an international arrest warrant to their names – become leaders of conflict parties negotiating for peace, the influence of the Court on conflict resolution efforts becomes visible. The main reason the ICC became an actor in conflict contexts is its institutional design. The ICC is a permanent court with a relatively broad and potentially global jurisdiction. It therefore has more possibilities to become active in ongoing conflicts than the international criminal tribunals created before.[1] The jurisdiction of these tribunals primarily lies with ensuring accountability in post-conflict phases. The ICC will in all likelihood increasingly investigate in conflict situations, especially when taking the rising number of ratifications of the Rome Statute into consideration. The Office of the Prosecutor of the ICC openly embraces this development, stating that:

> *[t]he ICC's mandate to select the most serious crimes committed after July 1, 2002, requires that we engage in judicial proceedings in relation to conflicts even before they have ended ... My Office is part of a new system dealing with a complex new reality: transitional justice during ongoing conflicts.*
> (Moreno Ocampo 2007b, p. 9)

If this involvement of the ICC in conflict situations proves to be a consistent trend, it will lead to a systematic global relevance of the question whether international trials and investigations can broker peace in conflicts (see Akhavan 2009, p. 625). While the increasing influence of international courts and tribunals in conflict contexts has been acknowledged by academics as well as practitioners in the last decades, there is little systematic assessment of its effect on conflicts. The opinions of how important this effect is – and whether it is helpful or harmful – differ. In order to understand this effect, we need to conceptualise the impact of international investigations in conflicts. In other words, we are in need of a theory.

One school of thought claims that future conflicts can be prevented through establishing (criminal) accountability, since a fair and just outcome is needed for successful conflict resolution (see Ambos et al. 2008, p. viii, Jeong 2008, p. 243, Wallensteen 2007, p. 295). These approaches tend to equalise accountability for the most serious crimes with a just outcome of a conflict. According to this school of thought, promoting international criminal justice in conflicts follows two ideas: (1) to deter future crimes by the threat of punishment everywhere and (2) to shape the future of post-conflict societies through addressing issues of guilt and retribution, thus avoiding that they contribute to renewed violence in post-conflict societies(Bassiouni 1996, p. 28, Unger and Wierda 2008, p. 246).

While equalising accountability with justice would surely be a simplification, accountability does clearly contribute to justice as a

[1] In fact, the ICTY was so far the only criminal tribunal that had started investigations while the conflict was still active.

compensation of wrongdoing through punishment. Much of the literature tends to discuss the question of how accountability measures and conflict resolution efforts influence each other along the lines of the relationship between peace and justice. The 'justice through accountability' school of thought claims that it is necessary to tackle justice in order to ensure a sustainable peace (e.g. Crowley 2010, du Plessis and Ford 2008b, p. X, Lederach 1995, Thony and Schneider 2003, p. 33, Van Acker 2004, p. 356), while others claim that pacifying measures at the cost of justice may be preferable (Kritz 2009, p. 21, Mamdani 2009c, Mendeloff 2004, Snyder and Vinjamuri 2003, Thakur 2006).

This debate has also reached the ICC. Its supporters believe it can contribute to peace through its investigations and trials. For example, Luis Moreno Ocampo, Chief Prosecutor of the ICC, claims that the ICC brings warlords to the negotiation table, focuses the debates surrounding the conflict on accountability issues, helps reduce crimes, weakens the support of spoilers by de-legitimisation and ensures harmony in post-conflict situations through dealing with past atrocities (Moreno Ocampo 2008a, p. 13).

Critics of the Court, on the other hand, suggest that investigations and prosecutions in conflicts could lead to an impasse in peace negotiations and other forms of peaceful conflict resolution efforts. Their main argument is that parties might reject a compromise out of fear of being tried after the conflict (Akhavan 2009, p. 625, Ambos et al. 2008, p. v, Sriram 2008, p. 306). Some authors go as far as claiming a connection between criminal prosecutions in conflicts and rising tensions or conflict intensity (Mendeloff 2004, p. 374, Osiel 2000). Roy Licklider, author of the Civil War Termination Database at the Rutgers State University of New Jersey, points out the risks of enforcing retributive justice in conflicts:

> *We are not just engaged in academic debates now; we are talking about other people's countries and other people's lives. And we do not know, in such a manner as to persuade others, what is true, what will work.*
>
> (Licklider 2008, p. 385)

Taking this debate as a starting point, this book will use theoretical frameworks from peace and conflict studies in order to analyse ICC investigations in conflicts as a concrete example of the relationship between peace and justice.

A number of crucial questions emerge from this approach. Some of them have been discussed extensively, others are relatively new: can quick and determined judicial reactions to human rights abuses in conflicts help to end them faster or to stop them from escalating? Can the application and enforcement of international criminal law from the outside help to defuse or even transform a conflict? Can the prosecution of leaders resorting to brutal methods of warfare help to isolate them by increasing the pressure on their external supporters?

Both critics and proponents have tried to answer some of these questions, but most of them lack empirical evidence to support their theses (also Akhavan 2009, p. 627, Hazan 2006, p. 19, Ryngaert 2009, p. VII). Some of the effects they claim directly contradict each other. Research on these claims is therefore urgently needed. The impact of investigations in *ongoing* conflicts in general remains under researched.[2] In fact, investigations of international crimes have often even been discussed without distinguishing between transition contexts (the aftermath of a transition from authoritarian rule) and conflict contexts. Yet, it is highly unlikely that these investigations will have similar consequences under these vastly different circumstances.

But analysing the impact of international investigations in the context of ongoing conflicts is difficult since it may take years until the final results of these investigations are clear. Nevertheless, the stakes of enforcing accountability in conflicts are high, and these questions are too pressing to ignore them due to methodological difficulties. The fact that the current stage of the research does not offer reliable advice on how investigations and trials affect conflict dynamics is a serious problem. The limits, the effectiveness, as well as the costs and utilities of international criminal tribunals are not understood at a crucial moment when the system is definitely entering its practice phase. The share of trials among transitional justice mechanisms conducted in conflicts or directly afterwards has risen to nearly 30 per cent since 1997, while it moved between 7 and 17 per cent in the fifteen years before. At the same time, the share of international and hybrid trials among trials in conflict contexts is steadily increasing. Both trends are clearly illustrated in the following graphs.

The graph (Figure 1.1) shows the number of different transitional justice mechanisms that have been implemented in conflicts or directly after the signing of a peace agreement. Each mechanism is included in

[2] Exceptions include (Kuovo 2009) on transitional justice during the conflict in Afghanistan, (Akhavan 2009) and (Kastner 2007) for cursory case studies on deterrence in ongoing conflicts and (Unger and Wierda 2008) for a more general approach. More recently, a blog has been started to tackle issues of justice in conflicts (JIC 2012).

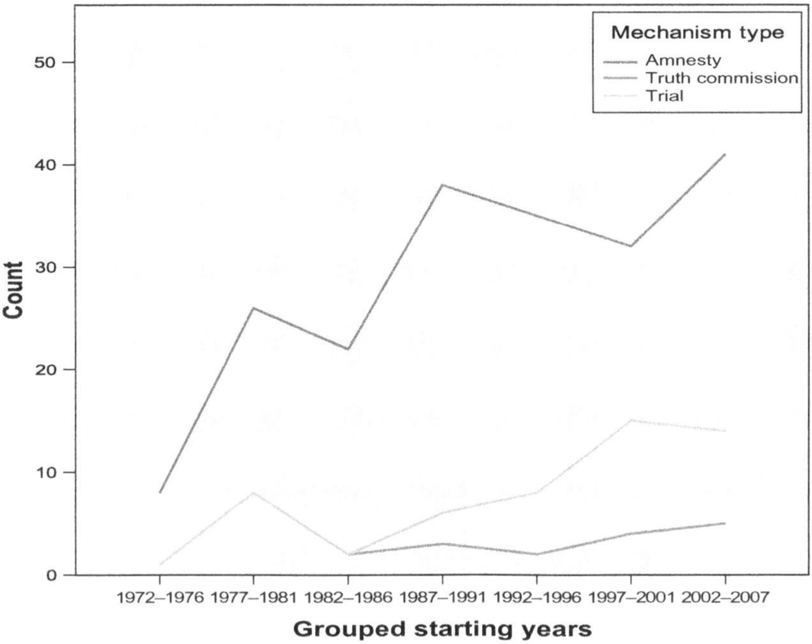

Figure 1.1: Transitional justice mechanisms in conflicts

the year in which its implementation started. The data is from the Justice in Conflict Database introduced in Chapter 3.

The graph (Figure 1.2) shows the number of domestic, hybrid and international trials that started each year in conflict contexts. The trend towards more international trials in conflicts is clearly visible.

Arguably this is the case because holding trials has become a mainstream demand of some Western civil society groups and NGOs in reaction to atrocities (e.g. Human Rights Watch, Amnesty International, Save Darfur, Invisible Children, to name a few). Additionally, some diplomats and practitioners are increasingly eager to use international trials and investigations as peacemaking instruments in international crisis management, even though furthering conflict resolution is not a mandate of these institutions.

1.2 Analysing the role of the ICC in ongoing conflicts

The following section will introduce the methodology applied in analysing the role of the ICC in ongoing conflicts.

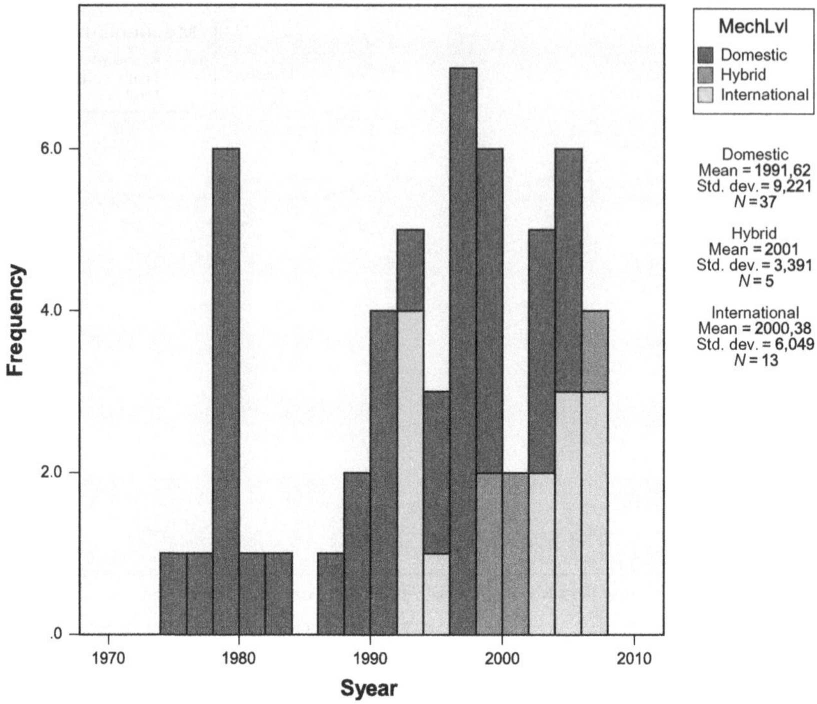

Figure 1.2: Type of trials started in conflict contexts

The approach combines a cross-case analysis of transitional justice measures implemented in conflicts with two in-depth case studies of ICC investigations during the LRA conflict in Uganda and the Darfur conflict in Sudan. The case studies rely on field research, expert interviews and a day-to-day analysis of the conflicts with the LexisNexis Database. LexisNexis was systematically analysed for both cases until 31 December 2011.

The idea is to compare theoretically informed cross-case findings (part 1) and empirical findings (part 2) in order to challenge both and highlight unresolved issues. The aim is to explain the mechanisms at work when the ICC investigates conflicts and shed some light on the complexities and pitfalls of criminal justice interventions in conflicts.

The cases chosen for the analysis in both parts of the book are armed intrastate conflicts. The term 'intrastate conflict' is a rather broad category. It includes classic civil wars fought between a state actor and a well organised rebel group vying for power in the central government.

But intrastate conflicts also include internationalised conflicts, in which external actors have intervened in a civil war (Bussmann et al. 2009, p. 13), or transnational conflicts in which several state and non-state actors fight each other across multiple state borders.[3] Focusing on intrastate conflicts is a logical choice because the ICC is mainly active in these conflicts. Additionally, the potential relevance of international criminal justice interventions is most obvious in contexts of weakened judicial systems often found in states afflicted by intrastate conflict.[4]

The respective strengths and weaknesses of cross-case and case study approaches make a combined approach most suitable to analyse the impact of ICC investigations in conflicts. For example, the results of some statistical and deductive research conducted so far have led to contradicting conclusions, pointing towards success (Kim and Sikkink 2009, 2010, Lie et al. 2007, Olsen et al. 2010), or failure (Meernik et al. 2010b, Snyder and Vinjamuri 2003, p. 5)of international trials to contribute to durable peace. This is largely due to the fact that the number of cases of international trials in conflicts is still too low to generate reliable statistical results.

On the other hand, most of the case studies conducted so far focus on specific aspects of transitional justice measures. For example, there have been case studies on the needs of victim groups in a single conflict area (ICTJ & HRC 2005, Wyrzykowski and Kasozi 2010), case studies on the implementation of traditional justice measures (Komakech and Sheff 2009) and cursory comparative case studies of several conflicts (Akhavan 2009). Yet, the method has rarely been used to present a comprehensive picture of the relationship between accountability measures and conflict resolution in one or more cases.

The comprehensive case studies informed by cross-case findings conducted here deliver a holistic analysis of ICC investigations in conflicts

[3] An example of an internationalised conflict would be the US intervention in the Afghan civil war in 2001, while the LRA conflict in northern Uganda is a good example for a transnational conflict. In the case of transnational conflicts, it might at times be difficult to distinguish them from international conflicts, as regional involvement and spill-over effects may involve several states (Busumtwi-Sam et al. 2004, p. 320, Omeje 2008, p. 68).

[4] The reason for this is twofold: first, there is often no other institution that could guarantee accountability; second, the potential contribution of accountability measures to justice is greatest here because grievances described as injustice are root causes for most intrastate conflicts.

rather than focusing on a specific effect. The analysis draws from the detailed information of specific but 'partial' case studies already available as well as from the contextual information of the cross-case overview conducted in Chapter 3. Cross-case and case study information is combined to paint the full picture of the impact of ICC investigations in conflicts. Finally, effects traced in the case studies are firmly rooted in conflict resolution theory, thus ensuring that the effects observed are relevant for furthering peace.

The main weakness of this approach is that the case studies have to rely on the findings of past research and develop creative indicators that allow measuring the effects identified in the cross-case section as precisely as possible with limited resources. It also restricts the book to two case studies because of the huge amount of information that has to be analysed. The results for the causal mechanisms are also not as precise as findings of case studies that focus on a single mechanism, but in return, they offer a much more comprehensive picture of the impact of ICC investigations in conflicts.

1.3 Structure of the book

The introduction is followed by a short chapter describing the institutional structures of the ICC and the Court's role in international relations. This is followed by the three main chapters of the book, namely the cross-case overview and the two case studies. The cross-case overview in Chapter 3 introduces the theoretical approach for the case studies and the causal mechanisms identified in the literature. The chapter then ends with a section that explains the reasons for selecting the LRA and Darfur conflicts as case studies. This leads to the second part of the book, in which the case studies are conducted. The Darfur and Uganda case studies are introduced subsequently in Chapters 4 and 5. Both start with a conflict analysis based on the conflict assessment guidelines developed by the UK Department for International Development (DFID) (Goodhand et al. 2002). The following sections of the case studies attempt to trace the causal mechanisms developed in the cross-case chapter. Chapter 6 introduces the conflict spectrum as a means to understand the potential impact of ICC investigations on peace by furthering justice through accountability. It also presents the most important third variable identified in the case studies. Chapter 7 then summarises the findings of the book and offers an outlook.

1.4 Key findings

In a nutshell there are five main findings of the book. Chapter 3 concludes that the current stage of research on the impact of international investigations is highly contradictory. A wealth of hypotheses concerning the possible impact of these measures is offered in the literature.

Second, even though a thinking of peace versus justice still dominates in the literature, there is a wide grey area between the two concepts. The research agenda needs to move beyond this dichotomy and explore the reasons why accountability mechanisms can sometimes strengthen efforts to reach peace while at other times, they become stumbling blocks. The book introduces the conflict spectrum as a model to understand how peace and justice relate to each other in conflicts and why justice furthers peace in general but accountability measures can still clash with conflict resolution efforts in specific contexts (Chapter 6).

Third, the case studies show that the impact of international investigations in conflicts is overestimated in much of the literature. Most of the mechanisms suggested in the literature could not be traced in the conflicts, even if they were explicitly claimed for that particular case. The conflict dynamics in each situation country are often overlooked and developments that took place independently of the ICC investigations are attributed to the ICC. The effects of ICC investigations in conflicts are also much more ambiguous than the current literature suggests and change over the course of a conflict. At the same time, expectations towards the role of the ICC in conflicts expressed in the literature are often unrealistic.

Fourth, the procedural decisions taken by the OTP and other organs of the Court, as well as local and regional perceptions of justice have an important impact on whether the ICC hampers or furthers conflict resolution efforts. Perceptions of justice are the views and opinions of stakeholders and actors about what kind of accountability should be implemented, and how it should be implemented in a specific situation. Both variables play important roles in the ICC investigations in Darfur and Uganda and have so far been neglected in the literature. A closer look at the procedural decision-making within the ICC shows that the decisions taken at the Court have important political implications, even though the practitioners of international criminal justice generally tend to describe these decisions as apolitical.

Finally, the book shows that there are grey areas between peace and justice and that the ICC can make use of this peace-justice divide by influencing the impact of its investigations through its investigation strategy and procedural decisions. The book thus concludes by suggesting that the ICC should aim to create in-house expertise for a political analysis of the conflicts in which the Court is active. Taking the impact of its investigations on conflicts into consideration may not be part of the mandate of the ICC, but protecting the victims of serious crimes is. Analysing the implications of its investigation strategy would make it possible for the ICC to actively navigate the peace-justice divide in order to maximise the positive effects of investigations, and avoid negative effects that can cost the lives of the very victims the Court strives to protect.

PART I

The International Criminal Court in conflicts

2

The ICC and its role in international politics

The time of absolute and exclusive sovereignty, however, has passed; its theory was never matched by reality.

(Boutros-Gahli 1992, § 17)

It would be neither sound morality, nor wise policy, to limit the world's options to watching the slaughter of innocents or to send in the marines. The magnitude of these ... crimes and violations demands early, preventive steps – and these steps should require neither unanimity in the Security Council nor pictures of unfolding atrocities that shock the conscience of the world.

(Ki-Moon 2008)

This chapter will provide an overview of the organisational structure of the ICC and the Rome Statute. It will also briefly describe the role of the ICC in the context of international politics.

2.1 The International Criminal Court – an overview

The following section will offer a brief overview of the ICC and the Rome Statute, the treaty establishing the ICC.[1] This overview is not comprehensive and focuses on the information and features relevant for the case studies.

The Rome Statute is the treaty adopted in 1998 that established the ICC. It grants the ICC extensive independence and prosecutorial discretion by allowing it to determine its own jurisdiction independently in the scope of Arts. 19 and 119 (see Nouwen 2013, p. 95f.). During the tenure of the first Chief Prosecutor, the Office of the Prosecutor (OTP) showed the ambition to use this independence to enhance the preventive and peace-securing functions of international criminal law in conflict situations. Chief Prosecutor Luis Moreno Ocampo made this explicit:

[1] Changes made to the Statute in the scope of the first Rome Statute Review Conference in May 2010 are included in this overview.

> *The International Criminal Court ... aims to confront centuries-old methods of behaviour – those of conflict and war, the abuse of civilians, women and children – and to reshape the norms of human conduct while violence is still ongoing, thus aiming, as stated in the Rome Statute, to contribute to the prevention of future crimes.*
>
> (Moreno Ocampo 2007b, p. 8)

Yet the ICC's mandate is to investigate the 'most serious crimes of international concern' (Art. 1) and is therefore much more narrow than the ambitious goals formulated by the OTP. These crimes are enumerated in Art. 5 I and include war crimes, crimes against humanity, genocide and acts of aggression. The ICC's jurisdiction on the crime of aggression was dormant since the drafters of the Statute could not agree on a definition. Only during the first Review Conference of the Statute in Kampala in May/June 2010, the States Parties managed to adopt a compromise concerning the crime of aggression. However, the jurisdiction of the Court for this crime will only kick in if the new definition is ratified by thirty states, and the States Parties activate the jurisdiction by vote in the Assembly of the States Parties (ASP). The earliest date at which the jurisdiction could be activated is 1 January 2017.

The organisational structure of the ICC largely follows the blueprint of the ICTY and ICTR, being composed of different chambers of judges, the OTP and the Registry. Finally, the States Parties are represented in the institutional structure through the ASP that appoints judges and key officials like the Chief Prosecutor, decides on the Rules and Procedures and the budget of the Court, and can amend the Rome Statute.

The eighteen judges are organised in the Presidency of the ICC, the Pre-Trial Division, the Trial Division and the Appeals Division. The divisions are further divided into different chambers according to Art. 39 II of the Statute.

The OTP is in charge of independently and objectively investigating core crimes within the jurisdiction of the Court and raising charges if there is sufficient evidence (Art. 42). The main difference to the offices of the prosecutor of the ICTY and ICTR is the objective role of the OTP. Its aim is to determine whether crimes have taken place and if the persons accused are responsible. The OTP is thus also collecting exculpatory evidence (Art. 54 I).

The Registry of the ICC is a neutral body responsible for the non-judicial administration of the Court (Art. 43 I), facilitating the access to court documents by the OTP as well as the defendants and making legal counsel available to defendants without sufficient financial means.

The Court is being funded through assessed contributions by the States Parties (Art. 115a), funds from the United Nations (Art. 115b) and voluntary contributions (Art. 116). In 2012, the ICC had a budget of 108 million USD. It remains to be seen if the ICC will be able to finance its work on this basis, especially since past experiences have shown that international criminal justice does not come cheap.[2] Whether the ICC can effectively pursue its tasks depends on the payments of the States Parties, which leads to a potential circumcision of the ICC's independence and impartiality.

2.1.1 Jurisdiction of the ICC

The Court's jurisdiction applies to the core crimes mentioned before and is limited to crimes committed on the territory of States Parties or by nationals of States Parties (Art. 12). These limitations do not apply if a case is referred to the Court through a UN Security Council Resolution. Interested non-States Parties may refer jurisdiction for a case to the ICC on an ad hoc basis, as was done by Côte d'Ivoire.

Since the Court has limited resources, the OTP developed a gravity threshold based on Art. 17 I d of the Statue in order to decide whether to initiate investigations in a particular case. For the threshold to apply, the crimes must have a social impact (large scale or systematic violations), they have to be particularly brutal or cruel and the investigations have to focus on those most responsible for the crimes (Ambos 2008, p. 73).

The jurisdiction of the ICC is based on the principle of complementarity, which means that the jurisdiction of the ICC is secondary to that of national courts. The principle of complementarity was the deal breaker at the Rome Conference since it allowed a compromise between state sovereignty and the international interest to combat impunity. In a first step complementarity means that a case is inadmissible if the state with jurisdiction is investigating or prosecuting the crimes, has already tried the suspect for the crimes or has investigated the crimes and decided not to prosecute them (Art. 17). In a second step, ongoing investigations or prosecutions in the state with jurisdiction do not lead to inadmissibility if

[2] The ICTY had a yearly budget of 120 million in 2005 (Zimmermann and Kloth 2005, p. 249). In 2000, the ICTY and the ICTR budgets made up 10 per cent of the total UN budget (Hofmann-van de Pol 2010, p. 283).

the state is unwilling or unable genuinely to carry out the investigation or prosecution (Ambos 2008, p. 76 and 81, Broomhall 2004, p. 89).[3]

Additionally, the jurisdiction of the Court has to be triggered by one of the mechanisms described in the Statute. A situation can either be referred to the ICC by the government of a State Party (Art. 14), by the UNSC under Chapter VII, or the prosecutor can take up investigations in *proprio motu* (Art. 15).[4]

While the OTP can immediately take up investigations if situations are referred by the UNSC or a State Party, a Pre-Trial Chamber has to approve *proprio motu* investigations (Art. 15 III).

The ICC's jurisdiction is additionally limited to persons who are at least 18 years of age, and to the time after 1 July 2002, when the Rome Statute came into effect. For more recent members to the Statute, the date of ratification determines the temporal jurisdiction. There is no personal immunity against ICC prosecutions and high officials may be held responsible for acts carried out by their subordinates according to the principle of command responsibility. The ICC is also not bound by amnesties or the decisions of truth commissions.

The only way to defer an ICC prosecution is through a resolution of the UNSC that can defer investigations for twelve months.

2.1.2 Enforcement

The question how arrest warrants issued by the ICC are being enforced is of high importance and remains one of the main challenges for the Court. The responsibility to enforce warrants of arrest in all cases remains with the States Parties. In establishing the ICC, the states created a system based on two pillars. The Court itself is the judicial pillar, while the operational pillar, including the enforcement of the Court's orders, belongs to the states. Even though the statute has a high potential for effectiveness due to the Courts competence to determine its jurisdiction and the prosecutor's *propio motu* powers, the ICC has met limited success in enforcing its arrest warrants. This challenge is especially obvious in cases in which individuals investigated by the Court are being protected by armies or states (Moreno Ocampo 2008a, p. 12).

[3] The most comprehensive legal analysis of complementarity to date can be found in Sarah Nouwen's recent book (Nouwen 2013, p. 34–110).

[4] In *proprio motu* means that the prosecutor takes up investigations independently.

States Parties to the Rome Statute do have a legal obligation to cooperate fully with the ICC under international law according to Arts. 86 to 102 of the Rome Statute. Still, at the end of the day, this obligation can only be enforced through other states with diplomatic or military means. Thus, enforcement largely depends on the willingness of the UNSC and the ASP to build pressure to ensure compliance with ICC rulings.

2.2 The ICC in the international system

The main weakness of the ICC lies in this reliance on its States Parties and the international system. It is forced to operate in an international environment dominated by powerful states and has to play by the rules of these states. It is already remarkable that states allow an international court to meddle in their internal conflicts.

Traditional notions of sovereignty do not leave space for an international organisation to interfere in the internal matters of a state. Only in recent decades entry points for limiting state sovereignty have emerged, international criminal law being one of them. International criminal law is directly applied to individuals. Since individuals used to be exclusively subject to the laws of sovereign states, tensions between sovereignty and international criminal law emerged when individuals increasingly became subject to international law.

These tensions between Westphalian notions of sovereignty and newly established principles of international law created pockets through which external intervention into state matters became gradually acceptable. This led to the ability of international organisations, like the ICC, to interfere in areas formerly shielded from outside intervention. The creation of these entry points for international law was furthered by the states themselves, which increasingly participated in international organisations. Additionally, the tendency was furthered from within the states, through the increase of citizen participation in state domains (Bell 2008, p. 38–39). Old notions of Westphalian sovereignty are increasingly being diluted through these processes. Gradually, the notion of sovereignty has ceased being a 'birth-right' of states, and has become a privilege that has to be earned by the states and granted by the international community by recognising that state (Fowler and Bunck 1995, p. 12, see Moghalu 2009, p. 71). As a result, the legitimacy of states in the eyes of their people and the legitimacy of states in the eyes of the international community have become interwoven. The states' internal configuration is therefore increasingly open to scrutiny from its citizens and from the outside (Bell 2008, p. 31–32 and 217).[5]

This new form of sovereignty has been termed 'sovereignty as responsibility' or 'sovereignty through membership' in international networks or organisation (Chayes and Chayes 1995, Thakur 2006, p. 251). Indeed, the protection of universal values is increasingly seen as both a state responsibility and an international responsibility of all states. The idea of international responsibility has led to a higher disposition of states to intervene in the internal matters of other states if values that have been declared as universal are in peril.

The values for which a collective responsibility of all states has arguably already been established are international peace and security as laid down in the UN Charter. But human rights are also values of growing importance, even though their universality is challenged by important international players like China and Russia. Ensuring the respect for human rights has become an issue of international concern, and the globalisation of knowledge about human rights violations has made non-intervention in cases of serious violations of human rights less acceptable (Bell 2008, p. 30 and 33, Rupprecht 2003, p. 267, Weiß 2004, p. 254).

The different forms of UN interventions (peacekeeping, peace enforcement), humanitarian interventions and the legal doctrine of the Responsibility to Protect (R2P) are examples that come to mind that illustrate these tendencies of intervening in internal affairs of states. Applying international criminal law to intrastate conflicts and the targeting of individuals through international courts and tribunals would be unthinkable without the emergence of these new forms of external interventions in state matters.[6]

The puncturing of state sovereignty is clearly a necessary precondition for the application of international criminal law in conflicts. The argument behind intervening to prosecute international crimes is that their exceptional nature has a destabilising effect on international peace (Broomhall 2004, p. 9). The very idea behind the term 'crimes against humanity' is that the perpetrators of such crimes should be seen as the

[5] The idea of state duties that stands behind this connection of external legitimacy with internal legitimacy is exemplified through UN General Assembly Resolution 59/2005, stating that '*It is [the states'] job to guarantee the rights of their citizens, to protect them from crime, violence and aggression, and to provide the framework of freedom under law*'.

[6] See (Mégret 2011) for an analysis of the rise of R2P and the creation of the ICC.

enemy of humankind, both philosophically and legally (Drumbl 2007, p. 4). This idea is also reflected in the second paragraph of the preamble of the Rome Statute ('atrocities that deeply shock the conscience of humanity'). On this basis, some argue that international crimes should be condemned universally, and that individuals can be held responsible for these crimes through external interventions (Drumbl 2007, p. 195). The normative condemnation of these crimes is an important basis for the legitimacy of the international community to prosecute them (May 2005, p. 21). Basically, international criminal courts were created to guarantee the compliance with norms seen as universal by threatening sanctions against individuals who violate them. Since humankind as a whole is concerned by such crimes, it has a right to intervene if the 'responsible' state does not prosecute.

But arguably there is a new tendency to go beyond these simple interventions into the spheres of state sovereignty. Transitional justice measures are increasingly used as a tool for peacemaking and for building the rule of law in conflict and post-conflict societies (see Dyzenhaus 2003, p. 169, Findlay and Henham 2010, p. 4, Goldstone 1995, p. 487, Heupel 2005, p. 39, Leebaw 2008, p. 103, Vinjamuri 2010, p. 192). International criminal tribunals were used by the international community to deal with atrocities committed in conflicts in Yugoslavia and Rwanda in order to further peace. More recent examples are the UNSC referrals of the situations in Darfur and Libya to the ICC, as well as the attempt to refer the Syrian case to the ICC. To a certain degree this development is even embraced by practitioners, as illustrated by the ambitions of Chief Prosecutor Moreno Ocampo to enhance the preventive and peace securing functions of the ICC. Also, the new Chief Prosecutor of the ICC, Fatou Bensouda, has called the ICC a tool to enforce the R2P (Bensouda 2012). With the establishment of the ICC, the role of international criminal justice in conflict contexts has gained importance, illustrated by the fact that the ICC is conducting seven of its currently eight investigations in conflict contexts.[7]

At the same time, the growing demands for accountability for international crimes limit the possibilities to grant amnesties at the end of conflicts. Yet, amnesties were the traditional way to end conflicts during much of world history (Bell 2008, p. 240).[8] Now there is a strong trend

[7] Two of these conflicts, namely the conflicts in Libya and Côte d'Ivoire, have meanwhile ended.

[8] Thirty of seventy peace treaties concluded between 1980 and 2006 included some kind of amnesty (Mallinder 2009a, p. 215).

towards limiting these amnesties so that they no longer include the most serious offences. Amnesties encompassing genocide, war crimes and crimes against humanity are even increasingly seen as violating international law. This view is shared by the UN Secretary-General,[9] and a growing number of states (Al-Hussein 2008, p. 534, Ambos 2008, p. 20 and 61, Bell 2008, p. 240–247, Freeman 2010). Judgements of international courts that support this trend include the ICTY decision in *Prosecutor* v. *Furundzija*, clarifying that amnesty does not suppress the *ius cogens* prohibition of torture, and the Inter American Court for Human Rights decision in *Barrios-Alto* v. *Peru*, stating that amnesties for war crimes are against the Inter American Convention for Human Rights. As will be shown in later chapters, the ICC's jurisdiction in many states has seriously hampered the possibilities of national parties and mediators to grant amnesty for the most serious crimes. To quote Christine Bell, amnesties within the jurisdiction of the ICC are 'no longer worth the paper they were written on' (Bell 2008, p. 249).

[9] Since the Lomé Agreement that ended the conflict in Sierra Leone, the UN has included internal guidelines for its mediators that amnesties on Rome Statute crimes should not be accepted. This has been reiterated by the UN Secretary-General in his report on transitional justice in post-conflict settings (UNSG 2004b, p. 21).

3

Cross-case overview

Restorative justice measures have a better track record than international justice institutions.

(Thakur 2006, p. 127)

Forms of legal accountability have a better track record than other measures.

(Moghalu 2009, p. 70)

This chapter includes the cross-case overview of transitional justice measures implemented in conflict contexts. The objective of the overview is to identify appropriate causal mechanisms describing the effects of ICC investigations in intrastate conflicts and identifying suitable cases for further study.

The basis for the cross-case overview is the Justice in Conflict Database. This database was developed by the author with the help of the Transitional Justice Data Base Project (Olsen et al. 2010) and includes all transitional justice measures implemented in conflict contexts. Based on the database, a list of relevant situation countries was created. A model from conflict resolution literature is used to frame the impact of the ICC investigations in conflicts. The centrepiece is an article by Thomas Ohlson on the causes of war and peace (Ohlson 2008).

With the help of this theoretical model, a number of causal mechanisms are developed to describe the impacts of the ICC on conflict resolution. These causal mechanisms can be divided into those furthering and those hampering conflict resolution efforts. In the process it becomes clear that the predicted impacts of ICC investigations are very diverse and often contradict each other.

The final sections of this chapter will describe the results and preliminary conclusions from the cross-case overview and explain the selection procedure that led to the adoption of the LRA and Darfur conflicts as suitable case studies.

3.1 Transitional justice measures and conflict resolution

This section will explain how the impact of transitional justice measures on conflicts can be understood by analysing how they affect the conflict parties. In one way or another, all transitional justice mechanisms influence the Reasons a party has to fight (grievances, issues, problems it wants to address), the Resources it can employ in the war effort (arms, manpower, financial means) and the Resolve of a party (will to fight and perceived lack of alternatives) (Ohlson 2008, p. 134). These in turn influence the probability of a peaceful solution to a conflict.

How ICC investigations exactly influence these three Rs is explained by causal mechanisms that are summarised in five groups. Three of them further durable peace and conflict resolution, while two of them are detrimental to conflict resolution and peace. The five types are (1) mechanisms that facilitate the emergence of the rule of law, (2) mechanisms that facilitate the reconciliation between conflict parties, (3) mechanisms that deter or isolate a conflict party not interested in achieving peace, (4) mechanisms that heighten tensions in a conflict and lead to further polarisation and (5) mechanisms blocking conflict resolution efforts.

The causal mechanisms were developed by analysing the impact of transitional justice measures in 103 conflicts included in the Justice in Conflicts Database. It includes all conflicts in which transitional justice measures have been applied, as part of a conflict settlement or immediately after a conflict. It thus includes cases in which the violence has already ended when transitional justice measures are introduced. Including these cases is justified by the very low number of international trials conducted during conflicts and the fact that the impacts of trials during a conflict and shortly after a conflict can be expected to be similar. Research has shown that fighting often stops only temporarily. Even for cases in which agreements or ceasefires were concluded, fighting often re-erupts within five years (High-level Panel on Threats 2004, Item 55, para. 85). This shows that the violent dynamics of conflicts continue for some time even if there is no longer actual fighting. In order to apply strict criteria, only transitional justice measures that were adopted during the first twelve months after the end of fighting were included in the overview.

Transitional justice measures included in the overview are trials, truth commissions and amnesties. The focus of the overview lies on international criminal tribunals and courts; cases of national trials, truth commissions and amnesties were included for comparative reasons.

The Transitional Justice Data Base (TJDB) Project (Olsen et al. 2010) serves as a basis for the Justice in Conflicts Database (JiCDB) with some modifications. The JiCD includes all countries that implemented transitional justice measures during or after internal conflicts.[1] The UCDP Non-State Conflict Dataset (Eck et al. 2010) and the UCDP One-sided Violence Dataset (Eck and Hultman 2007) were used to add cases of one-sided violence in conflict contexts and non-state conflicts not covered by the TJDB. The UCDP Conflict Termination dataset (Kreutz 2010) was used to remove military victories from the database since different impacts are expected from victor's justice.

The added value of relying on a data-led approach for the overview is a gain in scientific validity as opposed to conducting a mere literature review. Additionally, the JiCDB can serve as a data source for further research.

3.1.1 *Reasons, resources and resolve*

Thomas Ohlson introduced a useful theoretical framework grasping the most relevant factors causing the outbreak and the termination of war. In his model, the outbreak and the persistence of war is determined through the three Rs (Reasons, Resources, Resolve) of a conflict party (Ohlson 2008, p. 134). They include background reasons, meaning structural factors like inequality or discrimination, as well as proximity reasons. Background reasons are the long-term structural fault lines of a society along which conflicts tend to break out as soon as a triggering factor comes into play. These triggering factors are described as proximity reasons, meaning singular events that affect a conflict party. These are, for example, sudden price increases, disenfranchisement or a serious drought that threatens the lifestyle of the group (Bonacker and Imbusch 1996, p. 70, Mendeloff 2004, p. 375, Ohlson 2008, p. 136–138).

Resources include arms, money and soldiers, but also immaterial resources like connections to external supporters and the opportunity structures within the conflict state. Examples for opportunity structures are the existence of mountainous terrain suitable for guerrilla war, weak state capabilities to contain a rebellion or the proximity of a 'safe haven'

[1] The conflict information used in the Transitional Justice Data Base Project is based on the UCDP/PRIO Armed Conflict Dataset (Gleditsch et al. 2002). Thus, the definitions and measuring criteria of the UCDP/PRIO Dataset apply to the cross-case overview.

behind an international border (Fearon and Laitin 2003, p. 76, Ohlson 2008, p. 139).

Resolve finally explains the will of the actors to engage in fighting as well as their perception of a lack of possible alternatives. In order to build Resolve for fighting, conflict parties frame a situation in a way that fighting seems a logical solution. This process is usually steered by the leaders of a conflict party. During this process, leaders consider factors like the internal cohesion of their followers as well as inter-party cost–benefits calculations, determining whether they have a reasonable chance to achieve gains through an armed conflict (Jeong 2008, p. 179, Ohlson 2008, p. 141). But leaders also have to mobilise their constituency to follow them into an armed conflict (Ohlson 2008, p. 141, Walter 2004, p. 374). People are more likely to be mobilised if they have strong grievances that cannot be addressed through non-violent means, or if they perceive a lack of alternatives to engaging in the conflict in order to ensure their livelihoods (Sambanis 2005, p. 306, Walter 2004, p. 371).

Resolve plays a special role among the three factors as it can influence Reasons (through convincing framing) and Resources (through mobilising more fighters and donors). Yet, Reasons and Resources do in turn influence Resolve through a feedback effect, as actors are less likely to keep pushing for an armed conflict if Reasons and Resources are lacking (see Jeong 2008, p. 185, Ohlson 2008, p. 141).

If one or both conflict parties lack these three factors to a sufficient degree, a conflict has an increasingly high probability to end.

3.2 The ICC and the three Rs

The ICC can influence Reasons, Resources and the Resolve of conflict parties in a variety of ways modelled here through causal mechanisms. The five types of causal mechanism triggered by ICC investigations will be introduced in the following sections.

3.2.1 Facilitating the emergence of the rule of law

In hindsight, we should have put the establishment of the rule of law first, for everything else depends on it: a functioning economy, a free and fair political system, the development of civil society, public confidence in police and the courts.

(Paddy Ashdown, former UN High Representative for Bosnia and Herzegovina, cited in Chesterman 2005, p. 69)

> *One of the things I would do differently if I could return to Afghanistan in the year 2001 would be to prioritize the strengthening of the rule of law.*
>
> (Lakhdar Brahimi, former UN High Representative for Afghanistan, in Brahimi 2008)

The first set of causal mechanisms revolves around strengthening the rule of law in conflicts. Strengthening the rule of law in conflict situations is widely seen to be contributing to conflict resolution and durable peace in peace and conflict studies literature (Müller 2003, p. 227, Wallensteen 2007, p. 142–145, Weller 2004, p. 69), as well as in transitional justice (Coicaud 2008, p. 46, Hannum 2006, p. 589, Mallinder 2009a, p. 231), and peacebuilding literature (Sriram et al. 2011, p. 11). Several authors claim that the ICC can directly further the rule of law because it fights impunity, imports a minimal legal framework into the conflict situation, engages in rebuilding judicial institutions and promotes questions of accountability and judicial reform through issuing arrest warrants and maintaining outreach campaigns (e.g. Benzing 2007, p. 22, Leebaw 2008, p. 98, van der Merwe 2009, p. 122). These claims are translated into three causal mechanisms: furthering the respect for the law and human rights, combating a culture of impunity and furthering capacity building and legal reform in national justice systems.

Rule of law is defined here according to the Report of the UN Secretary-General on the rule of law and transitional justice in conflict and post-conflict societies. It

> *refers to a principle of governance in which all persons, institutions and entities, public and private, including the State itself, are accountable to laws that are publicly promulgated, equally enforced and independently adjudicated, and which are consistent with international human rights norms and standards. It requires ... measures to ensure adherence to the principles of supremacy of law, equality before the law, accountability to the law, fairness in the application of the law, separation of powers, participation in decision-making, legal certainty, avoidance of arbitrariness and procedural and legal transparency.*
>
> (UNSG 2004b, §6)

The connections between the rule of law and conflict resolution discussed in the literature are multi-layered and diverse. One of the core connections is that the rule of law provides predictability and planning reliability since people can count on clear rules (Broomhall 2004, p. 26 and 190, Dreier 1991a, p. 75, Okoye 2004, p. 72). This reliability of expectations and the mutual trust it creates within a society are key requirements for lasting peace (see De Greiff 2008, p. 346, Müller 2003, p. 219).

The rule of law also means that the law is enforceable in courts and applies to citizens and government officials alike. The rule of law is objective and counters the discrimination of certain groups, a typical Reason for conflict parties to fight. Unsurprisingly, rule of law deficiencies thus rank high among the structural reasons for the outbreak of conflicts (see Nhema 2008, p. 2, Poku 2008, p. 112).

In return, a political system with a functioning rule of law offers procedures and institutions to tackle background Reasons and solve conflicts peacefully (Bächler 2004, p. 13, Ibrahim 2007, p. 472), thus offering alternatives to an armed struggle and reducing the Resolve to fight.

Last but not least, many academics believe that the increase of conflict intensity is connected to the crumbling of legal and moral values. The escalation of violence in internal conflicts can be exemplified by the following steps: first, the rule of law and state capacities in internal conflicts crumble. The respect for the law decreases as it becomes a mere tool of the elites in power to defend their position. In later stages of the conflict, more and more moral taboos collapse in the course of an escalation towards total war.

The three most prevalent claims explaining the impact of ICC investigations on furthering the rule of law are introduced below.

a. Furthering the respect for the law and human rights

> *In all we do, human rights are at the core. . . . In our modern era, let us send a clear message: No nation, large or small, can violate the rights of its citizens with impunity.*
>
> (Ban Ki-Moon 2010b)

One of the key arguments of supporters of retributive justice is deterrence. Sentencing those found responsible for grave crimes can increase the respect for law and human rights in the society and lead to general deterrence. Many claim that ICC trials in conjunction with pressure from human rights NGOs and states can further the respect for the law and human rights in a situation country (Akhavan 2001, p. 21, Hazan 2006, p. 25, Minow 1998, p. 25, Stromseth 2003, p. 11, 2009, p. 97, van der Merwe 2009, p. 119). These effects are often termed the '*expressive function*' or the '*public education function*' of trials (Chapman 2009, p. 159, Drumbl 2007, p. 149, Rastan 2010, p. 592).

A growing respect for the law and human rights norms would have several effects on conflicts. Increased respect for law makes it harder to mobilise people, including state officials, for participating in an armed struggle and thus reduces Resources (Kim and Sikkink 2010, p. 958). This education function of trials is especially important when it targets the security services. If the security services themselves are guilty of atrocities and abuses, ordinary people have a Reason to take their protection into their own hands and start fighting (see Bächler 2004, p. 15).

The respect for law can diminish the Resolve of a party to take up arms, as lawful alternatives are seen as more attractive, or actions violating the law are per se seen as unattractive. This effect gains special importance because people involved in conflicts tend to think that legitimate war aims (e.g. defence or retaliation) legitimise the means, even when atrocities are involved (Davidson and Thoroddsen 2011, p. 114, Fiser 2010, Mani 2002, p. 91).

Sentencing perpetrators of serious human rights violations can also improve compliance with human rights standards. This is important since human rights violations are both causes and symptoms of conflicts and thus drive its cyclical dynamics (Bell 2006, p. 107–108, Parlevliet 2010, p. 5). Human rights violations are among the Reasons why parties take up arms in the first place; stopping them can diminish the Reasons of a party and thus contribute to conflict resolution. Several authors have claimed that trials and investigations contribute to increasing the respect for human rights (Kim and Sikkink 2010, Prunier 2005, p. 147, Olsen et al. 2010).

In the case studies, this mechanism will be measured through the human rights record of the conflict parties. Risse et al. suggest that an improvement of the human rights conduct of states can be measured by the ratification of important international treaties and the beginning of national codification and institutionalisation of the promoted norms. The possibility of filing individual complaints against infringements is a particularly strong indicator. Other indicators are statements supporting human rights made by regime officials, especially when they are made in front of the regime's followers (Risse et al. 2003, p. 42–43).

Accordingly, compliance with human rights will be measured by analysing reported human rights violations, the signing and implementation of new human rights treaties and reforms strengthening the rule of law. Clear indicators are orders or new rules of engagement that call on soldiers to respect human rights. The general increase in respect for laws should also result in a reduction of serious crimes after the ICC has taken action or published warrants.

b. Furthering judicial capacity building and reforms

The implementation of international crimes legislation provides an opportunity to modernize criminal procedural codes in countries around the world, resulting in better national laws with higher standards of justice and more complete jurisdiction over grave crimes.

(CICC 2011, p. 6)

I firmly believe that there can be no lasting peace in a society unless the criminal justice system is allowed to take its course.

(Former ICTY Chief Prosecutor Carla del Ponte cited in AI 2005, p. 9)

International investigations can further the rule of law by providing an impetus to local capacity building and reforms. The ICC can promote reform of national criminal laws when states decide to implement the Rome Statute in national law (e.g. in Germany). The ICC can also strengthen judicial capacities by offering training to judges or triggering the establishment of national courts for Rome Statute crimes as in Uganda. In Rwanda, the possibility to refer cases from the ICTR to national courts under Rule 11 bis sparked judicial reforms (Buckley-Zistel 2008b, p. 11, HRW 2009b, p. 99, Onsea 2009, p. 174–176, Stromseth 2009, p. 95). In the Democratic Republic of Congo (DRC), victim groups report that the ICC indictments have led to national reforms firmly implementing the crime of rape into the national penal code (Burke-White 2005, p. 559, VRWG 2010, p. 27). These effects have been claimed for several courts and tribunals in the literature (Bernaz and Prouvèze 2010, p. 298, HRW 2010c, p. 74, ICTY 2010, p. 19, Stromseth 2009, p. 95).

When the judicial system is strengthened, Reasons will diminish when discrimination is ameliorated through legal reforms, or the access to effective and independent courts. Providing a judicial path to remedy grievances also weakens the Resolve to join a rebel movement, as more attractive alternatives might be emerging. Additionally, prosecution techniques learned while enforcing international criminal law can also be applied to organised crime (HRW 2010c, p. 46). Capable prosecutors can undermine the basis of economies of violence through their work and thus cut the access to Resources, especially in non-state conflicts. Weak state capacities are also considered as part of the opportunity structures that facilitate insurgencies. The prosecution of international crimes furthers security sector reforms and state capacities which in turn indirectly affect the Resources of rebel movements (see HRW 2010c, p. 46).

The capacity building mechanism will be measured through several indicators, including the establishment of new courts or chambers due to the ICC's involvement, reforms in penal law and reforms of the court system connected to ICC activities, the passing of laws implementing standards from the Rome Statute, as well as improved performance of local courts due to cooperation with the ICC and the participation of local lawyers in ICC training programmes.

c. Combating impunity

> *Impunity is the torturer's most relished tool. It is the dictator's greatest and most potent weapon. It is the victim's ultimate injury. And, it is the international community's most conspicuous failure.*
>
> (Penrose 1999, p. 270)

> *The Court has become a pillar of hope in ensuring that crimes do not go unpunished.*
>
> (former German Foreign Minister Steinmeier 2008, p. 5)

Ensuring accountability, or combating impunity,[2] is one of the key aims of international criminal tribunals. One of the most persistent arguments of international criminal justice supporters is that accountability through prosecutions combats a culture of impunity and therefore tackles the roots of many armed conflicts (Hofmann-van de Pol 2010, HRW 2010c, p. 72, OHCHR 2010, §1022, Wierda 2010, p. 2). Investigations and trials lead to a public discussion of accountability issues and prevent them from being swept under the rug in negotiations (Hannum 2006, p. 592, Struett 2009, p. 131, Tolbert and Wierda 2010, p. 1).

In a culture of impunity,[3] violence reproduces itself as people take justice into their own hands (Akhavan 2009, p. 635, Davidson and Thoroddsen 2011, p. 113, HRW 2010c, p. 78, Robinson 2006, p. 223).

[2] The UN defines impunity as the '*impossibility, de jure or de facto, of bringing the perpetrators of human rights violations to account whether in criminal, civil, administrative or disciplinary proceedings since they are not subject to any inquiry that might lead to their being accused, arrested, tried and, if found guilty, convicted, and to reparations being made to their victims*' (Joinet 1997).

[3] In such a culture, government officials, the police and military, as well as ordinary citizens break the law without fear of punishment, for there is a shared understanding that each person will be silent about the other's abuses as long as the favour is returned (Crocker 1998, p. 506).

In terms of Ohlson's theoretical framework, impunity is one of the factors that make an armed struggle attractive. If there is a danger of being held accountable by courts for crimes committed during an armed struggle, peaceful alternatives may become more attractive. The Resolve of a conflict party is thus targeted by mechanisms that reduce impunity. This is especially true for the higher ranks in armed groups, as their responsibility for grave crimes is not adequately captured by ordinary national laws (HRW 2010c, p. 40). Additionally, impunity for privileged groups may exacerbate the perception of already existing inequalities, Reasons for the outbreak of many a conflict.

The effect of the ICC investigations on impunity in the case studies will be assessed according to a model developed by Hofmann-van de Pol (Hofmann-van de Pol 2010). She measured the effectiveness of combating impunity in several cases by comparing the actual progress of international investigations with a counter-factual scenario of what would have happened to the perpetrators in the absence of international investigations. This model will be complemented by information on whether the conflict parties have removed abusers from their ranks since the ICC started investigations (see Mallinder 2008, p. 412) and a qualitative analysis of the culture of impunity in the situation countries.

3.2.2 *Reconciliation mechanisms*

> *It will not be possible to re-establish a healthy and peaceful European community by simply covering the dead with a shroud without any investigation.*
>
> (Joshua DuBois, prosecutor at the IG-Farben trial, quoted in Steinmeier 2008, p. 5)

Criminal trials can arguably aid reconciliation and thus further conflict resolution efforts. Reconciliation in this context means both the transformation of the relationship between people living in the conflict region as well as the creation of a new relationship built on trust between the people and the government (Chapman 2009, p. 143). Trials and investigations can further reconciliation by countering notions of collective guilt through the identification of individual perpetrators and by addressing victim needs for justice that might lead to revenge killings if not addressed.

Ideas of reconciliation seem out of place in an ongoing conflict. After all, how are people supposed to put the past behind them while the killing is still going on? But the conflict history with its atrocities and mutually inflicted injuries does always play a role in protracting conflicts. Therefore, some degree of reconciliation, namely coming to terms with this conflict history, is necessary before the conflict has ended in order to make rapprochement and negotiations possible (Ali and Matthews 2004a, p. 418, Goldstone 2000, p. 60).

The effects of reconciliation may only become visible when a conflict has already ended or is close to a solution. Therefore, it is important to keep in mind for the case studies that these effects may be difficult to measure during conflicts or shortly afterwards (see Chapman 2009, p. 158, Finnström 2010b, p. 155).

a. Addressing victim needs

> *Victims, affected communities and communities under threat of future crimes should be the primary beneficiaries of the work of the ICC and the entire Rome Statute.*
>
> (Song 2010, p. 4)

International criminal justice is expected to contribute to reconciliation by addressing victim needs. Unaddressed atrocities are proximity Reasons that may drive revenge killings and thus new cycles of conflict (see Lu 2006, p. 194, Matwijkiw 2010, p. 230). International trials deal with these issues on a judicial level and reduce Reasons to fight, as some victims and their wider communities will only be ready to leave the past behind when their fundamental needs are acknowledged and addressed. These needs include an acknowledgement of the past (truth telling, establishing a historical record) (Mani 2002, p. 90),[4] compensation for past wrongs (Karbo 2008, p. 121), as well as some form of justice or at least closure (Ali and Matthews 2004a, p. 418, Malan 2008, p. 143). These effects have, for example, been claimed for the ICC in Colombia (ICC 2010a), the ICTY (ICTY 2010, p. 19) and the ICTR (Akhavan 2001, p. 9).

The effects concerning victims' needs will be measured by assessing the work of the Victim Trust Fund of the ICC, by determining how far concrete victim demands voiced by victim groups have been met, by determining the degree of victim participation in the trials and by consulting survey data on victim satisfaction with the work of the ICC.

[4] The importance of truth to victims has been documented in victim surveys in different countries (Vinck et al. 2008, p. 48, Vinck and Pham 2010, p. 37).

b. Individualising guilt

Only by clearly identifying the individuals responsible for these crimes can we save whole communities from being held collectively guilty. It is that notion of collectivity which is the true enemy of peace.

(Kofi Annan cited in Clarke 2009, p. 4)

Allegedly, international investigations and trials individualise guilt for atrocities committed by clearly naming the perpetrators. By making clear who is responsible – and who is not – notions of collective guilt are countered. Collective guilt ascriptions are used to paint the enemy as inhuman in order to mobilise people for an armed struggle through fear and hate. These emotional factors add to the Resolve of a party by reinforcing zero-sum thinking,[5] creating in-group out-group dynamics and negative stereotypes of the enemy (Jeong 2008, p. 55, 74–77). Thus, international criminal justice can further conflict resolution opportunities if it manages to address issues of hatred and reduce Resolve. Additionally, reducing notions of collective guilt can help to make negotiations more acceptable to the home constituencies of conflict parties (see Zartman 2005a, p. 296). The effect of personalising guilt has been claimed in the former Yugoslavia (ICTY 2010, p. 19, Stromseth 2003, p. 10) and Uganda (VRWG 2010), as well as in general terms (Grodsky 2009, p. 820, Lu 2006, p. 199, Malan 2008, p. 146, Rodman 2009, p. 107).

The individualisation of guilt will be measured by analysing press statements by the conflict parties. Indicators would be a reduced use of ethnically charged language and the formulation of differentiated views on the opposing party. Finally, statements ascribing responsibility for atrocities to particular groups are a strong indicator.

3.2.3 Deterrence and isolation

The International Criminal Court ... aims to confront centuries-old methods of behaviour – those of conflict and war, the abuse of civilians, women and children – and to reshape the norms of human conduct while violence is still ongoing, thus aiming, as stated in the Rome Statute, to contribute to the prevention of future crimes.

(Moreno Ocampo 2007b, p. 8)

[5] Zero-sum thinking describes a logic according to which the gains of one party are the losses of the other party. There is no mutually beneficial solution according to this logic.

International trials and investigations can contribute to conflict resolution by isolating and deterring parties that are not willing to find a negotiated solution to the conflict. By targeting the leaders of these parties, courts can pressure them to sit down and negotiate (Hazan 2006, p. 28, Vinjamuri 2010, p. 195). At the same time, the threat of being targeted by the ICC deters them from committing atrocities that would lead to an escalation of the conflict (Goldstone 1998, p. 201, Kim and Sikkink 2009, p. 29, Moreno Ocampo 2010e, p. 1). Additionally, it is claimed that the issuing of warrants can marginalise spoilers and hardliners within a party. These mechanisms are summarised as one set since they all rely on changing the calculations of specific conflict parties.

Generally, these mechanisms are hard to measure. Regarding deterrence, it is already difficult to assess how much the threat of punishment lowers the crime rate in national legal systems. The main difficulties lie in estimating how the crime rate would have developed if the threat of retribution had not existed. In internal conflicts, the measuring is even more complicated, as the motivations of armed groups are more complex than those of ordinary criminals.

a. Pressure and inducements to negotiate

The issuing of arrest warrants can bring leaders not interested in ending the conflict to the negotiating table or make certain commanders defect by the prospect that even a military victory would result in nothing but a trial (see Bell 2008, p. 34, Tolbert and Wierda 2010, p. 1, Vinjamuri 2010, p. 195). This causal mechanism directly targets the Resolve of the conflict party and its leaders in particular. For example, a rebel leader indicted by an international court has little prospects to form an accepted government in case of a military victory. As a result, the gains from a military approach are diminished and the alternatives to armed struggle become more attractive. First, the extra effort necessary for a military struggle and the risk of defeat it includes makes alternatives more attractive even if the gains are equally low. Second, the leader of a party may try to avoid being held accountable by cutting a favourable peace deal. The pressure stems in part directly from the arrest warrant, and in part from the increased international attention on a particularly brutal rebel group. Authors have, for example, identified this causal mechanism in the case of northern Uganda (Otim and Wierda 2010, p. 5, Tolbert and Wierda 2010, p. 3, Uganda Law Society and FES 2007, p. 2), Kosovo (de Waal and Stanton

2009, p. 335–336, Kerr 2004, p. 199), Yugoslavia (Meron 2006, p. 562) and Sudan (Baldo 2010, p. 6, de Waal and Stanton 2009, p. 342, Tolbert and Wierda 2010, p. 4).

This mechanism can be traced if the ICC activity triggers more pressure on the conflict parties. Indicators are increasing calls for negotiations by the international community, a rising number of statements concerning the conflict in general, increasing press coverage about the conflict, resolutions and decisions by international organisations as well as civil society actions demanding an end to the conflict.

b. Marginalisation of spoilers

In cases in which spoilers cannot be pressured or deterred, one of the few non-military options is to marginalise the hardliners within the 'spoiler party'. As Richard Goldstone put it, 'you don't have to accept leaders who are not trustworthy and who commit international crimes, you can change them through international and national pressure'. (Goldstone 1998, p. 206)

Isolating spoilers can be especially important but also difficult in modern intrastate conflicts, since the parties to the conflict are increasingly independent from foreign sponsorship and finance themselves through criminal activities like smuggling and the illegal extraction of resources found in the war theatre (Heupel 2005, p. 16–17). The access to these resources may at the same time be a key motivation for spoiling peace negotiations (Newman 2006, p. 146–147). In some cases, spoilers are thus able to uphold violent activity for much longer through the independent access to Resources. Accordingly, spoilers have been identified as key stumbling blocks in the implementation of negotiated settlements in peace and conflict research (Stedman 2002). In these difficult cases, international justice interventions may contribute to isolating spoilers by influencing the power balance within a party. A leader sought by arrest warrant will find it more difficult to mobilise his followers since the potential gains of an armed struggle are nullified through his international 'pariah' status. As a consequence, the Resolve of the rank and file may waver. In the best case, moderate forces will take over in order to negotiate a peace deal (Hayner 2010, p. 4, Jeong 2008, p. 151, Roth 2009). This mechanism has been claimed for the former Yugoslavia (Akhavan 2001, p. 21), Kosovo (Brubacher 2010, p. 265, de Waal and Stanton 2009, p. 335–336), Serbia (Brubacher 2010, p. 266, Darehshori and Evenson 2010, p. 37), Liberia (Darehshori and Evenson 2010, p. 37, Stromseth 2009, p. 92, Unger and Wierda 2008, p. 269), Rwanda (Akhavan 2001, p. 24, ICG 2001, p. 8), Sudan (Kastner 2007, p. 169) and northern Uganda (Akhavan 2005, p. 419, HRW 2009b, p. 31, ICG 2006c, p. 12).

In Bosnia, some authors claim that the isolation of Mladić and Karadžić through the indictments of the ICTY paved the way for the Dayton Agreement since Bosnian Muslims would never have negotiated with Mladić and Karadžić and both were not to be trusted to agree on a lasting peace (Akhavan 2009, p. 634, Goldstone 2000, p. 103, see Hazan 2004, p. 143).

Indicators for the increasing marginalisation of those who drive the war effort of a party are increasing opposition to leaders targeted by the ICC, dissent within a conflict party related to the arrest warrants or an increased number of desertions by the rank and file after the issuing of a warrant. In the case of indicted politicians, isolation can be measured by a reduction of their travel activity.

c. International isolation

ICC investigations can damage the reputation of an armed group severely. External supporters who no longer want to be associated with suspected war criminals will withdraw support. A supporting state might also be implicated in the crimes under investigation and sever all ties to the investigated party as quickly as possible to avoid loss of face or being investigated itself. External supporters will only stop their engagement if the loss of reputation connected to the investigations outweighs the gains of supporting a conflict party. A withdrawal of support translates in the loss of Resources like a safe haven in a neighbouring state, supplies or moral and political support. This might in turn prompt the party to negotiate or just undercut its ability to uphold armed violence or plan renewed aggression.

The effects of international isolation have been claimed for the cases of northern Uganda (Akhavan 2009, p. 641–646, Mendes 2010, p. 102, Moreno Ocampo 2010b), Serbia (AI 2005, p. 5) and Rwanda (Akhavan 2009, p. 634).

Indicators for international isolation are economic sanctions, the scaling back of verbal and economic support by former allies and statements as well as the voting behaviour of states in international bodies like the UNSC. These indicators then have to be connected to ICC's investigations through process tracing.

d. Prevention through special deterrence

> *Experience has taught us that . . . law is the only efficient way to prevent recurrent violence and atrocities.*
>
> (Moreno Ocampo 2008a, p. 13)

Many believe that deterrence contributes to the prevention of conflicts and their escalation because the threat of punishment can deter parties from initiating a violent conflict, escalating a conflict or committing grave human rights violations (see Goldstone 1998, p. 201, Kim and Sikkink 2009).

The idea behind deterrence is to influence the calculations of specific conflict parties. The threat of being investigated diminishes the possible gains for initiating or escalating violent conflicts and thus has a negative effect on the Resolve of conflict parties (see Jeong 2008, p. 179). Being investigated for war crimes often leads to international sanctions that directly affect the gains of armed struggles. Sanctions include travel bans, freezing financial assets in foreign banks and withdrawing international legitimacy, thus complicating the creation of a sustainable power base (Akhavan 2001, p. 12, Kim and Sikkink 2010, p. 942, Sikkink and Walling 2006, p. 42). While these calculations mainly affect the leaders of conflict parties, their followers' Resolve may also diminish when they see that their leader will have fewer possibilities to reward his followers.

Special deterrence is also believed to restrain the behaviour of combat forces, dissuading them from committing atrocities and breaking the rules of warfare (see Nitsche 2007, p. 69, Rupprecht 2003, p. 229). For example, a number of authors identify the deterrent effects of the ICC in Cote d'Ivoire, where militias were reportedly already in the countryside and hate speeches from radio stations were setting the field for violent conflict (Akhavan 2009, p. 625, HRW 2009b, p. 124, Mendez 2010a, p. 5). In other cases, authors have specifically named conflict parties that have restricted their military actions and boosted their efforts to avoid civilian casualties due to international investigations. These parties include the NATO forces in Kosovo (Heikkilä 2009, p. 44), the Ugandan Army in northern Uganda (Allen and Vlassenroot 2010, p. 16, Anderson 2006, Struett 2009, p. 128) and the Presidential Guards in the Central African Republic (CAR) (HRW 2009b, p. 124–125, 2010c, p. 71–72).

Solid theoretical foundations for measuring deterrence exist in the literature. The first step is to determine whether the theoretical prerequisites for deterrence exist in the cases. Prerequisites include that the targeted groups are aware of the relevant laws (Kim and Sikkink 2010,

p. 944, Robinson and Darley 2004, p. 175, Wippman 2006, p. 110), that they perceive a probability of being caught (Kim and Sikkink 2010, p. 943, Rothe 2010, p. 102) and that they see the applicable law as legitimate (Rothe 2010, p. 103). If these prerequisites are not fulfilled, it is improbable that a deterrent effect can gain traction. Deterrence itself will be measured through a decrease of the crimes investigated by the ICC and orders by commanders to their rank and file not to commit war crimes. A proxy indicator that will be used in the case studies is the development of the figures for battle-related deaths taken from reports and the ACLED Dataset (Raleigh et al. 2010).

3.2.4 Blocking conflict resolution

> *In seasons of insurrection or rebellion, there are often critical moments, when a well-timed offer of pardon to the insurgents or rebels may restore the tranquillity of the commonwealth; and which, if suffered to pass unimproved, it may never be possible afterwards to recall.*
>
> (Hamilton 1778)

One of the main arguments of the critics of international criminal justice is that investigations might block efforts of conflict resolution and management. On the one hand, it is claimed that indicted leaders may abstain from negotiations and go on fighting out of fear of being tried after signing a peace deal. On the other hand, retributive justice measures might complicate the starting of negotiations because they follow a confrontational logic and thus complicate a constructive dialogue. This set of causal mechanisms is the direct counter-claim to the pressure and isolation mechanisms introduced under Section 3.2.3c. In a nutshell, both sets of measures are based on rational calculations of conflict parties. Despite the similar approach, they predict fundamentally different reactions of conflict parties facing international prosecutions.

a. Blocking negotiations

Many critics of international trials and investigations claim that negotiations and prosecutions are fundamentally at odds with each other because (1) those most responsible for atrocities usually emerge as key figures in peace settlements since they are the leaders of conflict parties (Bell 2006, p. 14, Brubacher 2010, p. 264, Hayner 2010, p. 2) and (2) the logic of settling a conflict is one of compromise over accountability, while international criminal justice puts accountability first (Bell 2008, p. 239).

Armed conflicts end in three ways: through the military victory of one side, some sort of negotiated deal or by just gradually phasing out. Since decisive battles are increasingly being evaded by the parties in modern intrastate conflicts, negotiations gain further importance for conflict resolution (see Münkler 2002, p. 25).[6] Against this background, the claims that international prosecutions block negotiations are not to be taken lightly. This is emphasised by the fact that negotiations are already difficult undertakings without further complicating factors. As data shows, about half of the peace agreements concluded fail within five years, and 90 per cent of the rest are best described as ambiguous no peace, no war situations (High-level Panel on Threats 2004, Item 55, para. 85).

In practice, the mechanism of blocking negotiations works through boosting the gains of an ongoing military struggle as peaceful solutions would only lead to a trial for the prosecuted party. Conflict parties indicted at an international court might prefer to try to win the conflict as chances are considerably slimmer that they will be arrested in the case of a military victory. This results in the strengthened Resolve of the conflict party. An indictment perceived as unfair and biased may even add to the Reasons of a conflict party. If the court is seen to take sides with the adversary, the legitimacy of the investigation itself may become part of the contested issues of the conflict.

The causal mechanism of blocking negotiations implies that conflict parties cannot be deterred or pressured through indictments, as they have already been indicted and have nothing to lose. Some authors have pointed out that rebel groups might be turned into spoilers through this very mechanism (Kim and Sikkink 2010, p. 958, Sriram 2008, p. 307–308). Negotiations in these cases also pose special challenges to mediators. For example, they have to ask themselves whether it is appropriate to engage in mediation efforts with indicted war criminals (Unger and Wierda 2008, p. 284).

The effect of blocking negotiations has been claimed in a number of cases included in the overview. The SCSL indictment of Liberian president Charles Taylor is described as a monkey wrench thrown into the

[6] According to recent research, the share of ceasefires and peace agreements in conflict terminations has risen from 9.9 per cent in 1946–1989 to 38.1 per cent in 1990–2005. At the same time, the share of victories has dropped from 58.2 per cent to 13.6 per cent (Kreutz 2010, p. 246).

negotiations to end the Liberian civil war (Hazan 2006, p. 31, Rodman 2009, p. 100, Unger and Wierda 2008, p. 268). The African Union as well as the Arab League have called for a deferral of the ICC case against Sudanese president Omar al-Bashir, claiming that it blocks conflict resolution efforts (AL 2009, AU 2009). The AU has reiterated the same concerns in the case of Libya more recently (AU 2011, §6). In Uganda, civil society organisations have claimed that the ICC blocked the Ugandan peace process with the LRA (ARLPI 2009, Baines 2007, p. 91, Dolan 2009, p. 66, Schomerus 2007, p. 47).

The indicator for tracing this mechanism is the failure of negotiations due to ICC investigations or warrants, or a lack of progress in negotiations due to ICC actions. This can be measured through an in-depth qualitative analysis of the negotiations and by analysing official negotiation documents as well as academic literature that was published on the negotiations.

b. Hindering constructive dialogue and rapprochement

If international investigations can hamper negotiations, they might also be an obstacle in paving the way for peace talks. The Resolve of the conflict parties will only waver if other alternatives are attractive enough. Due to the deep distrust and hatred between the parties, some rapprochement between them is necessary before they can be expected to even consider negotiations (see Ali et al. 2004, p. 305, Jeong 2008, p. 56). Investigations, on the other hand, are a confrontational mechanism. There is an accused and a prosecutor. Especially in cases in which only one side of the conflict is being prosecuted, the investigations might reinforce the zero-sum mentality of conflicts so detrimental to negotiations (see Aggestam 2006, p. 26, Zartman 1995, p. 8, 2005a, p. 295).

Mahmood Mamdani and Alex de Waal have argued along these lines, saying that the ICC is reinforcing the zero-sum mentality in the Darfur conflict (Daly 2010, p. 308, de-Waal 2009, p. 125, Mamdani 2009a, p. 151, Peskin 2009b, p. 310). Yugoslavia (Kritz 1996, p. 143–144), Uganda (see Mahmood Mamdani, cited in Namutebi 2005) and Rwanda (Hansen 2011, p. 44, Wippman 2006, p. 121) have been named as other examples.

Indicators for this mechanism are the use of the ICC warrants in the propaganda of the conflict parties and a refusal to communicate with the other party due to the warrants.

3.2.5 Heightening tensions

The last set of causal mechanisms represents the strongest claims of the critics of international investigations. Some critics fear that international criminal justice interventions might in fact heighten the tensions in a conflict and lead to an escalation (Broomhall 2004, p. 55, Mendeloff 2004, p. 374). Their argument is that international criminal justice in conflicts is inevitably caught up in an ongoing power struggle. As it identifies perpetrators and victims, it becomes part of this power struggle and can reproduce or even exacerbate it. This could happen by triggering spoiler retaliation for the indictments (Olsen et al. 2010, p. 111), or by unwittingly bolstering the support for hardline factions on both sides (Jeong 2008, p. 172).

a. Triggering spoiler retaliation

International investigations might heighten the tensions in a conflict through triggering retaliation by the indicted party. In terms of Ohlson's model, the indictment might be seen as biased by the targeted party and the investigations would be perceived as another injustice that has to be fought, thus adding to the Reasons of a conflict party. Additionally, the indictment might lead to strengthened Resolve of the targeted party because it hopes to derail the investigations by destabilising the situation through further violence. Generally speaking, an increase of Reasons and Resolve is expected to lead to an uptick in violence and conflict intensity.

This causal mechanism has been claimed in the literature for the cases of Darfur (de Waal and Flint 2008, Mamdani 2009c, Weber and Tull 2008, p. 2), the former Yugoslavia (Snyder and Vinjamuri 2003, p. 12),[7] Bosnia and Herzegovina (Bojicic-Dzelilovic 2006, p. 213, Snyder and Vinjamuri 2003, p. 23), Croatia (Brounéus 2008, p. 208) Serbia (Wippman 2006, p. 119), Liberia (Hayner 2010, p. 5) and Uganda (Finnström 2006, p. 200, Hovil and Quinn 2005).

Measuring the backlash mechanism is pretty straightforward. If this mechanism applies, attacks would be conducted soon after the issuing of warrants. There would be aggressive reactions in stated retaliation to the

[7] In the case of Macedonia, the causal mechanism claimed by the authors is somewhat more complex. Albanian militias started destroying evidence of atrocities when they were targeted by ICTY investigators which in turn created a pretext for Macedonian nationalists to renew fighting in November 2001.

ICC actions; their targets would mainly be actors that are perceived to be supporting the ICC locally.

b. Bolstering support for hardliners

The ICC should avoid intervening in ongoing conflicts, since the instrumentalization of ICC intervention by states may lead to further militarization and violence.

(Branch 2007b, p. 195)

International criminal justice may boost the support for hardline factions in all conflict parties and perpetuate a conflict. This is the case because external pressure through ICC investigations can tighten the grip of a leader on his group when solidarity sets in or when the leader uses the external threat to stabilize his power by branding dissenting voices as 'traitors' (see Jeong 2008, p. 172). Additionally, indicted leaders will arguably start to cling to power to avoid arrest (Grono and O'Brien 2008, p. 17).

If the opposing party has been targeted by investigations, leaders who opt for a violent approach get tailwind. The indictments can be used as a propaganda tool against the enemy, and violence is more likely to be perceived as a legitimate means against indicted war criminals (see Cobban 2007, p. 51). Hardline leaders will argue that chances for victory have increased as the enemy will be isolated by the indictment and the chances for an external intervention against the indicted party have risen.[8] The investigations might also lead to a further polarisation through the clear identification of victim and perpetrator roles. In terms of Ohlson's model, the indictment would thus strengthen Resolve on both sides by facilitating the mobilisation of supporters by hardline leaders.

This mechanism has been identified in the former Yugoslavian Republics (Mendeloff 2004, p. 347, Nitsche 2007 p. 269, Schrey 2003, p. 63), in Darfur (Clark and Anderson 2010, p. 192, Thakur 2006, p. 282), in Ituri, DRC (HRW 2008a, p. 52), Rwanda (Cobban 2006, p. 28, Lu 2006, p. 199) and Uganda (Allen 2006, p. 186 and 191, Branch 2007a, p. 490, Nouwen and Werner 2010, p. 949).

[8] This mechanism is being discussed as the moral hazard of external interventions in intrastate conflicts. It is not explicitly coined on international investigations but describes the same process of emboldening rebel hardliners through external meddling (Kuperman 2008, 2009).

In tracing this mechanism, one would expect moderates within a party to lose their positions after ICC indictments. Additionally, followers (or the population in general) would start to rally behind indicted hardline leaders. An escalation in fighting and verbal attacks between the parties is an additional indicator.

c. Destabilisation, fragmentation, power vacuum

The priority of the Rome Statute is to prosecute[;] it's not here for political stability.

(Former ICC Deputy Prosecutor Serge Brammertz, quoted in Blumenson 2006, p. 821)

Some authors uphold rather broad claims that international criminal justice interventions may lead to a destabilisation in situation countries. If an indictment weakens the position of a head of state or a rebel leader sufficiently, he might lose control over his party. Rivals suddenly see a chance to take over and thus have a Reason to start fighting for internal control. At the same time, rivals and splinter groups may profit from better opportunity structures and an easier access to Resources due to the weakened control of the dominant parties. Additional rebellions might break out, extreme hardliners may challenge the leaders targeted by the ICC and the conflict might thus become even more complicated and bloody.

The causal mechanism has been explicitly claimed in the case of Sudan, where some authors have voiced the fear that al-Bashir's indictment might lead to a power vacuum and further destabilisation (de Waal et al. 2008, Odinkalu 2010, p. 16). Congolese officials also voiced fears of destabilising effects when national trials were discussed for the DRC in 2005 (Kerr and Mobekk 2007, p. 110). Other authors have claimed that the trial of former dictator Saddam Hussein in Iraq bolstered the intercommunity violence in Iraq (Bernaz and Prouvèze 2010, p. 386). Other cases mentioned include Bosnia (Brubacher 2004, p. 82), Côte d'Ivoire (Doria et al. 2010, p. 422) and Liberia (Brubacher 2004, p. 82).

The only way to trace this causal mechanism is to conduct a conclusive political analysis of the situation, linking a destabilisation to the ICC investigations.

3.2.6 Conclusions of the cross-case overview

The cross-case analysis has produced a total of fourteen causal mechanisms that can occur if the ICC starts investigations in ongoing conflicts.

Unfortunately, the literature so far provides only weak descriptions of the effects claimed and little empirical proof to sustain them. In many cases, the authors claimed the existence of causal mechanisms in general terms, often without even referring to a case to at least illustrate their claim.

The most important finding of the cross-case overview is the fact that most of the causal mechanisms from the literature are contested. Not only do many causal mechanisms contradict each other, but the literature often presents contradicting arguments as to whether the causal mechanisms can actually be traced in reality or not. In most cases, there are convincing arguments and counter-arguments speaking for and against the claimed effects.

How is it possible that the literature is so fundamentally divided about the impacts of international investigations and trials in conflicts? This is one of the key questions for the following case studies. There is no consensus about the impact of international investigations and trials in most of the cases included in the overview. In thirteen of the sixteen cases of international or hybrid trials addressed in the literature, both positive and negative impacts of trials on the conflict have been claimed. In twelve of the sixteen cases, even directly contradicting effects were claimed.[9]

It is not plausible that errors of judgement and measurement are the main reasons for this confusing picture. The most probable explanation is that international criminal justice indeed has contradicting effects in conflict situations and that these effects depend highly on context. The lack of accounting for important contextual factors, or third variables, would be a logical explanation for the contradictory findings in both the literature and the statistical surveys.

Case studies are the method of choice to shed light on the influence of these third variables through tracing causal mechanisms in reality. The sheer number of variables listed in the literature and the added complexities of internal conflicts make it impossible to account for all of them. One of the main tasks of the case studies was, therefore, to identify third variables that have a strong influence on the development of the causal mechanisms on the ground. Procedures (strategic decisions on how to investigate a conflict within the OTP) and perceptions (the views and opinions of stakeholders and actors about what kind of accountability should be implemented) will emerge as key factors in the case studies.

[9] The pairings of directly contradicting claims include special deterrence versus spoiler retaliation, pressure and inducement vs. blocking negotiations, individualising guilt vs. blocking rapprochement, as well as marginalisation vs. polarisation.

3.3 Case study selection

On the basis of the cross-case overview, suitable cases have to be identified in order to trace the mechanisms in situation countries on the ground. Due to the high number of causal mechanisms and the large amount of information that is needed for their analysis, the number of case studies has to be limited to two. The cases will be chosen among countries that are involved in ongoing intrastate conflicts and where there are active ICC investigations.

The ICC currently conducts investigations in the CAR, Côte d'Ivoire, the DRC, Darfur, Kenya, Libya, Mali and Uganda. At the same time, preliminary investigations are being conducted in Afghanistan, Colombia, Gaza, Georgia, Guinea (Conakry), Honduras, Nigeria and the Republic of South Korea. Preliminary investigations cannot be included since there is simply not enough data for in-depth case studies to be fruitful. Of the remaining cases, Darfur and Uganda are most suitable for further research. Both cases have been widely perceived as controversial and fraught with complexities. Additionally, a variety of the causal mechanisms identified in the overview has been claimed for both cases. Therefore, the situations in Uganda and Darfur can be expected to offer sufficient data for the tracing of the causal mechanisms as well as the analysis of external variables.

3.3.1 *Selection criteria*

Uganda and Darfur are confirmed ongoing intrastate conflicts according to information from the AKUF Database,[10] the Uppsala Conflict Data Project[11] and the Conflict Barometer of the Heidelberg Institute for International Conflict Studies (HIIK).[12]

[10] The AKUF Database is part of the Causes of War Project at the University of Hamburg. It includes all conflicts in which a state is the actor on one side of the conflict. Additional criteria are the existence of a central command exercising at least minimum control over each party as well as a certain continuity of hostilities (Wallensteen 2007, p. 20).

[11] The Uppsala Conflict Data Project 2010 based at the Uppsala University in Sweden includes armed conflicts including at least one state actor and reaching a threshold of at least twenty-five battle-related deaths.

[12] The Conflict Barometer of the HIIK includes non-violent as well as violent conflicts and rates them on a conflict intensity scale from one to five according to the degree of violence they exhibit.

Darfur and Uganda are the hardest cases that the ICC has taken up to date. This is illustrated by the extent of open criticism that the prosecution faced during its investigations in both conflicts. Additionally, the legitimacy of the Court has been openly challenged in both cases. In Uganda, there is a disagreement between the ICC and a portion of the local population about how justice should be implemented. In Sudan, a rift between the ICC and its supporters on the one side, and the AU on the other side has emerged over the Darfur investigations. Both countries therefore exhibit unfavourable preconditions for positive effects of the investigations. This means that a success in tracing positive causal mechanisms in the Darfur and Uganda cases would be a strong argument for their general validity. Additionally, the controversy connected to the cases and the advanced stage of investigations mean that a lot of data on the cases is available and relatively easy to access.

The conflicts in Darfur and northern Uganda were also chosen since their analysis adds to the relevance of the research question. Both conflicts are amongst the most intractable contemporary conflicts, and are generally considered to be especially harmful for the local population (Jeong 2008, p. 102). The need to understand how ICC investigations influence the conflict resolution opportunities for this conflict type is therefore high.

Finally, both conflicts are conflicts over government with an ethnic factor and a regional dimension that have lasted for several years. Both situation countries share a British colonial legacy. They are therefore comparable in many important aspects. Choosing similar conflicts allows for excluding several external variables and makes it easier to focus on the relevant variables.

Furthermore, the proceedings in Sudan against government officials, including President al-Bashir, may be the first of a growing number of cases referred by the UNSC. This would make the Darfur case, a case on the 'leading edge of change' (Schofield 2000, p. 82–83). The UNSC referral of the situation in Libya seems to confirm this tendency.

It is important to keep in mind that Darfur and Uganda are undoubtedly the hardest cases the ICC has tackled so far (even though the Kenya case has recently become equally challenging for the ICC). On the one hand, this means that the cases of Uganda and Darfur offer deeper insights into the dilemmas and complexities of ICC investigations in conflicts. On the other hand, the analysis of these particular cases may lead to a more sceptical assessment of the impact of ICC investigations.

PART II

The case studies

4

The ICC in Sudan: fighting impunity or heightening tensions?

Chapter 4 presents the case study conducted on the Darfur conflict in western Sudan that is subject to ICC investigations since a UNSC referral on 31 March 2005.

4.1 Conflict analysis - Darfur

The first part of both case studies is a conflict analysis following the conflict assessment guidelines developed by the UK Department for International Development (DFID) (Goodhand et al. 2002). As part of the analysis of the conflict actors, their Reasons, Resources and Resolve will be elaborated.

4.1.1 Conflict background and history

The Darfur conflict is characterised by the use of militias and a remarkable brutality against civilians. It broke out long before it received international media attention in 2004. The conflict is multi-layered and complex, involving rebels, the government and its affiliated militias. It is interwoven with conflicts in Chad and South Sudan.

Sudan is a former British-Egyptian Condominium, roughly two-thirds the size of Western Europe, that gained its independence in 1956. Sudan was long characterised by a marked north–south divide along geographic, economic, cultural and ethnic lines until South Sudan seceded in July 2011. The secession was a result of the Comprehensive Peace Agreement (CPA) between the Government of Sudan (GoS) and the Sudan People's Liberation Movement/Army (SPLM/A) rebel movement that ended decades of north–south civil war in 2005.

The conflict in Darfur first made headlines and received international attention in 2004. A veritable avalanche of articles, editorials and TV-features pushed the conflict into the media spotlight during 2004 and

2005. Yet, the Darfur conflict has a much longer history than most of the media reporting would suggest.

Darfur had been an independent sultanate from 1898 to 1922 when it was incorporated into the British–Egyptian Condominium under French pressure. Darfur has a tradition of rebellion. As early as in the 1950s and 1960s, Darfuri groups started criticising central domination, and in the 1980s, they forced the Numeiri regime to appoint a native governor in the province (Tanner and Tubiana 2007, p. 13). At the same time, tribal conflicts between nomads and settlers have been part of the political landscape of Darfur since the nineteenth century (Daly 2010, p. 131, Hoile 2006, p. 6). These conflicts have always been connected to the geography of the region. Darfur can geographically be roughly divided into three areas: the arid deserts of the north, the tropical area around the Jebel Marra mountain range in the centre and the southern savannah (Mamdani 2009c, p. 9–10). The slow desertification and recurring droughts in the thin Sahel zone at the southern fringe of the desert have made fertile land a precious and scarce resource in Darfur. The seasonal migration of nomads, who move through the fertile lands of the settled tribes, has always sparked some conflicts. Nevertheless, settlers and nomads coexisted peacefully most of the time (see de Waal 2007d, p. 2, Nielsen 2008, p. 439). Through various influences these traditional conflicts have been exacerbated gravely in the past decades.

The combination of increasing desertification, droughts, the influx of small arms from Chad and Libya and the increasing pressure through migration from the West led to a gradual increase in tribal conflicts. This development resulted in the Arab–Fur war between 1987 and 1989 (Flint 2007, p. 142, Mamdani 2009c, p. 259). Northern Arab tribes, mainly nomadic camel herders of the Abbala tribe, were pitted against the African Fur tribe, which was mainly sedentary. Militias organised by both tribes fought each other over access to fertile land and seasonal migration routes.

Then, in 1995, tensions between Arab tribes and the predominantly sedentary African Massalit tribe erupted (Mamdani 2009c, p. 249). The GoS was drawn into the conflict in the same year when it intervened militarily with gunships on the side of the Arab tribes. About 2,000 people were killed and 100,000 displaced during the ensuing fighting (Burr and Collins 2008, p. 287, Prunier 2005, p. 75). The current conflict in Darfur has to be understood against this background of recurring tribal conflicts.

The current Darfur conflict is extremely complex. In fact, it encompasses several conflict lines and different issues on the local, national, regional and international levels. It consists of three different conflicts: one between the government and Darfur rebel groups, one between the government-supported Arab militias and predominantly African civilians and finally the local conflicts between tribal communities (ICG 2004b, p. 1).

The Darfur conflict started after Arab militias attacked villages of the sedentary Zaghawa, Fur and Massalit tribes. The settled tribes started to see their common cause in 2001 and founded the first rebel group, the Darfur Liberation Front in the same year. The group was later renamed Sudan Liberation Army/Movement (SLA/M). As during previous conflicts, the government took the Arab side (Daly 2010, p. 259). After an internal split in the ruling Sudanese National Congress Party (NCP) between Omar al-Bashir and Hassan al-Turabi, the new opposition around Turabi started taking interest in the Darfur conflict as an opportunity to challenge the NCP. The national opposition thus got involved in 2002/3, which added a national dimension to the conflict (Mamdani 2009c, p. 16).[1]

There were several triggers that led to the 2003 escalation: the flaring of old ethnic tensions, the traditional competition for pasture lands, droughts, the failure of traditional reconciliation mechanisms as well as the GoS/SPLA negotiations that further marginalised Darfur within Sudan (Burr and Collins 2008, p. 284, ICG 2004d, p. 1, Prunier 2006, p. 195).

The conflict was relatively one-sided in the initial phase. There were at least eight major Arab militia attacks on Fur, Massalit and Zaghawa villages before the rebels even started their initial offensive by attacking el Fasher airport in 2003 (Hagan and Rymond-Richmond 2009, p. 208, Tanner and Tubiana 2007, p. 20). The government initially refused to acknowledge a rebellion in Darfur and described the rebels as armed bandits. It strongly underestimated the rebel movements and tried to quell the rebellion by exploiting the differences between the sedentary tribes in order to divide them (Daly 2010, p. 280). The rebels' fighting style relied on small and highly mobile units moving on 4×4 Toyota *Hilux* with mounted machine guns that outmanoeuvred the SAF with

[1] Many JEM members were members of the Turabi wing of the NCP before the party split. The JEM supreme commander Khalil Ibrahim himself led militias allied to the GoS in the civil war with Southern Sudan.

ease in the early phases of the conflict (Tanner and Tubiana 2007, p. 37). As the GoS attempts to split the rebels did not bear fruit, the rebels claimed a number of impressive military victories in the early phases of their campaign. In total, the rebels won thirty-four of the thirty-eight encounters with the SAF until mid-2003 (Flint and de Waal, 2008, p. 122).

In response to these early rebel victories, the government started to modify its counter-insurgency strategy by arming and supporting Arab militias (Burr and Collins 2008, p. 288, Daly 2010, p. 281–282). The government-supported militias in Darfur soon became known as Janjaweed. With their help, the government soon started displacing entire tribes that were perceived as rebel supporters in order to drain the support base of the rebellion (Flint and de Waal 2008, p. 157, Mamdani 2009c, p. 226, Prunier 2005, p. 102–103). The government-supported Janjaweed attacks on African villages were of a marked brutality and followed a pattern documented in detail in various studies and reports. The attacks described here are ongoing at the time of writing, even though with greatly reduced intensity.

It is beyond doubt that the attacks were not mainly aimed at the rebel movements, but at civilians belonging to the same ethnic groups as the rebels, especially the Zaghawa (ICG 2004a, p. 3, Markusen 2009, p. 101, Mohammed 2007, p. 211). In most cases, the Sudanese Armed Forces (SAF) initiated the attacks by bombing African villages. The SAF usually used crude carpet bombing techniques, rolling barrels filled with explosives and shrapnel off the ramps of transport planes. In other cases, the villages were attacked from the air with combat helicopters. Following the air attacks, Janjaweed militias surrounded the village and attacked on camels or horseback, sometimes supported by SAF troops. In some cases entire villages were exterminated, in others, selective killings and mass rapes were conducted (Prunier 2005, p. 99). In all cases the attackers burned the houses, deliberately destroyed the means of livelihood and polluted the wells (ICG 2004a, p. 1, Markusen 2009, p. 101 and 108). Fleeing refugees and stragglers were killed and there were reports of extreme atrocities like children being thrown into burning houses, gang-rapes, mutilations and branding of raped victims (Prunier 2005, p. 99). From the pattern that emerges it is clear that the attacks aimed at an ethnic cleansing of the targeted areas.[2] Even though they were meant

[2] A study by Médecins Sans Frontiers shows that Janjaweed attacks were the main reason for mortality among Darfuri civilians in the early phases of the conflict. Violence caused

to drain the rebel movements of their support, the use of Janjaweed drove more and more youths from the sedentary tribes into the arms of the rebel movements (Flint 2007, p. 153, Tubiana 2007, p. 75). According to field research conducted during 2006, the support for the rebel groups among the population had increased considerably after the brutal counter-insurgency (Tanner and Tubiana 2007, p. 38).

The counter-insurgency tactic employed by the GoS was successful militarily, but it came at the price of fuelling the Darfur rebellion. From 2004 onwards, the rebel movements started to splinter under the military pressure of the combined SAF and Janjaweed offensive and the GoS divide-and-rule strategy. Fighting between the two main rebel movements, the SLA and the JEM, erupted. At the same time both groups suffered from intensive infighting. The GoS also managed to exploit the rift between the Zaghawa and Massalit/Fur factions of the SLA. The splintering of rebel movements gained momentum during and after the peace negotiations between the government and the rebels in the Nigerian capital of Abuja. The signing of the Abuja Agreement by the mainly Zaghawa SLM-MM caused a rift between Fur and Zaghawa and more and more rogue rebel commanders started to emerge (Brosché 2008, p. 50, Mamdani 2009c, p. 265). The GoS played its role in this process by supporting some non-signatory groups and sending them to fight other non-signatory rebel groups (Tanner and Tubiana 2007, p. 45). The SLM-MM splintered quickly after the signature and its leader Minni Minawi lost most of his territory and support base (Tanner and Tubiana 2007, p. 41). The infighting in the SLA reached a new level after this split.

Increasingly, all parties involved in the conflict started to commit atrocities as the rebels became more and more criminal in their actions and started to retaliate against Arab civilians (Flint and de Waal 2008, p. 153 and 157). The rebel movements degenerated towards warlordism and began looting villages and attacking international aid convoys (ICG 2004b, p. 19, 2005d, p. 4). As a response, civilians have again become more reluctant to support the rebels and blame them for some of their suffering (Tanner and Tubiana 2007, p. 39).

At the same time, the international community remained largely passive. Five UNSC resolutions, some of them imposing sanctions or pronouncing threats to take up additional measures, were passed on

by the Janjaweed caused 50 per cent of deaths among those aged under five and 95 per cent of the deaths among those five years or older in the Mornei area in Darfur (MSF & Epicentre 2004).

Sudan while the conflict raged on. Resolution 1564 created an International Commission of Inquiry on Darfur (ICID). The report of the commission found systematic war crimes and crimes against humanity, and led to the referral of the Darfur situation to the ICC in resolution 1594 on 31 March 2005 under Art. 13 (b) of the statute, obliging Sudan to cooperate with the ICC.

The international community tried to tackle the conflict by deploying peacekeeping operations, albeit with limited success. In October 2004, the GoS accepted the AU mission AMIS in Darfur because a purely African peacekeeping mission with a limited mandate was acceptable to the government (Prunier 2005, p. 144–145). Yet, the AMIS mandate, its resources, as well as the international support for the mission proved to be insufficient to stop the conflict (Mansaray 2009, p. 37, Paes 2006, p. 30, Williams 2006). While the UN started to push for UN peacekeepers in Darfur, the GoS successfully blocked any deployment for many months, thanks to support from Russia and China. When the government finally accepted a hybrid mission of UN and AU troops, it repeatedly delayed deployment of UN peacekeepers (Fowler and Prendergast 2009, p. 157–158, Mansaray 2009, p. 38). Until this day the GoS has managed to keep any Western involvement in UNAMID at a minimum level (Cockett 2010, p. 231). UNAMID has still not managed to stabilise the security situation, even though a drop in direct fighting could be observed between 2007 and 2010 (Daly 2010, p. 308). In 2010, UNAMID had still only arrived at half of its authorised strength with 10,500 military and 1,800 police staff. International support for the mission is still lacking and UNAMID is short of vital equipment like transport helicopters (Cockett 2010, p. 133–134).

The GoS has found a way to target the rebel support base despite the deployment of peacekeepers by starving the displaced villagers and withholding medicine (Prunier 2005, p. 116). First of all, the internally displaced persons (IDPs) had to flee to remote areas where aid did not easily reach them (Weber 2008, p. 146). The government continues to hamper the access of aid workers to the IDP camps with bureaucratic tricks and through harassment, forcing NGOs and humanitarian agencies to apply for permits that are regularly delayed (Adam et al. 2011, p. 6, HRW 2006b, p. 15–16, Prunier 2005, p. 131–132). Additionally, the government started to recruit members of the same Arab militias that had displaced the African tribes into their security apparatus and stationed them at the IDP camps to 'protect' the refugees. An April 2004 UN mission found that the ex-Janjaweed and police in charge of security at the IDP camps were in fact starving the survivors (ICG 2004d, p. 2). IDPs leaving the camps to collect food or firewood are regularly attacked or raped by Janjaweed (HRW 2007a, p. 17, Kahn 2008, p. 28). The situation worsened further with increasing insecurity and banditry in Darfur. The transport costs for humanitarian goods skyrocketed due to the insecurity and the NGOs were generally underfunded (Natsios 2007, p. 1, Prunier 2005, p. 137–138). Apart from the deliberate failure of the GoS to protect humanitarian convoys, the SLA was blocking the flow of aid from government-controlled areas since it feared that SAF convoys would enter under the false pretence of escorting the aid trucks (ICG 2004d, p. 2). At the current stage of the conflict, NGOs and aid agencies are being attacked from all sides including the SAF, rebels, militias and bandits (Maguire 2011, p. 167). Even though the situation in the IDP camps is bad, the refugees at least have access to some aid there. To heighten the pressure on the African tribes in Darfur, the GoS thus soon started to close and attack camps in order to drive the IDPs home to their destroyed villages, knowing that they would not survive there (ICG 2004a, p. 5, 2005c, p. 8, Prunier 2005, p. 121).[3]

The Red Cross stated that the famine resulting from these deliberate actions was worse than the devastating Darfur famine of 1989 (Prunier 2005, p. 120). A UN investigation in Kaylak camp encountered a mortality rate 40–150 times higher than the threshold for emergency situations (Daly 2010, p. 285).

Between 2006 and 2010, the conflict dynamics again changed various times. In 2007/2008, fighting broke out between the GoS and the Janjaweed militias. Starting in 2008, clashes between Arab tribes over the spoils of the displacement of African tribes became the single largest cause of violent death in Sudan (AUPD 2009, p. 23). Again, the GoS allegedly played a role in fomenting the conflict in order to control the increasingly rogue Janjaweed (Flint 2010a, p. 5). In 2010, the conflict patterns of 2004 and 2005 started to re-emerge in lesser intensity as the GoS started new offensives with Janjaweed militias supported by the air force.

Currently, the conflict is characterised by renewed fighting between the GoS and the rebel groups, which recently reunited as a single military front in 2012. At the same time, Janjaweed groups are increasingly turning into insurgents, and tribal clashes between Arab tribes continue.

[3] There are some speculations that the reason the GoS started closing camps was that it feared that rebels might infiltrate them (ICG 2005c, p. 8).

The overall death toll in Darfur is disputed. In 2010, the UN assumed that 2,665,115 persons had been displaced by the conflict. The estimates for excess deaths range between 10,000 (President al-Bashir in Frost 2008b) and 450,000 (Markusen 2009, p. 95). The most reliable numbers were published by the Centre for Research on the Epidemiology of Disasters (CRED), a WHO affiliate that estimated the casualties at 158,000 including 131,000 excess deaths (Mamdani 2009c, p. 31–32). The official UN figure of conflict related deaths lies at 300,000 and has not been updated since 2010 (Sterling 2010).

4.1.2 Structural sources of the conflict

This section analyses the predominant social, economic, political and security causes of the Darfur conflict. Only if these causes are known, the impact of ICC investigations on the conflict can be fully understood.

a. Security

In terms of security, there are four factors that had an impact on the Darfur conflict. First, a number of conflicts in the region became increasingly interwoven and exacerbated each other. Second, international security issues and arms trade were among the triggers of the conflict. Third, the north–south conflict in Sudan worsened the security situation in Darfur. Finally, the general tendency of using militias in Sudanese conflicts and the accelerating collapse of state institutions had major security implications. The ICC could have some influence on these security factors, curbing illicit arms flows by isolating conflict parties and criminalising the acts of militias. For reasons analysed in the process tracing, the Court has largely failed to do so.

As an important regional player, Libya was involved in the different conflicts in Darfur for decades. During the Cold War, Kaddafi's Libya waged a proxy war against Hissène Habré's Chadian government, using Darfur as a staging ground. The influx of Libyan arms for proxies in Darfur made small arms easily available, which exacerbated the traditional conflicts between different tribes (Burr and Collins 2008, p. 238, Daly 2010, p. 3). In line with Kaddafi's ideology of Pan-Arabism, Libya even intervened in the Fur–Arab War by supporting Arab militias. The Libyan presence therefore aggravated the local conflicts already existing (Prunier 2005, p. 57).

Additionally, the Chadian civil war started to spill over into Darfur. Chadian nomads fled from the drought and the conflict to Darfur.

Fighting for survival, many nomads resorted to banditry and became a reservoir of recruitment for tribal militias (Haggar 2007, p. 119). The Sudanese region became deeply involved in Chadian power struggles. The Zaghawa, who live on both sides of the Darfur–Chad border, are involved in Darfur rebel groups while Chadians are fighting on both sides of the Darfur conflict (see Flint 2007, p. 153). Finally, the rebel groups in Darfur depended on supply lines and safe havens in Chad (ICG 2006d, p. 12, 2007a, p. 11).[4] It was only a matter of time until a feedback effect developed and the Darfur conflict started to exacerbate conflicts and worsen security in neighbouring Chad, CAR and South Sudan, creating a regional vicious circle of interconnected conflicts (ICG 2007a, p. 18, Jeong 2008, p. 126, SAS 2007).

The second international security factor is Russian and Chinese arms sales to the GoS, which contribute to upholding the steady influx of small arms that started during the Chadian and Libyan interventions. Even though China and Russia deny arms trade with Sudan, there are several sources that link Russian and Chinese arms to the conflict (AI 2012a, Cockett 2010, p. 277, DPA 2010).

A major national security factor influencing Darfur was the civil war between the north and the south. The SPLA initially supported the Darfur rebellion with arms, know-how and political expertise (ICG 2004b, p. 20, UNSC 2006a, p. 4). Even though most of the support stopped after the SPLA signed the CPA, the political support continues to this day. There were reports of intensified contacts between the SPLM and the JEM as well as the SLM-MM. JEM sources have confirmed these contacts (Abdelrahman 2010) and the group is currently involved in the South Sudanese civil war.

An important security factor is the massive use of militias that has led to large parts of the population being armed (see Mohammed 2007, p. 202). The National Congress Party (NCP) established a paramilitary group called the Popular Defence Forces (PDF) that is now intervening on the side of the Arabs in traditional land conflicts (de Waal 2005, p. 127). When the GoS later mobilised Janjaweed on a larger scale, it used existing tribal hierarchies as a chain of command for the militias. As a result, tribal militias became increasingly militarised and politicised (Abdul-Jalil et al. 2007, p. 59–60, de Waal 2007d, p. 30, Haggar 2007,

[4] The rapprochement between Sudanese president al-Bashir and Chadian president Déby between 2008 and 2010 led to a scaling back of this support, reducing the Resources of the rebels.

p. 139). The instrumentalisation of tribal militias and paramilitary forces led to a security dilemma between the tribes in Darfur. This forced all clans to join forces on a tribal level and create militias that were sufficiently big to ensure their protection (Mamdani 2009c, p. 255).

At the same time the GoS is failing to provide any security in Darfur (Flint and de Waal 2008, p. 18). Police forces failed to protect civilians and to hold the Janjaweed in check. In other cases they were even directly implicated in abuses against IDPs (HRW 2007a, p. 56). Additionally, police stations have been targeted during rebel attacks, further exacerbating the security meltdown in the region (UNSG 2004a, p. 4). Accordingly, the tendency to rely on militias has even increased with the post-Darfur Peace Agreement (DPA) violence (Fadul and Tanner 2007, p. 301). As part of the recruitment drive of militias, IDP camps in rebel-held areas and along the border have become militarised recruitment reservoirs (Kahn 2008, p. 15, Mamdani 2009c, p. 298). Aided by the easy availability of arms, the increasing use of militias has led to a general tendency to solve traditional conflicts over land and water by the gun (Ali-Dinar 2009, p. 105).

b. Political

There are several political constellations on the national, regional and local level that have facilitated the escalation of the Darfur conflict. On a national level, Darfur is politically marginalised and a victim of the ethnic divide-and-rule strategies of the GoS. The ethnic dimension of the conflict was further emphasised by international media, partly influenced by US grassroots activism through organisations such as Save Darfur. The ICC could in theory contribute to isolating the ruling elites in Sudan and further the emergence of moderates willing to end the marginalisation of Darfur. This is beyond the capacities of the ICC though, since the Court will only target those responsible for serious crimes in Darfur. The elite consensus to maintain control in Sudan is too strong to be shaken by arrest warrants issued against individuals. The relationship between the ICC and US grassroots activism is deeply problematic. As will be shown in the case study, the narrative the OTP uses in its prosecution of GoS officials aligns with the story told by US activists.

On the national level, Darfur is being politically marginalised by the centre in Khartoum. Both 'Arabs' and 'Africans' perceive this marginalisation in Darfur (Tubiana 2007, p. 80). At the same time, the ruling party is exploiting ethnicity in order to subjugate the periphery.

Neighbouring states have also supported Darfur's rebel movements on ethnic grounds.

Sudan has historically been an extremely centralised country with politically marginalised peripheries (see Johnson 2003, p. XVIII–XIX). Until 1981, there was no Darfuri in the higher ranks of the foreign or civil service of the independent Sudanese state. Not even the local administration in Darfur was left to native Darfuris (Daly 2010, p. 183 and 240, Tanner 2005, p. 13). The state is in fact run by the elites of the Arab tribes living along the confluence of the Nile Rivers. The so-called riverine tribes, about 30 per cent of the total population, rule all of Sudan (Prunier 2010, p. 124). The GoS has managed to establish shaky control over Sudan through a conscious approach of divide-and-rule in Darfur and other regions (Sharkey 2008, p. 36–37, Verhoeven et al. 2010, Ylonen 2005, p. 131). The power relations are never stable, but so far, the three central tribes have managed to stay in charge resorting to a balance of power approach. They are strong enough to maintain control, but not strong enough to pacify the country, sitting on top of a paralysed state while reaping all the benefits they can. But this approach comes at the price of general instability which is a further cause of the conflict (de Waal 2007d, p. 5, 2007e, p. 23). The combination of marginalisation and a lack of central control in the Sudanese political system have sparked rebellions and political tension in all parts of the country. The problem of political marginalisation has so far not been tackled. It has rather been covered up through some cosmetic reforms, like introducing federalism on paper in 1991.

It is broadly acknowledged that the political marginalisation of Darfur played a strong role in the genesis of the conflict (de Waal 2007d, p. 3, el Hassan 2008, p. 109, Mamdani 2009c, p. 191). The publication of the so-called *Black Book* is a good illustration of how rebels addressed this marginalisation to garner support. The book, allegedly published by JEM, contained statistical information illustrating the riverine domination of Darfur and the whole of Sudan (Abdelrahman 2010, Burr and Collins 2008, p. 290).

The political marginalisation described here affects all peripheries of Sudan, which means that the Darfur crisis is part of a bigger crisis of the Sudanese peripheries. This has led the AU High-Level Panel on Darfur (AUPD) to describe the conflict as a '*Sudanese crisis in Darfur*' (AUPD 2009, p. 3). Accordingly, the Darfur conflict is connected to other conflicts in the periphery, including the rebellion in Southern Sudan until 2005. The signing of the CPA in 2005 was a significant event for the Sudanese peripheries, particularly because the agreement was exclusive between the GoS and the SPLM. Darfur became doubly marginalised because it was excluded from the political benefits that the CPA brought the South (Elliesie 2007, p. 206). As a result, Darfuris were not only marginalised, but they increasingly felt abandoned since the SPLM was lost as a counter-weight to central Sudanese domination (Berg 2008, p. 75, de Waal 2007d, p. 3). In reaction, Darfuri rebels attempted to take action and unite with opposition forces in other marginalised parts of Sudan. The SLA, for example, signed a joint declaration with the eastern group of Beja Congress as early as 16 January 2004.

In order to maintain its domination, the GoS turns ethnic groups against each other (Idris 2005, p. 83, Nielsen 2008, p. 457). At the same time, it is following a nationalist agenda driven by the spread of Islam and Arabism (Idris 2005, p. 12, Sharkey 2008, p. 25, Ylonen 2005, p. 106). State formation and ethnicity are thus intertwined in Sudan, adding an ethnic factor to the conflicts in the country (see Idris 2005, p. 43). The situation in Darfur was interpreted in line with this Arab Islamist agenda of the centre. As a result, Darfur was never fully included into Sudan but was instead divided along ethnic lines (Ali-Dinar 2009, p. 104, de Waal 2009, p. 143, El-Tom 2009, p. 86).

Indeed, Darfur took up a key role in the struggle for the ethnic identity of the Sudanese state. The Darfur conflict broke out at a time when the NCP was still trying to impose its Arabic and Islamic model on predominantly Christian and African Southern Sudan. From the point of view of the GoS, the Darfur conflict was an alarming sign that the Muslim consensus on which the GoS based its domination was now also disintegrating in the north.[5] The GoS concluded that it had to close Arab ranks behind the regime and claimed that the Darfur rebels were 'Africans' who waged war against 'Arabs', thus further exacerbating the ethnic tensions (ICG 2004b, p. 19). The GoS started to manipulate the leaders of hostile tribes in an attempt to split them and tried to draw more Arab tribes into the conflict (ICG 2005c, p. 11).[6] The GoS then started to promote 'Arabs' to important positions in Darfur, thus triggering further resentment

[5] Sharkey describes how the conflict in Darfur challenged the linkage between Arab and Muslim identities and fortified the perception of an 'African–Arab divide' that threatened the unity of Sudan (Sharkey 2008, p. 27). Indeed, the divide ultimately led to the secession of South Sudan in 2011.

[6] To be more specific, the Arab cattle-herding Baggara living in the south have tried to stay out of the conflict, while the GoS have pressured them to join the counter-insurgency (Fadul and Tanner 2007, p. 300).

among the 'African' tribes (de Waal 2009, p. 135, el-Battahani 2009, p. 63). It even tried to further Arab influence by gerrymandering the Darfur regions to make sure that the 'African' Fur became minorities in each of the regions (Daly 2010, p. 261). Additionally, Chadian Arab migrants were given voting rights, which changed the political balance in western Darfur and alienated the 'African' Massalit tribes (Haggar 2007, p. 117, Prunier 2005, p. 75).

This resulted in a situation in which 'African' Darfuris are increasingly calling for autonomy while 'Arab' tribes are joining forces with the GoS in fear of being marginalised by an 'African majority' within Darfur (see Mamdani 2009c, p. 269). This tendency is being embodied by the Arab supremacist organisation 'Arab Gathering' that has aligned itself with the Janjaweed and Islamist elements within the NCP.[7] As a result of these developments, ethnicity and race have become essentially political identities in modern day Sudan (Idris 2005, p. 21).

Turning to international factors, US grassroots activism and the media attention surrounding the Darfur conflict have emphasised the ethnic aspects of the conflict described above. The narrative supported by these activists and much of the media describes the conflict as a government-supported Arab genocide committed against black 'African' Darfuris. The use of the genocide label has in turn led to demands for an interventions both in the media and among the activists which encourages the rebel movements to hold out for an international intervention (Hamilton and Hazlett 2007, Murphy 2007).

Libya, Chad and Eritrea have also been involved in the Darfur conflict at different points in time. At the time of writing, their role has diminished considerably and ceased to be a defining factor in the conflict. After a proxy war in 2005 and 2006, Chad and Sudan have meanwhile established a cooperative relationship.

c. Economic

The economic factors contributing to the Darfur conflict include the economic marginalisation of the region by the central government and the competition for scarce resources in Darfur, mainly for arable land and water. Additionally, a war economy that formed around armed

[7] The Arab Gathering aims at pushing back African influence in Darfur by enforcing Arab land claims and establishing an Arab domination in Darfur. Some authors have stated that there are personal connections between the Arab Gathering and the ruling NCP (el-Battahani 2009, p. 62, ICG 2007a, p. 14).

robbery, extortions and militia salaries is perpetuating the conflict. While it is difficult to fathom how the ICC could have an impact on the first two factors, the Court could play a role in undermining war economies through deterrence and improving the rule of law.

After independence, the consecutive governments of Sudan resumed the British colonial policy of spending exclusively on the central provinces while neglecting the peripheries (Cockett 2010, p. 27, Daly 2010, p. 162). The GoS also adopted the British approach of focusing spending on security, allocating the majority of its budget to the SAF and the National Intelligence and Security Services (NISS) (Cockett 2010, p. 262). Additionally, a significant share of Sudanese state revenues disappears in the patronage network of the government (Cockett 2010, p. 265).

Sudan has a history of economic exploitation of the peripheries by the centre. Foreign interests only furthered this tendency as even international development plans and IMF programmes focused on the central regions (Johnson 2003, p. XVIII–XIX, Tanner 2005, p. 13, Yongo-Bure 2009, p. 73). A diversified and industrialised economy that could have absorbed the poor rural population in arid areas and thus avoid rebellions was never developed (Yongo-Bure 2009, p. 81). The numbers impressively illustrate the extent of economic centralisation in Sudan: 50 per cent of the country's capital is concentrated in Khartoum, where 20 per cent of the population lives (de Waal 2007d, p. 8–9). The Darfur Province is suffering heavily from this economic marginalisation. It was ranked the poorest province in all of Sudan in 1967/8, 1982/3, 1999/2000 and 2011.[8] From 2000 to 2005, Darfur constantly received the smallest share of provincial funds by the GoS, and the figures were dropping further (Mamdani 2009c, p. 166 and 181–188, Radio Dabanga 2011l).

To add to the existing problems, the GoS does nothing to support the people of Darfur in coping with the consequences of economic marginalisation. It remained passive during the catastrophic famines that ravaged Darfur in 1984 and 1991; despite the fact that the famines resulted from heavy droughts and were thus predictable (see Tanner 2005, p. 13). The government even declined to accept foreign help for Darfur in order to avoid losing face (Daly 2010, p. 232 and 260–261). This economic disenfranchisement of Darfur is one of the Reasons for the conflict between the local tribes and the government.

[8] The poverty rate in the three Darfur states was at a staggering 93 per cent in 2011 (Radio Dabanga 2011l).

But economic Reasons are also having an impact on the local conflicts. Darfur's economy largely depends on herding and agriculture. Under the pressure of droughts and the advancing deserts, camel nomads from the waterless north like the Abbala and the Zaghawa started moving south towards the Jebel Marra mountain range, where water is more ample (el-Battahani 2009, p. 46, Mamdani 2009c, p. 9). As a result, conflicts over land and water developed in the 1960s. They exist until today and are fought along a north–south axis between landless nomads and settled tribes, as well as along a south–south axis between landless and land-owning cattle herders (Mamdani 2009c, p. 71). The government further exacerbated the land issue by supporting land grabs for mechanised farms that used the land intensively for a short time and left it exhausted (de Waal 2007d, p. 31).

The land factor is still playing an important role in the conflict. The resource scarcity has been exacerbated during the conflict because the SAF and the Janjaweed destroyed water holes and grazing land during their campaign. This in turn led to a massive numbers of livestock perishing and affected the economic outlook of the region (ICG 2005a, p. 2).[9]

Additionally, Arab groups and Janjaweed have started to occupy the empty land of displaced African settlers (HRW 2006a, p. 7, Tanner 2005, p. 28, Weber 2008, p. 148). By the end of 2006, there were reports of infighting between Arab tribes for the land left by the fleeing IDPs (Mozersky 2009, p. 165). The potential land claims of those displaced hold in store future conflict potentials for Darfur (Kahn 2008, p. 28, Tubiana 2007, p. 87). Fighting for land is an important economic motor of the conflict as gaining land rights implies the control of the resources (water, pastures) (Flint 2010a, p. 11). Both nomads and settlers see the current tribal conflicts as a struggle for survival (Tanner and Tubiana 2007, p. 14), which leads to a high Resolve on both sides.

Finally, the conflict disrupted Darfur's markets and trade system, which is vital for the local economy. At the same time, a war economy based on banditry, taxation, trade with stolen goods and extortion has emerged (Buchanan-Smith and Jaspars 2007, p. 57 and 60). Additionally, many poor Arab communities are joining the conflict on the side of the Janjaweed to get access to government support and militia salaries as a way to cope with the economic recession (Young et al. 2009). A reservoir

[9] During the first conflict year, the livelihoods of over one million people were destroyed (Buchanan-Smith and Jaspars 2007, p. 61).

of young fighters whose allegiance lies with money has emerged in the wake of the war economy (Flint 2010a, p. 29, Giroux et al. 2009, p. 13).

d. Social

Social factors in the emergence of the conflict include the legacy of ethnic and tribal tensions in Darfur, tensions triggered by the influx of migrants from Chad, the breaking down of traditional conflict resolution mechanisms and the lack of social services and schooling in Darfur. In the scope of reconciliation mechanisms, the Court could have an impact on alleviating the ethnic divides in Darfur. Individualising guilt and thus countering stereotypes would be an especially valuable contribution. As the case study shows, the investigations led to quite the contrary result because the OTP decided to adopt a narrative of genocide (see Section 4.2.2).

The Darfur conflict is often simplistically described as one between ethnic Arabs and Africans, while the Arabs are wrongly believed to be settlers and 'newcomers' in Darfur (Mamdani 2009c, p. 90 and 100). Therefore, it is important to emphasise that the Arabs of Darfur are also marginalised on a national level (Elliesie 2007, p. 200, Mamdani 2009c, p. 14, Mohammed 2007, p. 208). In fact ethnic differences between Africans and Arabs are difficult to trace in Darfur, as Arabs have acquired African physical features over the course of time (Daly 2010, p. 11–12). The long history of migration and generations of intermarriage in Darfur underline the artificial nature of ethnic division (see Idris 2005, p. 80–81, Prunier 2005, p. 6, Tanner 2005, p. 9). The fact that many Africans speak Arabic and have adopted an Arab culture and lifestyle further blurs the perceived differences (El-Tom 2009, p. 85). Even for experts the split between the local tribes is difficult to understand. It seems that there are some hardline elements who emphasise the ethnic fault-lines while the population is not as such split between 'Arabs' and 'Africans' (Expert Interview 2011h, ICG 2005g, p. 15).

Despite the absence of any clear ethnic indicators, people are being mobilised along ethnic lines and their identities have become increasingly racialised (Hassan and Ray 2009, p. 18, Idris 2005, p. 80–81). Broad alliances with 'Arab' and 'African' umbrella identities were formed when the conflict escalated in 2003 (Mamdani 2009c, p. 249). Even subtle differences like hues of skin colours became racially charged and groups that had been living together over generations were pitted against each other. At the same time, Arabs were described as being mainly pastoralists and Africans as being mainly sedentary. These simplifications were enforced by media reports and Western civil society groups focusing on the ethnic character of the conflict; at times, even demonising the Arab side (de-Waal 2009, p. 137, Hassan 2009, p. 162, Mamdani 2009a, p. 150).[10] Yet, the GoS is only supported by landless Abbala nomads in the north and some small tribes in the south. The settled Arab Baggara majority stayed neutral in the conflict since they already had land to settle on (Mamdani 2009c, p. 255).

While the tribal and ethnic tensions were increasing, the custom of living together was ignored and the social fabric started to disintegrate (Ali-Dinar 2009, p. 105, AUPD 2009, p. 27, Mamdani 2009c, p. 236–245). Traditional conflict resolution methods broke down due to the ethnic polarisation and the increasing use of violence. As a result, the tribal conflicts spiralled out of control. At the same time tribal leaders lost control of their youths who became increasingly prone to engage in looting and robbery (Flint 2009, p. 48–49).

Finally, Darfur is struggling with a number of social problems that add to the grievances of the local population. The health service and educational opportunities in Darfur are much worse than in the centre (Yongo-Bure 2009, p. 71–72). The figures concerning the schooling system illustrate this social marginalisation well. Shortly after independence, only 0.2 per cent of Darfuri boys attended an intermediate school, the lowest figure for all of Sudan (Daly 2010, p. 179). Due to the conflict, the schooling situation is again extremely bad in Darfur. Students in camps in northern Darfur share one classroom for 120 students and 1 textbook per 17 students (Radio Dabanga 2010l), in southern Darfur, 75 per cent of children are out of school (Radio Dabanga 2011l) and the illiteracy rate in western Darfur reached 45 per cent in May 2011, according to state officials (Radio Dabanga 2011o). At the same time, children are being affected psychologically by the conflict: 75 per cent of the children in Chadian refugee camps show signs of post-traumatic stress disorder (Radio Dabanga 2011a). The social marginalisation described here is repeatedly mentioned by IDPs as an important issue. It is seen as a conscious government policy

[10] Both African and Western media have bought into the ethnic polarisation of the conflict as Catherine Ray has demonstrated in an excellent article. Her citation of the Nigerian newspaper *This Day* is a telling example: '*It is bad enough that the black nations have not done anything to defend their people in Sudan but that we should be locked in a cozy embrace with these Arabs who have turned our people into hunting game is soul destroying.*' (Ray 2009, p. 179)

and thus adds to the grievances fuelling the conflict (see Hagan and Rymond-Richmond 2009, p. 5).

4.1.3 Conflict actors

This section will introduce and analyse the actors involved in the Darfur conflict and offer a brief analysis of their three Rs.

a. The Government of Sudan and the National Congress Party

Since the Islamist coup in 1989, Sudan has been ruled by a single party. The top personnel of the NCP and the GoS are identical until this day. Among its leaders during the coup were Omar al-Bashir, the current president of Sudan who has been targeted by an ICC arrest warrant, and Hassan al-Turabi, the ideological leader of the party. The NCP split in 1999 when Hassan al-Turabi was removed from the government and founded the Popular Congress Party (PCP).

Today's NCP is a very opaque organisation that is hard to assess. On the one hand, the NCP is described as a very disciplined party in which there are usually no arguments in public (Natsios 2010, at 14 minutes, Expert Interview 2011a). On the other hand, more and more authors are claiming that there are infighting and confusion in the GoS – partly connected to the Darfur issue (ICG 2004d, p. 8–9, Jaeger 2011, Prunier 2005, p. 109). Alex de Waal has convincingly shown that there has been a struggle between competing power centres during the entire history of the NCP (de Waal 2007e, p. 10). Yet, the party has always been united enough to avoid losing power to actors outside the NCP.

The exact role of President al-Bashir within the NCP is also disputed. Some say he is a mere figurehead for those who hold the real power (de Waal and Stanton 2009, p. 347, Expert Interview 2011h, Jaeger 2011), others say that the inner circle of the NCP and the GoS is fiercely loyal to al-Bashir and that he is the undisputed leader (Expert Interview 2011a).

The Reasons of the NCP and the GoS to fight the Darfur conflict are clear: they want to end the conflict without conceding significantly or undermining their dominance in the province (see ICG 2005g, p. 10). Experts have pointed out that the Darfur conflict will decide whether the power basis of the GoS is broad enough to ensure the dominant position of the centre (Mamdani 2009c, p. 297, Prunier 2005, p. 165). Because of the alleged connections between the JEM and al-Turabi's PCP the Darfur conflict goes right to the heart of elite competition in Khartoum.

Concessions over Darfur could be exploited by the enemies of the NCP in the centre; therefore, the Resolve of the GoS to fight the conflict out to its bitter end is high.

So far the GoS has consistently followed three main strategies in tackling the Darfur conflict. First, it has been trying to keep the conflict as quiet as possible, trying to stop any information flow to its own citizens and the international community. Second, it has so far focused on dividing and crushing the rebel movements through a brutal counter-insurgency involving attacks on civilians and attempts to buy-off rebel groups. Third, it has tried to minimise and delay any significant international involvement.

The attempts to keep the conflict quiet can be traced from its early stages. The government consistently called the rebels in Darfur 'armed bandits' and downplayed the situation as a tribal conflict (Prunier 2005, p. 91). The bad humanitarian situation was blamed on the insecurity caused by rebel attacks, while the marginalisation of Darfur was denied outright (e.g. Sudanese Embassy in the US 2004). Even during the conflict, al-Bashir said during an al-Jazeera interview that 90 per cent of Darfuris are leading a normal life and claimed that the region was better off than many others in Africa (Frost 2008b). This strategy of hiding the conflict was accompanied by media crackdowns within Sudan (Cockett 2010, p. 246, ICG 2004b, p. 15). As a part of this strategy, the GoS has also regularly accused Western press of leading a media campaign over Darfur and exaggerating the conflict (Hoile 2006, p. 128–152, IRIN 2003).

The GoS approach to crush the rebellion through violence and manipulation is in line with its approaches to conflicts in other regions of Sudan. Observers say that the hardliners within the NCP are used to solving conflicts mainly through the use of force (Expert Interview 2011a), which makes other alternatives less attractive and bolsters Resolve. At the same time, the GoS is actively trying to divide the Darfur rebel groups in order to weaken them. It has so far focused its efforts on exploiting the rift between the Fur and Zaghawa, especially within the SLA (ICG 2005g, p. 11). Internationally, the GoS is trying to delegitimize the rebels as Islamists or robbers, labelling them as 'Tora Bora'[11] in official press releases (Hagan and Rymond-Richmond 2009, p. 205). Additionally, the

[11] Tora Bora is the Afghan mountain range where Bin Laden and the Taliban fought their last battle before retreating to Pakistan. The term suggests that Darfur rebels are Islamists and terrorists.

NCP is describing the Darfur conflict as a coup attempt of Hassan al-Turabi, whom they paint as an Islamist and friend of Osama bin-Laden, thus trying to delegitimize the rebellion by suggesting al-Qaeda connections (Hoile 2006, p. 8–9).[12]

The GoS attempts to block any serious international interventions constitute a consistent trend that emerged during the LexisNexis analysis. The GoS tries to limit Western involvement to humanitarian aid in order to avoid an intervention and to appease international public opinion (ICG 2007a, p. 6, Prunier 2005, p. 130). Only after significant pressure did the GoS accept AU peacekeepers, and only in order to avoid the deployment of UN peacekeepers from Western nations. At the same, time, the GoS is consistently claiming that it is interested in solving the conflict peacefully and is determined to honour ceasefire agreements. The GoS is constantly buying time and delaying international actions through verbal cooperation. At the same time the government is completely rejecting any international intervention in Darfur in order to make sure that international involvement stays minimal if it has to compromise eventually. This can be illustrated by the deployment of a hybrid AU/UN mission to Darfur. The GoS resisted a UN deployment as long as necessary to achieve a compromise which led to the deployment of a mixed UN/AU force with a favourable mandate and composition. The GoS has also been consistently hindering the work of the peacekeepers (ICG 2006d, p. 16). Even though the GoS has so far managed to dodge a lot of the international pressure, the party's Resources are suffering to some extent from international isolation and economic sanctions.

b. The Janjaweed militias and the Arab tribes

The GoS decided to use Janjaweed militias in Darfur because the police and army proved ineffective in combating the rebellion (ICG 2004a, p. 8). The GoS also didn't fully trust the army because the army had many Darfuris in its ranks (Kastner 2007, p. 157, Prunier 2006, p. 196).[13] The

[12] The European Sudanese Public Affairs Council that published Hoile's paper is a London-based organization financed by the GoS. Sudanese Embassies have published reports by the institution on their homepages. Its publications promote the GoS view of the conflict and are thus used here as a source to show how the GoS tries to spin the perception of the conflict in the West.

[13] Apart from relying on tribal militias, the limited trustworthiness of the army apparently also made the use of mercenaries necessary. According to the former US Envoy to Sudan, Andrew Natsios, some bomber pilots involved in the bombing runs in Darfur were hired Egyptian officers or foreign mercenaries as Darfuri pilots refused to board planes (Natsios 2010).

use of militias was also seen as useful to cover the conflict behind a veil of tribal clashes and to avoid the loss of legitimacy connected to the brutal repression of civilians (Flint and de Waal 2008, p. 56, Johnson 2003, p. 141, Schlichte 2009, p. 258).

The composition and structure of the Janjaweed are not entirely clear. The term refers to a number of different militias without central command (el-Battahani 2009, p. 66). Estimates during the early phases of the conflict identified about 10,000–15,000 active Janjaweed (Tanner 2005, p. 19). It is clear that some of them enjoy GoS support, an important factor of Janjaweed Resources.

Each Darfur state has one official Janjaweed group and some unofficial ones (ICG 2004a, p. 8). The official Janjaweed groups are provided with a salary, uniforms and weaponry by the GoS (Prunier 2005, p. 97–98).[14] While some claim that the Janjaweed come mainly from Arab tribes in Darfur (ICG 2004b, p. 16, Tubiana 2007, p. 73), others say that they have a considerable number of foreigners from Mali, Mauritania, CAR, Cameroon and especially Chad in their ranks (Abdelrahman 2010, Brosché 2008, p. 76, Mamdani 2009c, p. 256). The native Darfuris recruited for the Janjaweed are mainly bandits, criminals pardoned for joining the Janjaweed, demobilised soldiers, young Arabs involved in land conflicts with African tribes, Arab supremacists and young unemployed (ICG 2004a, p. 8, 2005c, p. 8, Prunier 2005, p. 97–98). The main motivations of the Janjaweed are looting, ideological motivations and GoS promises of land rights (Cockett 2010, p. 296, ICG 2004a, p. 8, Tubiana 2007, p. 73). These factors explain the Resolve of the Janjaweed. When fighting for vital land, it can be expected that Resolve is especially high, as the alternative would be misery and starvation. Another important Reason to fight for the pastoralist Arab tribes is to preserve their nomad way of life that is under increasing pressure due to droughts and conflicts (Flint 2010a, p. 7–8). Regardless of the Janjaweed's motivations, it is pretty clear that the GoS exploited their economic and social marginalisation and raised fears of African rebel groups to mobilise them (Flint 2009, p. 11 and 23, see Tanner 2005, p. 20). These fears were backed by African rebel

[14] Some authors deny the existence of such a close link between the GoS and the Janjaweed. They say that the Janjaweed are bandits with changing allegiances who have temporarily aligned themselves with the GoS (Mamdani 2009c, p. 258, Weber 2008, p. 147). The nature of the support that the Janjaweed receive from the GoS is not entirely clear as the GoS denies ties to them. There are reports that the Janjaweed do not in fact receive salaries but have the permission to loot (ICG 2004b, p. 16).

attacks on Arab villages and herds, especially by the SLM-MM, that have seldom been reported in Western media or acknowledged by international observers (Flint 2009, p. 24 and 28).

There are no reasonable doubts that the GoS and the Janjaweed are cooperating in military attacks on villages of African settlers. According to International Crisis Group (ICG) figures, the Janjaweed were responsible for 75 per cent of all verified killings in the Darfur conflict until 2005 (ICG 2005a, p. 4). Yet, the GoS has constantly denied any direct links to the Janjaweed. Several high-ranking officials within the GoS have called them armed bandits or disorganised robbers (Frost 2008a, 2008b). Yet, the connections between Janjaweed and the GoS, including the chain of command, have been sufficiently proven.[15]

The GoS tried to distance itself from the Janjaweed under mounting pressure in 2004, but without losing them as a proxy. The government therefore started distinguishing between legitimate self-defence forces and 'criminal elements', arresting some petty criminals to underline their efforts to stop Janjaweed atrocities (Frost 2008a, ICG 2004a, p. 8–9). Additionally, the GoS started the integration of Janjaweed into the PDF, the Border Intelligence Units and the Central Reserve Police (Riot Police) to cover up the use of militias (ICG 2006a, p. 5, Prunier 2005, p. 115, Totten 2009, p. 190). There are estimates that up to 50 per cent of the Janjaweed were integrated into regular forces by June 2006 (ICG 2006a, p. 5), and some authors claim that the security institutions and the Janjaweed in Darfur had become virtually indistinguishable by the end of 2006 (Fadul and Tanner 2007, p. 295, Haggar 2007, p. 139). At the time of writing, the GoS has started to organise additional militias in the so-called Rapid Support Force (RSF). This strategy of deception shows that the GoS is unwilling to disarm the Janjaweed and stop the use of armed miltias.

Yet, rifts are emerging between the GoS and the Arab tribes. The Janjaweed are not sure about the ongoing support of the GoS, which

[15] There are documents proving that the SAF received orders not to intervene in Janjaweed atrocities (ICG 2004a, p. 9). Additionally, the Janjaweed leader Musa Hilal has said in an interview that the government told him to mobilise Arab tribesmen for the conflict (HRW 2005c). Former Presidential Advisor Salah Gosh admitted in an interview with Reuters that the GoS is bombing villages and integrating Janjaweed into the PDF (Cockett 2010, p. 241–242). Finally, the supposed main contact persons of the Janjaweed within the SAF, the generals Abdalla Ali Safi al Nur and Hussein Abdalla Jibril, have been identified (Tubiana 2007 p. 76). Human Rights Watch has documented SAF support during Janjaweed attacks in Darfur and in eastern Chad (HRW 2004, p. 30, 2005a, 2006a, p. 12).

affects their Resources. Additionally, they have not profited from the attacks to the extent that the GoS promised, which affects their Resolve. From the beginning, land-owning Rizeigat tribes rejected being recruited as the Resolve to fight in order to gain land was lacking (Tanner 2005, p. 22). The tribes avoiding to get drawn into the conflict were even attacked and displaced by Janjaweed in an attempt to coerce them into cooperation (Flint 2009, p. 20 and 26, ICG 2004a, p. 14). As a result, some Misseriya and Rizeigat Arabs have been fighting with rebels since the early phases of the conflict (ICG 2004a, p. 3). In August 2004, first rumours emerged that the Janjaweed might also be considering switching sides (ICG 2004a, p. 14). The Janjaweed – and indeed all Arab Darfuris – were further alienated when they were not being consulted at all during the DPA negotiations (Fadul and Tanner 2007, p. 291 and 296, Mamdani 2009c, p. 266).[16] While the rebels initially failed to formulate their agenda broadly enough to include Arab tribes, they have increasingly come to see the Arab tribes as another victim of GoS policy (Fadul and Tanner 2007, p. 294). As a result, some Arab tribes are signing treaties of cooperation with the rebels and have even started to establish their own rebel groups (ICG 2005c, p. 12, Mamdani 2009c, p. 266, Radio Dabanga 2010k, Weber 2008, p. 149).[17] Even hardline Arab leader Musa Hilal reportedly regrets the attacks he commanded on African tribes and blames the government for manipulating him, according to Wikileaks cables (Radio Dabanga 2011p). Reports of Arab groups fighting the GoS are starting to multiply. Several Arab fighters from Kordofan and Darfur were reportedly involved in JEM's May 2008 attack on Khartoum's twin city Ombdurman (El-faki 2010). Several incidents illustrate the increasing connections between Darfuri Arabs and the rebel forces. In May 2010, a number of Arab Gimr tribesmen were arrested by Sudanese military intelligence for allegedly supporting JEM (Radio Dabanga 2010a). There are also reports that the number of Arab rebels in the ranks of JEM are on the rise (Flint 2010a, p. 8).

The GoS on its part also has problems with its Janjaweed allies. On the one hand, they try to distance themselves from the Janjaweed due to Western pressure; on the other hand, they are pleased with Janjaweed

[16] The fact that Minawi, whom most of Darfur's Arabs hated, got a high ranking position for signing the DPA furthered this alienation (Flint 2009, p. 30).

[17] SLA-AW, for example, signed treaties with Baggara Rizeigat and Abbala Rizeigat around Jebel Marra after the Abuja talks. Some of them later spontaneously joined the SLA's forces (Tanner and Tubiana 2007, p. 62).

successes and fear a backlash if they decided to try to rein them in (ICG 2005c, p. 8). Reportedly, the government is also afraid to move against Janjaweed for fear that they could provide information to the ICC (ICG 2005g, p. 11). Yet, internal government reports and documents indicate that the Janjaweed organised in the PDF and the border guards are increasingly seen as security threats in Darfur (Radio Dabanga 2010j).[18] A recent government report confirms that some of the groups have become insurgents themselves (Flint 2009, p. 11). In private, GoS officials admit that they can control most of the Janjaweed only temporarily by offering more money and weapons (Flint 2009, p. 13). The complicated relationship between the GoS and the local Arab tribes proves how complex the conflict in Darfur is, and it clearly illustrates that the conflict belies simplistic 'Africans vs. Arabs' descriptions that are often published in Western media.

c. The Darfur rebel groups

The various rebel movements of Darfur are described in the literature as bottom-up movements founded mainly by young graduates and school dropouts (ICG 2004b, p. 19, Prunier 2005, p. 94–95). Their Reason to fight is to counter the marginalisation of Darfur (de Waal 2005, p. 128, ICG 2004d, p. 10).[19] While the rebels are inexperienced, they have no trouble in recruiting large numbers of fighters due to the atrocious counter-insurgency of the GoS, which boosts both Reasons and Resolve of potential recruits (ICG 2004d, p. 9). A general problem of the rebel groups is their splintering into ever smaller factions due to tribal and generational rifts, splits between intellectuals and field commanders, as well as GoS manipulation (Daly 2010, p. 281, Tanner and Tubiana 2007, p. 29). Additionally, the rebel groups are plagued by increasing warlordism, and the fact that many leaders put their personal agendas before the needs of the Darfuri population (ICG 2005g, p. 17). The assessment of their military capabilities (Resources) varies. Alan Kuperman claims that the rebellion does not stand a chance as the GoS/Janjaweed alliance is just too strong (Kuperman 2009, p. 289–290), while the former US Envoy for

18 For example, an official document from a government committee investigating a PDF raid on livestock concluded that the PDF did not obey orders of state authorities and should be brought back under the control of the GoS (AI 2012a, p. 12).

19 Their demands include an end to marginalisation, an equitable distribution of wealth and power, the unity of Sudan, rule of law, positive discrimination for Darfuris and compensation for damages (Toga 2007, p. 225).

Sudan, Andrew Natsios, claims that the JEM nearly toppled the GoS in its May 2008 attack on Omdurman (Natsios 2010).

The two main rebel movements are the Sudan Liberation Movement/Army (SLM/A) and the Justice and Equality Movement (JEM). Both groups have splintered into a number of smaller factions. Additionally, some smaller groups have been founded in the course of the conflict. Different factions of the rebel groups have also formed alliances and umbrella groups at several points during the conflict. Most of these alliances fell apart after a short time. At the time of writing, it seems that the rebel groups have been able to establish a durable alliance. They have united with northern splinters of the SPLA (SPLA-N) and with opposition groups in eastern Sudan, forming the Sudan Revolutionary Front (SRF). The most important groups will be briefly introduced here.

The JEM is a Zaghawa dominated rebel group that is often said to be close to Hassan al-Turabi and his Islamist ideology. The Zaghawa were long seen as loyal to Khartoum and some were even part of the Arab Gathering until the split of the NCP (Burr and Collins 2008, p. 289, Mamdani 2009c, p. 250). Accordingly, some JEM members had served in the Turabi wing of the NCP before the split (Flint 2007, p. 161, Salih 2005, p. 17).[20] As a result, the organisation is more politically mature and more apt at communicating its aims than other rebel movements (Tanner and Tubiana 2007, p. 31).

In contrast to many other rebel groups in Darfur, the JEM has an Islamist orientation and a national agenda. Its objective is to take power in Khartoum (Prunier 2005, p. 122). To this day, the JEM has a support basis in Kordofan and strong ties and a military presence in eastern Sudan (ICG 2005g, p. 6, 2006a, p. 12).

While the group was relatively small in the beginning, comprising 100 fighters in March 2003 (Tanner and Tubiana 2007, p. 31), its other Resources are ample. It has been supported by Chadian president Déby at various points during the conflict until late 2009 (Flint 2010b, p. 15, Mamdani 2009c, p. 226). Other supporters include Kaddafi's Libya and Eritrea (Flint and de Waal 2008, p. 115). Even though JEM leaders consistently deny it, many reports have also claimed ongoing support of the group by al-Turabi's PCP (Flint and de Waal 2008, p. 109, ICG

[20] JEM leader Khalil Ibrahim was reportedly an ally of the GoS during the anti-insurgency campaign in Southern Sudan where he led Arab militias against the SPLA (Mamdani 2009c, p. 70 and 251). A short list of important JEM members who had roles in the NIF can be found in (Tanner and Tubiana 2007, p. 32–33).

2005g, p. 6, Natsios 2010).[21] These sources of external support have boosted the importance of the group and the JEM became the most important and strongest group on the ground after 2009 (AUPD 2009, p. 41, Flint 2009, p. 13),[22] especially since substantial numbers of Arabs and ex-Janjaweed started to join it in 2006 (Flint 2010a, p. 8). At the time of writing, the strength of JEM is unclear. Their commander-in-chief Khalil Ibrahim was killed during a GoS air raid on Christmas 2012, and it remains to be seen if the JEM can recover from this important loss.

Even though JEM is better organised than other groups and has a relatively strong central command, it has also faced defections and splintering (ICG 2007a, p. 23). In 2004, the National Movement for Reform and Development (NMRD) split off and started individual negotiations with the GoS. Another faction, the JEM Wing for Peace split off after the Abuja talks (Weber 2008, p. 148). In October 2007, the JEM-Collective Leadership faction split off (Orchard 2009, p. 30). The rebel movement has the clearest national agenda and was the first to demand the national restructuring of Sudan (ICG 2007a, p. 1, Tanner and Tubiana 2007, p. 35). These demands have since gained importance on the agenda of all groups. While the JEM first mainly criticised the marginalisation of Darfur, it soon started to demand a regime change and some rebel officials have even declared that they are now fighting for an independent Darfur.[23] JEM has associated itself with the SRF at the time of writing.

The SLA was the second rebel movement at the side of JEM at the outbreak of the Darfur conflict. In terms of agenda and ideology, it is close to the African secularism of the SPLM, demanding a separation of religion and state and the introduction of a federal system in Sudan (ICG 2004a, p. 11). The movement was founded by the Fur Abdel Wahid al Nur in 2001 (Flint 2007, p. 141). The initial core of the movement was formed of existing Fur militias (ICG 2005g, p. 2, Prunier 2005, p. 93). Contrary to the JEM, they strongly focus on the marginalisation of

[21] The GoS is using these connections between the JEM and the PCP in order to delegitimize the rebellion as a hardline Islamist coup (see El-Tom 2009, p. 100).

[22] Reportedly, Nafie Ali Nafie, in charge of the Darfur dossier since September 2007, told UN officials that the JEM was more powerful than the SAF in 2009 (Flint 2009, p. 46). It reportedly had up to 3,000 fighters and 200 off-road vehicles in 2006 (Tanner and Tubiana 2007, p. 52).

[23] The demands for independence have been voiced by individuals belonging to JEM. It is not clear how far this is the official line of the rebels. The author's JEM contact maintained that the main aim was to reform the Sudanese state to achieve equal regional representation (Abdelrahman 2010).

Darfur and do not strive for central power (Marchal 2007, p. 195, Prunier 2005, p. 122). The SLA originally unified elements of the Fur, Massalit and Zaghawa tribes. Its strength peaked in 2005 when it reportedly had 11,000 men under arms (Flint and de Waal 2008, p. 85). The heterogeneity of the rebel group, traditional rifts between the Zaghawa and the other tribes as well as the divide-and-rule policy of the GoS led to a fast splintering of the SLA.

During the DPA negotiations in Abuja the split between the Zaghawa faction led by Minnie Minawi and the Fur faction led by al Nur deepened. The personal power struggle between al Nur and Minawi further contributed to the split (Flint 2007, p. 141). In the end, the SLA was represented by two different delegations at the Abuja talks. When the Minawi led delegation became the only rebel group to sign the agreement, the split into SLM-AW (Abdel Wahid) and SLM-MM (Minnie Minawi) was final.

Due to disagreements within the SLM-AW as to whether the DPA should be signed, the SLA-AW wing split further into the followers of Abdel Wahid and Abdel Shafi (SLA-AS) (Flint 2007, p. 166). Additionally, the SLM-Free Will faction split off at Abuja (Weber 2008, p. 148). In early 2006, another nineteen field commanders split from SLA-AW and formed the SLA-G19, which later became the SLA-Unity (Flint 2007, p. 168–169). At the end of this rapid disintegration, the SLA had broken into more than a half-dozen movements (Flint and de Waal 2008, p. 96).

International observers considered the SLM-MM to be the strongest movement on the ground during the DPA negotiations and thus an important partner to ensure peace in Darfur. Despite his bad human rights record, Minawi was thus supported internationally and even received by US president Bush after signing the DPA. Minawi received a position in the GoS and started to team up with the Janjaweed and the SAF, looting IDP camps and attacking other rebel factions (Flint 2007, p. 170–171). The cooperation between the SLM-MM and GoS forces was so close that the ICG described the SLA-MM as a paramilitary wing of the SAF after the DPA signature (ICG 2006b, p. 1). SLA-MM increasingly lost credibility in its northern Darfur stronghold due to its cooperation with the GoS and because it committed atrocities and arrested DPA critics (ICG 2006a, p. 11, Orchard 2009, p. 27). There are also some reports stating that the SLA-MM lost a lot of its military capacity as commanders started to defect after the DPA signature (Orchard 2009, p. 29). In early 2011, Minni Minawi re-joined the rebellion against the

GoS, blaming the government for not implementing the DPA. At the time of writing, both major SLA factions are united in the SRF.

The SLA-AW did not fare much better than its sister movement after the DPA signature. The SLA-AW support base and its military capacity narrowed down considerably with the DPA fracturing (Brosché 2008, p. 25, ICG 2006a, p. 11). The SLA-AW is now mainly representing IDP and refugee interests (Brosché 2008, p. 25, Kahn 2008, p. 24).[24] It has so far consistently rejected any negotiations since Abuja, hinting at a strong Resolve.

There are a number of smaller rebel groups that should be mentioned because they mainly draw their support from Arab tribes. These groups include the Popular Forces Army (PFA), an Arab rebel group that split away from the Janjaweed (Mamdani 2009c, p. 266) and the Revolutionary Forces Front. Both have unionist agendas and demand a federal organisation of Sudan (Elliesie 2007, p. 204).

A final rebel group that has gained some importance recently despite fielding only limited military capabilities is the Liberation and Justice Movement (LJM). It is a re-merger of various SLM factions led by Tigani Sese, a former Darfur governor (Baldo 2010, p. 6). For almost two years, it was the only rebel faction negotiating with the GoS in Doha. LJM finally signed an agreement with the GoS in July 2011. The LJM military commanders led by Ali Karbino have meanwhile joined the SRF. The Doha Agreement has thus largely failed to stop hostilities on the ground, much like the DPA in 2005.

4.1.4 Conflict dynamics

Analysing the dynamics of the conflict independently from the ICC investigations provides a counter-factual scenario of how the conflict can be expected to develop in the absence of any external influences. This facilitates the assessment of the ICC impact on the conflict by providing possibilities of comparison.

Clearly, the Darfur conflict has a strong influence on how Sudan will look in the future. Since South Sudan seceded, it has become even more improbable that the GoS will be ready for concessions concerning its domination over the rest of Sudan. Indeed, the facts seem to suggest that the GoS is sticking to its military approach in solving conflicts with its

[24] A 37 per cent relative majority of Darfuri refugees living in camps in Chad names the SLA-AW as the actor that best represents their interest (Darfurian Voices Project 2010, p. 22).

peripheries (ICG 2011b). The pressure to find a negotiated solution in Darfur has lessened since the demographic balance of the region has changed in favour of Arab tribes, as many thousands of 'Africans' have been killed and millions have been displaced during the conflict. This further strengthens the NCP's Resolve to fight the problem out.

At the same time, the unwillingness of the GoS to offer concessions is pushing Darfur further away from Khartoum. The lack of compromise has strengthened the Resolve of radical minorities calling for secession in all of Sudan's regions (Flint 2009, p. 48, Jaeger 2011). The future of South Sudan also remains hazy. While a new north–south war over disputed border provinces like Abyei and oil revenues was a distinct possibility during 2012 and 2013, South Sudan has meanwhile descended into civil war. Some of the Darfur rebel groups are active in the South Sudanese civil war and the Darfur conflict is increasingly merging with new conflicts along the border between Sudan and South Sudan. Northern splinters of the SPLM/A have risen in rebellion in Blue Nile State, Southern Kordofan and Abyei because they found themselves on the 'wrong' side of the border after the secession. The SPLM-N is now leading a coalition of Sudanese rebel movements called the Sudanese Revolutionary Front (SRF). Both major SLA splinters are members of the front, and the JEM is openly cooperating with the SRF. If hostilities between Sudan and South Sudan were to break out, these conflicts would soon merge and create a veritable quagmire of intractable conflicts in the region.

During 2011, the military escalation of the Darfur conflict has accelerated again, while the focus areas of the conflict have moved from the western areas of Darfur to the eastern parts (AI 2012a, p. 7). The rebel movements are uniting, while Arab scepticism of the GoS in the region is on the rise (see Mamdani 2009c, p. 267). Infighting between Arab tribes is also ongoing, dividing the main supporters of the GoS in the region, and banditry among former Janjaweed is increasing (Flint 2009, p. 48–49). All these factors point towards a protracted conflict in Darfur, including the possibility of an escalation in a new regional conflict if the South Sudan civil war spills over the border. The loss of South Sudan has put al-Bashir and his NCP supporters under a lot of pressure. Additionally, demonstrations started to flare up across Sudan in May 2011 and lasted most of 2011. The president is reacting by recruiting more and more tribal kin into key positions within the GoS (see Section 5.2.5c). He cannot afford a further erosion of power by conceding too much in negotiations over Darfur and the Resolve to fight is accordingly high.

The fact that the rebels are uniting again in the field also points toward renewed Resolve among the insurgents to fight the conflict until the bitter end.

As Mahmood Mamdani has pointed out, the Reasons of the rebel groups need to be addressed through a regional negotiated peace, a reform of the Sudanese power structure and a comprehensive land reform in Darfur in order to bring peace to Sudan (Mamdani 2009c, p. 16). Under the circumstances described above, it is improbable that the parties will arrive at a negotiated compromise tackling these issues. Indeed, the Doha Agreement signed in July 2011 left most of these issues unaddressed. New negotiations have become even less likely as the states in the region agreed to designate SLM and JEM as hostile rebel groups during a 15 December 2011 meeting of the Great Lakes regional group.

The most probable scenario for Darfur thus remains a military stalemate on the ground without comprehensive negotiations and with a distinct risk of a regional escalation if the conflict spills over to other marginalised regions or merges with a conflict along the border of South Sudan or the South Sudanese civil war.

4.2 The ICC in Darfur

The conflict in Darfur cannot be solved through criminal justice. It is a typical amnesty case.

(Expert Interview 2011a)

Against the background of the conflict analysis, an in-depth tracing of the causal mechanisms introduced in Chapter 3 will be conducted in this section. If the causal mechanisms do not fit the case for obvious reasons, an attempt to analyse them in detail is not undertaken. The Darfur case study largely relies on newspaper reports.

4.2.1 *Facilitating the emergence of the rule of law*

Today, Darfur is a lawless place, most of it beyond the control of either government or rebels, in which one third of the population is displaced and largely dependent on one of the world's largest humanitarian operations.

(de Waal and Stanton 2009, p. 331)

As shown in the conflict analysis, rule of law deficiencies are among the root causes of the Darfur conflict. One of the most striking examples is the grey area of land use, in which traditional land rights and legal regulations co-exist and conflict. The legal uncertainties contributed to sparking the conflicts over land (see Mohammed 2007, p. 211, Tubiana 2007, p. 113). Additionally, locals have described anarchy as the main problem in Darfur, thus raising rule of law issues (Fadul and Tanner 2007, p. 295). As the conflict dragged on, the rule of law became ever more tenuous. Increasing banditry committed by Janjaweed and splintering rebel groups, inter-tribal feuds, attacks on humanitarian staff and UNAMID troops and human rights violations of state and para-state actors were the most telling symptoms. By April 2007, the ICG spoke of a '*near total disruption of the rule of law*' (ICG 2007a, p. 27). According to Tanner, the police and the judiciary have been neglected and have become corrupted by the GoS in a longstanding process (Tanner 2005, p. 13). Ethical considerations were quickly left behind, together with restrictions of conventional warfare when the conflict spiralled out of control (de Waal 2007d, p. 33). Against this background, the ICC investigations could have a real impact on the conflict if they were able to support or encourage the re-building of the rule of law. The following sections will analyse whether the ICC has had an impact on the rule of law in Darfur.

a. Furthering the respect for laws and human rights

> *Of course there were crimes, even horrible crimes, but it's the same everywhere in the world where armed gangs cause trouble and oppose the government.*
>
> (President al-Bashir in an interview, Koelbl and Windfuhr 2010)

An analysis of the situation in Darfur quickly shows that the rate at which the most important violations of human rights were committed barely changed between the beginning of the ICC investigations in 2005 and the end of the observation period in 2012. The ICC has therefore clearly not had an effect on improving the human rights situation or the respect for the law. This is the case despite the fact that the OTP of the ICC tried to pressure the GoS to stop violations through a strategy of shaming. Main reasons for this failure were the skilled political manoeuvres of the GoS to deflect pressure as well as the lack of a consistent and unified position of the international community to back up the ICC's shaming strategy.

The baseline used for assessing the development of the human rights situation is the report of the International Commission of Inquiry on Darfur (ICID). The ICID had been instated by the UNSC to assess the human rights situation in Darfur. Its report was sent to the UN General-Secretary on 31 January 2005 and served as the basis for the later referral of the situation to the ICC. The report states that some Sudanese laws are '*grossly incompatible with international norms*' (ICID 2005, p. 147) and found that '*criminal acts were committed as part of widespread or systematic attacks directed against the civilian population*' and that '*serious violations of international human rights law and humanitarian law by all parties are continuing*' (ICID 2005, p. 5).

The rate of the crimes listed in the ICID report and the number of the violations most commonly reported in news sources and human rights reports were traced from 2005 to 2012. The ICID crimes consist of attacks on the civilian population accompanied by displacement, looting, destruction of property, raping, beating and killings. Other violations include illegal detentions and torture by security forces, violations of fair trial standards and free speech restrictions, as well as press censorship.

Analysing the pattern of criminal attacks in Darfur, Sudan experts have concluded that banditry has become normal for forces on both sides of the conflict since 2005 (Daly 2010, p. 306, Flint and de Waal 2008, p. 138 and 141, Mamdani 2009c, p. 261–262). A quick glance at newspaper reports between 2005 and 2011 shows beyond a doubt that the attacks described in the ICID report never completely ceased. There were lulls, and the intensity of the violations changed, but the same crimes were still being reported on a daily basis. Even in 2011 and 2012, rapes, beatings, looting, destruction of property, bombing of villages and forced displacement were being reported on a daily basis, if on a lower scale than at the height of the conflict (e.g. Radio Dabanga 2010m, 2011m, 2012a). Instead of helping, local security forces often were part of the problem in the area. Fadul and Tanner concluded that police officers trying to protect civilians were attacked, and in many cases, the police even fought alongside militias and the army (Fadul and Tanner 2007, p. 304–307). Research in 2011 suggested that security forces remained ill-equipped to guarantee security and resorted to violence against civilians instead (Maguire 2011, p. 163–164).

The picture is much the same for illegal detention and torture committed by Sudanese security forces. Arbitrary arrests have been reported regularly by human rights organisations, researchers and the media during the observation period. This includes mass arrests of journalists, protesters, opposition members and rebels, as well as cases of disappearances (HRW 2009a, p. 3, 2009c, p. 8, 2012a). In other cases, IDPs were held in custody by local authorities for more than six months without being allowed to see a lawyer (Adam et al. 2010). Researchers (Maguire 2011,

p. 163–164), human rights NGOs (ACJPS 2012, HRW 2011a, p. 23) and the UN Independent Expert for Human Rights in Sudan (Othman 2010b) all have reported similar cases in the observation period.

Reports of torture connected to these disappearances and arrests are also consistent (e.g. ACJPS 2012). The International Commission of Jurists accused police officers of torturing detainees in ghost houses[25] in 2007; some of the victims reportedly died (ICJ 2007, p. 43). Physicians for Human Rights, Redress and HRW have repeated allegations of torture as well as incommunicado detention and detention under inhumane conditions in 2009 (HRW 2009c, p. 8, Physicians for Human Rights 2009, p. 51, Redress 2009, p. 6).

Fair trial issues have also been raised continuously in recent years. On 7 August 2008, UNMIS voiced concern that trials of JEM members for their involvement in the Khartoum attacks may not have met international standards. Redress reported in 2009 that fair trial infringements were ongoing (Redress 2009, p. 6), and the UN Independent Expert for Human Rights in Sudan objected to executions after unfair trials in 2010 (Othman 2010b).

Last but not least, restrictions of the freedom of press and free speech have been constantly criticised by a number of actors (Cockett 2010, p. 263, HRW 2009a, Othman 2010b). The main targets have been newspaper journalists and human rights defenders. According to Freedom House, Sudan was one of the most repressive regimes for media in 2005, and it remains on rank 170 out of 197 in 2012 (Freedom House 2012). HRW estimated that about 200 articles were removed from newspapers between May and November 2008 alone (HRW 2009a, p. 10). Academics reported that radio and TV stations were directly controlled through military censors and that journalists were beaten and harassed (Chalk and Kelton 2009, p. 114). Repression and censorship have been stepped up again after the 2010 presidential elections. Radio Dabanga reported that newspapers were being permanently closed because journalists were allegedly implicated in coup plans (Radio Dabanga 2010n). Radio Dabanga's offices themselves were also shut down, which sparked a protest by the US on 3 November 2010. The LexisNexis analysis also showed that several newspapers were shut down during 2011 by either the GoS or the National Intelligence and Security Service (NISS).

If there were improvements in the human rights record at all, they were small, symbolic or temporary at best. For example, a National

[25] Ghost houses are unofficial detention facilities which location is kept secret from the public.

Commission for Human Rights (NCHR) was created by the government on 11 January 2012, as part of the Doha Agreement (ACJPS 2012, p. 8–9). Compliance with human rights standards otherwise has only been verbal.[26]

Academics (Elliesie 2010, Maguire 2011, p. 174), UN officials (e.g. Othman 2010a, UNSG 2010, p. 14–15), journalists (The East African 2011) and Western governments including the US (Sudan Tribune 2010b) agree that human rights progress has been minimal or that the situation has even worsened. A recent report by the Cairo Institute for Human Rights Studies even concludes that the human rights situation declined sharply during 2012 (CIHRS 2012). Against this background, it is clear that the ICC investigations have failed to stimulate an overall improvement of the human rights situation in Sudan.

Nevertheless, there is one area where the human rights record has improved and ICC influence is plausible, namely the use of child soldiers by rebel groups. This practice has generally stopped since 2007. On 11 June 2007, the SLM-MM became the first rebel group to announce that it would start to hand over child soldiers to UNICEF (UN News Service 2007). Similar agreements were made between UNICEF and the SAF on 25 December 2008 (Sudan Tribune 2008a), with JEM on 19 July 2010 (Radio Dabanga 2010u) and with SLA-AW on 6 October 2011 (Radio Dabanga 2011d). Taking into consideration that the ICC's first case against Thomas Lubanga, who was charged for the conscription of child soldiers, went to trial in 2006, a connection is at least possible. Combined with the fact that the Darfur rebel groups were eager to be seen cooperating with the ICC (see Section 5.2.5c), an impact of the ICC on the abolition of the use of child soldiers in Darfur is very plausible.

Still, the Darfur case is more interesting because all the human rights pressure has largely failed to produce progress in Darfur, especially since there was no lack of effort to influence the human rights situation on the side of the OTP. ICC Chief Prosecutor Moreno Ocampo followed a clear public shaming strategy in the case of Darfur since his UNSC briefing on 14 December 2006 when he first started hinting at Sudanese non-cooperation (de Waal and Stanton 2009, p. 333, Moreno Ocampo 2006a, p. 9–10, Peskin 2009a). This strategy became obvious in two of the prosecutor's public statements. He made his first statement on

[26] For example, Al-Bashir claimed on 16 October 2008 the he was fully committed to the rule of law and justice in Darfur. Several of these statements by high ranking government officials were cited in news sources during the observation period.

3 March 2011 when he called for more global cooperation in arresting war criminals in Doha, saying: '*Shame on Sudan and President Bashir, shame on the world [for failing to arrest al-Bashir].*' (Radio Dabanga 2011e). He made his second statement after the ICC issued an arrest warrant against the Sudanese Defence Minister Hussein, saying that the warrant aimed '*to promote a public discussion that may prompt the GoS to review its policy*' (Moreno Ocampo 2011, p. 2). The lack of coordinated international pressure and the skilled Sudanese efforts to deflect any pressure through the tactical manoeuvres analysed in Section 4.2.3a help to explain the failure of the human rights efforts.

The sobering result of the Darfur case study is an incentive to take a closer look at which external variables contribute to the success or the failure of international investigations in encouraging the respect for human rights. The results of this study point towards the importance of international support and pressure as a key variable for ensuring that investigations have an impact on the rule of law and the human rights records of particular states (compare with Section 4.2.3a).

b. Furthering judicial capacity building and reform

Progress in capacity building and legal reform has been low since the ICC started its investigations in Darfur (Maguire 2011, p. 163–164, Oette 2010a, 67, Othman 2010b). The ICC investigations stimulated the establishment of a number of national inquiry bodies and special courts, as predicted in the literature. But these institutions were mainly set up as a smokescreen by the GoS to undermine international support for the ICC investigations and to deflect incoming pressure to tackle the human rights situation in Darfur. This causal mechanism exemplifies the importance of justice perceptions on the impact of investigations, as the GoS modelled its judicial institutions according to Western expectations.

The state of emergency has been active in Darfur since 1997. Even if legal reforms are implemented, they are overridden by emergency laws. This leads to a situation where the effective prosecution of many crimes, like rape, committed in the Darfur conflict is simply impossible (AUPD 2009, p. 58). Analysing the situation in Darfur, the only incident that points towards some progress was the creation of Special Courts in Darfur to try war crimes and crimes against humanity.

It is obvious that the ICC played a role in the creation of Special Courts and inquiry bodies. The decisions to create these institutions were usually taken within days of important decisions of the ICC. Their creation was meant to support Sudan's argument that it was capable of trying the Darfur crimes on its own. For example, the new Special Criminal Court for Events in Darfur (SCCED), was created on 7 June 2005 (Baldo 2010, p. 3), just one day after the OTP announced that it would start full-scale investigations in Darfur. This was followed up with a Sudanese Fact Finding Mission for Darfur in August 2005 (ICJ 2007, p. 26). On 18 September 2005, a Specialized Prosecution for Crimes against Humanity Office was established in Khartoum (HRW 2006c, p. 9). During a visit of ICC investigators to Sudanese ministries on 17 November 2005, the GoS created further chambers and investigative committees at the Darfur Special Court, including a Committee Against Rape and the Unit for Combating Violence Against Women and Children (Baldo 2010, p. 3). On 26 February 2007, three days after the OTP applied for summonses to appear against its first two suspects in the Darfur case, the Minister of Justice set up another special court in western Darfur. In August 2008, after the OTP had applied for the al-Bashir warrants, Nimir Ibrahim Mohamed was appointed as prosecutor general for the crimes committed in Darfur since 2003, and the Justice Minister founded the Darfur Crimes Commission of Inquiry (Baldo 2010, p. 4, Flint 2009, p. 45). In November 2008, the GoS included by amendment international crimes in the Sudanese Criminal Act of 1991 (Oette 2010b, p. 349, Ssenyonjo 2010, p. 223).[27] Directly after the ICC had issued the first arrest warrant against al-Bashir in March 2009, the GoS announced that it would set up a new Darfur Special Court and promised to allow international monitoring of its work by the Arab League (AL), the AU, and the UN (Doria et al. 2010, p. 417).

While the ICC played an important role in the creation of these courts and bodies, as well as in encouraging legal reforms concerning accountability for international crimes, the effects of these measures were nearly non-existent or even harmful. The 2005 Fact Finding Mission for Darfur published the names of the victims who had provided the mission with information, which led to reprisals against them and their families (ICJ 2007, p. 26). On 16 December 2005, the UN Special Advisor on the Prevention of Genocide stated that the Darfur Special Court investigations were not satisfactory, a verdict that was confirmed by Sudan expert Alex de Waal in 2008 who termed the Darfur Special Court as '*wholly ineffective*' (de Waal 2008, p. 30). The AU High Panel for Darfur also

[27] The AUPD concluded that the new amendments might still be too imprecise to allow for an efficient prosecution of international crimes (AUPD 2009, p. 58).

concluded that the Special Courts did not investigate international crimes, and that major violations had yet to be subjected to any serious judicial process (AUPD 2009, p. 54–55).

It is clear that the ICC investigations encouraged some symbolic actions in the areas of capacity building and legal reform by the GoS, but these measures did not result in any tangible progress on the ground.

The case of judicial capacity building in Darfur shows how international perceptions of justice can have an influence on national accountability measures through the ICC. International demands for accountability, formulated by UN institutions as well as by the ICC and its supporters, led to the emergence of a national concept of accountability that focused on formal and retributive justice. The GoS formed an investigative commission, created a special court and appointed a special prosecutor to deal with the Darfur crimes when the ICC started investigating. Despite the fact that these institutions proved to be ineffective, their creation illustrates how international perceptions of justice influence nations like Sudan to adapt their approaches to accountability in order to create the impression that they are meeting international expectations.

Capacity-building claims in Sudan as brought forward by international criminal justice promoters like HRW (2010c, p. 74) do not withstand closer scrutiny. The case of Darfur illustrates that legal reforms and capacity building do not necessarily mean that a real impact is felt if the political will is lacking. The next section will elaborate how little change the legal efforts described in this section actually brought on the ground.

c. Combating impunity

> *Accountability is essential not only for Sudan's future, it also sends a powerful message about the responsibilities of all nations that certain behavior is simply not acceptable in this world; that genocide is not acceptable. In the 21st century, rules and universal values must be upheld.*
>
> (US president Barack Obama 2010)

> *Our armed forces are always acting in the scope of the law. Every member of the armed forces and the government who is violating the law will be brought to justice.*
>
> (al-Bashir in an interview with Koelbl and Windfuhr 2010)

Researchers and analysts agree that impunity is one of the main drivers of the Darfur conflict (e.g. ICG 2006d, p. II). As described in the conflict analysis, different economic gains feature highly among the main motivations of the Janjaweed militia to get involved in the conflict. A high possibility of being prosecuted for their involvement in the looting and displacement would affect both their Reasons and Resolve (see HRW 2009b, p. 74). The same is true to a certain degree for some rebel splinters that have degenerated towards armed banditry. The very fact that the ICC has issued arrest warrants against three government officials and one Janjaweed leader and has brought charges against three rebel commanders for attacking AU peacekeepers is a step towards combating impunity. In the absence of the ICC, the chances of a judicial investigation of these crimes would have been very low. Yet, the efforts of the GoS to shield all perpetrators against accountability have nullified the efforts of the ICC on the ground.

The analysis of the accountability mechanism has two steps – one, determining the efficiency of the ICC investigations using the model developed by Hofmann van de Pol (2010) and another, measuring the overall degree of accountability for crimes committed in Darfur.

Those mainly responsible for the worst crimes committed in Darfur were identified by referring to the ICC investigations, the reports of the ICID and the UNSC sanctions list. This information was verified through tracing the crime patterns reported in LexisNexis.

With the arrest warrant for former Minister of Interior and Minister of Defence at the time of writing, Hussein that was issued by the end of 2011, the ICC has now indicted the full chain of command on the government side allegedly responsible for the crimes: From the President, over the Minister of Interior and the State Minister of the Interior, to a Janjaweed commander. But a number of officials who could be considered mainly responsible for the crimes according to the news analysis have not been charged. Among them, two have attracted particular attention in the press and human rights reports, namely, the Janjaweed commander Musa Hilal and the former NISS Chief Salah Abdallah Ghosh. Musa Hilal is a notorious character in charge of recruiting tribesmen into the Janjaweed and the PDF in Central Darfur, while Salah Gosh is accused of having had command responsibility for widespread torture, harassment and arbitrary arrest in Darfur. On the rebel side, three commanders have been investigated for their alleged involvement in an attack on the African Union Mission in Sudan (AMIS) base in Haskanita in late September 2007. Attacks against UNAMID staff and humanitarian organisations are ongoing, but due to the splintering of the rebel factions and the banditry it is impossible to identify the individual rebel commanders 'most responsible' for these acts. But there have been consistent reports that the SLM-MM committed grave human rights violations after signing the DPA. The SLM-MM Commander Minnie Minawi is thus included in the circle of those most responsible for the violations committed in Darfur.

As described in Chapter 3, the efficiency of international investigations according to van de Pol's model is determined by comparing the actual investigations to a counter-factual scenario without international investigations. It is quite clear that national investigations would not have taken place on the government side in the absence of the ICC warrants considering the complete refusal of the Sudanese authorities to cooperate. None of the main suspects on the government side has been charged by national institutions; some of them even have been promoted despite ICC allegations. Ahmed Haroun was named governor of South Kordofan on 8 May 2009 (Mendes 2010, p. 59), former Minister of Interior Hussein became Minister of Defence and Musa Hilal was promoted from colonel to brigadier general in the General Security Services in November 2005 (ICG 2005c, p. 8). Hilal was even appointed as special advisor to the Ministry of Federal Affairs in early 2008 (Flint 2009, p. 18, Peskin 2009b, p. 311).

The cases of Salah Abdallah Gosh and Ali Kushayb are a bit more complicated. Salah Gosh was imprisoned by the GoS on 19 May 2011 after criticising al-Bashir for aspiring to stand for another term as president. He was again arrested on 22 November 2012 amidst accusation of plotting a coup. Yet, he was never charged or investigated for his involvement in violations committed in Darfur. Ali Kushayb, on the other hand, was initially imprisoned on charges not connected to the Darfur conflict. The GoS announced on 6 March 2007 that it would try him at the Darfur Special Court to prove that it was able to try the Darfur suspects itself. The trial was put on hold indefinitely the next day though, and Kushayb was released on 1 October 2007 (also Doria et al. 2010, p. 413, Peskin 2009b, p. 311). Kushayb was again arrested in October 2008, and again the GoS claimed that it had arrested him in order to put him on trial for crimes committed in Darfur (Akhavan 2009, p. 649, Arieff et al. 2011, p. 11). The most recent information available on the Kushayb case was published on 7 May 2009, when a Sudanese judge claimed that Kushayb was still '*under investigation*' in Sudan. The AUPD concluded that it was unlikely that Kushayb's crimes would come before a national court anytime soon (AUPD 2009, p. 56). The few, largely symbolic steps taken against Kushayb were due to international pressure and cannot be interpreted as a willingness to prosecute in the absence of ICC investigations.

Against this background, it is clear that none of those allegedly most responsible for the crimes in Darfur would have been investigated and tried on the government side in the absence of ICC investigations.

On the rebel side, three summonses to appear were issued by the ICC for those allegedly involved in the Haskanita attack on an AMIS base. An investigation of these rebels in the absence of the ICC is very unlikely as the GoS has no interest to improve the security of AU or UN troops on its territory. For years the main point of contention between the GoS and the international community was the presence of international observers and peacekeepers in Darfur. Since the Doha Agreement was signed, the GoS again has started arguing for finding an internal solution to the conflict. The GOS on 29 July 2011 reacted with hostility to the prolongation of the UNAMID mandate in the UNSC resolution 2003. Additionally, al-Bashir has made clear that the GoS would not hand over any suspects to the ICC, not even rebels, on 22 November 2008. He thus confirmed that there is no national will to prosecute rebels for attacks on peacekeepers.

That the ICC has not charged Minnie Minawi, Abdallah Gosh or Musa Hilal is either due to the limited resources at the ICC, or because the investigations did not confirm their supposed roles in the Darfur atrocities. Since the ICC does not publish the results of its investigations, it is impossible to say which is true.

The success of the ICC investigations in tackling the impunity of those allegedly most responsible for the crimes committed in Darfur is limited, but better than in the counter-factual scenario. The question whether the ICC investigations had a trickle-down effect on the 'culture of impunity' in Darfur will be analysed in the following paragraphs.

As shown above, the GoS indeed established some national bodies to counter impunity in Darfur in the wake of the ICC investigations. A before/after comparison shows that accountability measures for war crimes were not common in Sudan before the ICC started its investigations. The CPA for example did not include any accountability mechanisms and thus offered a de facto amnesty (Flemming 2010, Ibrahim 2007, p. 490, Oette 2010a, p. 67). Additionally, President al-Bashir dissolved the so-called Special Courts in 2004 and signed an amendment to the Armed Forces Act that granted immunity for all crimes committed in the line of duty in August 2005. This coincided with the beginning of the recruitment of Janjaweed militias. Presumably, the motivation behind passing the amendment and dissolving the court was to avoid national prosecutions of the Janjaweed (HRW 2005a, p. 70, Prunier 2005, p. 98).

According to reports published by HRW and ICG, a culture of impunity was taking hold in Darfur shortly before the ICC began its investigations (HRW 2004, p. 20–22, ICG 2005a, p. 1). The baseline for accountability is therefore low. Even a limited impact of the ICC might thus make a difference against the background of an otherwise total impunity for the crimes included in the Rome Statute.

Yet, a close look at the facts reveals that impunity was wilfully upheld during the ICC investigations by the GoS in order to ensure that tribal militias could be used without interference (Flint and de Waal 2008, p. 145). Apparently, the government issued a directive to the security forces to 'look the other way' when militias violated laws, and the UNHCR reported, on 27 July 2007, that the Janjaweed act without fear of prosecution (ABC 2007, Flint and de Waal 2008, p. 133).

State officials enjoy similar privileges, including legal immunity from prosecution as stated in the National Security Forces Act of 1999 (section 33), the Police Forces Act of 1999 (section 46) and the Armed Forces Act of 2007 (section 34) (AUPD 2009, p. 61). This immunity has to be lifted before investigations even become possible. So far complaints that were filed by victims of the Darfur conflict at police stations have remained without any consequence (Flint 2010a, p. 31). According to recent reports, the GoS has even started recruiting Janjaweed militias into the army and the Border Intelligence Guards in order to protect them from prosecution (Abdhalla et al. 2010).

The GoS has taken some steps to put an end to this impunity, but at a closer look, these measures turn out to be mere symbolic manoeuvres to deflect increasing international pressure (see Section 4.2.3a). Flint and de Waal report executions of regular criminals as 'Janjaweed' and fake disarmaments of Arab militias organised to deceive the international community in 2004 (Flint and de Waal 2008, p. 145, ICG 2004a, p. 2). When the threat of an ICC referral first arose in February 2005, the GoS claimed that it had brought charges against eighty Janjaweed and that it would investigate and try the Darfur atrocities. On 27 March 2005, the GoS added that it would prosecute 164 persons accused of atrocities in Darfur, and on 28 March, they announced that they had arrested fifteen army and security officers for crimes committed in Darfur (Totten and Markusen 2006, p. xxxvi). Yet, those declarations were not followed up with legal charges (AUPD 2009, p. 56). On 24 October 2005, the Darfur Special Court declared that it had found no evidence of systematic rape in Darfur, and that there had only been individual cases. Meanwhile, newspapers reported rape cases during the entirety of the Darfur conflict on a daily basis all over the region.

There is also a lot of evidence that the GoS was not interested in the Special Courts in Darfur working properly. When then Darfur Prosecutor Nimr Mohamed said on 14 March 2009 that he would question Haroun for his alleged involvement in crimes in Darfur, President al-Bashir stopped him by presidential decree (El-Gizouli 2009, p. 261, Sudan Tribune 2009). When the same prosecutor declared on 27 September 2010 that he would begin investigations into Janjaweed attacks on Tabra committed on 2 September 2010, he was replaced within three weeks by the Undersecretary of the Ministry of Justice, Abd Al Daim Zimrawi, ostensibly to 'strengthen' the position of the prosecutor (HRW 2010d, Moreno Ocampo 2010a, p. 4). On 27 December 2010, Zimrawi publicly admitted that he was being hindered by political interference in his work, especially in investigating the Haroun case (Miraya FM 2010). He then resigned for 'personal reasons' on 11 April 2011. HRW claims that the true reason was that the investigations in the Tabra case did not move forward (HRW 2011a, p. 24). The impression that the GoS was hindering the limited investigation efforts on the national level was confirmed by a statement of the then Minister of State at the Ministry of Justice (SPLM) on 26 January 2011, who said that the government was protecting Ahmed Haroun and Ali Kushayb against investigations (Radio Dabanga 2011j).

One of the very few cases in which the Darfur Special Courts delivered a ruling was the 5 May 2011 decision of the Nyala Special Court for Darfur that sentenced two car-jackers of a World Vision vehicle to ten years of prison. Until the time of writing, the GoS has remained active in creating investigative bodies and special courts. The GoS Minister of Justice appointed Ahmed Abdel-Motalib as new Special Prosecutor in charge of Darfur on 10 January 2012, while announcing a new Special Court to investigate the gravest crimes committed during the Darfur conflict as part of the implementation of the Doha Agreement. Abdel-Motalib also resigned from the post on 12 June 2012 without offering reasons (Radio Dabanga 2012b).

Again, the only possible conclusion from this overview is that Sudanese compliance with accountability demands remained symbolic or verbal[28] (also El-Gizouli 2009, p. 262–264, HRW 2005a, p. 1, Mendez

[28] For example, the Army spokesman Lieutenant-Colonel Khalid Alsawarmi was quoted as saying: '*If we find they are indeed border guards, it is our responsibility to curb and punish them... If the police for any reason say they cannot stop them from harming the people or violating their rights, they have to bring their complaints to the nearest military base so we*

2006, p. 1, Sriram 2009a, p. 327). As a consequence, the culture of impunity has prevailed (Buchanan-Smith and Jaspars 2007, p. 60, ICJ 2007, IRIN 2011b, Maguire 2011, p. 174, Ping 2010, p. 3–4, UNHRC 2009, §17 and 49). President al-Bashir himself has repeatedly made clear that he considers the reports of war crimes and rapes in Darfur as lies (AFP 2008, 2009f). If the official government line is that war crimes have not taken place, a lack of investigations and prosecutions is not surprising.

The analysis has shown that the success of the ICC investigations was rather limited after seven years, largely due to the total lack of cooperation by the GoS. The analysis of national accountability measures has shown that they are mere window dressing. Despite these clear findings, a number of authors have claimed that the ICC investigations in Darfur have helped to combat impunity (e.g. Akhavan 2009, p. 648–650). The findings presented here caution against expecting real progress just because there is activity on the surface. It also reveals one of the weaknesses of the quantitative methods currently used to measure the impact of international investigations and trials: indicators like the creation of national courts and charges brought against perpetrators would offer a wrong assessment of the situation in Darfur without deeper qualitative analyses.

4.2.2 Reconciliation mechanisms

a. Addressing victim needs

The Darfur conflict is a case in point that can be of tremendous importance to address victim needs to solve a conflict. Some rebel groups, in particular the SLM-AW, have large constituencies in the IDP camps in Darfur and the refugee camps in Chad to whom they have to explain themselves (Expert Interview 2011a, ICG 2006a, p. 9).[29] It is unrealistic to expect these groups to sign a negotiated agreement if the displaced cannot be convinced that the agreement would benefit them. For the rebel groups, the support from the displaced, largely 'African' population

can take action.' (Abdhalla et al. 2010). See also the citation of President Bashir at the beginning of this section.

[29] During negotiations, IDPs often organised demonstrations, voicing support for SLA-AW positions. The SLA-AW opposed both the DPA and the Doha Agreement and in both cases, IDPs demonstrated against the signing of the agreement in support of the SLA-AW.

is a key Resource. Rebels would never squander that support to sign an unpopular agreement with the GoS. The decay of Minawi's SLM-MM after signing the DPA has reminded the other rebel leaders how important it is to retain the support of the IDP and refugee camps. A negotiated solution thus depends on how well the needs of the victims of the conflict, particularly, those living in IDP and refugee camps across Darfur and Chad, can be addressed.

Security, accountability for crimes committed and compensation were consistently named as the most important needs of these constituencies. As shown in the preceding sections, ICC contributions to accountability have been low. While the ICC can pay compensation to the direct victims of convicted perpetrators, its resources are quite limited. Additionally, the ICC is far from starting a trial against any of the government suspects. The impact of the ICC in meeting victims' needs therefore has been low. Due to its involvement, the ICC may even block alternative approaches to ensuring accountability. Finally, it becomes clear that the ICC is in fact defining victimhood in the scope of its investigation strategy. It can therefore only meet the needs of *selected* victim groups.

Needs brought forward by victims and their representatives have differed somewhat over the course of the conflict, but the demand for prosecution of those responsible for their displacement and suffering is a constant factor in these demands. Security needs and re-establishing the rule of law were named as first priorities in early phases of conflict (Tanner 2005, p. 38–40). The demands for prosecution have gained importance over time, especially in the Chadian camps (e.g. AUPD 2009, p. 8, Darehshori 2008, Radio Dabanga 2010s). According to all sources, the victims of the Darfur conflict overwhelmingly supported al-Bashir's indictment by the ICC (AUPD 2009, p. 62, Cockett 2010, p. 288, Darfurian Voices Project 2010).[30] A 2010 survey among Darfuri refugees in Chad showed that nearly all respondents believed that the perpetrators of atrocities should be held accountable through criminal justice. Ninety per cent of them called for international trials and support for amnesties was near zero, even if only offered to the rank and file (Darfurian Voices Project 2010, p. 10). The existence of accountability demands has also been confirmed in expert interviews (Expert Interview 2010a, 2011h, Jaeger 2011). Finally, the civil society

[30] Newspapers reported celebrations in Darfur's IDP camps on 15 July 2008 after news about the issuing of an arrest warrant against President Bashir arrived. (McCrummen and Boustany 2008).

declarations made during the Doha negotiations also call for some form of accountability (Doha Declaration 2009, p. 8).

Another need that has often been identified over the years is for individual and collective compensation. The issue of compensation became one of the most contentious issues at Abuja (ICG 2007a, p. 10, Toga 2007, p. 236), and compensation demands have been repeated by IDP camp leaders on a regular basis (e.g. Radio Dabanga 2010i, 2010p). A survey among refugees in Chad showed that nearly all the respondents called for individual monetary compensations (Darfurian Voices Project 2010, p. 10). Again, the compensation demand is also included in civil society statements made during the Doha Negotiations (Doha II Declaration 2010, p. 4).

For a durable solution to the conflict, it is of key importance that the justice and compensation demands of the victims be met. The failure of the DPA underscores this as one of the main reasons for the rejection of the DPA among Darfuri refugees in Chad was the lack of justice provisions (Darfurian Voices Project 2010, p. 18). Darfur victims tend to react sharply when their needs are not taken into consideration. Refugees and IDPs refused to meet the US envoy for Sudan on 11 September 2009 and demanded the resignation of UNAMID Chief Ibrahim Gambari for downplaying the intensity of the Darfur conflict.

In principle, the ICC investigations align with the needs voiced by many victims. Some explicitly call for an ICC role in guaranteeing justice in Darfur. Traditional justice is seen as important by 90 per cent of Darfuri refugees in Chad, but a large majority do not believe that these mechanisms are sufficient to address the consequences of the conflict (Darfurian Voices Project 2010, p. 10).

Yet, the ICC impact in practice has been low. First of all, no arrests of GoS suspects have been ensured so far, so the justice needs remain largely unaddressed. Second, meeting the victims' needs for justice requires that they be able to take part in the proceedings in some way. Again, the ICC has so far not been very successful in guaranteeing that. By the end of 2008, only 11 victims were listed as participants in the ICC procedures in Darfur, compared to 171 in the DRC and 57 in Uganda (Flint and de Waal 2009, p. 2). A group of lawyers claimed that the victims did not receive enough legal support to take part in the ICC proceedings (Glassborow 2007). Additionally, refugees in Chad complained that they had not seen an ICC representative for more than a year (Anderson et al. 2012). Finally, the ICC has so far not been able to avoid negative repercussions of its investigations for victim communities. Especially, victims interested in taking part in the Haskanita trial are in a difficult position, as they have to move back to Darfur without any protection after having taken part in ICC proceedings (Uwineza 2011).

Expecting a real impact in terms of compensation from the ICC investigations is unrealistic due to the limited resources of the Court. Compensation is an issue that would have to be addressed in the scope of any agreement settling the conflict. Indeed, the Doha Agreement foresees compensations amounting to a total of 330 million USD. In terms of individual compensation, every displaced person who returns voluntarily to his village is supposed to receive 250 USD for facilitating his return (Radio Dabanga 2011n).

The analysis shows that success in meeting victim needs is not guaranteed just because the mandate of the ICC and the needs of victims on the ground coincide. In the case of Darfur, the ICC has so far failed to deliver on its mandate in a meaningful way, and there are even some perverse effects of the ICC investigations that penalise the very victims the ICC should support. The literature should shed more light on these potential adverse effects of international criminal investigations and trials and start to challenge the mantra that they are done for the victims. In the case of Darfur, the ICC investigations might paradoxically even block the adoption of meaningful justice mechanisms, as some hardliners among Darfur refugees and IDPs have rallied behind the demand that those most responsible should be tried by the ICC. As the AUPD rightly concluded, the ICC is currently dominating the discourse on justice in Sudan (AUPD 2009, p. 63), yet the GoS cannot be expected to compromise on justice issues as long as they are closely linked to the ICC investigations. It is therefore little surprising that the Doha Declarations of the Darfur Civil Society tried to circumnavigate the problem by demanding justice without mentioning the ICC. Decoupling the question of justice from the ICC's activities might therefore create better chances for the victims of the conflict to see some sort of justice.

Finally, the victim and perpetrator roles in the Darfur conflict are more complex than the mainstream discourse of an 'Arab' war waged on 'African' victims would suggest. Yet, the ICC has reinforced this interpretation (see Section 4.2.4b). Therefore, the majority of the Arab tribes – who tried to stay out of the conflict – are not accepted as victims of the conflict in the ICC's narrative.

But even the role of those Arab tribes that decided to join the Janjaweed is complex. The strategy of the prosecution currently focuses on shaming the Sudanese Government and their Janjaweed allies and is therefore blind to the needs of those Arab tribes that have been exploited by the GoS in the Darfur conflict. To some degree, these disillusioned Janjaweed are also victims of the conflict whose needs have to be addressed to find a durable solution (see Section 4.2.4b). The selective nature of how victimhood is defined by international criminal justice bodies deserves more scrutiny. In reality, international investigations and trials might very well only address *certain* victim needs of *selected* victim groups.

b. Individualising guilt

Taking the ethnic factors of the Darfur conflict into consideration, it is clear that individualisation of guilt for atrocities committed during the conflict would be helpful towards achieving peace in the region. Reasons and Resolve of both sides could be countered if fair and transparent trials were to establish the individual guilt of perpetrators of atrocities, thus avoiding that entire ethnic communities are blamed. The findings concerning this causal mechanism are inconclusive since there are not enough data available. The findings in other sections indicate, however, that the ICC has rather reinforced the perception of tribal identities.

The use of ethnic stereotypes has increased in the course of the Darfur conflict but is also more complex than one might expect. According to field research, only those tribes whose traditional and tribal leaders officially decided to join the militias were seen as responsible for the Janjaweed violence in the early phases of the conflict. This means that the people on the ground did not generally identify all Arabs as Janjaweed (Tanner 2005, p. 18 and 22). A 2010 survey with Darfur refugees living in Chad confirmed this finding. More than 80 per cent of them believed that the GoS or President al-Bashir were personally responsible for the violence in Darfur (Darfurian Voices Project 2010, p. 10). Nevertheless, more than 50 per cent of the respondents stated that they believed tribal groups involved in the violence were collectively responsible (Darfurian Voices Project 2010, p. 10). At the same time, 83 per cent associated the Janjaweed with specific Arab tribes (Darfurian Voices Project 2010, p. 24). These findings suggest that collective guilt assumptions are mainly connected to tribal identities, rather than broad ethnic categories.

Unfortunately, it is impossible to measure whether the ICC has had an impact on individualising guilt since not enough data on tribal stereotyping before and after the ICC investigations are available A conclusive answer could only be given with surveys on the use of ethnic and tribal stereotypes as well as hate speech before and after the start of the ICC investigations. Even though a definitive analysis cannot be done at the current stage, there is evidence that the ICC has rather reinforced the perception of tribal identities in Darfur by adopting a narrative of a genocide committed against the African tribes in its prosecution strategy. These aspects are discussed in depth in the sections on victim needs (Section 4.2.2a) and blocking rapprochement (Section 4.2.4b).

4.2.3 Deterrence and isolation

a. Pressure and inducement

At first glance, Darfur seems to be a perfect illustration of the pressure and inducement mechanism. In no other situation before the ICC has the OTP so explicitly and openly decided to follow a prosecution strategy of pressuring and shaming the Sudanese government in order to achieve cooperation to stop the commission of war crimes. It is therefore not surprising that several authors have brought forward claims of pressure and inducement in the Darfur case, claiming that the ICC investigations forced the GoS to negotiate in Doha (Baldo 2010, p. 6, Baldauf 2009, Jaques 2008, p. 8). The analysis shows that these effects were largely the result of international pressure on the GoS not connected to the ICC investigations. Contrary to the expectations of the literature, the ICC was rather used as an instrument by powerful states instead of shaping the pressure on the GoS. In some cases, the ICC even divided the international community over Darfur and thus undermined international pressure. The confrontational prosecution strategy of the OTP, especially the decision to issue a warrant against a sitting head of state, contributed to the failure of this mechanism.

In order to analyse the pressure mechanism in Darfur, two questions have to be answered. First, did the ICC play a role in augmenting the pressure on the GoS? Second, did this pressure reduce the Resolve to fight of the conflict parties?

At the time the Darfur conflict broke out, the priority of the international community in Sudan was to ensure the signing of the CPA between the GoS and the SPLM (e.g. Cockett 2010, p. 178, Daly 2010, p. 293–297, Prunier 2005, p. 143). Finding a solution for the Sudanese civil war took precedence over exerting pressure on the GoS to stop its attacks in Darfur. The GoS was aware of that and skilfully used the CPA negotiations to deflect any international pressure connected to the situation in Darfur (see Grünfeld and Vermeulen 2009, p. 230, ICG 2004b, p. 26–27). At the same time, the United States was sustaining a close intelligence cooperation with the GoS after the 9/11 attacks (Cockett 2010, p. 169).[31] Only after the signing of the CPA did the United States and the United Kingdom started putting pressure on Sudan over Darfur. China, Russia and a couple of other states, however, shielded the GoS from too much pressure over the coming years and months, softening the language of UNSC resolution drafts nine times until 2010 (Cockett 2010, p. 224). This has been the main weakness of international efforts to pressure the GoS ever since.

The international community has never been able to speak with one voice and effectively pressure the GoS into decisive concessions over Darfur (also Lanz 2008a). Harsh instruments were laid on the table by some individual states or officials, including US Secretary of State Powell's finding that genocide was ongoing in Darfur in 2004 (Kessler and Lynch 2004), Kofi Annan's call for a EU and NATO intervention in Darfur at the Munich Security Conference in 2005 (AFP 2005a) and British considerations about sending a EU 'Battle group' to 'African hotspots' to stop genocide in 2004 (Charter 2004).

Despite these strong words, Sudan managed to mitigate most of the pressure by exploiting divisions in the international community due to its contradicting priorities. China, Russia and others blocked any meaningful pressure by softening the phrasing of UNSC resolutions. For example, China decided to block the implementation of maritime sanctions against Sudan in order to not endanger its investments in the country (Peskin 2009b, p. 319).[32] The AL and the AU also played an important role in moderating the pressure on the GoS. The AL did so in the scope of its general policy of trying to protect its member states against Western intrusion. The AU on the other hand feared to be marginalised in its role as the primary African institution for conflict management (Grono 2006, p. 627). Additionally, the perception among many Africans that the ICC

[31] The GoS even claims that the cooperation went so far that the United States promised the GoS to remain acquiescent in order to allow the government to crush the Darfur rebels quickly and quietly in 2003 and 2004 (Cockett 2010, p. 180).

[32] The importance of China's role in mitigating international pressure on the GoS cannot be overstated. China is a key trading partner of Sudan and thus undercut many of the sanctions imposed on Sudan. It imported two-thirds of the Sudanese oil in 2007 (AP 2007), while 70 per cent of Sudanese exports went to China in 2006 (Economist 2006). Additionally, China has invested heavily in Sudan and is a major supplier of arms (Peskin 2009b, p. 319).

was acting like a neo-colonial institution encouraged the AU not to support the international pressure on Sudan connected to the ICC arrest warrants (see Section 4.2.3c).

Even in the resolutions that the UNSC managed to pass on Darfur (Table 4.1), the Council failed to react when the GoS did not comply with its demands. During a UNSC meeting in Nairobi that addressed the Darfur conflict, there was not even a mention of the obligations under previous resolutions that had been ignored by the GoS (ICG 2005c, p. 3). There is also a long list of cases from the LexisNexis analysis that illustrate how the majority of the international community blocked any increased pressure on the GoS. To name just a few, a UN General Assembly Committee blocked two resolutions on GoS human rights violations on 24 November 2004 and on 23 November 2005 (AFP 2005b, IPS 2004). In the UN Human Rights Council (UNHRC), a majority of states blocked the attempt to discuss the situation in Darfur on 6 October 2006 and watered down a resolution on SAF atrocities passed on 28 November 2006. Finally, on 30 March 2007, a majority of states prevented a UNHRC condemnation of Sudan.

But even the Western countries did not always speak with a unified voice concerning the Darfur issue. As de Waal has pointed out, the US and EU approaches towards Darfur were radically different in 2005 (de Waal 2007c, p. 19). France and the United States openly disagreed over whether the atrocities committed in Darfur amounted to genocide. Additionally, there were internal disagreements within both the United States and the EU about how the GoS should be approached over Darfur (Brosché 2008, p. 99, Jennings and Glassborow 2011). While the CIA was cooperating with the GoS in the scope of the war on terror, the Congress and the White House were bashing the GoS for its Darfur policy (Cockett 2010, p. 297, de Waal 2007c, p. 18). The EU could not agree on a common policy towards Darfur in the initial stages of the conflict either (Prunier 2006, p. 198). On 23 August 2004, the British Foreign Minister said that '*no options are ruled out*' in Darfur, while the French Foreign Minister emphasised that there could only be a political solution.

The Western lack of will to intervene strongly in Sudan has several reasons, including energy security, geopolitical considerations of ensuring regional stability and the need to obtain Sudanese cooperation in the war on terror (Akhavan 2009, p. 635, Paes 2006, p. 30). Several examples illustrate this. After al-Bashir expelled fourteen international aid organisations due to the ICC warrant issued against him, diplomats focused on regaining Sudanese cooperation to ameliorate the situation of the IDPs

Table 4.1: *UNSC resolutions passed on Darfur between Late 2004 and 2011*

Date	Resolution	Measures
19 November 2004	1574	Demand to cease violence and attacks but no sanctions foreseen
29 March 2005	1591	Ban of offensive military flights, GoS has to ask for permission when moving military supplies in Darfur, sanctions of freezing assets and travel restrictions for individuals, arms embargo
31 March 2005	1593	ICC referral
21 December 2005	1651	Call on parties to respect ceasefire, says violators will be held accountable. Four-member panel of experts for individual sanctions asked to identify individuals for travel bans and asset freezing.
25 April 2006	1672	Urges accord by end of month, passes sanctions for Major General Gaffar Mohamed Elhassan, Commander of the Western Military Region for the Sudanese Air Force; Adam Yacub Shant, Commander of the SLA; Gabril Abdul Kareem Badri, the Field Commander of the NMRD; and Sheikh Musa Hilal, the Paramount Chief of the Jalul Tribe in North Darfur
31 August 2006	1706	Call for UN deployment with GoS consent
31 July 2007	1769	Transfers authority to hybrid UNAMID mission
31 July 2008	1828	Prolongs the UNAMID mission under a Chapter VII
30 July 2010	1935	Extending UNAMID mandate with focus on protecting civilians and ensuring humanitarian access. Call on rebels to join talks.
29 July 2011	2003	Prolongs UNAMID mandate by one year, condemns all violations and calls for accountability

instead of pressuring Sudan to hand over al-Bashir (Peskin 2009b, p. 309). In 2010, the international community focused on ensuring peaceful presidential elections in Sudan. The international community was even ready to leave the Darfur issue off the agenda to ensure that the situation remained stable, much as it had done during 2003 and 2004 to secure the signing of the CPA. After the election issue was off the table, the international community worried about the South Sudanese independence referendum in early 2011,[33] and the peaceful implementation of the actual secession in July 2011 (also Adam et al. 2011, p. 13, Flint 2010b, p. 41 and 43). Again, the Darfur problem was ignored due to more pressing concerns.

There were four factors that hindered the emergence of any consistent pressure on the GoS to solve the Darfur conflict. First, important players like China, Russia, the AL and the AU mitigated the pressure on Sudan. Second, the international community did not insist on the GoS fulfilling past demands. Third, even Western countries were often divided over their policy towards Darfur. Fourth, conflicting interests in Sudan led the Western powers to ignore the Darfur issue if other hotspots in Sudan threatened to emerge.

Due to these four factors, the pressure on the GoS was never consistent or credible enough to achieve tangible changes in GoS policy (also Expert Interview 2011h). Authors have aptly described the international policy towards Darfur as '*barking without biting*' (Brosché 2008, p. 107) or '*empty talk without action*' (Totten 2009). Even the small measures taken by the international community have so far not been enforced. The arms embargo imposed on Darfur is a good example. Both the UN Panel monitoring the embargo as well as the AI have reported that it has remained '*without discernible impact*' (AI 2012b, UN 2011, p. 4). The GoS used the space of manoeuvre that emerged from the lack of unity in the international community with utmost efficiency (also Elliesie 2007, p. 212, ICG 2007a, p. 1). For example, it started a major offensive in Darfur when the Tsunami in south-east Asia pushed the Darfur issue from international headlines in December 2004.[34] It also managed to

[33] US Senator Kerry offered Bashir to take Sudan off the US terrorist sponsor list if the South Sudan referendum went down smoothly, without demanding an end to the Darfur conflict first, as in the past (Fick 2010, Perras 2010). The United States was unable, however, to remove Sudan from the list after South Sudan's secession due to pressure from the public and the Congress.

[34] The GoS is also actively trying to reduce attention for the conflict. For example, a Sudanese diplomat at the London embassy claimed that '*Darfur is off the focus because*

block the deployment of any meaningful international component in the African-dominated UNAMID mission.

At the same time, the GoS cannot really afford to give in to international pressure after the signing of the CPA and the later secession of South Sudan. The GoS is under strong pressure from internal critics and is doing everything to cling to power. Compromising over Darfur in such a delicate situation would weaken its position (de Waal 2007c, p. 18–21, Natsios 2008, p. 3). The GoS will thus only yield if there is strong and consistent pressure.

An example from 2008 illustrates that this kind of unified and persistent pressure could indeed force a change in GoS policies. Starting in 2007, Sudan's main supporter China got caught in a media campaign calling for a boycott of the Olympic Games in Beijing over the lack of Chinese pressure on Darfur. At the height of the campaign in February 2008, the famous American movie director Steven Spielberg quit his position as artistic advisor on the Chinese organisation team for the Olympics. During the same month, the US House, a group of Nobel Prize Laureates and International Olympic Committee Chief Rogge asked China to apply more pressure in the Darfur situation. On 17 March 2008, the EU disinvested from the Chinese oil firm Petrochina due to its Darfur involvement (Sengupta 2008). These combined measures finally pushed the Chinese Government to exert some pressure on the GoS to stop its blockade of the deployment of UNAMID. The Chinese Special Envoy for Darfur issued a stern warning to Sudan and there were reports of behind-the-scenes pressure by China (Baldauf et al. 2009, p. 129). This pressure led to a more speedy deployment of the UN support packages for UNAMID (also Brosché 2008, p. 60, Cockett 2010, p. 230). The example illustrates that only coordinated and common pressure can make a difference in the case of Darfur.

The pressure exerted by the ICC investigations can only be understood against this background. Considering the inability of the international community to find a coordinated and effective approach vis à vis the Darfur problem, and keeping in mind that the ICC relies on state cooperation for enforcing its warrants, it is clear that efficient pressure from the ICC investigations cannot materialise at a time when the

there is nothing to talk about in Darfur. As simple as that.' (Peled 2010). Along similar lines, the GoS took advantage of the focus of Western attention on the Libyan civil war to harden its stance in the border conflicts with South Sudan in the second half of 2011.

combined pressure of a large part of the international community fails to render tangible results. The ICC still might have helped to increase the pressure on the GoS, for example, by focusing even more media attention on the conflict or by becoming a rallying point for critics of the GoS. The final parts of this section will thus focus on analysing whether the ICC had an impact on media reporting on the Darfur conflict and whether it served as a catalyst for the pressure of the international community on the GoS.

As mentioned above, the OTP followed a conscious approach of pressuring and shaming the GoS since about 2006 (also Peskin 2009b, p. 315). In June 2008, Moreno Ocampo even extended that approach to the UNSC and started shaming the states represented in the Council for their passivity on the Darfur dossier saying that '*It takes a lot to commit massive crimes. It takes commanders and many executioners. But mostly, it requires that the rest of the world look away and do nothing*' (Moreno Ocampo 2008b).

The OTP itself claims that its pressure on the GoS rendered some results. Moreno Ocampo claimed that the GoS considered turning in Haroun to the ICC and would have done so if the international pressure had been stronger (Peskin 2009b, p. 314). The OTP also claims that its pressure on the GoS helped to start a peace process in Doha and sped up the deployment of UNAMID (Mendez 2010b, p. 5–6).

At a closer look, these OTP statements are too optimistic. The ICC in fact only played a secondary role. As shown in Figure 4.1, the media reporting on Sudan peaked in the second quarter of 2004. The reporting reached another peak in the second quarter of 2007, when the ICC issued its first arrest warrants in the case. Yet media reporting does not statistically correlate with important ICC decisions like the issuing of warrants and the opening of investigations. The generally accepted correlation tests result in very low correlations of 0.11–0.13 without reaching relevant significance levels. The correlation even drops to 0.09 when controlling for other events in the context of the Darfur conflict that sparked major news coverage.

The LexisNexis analysis shows that the Darfur conflict triggered exceptional interest and media reporting between mid-2004 and late 2008 (also Kahn 2008, p. 21). Yet, most reports did not revolve around the ICC investigations. The media interest started dropping for good in the second quarter of 2007 and even the spectacular decision to indict Sudan's sitting president al-Bashir and charge him with genocide only temporarily slowed this trend.

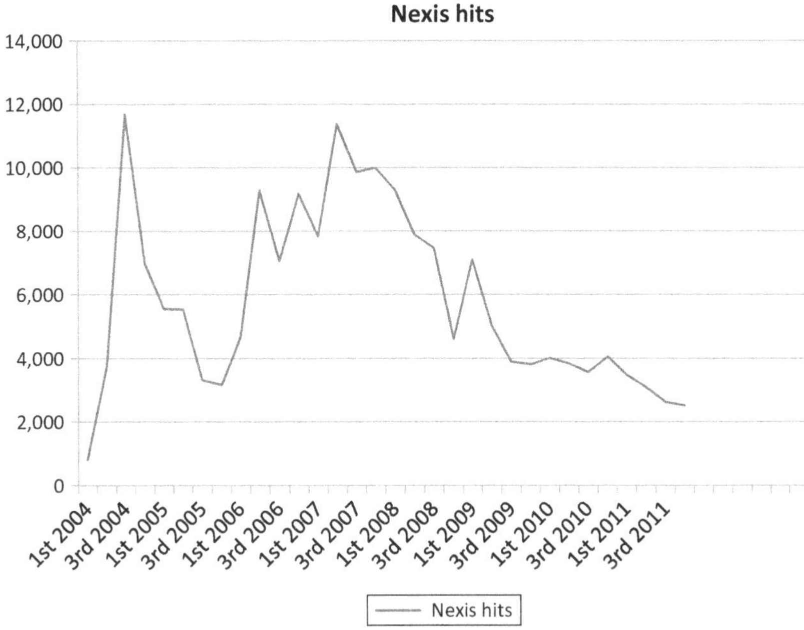

Figure 4.1: Number of hits per quarter for 'Darfur' on the LexisNexis Database

At the same time, an analysis of the international pressure exerted during the Darfur conflict shows that it is implausible to claim that the ICC was a catalyst for it. The ICC was rather used as leverage by those states that tried to pressure the GoS into cooperation. This can be illustrated in several ways. For example, both the UN and Western countries threatened further ICC investigations if Sudan refused to move on the Darfur issue. The UN threatened further ICC investigations after a joint SAF/Janjaweed attack on IDP camps on 1 October 2005 (AP 2005), the United States repeatedly threatened the GoS with further ICC actions if it did not compromise on the Darfur issue and France told the GoS that declaring a ceasefire was 'not enough' to stop an ICC indictment of President al-Bashir on 13 November 2008. At the same time, these countries did not insist on the implementation of the ICC warrants if they did not fit into their current Darfur policy. A UNSC mission to Sudan in June 2007 did not even mention the ICC and the issue of Sudanese non-cooperation (HRW 2008a, p. 227). The UNSC generally remained passive on the ICC question, making only two references to the ICC before June 2008. The council didn't even include the duty to cooperate with the ICC in a list of demands to the GoS; instead, it stressed that justice was a *domestic* responsibility of the GoS (Peskin 2009b, p. 316). France and the United Kingdom even showed readiness to defer the ICC case against al-Bashir if Sudan showed more willingness to cooperate (also Akhavan 2009, p. 649, Oette 2010b, p. 356, Peskin 2009b, p. 318, Sarro 2010). While the EU supported the ICC verbally, it did not demand the extradition of President al-Bashir nor did it follow up on its sanction threats spelled out in June 2008 (Peskin 2009a, p. 675–676). A leaked diplomatic cable from the United Kingdom dated March 2009 voiced fears that additional attempts to heighten ICC pressure at the UNSC could lead to a backlash and more support among sceptical states for a deferral of the ICC investigations on humanitarian grounds (Jennings and Glassborow 2011). Finally, the Norwegian Foreign Minister Stoere said that European countries should engage the Sudanese government in the run-up to the January 2011 referendum on South Sudan despite the ICC warrants against al-Bashir in order to prevent a possible escalation (McDoom 2010).

These examples show that even the ICC's main supporters were ready to compromise on the warrants under certain conditions. Instead of augmenting and focusing the pressure of the international community, the ICC was used as an instrument. To some degree, the UNSC used the ICC referral as an excuse to not take any more drastic steps in the face of the high media attention and the domestic pressure, especially in the US. The UNSC referred the case of Darfur to the ICC to make sure it was *seen* to be doing something – *anything* – in the Darfur issue (also Akhavan 2009, p. 646–647, Peskin 2009b, p. 316).

Even though the ICC clearly did not play a defining role in terms of pressuring the GoS, there are two incidents in which a contribution of the ICC towards pressuring the GoS is plausible. First, the ICC may have changed the cost calculation of the GoS towards starting the Doha Negotiations in February 2009. The ICC was just about to issue the first arrest warrant against al-Bashir at that point and it had been public knowledge for nearly a year that the OTP was pursuing a warrant against al-Bashir. In that light, the claims that the ICC played a role for President al-Bashir to start the Doha Negotiations are very plausible. The GoS had to show the international community that peace was possible with al-Bashir in order to avoid an enforcement of the upcoming warrant (Baldauf 2009). The second concession in which the ICC might have played a role is the faster deployment of the UN packages of UNAMID. A diplomat working on Sudan suggested that the ICC played a role in helping to enforce a more rapid deployment of the rest of UNAMID (Expert Interview 2011a). Indeed, the GoS started to let more and more UN units into Darfur after the OTP applied for an indictment of al-Bashir in July 2008, presumably in order to reduce the pressure on President al-Bashir. But China's pressure on the GoS due to the threats of a boycott of the Olympic Games during 2008 cannot be ignored here. Since the GoS did not care to cooperate with the ICC in other instances, the Chinese factor probably played a more important role. This view is supported by al-Bashir's defiant behaviour at the time, telling a UNSC delegation on 5 June 2008 that he would cooperate with the ICC '*over his dead body*' (Peskin 2009b, p. 309).

The ICC pressure failed mainly due to the lack of consistent support of the investigations from powerful states. If the ICC had been able to mobilise state pressure on Sudan instead of being used as an instrument, it might have made a real difference. Yet, instead of catalysing or harnessing the pressure of the international community in the Darfur issue, the ICC arguably divided the international community over Darfur (also Flint 2010b, p. 26). This can be seen in the reactions to the indictment of Sudanese president al-Bashir, but also in the voting and negotiation behaviour of the states in the UNSC. When the first ICC warrant for al-Bashir was announced, it was only fully supported by Canada and France. The US, UN institutions and Germany reacted cautiously, while Uganda showed some scepticism. The African Union, the Gulf Cooperation Council, the Arab League as well as Egypt, Ethiopia, China, Lebanon, Libya, Qatar, Russia, Syria, Yemen and the president of the UNGA reacted negatively. As a result, Russia, Libya, South Africa and China tried to support the GoS by including an ICC deferral in resolution 1828 of the UNSC that prolonged the UNAMID mandate (Baldo 2010, p. 5). Even though the attempt failed, a unified response to the Darfur situation was more distant than ever, with the United States abstaining because of a paragraph mentioning a possible future deferral of the ICC (Arieff et al. 2011, p. 28) The resolution also mentions concerns of some states regarding the ICC investigations (Clark 2010, p. 83).

The reasons for this controversial role of the ICC can be found in the confrontational strategy of the OTP. It started shaming both the GoS as well as 'passive' states. The decision to directly indict a sitting head of state, instead of following the chain of command and indicting the former Defence Minister Hussein first, was a deliberate escalation of this strategy. As shown in the polarisation section, this confrontational approach of the OTP lost the ICC a lot of support among African Member States, and even ICC supporters like HRW criticised the decision to skip mid-level suspects (HRW 2011b, p. 35). Some authors have also accused the Chief Prosecutor of misrepresenting statistics to arrive at a higher death toll in Darfur (Flint and de Waal 2009, p. 3 and 7, Mamdani 2009c, p. 272). But the Chief Prosecutor did not stop there. On 23 March 2010, he compared the upcoming Sudanese presidential elections with the 'Hitler elections' (AFP 2010). At the same time he started claiming publicly that genocide was ongoing in Darfur (AFP 2009b, Moreno Ocampo 2010d), even though there had not been a confirmation of charges in the al-Bashir case and al-Bashir was legally to be considered innocent until proven guilty. Considering that the OTP is supposed to work like prosecutors in the continental law tradition, collecting both incriminating and exculpatory evidence, his public claims of genocide have to be considered unprofessional to say the least. It also gave the GoS the possibility to attack Moreno Ocampo for politicising the case (AFP 2009b). The Sudan Workers Trade Unions Federation and the Sudan International Defence Group lodged a complaint against Moreno Ocampo's genocide claims. The organisations stressed the potential negative impact of these claims on the situation in Sudan, especially since they were not legally proven (ICC 2010b).[35] The Pre-Trial Chamber of the ICC declared the request inadmissible on 24 August 2010 (ICC PTC I 2010), and Moreno Ocampo repeated his genocide claims on France 24 on 20 October 2010 (Perelman 2010).

On 12 December 2011, the Pre-Trial Chamber of the ICC escalated the disagreements between the AU and the ICC by essentially declaring the AU's resolution not to cooperate with the ICC in arresting President al-Bashir as illegal (ICC PTC I 2011, p. 9 and 18). Finally, Moreno Ocampo recently threatened to investigate Ali Osman, the UN Ambassador of the GoS, for rejecting the Prosecutor's statements about crimes in Darfur. Ocampo was quoted by AFP as saying: '[Ali Osman's] *activities denying the crimes in Darfur could be considered part of the crimes,*... [the ICC will] *investigate if Mr ... Ali Osman's denial of the crimes committed could be considered a contribution to the perpetrators, acting with a common purpose*' (AFP 2012). By threatening to investigate political remarks made during a session of an international institution, the Chief Prosecutor is fostering the perception of the AU and other

[35] It is unclear whether the groups are genuine civil society organisations or acting as GoS proxies.

critics that he is overstepping the borders of his mandate and meddling in political affairs. His statement is clearly part of a shaming strategy that is likely to do more harm than good as it helps those who question the ICC's legal professionalism.

This analysis has shown that claims of effective ICC pressure on the GoS are vastly overstated. The ICC alone was not able to exert sufficient pressure on the GoS, and it was even used as an instrument by powerful states. Additionally, the peak of external pressure on the GoS was reached in 2005/2006, when some states were still discussing a possible intervention in Darfur and before worries concerning the South Sudan referendum took centre stage (Grünfeld and Vermeulen 2009, p. 232). The ICC had not even issued an arrest warrant at that point and was thus not able to play an important role in pressuring the government. Even though the ICC helped to start the Doha Negotiations by indicting President al-Bashir, the overall impact was limited and came at a high price. Throughout the investigations, Sudan has remained essentially defiant. First, the GoS promoted those accused of having committed crimes in Darfur into high government positions (see Section 4.2.1c), then al-Bashir reacted to the issuing of the ICC warrant against him by telling the Court it should 'eat' its warrant (The Vancouver Sun 2009). At the same time, the ICC warrant deepened the division between the different camps in the international community that were disagreeing about how to proceed in the Darfur issue. The procedural decisions taken by the ICC organs played an important role in this, particularly the decision of the OTP to go directly for al-Bashir.

These findings stress the importance of the interplay between pressure exerted by the international community and by international trials and tribunals on conflict parties. The pressure exerted through international investigations can lead to a fragmentation of international pressure, especially when the role of the Court is perceived as inappropriate meddling in the internal affairs of another state by one part of the international community. Accordingly, the international pressure did not render results. UNAMID has been deployed, but Sudan is increasingly challenging the mandate of the operation. At the same time, the Doha Negotiations only led to a partial peace agreement, signed by the political wing of one small rebel group. The Darfur conflict remains essentially unresolved.

b. Marginalisation of spoilers

The marginalisation mechanism predicts that hardliners within a conflict party who are opposed to a negotiated settlement will be weakened through international investigations and prosecutions, which would in turn lead to the takeover of a moderate party more willing to negotiate a solution to the conflict. In the case of Sudan, the prosecutions were targeted against President al-Bashir and his chain of command responsible for the handling of the Darfur dossier.

While the ICC arrest warrant against al-Bashir initially deepened the rifts within the ruling elite, the president has fully re-established his position at the time of writing. He was even able to use the ICC warrants as a rallying call to unite the elites around him (see Section 4.2.5b). Additionally, there is no real moderate faction within the NCP that is willing to tackle the root causes of the Darfur conflict. The marginalisation effect thus did not gain traction and the ICC even contributed to obfuscating the root causes of the conflict by focusing on the role of the president. Yet, somewhat unexpectedly, the ICC investigation led to a marginalisation of the NCP in Darfur and to a rift between the GoS and its Janjaweed allies. The strategic decision of the OTP to apply a confrontational approach focusing on al-Bashir was crucial for both outcomes.

How to deal with Darfur has been controversial within the GoS since the early phases of the conflict. Some authors report first splits over the hardlinc approach relying on tribal militias and the displacement of 'African' tribes as early as 2004 and 2005 (ICG 2004a, p. 4 and 12, 2004d, p. 8, Tanner 2005, p. 33). Moderates and hardliners mainly disagree about how to solve the Darfur conflict. While the hardliners support the military approach and want to keep the international influence in Darfur minimal, the moderates are ready to accept an UN involvement in Darfur and are willing to compromise in order to resolve the crisis (ICG 2006b, p. 4, 2007a, p. 8). According to several sources, the moderates within the NCP are Vice President Ali Osman Taha, Presidential Advisor Ghazi Salah al-Din al-Atabani and Major General Salah Abdallah Gosh (Cockett 2010, p. 242, ICG 2007a, p. 8), while the hardliners are Presidential Advisor Magzoub al-Khalifa (who was killed in a 2007 car accident), Presidential Advisor Nafie Ali Nafie, as well as President al-Bashir (ICG 2005c, p. 9, 2007a, p. 8).[36]

Several rifts have emerged between these two groups over the course of the Darfur conflict. Disagreements emerged, for example, over the UN

[36] According to a senior commander and founding member of JEM, a group around Nafie Ali Nafie constitutes the hardline faction of the NCP. According to him, Nafie is 'even more radical than al-Bashir' (Abdelrahman 2010).

role in UNAMID in 2006 (ICG 2006b, p. 4), which led to a public declaration of President al-Bashir denying rumours that there was a rift between him and his Vice-President Taha (BBC 2006a). The fact that al-Bashir found it necessary to deny these rumours explicitly, arguably shows that they were not completely baseless. The disagreement between hardliners and moderates about whether to implement the CPA and whether to resolve the Darfur and Abiyei crises through negotiations reportedly persisted after 2006 (ICG 2007a, p. 8).

The ICC activity in Sudan has clearly emboldened the opposition within the country. With the indictment of President al-Bashir, the opposition started to openly criticise the NCP and al-Bashir himself. A senior member of the DUP opposition party and PCP leader Hassan al-Turabi were detained during 2008 and 2009 for supporting the ICC indictment against al-Bashir (AP 2008a). According to some sources, the ICC indictments for some time seriously threatened to undermine al-Bashir's position (e.g. de Waal and Stanton 2009, p. 331). Some sections within the NCP said al-Bashir's ICC indictment was a liability for the presidential election and asked him not to run for president (ICG 2009, p. 11–12). Leaked diplomatic cables show that Ali Osman Taha and Salah Gosh were contemplating to get rid of al-Bashir in the wake of the ICC indictment for the same reason (Sudan Tribune 2011e).

Some incidents reported in the newspapers also illustrate the splits within the NCP. An Arabic newspaper reported on 3 October 2009 that al-Bashir was trying to appoint a new vice-president in order to get rid of Osman Taha (Al-Sharq al-Awsat 2009). Another split over the role of the Paramilitary Border Guards (PDF) was reported in 2010, when a military committee in southern Darfur identified the PDF as a security threat (Radio Dabanga 2010d, 2010j). On 5 December 2010, a Sudanese university professor wrote an op-ed calling on al-Bashir to step down, arguing that the president's isolated position due to the ICC indictment hampered Sudan's international standing (BBC 2010b). Finally, disagreements emerged within the NCP after al-Bashir's re-election. One group of NCP functionaries demanded that the governing party open up to the opposition, while the hardliners thought they could control the situation without sharing power (ICG 2011b).

The pressure on the Sudanese Government again increased in the scope of the Arab Spring during 2011, when reports of several protests due to price hikes in commodities like sugar and fuel emerged. The PCP opposition party and Darfur refugees called on al-Bashir to step down several times during that period, and demonstrators in areas like Darfur and Blue Nile publicly called for al-Bashir to face justice or to turn himself in to the ICC (Sudan Tribune 2011e). Al-Bashir was forced to declare that he would not run for the 2015 elections when the pressure peaked on 22 February 2011 (see Perras 2011, p. 9), but it is unclear whether this declaration still stands today. Reports of ongoing pressure on President al-Bashir over the economic situation persist at the time of writing (e.g. El Gizouli 2012, Jennings 2012).

The analysis shows that the ICC had an impact on the divisions and splits within the NCP, particularly shortly after the issuing of the ICC arrest warrant against President al-Bashir. Critics of al-Bashir, both within and outside the party, used the ICC indictment to increase the pressure on him. Yet, al-Bashir has meanwhile been able to consolidate his position by skilfully using the ICC warrants as a rallying call. This is illustrated by the fact that he was able to get rid of 'moderates' like Salah Gosh, who was arrested on 19 May 2011 and again on 22 November 2012 (Radio Dabanga 2011b). He was also able to weaken the 'moderate' vice-president Taha by appointing the Darfuri NCP member Adam Yousef as another vice-president in the scope of the Doha Agreement.[37]

While the ICC investigations at least temporarily marginalised al-Bashir within the NCP, it is unclear whether this marginalisation actually increased the chances of a peaceful solution of the Darfur conflict. There are simply no moderates around who would have been willing to tackle the root causes of the Darfur conflict in peaceful negotiations. First, 'moderates' is a very relative term in Sudan. People like Vice-President Taha and Salah Gosh, who are described as moderates by Sudan experts, are mentioned in ICC documents for their role in crimes committed in Darfur. As shown in Section 4.2.1c, Gosh can even be considered to be amongst those most responsible for these crimes. Second, the moderates are part of the dominant central elites who exploit the peripheries of the Sudanese state. If al-Bashir were to be marginalised and replaced, the same old elites would stay in control and the root causes of the conflict would not be tackled. Whether the 'moderates' would achieve a negotiated settlement is doubtful, as they would not be ready to cede the same degree of autonomy to Darfur that the rebels demand. That said, starting negotiations would have become simpler with al-Bashir's marginalisation

[37] A more detailed analysis of al-Bashir's consolidation of power is conducted in Section 4.2.5c.

since many victims want him to be handed over to the ICC as a prerequisite to negotiations.

Unexpectedly, a secondary effect of the ICC warrant against al-Bashir that contributed to the increased marginalisation of the NCP within Darfur was identified in the analysis. The Janjaweed who cooperated with the GoS have lost their seasonal migration routes in the conflict and are cut off from humanitarian aid. At the same time, they say that the GoS has not fulfilled promises of rewarding their support (Flint and de Waal 2008, p. 257–258, Tajeldin 2009). Reportedly, Janjaweed commanders are also increasingly afraid that the NCP is going to use them as scapegoats to deflect pressure resulting from the ICC investigations. These fears have been nurtured by the repeated arrest of the ICC-indicted Janjaweed Commander Ali Kushayb (Arieff et al. 2011, p. 11, Flint and de Waal 2008, p. 257–258). As a consequence, a number of Arab leaders have started to disassociate themselves from the government since 2008 (Flint 2009, p. 25 and 28, Tajeldin 2009). In several instances, former Janjaweed fighters have joined Darfur rebel groups (Flint 2009, p. 32, Radio Dabanga 2010f, 2010o). Additionally, two Arab rebel groups, the Popular Democratic Front and the Nomads and Herders Movement, emerged in October 2010 (Radio Dabanga 2010c, 2010k). This illustrates that the NCP is increasingly losing the support of the Arab tribes in Darfur.

The example of Darfur shows that the marginalisation mechanism cannot work as predicted if there are no real moderates within the targeted party. There is no reason to believe that the so-called moderates would have been ready to really compromise on the Darfur issue. By indicting al-Bashir, the ICC has focused the attention on one particular actor, which is not necessarily helpful for solving the conflict since the very structure of the Sudanese state is at the centre of the conflict. The attempts to marginalise al-Bashir ignore the fact that the problem of central elites exploiting the peripheries would remain even if the president changed.

At the same time there has been a secondary effect of the ICC warrants against al-Bashir that could not be predicted from the findings in the literature, namely the marginalisation of the NCP within Darfur. The prosecution strategy of the OTP played a defining role in this context. The decision to focus on al-Bashir and isolate him was a deliberate strategic approach. This is illustrated by the fact that the Chief Prosecutor, in his December 2008 report at the UNSC, offered the inner circle of the NCP immunity from investigations if al-Bashir was handed over (Peskin 2009a, p. 674). The decision of the OPT to focus on al-Bashir, however, neglected the real root cause of the conflict: the marginalisation of the Sudanese peripheries. Another OTP decision was to frame the Janjaweed tribes in Darfur as the 'bad guys'. While this might have contributed to deepening the tribal fault lines in the conflict (see Section 4.2.4b), it also contributed towards deepening the distrust between the GoS and its Janjaweed allies, thus marginalising the GoS in Darfur.

c. International isolation

Being targeted by the ICC may cause conflict parties to lose international legitimacy and thus access to Resources to maintain armed conflict. In the case of the Sudanese Government, key Resources are investments from China and India that counteract US sanctions, as well as the political support from a number of countries in the UNSC that block any drastic resolutions. The OTP has made clear that it is trying to isolate the GoS to make an enforcement of its warrants against al-Bashir more likely. ICC officials have publicly claimed progress in these efforts. For example, the Chief Prosecutor claimed that al-Bashir had been further isolated by the ICC warrants and his travels had been complicated (Moreno Ocampo 2011, p. 11, Radio Dabanga 2011i). The ICC has met some success in isolating al-Bashir, as evidenced by the number of state visits that had to be cancelled due to the ICC warrants. But in the long run, the AU and the AL closed their ranks behind al-Bashir to support him against the warrants. At the same time, key sponsors like China have upheld their close relations to Sudan. The isolation mechanism has thus ultimately failed, mainly due to the perception among Sudan's African and Arab peers that the warrant issued against al-Bashir is a manifestation of a neo-colonial bias of the ICC.

The ICC warrant against Sudanese president al-Bashir has to be regarded as a litmus test for the isolation claims in Darfur. If al-Bashir lost the support of other states, he would no longer be able to deflect the international pressure on his regime and would eventually have to cede on Darfur. The importance of international supporters for the Sudanese policy in Darfur has been explained in detail above. The GoS is thus not immune against attempts of isolating it internationally. The regime's diplomatic manoeuvres when feeling under pressure suggest that the GoS is actively seeking to avoid international isolation over Darfur (ICG 2006b, p. 6).

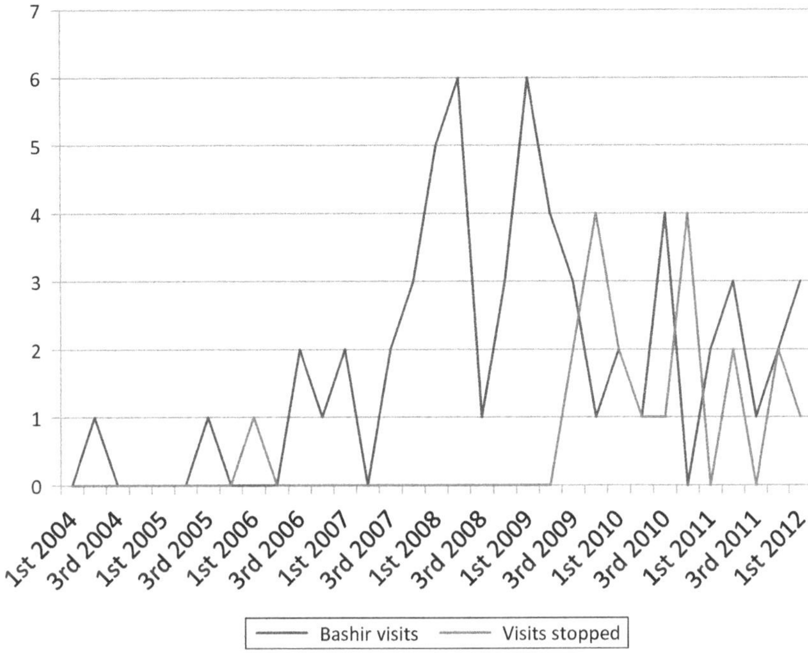

Figure 4.2: Official trips conducted by President al-Bashir since his indictment

A strong indicator for isolation would be a measurable reduction in travels of the president after the issuing of the warrants. The number of state visits conducted by President al-Bashir before and after his ICC indictment reveals that he travelled a lot directly after the warrant became public (Figure 4.2). This was obviously a political decision, meant to show that the president would not be affected by the warrant. He conducted ten trips without any obvious interference due to the ICC warrant during the first six months of 2009. Yet, starting in the third quarter of 2009, al-Bashir had to cancel a number of conference trips and official state visits to different countries. Of course, the GoS always presented an excuse on these occasions. Yet, taking into consideration that every successful trip abroad is a political triumph for President al-Bashir, it is clear that he did not cancel those trips voluntarily. The percentage of official trips that al-Bashir was forced to cancel is rising continuously since 2009. While he had to cancel 30 per cent of his trips in 2009, the share rose to 42 per cent in 2010 and 50 per cent in 2011.

Yet it is important to consider that al-Bashir was able to travel to a number of ICC State Parties, including Chad, Djibouti, Kenya and Malawi. Taking into consideration that State Parties are under the legal obligation to arrest ICC suspects – according to the Court's interpretation of the Rome Statute – and remembering how much the ICC depends on state cooperation, these trips were victories for President al-Bashir. But these triumphs came at a price and may have been short-lived. As shown below, the trips to Kenya and Malawi sparked developments that made future visits of al-Bashir to these countries impossible.

The number of trips is one important indicator, but the fact that al-Bashir has been able to make some important trips to ICC State Parties shows that isolation in this area has so far been a partial success at best. An evaluation of al-Bashir's trips can therefore not conclusively clarify whether isolation worked. Accordingly, the relationships between the GoS and other states have to be analysed in more detail.

The increasing political isolation of Sudan over the Darfur conflict could be felt even before the warrants against al-Bashir were issued. The Sudanese president tried to become Chairman of the AU twice in January 2006 and 2007. On both occasions, he failed to get the necessary votes, partly due to African NGO pressure over the situation in Darfur (also Baldauf et al. 2009, p. 131).

Despite the fact that al-Bashir travelled without interference after the issuing of the ICC warrant, its impact could be felt as the presidents of Brazil, Chile and Colombia actively dodged al-Bashir at a summit in Qatar (Simons 2010, p. 2). Additionally, Presidential Advisor Salah al-Din admitted on 29 September 2009 that the ICC warrant had restricted al-Bashir's movements (BBC 2009e). During the first year, al-Bashir therefore avoided visiting any ICC State Party and instead focused his efforts on galvanising the support of states and international bodies against the ICC. While the AU as an organisation supported al-Bashir from the beginning, this support was not unanimous as South Africa, Nigeria, Uganda and Botswana stated that they would arrest him should he set foot in their countries (Akhavan 2009, p. 649, Baldauf et al. 2009, p. 131).

In order to rally the support of Arab and African countries, the GoS started a campaign against the ICC, labelling it a '*white man's court for Africa*' and calling the ICC warrant against al-Bashir an imperialist plot, thus trying to drive a wedge between the ICC and its thirty African State Parties (Lauria 2009, Peskin 2009a, p. 677, Ssenyonjo 2009, p. 419). Similar efforts were made to gain AL support by claiming that the warrant was part of an anti-Arab campaign (de Waal 2009, p. 140). These efforts aligned with the earlier efforts of the GoS to criticise the UNSC referral of the Darfur situation as biased and politically motivated in 2007. The main point of criticism was that the United States had designed the referral resolution to exclude any ICC jurisdiction for US citizens in Sudan, while Sudanese citizens could be targeted even though Sudan was not a State Party to the Rome Statute, either (Isma'il 2007).

The GoS also tried to foster worries in the international community that the ICC might endanger peace efforts (Peskin 2009b, p. 308). After the al-Bashir warrant was issued, the GoS even intensified its campaign against the Court. This included mobilising demonstrations against the ICC and UN peacekeepers in Khartoum and Darfur, and issuing threats against the safety of UN personnel in Sudan. The GoS went as far as claiming that Western powers were using the ICC as an instrument in a conspiracy for regime change in Sudan (Chalk and Kelton 2009, p. 121–122, Nouwen and Werner 2010, p. 956, Peskin 2009b, p. 309).

This campaign started to bear fruits soon, as several African and international officials adopted Sudan's arguments (AFP 2009a, 2009d, Lauria 2009). A joint Sudanese–Libyan campaign to persuade African states to 'unsign' the Rome Statute failed (Peskin 2009b, p. 307), but the attitude of the AU towards the Court has changed considerably since the Sudanese propaganda campaign started. In its 2004–2007 Strategic Action Plan, the AU was still calling on all member states to ratify the Rome Statute (Clarke 2009, p. 72). Now, the AU shares many of the allegations of an anti-African bias of the ICC and criticises the role of the UNSC in the ICC referral system (Abdulai 2010, p. 10, de Waal and Stanton 2009, p. 332, du Plessis 2010, p. 14, ICG 2006d, p. 21).[38] Most notably, the AU decided at its July 2009 summit in Libya that no country on the continent should cooperate in arresting al-Bashir even if they had ratified the Rome Statute (AU 2009). This decision rendered visits of President al-Bashir to African ICC member states possible and led to visits in Chad, Kenya and Malawi. The AU made clear that its decision not to arrest al-Bashir was binding for AU member states and defended Chad, Kenya and Malawi for receiving al-Bashir (Kezio-Musoke 2010). In the meantime, there has been an ICC decision declaring the non-cooperation resolution of the AU as illegal. This ruling has only fanned the discord between the AU and the ICC. The AU ended up supporting

[38] The recent controversy surrounding the ICC indictment of Kenya's current president has further deepened the rift between the AU and the ICC.

several attempts by African states to obtain a UNSC deferral of the ICC investigations in Darfur, Libya and Kenya (Ero 2010, p. 12–13).

To sum up, the GoS has managed to exploit and amplify Arab and African scepticism towards ICC investigations in Sudan and to partly break the international isolation of Sudan (Baldo 2010, p. 1, Mendes 2010, p. 92). This tendency has been confirmed by more recent AU criticism of the ICC's role in Libya and Kenya. Yet, it is important to acknowledge that the AU is not a homogenous block. The same applies for its relations to the ICC (Ero 2010, p. 11–12). Some AU countries, including Benin, Botswana, Chad, Ghana and Uganda[39] later distanced themselves quietly from the non-cooperation decision and warned al-Bashir not to visit their country and risk arrest (Peskin 2009b, p. 308, Sudan Tribune 2010a). South Africa joined the position of these countries under civil society pressure on 3 August 2009, when it clarified that its national law obliged it to arrest al-Bashir if he visited (BBC 2009c). Additionally, visits by al-Bashir to CAR and Kenya have been blocked repeatedly due to civil society outrage (CICC 2011, p. 7). The Kenyan High Court issued a domestic arrest warrant against al-Bashir on 28 November 2011 after civil society groups had sued the government for inviting al-Bashir (Wegner 2011b). Finally, the new Malawian president changed the policy of her country in May 2012 by stating that the Sudanese president would no longer be welcome at conferences in Malawi, thus causing the relocation of a planned AU summit (BBC 2012).

The support of al-Bashir from the AL and the Muslim world is also not as unified as the GoS suggests. While a number of countries reject the ICC warrant outright, others have so far not voiced an official opinion on the issue, including Bahrain, Egypt, Iraq, Lebanon, Libya, Morocco and Palestine (AL 2009). Additionally, a majority of the population in four Muslim countries showed support for al-Bashir's indictment in a 16 July 2009 poll (WPO 2009).

On the side of Western countries, the warrant indeed deepened Sudan's isolation. France, Germany, Canada, the United Kingdom, the EU and Denmark started calling on Sudan to cooperate with the Court (Arieff et al. 2011, p. 13). France even moved the France–Africa summit from Egypt to France in order to keep al-Bashir away in December 2009 (BBC 2009b). After al-Bashir was re-elected on 26 April 2010, the only

[39] Uganda president Museveni has, meanwhile, again become an increasingly vocal critic of the ICC.

heads of state or government who attended the inauguration were from Chad, Djibouti, Ethiopia, Malawi and Mauritania. It is particularly striking that no Arab leaders attended the inauguration (see Rice 2010). The fact that the heads of the UNAMID and UNMIS missions attended the ceremony caused a controversy.[40] As a result, the UN later admonished UNAMID head Gambari for attending Chadian president Déby's wedding in Khartoum at which al-Bashir was present in February 2011.

Nevertheless, Sudan's main supporters, which include China, Russia, etc. stayed by Sudan's side. This is being illustrated by the fact that President al-Bashir was received in China with full military honours during a state visit in June 2011, despite a second arrest warrant for genocide being issued by the ICC (Branigan 2011). The AU and the AL are supporting President al-Bashir in official declarations, and the GoS has been able to reduce its isolation by creating divisions between the ICC and its African member states. On the international level, a certain degree of ambivalence towards al-Bashir prevails. This is partly due to the fact that the international community needed al-Bashir to guarantee the stability during the secession of South Sudan and beyond (also Assal 2009, p. 294, Expert Interview 2010b).

The Darfur case shows that the isolation mechanism does not always work even when it is used as a conscious approach, as was the case in the ICC's Darfur prosecutions. Again, the strategic decisions at the OTP and perceptions of justice determined the outcome of the isolation mechanism. The OTP decision to directly indict al-Bashir and the African and Arab reactions to this step – defined by perceptions of a biased Court – largely explain why the isolation attempts failed in Darfur. The strategic decisions taken at the OTP and the regional perceptions of (in)justice went hand in hand here and undermined the ICC efforts to isolate the GoS internationally.

d. Prevention through special deterrence

Special deterrence would lead to a reduction of the crimes being investigated by the ICC in the Darfur conflict, especially in cases where the perpetrators have not yet been targeted by the Court. At first glance, the reduction of the number of battle related deaths since the inception of the ICC investigations suggests that this is indeed the case. However, an

[40] The UN clarified that its personnel was required to keep contact with al-Bashir to a minimum but that presence at the inauguration was unavoidable due to their duties (Worsnip 2010).

analysis of the situation shows that the GoS merely changed its modus operandi in late 2004, trying to starve the African population instead of attacking it directly. The systematic use of militias and the targeting of the ICC population have not stopped, despite ICC investigations. The same is true for rebel attacks on UNAMID personnel, another crime under investigation by the ICC. Additionally, the attacks from the early phases of the Darfur conflict re-ignited in 2008, thus undermining deterrence claims.

Both a comparison of the situation before and after the ICC referral as well as between the different stages of the investigations is helpful to determine whether the ICC investigations have had a deterrent effect on the ground. The analysis will be guided by the criteria for efficient deterrence described in Chapter 3. There have been a number of deterrence claims in the literature and also some more specific claims brought forward by people involved in the conflict. A high ranking JEM commander claimed that many foreign Janjaweed had left Darfur again due to fear of the ICC, and the UNAMID chief claimed that attacks on peacekeepers had diminished due to new rules of engagement and the threat of ICC prosecutions (Abdelrahman 2010, Gambari 2010). Additionally, the OTP has made clear that it is aiming to deter the commission of more crimes in Darfur (Moreno Ocampo 2006a, p. 2).[41]

The violence in the Darfur conflict peaked in late 2003, before the case had been referred to the ICC. The crimes that would have fallen under the jurisdiction of the ICC that were committed during this time include attacks against civilians, looting, summary execution and rape (HRW 2004, p. 32–36). Active fighting started to subside during 2004. Human rights advocates and researchers agree that the worst violence of the early conflict had ended by November 2004, simply because most of the villages directly targeted by the GoS and the Janjaweed were already deserted at that point (de Waal and Stanton 2009, p. 341, HRW 2004, p. 1). All existing data on battle-related deaths confirm that direct violence had lessened considerably by the time the ICC started to investigate in 2005. This is illustrated by the number of battle-related deaths from the UCPD datasets displayed in Figure 4.3.

The GoS then changed its approach of targeting the 'African' tribes by blocking humanitarian aid to the IDP camps. A warrant for genocide has

[41] The OTP seems to believe that these efforts have shown some success in Darfur. It has prepared a graph showing a decreasing number of killings in Darfur with the caption 'quantitative analysis of the deterrence impact' (Mendez 2010b, p. 9).

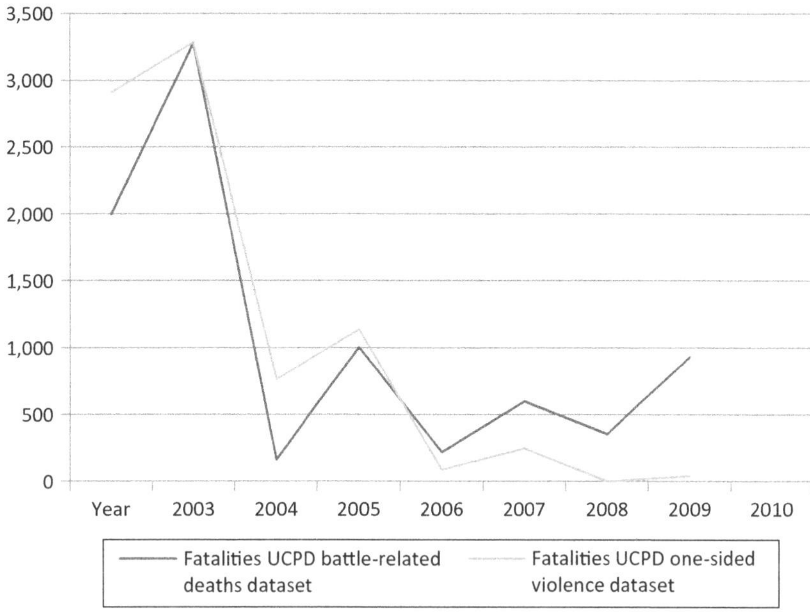

Figure 4.3: Battle-related deaths according to the UCPD datasets

been issued against President al-Bashir by the ICC for this indirect approach allegedly aimed at exterminating the African population in Darfur. The statistics for battle-related deaths do not count these indirect victims of the Darfur conflict; but there are some estimates based on UN figures which include excess deaths from malnutrition and diseases. Even though these figures are far from exact, they better reflect the number of lives lost during the Darfur conflict than the battle-related death figures. According to these figures, the number of deaths had reached about 150,000 in March 2005 and then steadily climbed to 300,000 in early 2008 (Grünfeld and Vermeulen 2009, p. 230). There have been no reliable new estimates of the death toll in Darfur since.

Accordingly, one has to distinguish between the direct attacks and the indirect starving of IDPs in order to determine the deterrence effect. If deterrence worked, direct attacks against the civilian population, for which Haroun and Ali Kushayb have been indicted by the ICC, would not intensify again now that the OTP is monitoring the situation. Yet, there are consistent reports that the IDP populations were still being attacked after 2005 (e.g. Kahn 2008, p. 16). Additionally, a new GoS offensive was reported in February 2008. HRW described it as a '*vicious reprise of "scorched earth" counterinsurgency tactics from 2003 to 2005*' (HRW 2008b, p. 2, Reeves 2009, p. 172). GoS officials and their allies thus applied the same tactics for which the ICC had issued warrants of arrest in 2007. More recent reports also indicate that the situation has again deteriorated sharply since December 2010. According to UN and HRW information, both rebels and the GoS are again targeting civilians based on their ethnicity and have so far displaced another 40,000 civilians (HRW 2010e, IRIN 2011a). HRW also reported in 2011 that the conflict patterns known from the earlier years of the Darfur conflict have re-emerged (HRW 2011a, p. 1). There are numerous other reports of ongoing attacks following the same patterns as the 2003–2005 attacks, including the execution of seventeen civilians by a militia firing squad in Zalingei (Moreno Ocampo 2011, p. 5). At the time of writing, there are reports of the GoS Rapid Support Force militias committing similar violations as the Janjaweed in the early phases of the conflict (SCR 2014).

The attacks investigated by the ICC thus continue at a lower level. The extent of the attacks is much lower than in 2003 and 2004, simply because the conflict has entered a different phase. That there has been a new escalation between 2008 and 2010 points to the fact that ICC deterrence in this area has largely failed. Arguably, the limited successes in protecting the civilian population are mainly due to increasing UNAMID patrols rather than an ICC deterrence effect (see Kahn 2008, p. 50).

There are several incidents that underscore that the GoS has not stopped using tactics applied during the early phases of the Darfur conflict despite the ICC warrants. One example is the ongoing use of tribal militias to target civilians. A UN panel of experts reported in October 2006 that the GoS had upgraded Janjaweed militias with pick-up trucks and rocket-propelled grenades (RPGs) instead of disarming them (UNSC 2006b, p. 3). This continued after the ICC had issued its first warrants in May 2007. AFP reported on 17 November 2007 that al-Bashir opened new paramilitary training camps in Darfur (AFP 2007), and the GoS also started a new recruitment campaign for Janjaweed after the JEM offensive on Ombdurman (Flint 2009, p. 46–47). It is important to consider that the OTP had already applied for an arrest warrant against President al-Bashir when this recruitment campaign started. The theoretical pre-conditions for deterrence were thus clearly there: the ICC had issued warrants against suspects of the combined Janaj-weed/SAF attacks in 2007. It was directly targeting the president in its current investigations but had not yet issued an arrest warrant. The theory would thus expect al-Bashir to avoid committing any acts that might encourage the issuing of an arrest warrant, yet the president remained defiant. He was quoted on 12 November 2008 as saying that for him the possible ICC indictment was '*similar to mosquito buzz*' (Sudan Tribune 2008b).

Indeed, reports emerging a couple of months later in March 2009 indicated that new Janjaweed groups were emerging (BBC 2009f). This pattern of further militia recruitment can be traced until early 2011, with a new recruitment wave reported on 27 January 2011 in Darfur (Radio Dabanga 2011h). Tribal militias are also increasingly used in the emerging border conflicts with South Sudan in the states of Southern Kordofan, Abiyei and Blue Nile (Sudan Tribune 2011d). Interestingly, Ahmed Haroun, who has already been indicted by the ICC, again plays a role in this context as the current governor of South Kordofan (Al Jazeera 2012). At the time of writing, the GoS has deployed additional militias under the so-called Rapid Support Force.

The blocking of humanitarian aid and the harassment of people in IDP camps, incidents that the OTP cited in its applications for the warrant of arrest for President al-Bashir, were also ongoing, despite the ICC prosecutions. Examples include the expulsion of foreign NGOs and humanitarian aid organisations working with IDPs and victims of violence in Darfur after the ICC warrants were issued. Additionally, NGOs and humanitarian agencies report ongoing and permanent attacks from rebels, bandits and government militias (IRIN 2011b). Finally, there are daily reports on Radio Dabanga about violence in the camps, harassment and rape of IDPs by government militias and attacks by government militias on civilians, markets and livestock in the camps (also AI 2012b, p. 13).[42] A particularly extreme situation emerged in Kalma Camp in 2010, after clashes over the Doha Agreement broke out between supporters and critics of the peace process. The GoS sealed off the camp, blocking humanitarian aid from reaching 82,000 IDPs (Radio Dabanga 2010e, 2010t). The GoS then tried to dismantle the entire camp, which led to a conflict between the GoS and UNAMID during which the camp was cut off from humanitarian aid for an additional two weeks. A similar situation developed in January 2011 in Zamzam IDP Camp (Radio Dabanga 2011m). The humanitarian situation in the IDP camps has

[42] The timeline from the LexisNexis analysis is full of incidents of reported attacks in the IDP camps, for example on 25 March 2009 and 2 September 2010.

improved since 2005,[43] but the ongoing security incidents show that this is a development connected to the reduced conflict intensity rather than deterrence through the ICC investigations. This is underscored by al-Bashir's decision to expel the fourteen most important international aid agencies after being indicted, thus further impairing the work of aid agencies in the camps. The GoS again reacted with defiance instead of being deterred.

Finally, the ICC is prosecuting a number of rebel leaders for their alleged role in an attack on the AMIS base in Haskanita. The OTP made clear that it wanted to prosecute those responsible for the attack to show that targeting peacekeepers is inacceptable (ICC OTP 2009, p. 6). The case of the rebel commanders allegedly responsible for the attack on the Haskanita base is so far the only case that has moved to the trial stage. It would thus in theory have a higher probability of creating a deterrent effect. Yet, UNAMID patrols are still being attacked at the time of writing. The number of peacekeepers killed has decreased from eleven in 2008 to five in 2010, but the attacks are ongoing (Center on International Cooperation 2012, p. 231). Between January and September 2011, three more peacekeepers were killed, and JEM briefly abducted fifty peacekeepers in February 2012 (Center on International Cooperation 2012, p. 231, Wegner 2012b). Taking these facts into consideration, deterrence against attacks on peacekeepers is at best very limited, and the lower number of incidents is in all likelihood again connected to the generally lower intensity of the conflict.

For deterrence theories, this failure does not come as a surprise. As shown in Chapter 3, the deterrence of the rank and file of conflict parties is generally difficult. These considerations are particularly true for the Janjaweed in Darfur since their motivations to attack are looting, revenge and fighting for what they see as their 'fair share' of land rights (see Flint 2009, p. 14, Hagan and Rymond-Richmond 2009, p. 122). Additionally, the probability of punishment is perceived as low. The fighters are aware of the immunity of government army and militia units under the Sudanese law and seek to be integrated into these units to profit from GoS protection against the ICC (see Flint 2009, p. 46).

On the rebel side, recruitment in Darfur is driven by the victimisation of entire groups. It is a typical behaviour known in criminology that

[43] The only area in which the humanitarian access remains extremely restricted in Darfur is the Jebel Marra area. Otherwise the focus of the humanitarian emergency has moved towards Southern Kordofan and Blue Nile (see UNOCHA 2012, p. 3).

young men in victim groups react with defiance and take up arms to fight back violently (Hagan and Rymond-Richmond 2009, p. 204–214). Additionally, the ICC is perceived by the rebels to be largely targeted against the GoS (see Section 4.2.5c). The perceived probability of being held to account by the ICC is therefore low.

Finally, a pre-condition for deterrence is the knowledge of the law among the rank and file. As authors have pointed out, the knowledge of even the relevant national laws in Darfur is low (Robinson and Darley 2004, p. 176). The knowledge of the Rome Statute is even lower, especially in the absence of any outreach efforts by the Court in Darfur. Under these circumstances a deterrence effect on the rank and file of both sides is only a remote possibility.

Achieving deterrence through targeting the commanders is also not likely to work in the context of Darfur because theoretical pre-conditions for deterrence are lacking. The GoS side repeatedly decided to stop efforts to rein in the Janjaweed militias because their sheer military efficacy made their use worthwhile in the cost calculations of the GoS (Flint 2009, p. 46).

But even if the motivation among commanders on both sides to stop violations was higher, they would probably not be able to control their troops. On the rebel side, banditry is on the rise since 2005 and the commanders have increasingly lost control of their troops (Burr and Collins 2008, p. 306). On the GoS side several experts have concluded that the GoS would not be able to disarm the Janjaweed (AUPD 2009, p. 23, Flint 2009, p. 14 and 50, Pronk 2004). This lack of control has even increased in the course of the conflict. In 2007, UN envoy Eliasson said that the Janjaweed are no longer a discernible group due to mutinies (Reuters 2007).

The motivation of the commanders to rein in violations of their rank and file is also low since the probability of being punished is too low. Experts emphasised the lack of any consequence of the ICC warrants for those commanders indicted (Expert Interview 2011h). For example, Musa Hilal openly stated that he was not afraid of ICC prosecutions in an interview with HRW in March 2005 despite being on the UN list of suspected war criminals (HRW 2005c). Additionally, the incoherent international pressure on the GoS undermined deterrence since it can only work in tandem with strong coercive diplomacy (see Rodman 2008, p. 556).

Deterrence theories expect zero impact if only one factor of deterrence fails (Robinson and Darley 2004, p. 196). It is therefore not surprising that ICC deterrence failed in Darfur. The Darfur case is a strong example illustrating that deterrence is very difficult to achieve in ongoing conflicts. Yet, there are many publications claiming deterrence effects, even in the scope of quantitative studies. Indeed, analysing the figures for battle-related deaths would suggest a deterrent effect of the ICC investigations in Darfur. But a contextual analysis reveals that the very same crimes that the ICC is prosecuting are still being committed on a smaller scale. Taking the conflict dynamics into consideration, it becomes very clear that it is the reduced intensity of the conflict rather than the ICC investigations that led to a reduction of the violations.

4.2.4 *Blocking conflict resolution*

a. Blocking negotiations

Some authors claim that ICC warrants are an obstacle to peace negotiations, especially if indicted leaders of a conflict party are in danger of being arrested after signing a peace agreement. Several negotiation attempts failed during the Darfur conflict or led to partial agreements that proved to be inadequate to end the fighting. Taking into consideration that the ICC indicted the Sudanese president, who is a leader of one of the conflict parties, an impact of the ICC investigations on the Resolve of the GoS seems probable. This view has also been brought forward by some authors (e.g. Rodman 2008, p. 557–559) and even by officials of the AU and the AL (AL 2009, AU 2009). The GoS quickly took up these worries and started claiming that the ICC was jeopardising a settlement in Darfur (Peskin 2009b, p. 309). An analysis of the different negotiations shows that there is no solid foundation for these claims. Negotiations rather failed due to the splintering of the rebel forces or important disagreements between the conflict parties regarding the status of Darfur. In the early phase of its investigations, the ICC was even used as a neutral institution to defuse the question of accountability for crimes committed in Darfur.

Negotiations conducted since the inception of the ICC investigations are the Abuja Talks between 23 August 2004 and 5 May 2006, the Sirte Talks in late 2007 and the different rounds of the Doha Talks between 9 February 2009 and the signing of the resulting agreement on 14 July 2011. These negotiations will briefly be analysed in the following section.

When the Abuja Talks started, the Darfur situation had not yet been referred to the ICC. The Court only became relevant after the UNSC referral on 31 March 2005, and thus could only influence the later stages of the talks. Yet the ICC did not issue any arrest warrants during the talks and the OTP's strategy was focused on obtaining cooperation from the GoS during the Abuja negotiations.

The Abuja Talks have been covered widely in scientific literature (e.g. Fisas 2010a, p. 60, Lanz 2008c, Toga 2007, p. 233), and extensive accounts of the talks have been published by insiders involved in the negotiation efforts (e.g. de Waal 2007a, 2007b). None of these accounts mention the ICC warrants as having a prominent role. Indeed, the issue of the ICC warrants was overcome in the early stages of the talks. In early 2005, the rebels demanded international investigations of alleged war crimes committed by the GoS as a pre-condition to negotiations (Fisas 2010a, p. 60, Toga 2007, p. 223). The mediators were able to circumnavigate this potential impasse by arguing that the ICC would tackle the issue of accountability independently. As a result, the Abuja Agreement remained silent on the question of accountability (de Waal 2008, p. 33, ICG 2005c, p. 14–15, Oette 2010a, p. 67). The ICC investigations did not re-emerge on the agenda of the talks. A comprehensive agreement finally failed in early 2006 as only one rebel splinter faction, the SLA-MM, signed the Abuja Agreement under heavy international pressure on 5 May 2006.

The Abuja case illustrates that ICC investigations are not an issue for peace negotiations as long as warrants for high ranking members of the conflict parties have not been issued. Quite the contrary, the ICC investigations even helped to circumnavigate the thorny issue of accountability for war crimes during the talks, as mediators skillfully removed accountability from the agenda by referring to the ongoing ICC investigations.

A detailed discussion of the Sirte Talks in this context is not necessary as they never really gained traction. Most rebel movements did not participate and the mediation was described as incompetent by UNMIS staff (Cockett 2010, p. 240, Fisas 2010a, p. 65, Flint 2010b, p. 24–25). An analyst concluded that the GoS had no interest in real negotiations at Sirte but wanted to show commitment to a peaceful solution, while the rebels were mainly interested in the free hotel accommodation (Daly 2010, p. 288 and 306).

By the time the Doha negotiations began in February 2009, the ICC had indicted the former Minister of State of the Sudanese Ministry of the Interior, Ahmed Haroun, as well as the Janjaweed leader Ali Kushayb. The ICC would also issue two arrest warrants against President al-Bashir during the early phases of the negotiations. The issuing of the first arrest warrant against al-Bashir in March 2009 dominated the first round of the talks. The parties talking at Doha were the GoS and the JEM, which had become, militarily, the most powerful movement by the time. When the ICC issued the warrants against al-Bashir, the JEM apparently hoped that the GoS would be weakened by the ICC. It therefore withdrew from Doha, saying it would not negotiate with an indicted war criminal (Cross and Williams 2009, p. 278, de Waal and Stanton 2009, p. 342, Flint 2010b, p. 33–34). The ICC indictment of President al-Bashir apparently led to a re-evaluation of the situation by the JEM. The rebels started hoping that al-Bashir might become isolated and would possibly even be toppled by an international intervention in the wake of the warrants. The indictments thus increased the Resolve of JEM.

The ICC warrant clearly had an impact on the negotiations. Yet, analysing the later stages of the negotiation shows that it was not the ICC that led to the failure of the Doha Talks. JEM declared already on 10 March 2009 that it would resume the Doha negotiations with the GoS. It had thus only interrupted the talks for five days due to the warrants. While JEM suspended the talks again on 21 March 2009, they did so due to the expulsion of international aid agencies and because their prisoners had not been released as agreed. The ICC warrants were not the reason for the second suspension.

Despite the ICC warrant, the talks led to the signing of a ceasefire between the GoS and JEM on 24 February 2010 after long interruptions. Yet, both parties were not so much interested in finding a negotiated solution to the conflict, but rather pursued their own aims with the talks (Abdulai 2010, p. 10, Expert Interview 2011h, Flint 2010b, p. 33–34, ICG 2007a, p. 6). While the GoS engaged in the talks because they needed to show that the indicted al-Bashir was not blocking peace efforts, the JEM was interested in being recognised as the only negotiation partner on the rebel side (Baldauf 2009, Daly 2010, p. 306, ICG 2009, p. 9).[44] The talks never reached a stage at which a real commitment of the two parties could be seen. For example, the GoS immediately started a large-scale offensive against the non-signatory SLA-AW in Jebel Marra after signing

[44] JEM leader Ibrahim made this aim clear in a statement published in newspapers on 16 March 2008, in which he called for one-on-one negotiations between JEM and the GoS. He argued that there were no other 'real' movements on the ground. Additionally, JEM threatened to withdraw from the talks on 7 July 2009 if other rebel groups joined as separate parties. On 25 February 2010, JEM again threatened to withdraw because the GoS considered taking up talks with the LJM.

the ceasefire with the JEM on 24 February 2010, followed by an offensive against JEM itself in May 2010 which led to the interruption of the talks (UN 2010, p. 1). At the same time, JEM left and re-joined the negotiations in Doha at least five times between February 2009 and February 2011. The main sticking points that emerged during the later stages of the talks and prevented an agreement between the parties also revolved around issues not connected to the ICC investigations. Issues of contention were the administrative status of Darfur,[45] the rebel demand of appointing the vice-president,[46] and most importantly, JEM's demand to negotiate the solution of the Darfur conflict as part of a broader agreement tackling the issue of the marginalisation of the peripheries in the Sudanese state (JEM 2010, Radio Dabanga 2010r).[47]

Admittedly, some accountability demands were occasionally brought forward by JEM and other rebels groups (JEM 2009, Mirmar 2011, NRF 2009). The most recent demands were brought up by the JEM and the LJM at the Doha negotiations on 23 March 2011, when the movements signed an agreement to coordinate their positions in Doha and called for the punishment of those indicted by the ICC. This position was reiterated by the parties on 24 May 2011, when they demanded 'prosecutions of war crimes' more generally.

These demands illustrate that the ICC warrants might have become a sticking point in later stages of the talks if JEM and the GoS had been able to solve the other differences. An expert working as an external trainer for the GoS emphasised how important it was for the GoS to keep the ICC out of any agreements (Expert Interview 2011h). It is difficult to say whether JEM would have upheld the accountability demands had the GoS been willing to compromise on the main points of contention. This remains a purely academic question as the rebels have so far always seen a realistic chance to decide the conflict militarily in their favour, and were as little inclined to compromise as the GoS.

After the talks between JEM and the GoS failed, the government focused on negotiating with the LJM. Even though mechanisms for transitional justice and compensation payments remained contentious

[45] JEM left the Doha negotiations again on 5 April 2011 because al-Bashir issued a decree stating that the administrative status of Darfur should be determined by referendum rather than in negotiations with rebels.

[46] On 30 March 2010, newspapers reported that the talks between the GoS and JEM got stuck on power-sharing demands by the rebels.

[47] JEM specifically demanded several times to include Kordofan in the framework of the peace negotiations, for example, in a meeting with the US envoy in Doha on 2 May 2011.

in the late stages of the talks (Radio Dabanga 2010g, 2010q), the parties were able to solve the issues and the Doha Agreement between the LJM and the GoS was signed in July 2011. This shows that the justice issue can be circumnavigated if both sides are committed to a peaceful solution.

The question whether a durable and comprehensive agreement to end the Darfur conflict is possible despite the ICC investigations cannot be answered conclusively though since the Doha Agreement is as partial and fragile as the DPA was. The main military factions of the LJM split off when it became clear that LJM leader Tigani Sese would sign a deal, thus further undermining the impact of the agreement on the ground. Major constituencies in the IDP and refugee camps in Darfur and Chad have also rejected the agreement (Radio Dabanga 2011c, 2011g).

To sum up, the situation in Darfur remains such that the parties with relevant military capabilities are currently not interested in negotiating in earnest. The rebels are no longer willing to negotiate the issues in Darfur as a separate question, but have largely united behind the JEM demand that the marginalisation of the Sudanese peripheries has to be tackled in a comprehensive agreement. This is the direct consequence of the emergence of the SRF, an umbrella movement that unites rebels from Darfur, eastern Sudan and the border areas to South Sudan.

The GoS, on the other hand, does not want to negotiate as long as it sees a chance of defeating the rebellion (also Cockett 2010, p. 235). After having lost South Sudan to the secession in July 2011, al-Bashir cannot afford to strike more compromises in other areas of Sudan if he wants to stay in power (also de Waal 2007c, p. 21). He is now clearly trying to reduce the international involvement and the UNAMID presence in Darfur through the new '*Peace from within Approach*' adopted by the GoS (see HRW 2011a, p. 6–8). He has also made clear that there will be no talks with international mediation after Doha (Sudan Tribune 2011b). The ICC warrants have so far not been a stumbling block to the negotiations because there are other important incompatibilities between the parties that block any real progress.

The analysis of the different peace talks in Darfur has shown that sweeping statements concerning the impact of international investigations on negotiations are hard to make. The impact depends on the stage of the prosecution efforts, as well as on the question of who is being targeted. Another factor is how far the negotiations have already progressed by the time the warrants are issued. If investigations are in an early phase and no warrants have been issued, they can even serve to defuse potentially divisive accountability issues, as was the case during the Abuja negotiations in 2005.

b. Hindering constructive dialogue and rapprochement

> *The longer the Darfur conflict goes on, the more it takes on an awful complexity, for which the notion of genocide may be too dangerously simple.*
>
> (Polgreen 2006, p. 3)

The hindering rapprochement mechanism expects ICC investigations and prosecutions to complicate conflict resolution by making negotiated solutions less attractive and thus heightening the Resolve of the conflict parties. According to the analysis, the ICC has indeed hardened the stance of the conflict parties through its prosecution strategy. By adopting the Western mainstream narrative of an 'Arab' genocide committed against 'African' villagers, it has applied clear 'victim' and 'perpetrator' labels. This encourages a piecemeal approach to conflict resolution that ignores the root causes and focuses on stopping the fighting at all costs. Second, this has contributed to the exclusion of the Arab tribes of Darfur in all important peace negotiations, while reaching a lasting solution without them will be all but impossible. Finally, victims of al-Bashir's Darfur policy have been encouraged by the ICC's narrative to uphold their demands of an arrest of al-Bashir. Rebel groups depend on these constituencies, which has led to some groups – like SLA-AW – to refuse negotiations with al-Bashir entirely.

The OTP tries to portray the Darfur conflict in a way that benefits its efforts to enforce the warrants issued against GoS officials. The narrative brought forward by the OTP focuses on the attacks of the GoS and its allied militias (the perpetrators) on African civilians (the victims) (e.g. Moreno Ocampo 2006a, p. 4, 2008b, p. 4, 2010e, p. 6). The OTP thus promotes a reading of the Darfur conflict that focuses on a specific symptom (violence perpetrated against African civilians), rather than on the root causes.

The OTP's interpretation of the conflict is only applicable – and then in part – to the period between 2003 and early 2005. The OTP ignores that the conflict has degenerated into banditry accompanied by tribal clashes, including infighting between the 'Arab perpetrators', in 2007 and 2008. It uses this narrative of the conflict in order to pressure others into enforcing the ICC warrants by creating a sense of urgency. When the genocide charges against Sudanese president al-Bashir were confirmed in

July 2010, the Chief Prosecutor stated: '*The problem is the victims have no time. The victims are living for the last five years in camps – no education, no future for them, destroyed. They have no time. We have to rescue them now*' (Barchfield 2010).

This narrative enforces an approach focusing on peacekeeping or forcing some sort of quick settlement of the conflict. It ignores the root causes of the conflict and encourages the recipes the international community has followed over the past years – to no avail. Neither peacekeeping nor forcing partial settlements has proved suitable to address the problem in its entirety. The ICC thus furthers the piecemeal approach to conflict resolution that has failed to end the conflict during the last nine years.

The OTP has identified the Fur, Masalit and Zaghawa as victims of the conflict in several reports and press statements (e.g. Moreno Ocampo 2008b, p. 2, 2010d). At the same time, the decision to bring genocide charges against al-Bashir implies that an Arab government and Arab militias are trying to exterminate an African population. Arguably, the decision to bring genocide charges is in itself a confirmation of the racial and ethnic labels used by the conflict parties, as the definition of the crime requires targeting of victims based on their ethnicity. Unsurprisingly, the Arab population in Sudan saw the genocide charges as another unfair denigration of Arabs by the West (de-Waal 2009, p. 141, Mamdani 2009a, p. 151). This goes hand in hand with US civil society activism advocating an intervention in Darfur.

As described, the role of the Arab tribes in Darfur is far more complex than this narrative suggests. Painting the Arab tribes as perpetrators has had a tangible negative impact on the possibilities to solve the land issues in Darfur peacefully, because it has led to the exclusion of the Arab tribes at the negotiations in Abuja, Sirte and Doha (Flint and de Waal 2008, p. 214, Mamdani 2009c, p. 292).

Arab tribes have explicitly complained that the international community has demonised them and that they have been marginalised in efforts to solve the conflict (BBC 2007b). At the same time, it is clear that a real negotiated solution can be found only with Arab inclusion.

Finally, the narrative of the Darfur conflict presented by the ICC has encouraged and radicalised the Darfuri IDPs and refugees in their victim role. The OTP focuses on attacks and blockades of the IDP camps (e.g. Moreno Ocampo 2007a, p. 6, 2011, p. 8–9). But it does not mention the fact that some IDP camps have become radicalised and are now recruitment reservoirs for the rebel movements. Refugees in Chad now demand al-Bashir's extradition to the ICC as a pre-condition to negotiations. Finding a peaceful solution to the Darfur crisis with the current government is impossible if these demands are upheld. The rebels in turn are trapped by the radical demands of their constituencies and cannot drop the ICC prosecutions. According to a diplomat working on the Darfur dossier, the rebels are thus using the ICC indictments as a convenient excuse to not accept the GoS as a legitimate negotiation partner (Expert Interview 2011a).

The Darfur case study shows how the narratives of a conflict produced by the ICC can shape the conflict and the demands of conflict parties. Through the victimisation of certain groups and the attribution of guilt to other groups, the ICC is creating new Reasons for the parties to fight (e.g. al-Bashir's extradition to the ICC). For the Janjaweed and the Arab tribes, who are being marginalised as perpetrators, the ICC is increasing the Resolve to fight the problems out as they will not be included in political negotiations.

Again, the decisions on the prosecution strategy taken at the ICC emerge as a neglected factor for explaining the impact of international investigations. The way an international court chooses to describe a conflict can have a real impact on the ground. Of course, the ICC did not cause these developments alone. It rather reinforced tendencies that already existed. Civil society movements calling for an international intervention to 'save' the African civilians in Darfur also played a role here (e.g. Save Darfur 2012). Nevertheless, the narratives used by international criminal law institutions in their investigations deserve additional attention as they can have important repercussions on the ground.

4.2.5 Heightening tensions

a. Triggering spoiler retaliation

The spoiler retaliation mechanism expects conflict parties to react defiantly to international investigations, causing a backlash against international actors on the ground or an intensification of the violence as a negotiated solution becomes less attractive for the targeted conflict party. The arrest warrants issued against Omar al-Bashir did indeed trigger the expulsion and additional harassment of aid NGOs working in Darfur. But if these immediate reactions to the warrant are seen in the context of the GoS' attempts to hinder the work of these NGOs in Darfur, it becomes clear that the warrants only served as a convenient excuse for President al-Bashir to intensify the harassment. The ICC did not cause or provoke this policy of the GoS.

Only hours after the president had been indicted on 4 March 2009, he started expelling international aid agencies (de Waal and Stanton 2009, p. 346). In the end, he expelled a total of fourteen international aid agencies. In the following days and weeks, he additionally shut down three national human rights organisations and intensified the surveillance of opposition and human rights organisations (de Waal and Stanton 2009, p. 341, Flint 2010b, p. 26). The consequences of these expulsions were soon felt, as the expelled NGOs provided approximately 40 per cent of the humanitarian aid and assistance to the IDPs in Darfur. Malnutrition rates and food shortages increased according to camp leaders and aid workers (Adam et al. 2011, p. 6–7). Al-Bashir justified the expulsion of the aid agencies by claiming that they were spying for the ICC (Peskin 2009b, p. 309).

After the issuing of the warrants, some people warned that al-Bashir might go even further. There were fears of an escalation of the Darfur conflict and revenge attacks against IDPs and of a disruption of the implementation process of the CPA. Others warned that the expulsion of Western diplomats and UN staff might follow, as well as further attempts to sabotage humanitarian aid efforts and the deployment of UNAMID (CBC News 2009, p. 76–77, Weber and Tull 2008, p. 2).

The timing and al-Bashir's statements leave no doubt that the expulsion was a direct reaction to the ICC indictments. Yet, when analysing the policy of the GoS towards aid agencies, it becomes clear that the decision to expel the agencies was part of a consistent policy that was followed both before and after the issuing of the warrant and even before the ICC had begun its investigations in Darfur.

President al-Bashir called Western aid agencies the '*enemies of Sudan*' as early as 28 October 2004, arguing that the organisations were conspiring against the Sudanese state (AFP 2004). The newspapers on LexisNexis are filled with similar statements by the GoS and state media from the following years. On 10 March 2005, the GoS accused Oxfam, MSF and the Norwegian Refugee Council of conducting a political campaign on rape in Darfur and arrested MSF staff members (Chalk and Kelton 2009, p. 115). These statements soon turned into an official policy of harassing aid agencies and hindering their work. On 21 February 2006, the GoS passed the Organization of Humanitarian and Voluntary Work Act, requiring NGOs to register with the

Humanitarian Aid Commission (HAC), which started obstructing the work of the agencies by different bureaucratic means (HRW 2006b, p. 21, IRIN 2010b). Sudan experts reported that in 2007, President al-Bashir started to encourage attacks on humanitarian aid workers (Flint and de Waal 2008, p. 197).

The expulsion of aid agencies in 2009 was also not the first incident of this sort. On 3 April 2006, the GoS threw out the Norwegian Refugee Council, followed by threats in July 2006 and in 2007 to expel UN staff (BBC 2006b, 2007e). The list of comparable incidents is long. The GoS expelled the heads of UNOCHA and Care in 2008 (Kahn 2008, p. 55), and suspended the work of MSF-Holland, the International Rescue Committee, International Medical Corps and the Norwegian Aid Organization on 8 July 2008, shortly before the OTP applied for the al-Bashir warrant (BBC 2008b). On 21 October 2008, the GoS said it was probing the alleged collaboration of UNMIS with the ICC (BBC 2008c), and started issuing threats against UNAMID in connection with the possible ICC warrant.

These incidents show that the expulsion of fourteen aid agencies in March 2009 was just the culmination of a long-standing GoS policy. This policy continued after the issuing of the warrants. For example, the GoS withdrew the permits of another twenty-six organisations in January 2010 (Adam et al. 2011, p. 7). Additionally, the GoS has so far arrested twenty NGO staff for allegedly cooperating with the ICC (Baldo 2010, p. 7). Finally, UNAMID and aid NGOs have been attacked by government-affiliated militias due to alleged ICC links (Glassborow 2009). On 27 April 2011, aid NGOs complained that harassment and threats by the GoS had reached unprecedented levels (Jennings and Glassborow 2011), and on 12 July 2011, the GoS again threatened to expel aid organisations from Southern Kordofan and Darfur (Sudan Tribune 2011a).

The analysis clearly confirms that the ICC warrants against al-Bashir triggered a direct reaction, but it also shows that the GoS has pursued its policy of harassing aid agencies independently of ICC activity. It would thus be wrong to claim that the ICC significantly worsened the situation in Darfur. The arrest warrants rather offered a convenient excuse to step up a policy that the GoS had been following for years. Al-Bashir's decision to expel humanitarian organisations has to be seen in the context of his campaign against the ICC. In his propaganda efforts he had been claiming that the Court was complicating a peaceful resolution of the Darfur conflict.[48] It is reasonable to believe that al-Bashir expelled the organisations to underscore this argument (also Peskin 2009a, p. 675–676).

The retaliation mechanism in the Darfur case shows that even if an ICC warrant causes direct reactions, the ICC may not be at the root of these actions. Critics of ICC investigations need to analyse the impact of warrants in the light of the conflict history. If the context of these incidents is ignored, wrong causal links are easily assumed.

b. Bolstering support for hardliners

> *We cannot waste our time and efforts to conclude a partial peace agreement the regime will never honour. Instead, I call upon the international community to support us to establish a democratic and secular state in Sudan.*
>
> (SLA-AW Commander Abdel Wahid al-Nur cited in Sudan Tribune 2012)

> *Everything that is being claimed about reputed attacks of the Janjaweed militias abroad has the aim to pervert the facts.*
>
> (al-Bashir in an interview with Koelbl and Windfuhr 2010)

Polarisation claims expect the ICC investigations to heighten the Resolve of the conflict parties or to add to their Reasons by increasing their mutual hatred, thus increasing the support for violent approaches. The following analysis shows that the ICC has had these effects on both the rebels and the GoS. The rebels used the ICC warrants and in particular, the genocide charges to legitimise their fight and argue for an external intervention in Sudan. The ICC warrants also increased their hopes that such an intervention would take place and strengthened their Resolve. On the side of the GoS, al-Bashir managed to use the ICC investigations in a propaganda campaign to close the ranks of the ruling elites around him and galvanize their support for his violent approach in Darfur.

The disunity of the Darfur rebels and their far-reaching demands make it difficult to achieve a negotiated solution to the conflict. Some authors have argued on that basis that the rebels are blocking a negotiated solution because they are speculating on an external intervention (Kuperman 2009, Natsios 2010).

This claim can be confirmed by analysing rebel statements that have been issued over the course of the conflict. The rebels have consistently

[48] For more details on the GoS campaign against the ICC please refer to the polarisation section (Section 4.2.5c).

described the attacks by the GoS and the Janjaweed as criminal acts. This began in the first quarter of 2004, when an opposition radio first called the attacks on African villages, genocide. Accordingly, JEM soon demanded international investigations (Fisas 2010a, p. 60). At the same time, JEM and student demonstrators in Darfur demanded an international intervention. During the Abuja negotiations, the rebels demanded the deployment of a NATO or UN force (Kuperman 2009, p. 294). The AUPD concluded that the main motivation of the rebels in Abuja was to appeal to the international community to obtain recognition and support (AUPD 2009, p. 39).

There are a number of other examples that illustrate how rebels banked on an international intervention. SLA leader Abdel Wahid al-Nur repeatedly demanded an intervention, once as a direct reaction to the ICC genocide warrant (Radio Dabanga 2010b). Later, on 14 April 2011, Al-Nur called for the enforcement of a no-fly zone over Darfur (AFP 2011). The rebel calls for interventions have also been described consistently by a number of authors analysing the conflict (Darfurian Voices Project 2010, p. 35, Markusen 2009, p. 109).

These intervention demands soon found an echo both within Sudan and on the international stage. On 21 May 2004, the opposition politician al-Mahdi warned that the Darfur conflict could lead to an international intervention (BBC 2004). On 17 June 2004, UN General-Secretary Annan raised the possibility of an intervention in Darfur to protect civilians. On 22 July 2004, UK PM Blair asked his officials to prepare plans for an intervention in Darfur, and on 1 August 2004, the Dutch Parliament called the GoS attacks in Darfur genocide and called for an intervention. On 3 February 2005, NATO offered 'help' in Darfur if necessary; Kofi Annan again called for an EU and NATO intervention in Darfur during the Munich Security Conference on 13 February 2005; France, the United Kingdom and the United States considered a NATO involvement in the planned UN takeover of AMIS in early 2006.These reactions show that the rebel groups could realistically hope for an international intervention in Darfur at several points. Unsurprisingly, local actors and opposition parties soon joined the calls for intervention (de Waal 2007c, p. 21, Mamdani 2009c, p. 292–293). The Guardian reported in January 2009 that the GoS was increasingly worried about a possible US intervention in Darfur (Guardian Unlimited 2009).

In particular, the rebel movements used the genocide charges to argue for an international intervention. The Darfur rebel groups immediately welcomed US Secretary of State Powell's use of the term 'genocide' and called for the prosecution of those responsible in 2004. They soon began raising genocide allegations themselves. JEM emphasised that al-Bashir had a 'genocidary intent' in an April 2011 statement (Radio Dabanga 2011f). On 6 April 2011, SLM-MM described a new GoS offensive as a '*second genocide*' and called for an international intervention (Radio Dabanga 2011k). This analysis indicates that the use of the genocide label has emboldened rebel groups who hope for an international intervention and thus prefer not to negotiate (also Wax 2009, p. 43).

The analysis shows that the Court played a role in strengthening rebel hopes for an intervention. Rebels had already called for criminal investigations of the SAF/Janjaweed attacks in the early phases of the conflict. It is therefore not surprising that they would interpret the referral of the Darfur situation to the ICC as a first sign that the international community was starting to support them. Accordingly, the rebel groups greeted the referral as a '*victory for humanity*' in a statement on 1 April 2005. The rebels soon started combining their intervention demands with statements supporting the ICC (e.g. BBC 2007a, 2007d). The clearest examples for the ICC actually emboldening the rebels can be found shortly before and after the ICC issued its first arrest warrant for President al-Bashir. On 24 February 2009, JEM – having entered negotiations with the GoS recently – declared that it would re-focus on toppling al-Bashir if the ICC issued a warrant (AFP 2009e). Indeed, JEM broke off the negotiations with the GoS after the ICC issued the warrant and even declared that they would march on Khartoum, arrest al-Bashir, and hand him over to the Court (Baldo 2010, p. 6). Shortly after the warrant was issued, on 27 April 2009, SLA-AW leader al-Nur called for protests across Darfur until al-Bashir was toppled and handed over to the ICC.

The genocide finding of the ICC against al-Bashir was perceived as a victory by the rebels, since JEM had been lobbying for the use of the term 'genocide' (see Flint and de Waal 2008, p. 101). The tendency illustrated here can be backed up with figures. The rebels regularly issued declarations calling for an international intervention in the Darfur conflict (Figure 4.4), and unsurprisingly, these declarations peaked around the time when the first ICC warrant against al-Bashir was issued.

Rebel calls for additional ICC investigations or accountability measures show that they tried to use the Court to increase pressure on the GoS (e.g. BBC 2007c, JEM 2009, Radio Dabanga 2010h, 2011m). The statements of a senior JEM commander were particularly illustrative of the relationship between the Court and the rebel movements. He said that

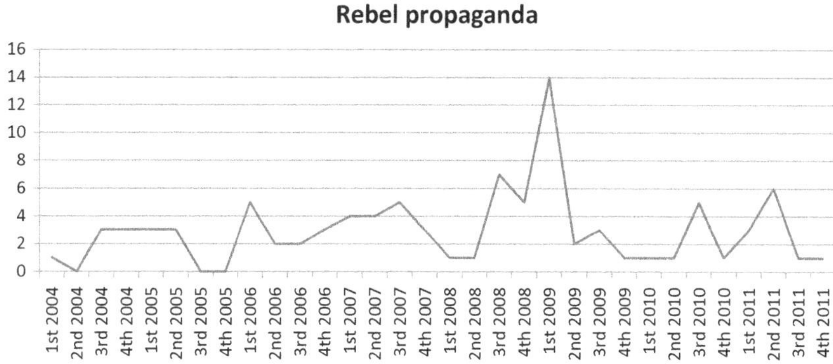

Figure 4.4: Calls for international interventions in Darfur issued by rebel officials

the ICC was '*like gold from the sky*', that the Court offered a big hope for democratising Africa, and was giving people a voice against dictators (Abdelrahman 2010).

The ICC involvement fell in line with the rebels' interest in internationalising the Darfur conflict. With increasing chances of an internationalisation of the conflict, the Resolve of the rebels also increased. The ICC furthered the perception among rebels that it was an ally in the fight against the GoS. In his reports to the UNSC, Moreno Ocampo increasingly supported a view that painted the GoS as the 'bad guys', while the rebels were seen as good. The Chief Prosecutor compared the GoS to the Nazi Regime (Moreno Ocampo 2008b, §3) and claimed that the entire Sudanese state apparatus was involved in the commission of the crimes (ICC PTC I 2008, §269). At the same time he emphasised the rebels' willingness to cooperate with the Court (Moreno Ocampo 2009a, §22, 2009b, §5). The impression that the ICC might be favouring the rebels over the GoS reached its apex in February 2010, when the Court decided to re-evaluate the initial rejection of genocide charges against President al-Bashir, while simultaneously dismissing the charges against rebel commander Abu Garda for lack of evidence. It was a mere coincidence that both decisions were taken during the same month, but they nevertheless sent a clear signal to both the GoS and the rebel movements.

The decision of the OTP to bring genocide charges against al-Bashir furthered the ICC's role in involuntarily emboldening the rebels. Bringing up the highly charged genocide issue adds a political dimension to any legal proceeding, since the international community and particularly civil society in Western states are instantly mobilized when the 'G-word' is used. The failure of the international community to stop the genocide in Rwanda and the massacre in Srebrenica has encouraged many actors to demand a humanitarian intervention as soon as the first signs of genocide are identified.

The ICC was not the only factor emboldening the rebels, but it played a role in furthering an emerging international public opinion that something should be done about the Darfur conflict. The demands for an intervention by the Save Darfur campaign in the US, the AU and UN deployments in Darfur and the sanctions issued by the UNSC all encouraged the hopes of rebels that an international intervention could take place in Darfur (Flint 2010b, p. 12, Kuperman 2009, p. 293). The positive image of the Darfur rebels spread by US activists and international media – and confirmed by the OTP in its briefings – led to a lack of pressure on the rebels to find a non-violent solution to the conflict (Cockett 2010, p. 222 and 239).

The effects of the ICC investigation on the government side were completely different, even though the outcomes were similar. The ICC investigations of high ranking GoS officials triggered a rallying effect behind al-Bashir, even though the effect might have been temporary. When the ICC decided to indict al-Bashir, the GoS had already been waging a political campaign to paint Western pressure over Darfur as a neo-imperialist or Zionist attempt to change the regime in Khartoum and gain access to the oil wealth of the country (e.g. ICG 2006b, p. 16). The GoS claimed that the Sudan policy of many Western states was part of a campaign against Muslims and Arabs who, the GoS claimed, had constantly been vilified since the 9/11 terrorist attacks. Some statements illustrate this campaign. A Presidential Advisor of al-Bashir said on 1 May 2008 that the Western media campaign around the Darfur conflict served to cover up the US failure in Iraq. On 17 July 2010, al-Bashir himself said that '*Crusaders and Zionists*' were targeting Muslims all over the world (BBC 2010a).

The referral of the Darfur situation to the ICC and the Chief Prosecutor's shaming campaign against the GoS fitted well into Sudan's propaganda efforts. Initially, the GoS argued against the ICC investigations on legal grounds, claiming that the Court had no jurisdiction in Sudan since Sudan was not a State Party. The government said that it would investigate alleged crimes in Darfur itself and it cooperated with the ICC by allowing a number of OTP delegations to conduct interviews in Sudanese ministries. This changed when the OTP took up a more offensive strategy by publicly shaming the GoS for non-cooperation, starting in December 2006 (Peskin 2009b, p. 306). When the ICC escalated this approach by indicting the president of Sudan, the GoS launched a massive diplomatic campaign against the ICC, blaming it for exacerbating the conflict (Baldo 2010, p. 3), being part of a Western plot to overthrow the regime (AP 2008b, Ssenyonjo 2009, p. 430), increasing the chances of a hardline Islamist coup in Sudan (AP 2009) and emboldening rebel groups to keep on fighting (Chalk and Kelton 2009, p. 130).

There is a wealth of other examples of how the GoS managed to make the ICC part of its propaganda campaign against an alleged Western conspiracy through statements (BBC 2008d) or by orchestrating anti-ICC rallies (Radio Dabanga 2010h).

The ICC warrants also increased al-Bashir's motivation to remain president of Sudan and defend his position at all costs to protect him from the ICC indictments. This is illustrated by the orders of the western Darfur security chief to meet any demonstrations in support of the al-Bashir warrants with bullets (HRW 2009a, p. 9), and the general hardline stance that the GoS has taken against those supporting the ICC indictment in Sudan, including censoring press articles, and arresting and torturing advocates of the ICC (Arieff et al. 2011, p. 14).

There are signs that al-Bashir has stabilised his position, at least until mid-2012. The ICG reported in 2006 how the GoS skilfully used external pressure to silence critical civil society, the opposition, as well as the national media (ICG 2006b, p. 2). The ICC indictment has furthered this approach by weakening the moderate forces within the NCP (Natsios 2010). In the current situation, opposing al-Bashir is interpreted as betraying Sudan. The rally effect for al-Bashir can be measured in the loss of influence of the comparatively moderate Vice President Ali Osman Taha, who was very powerful between 2005 and 2007 after he successfully concluded the CPA negotiations with the SPLM. He was later eclipsed by presidential advisor Nafie Al Nafie, a hardliner and one of the major supporters of the violent GoS strategy in Darfur (de Waal 2008, p. 34).

The progress of the hardliners in securing key positions in the regime has gained momentum since al-Bashir was indicted by the ICC. Journalists have reported that political enemies started closing ranks behind al-Bashir (Simons 2009), and that the president replaced people in several important positions close to him with loyalists, while suppressing criticism at the 2009 NCP convention (ICG 2009, p. 11–12). He was able to affirm his position as the presidential candidate of the NCP as nobody wanted to run against him, afraid that disunity within the NCP could permanently divide Sudan (ICG 2009, p. 13). The 2010 presidential elections and the 2011 independence referendum in South Sudan were critical junctures for al-Bashir's political future. After he had managed to weather both, he started to increasingly centralise power in northern Sudan by appointing close companions and tribal kin to central positions (ICG 2011b). As a result, a rift between the pragmatist wing and the hardliners around al-Bashir emerged about whether the GoS should seek a dialogue with opposition parties or consolidate its grip on power (ICG 2011b, Sudan Tribune 2011c). On 19 May 2011, Al-Bashir overcame this rift by arresting Salah Gosh, a key figure who was standing for the pragmatic approach within the NCP (Radio Dabanga 2011b).[49]

Apart from consolidating his grip on the ruling party, al-Bashir was also successful in fanning popular support in Sudan by using the ICC indictments in his propaganda efforts. According to a consultant working with the Sudanese government, the UNSC referral is increasingly seen as imperialistic among the political class in Sudan. In general, large parts of the population, even among the opposition, saw the indictment of al-Bashir as an attack against Sudanese sovereignty or criticised it for destabilising the situation (Expert Interview 2010b, Simons 2009, Srinivasan 2010, p. 51).

In general, more and more people started supporting al-Bashir after he had been indicted. According to most experts, this also played a role in his re-election (Expert Interview 2011h, Jaeger 2011, Scheen 2010). The ICC indictments proved to be helpful because al-Bashir managed to whip up anti-imperialist sentiments when the ICC intervened in Sudan (Cockett 2010, p. 268). After the warrant was issued, thousands rallied in Khartoum to show their support for the president (Al-Arabiya 2009), and the army as well as several Arab tribes in Darfur swore personal oaths of allegiance to al-Bashir (BBC 2009a, 2009g). Finally, AFP reports an increasing number of pictures of al-Bashir on the streets in Khartoum on 7 April 2009 (AFP 2009c). A similar effect took hold on the regional and international stage where al-Bashir was able to rally AL and AU support (see Section 4.2.3b).

Last but not least al-Bashir was also able to – at least temporarily and in part – close the lines of the opposition parties behind him due to the

[49] See also Section 4.2.3b for additional information on al-Bashir's efforts to consolidate his grip on the NCP.

ICC indictment. DUP leader al-Mahdi warned about the consequences of a warrant against al-Bashir on 12 June 2008 (BBC 2008a). After the al-Bashir warrants, the GoS explicitly called on all political parties to maintain the internal 'front' against the ICC on 10 March 2009 (BBC 2009d, Expert Interview 2011h). Even the SPLM declared that al-Bashir needed support in this hard time because they were concerned about the impact of the warrants on the implementation of the CPA (Arieff et al. 2011, p. 15). The apex of this development was reached in November 2011, when the DUP joined the NCP in government after South Sudan had seceded.

Yet, there are increasing demonstrations against the GoS in the aftermath of the Arab Spring and rising commodity prices, so al-Bashir's success in uniting the Sudanese population may be crumbling. An illustrative example is the arrest of over 100 demonstrators at Nyala University after they called for al-Bashir to face justice on 20 April 2011 (HRW 2011a, p. 21). The elite consensus is also disintegrating: at the time of writing, DUP chief Sadiq al-Mahdi has been arrested by the GoS for speaking up against human rights violations committed against civilians in Darfur.

The Darfur case clearly shows that there is a danger of ICC investigations causing a rallying effect and bolstering the position of hardliners, especially when investigations are polemical and align with the interest of one conflict party. The procedural decisions of the ICC organs again played an important role in this mechanism, as the shaming strategy of the OTP enabled the rebels to use the ICC for their propaganda efforts. As shown in the pressure and inducement section, some OTP statements were one-sided and legally not well founded, which allowed the GoS to mobilise Sudanese and regional (AL, AU) sceptics against the ICC. The fact that the OTP had not conducted investigations on the ground in Darfur for security reasons,[50] as well as allegations that the OTP used inflated mortality figures for the Darfur conflict, made it easy for the GoS to claim that the investigations were based on hearsay and rebel sources. In terms of Ohlson's theory, President al-Bashir was able to use the ICC in a political campaign and thus increase the Resolve of his followers.

[50] The decision of the OTP to not conduct investigations in Darfur has been criticised sharply by the High Commissioner for Human Rights and the head of the ICID (Arbour 2006, p. 2, Cassese 2006, p. 5–6).

c. Destabilisation, fragmentation, power vacuum

Darfur is a prime example of a case in which a range of fears were voiced regarding the consequences of ICC investigations. Some believed the issuing of warrants against al-Bashir would destabilise the situation and lead to a dangerous power vacuum in Sudan.[51] There were worries that the ICC might disrupt the implementation process of the CPA, especially the South Sudan referendum (AUPD 2009, p. 62, Badiey 2008, Weber and Tull 2008, p. 2).

From the point of view of conflict resolution theory, these fears were well founded, as the ICC indictment questions the continued existence of one of the conflict parties, namely the NCP around President al-Bashir. At the same time, al-Bashir was the main guarantor for the implementation of the CPA. In conflict resolution theory, the ICC indictment would therefore be understood as a dangerous conflict trigger (see Odero 2011, p. 152).

The developments on the ground have disproven these claims. South Sudan seceded largely peacefully in July 2011 and the Sudanese state did not implode. Al-Bashir may be under pressure, but he is still in control. Contrary to the fears, conflicts did not emerge due to a power vacuum in Sudan, but because the north and the south disagree over how to share the oil revenues and over the status of the provinces Abiyei and Blue Nile. In conclusion, the destabilisation claims were unfounded.

4.3 Conclusion of the Darfur case study

Sudan remains a violent place in which conflicts are addressed through the use of force. On balance, the ICC has rather increased the polarisation between the parties and the readiness to use violence to solve conflicts instead of furthering peace. Yet, it is important to acknowledge that the initial conflict analysis yielded a bleak outlook for the conflict anyway. It is unlikely that the chances for achieving peace in Darfur would be significantly higher in the absence of the ICC investigations.

[51] According to leaked diplomatic cables, Chinese diplomats told US diplomats that they were extremely worried about a possible destabilisation of Sudan through the ICC indictments (Fernandez 2008), and the Ethiopian PM told US representatives in January 2009 that if there was no quick coup against al-Bashir, the warrants would leave the regime '*a wounded animal that is more desperate than ever*' (Radio Dabanga 2011p).

The literature on Darfur has brought forward a considerable number of claims concerning the impact of the ICC investigations. Ten of the fifteen causal mechanisms from the literature overview were claimed for the Darfur conflict. After a careful analysis, only two of these mechanisms could be confirmed convincingly, namely, the blocking rapprochement and polarisation mechanisms. Other mechanisms developed a very limited or temporary effect on the conflict. Table 4.2 gives an overview of the different effects and when they played a role in the conflict.

Since the beginning of the conflict, rebel leaders used the ICC investigations as a rallying call for their supporters and as an argument for an external intervention in Darfur (furthering hardliner support). When the GoS understood that the international pressure to stop attacks on the 'African' population on Darfur aligned with the ICC investigations, it changed its modus operandi and tried to target the perceived rebel supporters through hindering the access of humanitarian aid. Even though direct attacks were scaled down considerably, they were not stopped completely and increased again for some time in 2010 and 2014 (special deterrence). When the investigations were finally opened, the OTP narrative of Arab attacks on African villages reinforced the conflict lines between the parties and complicated rapprochement. The decision of the ICC to switch to a public shaming approach in attempts to prosecute GoS officials further strengthened hardliner support and complicated rapprochement. The conscious decision to further escalate the conflict with the GoS by personally arresting al-Bashir had several simultaneous effects. It blocked the Doha negotiations briefly, pressured the GoS to compromise on deploying UNAMID through increasing the pressure on its main supporter China and temporarily weakened al-Bashir within the NCP. The warrant led to a partial isolation of al-Bashir on the international stage. All of these impacts of the al-Bashir arrest warrants were quite short lived.

These findings contradict the literature in many ways and illustrate how much the analysis of ICC impacts in conflicts still relies on shaky claims rather than on empirically well-founded research. There are several reasons why the claims of ICC impacts in Darfur prove to be incorrect at a closer look. Many ignore the history and the local context of the conflict. This is particularly true for the claim that the ICC triggered the hostile GoS policy towards international aid agencies and NGOs. As shown above, the ICC is more appropriately described as a convenient excuse for an existing GoS policy in this context. Another example is the destabilisation claim that expected al-Bashir to lose

Table 4.2: *Overview of ICC Effects in the Darfur conflict (a grey shade is a partial effect, black shade a strong effect)*

Investigation phases	Referral to opening investigations		Investigations to issuing of warrants		First warrants in force		Second set of warrants		
1. Rule-of-law mechanisms									
Human rights protection and respect for law									
Capacity building / reforms									
Counter-impunity									
2. Reconciliation and transformation									
Meeting victim needs									
Individualising guilt									
3. Isolation and deterrence									
Pressure and inducement									
Marginalisation									
International isolation									
Special deterrence									
4. Blocking conflict resolution									
Blocking negotiations									
Blocking rapproachment									
5. Heightening tensions and polarisation									
Triggering spoiler retaliation									
Reopening wounds									
Furthering hardliner support									
De-stabilisation									
Conflict phases	**Starving tactics of GoS, medium intensity warfare**	**Abuja negotiations**	**Abuja negotiations**	**Post-DPA conflicts, rebel offensive**	**Low-intensity conflict, splintering of rebels, Arab infighting**		**Doha negotiations**	**Doha negotiations, renewed SAF/ rebel fighting**	**Post-Doha conflicts, rebel unifications**

control in Sudan and predicted an implosion of the state. The claim ignored the fact that al-Bashir was in fact able to use the ICC warrants to rally support on a national level and strengthen his position, at least temporarily. Finally, there is a reasonable basis for claiming that the ICC has deterred crimes in Darfur when focusing on the data of battle-related deaths. At a closer look, all that changed was the modus operandi of the government forces that targeted African civilians.

Another finding of the Darfur case study is that the effects of ICC investigations differ across the conflict parties. While the rebels have been emboldened by the ICC investigations, the GoS came under pressure and tried to turn the table by painting the investigations as biased. The dominant country-level approaches in the literature fail to grasp the different effects of international trials and investigations on the conflict parties. The deterrence effect is another example of the variation of effects across parties. The OTP has been concentrating on a number of clearly identified, specific crimes in the Darfur conflict. On the government side, that was the use of tribal militias against the civilian population in Darfur, an integral part of the GoS war effort. On the rebel side, the ICC only targeted those rebel commanders who attacked international peacekeepers. Deterrence thus works very differently for both sides. On the rebel side, it may prove to be more successful in the long run as the ICC investigations only target attacks against peacekeepers and thus do not have an impact on the overall rebel war effort. The GoS, on the other hand, heavily relied on the Janjaweed militias to rein in the Darfur rebellion in the early stages of the conflict and would have a lot to lose if it cooperated with the ICC investigations.

The case study has also illustrated the critical importance of external variables to the impact of ICC investigations. The OTP has done its utmost to pressure and shame the GoS and to deter the commission of future crimes. Yet, the effects of these efforts have remained negligible because the international community remained divided over the Darfur issue and was barely ever able to exert coordinated pressure on the GoS, thus also failing to enforce cooperation with the ICC. At the same time, the Darfur case has shown that the ICC is in many cases more a tool than an actor in conflict contexts. The isolation section has shown how particularly Western powers used the ICC to push the GoS towards more concessions but also offered a deferral of the investigations as a carrot in negotiations. The role of the UNSC in the ICC referral system should be judged very critically in this context. A comparison between the LRA and Darfur investigations suggests that those who refer the case to the ICC have a particular influence on the effects of the investigations. This is the case because the referring party usually has a particular stake in the investigation, and thus plays a crucial role in enforcing the warrants resulting from it. Additionally, the ICC investigators rely on outside support in order to be able to conduct their investigations safely with the limited resources available at the Court. In the LRA conflict, the main supporter was the GoU, for Darfur it was the UNSC and the P5. The weak impact of the deterrence and isolation mechanisms largely can be explained by the fact that the UNSC and the P5 were divided over the investigations.

Finally, the Darfur study showed that two external variables that are nearly absent in the literature played an important role in many causal mechanisms. These variables are the strategic and procedural decisions taken by Court organs, as well as justice perceptions connected to the investigations. The local and regional perception of the ICC's work played a strong role in the polarisation and isolation mechanisms. Because the ICC was seen as an imperialist actor, the NCP was able to rally the Sudanese population behind al-Bashir and drive a wedge between the ICC and its African States Parties. This rift between the AU and the ICC still has not been overcome, despite the first African Chief Prosecutor taking charge at the OTP at the time of writing.

These perceptions were caused in part by the procedural and strategic decisions taken by the OTP. Moreno Ocampo's approach to paint the GoS as criminals by using Nazi analogies and to shame the GoS to a point that some doubted his judicial professionalism and impartiality (e.g. Flint and de Waal 2009) made it easier for the GoS to criticise the OTP's approach. Additionally, the decision to focus on a shaming strategy contributed to the polarisation between the conflict parties.

Ten years after the start of the conflict and eight years into the ICC investigations, the Darfur conflict remains intractable. The marginalisation of the Sudanese peripheries, one of the main causes for the conflict, has not been addressed. It is therefore unsurprising that the Darfur conflict has started to merge with conflicts in other marginalised areas. The Darfur rebels have forged an alliance with the SPLM-N in the provinces along the border with South Sudan and the Beja Congress in eastern Sudan. The impact of the ICC investigations on the conflict dynamics has been surprisingly small, especially taking into consideration the sheer number of claims brought forward in the literature. For most mechanisms, the conflict dynamics and the policy of the UNSC towards Darfur superimposed whatever effects the ICC investigations might have had. Only for a short period after the indictment of President al-Bashir did the ICC have a strong influence on the conflict in terms of international isolation and marginalisation. A long-term impact in these areas could not develop due to the disunity among the P5 and the ICC State Parties over Darfur. As shown above, the ICC itself played a role in fostering this disunity through its polemical approach to its Darfur investigations. Unfortunately, the only lasting impact of the ICC in Darfur to date has been to complicate the rapprochement between the conflict parties and to increase the polarisation in the conflict. The sceptical views of international justice critics have thus been largely confirmed in the Darfur case.

5

The ICC in Uganda: isolating spoilers or blocking negotiations?

The following chapter presents the case study conducted on the conflict between the Lord's Resistance Army (LRA) and the Government of Uganda (GoU) in northern Uganda. The conflict later spread to the border areas of Southern Sudan, the Democratic Republic of Congo and CAR. Hostilities are exclusively taking place outside of Uganda at the time of writing. Nevertheless, the initial analysis of the conflict focuses on Uganda because the root causes of the conflict undoubtedly lie in Uganda's history of tribal divisions and patronage. The conflict was referred to the ICC by the GoU in December 2003 and became the first case ever referred to the Court.

For the Uganda case study, an analysis of the local notions of justice in northern Uganda is included in the conflict analysis. This is necessary because differing perceptions about justice became a key point of contention between local and international interest groups. In the second section of the study, the ICC impacts are traced based on the causal mechanisms identified in Chapter 3.

5.1 Conflict analysis

5.1.1 Conflict background and history

Until its independence in 1962, Uganda was a British colony. While the north was primarily used as a recruitment reservoir for the army, all profitable crops were planted in the south (Apuuli 2008b, p. 53, Dolan 2009, p. 41–42). The British colonial administration thus laid the foundations for a north–south divide prevalent in Uganda until the present day. Shortly after independence, Milton Obote, a member of a tribe from northern Uganda, took power in 1966 and established a one-party system. In 1971, Obote was ousted through a coup led by General Idi Amin who counted on support from the army and the Buganda Kingdom (Risse et al. 2003, p. 102–103).

After taking power, Idi Amin, who hailed from the north-west of Uganda, massacred the Lwo-speaking Acholi and Langi in northern Uganda, accusing them of being Obote supporters (Allen 2006, p. 28, Doom and Vlassenroot 1999, p. 9). A move to attack Tanzania in order to garner domestic political support led to the downfall of Amin. He was ousted by Milton Obote with support from the Tanzanian army in 1979. After returning to power, Obote once again established his regime relying on an army dominated by Acholi and Langi soldiers from the north (Allen 2006, p. 29). When Obote was confirmed as president in elections in 1980, a southern rebel group named the National Resistance Movement (NRM) started an insurgency, accusing Obote of having rigged the elections.

Obote was ousted by his own army in 1985 because he failed to control the rebellion and the Acholi general Tito Okello took power. Despite signing a power-sharing agreement with the new government, the NRM continued to march on Kampala and finally took the capital in 1986, making their leader Yoweri Museveni the new president.

The new NRM government quickly managed to appease the southern and western parts of Uganda. But the former government army, the northern dominated Uganda National Liberation Army (UNLA), was angered by the fact that Museveni did not honour the power-sharing deal he had signed with Okello. The UNLA fled Kampala and retreated to the northern areas populated by their fellow Acholi and Langi. Since the UNLA fled with a considerable stockpile of arms, Museveni interpreted them as a danger to his newly established rule and ordered his NRA to advance north (Eichstaedt 2009, p. 151).

The Acholi of the north on the other hand felt marginalised by the NRM government. Many northern civilians even feared revenge attacks when they heard that the NRA was marching north, in particular because Acholi soldiers were accused of massacres in Uganda's central region of Luwero (see Van Acker 2004, p. 340–341). Indeed, the NRA started to wage an atrocious counter-insurgency campaign in the north because they expected the Acholi population to support the UNLA. Ironically, the NRA's methods ended up creating the insurgency they were supposed to stop as several rebel groups emerged out of the UNLA, among them the Lord's Resistance Army (LRA) (Branch 2005, p. 10, 2010a, p. 33, Finnström 2006).

Some of these movements, particularly the Holy Spirit Movement (HSM), managed to mobilise strong local support (Branch 2010a, p. 37, Komakech and Sheff 2009). Yet, most rebel movements finally surrendered in 1988 and accepted an amnesty offered by the government. The few remaining rebels joined a number of spiritually guided movements emerging from the HSM, including the LRA (Allen and Vlassenroot 2010, p. 9). Due to the NRA's bad human rights record during the northern counter-insurgency campaign and due to large-scale cattle rustling perpetrated by the army, some Acholi perceived the NRA offensive as an attempt to permanently marginalise the Acholi. Since the LRA was the last remaining rebel group after 1988, it therefore enjoyed some local support (Finnström 2008, p. 72). The LRA soon started to attack the Acholi civilians itself though, committing massacres and unspeakable atrocities. In the end, neither the NRA nor the LRA could count on any real popular support in the north and a stalemate started to emerge. The LRA had to replenish its ranks by regularly abducting young Acholi, while the NRA was not able to collect sufficient intelligence from the hostile local population to track the LRA down.

Meanwhile, Yoweri Museveni forged a new state dominated by his NRM (Poku 2008, p. 98).[1] He prolonged his rule unilaterally in 1989 and 1994 and then emerged victorious in the 1996 general elections which he won with 70 per cent since they were held at the apex of his popularity (Ali and Matthews 2004a, p. 413).

The current conflict between the LRA and the GoU started in 1991, when the NRA started its first offensive against the LRA, called Operation North. As in the case of Darfur, several conflict lines are interwoven in the LRA conflict. On the one hand, there is a conflict between the marginalised Acholi and the GoU dominated by western and southern tribes. This conflict is embedded in a greater north–south dichotomy in Uganda. Second, the LRA is attacking Acholi civilians, creating a second conflict between the rebels and the local population. Finally, Sudan and Uganda were waging a proxy war across northern Uganda and Southern Sudan for several years, adding a third layer to the conflict (Apuuli 2005, p. 37, 2008b, p. 52–53, ICG 2004c, p. I). The conflict has regional and international dimensions due to the involvement of Sudan and the fact that the LRA has now spread out across the tri-state area of CAR, DRC and South Sudan.

During Operation North, the government army further alienated the local population because it acted repressively and failed to protect

[1] Museveni introduced the so-called Movement System in which parties could be established but were not allowed to compete in elections, only individual candidates were allowed to run (Risse et al. 2003, p. 129).

civilians. In an attempt to address this problem, the newly appointed Minister of State for the Pacification of Northern Uganda, Betty Bigombe, tried to create local self-defence forces in the affected areas (Allen 2006, p. 47–48). Yet, the self-defence forces were badly armed and thus bore heavy losses when attacked by the LRA (Dolan 2009, p. 47). Betty Bigombe then attempted to negotiate with the LRA in 1994. The conflict transformed for the first time when the negotiations failed and the LRA became a proxy of the Government of Sudan (GoS). Sudan started to support the LRA in retaliation of the political support that the SPLA received by the GoU. It also used the LRA as a proxy force in the Sudanese civil war to attack the SPLA behind the frontlines. The LRA conserved its independence and cultivated ties with the Southern Sudanese rebel group Equatoria Defence Forces (EDF) when support by the GoS started to falter (Dolan 2009, p. 82–83). Thanks to massive GoS support between 1994 and 2002, the LRA became a well-trained force equipped with modern weapons (Van Acker 2004, p. 338). It is not clear how much support, if any, the LRA received from the GoS beyond 2002.

In an attempt to drain the LRA of local support, the NRA started to force the Acholi population into 'protected villages' in 1996 (Allen and Vlassenroot 2010, p. 14, Dolan 2009, p. 47). The NRA enforced this policy by issuing ultimatums to the rural population, demanding that they move to the camps. After the ultimatum had passed, the NRA started shelling and bombing the designated areas or forced the remaining villagers into the camps at gunpoint (Branch 2004, p. 2, Dolan 2009, p. 110, Finnström 2008, p. 11 and 139).

Once forced into the camps, the IDPs were shot at by Ugandan soldiers if seen outside the camps farming or hunting because the army perceived everyone outside the camps as a rebel (Finnström 2008, p. 233, ICG 2005b, p. 7). The LRA in turn started to attack and target the camps because they feared that the government would mobilise the civilians as militias and undermine LRA propaganda efforts by cutting off their access to the population (Branch 2005, p. 21).

The most extensive account of the IDP camp system has been written by John Dolan, an anthropologist who has been studying the situation in Uganda for several years. He concluded that the camp system violated the rights of the IDPs to health and education, as well as their economic rights without providing adequate protection in return. The lives of the IDPs were dominated by insecurity in all the areas mentioned above (Dolan 2009, p. 151).

In 2000, the GoU issued an amnesty for all rebels in Uganda under heavy pressure from civil society organisations and MPs from the northern region (Eichstaedt 2009, p. 168). Even though Museveni was reluctant to implement the amnesty and repeatedly delayed it, the Amnesty Act eventually entered in force (Finnström 2008, p. 92). The amnesty offers were broadcast in northern Uganda via the regional radio station Mega FM. Yet, the LRA initially managed to discourage the rank and file from making use of the amnesty by cutting them off from radios, by spreading rumours that those who had taken the amnesty offers were shot or put on trial, and by attacking villages that had accepted LRA returnees (Allen 2006, p. 74–76 and 123). Additionally, the 2002 Anti-Terrorism Act in Uganda practically nullified the amnesty for LRA members (Allen and Vlassenroot 2010, p. 15, Dolan 2009, p. 53).

In 2002, the NRM started its next attempt to solve the situation in northern Uganda militarily. It started Operation Iron Fist that involved the deployment of 10,000 Ugandan People's Defence Force (UPDF)[2] soldiers in Southern Sudan with GoS permission. The offensive inflicted heavy casualties on the LRA and drove it from Southern Sudan back to northern Uganda. All the while the LRA quickly replaced its losses through a higher rate of abductions. Itthen outflanked the UPDF and spread the war to previously untouched districts of northern Uganda (Allen and Vlassenroot 2010, p. 14). When the operation began, there were about 150,000 IDPs in northern Uganda; by August 2002, there were 1.8 million and nearly 90 per cent of the population in the affected areas had been displaced (HRW 2005b, Mwenda 2010, p. 52). In 2003, Uganda became the country with the largest IDP population in the world due to this development (Allen 2006, p. 60). At the same time, about 40,000 children commuted from the IDP camps to the urban centres of northern Uganda every night to avoid LRA abduction (Latigo 2008, p. 94).

One reason for the difficulties the UPDF faced when trying to root out the LRA was the weakness of the army in the early 2000s. UPDF soldiers were undisciplined, their morale and their salaries were low, they were badly equipped, many soldiers suffered from illnesses and alcoholism and the army was plagued by operational inefficiencies (Dolan 2009, p. 73, ICG 2004c, p. II, Van Acker 2004, p. 353). The lack of expertise within the army led to a pure body count mentality that proved ineffective to

[2] The NRA became the official army of the Ugandan state and was renamed Ugandan People's Defence Forces.

decide the conflict as most LRA fighters were abductees and could be easily replaced (ICG 2005b, p. 2). At the same time, the army completely failed at protecting the local population against LRA attacks (Hovil and Quinn 2005, p. 3, ICG 2004c, p. I). Only during Operation Iron Fist II in 2005 the UPDF was able to improve its performance in counter-insurgency operations (ICG 2005b, p. 2).

Operation Iron Fist II that started in March 2004, pushed the LRA out of Uganda and back into Southern Sudan and led many LRA fighters to accept the 2000 amnesty (Allen 2006, p. 52, Allen and Vlassenroot 2010, p. 15). The LRA's leader Joseph Kony himself narrowly escaped UPDF forces and the LRA's position was even further weakened when its one-time ally the EDF also started to turn against them in Southern Sudan (Brubacher 2010, p. 270, Lomo and Hovil 2004, p. 18). Even though LRA commanders defected or were captured in significant numbers in early 2005, the rebels managed to reorganise and restructure in order to cope with the new situation (ICG 2005e, p. 2).

Under the increasing military pressure and due to the ebbing support from the GoS, the LRA started to negotiate with the GoU in 2006. Many observers described the 2006 talks as the first serious negotiations between the conflict parties. Yet, under circumstances that will be analysed in detail in the second part of the case study, the negotiations finally failed in late 2008.

The LRA used the breathing space of the negotiations to withdraw into the DRC and established bases in the Garamba National Park in the north-east of the country, close to the Sudanese border. When negotiations faltered, the UPDF started to plan a final offensive on the new LRA positions in the DRC. The operation, dubbed Lightning Thunder, was not kept secret enough though and Kony got wind of the operation. Bad luck did its part when the weather made the planned use of MiG jets impossible and the UPDF had to use attack helicopters that could be heard approaching from miles away (ICG 2010, p. 3). Additionally, the attack was badly organised. Ground troops that were supposed to clear out the LRA positions after an initial round of airstrikes arrived too late, so the LRA was able to dodge the advancing UPDF troops and retaliate against Congolese civilians.

By January 2009, six weeks after the start of Operation Lightning Thunder, most of the LRA fighters had escaped, killing 1,000 civilians and abducting 700 in the process (Allen and Vlassenroot 2010, p. 1 and 19). The LRA reportedly dispersed into four groups, one of which stayed in the DRC, two of which moved to Southern Sudan and one moving to

CAR, all of them with orders to retaliate against civilians (Allen et al. 2010, p. 284). The rebels gave up the idea of maintaining a permanent headquarters and moved in small groups. According to reports, Kony and 200 of his men even temporarily moved to Daffak in Darfur in 2010 (Radio Dabanga 2010v), and some sources maintain that he remains there under SAF protection (Enough Project 2010). As a result, the conflict was pushed out of northern Uganda and spread across the whole region. Operation Lightning Thunder has meanwhile become a roaming hunt for small LRA groups across the entire region. The UPDF is now relying on a combined strategy of hunting down the LRA rebels and encouraging defections through radio messages and leaflets (ICG 2010, p. 5). Additionally, self-defence groups are springing up in DRC, South Sudan and CAR in attempts to defend villages against LRA attacks and abductions (ICG 2010, p. 13–14). The US Army has meanwhile deployed a number of armed military advisors to the region in order to support the hunt for the LRA.

The complete impact of the conflict on the region is hard to assess. Estimates for northern Uganda put the death toll at 100,000 until 2006. These figures include deaths caused by the unbearable living conditions in IDP camps (Eichstaedt 2009, p. 3, Oketch 2010b). During the conflict, 3,500 people were dying each month in the north, a death rate three times higher than mortality in Iraq in the months after the US invasion and three times higher than the mortality rate in Darfur in October 2005 (CSOPNU 2006, p. 7). Additionally, between 1.3 and 1.8 million civilians were permanently displaced from their villages, amounting to 90 per cent of the entire population of northern Uganda, leaving an area the size of Belgium depopulated (Clarke 2009, p. 124, CSOPNU 2006, p. 7, Mwenda 2010, p. 52). In total, about 8 per cent of the Ugandan population was negatively affected by the conflict in 2006 (CSOPNU 2006, p. 7–8). Figures for the impact of the LRA conflict on the civilian population in CAR, DRC and South Sudan are harder to come by. The International Crisis Group (ICG) estimated that the LRA has displaced 440,000, killed more than 2,400 and abducted more than 3,400 civilians since the failure of the Juba Talks in 2008 (ICG 2011a, p. I).

5.1.2 Structural sources

Many researchers working on the LRA conflict have complained about the tendency in the media and even among other academics to paint the conflict as the typical 'Heart of Darkness' story, describing the LRA as a crazy religious terrorist sect that is committing bizarre and brutal atrocities in the jungles of Africa. Authors like Peter Eichstaedt claim that the war in northern Uganda defies logic and thus overlook the real grievances at the core of the conflict (Eichstaedt 2009, p. 5). This lack of understanding of the situation on the ground is even plaguing ICC investigations in northern Uganda, as is shown in the second part of the study.

Yet, the grievances in northern Uganda concerning the economic situation, the lack of security and bad educational opportunities are very real. For a long time, the population in the north has felt equally abandoned by the LRA and the GoU (Finnström 2010a, p. 82). Even though the LRA is objectively not helping to address the issues in the north, Kony has claimed in LRA pamphlets and interviews that the LRA is fighting to address the marginalisation of northern Uganda (Schomerus 2010b, p. 115). The tendency of some journalists and academics to ignore this aspect of the LRA is especially dangerous when taking into consideration that the GoU used the very same arguments to defend their military focus in combating the various rebellions in Uganda. For a long time, the GoU did very little to tackle the root causes of the conflict and denied that the rebels had a real agenda (Hovil and Quinn 2005, p. 7). The following section will detail the root causes of the northern Uganda conflict including ethnic polarisation, economic marginalisation and the abuse of power (Latigo 2008, p. 89). A picture of self-sustaining conflict dynamics emerges as the fighting constantly creates new conflict issues through its destructive impact.

a. Security

A number of different security factors contributed to the outbreak of the conflict in northern Uganda. They include a legacy of armed conflicts in the area, past human rights abuses, the proliferation of armed groups and small arms, as well as the weak borders and state structures in the region. The ICC could alleviate these issues by deterring armed groups in the region and stimulate accountability measures to deal with the legacy of past human rights abuses.

The legacy of past conflicts is arguably the most influential security factor. Uganda has a history of ethnic groups vying for power in the central state, as a result of which a dichotomy between the north and the south developed. The governments that emerged from these struggles often used their respective armies to commit massacres against other ethnicities (Van Acker 2004, p. 336 and 338). An important root cause is the atrocious counter-insurgency campaign that the NRA conducted in Acholiland during the late 1980s (Van Acker 2004, p. 335). Serious human rights violations by both sides have been reported for that period, and both parties retaliated against the civilian population for allegedly supporting the other side (Branch 2005, p. 13, Dolan 2009, p. 40–44, Finnström 2008, p. 71). The conduct of the thirty-fifth NRA battalion in northern Uganda sticks out as particularly brutal (Apuuli 2008b, p. 53). There are reports of rape of male civilians by NRA soldiers (Dolan 2009, p. 212, ICG 2004c, p. 3, OHCHR 2007, p. 7), massive human rights abuses (Dolan 2009, p. 152), cattle rustling and teak logging. The local population even raised genocide accusation against the NRA (Branch 2005, p. 11). Until this day, IDPs believe that the beginning of the LRA uprising was justified by the NRA's brutality (Wyrzykowski and Kasozi 2010, p. 21).

The legacy of this atrocious counter-insurgency was later complemented by human rights abuses committed by the NRA and later the UPDF in northern Uganda. In 1997, the army started to carry out large-scale population screenings that led to mass arrests of alleged LRA supporters (Dolan 2009, p. 47, Finnström 2008, p. 176). The Acholi were also forcibly recruited as home guards for the camps and forced to participate in anti-LRA demonstrations (Finnström 2008, p. 11 and 91). At the same time, the UPDF consistently showed up too late when IDP camps were attacked (Dolan 2009, p. 145, ICG 2004c, p. 14). Combined with the impunity for UPDF violations, this led to the perception among locals that the government was against them (Dolan 2009, p. 103 and 153). The LRA could not profit from these grievances though as the brutality of the rebels undercut the possibility of a mass rebellion in the north. Still, the NRA/UPDF violations helped to spark the initial rebellion and the lack of accountability for these crimes remains a sore thumb that could cause further tensions in the future (Lomo and Hovil 2004, p. 7).

Another trigger for the conflict was the easy availability of recruits for armed groups. Potential rebels had access to an ample reservoir of young, untrained soldiers that was created through the many coups in Uganda's history (Van Acker 2004, p. 336 and 338). This security problem has been perpetuated through the creation of militias and self-defence forces in the course of the LRA conflict. The UPDF started forced recruitment into the home guards which were supposed to defend the IPD camps. Many of the recruits were later forced to join the UPDF in the Congo War or in fighting the LRA in Uganda (Branch 2005, p. 20, Dolan 2009, p. 144, Finnström 2008, p. 11). The numbers of the home guards and soldiers meant to protect the camps were wholly inadequate.[3] Additionally, those meant to protect people often became a source of violence and insecurity themselves (Dolan 2009, p. 148, ICG 2006c, p. 5, Weeks 2002, p. 2). John Dolan has described systematic harassment and abuses of IDPs by the UPDF and the home guards in camps, and others even accuse the security forces of torture, assaults, rape and murder (Dolan 2009, p. 109, Williams 2007, p. 3). There were reports of UPDF soldiers who started raiding and stealing in the camps disguised as LRA members (Dolan 2009, p. 147–149). This led the ICG to conclude that the conditions in the camps were a greater threat than the LRA attacks (ICG 2007c, p. 1). Unsurprisingly, the civilians therefore started to fear and distrust both the LRA and the UPDF (Dolan 2009, p. 146, Hovil and Quinn 2005, p. 8–9). Many IDPs have accused the government of not protecting them adequately (Wyrzykowski and Kasozi 2010, p. 27). They feel betrayed by the government, and some even accuse the UPDF of collaborating with the LRA (OHCHR 2007, p. 22 and 26).

It is important to acknowledge that the security situation has improved dramatically over the years, especially since the LRA was pushed out of northern Uganda. In 2010, 90 per cent of the people felt safe when going to work or collecting firewood and 80 per cent felt safe walking at night (Pham and Vinck 2010, p. 2).

Apart from the recruitment of home guards, the GoU also decided to tap the reservoir of young men to form local self-defence groups which were supposed to fight the LRA. The NRM initially understood the LRA as a local problem and thus concluded that local self-defence groups should deal with them (Finnström 2008, p. 106). But the UPDF often failed to support these self-defence groups against LRA retaliation, and the government was reluctant to arm them adequately since they distrusted the Acholi population (ICG 2004c, p. 15). Despite these problems, self-defence groups were used with success in the Teso and Langi districts that border the Acholi districts in the east during the LRA invasion after Operation Iron Fist.

As with the home guards, some of these self-defence groups later became part of the security problem. Questions were raised whether these groups would disarm voluntarily and there were worries that the arming of civilians could lead to increased banditry or clashes between

[3] In one camp, fourteen militia soldiers were supposed to protect 15,000 IDPs, in another, forty-five home guards were deployed for a camp of 50,000 (Branch 2005, p. 20, Mwenda 2010, p. 55).

tribes (Apuuli 2005, p. 41, Lomo and Hovil 2004, p. 40). A 2003 report by HRW listed a number of human rights violations committed by paramilitary groups close to the government (HRW 2003, p. 48–50) and in July 2008, there were reports of a series of robberies and murders committed by former militia members, former LRA fighters and possibly even UPDF members (Baines 2008, p. 3, Mallinder 2009b, p. 16).

Self-defence groups have also been used against the LRA in the DRC and South Sudan. In South Sudan, there are worries that militias might spark tribal conflicts, while the Congolese groups have increasingly become bandits according to UN reports (Gordon et al. 2007, p. 48, ICG 2011a, p. 9, IRIN 2010a).

The easy availability of weapons also contributed to the outbreak and perpetuation of the conflict. Small arms were easily available in Southern Sudan thanks to the weapons that many governments sent there to support some faction or militia involved in the Sudanese civil war. The LRA thus never had problems in replenishing its weapons supplies and was additionally supplied directly by the GoS. Even in northern Uganda, weapons were easily available, as fleeing UNLA forces hid weapons stockpiles in the northern districts (Schomerus 2007, p. 41).

Two final factors contributing to the security problems in the region are a lack of state capacity and weak borders. For many years, the LRA has exploited these regional weaknesses to withdraw from UPDF pressure, first to Southern Sudan, later to the DRC and the CAR. The existence of safe havens in neighbouring states has greatly contributed to the survival of the LRA rebellion. At the moment, CAR is the weakest link in the region as its army is unable to control the state territory and the borders. Only few soldiers are stationed in the southeast where the LRA is roaming because most of CAR's armed forces were bound in the north where they fought a rebellion that finally overthrew the government in mid-2013 (Cakaj 2010b, p. 2, ICG 2010, p. 8). CAR has become the main battleground in the LRA conflict due to Kony's alleged presence there and the high number of LRA attacks (ICG 2010, p. 9).

On the other side of the border, in the DRC, the situation is similar. Only 1,000 of the 18,000 United Nations Organization Stabilization Mission in the Democratic Republic of the Congo (MONUSCO) soldiers are stationed in the area affected by the LRA (Oxfam 2010).

In the LRA-affected regions of South Sudan, there is some United Nations Mission in Sudan (UNMIS) presence, but the peacekeepers are largely ineffective in stopping LRA raids while state security forces are often stationed at least half a day away from the affected areas (Gordon et al. 2007, p. 46, HRW 2010b).

The whole tri-state area between South Sudan, DRC and CAR is practically ungoverned, and a security vacuum and the lack of infrastructure make hunting the LRA a difficult endeavour (ICG 2010, p. 5). The conflict itself has become a menace for the security of the whole region and threatens to spark new conflicts. LRA incursions have already disrupted peace processes in the DRC and in Sudan (ICG 2006c, p. 1), and the LRA has become an arms conduit for different groups, thus fuelling conflicts all over Central Africa (Rupiny 2010).

b. Political

The political root causes of the conflict are the political marginalisation of the north, and the political and military exploitation of ethnicity. On the regional level, the GoS support of the LRA and the proxy war dynamics played an important role. International political support of the GoU has entrenched the government approach to deal with the LRA insurgency militarily. A contribution of the ICC can be expected on the regional level by isolating the LRA from GoS support.

While the government has meanwhile managed to 'appease' the northern districts, it has used ethnic stereotypes of 'warlike' northerners to mobilise electoral support by painting itself as the protector of the southern tribes. Based on this campaign strategy, some authors have also accused the GoU of deliberately prolonging the conflict in the north in order to keep the region marginalised. These political factors on the national level are joined by others on the regional and international levels. The GoS discovered the LRA as a tool for waging a proxy war against Uganda in 1994. International support, provided mainly by the United States, encouraged the GoU to pursue a strategy that focused heavily on a military approach to defeat the LRA rebellion. As a result, the government took a long time to tackle the root causes of the conflict and to engage in serious negotiations.

The mishandling of power by the GoU has been identified as an important root cause of the conflict (Hovil and Quinn 2005, p. 3). The Ugandan state has always been dominated either by the northern or the southern tribes of Uganda. This pattern continued with the victory of the NRM, which largely excluded the northern population from leading positions in government and army. This marginalisation is a real grievance which contributed to the outbreak of the conflict in the 1980s and led to general mistrust among the northern population vis à vis the GoU.

The ongoing marginalisation of the north confronted the GoU with an unforeseen problem: in order to be perceived as a legitimate government, the NRM had to establish control of the north and stop the ethnic fragmentation of the country (Dolan 2009, p. 63). As long as the government does not establish its legitimacy, more rebellions will likely keep springing up in the peripheries. This is being illustrated by the fact that the NRM has so far faced seven to twenty-two different rebellions, depending on how they are counted (Latigo 2008, p. 87, Lindemann 2011, p. 388). It is thus clear that Uganda is paying a high price for non-inclusive governance.

It took the NRM until 2006 to fully grasp the problem and start to address the marginalisation of the Acholi people. In the early years of his rule, Museveni openly identified the Acholi as enemies of the NRM (Buckley-Zistel 2008a, p. 66). Later, he started claiming that the LRA conflict was a conflict between northerners, thus denying the national north–south dimension of the conflict (Eichstaedt 2009, p. 136). On another occasion, Museveni declared that he aimed at creating a Bantu-speaking Africa, thereby verbally marginalising the Luo and Langi speaking northerners (Finnström 2008, p. 117). As a result, divisions between north and south were enforced over decades (Lomo and Hovil 2004, p. 7).

Complementing the political marginalisation of northern Uganda, Museveni is often accused of having a personal motivation in keeping the LRA conflict going (e.g. Allen 2006, p. 48, Dolan 2009, p. 102, Williams 2007, p. 10). According to these critics, Museveni is on purpose maintaining a situation of instability in the north to neutralise political opposition (Branch 2005, p. 3, Finnström 2008, p. 13, Mwenda 2010, p. 51–54). Indeed, Museveni has even actively used the war in the north to keep the national opposition small, for example, by labelling opposition politicians like Kizza Besigye as LRA terrorist supporters (ICG 2004c, p. I, Schomerus 2010b, p. 114). Since his power base is the south, he can afford to leave the northern population at the mercy of the LRA and can even present himself as a protector of the south against northern rebels (Allen 2006, p. 48–49, Mwenda 2010, p. 51–54, Van Acker 2004, p. 353).[4] Some observers and locals claim that the UPDF therefore never tried in earnest to root out the LRA (Eichstaedt 2009, p. 138, Lomo and Hovil 2004, p. 43, Oxfam International 2007, p. 14). Others have

[4] Even during the 2011 presidential elections, NRM posters for Museveni suggested that his military track record of having defeated '28 *rebellions*' was an argument to vote for him.

suggested that a permanent conflict in the north is useful for maintaining, controlling and keeping busy Uganda's large army (Dolan 2009, p. 213, ICG 2004c, p. I, Mwenda 2010, p. 51–54).

The final political factor on the national level is the politicisation and militarisation of ethnicity and tribal identities during a series of ethnically based coups and counter-coups (Branch 2005, p. 9). During Obote's and Idi Amin's regimes, ethnicity became a dominant factor in national politics due to the northern dominance in military and security services (Branch 2010a, p. 29, Mbazira 2011, p. 199). The ruling elites have politicised ethnicity to achieve and secure power in Uganda ever since (Latigo 2008, p. 89). After taking Kampala, the NRM followed this pattern by identifying the Acholi tribe as a threat and excluding its members from government and army positions (Branch 2010a, p. 33, Lindemann 2011, p. 395). Northern groups in general, and especially the Acholi, have also been discriminated against in civil service appointments. Western Ugandans hold 44 per cent of the top public appointments and occupy 76 per cent of the top army positions while representing only 26 per cent of the total population. The top seven positions in the army are exclusively held by western Ugandans. The most favoured group, the Baganda, even holds 30 per cent of the top public positions while making up 17 per cent of the population (ICG 2008, p. 6, Lindemann 2011, p. 404).

On the regional level, the GoS support for the LRA starting in 1994 played an important role. Uganda and Sudan waged a proxy war in northern Uganda and Southern Sudan for several years (Dolan 2009, p. 45). Due to its political interests in the area, the GoS supplied the LRA with arms, supported it with equipment, treated its wounded soldiers and offered a safe haven from the UPDF pursuit in Southern Sudan. Starting in 2004, this support has been gradually receding, but there are still rumours that the LRA is being supported by elements within the Sudanese military intelligence.

Another political factor in the region is the tense relationship between DRC and Uganda after the UPDF invaded eastern Congo during the Congo Wars. As a consequence, the DRC is deeply distrustful of the UPDF. Of all places, the LRA moved their main base to the DRC between 2006 and 2008. During that period, Uganda was constantly threatening to invade the DRC in pursuit of LRA groups (see ICG 2007c, p. 7). Clearly, a coordinated regional answer to the LRA threat is needed, but the complex political situation in the region is complicating this endeavour (ICG 2007c, p. 16). The allegations of Ugandan and Rwandan involvement in the M-23 rebellion in eastern Congo in 2013 show that the situation remains complicated.

Finally, the influence of international powers played a role in the perpetuation of the conflict. First, the international donor community was indirectly funding the internment strategy of the NRM in northern Uganda by providing the camps with humanitarian aid while leaving the GoU in full control of the camps (Allen 2006, p. 60, Eichstaedt 2010, Perrot 2010, p. 204). Uganda was able to uphold this strategy over several years by skilfully dividing the international donors (Perrot 2010, p. 200). For example, Museveni proved his strong political instinct by aligning himself with the US war on terror after the 9/11 attacks in branding the LRA a terrorist organisation. The Ugandan military soon started to profit from US support as an important regional ally in the global war on terror (Finnström 2010b, p. 137). Uganda also started to serve as the US conduit for supporting the SPLA in its war against the GoS, which further strengthened the proxy war dynamic in the region (Mwenda 2010, p. 49).

The role of the US policy in the conflict has changed in the last few years as US civil society movements like Invisible Children started to push the agenda of ending the LRA conflict. These organisations started to lobby for a US Act to stop the regional menace of the LRA and also helped to mount the pressure for achieving a negotiated solution during the Juba Talks in 2006 (Allen and Vlassenroot 2010, p. 1, Finnström 2010a, p. 80).

c. Economic

There are a number of economic grievances that played their role in fuelling the rebellion in northern Uganda. During the early stages of the conflict, the entire economic basis of the northern districts was destroyed, leaving northern Uganda in the worst state since independence. At the same time, people connected to the GoU and the army took advantage of the situation to enrich themselves during the conflict. The ICC has no means of directly influencing these economic root causes.

In economic terms, Uganda is defined by a glaring inequality between its northern and southern districts (Dolan 2009, p. 65). During the NRA invasion in the late 1980s, large-scale cattle rustling and slaughtering broke the economic backbone of the Acholi communities. The survivors were not even left with enough resources to maintain traditional rituals of marriage, burial and compensation, let alone to invest money for economic purposes (Dolan 2009, p. 222, Van Acker 2004, p. 343). Today, about 2 per cent of the pre-war cattle remain (Finnström 2008, p. 34). The loss of northern Uganda's huge cattle herds and the near total displacement of its population have left 30 per cent of the local population in chronic poverty, compared to a 7 per cent on the national level. Poverty levels in northern Uganda were about 30 per cent over national average (Ginifer 2006, p. 14, Ugandan Ministry of Finance, Planning and Economic Development 2003). While the rest of Uganda has developed economically since the NRM took power, the conflict sapped northern Uganda of all economic progress for years. As a result, the economic divide in Uganda deepened during the conflict with each passing day. According to a 2006 report of local civil society organisations, at least 100 million USD were lost every year at the height of the conflict. In total, the conflict cost up to 1.7 billion USD during the first twenty years of the LRA insurgency, equalling about 3 per cent of Uganda's GDP growth during the period (CSOPNU 2006, p. 22).

While the rest of Uganda witnessed rapid development between 1990 and 2000 (Ali and Matthews 2004a, p. 406), 84 per cent of the households in northern Uganda depended on food aid in a region that is blessed with some of the most fertile soils in Africa (CSOPNU 2006, p. 17). One reason for this development was the fact that there was barely enough room to cultivate in the IDP camps while curfews and restrictions made cultivation outside the camps impossible (Dolan 2009, p. 108 and 162).[5] Alternative means of subsistence scarcely existed as unemployment was rampant in the area until recently (Borzello 2007, p. 402).

In conclusion, the IDP camp system crippled the economy in northern Uganda for the duration of the conflict, thus adding to the economic grievances (Weeks 2002, p. 31). A similar situation has arisen in the regions in which the LRA is active today. Reports from Western Equatoria, for example, indicate that most communities were not able to engage properly in agriculture due to the insecurity in recent years. Many farmers were thus not able to sell their surplus produce to cover their other bills and some were even forced to eat the seeds kept for future harvests (Gordon et al. 2007, p. 34–35).

For a long time, the government did little to tackle these problems. Instead, the GoU funnelled large sums into attempts to eradicate the LRA militarily. It was not until 2010 that President Museveni changed this

[5] Seventy-eight per cent of households had no access to land (CSOPNU 2006, p. 17).

approach and launched the Peace, Recovery and Development Plan (PRDP) that aimed at revitalising the northern economy (Museveni 2010).

Another economic factor that prolonged the fighting was the profit that some army and government members extracted from northern Uganda during the conflict. Individual soldiers and officers profited from the war since they were able to engage in cattle rustling, teak logging, illegal trade in Southern Sudan and other activities to fill their pockets (Allen 2006, p. 48–49, Dolan 2009, p. 45 and 146, Van Acker 2004, p. 353). Some UPDF generals allegedly received personal allotments of foreign aid money, or profited from corruption in weapons deals (Eichstaedt 2009, p. 33 and 139, 2010, Mwenda 2010, p. 48).[6] Up to this day, some locals are claiming that members of the GoU are grabbing Acholi land by displacing the former inhabitants (Branch 2005, p. 3, Finnström 2008, p. 177, Van Acker 2004, p. 343).

The unsolved question of land ownership also illustrates how economic factors continue to influence the conflict until the present day. Ownership issues threaten to sow the seeds of future conflicts as returnees from the camps increasingly fight with their neighbours and newcomers over the borders of their ancestral land (see Pham and Vinck 2010, p. 2). Indeed, many locals voiced worries about future land conflicts when the dismantling of the IDP camps began (Oxfam International 2007, p. 21).

d. Social

Social factors that have led to the outbreak and perpetuation of the conflict include longstanding ethnic and tribal tensions in Uganda, the near-complete destruction of the traditional way of life of the Acholi people and the social traumata caused by the high levels of exposure to violence. By dealing with LRA atrocities, the ICC can contribute to remedy stereotypes of northern Ugandans in investigating the individual guilt of LRA commanders. Dealing with past atrocities could help to heal the prevalent social traumata.

The Ugandan north–south split described above is reinforced through ethnic categories attached to southern Bantu speakers and northern

[6] According to one author, the GoU even accepted this practice of individuals enriching themselves in the conflict since it allowed the government to cut the wages of the army for reasons of austerity, expecting that members of the army compensated the cuts by profiting from the conflict economy (Mwenda 2010, p. 48).

speakers of Nilotic and Sudanic languages (Allen and Vlassenroot 2010, p. 6). Since colonial times, the people of Uganda's north – and in particularly the Acholi – have been stereotyped as violent warriors without a real culture (Finnström 2008, p. 48 and 61, Lomo and Hovil 2004, p. 10). In line with these stereotypes, they were later made collectively responsible for massacres in the Luwero Triangle during the counter-insurgency campaign of Obote's second regime against the NRM (Finnström 2008, p. 74–75). Even today, these prejudices against the Acholi prevail in central Uganda; many southerners perceive them as synonymous with the LRA or generally as inferior (Dolan 2009, p. 202, Finnström 2006, p. 204).

These prejudices can even be found in the ranks of the UPDF and the Ugandan government. For example, the former Army Commander James Kazini told HRW in 1997 when explaining the conflict in the north that '*It's the cultural background of the people here; they are very violent. It's genetic.*' (HRW 1997, p. 67). According to the local press, Museveni described the Acholi as grasshoppers trying to get out of a bottle, but eating each other before finding a way out (Latigo 2008, p. 89).[7] These stereotypes humiliate the Acholi population and blame them for their own plight. People argue that northerners are 'passive' or even supporting the LRA, while ignoring the real grievances of the north (Dolan 2009, p. 238, Eichstaedt 2009, p. 107, Lomo and Hovil 2004, p. 33 and 48).

As a result, the NRM did not manage to unify the country. The Acholi were not feeling part of the Ugandan society, and especially some diaspora elements of the Acholi remain pro-LRA (ICG 2004c, p. 23, Lomo and Hovil 2004, p. 34). One of the consequences is that the Acholi population in the north denied the UPDF vital intelligence for the counter-insurgency (ICG 2005b, p. 7). Even though the situation has improved, 50 per cent of the Acholi still felt not understood by Ugandans in the south in 2010 (Pham and Vinck 2010, p. 31). In the 2011 presidential elections, Museveni managed to get a majority of votes in the northern districts for the first time, another indication that the social divisions in the country may be healing five years after the LRA was driven out of northern Uganda.

[7] Another example was the president's speech at the opening ceremony for the Barlonyo massacre memorial in northern Uganda. Attendants felt the president was describing the event as some sort of cosmic justice due to northerners' involvement in the Luwero triangle massacres during the 1980s (Hopwood 2011, p. 12).

The violence in northern Ugandan has badly damaged the social fabric of the region and hindered the emergence of local solutions to the conflict. According to two surveys held in 2005 and 2007, the exposure to violence in the north was extremely high, with 40 per cent of the respondents having been abducted (37 per cent in 2007), 45 per cent having witnessed family members being killed (76 per cent in 2007) and 23 per cent having been victims of mutilations (ICTJ and HRC 2005, p. 4, Pham et al. 2007, p. 2 and 28). Twenty-five per cent of the children aged ten are orphans or have lost at least one parent (CSOPNU 2006, p. 13).

The living conditions in the camps further exacerbated the impact of the violence on the population. These living conditions have been well documented and described as unspeakable. Population density reached figures of up to 1,700 people per hectare (CSOPNU 2006, p. 7). Life was dominated by off-the-chart malnutrition and mortality rates[8] as well as exposure to illnesses and violence (Allen 2006, p. 53–56, Apuuli 2008b, p. 55 and 59). A 2005 health and mortality report co-authored by the GoU stated that the displaced persons in the districts of Gulu, Pader and Kitgum suffered a very serious humanitarian emergency that affected over 90 per cent of the population (WHO 2005). According to the GoU's own figures, there were 1,000 excess deaths per week in the camps (WHO 2005, p. II). Other estimates found overall mortality rates of 1.54, 2.79, or 5.4 per 10,000 inhabitants per day respectively, while the rate in the south was 0.46 per 10,000 (CSOPNU 2006, p. 14, MSF-Holland 2004a, 2004b). Even in 2010, 50 per cent of respondents still judged the health situation to be bad or very bad in Acholiland (Pham and Vinck 2010, p. 26).

There was a rising number of suicides and increasing gender violence (rape) in the camps, while prostitution had increased significantly, and alcoholism had become a major problem (Borzello 2007, p. 402, Dolan 2009, p. 166–167, Otim 2010). The camps were crammed in a small area to better protect the people, which worsened the living conditions and led to the quick spread of fires. Also, there were not nearly enough latrines for the number of people living in the camps, and even Ebola and an HIV epidemic eventually broke out (Bevan 2006, p. 280, Dolan 2009, p. 112,

[8] In 2004, an MSF-Holland survey found a 'severe acute malnutrition rate' of 4.4 per cent with nearly double the rate for children between five and fifty-nine months. The overall crude mortality rate in the camps lay between 2.79 and 5.4/10,000/day. Any figure above one is considered as an emergency rate. Additionally, 79 per cent of the population in Pader district had witnessed torture, 40 per cent had witnessed killings, 5 per cent were forced to harm other people and 62 per cent of the female population was considering suicide in 2004 (MSF-Holland 2004a, 2004b).

128 and 184). Most children in the camps were uneducated because the teacher–pupil ratios were catastrophic and 60 per cent of the schools in the area had been closed (Bevan 2006, p. 280, CSOPNU 2006, p. 8, Dolan 2009, p. 132). All the while, the IDPs were constantly under threat of further LRA attacks or abductions. Even though some of them wanted to return home, the UPDF did not let them (Dolan 2009, p. 128). As a result, traditional cultural and moral values started to break down (Dolan 2009, p. 169–178, Oxfam International 2007, p. 11). Chris Dolan has fittingly described the IDP camp system in northern Uganda as a form of 'social torture' (Dolan 2009).

Some authors interpret the northern Uganda conflict as a symptom of the breakdown of the traditional Acholi society (Branch 2010a, p. 25–26, Meier 2011, p. 201). Similar social impacts can be observed in other areas of LRA operations. In Western Equatoria, for example, community coping mechanisms are crumbling under the pressure of LRA attacks (Gordon et al. 2007, p. 37).

5.1.3 *Conflict actors*

a. The Lord's Resistance Army

The Lord's Resistance Army (LRA) has waged one of the longest insurgencies on the planet, entering its twenty-seventh year at the time of writing. Much has been written about the rebel movement. It has often been mystified for its Christian-spiritual orientation and the grotesque massacres it has committed in the course of the conflict. It is very hard to make sense of the LRA as little is known about its leaders, structures, aims and motivations.

The strength of the rebel movement has been estimated at anywhere between 200 (UPDF) and 5,000. It is probable that the LRA commanded more than three thousand soldiers at the peak of its strength when it received GoS support in the late 1990s (Allen and Vlassenroot 2010, p. 10). In 2004, the ICG still estimated its strength at 3,000 soldiers (ICG 2004c, p. 5); current estimates assume 200–400 armed soldiers plus hundreds of abductees (Cakaj 2010a, p. 4, HRW 2010b, Young 2010).[9] Current numbers are especially hard to verify since the LRA has spread out in small groups and abducts new fighters in DRC, CAR and Sudan all

[9] New 2012 figures based on information gained from LRA returnees put the strength of the LRA at 250–800 fighters with guns (Lezhnev 2012, p. 3). The UN estimates that there are around 60–70 LRA fighters in the DRC (UN Source 2011).

the time. It seems to be clear though that their forces are gradually decreasing (ICG 2006c, p. 4).

The origins of the LRA reach back to the rebel movements that sprung up in Acholiland when the NRA invaded in the late 1980s (Apuuli 2008b, p. 54). The movement was founded by an *ajwaka*, a traditional witch doctor, named Joseph Kony (Eichstaedt 2009, p. 81). As the name suggests, Kony established his organisation based on Christian ideas but also included traditional Acholi spiritualism into the mix. These spiritualist ideas are entrenched in northern Ugandan culture, even though less so amongst the young generation (Allen 2006, p. 31–33 and 156). Concerning the use of spiritual elements, the LRA is a direct successor of the HSM, a rebel group led by Alice '*Lakwena*' Auma. Locals generally attributed strong spiritual powers to Lakwena (Dolan 2009, p. 93). Her movement was surprisingly successful and by the end of her campaign, she commanded as many as 18,000 soldiers. The HSM was finally beaten after initial successes in swamps east of Jinja in 1987, only eighty miles from Kampala. Alice Lakwena managed to flee by bicycle to the DRC and died in a Congolese refugee camp a couple of years ago (Allen 2006, p. 33–36). Like Alice Lakwena, Kony claims that he is possessed by various spirits who guide his actions (Dolan 2009, p. 80).[10] His men believe that Kony has supernatural powers. One of his officers stated during a TV interview that he was convinced that Kony would not die if shot (Journeyman Pictures 2007). The LRA interprets the whole conflict with the NRM in spiritual terms and claims that bad *ajwaka* are fighting on the side of the UPDF (Titeca 2010, p. 66–68).

The ideology of the LRA complements Christian beliefs with traditional Acholi spirituality. The Ten Commandments play a central role in the spiritual and religious views of the LRA. Indeed, one of their key demands is the establishment of a new political system in Uganda that is based on the Ten Commandments. The spiritual and Christian elements of the LRA ideology partly explain the high Resolve of the LRA rank and file.

Apart from mimicking some of the spiritual aspects of the HSM, the LRA initially also adopted the military approach of Lakwena. LRA

[10] Many locals believe Kony is possessed by several spirits. Some say that evil spirits actually make him commit the atrocities. Even the battle command is reportedly taken over by the spirit '*Who Are you?*". Some locals believe that Kony is no longer possessed by spirits; others say that the LRA can only be stopped by cleansing Kony's spirits (Allen 2006, p. 38–39 and 42).

fighters were not supposed to take cover as they were told that holy water and the spirits had made them immune to bullets (Nyeko and Lucima 2002, p. 22, Van Acker 2004, p. 348). Chanting groups of rebels advanced without cover towards the enemy. This tactic was initially successful as the NRA soldiers seemed to be scared by the fearlessly advancing columns.

Since the Acholi were leaderless as a people, spiritual leaders like Kony and Lakwena could fill a power vacuum, especially as both movements were dominated by the young generation, which had lost trust in their elders (Van Acker 2004, p. 342 and 344). Apart from those who joined the LRA looking for guidance, many ex-UNLA soldiers and rebels from the UPDA initially joined the movement because they had no other vocation than soldiering and were not accepted back by their home communities (Allen 2006, p. 38, Van Acker 2004, p. 339–340). Also, former UNLA forces under Odong Latek joined Kony in 1988 and brought professional military experience and tactics to the organisation (Allen and Vlassenroot 2010, p. 10, Gordon et al. 2007, p. 21, Van Acker 2004, p. 348).

It remains one of the secrets of the LRA on how much popular support it could count on at the beginning of its campaign. There are rumours and reports of an unfinished blessing ceremony conducted by Acholi clan leaders that legitimised one of Kony's commanders to go to war with the NRA in the name of the Acholi (Eichstaedt 2009, p. 230–233, Finnström 2008, p. 211–212). Additionally, most authors claim at least initial public support for the LRA insurgency in the north (Branch 2004, p. 2, Cakaj 2011, p. 3, Finnström 2008, p. 73, ICG 2007c, p. 11). Still, most authors agree that the LRA received less popular support than other northern groups before it (Branch 2010a, p. 39, Doom and Vlassenroot 1999, p. 22). This posed a challenge to the LRA since it had to fight to get access to Resources.

As support by the population was not forthcoming or quickly dwindling, Kony had to coerce people into supporting him from the start (Branch 2010a, p. 39). The LRA started attacking Acholi villages and committed massacres and mutilations while abducting people, forcing them to join their rebellion (Apuuli 2008b, p. 61, HRW 2005b, p. 20). Kony justified these attacks on his own people by claiming that he wanted to purify the Acholi through his brutal campaign. Another motivation was to punish them for their alleged support of the Museveni government and for not accepting Kony as their 'prophet'

(Allen 2006, p. 40, Eichstaedt 2009, p. 100).[11] In his interpretation, Kony is saving his people, creating the 'new Acholi' by purging the 'impure' – those who are allegedly supporting the GoU (Branch 2010a, p. 41–42, Titeca 2010, p. 69). As the government had forced the Acholi into camps to drain the support basis of the LRA, the rebels saw camp inhabitants as government agents and targeted them accordingly (Finnström 2008, p. 136). From the LRA's point of view, the Acholi asked them to stave off the NRA incursion, only to later abandon the LRA in its fight against the UPDF (Finnström 2008, p. 214, Liu Institute for Global Issues 2005, p. 52). These messianic elements of the LRA ideology add to the Resolve of the LRA since perceiving the conflict as a religious mission reduces the appeal of an alternative negotiated solution.

The modus operandi of the LRA has remained consistent in the twenty-seven years of its existence. It is attacking local villages in order to loot food and supplies and to abduct adolescents, young men and sometimes children to fill its ranks. Girls and young women are also abducted and later given to LRA commanders as 'wives' (Allen 2006, p. 112–113, Dolan 2009, p. 81). A large number of people have been abducted by the LRA over the course of the conflict. Estimates from the year 2005 put the figure at 30,000 abductions; more recent estimates reach 66,000 abductions in total (Blattman and Annan 2010, p. 135, Hovil and Quinn 2005, p. 3). In Pader district in northern Uganda, approximately two-fifths of the youth have been abducted over the course of the conflict, yet only one-third of them were taken for more than two weeks (Blattman and Annan 2010, p. 133–134). The reason for these short-term abductions is that the LRA abducts large numbers of young men and children to help them carry the goods they loot in the villages to their bases (AI 1997, p. 13, Dolan 2009, p. 78).[12] These short-time abductees are freed afterwards, provided that they can keep up with the rebels while carrying supplies, since those who cannot are often severely beaten or killed (AI 1997, p. 24, HRW 2010a).

[11] Kony himself said, according to an ex-LRA member interviewed by Tim Allen that: '*If you picked up an arrow against us and we ended up cutting off the hand you used, who is to blame? You report us with your mouth, and we cut off your lips. Who is to blame? It is you! The Bible says that if your hand, eye or mouth is at fault, it should be cut off!*' (Allen 2006, p. 42).

[12] John Dolan claims that 80 per cent of the abductees are taken for less than one year by the LRA (Dolan 2009, p. 78).

It is clear that the LRA mainly consists of abducted civilians, even though the exact composition remains unknown. While World Vision claims that more than 80 per cent of the LRA consists of child soldiers, UNICEF reports state that two-thirds of those abducted between 1990 and 2001 were over eighteen (Allen 2006, p. 112–113, World Vision 2004, p. 18).[13] A research team that analysed the abduction pattern of the LRA concluded that the bulk of the LRA probably consists of adolescent 'child soldiers' (Blattman and Annan 2010, p. 139). The abductees are co-opted into the LRA ranks through a mixture of promises of future gains, brutality, disorientation, misinformation, indoctrination and the use of spirituality (Blattman and Annan 2010, p. 140–141, Lancaster et al. 2011, p. 19–20). Thanks to this abduction and indoctrination approach, the LRA can recover relatively quickly from military blows. The approach also serves to further undercut Acholi support for the government as the population is not willing to fight their own abducted family members (ICG 2004c, p. 6).

As mentioned above, the attacks on the villages are often accompanied by atrocities, mutilations or even massacres. The reports of these atrocities are gruesome and much of the media reporting on the conflict focuses on these acts, betraying a morbid fascination for the LRA's crimes. In its massacres, the LRA kills men, women and children, in most cases using machetes or clubs in order to save ammunition (Allen 2006, p. 65). Mutilations like the cutting off of limbs or the lips and noses have been reported for a majority of the attacks (Apuuli 2008b, p. 54, Wyrzykowski and Kasozi, 2010, p. 20). The LRA is also known for lining roads with the cut-off heads of their enemies (Baines 2009, p. 172). There are also unspeakable stories of babies pounded alive in grain mills and forced cannibalism, yet it is not clear whether some of the most gruesome stories are true or rumours and government propaganda (Dolan 2009, p. 85, Wyrzykowski and Kasozi 2010, p. 20). The mutilation approach was not used consistently. It peaked in 1991 and 1996 and again started to rise in 2005 (Dolan 2009, p. 79).

The LRA often forces young abductees to mutilate and kill members of their home community or even their own family and drink their blood as part of the initiation into the LRA (Wyrzykowski and Kasozi 2010, p. 23).[14]

[13] World Vision has meanwhile corrected its position and now states that most of the abductees are adolescents (WV Uganda 2011).

[14] While many accounts have emphasized the fact that children are forced to kill their friends and family, it reportedly happens 'only' in 8–14 per cent of the cases (Blattman and Annan 2010, p. 141).

The abductees are forced to commit these acts to separate the children from their communities and discourage them from ever trying to return (AI 1997, p. 1, Allen 2006, p. 1). The killing and mutilation of civilians and enemy soldiers is encouraged among the new recruits from the beginning as they lead to promotions, and higher ranks in turn lead to more security and better access to food, 'wives' and other commodities (Allen 2006, p. 141, Baines 2009, p. 174, Pham et al. 2007, p. 15).[15] The individual Reasons and the Resolve to fight are thus strengthened through LRA indoctrination.

In waging its guerrilla war, the LRA has become a highly professional organisation over its twenty-seven years of existence. According to the ICG, the LRA is tightly managed and has good record keeping. When infiltrating an area, it splits into ever smaller groups in order to avoid detection.[16] It applies decentralised ambush tactics using GPS, radios and mobile phones to coordinate (Cakaj 2010a, p. 18, ICG 2004c, p. 5–6). Its attacks are described as well planned and sudden and its commanders are skilled at guerrilla fighting (ICTJ and HRC 2005, p. 15, Sai 2010).[17]

The LRA is also very apt at using safe havens across regional borders. Especially their bases in areas of Southern Sudan were of key importance for the LRA's early survival (Akhavan 2009, p. 642). The support of the GoS had a deep impact on the LRA as its Resources were multiplied and it became independent from faltering local popular support. Since the GoS expected the LRA to fight both the UPDF and the SPLA, it grew in size considerably through abductions, and attacked civilians even more indiscriminately (Allen and Vlassenroot 2010, p. 12, Mwenda 2010, p. 49). The start of the GoS support also finalised the LRA's transformation from a spiritual to a military organisation (Titeca 2010, p. 72). Some analysts and UPDF sources say that the LRA was better equipped and more professional than the UPDF at that time (Atkinson 2010, p. 205–206, Schomerus 2007, p. 41).

15 The LRA 'wives' are young girls abducted from villages and given to high ranking officers. Kony himself reportedly had forty wives. Low-ranking LRA soldiers in contrast are not allowed to have sex without permission. Rapes during attacks are thus an uncommon crime for LRA (see Allen 2006, p. 59 and 65). See (AI 1997, p. 20) for a report that claims a high number of rapes during LRA attacks.

16 According to reports, the LRA is now carrying out ambushes in groups of less than ten (ICG 2011a, p. 2).

17 The LRA reportedly even uses spies and abducts informants before attacking a location (Cakaj 2010a, p. 16).

Despite this professionalism, the LRA is often described as an insane cult or a group of religious terrorists by journalists, officials of the GoU, diplomats and even academics (Finnström 2010a, p. 74 and 80, Titeca 2010, p. 59, Van Acker 2004, p. 350). This is due to the spiritual and religious elements as well as the LRA's extremely brutal modus operandi. The perception of the LRA as a cult leads to a lack of understanding for the credibility of the LRA's agenda in the Ugandan north–south context (Allen 2006, p. 25). Kony himself has rejected the characterisation of the LRA as a Christian fundamentalist or terrorist organisation as government propaganda, while other LRA leaders like Brigadier Sam Kolo have described themselves as freedom fighters (Finnström 2010a, p. 84, Latigo 2008, p. 92, Schomerus 2010b, p. 114 and 123). At a closer look, the 'insane cult' thesis is indeed too simple to bear up to the facts.

For example, the mutilations and atrocities committed by the LRA can be understood as a strategic instrument, and not a mere act of savagery (see Mergelsberg 2010, p. 169). Even though the LRA violence is deeply shocking and seems grotesque and senseless, the atrocities committed by the LRA have a practical function as propaganda of the deed, showing the strength of the LRA and disproving GoU claims of winning the conflict (ICG 2005b, p. 2). They also serve the political function of meting out collective punishment to the alleged supporters of the GoU, thus deterring future support. At the same time, the faith of the Acholi in the government is undermined, which in turn limits the Resources of the government (see Branch 2005, p. 6, Lomo and Hovil 2004, p. 22).[18]

As a result of this strategy, the LRA was never able to mobilise real support in the later stages of the conflict, but it was successful in creating an ambiguity towards both the NRA and the LRA among the local population that made a military solution of the conflict more difficult (Branch 2005, p. 2, ICG 2004c, p. 9–10). The GoU was only initially able to mobilise the Acholi population in self-defence groups against the LRA in 1991 and 1995. Both times, the UPDF did not support the militias adequately and left them to bear the brunt of LRA retaliation attacks.

[18] Interestingly, Joseph Kony himself has denied LRA atrocities and even the fact that the LRA is abducting child soldiers on various occasions. He claims that the government is committing the crimes and blaming the LRA in order to tarnish its image (Okidi 2011). A former LRA Commander went as far as claiming that mutilations were never part of the LRA's official policy. According to his version, Joseph Kony killed commanders responsible for atrocities for '*bringing up the entire world against the LRA*' (LRA Commander 2011).

Since then, the Acholi have not been willing to mobilise against the LRA (Branch 2005, p. 4).

The religious rules and rituals of the LRA also fulfil strategic functions. They provide structures and hierarchies, keep abductees controlled and prevent escapes and serve to integrate fighters and boost their Resolve (Cakaj 2010a, p. 5, Titeca 2010, p. 60–64). Indeed, LRA returnees have reported that they considered fleeing for a very long time but did not do so out of fear of Kony's supernatural powers (Mergelsberg 2010, p. 164). Additionally, their spirituality also serves the LRA on the battlefield. Soldiers from the UPDF and the SPLA often also believe in spiritual powers and are afraid of the LRA. Many claim that it takes 10–30 bullets to kill an LRA soldier in battle (Titeca 2010, p. 70). The spiritual character of the LRA is also linked to the Acholi culture and its animist beliefs, and adds to the LRA's local credibility (Dolan, 2009, p. 95). Unlike the media reports suggest, spiritualism is not a crazy abnormity unique to the LRA, but is also used by other African guerrilla movements, for example in Zimbabwe (Dolan 2009, p. 95, Royo 2008, p. 9).

It is important to note that these spiritual factors are losing importance, particularly since Operation Iron Fist (Borzello 2007, p. 394). They did not play any role during the Juba negotiations between the LRA and the GoU in 2006–2008.

The fascination with the spiritual background of the LRA and its brutal mutilations often overshadows the agenda of the rebel group. This agenda may be incoherent but it still exists. Even in the earliest phase of their rebellion, Joseph Kony and Odong Latek argued for Acholi nationalist aims in a joint public letter (Van Acker 2004, p. 348). Further political manifestos were published in 1996, 1998 and 1999 (Finnström 2008, p. 121 and 127, Latigo 2008, p. 91).[19] Initially, the LRA even had a radio station called Radio Free Uganda which was quickly blocked by the government (Allen 2006, p. 43–44). The LRA demands that a National Conference should be convened to pave the way for new national elections. It demands the establishment of a Religious Affairs Ministry, the rehabilitation of the Ugandan infrastructure and economy, the realisation of national unity, access to education for everyone, an independent judiciary, the balanced composition of public institutions (especially the army) and improvement of the relations with Uganda's neighbours, as

[19] There is some polemic surrounding these documents as many claim that they are artificial diaspora creations, yet they are taken seriously on the ground and are attributed to the LRA in the population (Finnström 2010a, p. 84–85).

well as the moving of the state capital to the north-western municipality of Kigumba (Allen 2006, p. 43).[20] Other demands include the creation of a multi-party federal system, the furthering of the socio-economic balance in Uganda, and nationwide peace and security (Finnström 2008, p. 122, Latigo 2008, p. 92). Finally, the rebels accuse Museveni of overstaying in power and misusing government funds (Allen 2006, p. 43–44).

The manifestos include detailed criticism of specific policies, for example the IMF programmes in Uganda are criticised for causing deflation (Finnström 2010a, p. 86–87). Both Kony and his second-in-command Vincent Otti managed to phone in on live radio broadcasts and propagate their aims (Allen 2006, p. 43–44). The demands of the LRA described here echo many of the grievances analysed in the preceding section and constitute some of the main Reasons for the LRA to fight.[21]

Many academics working in the field in northern Uganda have identified political motivations of the LRA and attempts to communicate politically with the local population (Allen 2006, p. 44, Branch 2010a, p. 41, Dolan 2009, p. 85). The LRA has also made specific efforts to present a political agenda at the Juba negotiations (Finnström 2010a, p. 88, Pham et al. 2007, p. 16). Yet, even a renowned think tank like the ICG has failed to consider the LRA demands seriously, describing the LRA as a self-sustaining war machine without an agenda (ICG 2004c, p. 5–6).

Naturally, it is important to keep in mind that the stated aims of the LRA are at complete odds with the behaviour of its fighters on the ground, who abduct children and thus impede their access to education, pillage villages and thus hamper economic rehabilitation, and attack civilians in neighbouring states and thus threaten Uganda's good relations with its neighbours. Some explain this contradiction by claiming that the LRA has lost its political agenda in the course of the conflict, carried away by the increasing violence (Eichstaedt 2009, p. 176, Finnström 2008, p. 100, Van Acker 2004, p. 351).

The contradictions between the stated aims and the behaviour on the ground illustrate that the LRA and its motivations are very difficult to

[20] Kigumba had approximately 40,000 inhabitants in 2008, compared to the current capital Kampala's estimated population of 1.4 million people.

[21] Ayena Odong, a member of the LRA delegation during the Juba talks, reported that Kony described the cattle rustling, the abuses committed by the NRA, as well as the marginalisation of the north as reasons for his armed struggle (Odong 2011b).

assess. It is not clear whether Kony can be trusted in negotiations or whether he is an insane, paranoid madman as many claim. The possible irrationality of the LRA leadership figures into the Resolve of the movement. It is clear though, that Kony's role is central for the cohesion of the Lord's Resistance Army in terms of hierarchy, tactics and ideology (ICG 2004c, p. II). Without him the organisation would unravel, leaving scattered LRA groups to abduct, roam and loot in the region (ICG 2005e, p. 4, 2010, p. 12, Prendergast 2005, p. 4).

After its first transformation when becoming a proxy of the GoS, the LRA had its second defining moment with the failure of the Juba Talks in late 2008. In the final stages of the peace talks, a rift emerged within the LRA leadership. Some members around Kony's second-in-command Vincent Otti were apparently in favour of signing the Juba Agreement. In order to reassert his authority, Kony killed Vincent Otti and managed to contain the split shortly afterwards, renewing the LRA's Resolve to fight and minimising the chances for a future negotiated solution (Brubacher 2010, p. 276). The LRA then had to disperse in order to avoid the UPDF Operation Lightning Thunder. The rebels broke up into small independent groups that were much more difficult to chase (Eichstaedt 2009, p. 21, Finnström 2008, p. 197). In combination with the increasing number of killed and captured Acholi commanders, this fragmentation led to a partial breakdown of LRA command structures (Cakaj 2010a, p. 21, ICG 2010, p. 10). This does not mean, however, that the LRA has ceased to exist as a conflict party, as HRW found transcripts and other information indicating that Kony is still orchestrating the LRA campaigns and is in contact with at least some of his commanders (HRW 2010a).

Despite having been driven from their Ugandan homeland for good, the rebels have adapted to the new situation and are securing their survival through smuggling and by exploiting gold and ivory in the DRC and CAR. The LRA has reportedly also forged alliances with local militias to pursue these activities (Allen and Vlassenroot 2010, p. 20, ICG 2008, p. I and 15, Perrot 2010, p. 203). This access to new modes of economic reproduction has provided the LRA with new Resources and economic Reasons to continue the fight. The LRA has now created a safe corridor stretching from the DRC westwards to CAR, where it can move safely and evade intelligence gathering (ICG 2008, p. 14). Within this corridor, they move by changing clothes to blend in with the local population. They shake off UPDF patrols by taking off their shoes and spreading out when being chased (IRIN 2011c).

The LRA has also evolved considerably concerning its composition. The ICG estimates that by 2008, a majority of the LRA fighters were Sudanese (ICG 2008, p. I). Even though there are rumours that the LRA wants to return to northern Uganda, the group is no longer a threat to Uganda itself for the time being. Instead, it has become a threat to regional stability in the tri-state area (ICG 2008, p. 20).

b. The National Resistance Army/Movement and the Uganda People's Defence Forces

The NRM is a former rebel group from southern Uganda that took power from the Obote Regime in 1986. Uganda's current president, Yoweri Museveni, was the leader of this rebel group. He first prolonged his term unilaterally several times and was then repeatedly re-elected as president, most recently in February 2011. Even though the elections were largely free and fair, the NRM used state resources to gain the upper hand over the opposition parties and has also intimidated opposition supporters during the electoral campaign.

The NRM based its power on southern Uganda after taking Kampala. It has exploited the history of ethnic animosity between the north and the south in order to fortify this power base. The north was subdued through maintaining a counter-insurgency campaign for decades and driving the local population into tightly controlled IDP camps.

The NRM and the UPDF have consistently seen the LRA insurgency as a local problem and have thus advocated a local solution through the creation of self-defence groups. Due to the lack of government support for these local militias in combating the LRA, this approach has largely failed.

Even though Museveni first underestimated and downplayed the LRA insurgency in the north, he always followed a clear military approach towards solving the conflict (e.g. Ginifer 2006, p. 15).[22] President Museveni has personally contributed to the failure of negotiations with the LRA in 1994 and 2004 through hostile statements or through pronouncing ultimatums. In 2000, President Museveni also tried to delay the passing of an amnesty for Ugandan rebel groups, even violating the

[22] President Museveni himself has stated in an interview that he focuses on the military factors of the northern conflict and is not too much aware of the humanitarian situation (IRIN 2005c). An internal DFID review found that only '*most determined leverage or conditionality*' would persuade the GoU to focus on tackling the root causes of the conflict (Ginifer 2006, p. 13).

Ugandan Constitution in doing so. The Juba negotiations between 2006 and 2008 are perceived as the only genuine GoU attempt to end the conflict peacefully. After the failure of the Juba Talks, the government is again firmly pursuing a military solution of the problem. Since the LRA was driven out of Uganda, the GoU is celebrating its victory, stating that the pacification of the whole country has been achieved (Mpagi 2010). The conflict history is thus indicating a strong Resolve of the NRM to fight.

The government has also managed to secure considerable Resources by tapping into international economic aid, US military support, as well as regional support by coordinating military actions with its neighbours.

At the same time, the government has consistently denied the real grievances in the north (Lomo and Hovil 2004, p. 12).[23] It has emphasised time and again that it does not see the LRA as a legitimate representative of northern political demands and initially refused to discuss the root causes of the conflict even during the Juba Talks. The GoU essentially denies the existence of any legitimate political agenda of the LRA (Finnström 2008, p. 121 and 127). It has gone to exceptional length in order to hinder the distribution of LRA leaflets and to undermine LRA propaganda in northern Uganda, even imprisoning people in possession of leaflets (Finnström 2010a, p. 85, Schomerus 2007, p. 14).

To sum up, the GoU has contributed to the root causes of the conflict through ethnic manipulation and by marginalising the north. At the same time, it denies the existence of any grievances and paints the LRA as a terrorist organisation. Its will to negotiate is therefore very limited and it would only sign an agreement in which the LRA basically surrenders and accepts a government amnesty and reintegration package.

Only recently has the GoU started to address the marginalisation of the north (ICG 2007c, p. 3, Bayne 2007, p. 19).[24] Yet, it still doesn't accept any strong political opposition in the country. This has been illustrated by the events in spring 2011 when the opposition leader Kizza Besigye started to stage the so-called Walk to Work Protests against rising living costs in Uganda. The police dissolved the demonstrations

[23] A Parliamentary Committee instated by the GoU to investigate the LRA conflict failed to identify any causes for the LRA's struggle in its report (Ugandan Parliamentary Committee on Defence and Internal Affairs 1997, p. 21).

[24] This is, for example, reflected in the Poverty Eradication Action Plan (PEAP) of the GoU (The Republic of Uganda 2004).

on several occasions, at times violently and under the use of firearms, while Besigye was repeatedly arrested.

5.1.4 *Conflict dynamics*

> *I was very surprised when Operation [Lightning Thunder] was launched. For me, I thought I would just wake up one morning and hear Joseph Kony was arrested or killed with his senior commanders and that would be the end of the war. But . . . to my surprise, I was seeing in the papers that . . . they were talking [about having found] maybe a blanket: 'We got a real blanket of Joseph Kony that he was covering himself with, we [also] brought some bags of Simsim.' Now what is that?'*
>
> (Former LRA fighter during an interview)

> *Within minutes it was all too apparent how impenetrable these forests are – and what a haven they represent to the LRA. This is thick, thick foliage. I'm absolutely soaking wet. I've lost the soldiers. Where are they? They're five yards ahead of you and you wouldn't know they are there.'* Voice of America journalist Ivan Broadhead, embedded with the UPDF.
>
> (Broadhead 2011)

After having endured twenty-two years of conflict, it seems that peace has finally returned to northern Uganda. The IDP camps are already closing and up to 92 per cent of the displaced people have returned to their villages and started to cultivate their land (Allen et al. 2010, p. 282–283, Pham and Vinck 2010, p. 10).[25] Incidents of violence were reported very sporadically in 2010 (Pham and Vinck 2010, p. 23). There are also some hopeful signals that the economic marginalisation of northern Uganda is ending. The government started a three-year strategy with donor funds to improve emergency relief, health care, education, the judiciary and the police services in October 2007. The plan also includes the construction of new railway lines, sugar factories and a dam (ICG 2008, p. 7). The region has become a gateway for the booming trade between South Sudan and Uganda. Gulu, the largest city of the north, is profiting most from this and has become a veritable boomtown (ICG 2010, p. 21). The GoU is discovering the untapped economic potential of its northern districts and is starting to support development in the area

[25] Unfortunately, this process was not completely voluntary in the beginning. There were complaints in late 2006 that the government was trying to force IDPs out of camps and back into villages and blacklisting NGOs that kept on supporting camps marked for closure (Oxfam International 2007, p. 20)

(Allen et al. 2010, p. 279). Additionally, oil was recently discovered in Amuru in the north-west. Estimates expected 600–800 million barrels in 2008 (ICG 2008, p. 8). Last but not least, the strategic interest of the United States in the region is growing with the recent independence of South Sudan, Uganda's role as the lead nation in the AU mission in Somalia and increasing civil society pressure in the United States to crack down on the LRA. At the same time, the level of local government, the so-called local councils, has been strengthened by Museveni. As a result, local elites now have some access to political positions which counters the political marginalisation of the north (Lindemann 2011, p. 407). The majority of the population is also happy with the improved security in the area (Expert Interview 2011c, Pham and Vinck 2010, p. 2). It is fair to say that many of the Reasons for a rebellion in the north are thus diminishing.

It is also a positive signal that the rest of Uganda is seemingly starting to overcome stereotypes and accept the investment programme in the north. Sixty-three per cent of Ugandans who took part in the 2008 Afrobarometer survey said that investing in northern Uganda and resettling the IDPs there should be a priority even if money for other tasks had to be pulled off (Afrobarometer 2008).

Even though the overall outlook is positive, there are also some bleak spots. The GoU has tried to speed up the return of people from the IDP camps and has partly forced them to return to their home villages even though the infrastructure in return zones is bad and the harvest may not be enough to feed the population (Wyrzykowski and Kasozi 2010, p. 9). Additionally, the development plan has been delayed by one year. The total budget allocated to the north within the plan is rather small and has to be shared between all districts north of Karuma falls, which means the war affected districts share the funds with numerous other districts that were not affected (Allen et al. 2010, p. 284, ICG 2010, p. 20–21). Finally, the return of IDPs has also triggered conflicts over land which means that the peace in the north remains fragile (Lenhart 2009, p. 1).

There are still few signs for a genuine effort by the GoU to tackle the marginalisation of the north on a national level (ICG 2008, p. 20). The trust in the government remains lower in the Acholi regions than anywhere else in Uganda, and people are not happy with the government track record in social issues (Pham et al. 2007, p. 26, Pham and Vinck 2010, p. 2). Yet, only 30 per cent of the Acholi still feel marginalised by the central government and Museveni managed to obtain a majority of votes in the northern districts for the first time in the 2011 presidential elections (Girke and Kamp 2011, p. 54, Pham and Vinck 2010, p. 31). The ICG warns that some root causes still need to be addressed to avoid the possible emergence of new rebel groups (ICG 2010, p. 20–21). Other experts don't see any real danger of a renewed insurrection at the current development level (Expert Interview 2011a).

Regarding the LRA, most observers agree that the rebellion has no longer an impact on the situation in northern Uganda (ICG 2008, p. I).[26] According to diplomatic sources, the LRA has been reduced to a mere security problem in the region and is fighting for its survival. Its importance has reportedly dropped so far, that experts suspect that some of the recent LRA attacks are in fact ambushes carried out by bandits who use the LRA activities as a cover to conduct their own attacks (Expert Interview 2011a, Schomerus 2007, p. 17, UN Source 2011).

The overall outlook for the conflict is thus positive, yet it is improbable that the conflict will end for good soon since the LRA has gained access to natural resources and needs little more than small arms and abducted fighters to survive. Even without external support, LRA weapons stockpiles are believed to be plentiful, and defections after Operation Lightning Thunder have been relatively low (Bevan 2006, p. 273, Resolve Uganda & Enough Project 2009, p. 2). Kony's personal Resolve to go on fighting has also been described as very high (Cakaj 2010a, p. 10). The current instability in CAR due to the resumption of hostilities by the Seleka rebels in 2014 further complicate efforts to crack down on the LRA. The most realistic scenario is that the conflict will continue at a low level, at the cost of innocent civilians in the DRC, CAR and South Sudan. The possibilities of a renewed rebellion in northern Uganda are currently remote. According to reports, the UPDF is also increasingly closing in on the commanders of the LRA. More and more are getting killed or captured and Kony himself has been close to being captured in the CAR (Cakaj 2010b, p. 1). Reportedly, the UPDF also still has a strong presence in DRC despite its official withdrawal in 2009 (HRW 2010f, p. 53). Additionally, US combat advisors have recently joined the UPDF in its hunt for the LRA and the affected countries have started to form a joint AU brigade targeting the LRA. The rebels also feel the pressure of a campaign organised by MONUSCO that is dropping leaflets to encourage LRA defections (Dalby 2011). The consensus among observers is that the LRA is currently operating in survival mode (Lancaster et al. 2011,

[26] The then UN Secretary-General Annan stated already in June 2006 that the LRA is no longer a credible military threat (UN Secretary-General 2006, §7).

p. 2). It is still far from clear if the new efforts will be enough to track down and end the threat of the LRA since the rebels are now operating in small groups on a terrain of 115,000 square miles, a territory half the size of France (Wegner 2012a).

Should the command structure of the LRA break down under this increased pressure, a degeneration of the conflict to low-level banditry committed by uncoordinated LRA splinters is probable. There are two rather improbable worst case scenarios in which the conflict could gain traction again. First, there are rumours that the LRA is trying to return to northern Uganda. Should they make it back into Uganda, the current development of the region could unravel and northern Uganda might plunge back into civil war. The fact that up to 40 per cent of the Acholi population believes peace is only temporary reflects the local fears of such a development (see Pham and Vinck 2010, p. 17). Considering that the UPDF is now hunting for the LRA deep within the CAR, and keeping in mind that the UPDF has become a lot better at counter-insurgency, this scenario is unlikely.

Second, a new conflict in South Sudan could break out between the GoS and its newly independent southern neighbour. In a war scenario between the two Sudans, renewed support by the GoS for the LRA is probable. Such a scenario would greatly boost LRA Resources, and the recent developments in Abiyei, the Blue Nile and South Kordofan provinces have shown that such a scenario is not out of the question. The outbreak of civil war in South Sudan has already improved the situation for the LRA by providing new safe havens in the war-torn country. Additionally, the breakdown of South Sudan has affected the economic outlook of northern Uganda. Yet, only renewed ties to the GoS could significantly strengthen the LRA in the current situation and so far, Sudan has steered clear of any involvement in the civil war.

5.1.5 Ugandan justice perceptions[27]

In the Ugandan case, a closer look at the justice perceptions in northern Uganda is necessary, because the ICC investigations triggered heated public discussions about how to ensure accountability for LRA atrocities. Local civil society organisations as well as traditional authorities in the north started championing values of traditional justice and reconciliation

[27] This section was part of a paper presented by the author at the 40th ECPR Joint Sessions of Workshops in April 2012 in Antwerp.

as an alternative to ICC prosecutions. This section will focus on describing notions of traditional justice prevalent in northern Uganda. The tracing of causal mechanisms in the following section will then illustrate why these justice perceptions played an important role in the impact of the ICC investigations in some areas.

Many local civil society organisations and authors claim a general cultural preference for reconciliation among the people living in the northern districts of Uganda, especially among the Acholi (e.g. Hovil and Lomo 2005, p. 10, New Vision 2011). Reconciliation in this context means offering LRA returnees amnesty and using traditional justice rituals for reconciliation and reintegration.

As a consequence of northern Ugandan lobbying efforts, the Parliament of Uganda passed the Amnesty Act in 2000, which allowed all rebels who laid down arms and renounced rebellion to receive amnesty. According to recent figures, 22,520 rebels have accepted the amnesty offer since the act was passed, approximately 48 per cent of them being former LRA fighters. Local support for the amnesty law also remains high, with 98 per cent in Acholiland supporting the amnesty approach in December 2011 (Otwili et al. 2011, p. 1–2).[28] Despite this strong local support, the Amnesty Act was not prolonged and expired in May 2012.

Traditional leaders and some local NGOs also promote the Acholi reconciliation ritual known as *mato oput* as an alternative to ICC trials or retributive justice in general. The ritual is designed to cope with murder on an individual level. It involves the perpetrator asking for forgiveness, complex compensation negotiations between the clans of the victim and the perpetrator and a final reconciliation ritual in which a goat is slaughtered and the perpetrator and a representative of the victim's clan drink a brew mixed from goat blood and the bitter juice of the eponymous *oput* root. After the ceremony, the clans share food and drinks to symbolise their reconciliation. The most detailed descriptions of a *mato oput* ceremony can be found in reports by Erin Baines and Stephen Lamony (Baines 2005, p. 57–63, Lamony 2007).[29] The involved clans will act as if the crime had not occurred after having completed the ritual which allows them to co-exist in the future. Between 2004 and 2006

[28] Also, 80 per cent of northern Ugandans preferred peace with amnesties to peace with trials in 2007, while 33 per cent thought pardoning was necessary to avoid future conflict (Pham et al. 2007, p. 4 and 31).

[29] Some video footage of a *mato oput* ritual has also been shown in a documentary by al-Jazeera (Negara 2011).

alone, USAID has funded fifty-four of these ceremonies (Latigo 2008, p. 105). Ugandan researchers claim that the local population wants their values of reconciliation to be reflected in the national transitional justice policy, even though the population does reportedly not insist on any specific rituals (Komakech and Sheff 2009, p. 39 and 43).

It is undeniable that the amnesty and the use of reconciliation rituals are of importance for the people in northern Uganda, and that they represent a local restorative approach to justice to some degree.[30] Still, it is important to acknowledge the limitations of this 'restorative justice' culture. While the amnesty is widely supported in the north, the support is given in the hope that it will lead to peace and out of fear that retributive justice measures might undermine it (Hovil and Quinn 2005, p. 34, Pham et al. 2007, p. 34). Additionally, there is a lot of cultural pressure among northern Ugandans to support the amnesty (Allen 2006, p. 138, Oxfam International 2007, p. 16). Some persons, particularly direct victims of the LRA, are extremely opposed to the amnesty and see it as a scandal that some former LRA commanders are now allowed to live in relative luxury (Clarke 2009, p. 131, Hovil and Quinn 2005, 34, HRW 2005b, p. 40 and 60). Still, most of these critics would not openly voice their opinion.[31] Additionally, surveys suggest that the local population wants to use traditional justice mainly to re-integrate LRA returnees.[32] They do not expect traditional justice measures to solve accountability issues.

Public opinion on these issues also seems to change according to the situation. When there are negotiations, people want the ICC to lay low. After negotiations failed, calls were made for the ICC to arrest the LRA 'already' (Glasius 2009, p. 512). Accordingly, many more recent reports claim that there is now a majority in northern Uganda in favour of trying

[30] This does not automatically exclude the fact that Ugandans also want to see those who committed the crimes punished. In fact, the opinions gathered so far are very complex. According to a 2005 survey, 66 per cent in northern Uganda are calling for punishment as an accountability measure (ICTJ and HRC 2005, p. 26). Yet, the public shaming involved in traditional justice and guilt felt by the perpetrator is also seen as a form of punishment.

[31] There are some exceptions, like a number of politicians from northern Uganda who were arguing openly against dropping the ICC warrants as Kony had not made use of past opportunities to make peace (Apuuli 2005, p. 53).

[32] Most northern Ugandans saw traditional justice as useful for dealing with the LRA and 32 per cent see reconciliation as the main contribution of traditional justice (ICTJ and HRC 2005, p. 32, Pham et al. 2007, p. 40). Interviews during field research also suggest that the contribution of traditional justice is mainly seen in the re-integration of returnees.

those most responsible for atrocities (Nouwen 2013, p.158, OHCHR 2007, p. 30 and 54, Registry of the ICC 2010, p. 7).

5.2 The ICC investigations in Uganda

You cannot have justice if you don't have peace.

(Norbert Mao, Gulu Politician, Daily Monitor 5 December 2006)

The second part of the case study will trace the causal mechanisms developed in the cross-case overview. If the causal mechanisms do not fit the case for obvious reasons, a full process tracing is not conducted. The analysis is based on a detailed daily timeline of the conflict that has been verified through triangulation with other sources (interviews, survey findings and statistics) whenever possible.

5.2.1 Facilitating the emergence of the rule of law

a. Furthering the respect for laws and human rights

The LRA conflict followed escalation patterns typical for armed conflicts that led to the breakdown of moral rules and cultural taboos. This breakdown manifested itself in the brutal atrocities committed by the LRA as well as the degrading treatment of civilians by the UPDF (OHCHR and UHRC 2011, p. 38, Wyrzykowski and Kasozi 2010, p. 38). Addressing this degradation of the respect for laws and cultural norms is a key issue for ensuring lasting peace. Strengthening the rule of law is also important for winning back the trust of the northern population in the GoU, which has been lost due to mass arrests and violations committed by UPDF soldiers (Bradbury 1999, p. 29, Van Acker 2004, p. 356). An analysis of the human rights record of government institutions shows that some progress has been made but the human rights situation remains an issue. Contrary to the expectations in the literature, the ICC did not contribute to the little improvement that Uganda has seen in the area of human rights. Rather, the ICC was deftly used by the GoU to focus all attention on LRA atrocities and to claim that there have been no serious violations on the government side.

Progress in respecting the law and human rights is measured by analysing the human rights records of state institutions, the ratification of protocols and treaties for human rights protection and legal reforms. This section will focus on the human rights record of the GoU as this mechanism is mainly relevant for state actors. The impact of the ICC investigations on LRA crimes will be analysed in the scope of the deterrence mechanism.

The Museveni government has ratified a number of relevant human rights documents, namely the Anti-Torture Convention (1986), the African Charter on Human and Peoples' Rights (1986), the International Covenant on Civil and Political Rights (1995), the UN Principles to protect children against recruitment in armed forces (2006) and the African Charter on Women's Rights (2010). The government has also started to legally implement these treaties, including the Additional Protocol I, II and III to the Geneva Conventions and the Anti-Torture Convention (Wandera 2010). But there have been implementation and compliance problems connected to some of these treaties. The committee against torture asked Uganda to investigate allegations of torture in June 2006 and HRW and AI criticised the government for taking so long to implement the anti-torture convention (AI 2008, p. 8, HRW 2011c). Human rights organisations interviewed during the field research suggested that torture remains a problem both in police and in military detention facilities until today (Expert Interview 2011e, 2011j). This is confirmed in the 2013 report of the Ugandan Human Rights Commission (UHRC 2014, p. XXX).

Some improvement of the human rights record of state institutions in Uganda is measurable, but the record remains mixed. Due to the important role of army human rights violations in the conflict, the analysis will focus on the UPDF.

Especially the early military operations conducted by the NRA were marked by atrocities and even sporadic massacres against the civilian population, most notably during Operation North (also known as Operation Simsim) in 1991 (Mallinder 2009b, p. 12). Until the LRA was pushed out of Uganda between 2005 and 2006, violations committed by government forces in the north included raping and beating of civilians, arbitrary arrests, illegal detention and torture, extrajudicial killings of civilians, as well as looting and destruction of property (AI 1999b, Dolan 2009, p. 61 and 109, Finnström 2010b, p. 138, HRW 2005b).[33]

The UPDF has been found responsible for similar behaviour in the DRC by the International Court of Justice (ICJ), including '*killing, torture*

[33] These allegations are well documented in the literature and were also brought forward in all the interviews conducted with human rights organisations during the field research (e.g. Expert Interview 2011e, 2011j, Sekindi 2011).

and other forms of inhumane treatment' of the civilian population while inciting '*ethnic conflict*' and failing '*to take measures to put an end to such conflict*' (ICJ 2005). A 2010 report of the OHCHR accused the UPDF of being complicit in serious human rights violations including killings, rape and recruitment of child soldiers during the DRC war between 1993 and 2003 (OHCHR 2010, United Nations 2002, §97–138). The Congolese army (FARDC) is accusing the UPDF of faking LRA attacks in order to justify their presence in the DRC so they can exploit the natural resources in the region (Cakaj 2011, p. 9, ICG 2011a, p. 7).[34] Civilians living in the LRA-affected areas in DRC have also named the UPDF as a perpetrator of rape and looting, even though on a much lesser scale than the LRA, the FARDC or even other civilians. Most civilians in the DRC rather perceive the UPDF as a protector (Oxfam 2011, p. 4).

Another hotspot of alleged UPDF abuses is Karamoja, a region in the north-west of Uganda, infamous for its armed cattle rustlers. There have been reports of torture and killings as well as rape in the national media, and some reports accuse the UPDF of systematic brutality in the region (Barigaba 2010). The Ugandan Human Rights Commission (UHRC) is currently investigating in Karamoja and has reportedly found some evidence of UPDF human rights violations. The UPDF spokesperson, on the other hand, has denied the allegations (Mugerwa 2010). HRW has published a report on the UPDF's Karamoja operations that includes allegations of unlawful killings, arbitrary detentions, destruction of property, excessive use of force and torture (HRW 2007b, p. 36). During the field research, some informants gave information about massive human rights violations committed by UPDF soldiers that were allegedly still ongoing in Karamoja but preferred to remain anonymous.

Reports of UPDF abuses have also emerged in the areas where its forces are currently hunting the LRA. In the South Sudanese region of Eastern Equatoria, Acholi civilians complained that '*[the UPDF] turned their guns on the civil population, shooting, looting, raping, and burning their huts in pretext of chasing the LRA*' (cited in Schomerus 2007, p. 29–30). Others have also reported accusations of abusing civilians and logging teak trees in Southern Sudan against the UPDF (Borzello 2007, p. 410, ICG 2010, p. 1).

[34] It is impossible to say whether these allegations have any real foundation or were just used as a pretext to get rid of the UPDF presence. Ugandan troops on DRC soil were an inconvenience for President Kabila during his election campaign.

Similar reports emerge from CAR. ICG reported worsening relations between the UPDF and locals due to indiscipline of UPDF soldiers and a lack of progress in the hunt for the LRA (ICG 2011a, p. 6). In recent reports, locals in Obo accused UPDF soldiers of rampaging drunk in town and abusing civilians (Boswell 2012, Small Arms Survey 2012). There have also been ongoing accounts of rape of civilians and looting by UPDF soldiers (Cakaj 2011, p. 1, Colombant 2012).

Despite this very mixed record, think tanks, human rights groups, UN staff and experts all agree that there has been some real progress (Expert Interview 2011d, 2011j, ICG 2010, p. 6–9, Ronan 2011, UN Source 2011). There have been institutional reforms within the UPDF to increase compliance with human rights, efforts to ensure accountability of UPDF members who commit violations, as well as an increased responsiveness to human rights issues among UPDF commanders (Babalanda and Kyama 2011, p. 8, Expert Interview 2011d, 2011k, HRW 2007b, p. 68–69, ICG 2010, p. 6, Sekindi 2011).

The human rights record of the GoU more broadly remains problematic. The GoU has used terrorist charges to target opposition politicians and critics. Additionally, the government has occasionally targeted media for unpleasant reporting (ICG 2011a, p. 4, Tripp 2004, p. 9–10). More recent analyses accused the GoU of using the army to intimidate voters during the 2011 elections, and the ICG concluded that the Museveni government is slowly but steadily moving towards repression and patronage strategies comparable to the Amin and Obote regimes (ICG 2011a, p. 4, 2012). This analysis is shared by opposition politicians (Okumu 2011), and illustrated by events on the ground. In 2009, there were violent crackdowns against demonstrations in favour of the Buganda Kingdom during which up to forty civilians were killed (HRW 2010g). Additionally, there have been army-led crackdowns against the so-called Walk to Work demonstrations in 2011 and 2012 during which at least 9 people have been killed, 700 arrested and 47 injured (ICG 2012, p. 32). The US State Department as well as the British House of Commons recently voiced concerns about an increasingly repressive GoU (Mpuga 2012), and the most recent human rights report of the US State Department accuses Ugandan security forces of killing and torturing civilians (USDOS 2012). The situation has continued to degenerate during 2013 to a point that EU Member States were considering joint action to address the GoU human rights record. The recently passed legislation penalising homosexuality finally led to several states stopping their official donor assistance to Uganda (Reuters 2014).

Nevertheless, it remains to be seen whether this is a temporary problem or a long-term trend. After all, safeguards for human rights protection have been implemented in Uganda, including the Ugandan Human Rights Commission (UHRC), which has an extensive mandate and has been reporting violations openly.

The sequence of events suggests that the ICC contributed to the improved human rights record of the UPDF since most of the progress has been made since the ICC started its investigations in 2004. The logical assumption would be that the ICC increased pressure on state institutions to improve their human rights record since the Court was investigating on their territory. But did the ICC really contribute to public pressure on the UPDF to improve its human rights record?

Researchers have identified growing pressure from human rights campaigners to address the human rights violations of the LRA and – to a lesser extent – the NRA and UPDF since 1997, also in the context of the Congo war (Bradbury 1999, p. 13, Risse et al. 2003, p. 130–131). At around the same time, the UHRC started its work in Uganda, and in 1997, a Parliamentary Committee criticised the UPDF for their poor human rights record (Ugandan Parliamentary Committee on Defence and Internal Affairs 1997). According to Chris Dolan, international NGOs were very reluctant to report human rights abuses, particularly those committed by the government, in the early phases of the conflict. It was mainly local organisations that addressed human rights issues and national organisations joined in around 2003 (Dolan 2009, p. 229).

The newspaper analysis confirms this, as the first statements by international human rights organisations concerning the LRA conflict were cited in the press in the third quarter of 2002. The statements by international NGOs reached their apex between the fourth quarter of 2005 and the fourth quarter of 2009 with 2–3 statements issued per quarter. AI published its first reports of human rights violations committed in the LRA conflict in 1999, HRW in 2003. The newspaper analysis shows a clear trend of increasing human rights statements by third states, international organisations, as well as NGOs. Interviewees from organisations working in the human rights sector also confirmed that the international pressure on the government to improve its human rights record started to mount during the 2000s (Expert Interview 2011e, HURIFO 2011).

Some of the pressure was significant, for example, the US Army put its funding of the UPDF on hold after the 2003 State Department country report on human rights accused the UPDF of violations (ICG 2004c,

p. 21). In another case, the United States threatened to stop its support of anti-LRA operations due to accusations against the commanding officer of the operation, Brigadier Charles Otema, of having executed a prison inmate (Kulayigye 2011).

Further cases of direct external pressure included a reprimand by the UN Committee Against Torture and Uganda being blacklisted as a country that violates the rights of children in June 2006 (UNCAT 2005). In the latter case, President Museveni immediately agreed to implement UN principles to protect children against recruitment. Indeed, the fact that the UPDF completely stopped using child soldiers since around 2003 is one of the key successes of human rights pressure in Uganda. General pressure to improve human rights protection in Uganda was thus already measurable before the ICC came into play in 2004.

Still, most of the public pressure focused on LRA violations. During the active phase of the conflict, UPDF human rights violations were addressed or mentioned in the media on average once a quarter. Yet, the reports of HRW (2005b) and AI (1999b) suggested that some violations by government troops, like rape, were frequent. Chris Dolan estimates that about one-third of the violations committed during the LRA conflict were perpetrated by the UPDF (Dolan 2009). Against this background, the human rights pressure reflected in media reports seems one-sided. It is beyond a doubt that LRA violations were a lot worse and more frequent than alleged GoU violations, yet this should not cloud the vision of human rights watchdogs and media concerning the human rights record of the government side.

One reason why the GoU violations were not addressed prominently in news sources is press censorship in Uganda. The government at times closed down national media outlets that caught their attention with unpleasant reporting, and some of the international human rights organisations working on the ground have been threatened with expulsion by the GoS after publishing critical reports (Okumu 2011).[35] It is no secret that the GoU was very displeased with the publication of the UNHCHR report on the UPDF conduct in the DRC (OHCHR 2010). Some journalists reported self-censoring among their colleagues when it came to the human rights record of government forces (Oketch 2010a).

[35] According to opposition politician Reagan Okumu, Human Rights Watch's Maria Burnett faced near deportation by the GoU over some of her reports on the UPDF's human rights conduct.

The analysis suggests that the ICC even furthered this tendency of neglecting the human rights record of the GoU. From the moment when the case was referred to the ICC, it seemed that the OTP and the GoU were cooperating closely. The Ugandan government issued a self-referral, specifically asking the ICC to investigate the *crimes of the LRA* in northern Uganda. Additionally, the referral was announced at a joint press conference of President Museveni and Chief Prosecutor Moreno Ocampo. This created the perception – especially in the LRA-affected areas – that the ICC was being used as a tool by the GoU to isolate the LRA internationally (Dolan 2009, p. 100, Drumbl 2007, p. 145, Mégret 2010, p. 28). Indeed, it is hard to challenge claims that the main motivation of President Museveni's referral was to use the ICC in order to mobilise world opinion against the LRA (e.g. Branch 2007a, p. 488). Some interviewees also voiced the opinion that Museveni was directly targeting the Government of Sudan (GoS) for its support of the LRA by referring the case to the ICC (Expert Interview 2011i, Okumu 2011). President Museveni later personally hinted that this was part of his motivation, stating that pressure on Sudan to pursue Kony had increased since the issuing of the ICC warrant (Museveni 2005). The impression that the GoU was using the ICC is being reinforced by the fact that the government has always been confident that it will not be targeted itself. The former Defence Minister said already at the beginning of the investigations in 2004 that he only expected five LRA leaders to be indicted (Mbabazi 2004). Also, it was telling that the Ministry of Defence initiated the ICC referral within the GoU, and not the Ministry of Justice or the Department of Public Prosecutions (Nouwen and Werner 2010, p. 948–949).The army has also made clear that it wants to avoid ICC investigations of UPDF crimes: '*Our position is if they come across any allegations against government officials, they should let them be tried by the government*' (Daily Monitor 2004).

The ICC tried to counter this perception later by clarifying publicly that the government side was also under investigation, e.g. in July 2004 and in February 2005. The OTP argued that it had started its investigations on the LRA side, because their crimes were of a higher gravity. The prosecution also added that investigations of the GoU were still ongoing (ICC 2010c). Yet, the OTP has consistently declined to offer further details concerning these investigations. Requests for information, e.g. by HRW and the author, have been declined for reasons of confidentiality (HRW 2011b, p. 28, Rastan 2011b). Additionally, the ICC investigators depended on the UPDF to ensure their security during investigations (see Unger and Wierda 2008, p. 277). This has furthered the widespread perceptions of one-sided investigations in northern Uganda,[36] particularly among victims (HURINET et al. 2010, p. 8, VRWG 2010, p. 14). Additionally, the local population has been consistently calling for investigations of both sides in surveys conducted since 2005 (ICTJ and HRC 2005, p. 5, OHCHR 2007, p. 21, Pham et al. 2007, p. 3, Pham and Vinck 2010, p. 3). Even ICC advocates and human rights organisations on the ground did not believe that the ICC did a good job in investigating alleged government crimes (Expert Interview 2011e, Freda and Aceng 2011, HURIFO 2011). This culminated in a Ugandan newspaper report which wrongly declared that the UPDF and the government had been 'cleared' by the ICC (Nouwen and Werner 2010, p. 951).

Neither the Ugandan government nor the Ugandan population believe that the government has anything to fear from the ICC. The UPDF spokesperson stated that the ICC had not found sufficient evidence to link the UPDF to atrocities committed in northern Uganda (Kulayigye 2011). Even though the ICC keeps emphasising that the investigations of the UPDF remain open, the army feels it has been cleared.[37] The fact that the ICC has not disclosed any information on its GoU investigations has even reinforced the perception both among the army as well as in the population that the UPDF can keep up the current modus operandi without fear of repercussions from the ICC or the international community more broadly.

It is unlikely that much will come out of the ICC investigations of the GoU. First, the ICC has not published any relevant document on the GoU investigations in the first ten years of its investigations. Second, the court has now reduced the resources for the Ugandan situation from 3.5 million EUR and twenty-seven staff members in 2006 to 111,200 EUR and one staff member in 2012 (HRW 2011b, p. 26). Under these circumstances, it is clear that there was no ICC contribution towards human

[36] Bias allegations against the ICC were regularly mentioned during interviews with local stakeholders (Loum 2011, Mapenduzi 2011) and have also been reported in academic literature (Carayon 2010, p. 12, Drumbl 2007, p. 145).

[37] This is consistent with past reactions of the UPDF and the government towards allegations of human rights violations. When confronted with accusations of human rights violations by HRW, the GoU answered that accusations of UPDF mistreatment come mainly from the opposition and are thus political. The government also emphasised that civilians who were allegedly killed by the UPDF had in reality died in crossfire with the LRA (HRW 2005b, p. 41).

rights pressure on the government, despite claims to the contrary (e.g. Allen 2010, p. 262).

At this point, ten years into the ICC investigations in Uganda, the picture that emerges suggests that the ICC is even undermining the human rights pressure on the government side. Arguably, the ICC has been increasing the Resources of the GoU, since the government uses it as a tool to boost its legitimacy and as a 'proof' that its human rights record is clean. Additionally, the ICC referral was part of the GoU propaganda strategy to label the LRA a terrorist group. By aligning their fight with the global war on terror, it was easier for the UPDF to justify their pronounced military approach internationally (Dolan 2009, p. 239).

This is an unexpected finding as none of the theoretical models discussed in the literature predicted a potentially negative impact of international investigations on human rights pressure as was the case in Uganda. This mechanism was only recently identified and fully traced in the case of Uganda (Rodman 2013). Critical human rights literature in International Relations would predict a similar outcome in Uganda, as the logic of the conflict is strengthened if human rights violations are discussed one-sidedly (e.g. Pia and Diez 2009, p. 2). It would be of utmost importance for the research agenda to ascertain whether similar processes have unfolded in the context of other international investigations.

The rule-of-law mechanism analysed here is also helpful to illustrate the role of justice perceptions for the impact of ICC investigations. Despite a local culture of restorative justice, the ICC is pursuing retributive justice. The resulting clash between international efforts to prosecute and local efforts to reconcile will undermine the education effects of trials. If local stakeholders feel that their approach to accountability and reconciliation is not taken into account by the ICC, they might very well become passive in the whole process of seeking justice. Various authors have criticised the ICC along these lines as disempowering the Acholi people (Branch 2007a, p. 480 and 508, Buckley-Zistel 2010, p. 111, Lomo 2006, p. 4). A number of interviewees stated that they had the impression that the ICC staff did not understand traditional justice mechanisms in northern Uganda and did not even bother to try to understand them (Expert Interview 2011e, Loum 2011, Okidi 2011). Additionally, local civil society organisations have blamed the ICC for blocking the use of traditional justice in dealing with LRA crimes (Uganda Victims Foundation 2010, p. 23). A local expert on the topic concluded that all local accountability alternatives were now being constructed to pass the ICC complementarity test and that international donors were biased towards funding only prosecutorial accountability mechanisms (Oola 2010, p. 11). This shows that rule of law efforts will not gain traction when local initiatives and international investigations are at odds with each other.

The same is true for the pressure to improve the human rights record. In northern Uganda, the ICC investigations are perceived as biased by the people and as harmless by the government and did thus not generate pressure to improve the human rights record on the government side. Justice perceptions thus determine how far the ICC can be effective in furthering the rule of law and human rights protection.

How local perceptions and investigations relate to each other very much depends on the procedural decisions taken by the Office of the Prosecutor of the ICC. The decision to announce the start of investigations at the side of President Museveni, as well as the decisions to focus on LRA crimes and not to publish information about investigations of the government side, created and reinforced perceptions of bias among the population and confirmed government expectations that the ICC investigations were mainly targeting the LRA. The Court's decision to not accept traditional justice as an alternative to ICC trials under the complementarity system of the Rome Statute (see Section 5.2.4a), as well as the lack of interest of ICC prosecutors for traditional justice measures led to the perception that the ICC does not care about local notions of justice and undermined the legitimacy and thus the effectiveness of the ICC in terms of its 'education function'.

b. Furthering judicial capacity building and reform

The capacity-building effects triggered by the ICC do not have a direct impact on the LRA. First of all, the LRA moved out of Uganda in 2006, so capacity building in Uganda does not have an influence on their opportunity structures. Second, LRA forces are indoctrinated and cut off from all communications, so an impact on their Resolve is unlikely. Nevertheless the introduction of international standards through the national implementation of the Rome Statute and the development of a national transitional justice concept helped to address the root causes of the conflict. The ICC also played an important role in founding the International Crimes Division (ICD) of the Ugandan High Court and improving its capacity through training and information sharing. The existence of the ICD reduces the probability of new rebel movements emerging, as there is a credible threat that commanders will be tried and held accountable by the ICD instead of receiving amnesty as in the past.

Capacity building and judicial reform triggered by the ICC are largely limited to the area of criminal law. These effects are indirect, since the ICC has neither the mandate nor the resources to directly engage in capacity building or in influencing a local justice system. But there are obvious indirect effects. The Rome Statute binds its state parties to make sure that the crimes included in the Statute are prosecuted. In order to do so, the Rome Statute has to be domesticated, the national prosecutors need to be trained how to prosecute these complex crimes and competent courts for trying these crimes have to be established.

The main impact of the ICC in Uganda was its contribution to the founding of the International Crimes Division of the Ugandan High Court (ICD). The division has the mandate to try Rome Statute crimes as well as international crimes and terrorism. The founding of the ICD is one of the consequences of the extensive accountability discussions during the Juba Talks (also Ajok 2011, Expert Interview 2011i, Tolbert and Wierda 2010, p. 5). The ICC warrants for the LRA commanders were already public when the Juba Peace Talks started in July 2006, and one of the key demands of the LRA was the lifting of these warrants. Therefore, accountability issues took centre stage in the later phases of the talks starting in spring 2007. Accountability was not discussed during earlier talks, which illustrates that the ICC warrants played a role in the new accountability focus. The parties attempted to forge an accountability agreement geared towards finding an accountability solution beyond the ICC,[38] and the ICD emerged as an alternative. The need to develop accountability measures that would meet the complementarity criteria of the ICC led to the proposal to create a division capable of judging the LRA commanders for war crimes. The founding of the ICD is therefore in many ways a direct result of the ICC warrants. Several interviewees working at human rights organisations or the ICD shared this view (Babalanda and Kyama 2011, p. 7, Expert Interview 2011f, p. 2, Odong 2011a).

The ICD has the potential to benefit judicial reforms in Uganda on a broader scale by introducing the international standards from the Rome Statute in the legal system. This could lead to a trickledown, leading, for example, to a better protection of the rights of the accused and the abolition of the death penalty in the national system.

At the moment, these international standards still need to be fully implemented by the ICD. This is demonstrated by the ICD's first trial of

[38] For a more detailed analysis of the Juba Talks and the Accountability Agreement with its annex, please refer to Section 5.2.4a below.

the mid-level LRA commander Thomas Kwoyelo in summer 2011.[39] Since the creation of the ICD is an unprecedented development in Africa, it is not surprising that the proceedings have met some challenges. Apparently, clear rules of procedures have not yet been fully established. One informant within the ICD heavily criticised the judicial standards of the institution (Expert Interview 2011g). The Kwoyelo trial has shown that there are a lot of due process issues including problems of sharing information with the defence, protecting witnesses, as well as allegations that the ICD was given a fixed budget and time frame within which it was expected to deliver a sentence by the GoU (Baxter 2011). Finally, the first defendant of the court, Thomas Kwoyelo, is still being held by the Department of Public Prosecutions (DPP) despite several court rulings that he should receive amnesty under the Ugandan Amnesty Act.

Closely connected to the work of the ICD was the adoption of the ICC Act by the Ugandan Parliament in 2010. The ICC Act essentially domesticated the Rome Statute and made it possible for the ICD to try Rome Statute crimes like genocide and crimes against humanity that had so far not been adequately incorporated into the national criminal laws (see Bekou and Shah 2006, p. 509, Mbazira 2011, p. 215–216). Additionally, the principle of command responsibility – so far unknown in Ugandan law – was included through the ICC Bill. The act was drafted and passed due to Uganda's international legal obligations from the Rome Statute and is thus a clear product of the ICC's existence.

Other laws that were influenced by the ICC's presence in the country, according to parliamentarians and human rights activists, are the new witness protection legislation that is currently being developed as well as a draft reconciliation law (Freda and Aceng 2011, Odong 2011b, Okumu 2011).

Finally, the accountability agreement made at the Juba Talks also sparked the development of a broader transitional justice concept. Despite the LRA's failure to sign the agreement, the GoU and donors started implementing some of its provisions (Oola 2010, p. 11). One result was the forming of a Transitional Justice Working Group in the scope of the Justice Law and Order Sector (JLOS)[40] of the GoU. Through bringing

[39] For a number of articles that provide a detailed overview and a deeper analysis of the Kwoyelo trial, please refer to (Justice in Conflict 2012).

[40] JLOS comprises the ministries relevant for justice issues, including the Ministries of the Interior and Justice, as well as the DPP, the courts and the police.

accountability to the fore at the Juba negotiations, the ICC thus served as a catalyst for several national projects strengthening the capacity of the Ugandan state to try war crimes and deal with past wrongs through a national concept of transitional justice (Freda and Aceng 2011, Odong 2011b, Okumu 2011). Indeed, the demands of the LRA during the talks to include traditional justice measures and a truth commission ensured that a broad transitional justice concept was designed that could serve as a blueprint for post-conflict transitional justice in other countries. The scope of this comprehensive concept is impressive on paper, including amnesties, a truth commission, re-integration through the use of traditional justice and trials for those most responsible. Notably, JLOS has been conducting population surveys to determine which kind of transitional justice concept is needed. It yet remains to be seen how far the concept can be implemented.

Local human rights organisations have claimed that the ICC involvement in Uganda has led to a great increase in interest and knowledge concerning international criminal law, including the introduction of courses on the topic at Makerere University. They also claim that the national judicial reform process is being monitored more closely since the ICC has become involved in Uganda (HURINET et al. 2010, p. 32–33). A transitional justice expert also stated that the ICC involvement in Uganda has led to many reform suggestions to criminalise different forms of rape and other sexual crimes based on the Rome Statute and ICC proceedings (Expert Interview 2011i, p. 2).

Apart from these indirect impacts of the ICC, the Court has also had a more direct influence on national capacity building. According to the yearly report of the Registry, the outreach programme of the Court held seminars for lawyers informing them about the ICC and encouraged applications of Ugandans to the internship and visiting professionals programmes of the Court (Registry of the ICC 2010, p. 15). The OTP also directly supported the Ugandan DPP in prosecuting LRA commander Thomas Kwoyelo at the ICD. Moreno Ocampo met the Ugandan Attorney General personally in the scope of this cooperation (Ajok 2011, OTP 2010). There has also been information sharing between the ICC and the ICD, and three visits by several judges to the ICC have been organised for training purposes (Expert Interview 2011b, Kamara 2011, p. 4).

In general, however, the ICC is very reluctant to engage too much in direct capacity building in situation countries. Capacity building through the ICC is not foreseen in the Rome Statute and the Court wants to avoid financial requests from national institutions for capacity building purposes.

To sum up, the ICC has clearly had an impact on judicial capacity building in Uganda, particularly in the area of prosecuting international crimes and developing a national concept for transitional justice. The ICC arrest warrants against the LRA have served as an impetus for a host of activities connected to accountability in the scope of the Juba Talks. The claims from the cross-case overview have thus been largely confirmed. The impact of this capacity building on the LRA conflict is limited for the reasons described in the initial paragraphs of this section. Nevertheless, the reforms sparked by the ICC have limited the opportunity structures for armed groups. Additionally, the Resolve of commanders and fighters to join an armed rebellion is reduced since they are more likely to be prosecuted for acts committed during the rebellion.

c. Combating impunity

Local researchers have identified impunity for atrocities committed in the LRA conflict as a driver for renewed conflict cycles (Lomo and Hovil 2004, p. 8). Being held to account for atrocities committed during conflicts might also reduce the Resolve of fighters to join a rebellion. The ICC has met some success in ensuring accountability for those most responsible. Prosecutions of LRA commanders would have been improbable in the absence of the ICC due to national amnesty laws. On the GoU side, the ICC has not contributed to accountability efforts since no findings from its investigations have been published. There is no discernible effect of combating impunity for the rank and file of both conflict parties. For the LRA, this is due to the indoctrination and isolation of the fighters. On the UPDF side, there is no credible threat of being held to account because of the ICC investigations.

When tracing the impact of the ICC investigations on accountability in the LRA conflict, it is important to distinguish between the LRA and the GoU. Since the ICC is concentrating on LRA atrocities so far, it is no surprise that the impact differs for the two sides.

On the side of the LRA, the ICC has issued arrest warrants for the Chairman Joseph Kony and four of his top commanders. According to the ICC investigations, those are the persons most responsible for LRA atrocities committed in northern Uganda since July 2002. The effectiveness of the ICC in combating impunity can be estimated by comparing the performance with a counter-factual scenario without an ICC referral. Uganda passed a blanket amnesty in 2000 that remained in force until as late as May 2012. It upheld the amnesty law even though it was obviously clashing with its legal obligations under the Rome Statute to prosecute war crimes, crimes against humanity and genocide. The fact that the GoU decided to stick to the amnesty law despite its international obligations for so long, shows that it is very unlikely that the amnesty law would have been abolished in the absence of ICC investigations since there would have been even less pressure to do so.

Additionally, the case of Thomas Kwoyelo shows that it was not possible to effectively try LRA commanders for their crimes as long as they were legally entitled to receive amnesty. The LexisNexis analysis shows that President Museveni has been consistently offering amnesty to Joseph Kony and his top commanders, thus making explicit that the Amnesty Act also included the top commanders. Amnesty offers were, for example, made on 7 March 2000, 9 March 2003, 7 June 2005 and as late as 9 February 2009. The Amnesty Act includes a procedure to bar certain individuals from receiving an amnesty if the Parliament decides so on request of the Ministry of the Interior. An attempt to exclude Joseph Kony and his top commanders from amnesty failed on 13 April 2010 after massive protests by MPs. This clearly shows that the probability of the LRA commanders being charged for their atrocities in the absence of the ICC is extremely low. Additionally, the DPP would have had practical difficulties charging Kony and his top commanders as the Ugandan criminal law did not cover crimes against humanity and command responsibility before the ICC Act was passed.

We can therefore assume that the LRA would have been accused of atrocities in the absence of the ICC, but the matter would probably not have been brought before any court. All five LRA commanders are legally entitled to amnesty in the counter-factual scenario. In reality, these commanders face an arrest warrant, but none has been arrested so far. The ICC has therefore made limited progress in combating impunity on the LRA side.

On the side of the UPDF and the GoU, there have been several allegations, especially against individual UPDF soldiers as described in Section 5.2.1a. Since the ICC jurisdiction began in July 2002, only crimes committed after that date can be taken into consideration to determine the effectiveness of the ICC in combating impunity. Crimes committed during the relevant period, between July 2002 and the end of 2011, include rape, extrajudicial executions, torture and the abuse of civilians. Additionally, the northern population, opposition politicians and church authorities have accused the GoU and Museveni personally of committing genocide against the Acholi people by forcefully displacing the majority of the northern population and herding them into 'protected camps' in which they lived under grievous conditions (Dolan 2009, p. 6, Finnström 2008, p. 170, Otunnu 2006, Lawino 2012).

Who can be considered responsible for this policy on the GoU side? Taking into consideration the chain of command within the Ugandan government and army, the commanders of the Fourth and Fifth Division of the UPDF that are based in the conflict region in Gulu and Pader, the Chief of the Defence Forces, as well as President Museveni himself as Commander in Chief are responsible for the alleged violations. The ICC has started investigations of the government side in the conflict, and according to statements of the OTP, these investigations are ongoing to date. The OTP has not given any specific information about these investigations, but it is probable that it has looked into the responsibility of the UPDF commanders in charge in the region as well as their superiors in Kampala. Due to the lack of any relevant information on these investigations, their effectiveness in combating impunity remains low.

For the counter-factual scenario, a number of relevant factors have to be discussed. The Ugandan amnesty only covers rebel groups and would thus not apply to the government side. Yet, there have been no domestic attempts whatsoever to investigate those in charge of the UPDF and the government policy in northern Uganda. If investigations of crimes in northern Uganda were reported in the newspaper, they related to individual rape cases or to commanders who were charged for failing to protect the camps from LRA attacks. There is no indication that there would have been genuine investigations of the higher echelons of the UPDF chain of command in the absence of ICC investigations. Since a complete absence of credible investigations is the most probable counterfactual scenario, the ICC has at least ensured that there are independent investigations of the accusations. Meanwhile, the budget for the Ugandan situation has been cut heavily by the ICC, and further progress in investigations apart from the possible arrest of the three remaining indicted LRA commanders is remote. The ICC will thus not reach a significantly better impact in the short to mid-term.

It remains to be seen if these investigations of the most responsible have had an impact on the 'culture of impunity' in the conflict area more broadly. A closer look at accountability measures for individual soldiers and officers below the command level is therefore necessary. There is some evidence that the ICC has strengthened local calls for accountability in Uganda by essentially becoming a buzzword for accountability. Several examples from interviews and newspapers illustrate this. The opposition has been explicitly calling for ICC investigations of government conduct in northern Uganda, in particular in connection with the camp policy. The East African Law Society warned the GoU of triggering ICC investigations due to the crack downs against Walk to Work protests in April 2011. A large number of interview partners agreed that the ICC had created a lot of publicity around the issue of accountability and was regularly mentioned in these discussions (e.g. Babalanda and Kyama 2011, p. 7, Expert Interview 2011i, 2011b).[41] The Juba Talks are another example of the connection between the ICC and accountability, since accountability questions received a high priority for the first time due to the ICC warrants.

Due to several factors, this has no impact on the three Rs of the rank and file of the conflict parties though. LRA fighters cannot be deterred from joining the rebellion because they are abducted. Additionally, the isolation and indoctrination of the LRA rank and file made sure that the accountability discussion did not reach them.

On the UPDF side, there are allegations against the rank and file of widespread rape and torture as well as allegations of genocide. The ICC has not issued any warrants on the government side and many even believe that the ICC has cleared the government. As shown in Section 5.2.1a, the ICC might even have undermined local calls for accountability. For example, an interview partner from a local human rights NGO stated that there was little hope of addressing the impunity of government crimes: '*The ICC has cleared the UPDF anyway, then who are you to bring a case which has already been cleared?*' (Expert Interview 2011i, p. 4). Historically, impunity for violations has been the norm in Uganda; this is also true for individual UPDF soldiers and officers. During the conflict, analysts and human rights groups said that individual UPDF soldiers were committing abuses against civilians with impunity. According to human rights organisations, the worst consequences the perpetrators had to fear was being transferred to another unit and region (AI 2008, p. 5, Expert Interview 2011e, HRW 2005b, p. 37, Weeks 2002, p. 21 and 28). To illustrate this, eighty-six soldiers were charged with serious offences against civilians between January

[41] ICC outreach staff in Kampala claimed that even school-level children are increasingly conscious about the institution and that it stands for accountability in their perception (Kamara 2011, p. 9).

1996 and April 1998, yet only two soldiers and four home guards were brought to trial later (AI 1999a, p. 71). In cases in which soldiers have been held accountable, the UPDF has been dealing with the violations internally in court martials that have been criticised for lack of transparency (Babalanda and Kyama 2011, p. 3, Expert Interview 2011e). The systematic use of court martials to hold individual UPDF members accountable began around 2004 and was partly a reaction to US pressure to improve the human rights record of the US-funded UPDF (Allen 2006, p. 74, Dolan 2009, p. 150).While the UPDF remains legally subjected to the regular courts of law in Uganda, the use of military court martials remains the norm in practice (Expert Interview 2011b, Odong 2011a). Even the accountability discussions during the Juba Talks could not change this, as no new accountability measures for UPDF soldiers were implemented (Royo 2008, p. 18, Odong 2011a). Human rights organisations and researchers have also criticised ongoing impunity for extrajudicial UPDF killings during the September 2009 Kabaka riots in Kampala (Burnett 2011, HRW 2010g), for crimes committed in cordon and search operations in Karamoja (Burnett 2011), for rapes and looting committed in CAR (Cakaj 2011, p. 10), for killings during the 2011 Walk to Work protests (HRW 2012b), and for torture and ill treatment (HURIFO 2011, Odong 2011a). Experts thus conclude that the UPDF does not feel the need to be accountable to the citizens of Uganda (Burnett 2011, Expert Interview 2011e). The latest human rights report of the US State Department goes even further by concluding that Ugandan security forces are killing and torturing civilians with near impunity (USDOS 2012).

The army, on the other hand, claims that 123 officers were executed after court martials for grave human rights violations between 1986 and 2005 and that no proven rape or murder cases went unpunished. According to the spokesperson of the UPDF, the claims that UPDF soldiers and officers committed crimes with impunity are politically motivated (Kulayigye 2011). Newspaper reports seem to confirm that at least some perpetrators were tried, as articles that mention UPDF violations usually include the information that the suspected perpetrator was arrested. Yet, the press might simply not be reporting cases that ended with impunity for the perpetrator. Weighing the high number of detailed and credible reports of violations committed by individual UPDF soldiers who were not held accountable, the evidence indicates that impunity for crimes committed by individual UPDF soldiers and officers remains a problem despite UPDF assurances and media reports to the contrary.

As mentioned in Section 5.2.1a, there is a distinct possibility of self-censorship of the media concerning UPDF violations.

To sum up, several reports of UPDF impunity in different contexts show that the calls for accountability connected to the ICC investigations have not yet led to significant changes in practice. An impact on the Resolve of the UPDF can thus not be expected.

Despite some successes in fighting impunity and promoting accountability, the practical impact of the ICC investigations remains very limited. This shows that a trickledown effect of investigations does not occur if the rank and file is isolated from the accountability measures – quite literally as in the case of the LRA, or through a parallel system of martial law as in the case of the UPDF. The case of northern Uganda shows that it is not sufficient to analyse whether an international court or tribunal is efficient in combating impunity, rather a second step is needed to assess whether the possible trickling-down effect leads to real progress on the ground.

Again the procedural decisions of the OTP and the perceptions of the investigations on the ground had an influence on the impact of the ICC investigations. The failure of the OTP to publish any information on its investigations of the government side undermined the possible effect of the ICC to address the issue of impunity for government crimes. The decision to not publish this information was probably among the most momentous procedural decisions taken during the ICC investigations in northern Uganda. This effect was reinforced by the fact that the ICC investigations were locally perceived as one-sided and as having cleared the government of any allegations. As a consequence, the ICC investigations will not affect the government's Resolve as long as they are mainly targeted at the LRA and perceived to be one-sided.

5.2.2 Reconciliation mechanisms

Root causes of the conflict like tribal tensions, north–south animosities[42] and revenge feelings[43] are still present in Uganda (Charles 2011, ICG 2012, p. 10, Latigo 2008, p. 91, OHCHR 2007, p. 28–29). This bitterness and animosity has even sometimes led to physical attacks, for example

[42] Prejudices and stereotypes towards northern Ugandans also came up during conversations with interviewees from western and southern Uganda at times.

[43] Some northern Ugandans openly demanded that Kony should be killed, being on camera in an Al-Jazeera documentary (Negara 2011).

against Kony's brothers or former LRA commanders living in northern communities (Prendergast 2007c, p. 4). There have also been newspaper reports of mob justice against suspected LRA fighters and collaborators. In one case, tensions even peaked in repeated clashes between clans. Violence between different clans erupted in Kitgum in 2002 and early December 2007 over the involvement of individual members of the different clans in LRA massacres committed in the region. There are also reports of tensions between the Acholi tribe and its neighbouring tribes within and beyond the borders of Uganda. Most neighbouring tribes see the LRA as an Acholi group and some blame the Acholi for the massacres of the rebels (Odama 2011, Rodriguez 2009, p. 111 and 216). This is, for example, illustrated by stronger demands for retributive justice among non-Acholi victims of the LRA (Williams 2007, p. 7). Acholi victims are more likely to call for restorative justice as nearly everybody has lost a relative to the abduction spree of the rebels.

Additionally, reconciliation on the individual level – between LRA returnees and the affected communities – remains a challenge. Many interviewees working with formerly abducted persons reported ongoing stigmatisation or even mistreatment of their clients (Al 2008, p. 10–15, Baines 2009, p. 166, Nono and Acan 2011). Others described serious problems that returnees face when trying to find a way back into civilian lives (Allen 2006, p. 170–171, Babalanda and Kyama 2011, ICG 2011a, p. 8, Schomerus 2010a, p. 95).[44] Especially in DRC and CAR, returnees even risk being killed by the affected communities (EurAc 2010, Lezhnev 2012, p. 8).

Finally, LRA fighters and officers are reportedly still being indoctrinated against the GoU. The LRA commanders claim, in their internal propaganda efforts, that Museveni and his Banyankole dominated regime are repressing and marginalising the northern tribes (Lancaster et al. 2011, p. 33)

The overall effect of these numerous simmering tensions is fear and distrust. The villagers in the conflict region are more distrustful and hostile towards outsiders, which creates new conflict potentials (ICG 2011a, p. 8). It is therefore clear that reconciliation efforts in Uganda and the LRAaffected areas are of a high importance, both to deal with the root causes of the LRA conflict and to solve new conflict potentials.

[44] Yet there were also positive accounts of successful re-integration efforts of former LRA fighters and progress in reconciliation between the tribes (Borzello 2007, p. 399, JPC 2011, Freda and Aceng 2011, MDRP 2008, p. 3).

a. Addressing victim needs

Revenge feelings among victims against both LRA and UPDF perpetrators of crimes could be addressed by the ICC. This would help the victims to move on and forget. Victim and perpetrator roles are very complex in the LRA conflict, mainly due to the abduction policy of the LRA. The ICC contribution to meeting the needs of victims is low, because security and livelihood needs take precedence over justice needs. Demands for justice are mainly voiced in connection with NRA and UPDF violations. Since the ICC has declined to publish any information on its investigations of UPDF violations, it has failed to meet these justice needs.

A huge majority of people living in the north of Uganda – and especially in Acholiland (98 per cent) – perceive themselves as victims of the conflict (New Vision 2011, Pham and Vinck 2010, p. 44–45). These people can be considered as the war-affected communities. Apart from the communities that have been affected in general terms, there are direct victims of the violence like orphans, widows and disabled who are in need of targeted support (Oxfam International 2007, p. 19).

On the side of the perpetrators and collaborators, the roles are equally complex. Some civilians, who notably see themselves as victims of the conflict, have become LRA collaborators in order to profit from the conflict financially or in order to protect themselves (Baines 2007, p. 95). LRA fighters who committed atrocities during the conflict were often abducted as children or adolescents, forced into the LRA, and indoctrinated by the officers and commanders.[45] For outsiders, it may be hard to understand that even the LRA fighters perceive themselves as victims and are also widely seen as victims by the war-affected communities in Acholiland (OHCHR 2007, p. ii, Wyrzykowski and Kasozi 2010, p. 24).[46] Indeed, some researchers point out that the abductees are best described as collaborators rather than victims (Allen 2006, p. 61–63, Mergelsberg 2010, p. 159–169, Wyrzykowski and Kasozi 2010, p. 21).

Research conducted with the direct victims and those affected by the LRA conflict in northern Uganda has shown that the needs of both

[45] This is even the case for some of the LRA's mid-level and top commanders. Dominic Ongwen, who faces an arrest warrant of the ICC, was himself abducted when he was ten years old (Wyrzykowski and Kasozi 2010, p. 20) and Thomas Kwoyelo, now being tried by the ICD, was abducted when he was fifteen (IRIN 2011d).

[46] Former LRA officers interviewed by the author also described themselves as victims of the conflict (Charles 2011).

groups focus on economic and livelihood issues,[47] followed by public acknowledgement of their suffering (Murithi and Ngari 2011, p. 5, Nono and Acan 2011, OHCHR and UHRC 2011, p. IX, Pham et al. 2007, p. 23).[48] Concrete compensation demands for losses endured during the conflict have been brought forward by victims (ICTJ and HRC 2005, p. 36, OHCHR 2007, p. 47, Pham et al. 2007, p. 4). The same needs have been reported for LRA returnees (Baines 2008, p. 5, WV Uganda 2011). During the conflict and immediately afterwards, the main needs of the northern population were the access to food and securing peace (ICTJ and HRC 2005, p. 4, Pham et al. 2007, p. 3).

Justice, on the other hand, was not voiced as an immediate need by the northern population in 2005 (ICTJ and HRC 2005, p. 25). If demands for justice are being voiced at all, they usually come from the direct victims of LRA or GoU abuses and not so much from the broader war-affected community (OHCHR 2007, p. 21, VRWG 2006, p. 1). According to several sources, victims of UPDF and government crimes attach particular importance to seeing their tormentors being held to account, partly because they have better chances to get compensated if a government official is to blame for the abuses. LRA perpetrators, on the other hand, are attributed less responsibility for their deeds since they are abductees (Babalanda and Kyama 2011, p. 4, Branch 2005, p. 21, Nono and Acan 2011, OHCHR 2007, p. 47). Justice needs therefore seem to play a less important role for the majority of the victims. Even interviewees working with direct victims of atrocities disagreed whether it was important for them to see the perpetrators of atrocities being held to account (Expert Interview 2011k, HURIFO 2011).

Since the ICC's primary mandate is to deliver justice, it is hard to conceive how the Court could play a meaningful role in meeting victim needs if justice is only of secondary importance to them. At the same time, the ICC is struggling to even deliver on its justice mandate as no arrests are forthcoming on the LRA side and no information on alleged GoU crimes has been made public. Consequentially, there is an increasing sense of disappointment among the victims who say that the ICC is

[47] The different economic needs of those affected by the LRA conflict are described in a UN report from Uganda (IRIN 2012a).

[48] Ninety-five per cent of northern Ugandans wanted acknowledgement of their suffering through a written historical record in 2007 (Pham et al. 2007, p. 6). See also (Otwili et al. 2011, p. 2) for other victim calls for acknowledgement.

working slowly and not delivering tangible results (Carayon 2010, p. 12, Kamara 2011, p. 7–8, Nakumbi 2011).

The ICC is therefore unable to – or has failed to – meet the primary needs of the victims and affected communities. The ICC does not have the resources to pay compensation for large parts of the affected population and it is definitely not part of the Court's mandate to further the development of northern Uganda economically. Even though the ICC Trust Fund for Victims (TFV) does fund organisations that work with victims, this support can only reach a small percentage of them. Organisations funded by the TFV are, for example, providing plastic surgery for those mutilated by the LRA. Compensation payments, one of the concrete demands of victims, could only be ordered by the ICC if one of the LRA commanders was to be found guilty. And even then, only his direct victims would profit from payments.

The ICC has also failed to deliver on the justice demands of victims of UPDF violations since it has not published any information on its government investigations. It is hard to understand why a Court that is supposed to be victim-centred would decide to not publish this information because of confidentiality.

The analysis has shown that victims of conflicts do not automatically voice justice demands. In the case of northern Uganda, development initiatives would be more helpful to address the unresolved issues of victims and waraffected communities. Since international justice does not come cheap, the dogma that victims want justice should be reviewed on a case-to-case basis. Funds might be better used to compensate victims or finance development projects.

The analysis also confirms that the impact of investigations changes over the course of the conflict. While justice needs were barely voiced at all as long as fighting was ongoing in northern Uganda, some demands were voiced in later stages. Therefore, an impact of ICC investigations in terms of meeting victim needs could only have materialised in later stages of the conflict.

b. Individualising guilt

The complex status of LRA combatants as both victims and perpetrators poses a key challenge for re-integration efforts of former fighters. Additionally, the conflict has created new animosities between the Acholi tribe and its neighbours who collectively blame the Acholi for atrocities committed. Furthermore, UPDF and government officials often accused the civilian population of collaborating with the

LRA.[49] Last but not least, members of the northern tribes most affected by the war often perceived the Museveni government as a southern aggressor trying to subjugate the north. The ICC could assist in tackling these issues by clarifying who is individually responsible for the violations committed during the conflict and countering perceptions of collective guilt. Particularly, the re-integration of former abductees is a key challenge that has to be overcome to ensure lasting peace. Interview research with returnees has shown that most of them would take up arms again to survive in a renewed conflict. Some are even having second thoughts about returning to the bush due to the difficulties they face in their re-integration efforts (Allen 2006, p. 170–171, Baines 2008, p. 4, Schomerus 2010a, p. 95). They thus potentially provide manpower (Resources) for future rebellions.

But the ICC has so far failed to clarify questions of guilt in the LRA conflict. On the government side, it has not published any information on its investigations. The question of how much responsibility should be ascribed to mid-level commanders and officers of the LRA also remains unaddressed.

In the case of the LRA, the ICC has made clear that it considers the five indicted top commanders of the LRA as those most responsible for the atrocities committed by the rebels. While the OTP has hinted that it would not prosecute mid-level commanders, the question of guilt and accountability of mid-ranking LRA commanders and officers remains open. This is illustrated by the charges the DPP brought against Thomas Kwoyelo, a mid-ranking LRA commander who was abducted as a child. Former LRA officers have also stated that they are still afraid to be charged for their role in the LRA massacres. The ICC investigations have therefore not yet helped to provide an answer to the question of how to deal with LRA perpetrators that were abducted as children.

Again local notions of justice play an important role when assessing this mechanism. The expectations of individualising guilt brought forward in the literature might not fit the specific case of northern Uganda, as traditional justice in Acholiland emphasises responsibility of the clan of a perpetrator (Hovil and Quinn 2005, p. 12, Komakech and Sheff 2009,

[49] For example, an UPDF intelligence officer was quoted in the news on 11 March 2000 saying that the LRA war might take thirty years if the Acholi '*don't change their attitude towards the UPDF*'. A similar statement suggesting Acholi collaboration with the LRA was made by a government official on 5 September 2003, and Museveni called Kony a '*symbol for northern backwardness*' on 14 March 2003 (see annex VI).

p. 12 and 16, Mapenduzi 2011). When a murder happens, the clans of the victim and the perpetrator traditionally stop all interaction until the relationship between the clans is re-established through *mato oput*. Compensation for the murder is also paid by the entire clan of the perpetrator. From a Westerner's perspective, collective guilt ascriptions are clearly at work here. The idea of individualising guilt might just not work in the northern Ugandan context. Again, the case study raises the question of whether broad claims for the effects of international trials can be made across cultural contexts as the literature tends to do. Western concepts of justice cannot just be transferred to other regions while expecting similar impacts.

5.2.3 *Deterrence and isolation*

a. Pressure and inducement

Pressure and inducement claims were regularly brought forward by interview partners in Uganda (Ajok 2011, Bigombe 2011, p. 1, Expert Interview 2011i, HURIFO 2011, JPC 2011, Kamara 2011, p. 8, Mapenduzi 2011, Rastan 2011a, UN Source 2011).[50] Most people ascribe a role to the ICC in the initiation of the Juba Talks in 2006, but a number of authors claim that the ICC investigations already compelled the LRA to negotiate with the government in 2004 (Allen and Vlassenroot 2010, p. 17, Hayner 2009, p. 17, Mwenda 2010, p. 57). The most commonly held view is that the Court increased the international attention for the LRA conflict and thus increased the pressure on both parties to negotiate. Yet, the analysis shows that the international attention on the LRA conflict increased independently of the ICC investigations. At the same time, it was the mounting military pressure on the LRA that forced it to the negotiation table, and not the ICC warrants. Nevertheless, the ICC contributed to the decision of some individual officers to desert the LRA.

It is certainly true that the LRA conflict was neglected, if not to say ignored, on the international scene until the early 2000s. An increase of international attention and increased pressure on both conflict parties to negotiate is clearly measurable by three indicators. First, there was an

[50] The idea that the ICC pressured the LRA to negotiate is even widely shared in the population. Thirty-five per cent of those who think the ICC helped to alleviate the situation in northern Uganda believed that the ICC investigations had enforced negotiations (Pham and Vinck 2010, p. 43). The diplomatic community also shared this view (HRW 2009b, p. 33, Peskin 2009a, p. 680).

increase of activities of states and international organisations aimed at addressing the LRA conflict. Second, the attention the conflict received in the media started to build up; and third, the number of statements by NGOs, international organisations and states concerning the LRA conflict multiplied.

In the early 2000s, the UN was very reluctant to take any action in northern Uganda (Rodriguez 2009, p. 187–188). Until 2001, the UN and its organisations had remained basically silent concerning the LRA conflict. The UNHCR was the first UN body to become active by condemning the LRA attacks on the civilian population on 27 April 2001. While different UN agencies, including UNOCHA, UNHCR and UNICEF started issuing statements on the LRA conflict, it took the UNSC until April 2004 to issue its first statement condemning LRA atrocities. In December 2005, Britain became the first permanent member to take an interest in the issue and started to push for a UNSC resolution on the LRA. On 27 January 2006, the Council finally passed its first resolution (1653) mentioning the LRA (Ssenyonjo 2007, p. 66).

At the same time, the major donors of the GoU also started taking interest in the conflict. The United States started pressuring Sudan to allow the UPDF to crack down on LRA bases in southern Sudan between 2000 and 2003 (Latigo 2008, p. 93). In the second half of 2005, international donors like Ireland, United Kingdom, Denmark, Sweden and the Netherlands cut their support to the GoU, demanding non-military approaches to tackle the LRA conflict (Royo 2008, p. 18). Especially the US involvement in the conflict has increased over time. President Bush personally called Presidents Salva Kiir (then southern Sudan) and Kabila (DRC) to persuade them to cooperate with the GoU in the scope of Operation Lightning Thunder (ICG 2010, p. 2). Pushed by constant civil society pressure, President Barack Obama signed into law the LRA Disarmament and Northern Uganda Recovery Act in May 2010, essentially pledging that the United States would help to end the conflict and commit itself to support the development of the LRA-affected areas in northern Uganda. A UN source confirmed that the United States was increasingly taking interest in the LRA during the course of 2011, supporting regional governments in coordinating their fight against the LRA (UN Source 2011). Additionally, both the United States and a number of individual AU Member States pressured the AU to become active in the LRA conflict in 2010 and 2011 (ICG 2011a, p. 11). These activities culminated in the October 2011 deployment of hundred

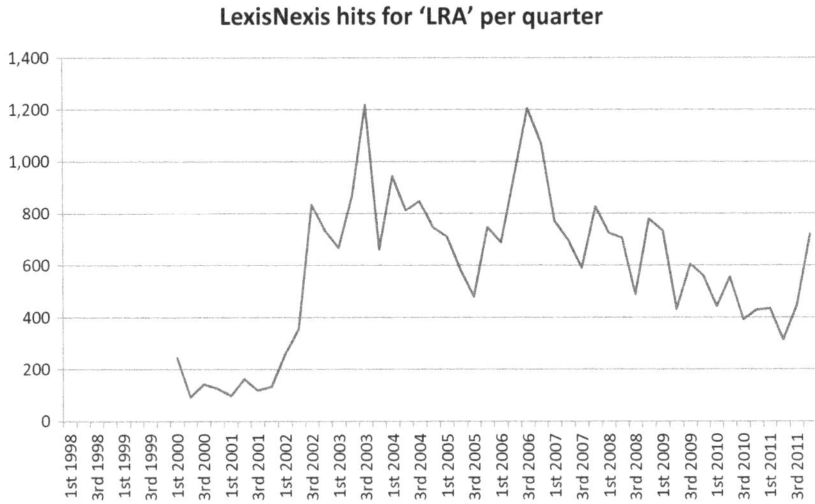

Figure 5.1: News reports on the LRA in the LexisNexis Database

combat armed US military advisors in Uganda and in LRA-affected areas in CAR. The US deployment was quickly followed by an AU decision to form a 5,000 man joint brigade of Ugandan, Congolese, Central African and South Sudanese soldiers in early 2012 to hunt down the LRA. The international attention for the conflict peaked with the release of an advocacy video by Invisible Children that went viral on the internet in March 2012.

Finally, statements by international and local NGOs calling for more attention for the LRA conflict increased steadily. Figure 5.1 shows that the activities started to increase in late 2003 and that they peaked for the first time right before and during the Juba Talks. At the same time, the number of news articles mentioning the LRA in the LexisNexis Database quadrupled from below 200 in the year 2000 to over 800 by 2002. Media attention peaked in the third quarter of 2003 and the third quarter of 2006 and remained well above the initial level for the rest of the observation period.

This increased media attention was not a direct result of the ICC activities though. Media reports peaked in the third quarter of 2003, before the case was even referred to the ICC in December 2003. Additionally, correlation tests between key ICC decisions and media reports delivered results around 0.25 without reaching significance levels in two-tailed tests. The correlation between ICC decisions and Western media statements is slightly higher with 0.28.[51] Key ICC activities had some influence on the number of NGO statements (0.42**), as well as actions and statements of international organisations (0.28*). In the case of the NGO statements, this is not surprising, since ICC decisions are often followed by supporting statements from the significant number of NGOs that are organised under the umbrella of the Coalition for the ICC. But correlation testing suggests that increased activities by states, NGOs and international organisations were rather a reaction to increased media coverage than to ICC activity. Correlation results range between 0.43** and 0.59** and are significantly higher than the correlation with key ICC decisions. Especially states and international organisations are apparently reacting to the increased media reporting, and not that much to ICC activities. In general, media reporting on the LRA conflict seldom focused on ICC activities. The only exception is the fourth quarter of 2005, when there was significant news coverage about the ICC warrants. All things taken into consideration, the figures suggest that the ICC did not have a strong influence on the increase of international attention for the LRA conflict.

But the issuing of the ICC warrants might still have prompted LRA commanders to negotiate as suggested by many interviewees and authors. An analysis of the conflict dynamics in the run-up to the negotiations sheds some light on the likely motivations of the LRA leadership to engage in the talks.

Conflict resolution theories offer a variety of alternative explanations as to why the LRA would decide to engage in talks in early 2004 and again in mid-2006. The military pressure on the LRA increased significantly in the run-up to both talks (also Prendergast 2005, p. 3). In January 2004, the LRA was driven out of the Teso Districts by the UPDF (Baines 2009, p. 173). Shortly after that, in March 2004, Operation Iron Fist II started and put the LRA under a lot of military pressure. At the same time, the EDF – a militia formerly allied with the LRA – switched sides and started to attack the LRA (ICG 2004c, p. 24). In the following months, the UPDF improved their counter-insurgency operations and finally pushed the LRA out of most Ugandan districts, containing the LRA activities to ever smaller pockets in Gulu and Pader districts. At the same time, the GoS allowed the UPDF to penetrate deeper into Southern

[51] The correlation between ICC decisions and newspaper reporting was controlled for major events in the LRA conflict that led to a lot of reporting like the Barlonyo Massacre, the Makombo Massacre, as well as the deployment of US military advisors.

Table 5.1: *Information on defections and arrests of LRA members from LexisNexis*

Quarter	Amnesty applications	Defections and arrests of LRA commanders/officers
2nd 2001	0	1
3rd 2001	0	1
2nd 2002	400 amnesty applications until April 2002	0
4th 2002	0	1
1st 2003	0	steady trickle of junior commanders (Rodriguez 2009, p. 148)
3rd 2003	0	6 officers
4th 2003	10,000 across all rebel groups until late 2003	0
1st 2004	0	Exodus of high and mid-level commanders between 2004–2006 (LRA Commander 2011)
2nd 2004	139 LRA surrender, Reception centres overwhelmed by Influx	2 officers
3rd 2004	18 Fighters, total of 400 rebels between April and August, high numbers	1 Major, 1 2nd Lieutenant, 2 Captain, 1 Lieutenant Colonel
4th 2004	0	1 Major
1st 2005	A number of 14,700 amnesty applications is reached (including other rebel groups)	1 Brigadier, 1 Commander, 1 Lieutenant, 1 Captain
2nd 2005	0	1 Lieutenant, 1 2nd Lieutenant, 4 Officers
4th 2005	0	1 Major
1st 2006	0	1 Captain, 1 Commander
4th 2007	300	4 Commanders
4th 2009	107 fighters	1 Lt. Colonel, 1 Captain

Sudanese territory to attack the LRA bases there in mid-2004. As shown in the isolation section below, Sudan had also stopped most of its support to the LRA at that point. Finally, an increasing number of LRA fighters and officers were killed or deserted.

All of these tendencies can be illustrated with numbers (Table 5.1). Vincent Otti was number 27 in the LRA hierarchy in 1993 and became number 2 in 2005. This clearly shows how many senior commanders, the LRA lost in this twelve-year period (HRW 2005b, p. 10). At the same time, the LexisNexis analysis and other sources show that the number of rebels accepting amnesty went up by nearly 50 per cent during 2004 (from 10,000 to 14,700), and an increasing number of mid-level commanders and officers deserted between 2004 and the beginning of the Juba Talks (ICG 2005e, p. 2, LRA Commander 2011, UN OCHA 2005, p. 5).

The military pressure, the drain of manpower caused by the amnesty, as well as the reduced GoS support clearly reduced the Resolve and the Resources of the LRA to fight, thus making them much more likely to negotiate. When the Juba Talks were initiated, the emergence of the GoSS as a credible mediator was an additional factor triggering the talks. Indeed, some analysts and interview partners concluded that the GoSS' role in initiating the Juba Talks was the most important factor that led to the negotiations (Atkinson 2010, p. 211–212, Oulanyah 2011).

As pointed out above, there were several factors that pushed the LRA towards initiating peace negotiations both in 2004 and 2006. Applying the three R model, the LRA's loss of key sponsors, the drain in troop numbers and officers, as well as the heavy military pressure they were facing were factors that would have prompted the LRA to negotiate even in the absence of ICC warrants. It cannot be excluded that the existence of the warrants played a role in the decision of individual commanders to negotiate, but from a perspective of conflict resolution theory, it was hardly the main reason (also Expert Interview 2011a). Another detail that speaks against an ICC influence during the 2004 talks is that the Court did not play a role in the negotiations. The LRA would have brought up the ICC on the agenda of the 2004 talks if the Court's investigations had been a key reason for engaging in talks.

Nevertheless, the ICC had an impact on the decision of individual commanders to desert the LRA. The commanders had the choice between accepting the GoU amnesty now or risking that a future ICC warrant could permanently bar the possibility to receive amnesty. Indeed, at least in one case, the motivation to dodge an ICC warrant has been confirmed as the reason for the defection of an LRA commander (Mullins and Rothe 2010, p. 785). Former LRA officers confirmed that the issuing of the ICC warrants were known within the LRA, and the officers interviewed were clearly still worried about being indicted by the ICC today, even after defecting (e.g. Charles 2011, Okello 2011). This confirms that the ICC did play a role in individual calculations.

Summing up the findings of this section, the claim that the LRA was forced to negotiate by the issuing of the ICC warrants cannot stand against closer scrutiny. The analysis has shown that there were many factors that decisively reduced the three Rs of the LRA, while a direct connection between the ICC warrant and a reduction of the LRA's Resolve cannot be proven. The less extensive claim that single LRA commanders and officers reacted to ICC pressure, on the other hand, is plausible.

Statistical correlations show that it was a mere coincidence that the warrants against the LRA were issued at a time at which the conflict was gaining attention in the media and the LRA was starting to face increased military pressure. Again, context is an important factor in determining whether causal mechanisms can be traced in a conflict.

b. Marginalisation of spoilers

In the context of the LRA conflict, marginalisation claims refer to the situation of the ICC indicted top commanders of the LRA. If marginalisation worked, one would expect them to lose support of the rank and file. This has been claimed by some authors (Akhavan 2005, p. 419, HRW 2009b, p. 31, ICG 2006c, p. 12). Other mid-level commanders would reconsider their situation after hearing about Kony's indictment. They might consider challenging Kony for fear of being stuck with a wanted man. They would try to organise an internal coup in order to negotiate a beneficial settlement for themselves. But the ICC warrants have targeted the whole inner circle of the LRA. Ongwen and Odhiambo, the other LRA commanders who are targeted by the ICC, are popular among the rank and file. Vincent Otti, the only commander willing and able to challenge Kony, was killed during the Juba Talks. As a result, the ICC has not contributed to the marginalisation of Kony.

There was indeed some potential for a palace coup within the LRA during the Juba Talks. The fact that Joseph Kony killed his second in command Vincent Otti is a clear indicator of disagreements within the LRA leadership. The execution led to defections of several commanders and officers close to Otti. According to newspaper reports, more than 300 rebels and four commanders defected in the aftermath of the execution. LRA experts have also reported that Dominic Ongwen, one of the LRA indictees, has been operating independently since Otti's death, and is currently refusing to take direct orders from Kony (Lancaster et al. 2011, p. 24).

Despite this obvious splintering of the LRA, all groups that remain in the jungle today are likely to keep on fighting since both Ongwen and

Kony have been indicted by the Court. Kony's current second in command, Odhiambo, has also been indicted. Since the whole inner circle has been indicted, there is not a lot of room for a palace coup (also Charles 2011). A former LRA officer emphasised that Ongwen and Odhiambo are very popular with their fighters. Since both of them face the ICC warrants alongside Kony, a rift between the rank and file and the leadership is unlikely (Charles 2011).

Additionally, most LRA fighters were abducted at a young age and have been indoctrinated for a long time, making the emergence of a rift between the leadership and the officers and fighters less likely (Branch 2007a, p. 486, 2007b, p. 183). Finally, Kony's central role in the LRA can hardly be overestimated (Lancaster et al. 2011, p. 22). It is very hard to isolate the leader of a conflict party with such absolute power and influence over his followers. Kony's inner circle consists of commanders that have been abducted and who have fought alongside him since childhood. LRA fighters and officers still fear him for his spiritual powers. After visiting Kony's camp in the Garamba National Park, the ICG concluded that the pressure on the rank and file to defect is low. The analysts reported that morale in the camp was high and that the fighters saw little prospects of returning to northern Uganda (ICG 2007c, p. 8). Additionally, the LRA has moved into areas far away from Uganda, where they are surrounded by tribes that are deeply hostile to the Acholi LRA fighters. Accordingly, defection has become considerably more difficult.

Again, procedural decisions taken at the OTP played a role in the context of this causal mechanism. According to authors, the ICC consciously tried to drive a wedge between the LRA rank and file and the high command to promote an internal split within the LRA (Allen and Vlassenroot 2010, p. 18, Schomerus 2007, p. 38). The ICC has also publicly indicated that there are no remaining sealed warrants in order to encourage the defection of non-indicted LRA commanders (ICG 2006c, p. 8). Yet, the indictment of Kony's entire inner circle proved to be a mistake if the ICC was indeed hoping to encourage a split within the rebel group. Especially Odhiambo and Ongwen are apparently popular with the fighters, so their indictment led to more cohesion within the LRA.[52] If the ICC takes strategic decisions to indict a certain number of people in order to encourage rifts and defections within a rebel group, it

[52] There would have been valid arguments against indicting Ongwen since he had himself been abducted as a child before climbing the ranks of the LRA. The OTP could have

has to make sure to collect the necessary information who to indict in order to achieve this result. Since the ICC does not have the capacity to analyse a conflict situation in-depth, it should probably refrain from taking procedural decisions based on objectives like marginalising rebel leaders. The findings in Section 5.2.5c suggest that Kony has been able to use the ICC indictments as an additional tool to control his followers and scare them into staying with the LRA.

c. International isolation

The international isolation claim is another of the most repeated claims for ICC investigations in the LRA conflict (e.g. Babalanda and Kyama 2011, p. 11, Mapenduzi 2011, Okumu 2011).[53] These claims focus on the connection between the GoS and the LRA since 1994. The GoS supplied the LRA with significant amounts of cash, uniforms, arms, training and most importantly provided a safe haven for the LRA in southern Sudan. The analysis shows that the international pressure described above was the main reason the GoS stopped its support for the LRA. The ICC did not trigger this pressure on the GoS but at most played a role by galvanising the already existing pressure. The fact that there are increased indicators of renewed GoS support to the LRA after 2006 confirms that the ICC was not the main reason for the GoS to cut LRA support.

It is hard to overestimate the amount of Resources that the LRA drew from GoS support. Analysts and authors agree that Sudanese support was vital for the LRA (ICG 2004c, p. 24, Lomo and Hovil 2004, p. 18). Many authors claim that the ICC warrants forced the GoS to reconsider this support and to ultimately scale it down considerably. As described in Section 5.2.3a, the loss of the Sudanese support and safe haven played a key role in the LRA's decision to negotiate. In order to ascertain whether there was an ICC influence in stopping the GoS support to the LRA, it is necessary to trace this support over the course of the conflict.[54]

Large-scale support for the LRA started after the 1994 talks between the GoU and the LRA failed. Museveni issued an ultimatum to the LRA, claiming that the group was trying to acquire support from the GoS.

decided to argue that somebody abducted as a child and forced to fight cannot be considered to be among those 'most responsible'.

[53] Again, the diplomatic community shares the claims that the ICC investigations led to the halt of GoS support to the LRA (Peskin 2009a, p. 680).

[54] All the information used for tracing the GoS support of the LRA is taken from the LexisNexis newspaper analysis if not otherwise indicated by citations.

The main conduit for GoS support to the LRA in this early phase was the SPLA-Nasir faction of William Nyuon that was allied with the Khartoum Government. Analysts agree that the support provided by the GoS turned the LRA into a very capable force, supplied with better uniforms than the NRA and equipped with several guns per fighter (Branch 2005, p. 18, Cakaj 2011, p. 3). Around the same time, in February 1994, the LRA set up its first bases in southern Sudan (O'Kadameri 2002, p. 41). The apex of GoS support was reportedly reached in 1996, when the GoS brought several carloads of food to the LRA headquarters in 3–4 months intervals and regularly airdropped ammunition (Schomerus 2007, p. 25).

In the first years, there was practically no international attention for this GoS support, and no pressure to stop it. The GoS support drew some international attention through the kidnapping of the Aboke girls by the LRA in October 1996 (Allen and Vlassenroot 2010, p. 13–15).[55] The first public condemnation of GoS support in the newspaper database was identified in 1997 (AI 1997).

Many sources claim that the official support from the GoS already stopped in the late 1990s when the GoS and the GoU signed the Nairobi Agreement brokered by the US Carter Center, in which they agreed to stop the support of each other's rebel groups (Neu 2002, Otto 2002, p. 56). Carter Center staff claims that Sudan decided to stop LRA support in order to gain a better international standing. LRA deserters returning around that time confirmed that most of the GoS support stopped after the agreement (Bevan 2006, p. 275, LRA Commander 2011, Nyeko and Lucima 2002, p. 18–19).

A number of authors confirm that the relationship between the GoS and the LRA worsened after the Nairobi Agreement had been signed (Dolan 2009, p. 285, Nyeko and Lucima 2002, p. 23, Schomerus 2007, p. 26). Roughly at the same time, AI also reported increasing pressure on Sudan to stop the support for the rebels (AI 1999a, p. 100). It is plausible that the GoS was ready to act on that pressure since it wanted to improve its image abroad to find buyers for its recently discovered oil resources (see Bradbury 1999, p. 4). According to the LRA commander in charge of the GoS–LRA relations, official support by Sudan stopped after the Nairiobi Agreement and the LRA received a farewell package of 20,000 guns and millions in cash. After the farewell package was delivered,

[55] The LRA kidnapped 139 female secondary school students from a boarding school in Aboke, which provoked significant international news coverage on the LRA and the GoS support of the group (e.g. Knox 2000).

reduced support was provided by rogue elements within the Sudanese army and security apparatus (LRA Commander 2011). The GoS officially distanced itself from the LRA in April 2000. In September 2000, the GoU and the GoS re-negotiated parts of the Nairobi Agreement and Sudan renewed its commitment to stop the LRA support. In August 2001, Sudanese President al-Bashir stressed that the GoS had stopped LRA support as agreed and called on the GoU to also stop supporting the SPLA. At the same time, the Sudanese Armed Forces (SAF) lost soldiers to LRA attacks in Southern Sudan and declared that they would step up military efforts against the LRA.[56] An SAF offensive against the LRA in reaction to the attacks was reported in news sources in March 2002. According to newspaper reports, another LRA deserter confirmed in early 2001 that Sudanese support to the group had stopped. The GoU and the GoS re-established diplomatic relations in April 2002.

After the terrorist attacks on the World Trade Center in New York in September 2001, the LRA was put on the international terrorist list of the US Government. The US War on Terror and the Bush doctrine[57] significantly increased the pressure on the GoS to stop any remaining support to the LRA (also HRW 2009b, p. 32, Prendergast 2007a, p. 8). In January 2002, the United Kingdom, Sudan and Uganda agreed on an UPDF incursion into Sudan in the scope of an anti-terror crack down (Dolan 2009, p. 53). In September 2002, the GoS accused the LRA of binding the Equatoria Defence Forces (EDF) – a militia that was allied with the GoS – in skirmishes, thereby facilitating an SPLA offensive that led to the fall of the strategically important town of Torit. According to a number of concurrent reports, GoS support for the LRA was briefly revived in October 2002, when the LRA helped to re-take Torit (Borzello 2007, p. 391, HRW 2003, p. 4, ICG 2004c, p. 7). But already in January 2003, the GoS returned to its approach of fighting the LRA, agreeing with the government of Uganda to jointly '*finish off*' the LRA.

The GoS was still regularly accused of supporting the LRA by the Ugandan Government (November 2002, June 2003) and the Catholic Church (June 2003). A number of analysts also claim ongoing LRA support by Sudan after 9/11 (Atkinson 2010, p. 206–207, HRW 2003, p. 14, Lomo and Hovil 2004, p. 18–19). Against the background of the newspaper analysis and the interview findings, it is possible that single elements within the security apparatus of Sudan upheld contacts with the

[56] LRA attacks on SAF convoys were reported in June 2001 and March 2002.

[57] '*Either you are with us or you are with the terrorists*' (Bush 2001).

LRA, and managed to provide some limited support to the rebels. All the facts, however, speak against large-scale, official support. GoU accusations of LRA support are in fact also levelled at '*some members of the Sudan Peoples' Armed Forces*' rather than the GoS as such (New Vision 2003a). The GoS confirmed in a statement on 31 July 2003 that single SAF elements supported the LRA without government authorisation (New Vision 2003b). ICG also reported at different points that individual military intelligence and SAF elements were supporting the LRA even until 2005 and 2006 (ICG 2005e, p. 5, 2006c, p. 1). Sudan promised to crack down on these officers and withdrew some of them from Southern Sudan in October 2003. The ICC, on the other hand, only got involved in the LRA conflict in December 2003. An immediate impact of the ICC investigations on GoS support to the LRA is improbable considering the timing, especially since it was not even clear in the initial stages of the investigations whether the Court would conduct a full investigation of the situation, let alone who would be charged.

The relations between the GoS and the LRA seemed to worsen further in the following years. In February 2004, the Sudanese ambassador in Kampala said that the GoS would eradicate the LRA in retaliation for attacks on villages in Southern Sudan. President al-Bashir declared the LRA a terrorist group during a meeting with the GoU on 3 March 2004 and soon afterwards allowed Uganda to use warplanes in Southern Sudan. Even the Ugandan Foreign Minister said in April 2004 that the LRA was now '*a common enemy*' of the GoS and Uganda. Considering the deep mistrust between these two governments, this declaration by the Ugandan Foreign Minister was a strong sign that Sudanese efforts to stop LRA support were perceived as genuine by the GoU. After the GoU brought forward allegations that the LRA was camping close to an SAF base behind the red line in Southern Sudan beyond which the UPDF was not allowed to operate, Sudan allowed the Ugandan army to advance beyond that line on 29 July 2004 (Brubacher 2010, p. 270).

Only one day before, on 28 July 2004, the ICC had authorised full investigations in the Uganda situation. Only after this point would it be realistic to assume that the ICC investigations could create some pressure on the GoS to stop supporting the LRA. Yet, assuming a direct connection between the start of the ICC investigations and the Sudanese authorisation to the UPDF to pass the red line one day later would be rushed. This is illustrated by the findings of the Darfur case study. Massive ongoing pressure on the GoS was needed to persuade it to even budge slightly in Darfur. It is simply not believable that a government that withstood the pressure of the international community over its Darfur counter-insurgency strategy for months would halt its support of a proxy group from one day to the next just because a recently established international court started investigations in Uganda.

As shown above, the pressure on the GoS to stop LRA support was already very high before the ICC started investigations, particularly due to the US War on Terror. According to credible sources, full official support of the LRA had already stopped in 1999. The increased pressure after 9/11 forced the GoS to further crack down on rogue elements that were still supporting the LRA. Cooperation between the governments of Sudan and Uganda was already solid when the ICC investigations started. Additionally, the 29 July 2004 decision to extend the red line for UPDF operations in Southern Sudan was not the first of its kind. Analysts and Ugandan officials (including the Ugandan president) agree that there was an almost complete cessation of support by the early to mid-2000s (Hovil and Moorehead 2002, p. 6, IRIN 2005c, Kulayigye 2011).[58] Any ICC impact beyond this point would only reinforce the isolation gains already made since 1999. The ICC did therefore not play a decisive role in isolating the LRA. Yet, one could argue that the ICC at least had an impact in increasing and upholding the pressure on the GoS to not start supplying the LRA again at a later point.

In January 2005, the reasons for the GoS and its rogue elements to support the LRA diminished as the CPA between the government and the SPLM was signed, ending decades of civil war in Sudan (Mwenda 2010, p. 57, Otim and Wierda 2008, p. 22). On 31 March 2005, the UN Security Council adopted resolution 1594, referring the crimes allegedly committed in the scope of the Darfur conflict to the ICC. The enormous international pressure on the GoS in connection to the Darfur conflict was now directly linked to the ICC. As shown in Chapter 4, the GoS initially tried to cooperate with the ICC to avoid full-scale investigations of its officials for crimes committed in Darfur. The international pressure and the threat of ICC investigations in Darfur made it even more important for Sudan not to be perceived as an international pariah and to uphold the efforts to crack down on the LRA (see Allen 2006, p. 192, O'Brien 2007). On 15 April 2005, the OTP and a delegation from the

[58] Confirming these analyses, Father Carlos Rodriguez, based in the war-affected areas in northern Uganda, reported in 2004 that the GoS was not supporting the LRA anymore (Allen 2005, p. 58).

LRA-affected areas in northern Uganda called on Sudan to continue cooperating with the GoU against the LRA (OTP 2005).

In May 2005, al-Bashir promised to boost his cooperation with the GoU to stop the LRA after renewed attacks in Southern Sudan. This led to the signing of a bilateral cooperation protocol between Uganda and Sudan (ICG 2005b, p. 7). In June 2005, Moreno Ocampo declared in a newspaper interview that the GoS support of the LRA could fall within the jurisdiction of the Court (IRIN 2005b). In September 2005, al-Bashir proposed a meeting of defence ministers over the LRA threat, which led to joint UPDF/SAF operations against the LRA in November 2005 and to an authorisation for the UPDF to cross the red line and go even deeper into southern Sudanese territory (ICG 2006c, p. 5, Royo 2008, p. 15). In October 2005, Sudan signed a cooperation agreement with the ICC in which it assured the Court of cooperation in arresting the LRA leadership (OTP 2006, p. 17). Even though the Sudanese cooperation had already reached high levels before the ICC entered the scene, the ICC investigations in Darfur as well as statements made by the OTP galvanised GoS cooperation against the LRA and even led to further concrete steps like the signing of bilateral protocols and the planning of joint operations with Uganda. President Museveni personally stated that he believed that the ICC helped to pressure Sudan into cooperating with Uganda in hunting the LRA (IRIN 2005c). On 8 January 2006, President al-Bashir threatened to eliminate the LRA in Sudan if they would not agree to negotiate with the GoU.

Yet, the GoS support in fighting the LRA slowly began to unravel during 2006. According to newspaper reports and accounts by people involved in the negotiations, participants at the Juba Talks sighted new weaponry at LRA assembly points in September 2006 and at later points during the talks (Borzello 2007, p. 396, Pham et al. 2007, p. 17, Rodriguez 2009, p. 134).[59] In October 2006, Sudan rejected to prolong the authorisation of UPDF operations in Southern Sudan, even though UPDF troops stayed, based on a '*gentleman's agreement*'. In November 2006, the relations between the governments of Sudan and Uganda deteriorated again amongst reports that the UPDF was providing training to Darfur rebels, which led to the demand of the Sudanese Parliament that the UPDF should retreat from Southern Sudan on 24 November 2006. After the OTP applied for the first ICC arrest warrants in its Darfur case

[59] Allegedly, the weapons bore Arabic markings, which hint at a Sudanese origin (see Gordon et al. 2007, p. 21).

on 27 February 2007, the GoS cancelled its cooperation agreement with the ICC to help arrest the LRA on 20 March 2007.

From now on, reports of renewed LRA attempts to re-kindle contacts with the GoS started to multiply. Failed LRA attempts to re-establish GoS support were reported in March 2006 (Schomerus 2007, p. 25). Then, during the first quarter of 2007, LRA Commander Odhiambo undertook several failed attempts to contact the SAF in south Darfur (Cakaj 2010a, p. 21). A former member of the LRA delegation believes that some members of his delegation were sent to re-establish contact with the GoS in the later stages of the Juba Talks under Kony's instructions (Odong 2011b). Further attempts were undertaken in 2009 (Lancaster et al. 2011, p. 25) and 2010 (Cakaj 2010b, p. 13, Charles 2011, Okello 2011). The ICG and the Enough Project claim that the LRA received small amounts of GoS supplies via CAR in May 2007 (ICG 2007b, p. 6, Prendergast 2007a, p. 2). There are thus many signs that the GoS might have resumed its support of the LRA during 2006.

There are three reasons for the unravelling of the Sudanese commitment to isolate the LRA. First, the GoS did not gain international legitimacy by accepting the CPA with the SPLM as it had hoped. Due to the Darfur situation, Sudan remained an international pariah and felt betrayed by the United States and other Western powers who had promised to mend their relations with Sudan if the CPA was implemented. Second, the ICC investigations were ongoing and could not be dissuaded through limited cooperation. The Chief Prosecutor had even started to openly criticise the GoS for lack of cooperation, which meant that the Sudanese strategy of limited cooperation with the Court had failed. Finally, a crisis in the unity government of the NCP and the SPLM emerged in 2007, which made the LRA more useful as a proxy again (Lanz 2008b, p. 63). Fears of renewed GoS support were especially high in the run-up to the 2011 independence referendum of South Sudan and the date for the final independence in July 2011 (UN Source 2011).[60]

There has so far not been a smoking gun proving renewed GoS support to the LRA, but the reports are multiplying and everybody familiar with the situation – from UN sources to former LRA commanders and UPDF officials – agrees that renewed support is a distinct possibility (e.g. Kulayigye 2011, LRA Commander 2011). Former LRA

[60] According to the assessment of a UN source, the fact that the situation during the referendum and the independence of South Sudan remained calm suggests that the LRA was not able to obtain GoS support (UN Source 2011).

officers as well as some analysts even claimed that official GoS support has resumed again (Charles 2011, New Vision 2010, Okello 2011, The Indian Ocean Newsletter 2006). Renewed support is even more plausible in the light of the recent tensions between Khartoum and the newly independent South Sudan. Uganda has already declared that it would intervene in a war between the two Sudans to support South Sudan, which makes the LRA an interesting ally for Khartoum. There has been a lot of speculation about how the GoS might now be supporting the LRA. Some analysts have pointed out LRA connections to the CAR rebel group Union des Forces Démocratiques pour le Rassemblement which is supported by the GoS and may serve as a new conduit for GoS support to the LRA (ICG 2007c, p. 8, Royo 2008, p. 16). Another report has named Chadian rebels supported by Khartoum as a possible conduit (ICG 2008, p. 14). Other possibilities that are discussed are GoS airdrops to the LRA base in Garamba during the Juba Talks (Allen and Vlassenroot 2010, p. 2, Borzello 2007, p. 396, The Indian Ocean Newsletter 2006), or the use of Mbororo nomads living in the area as a GoS conduit to supply the LRA (Charles 2011).

The United States is one of the few countries that have kept up visible pressure on the GoS not to support the LRA, even though this pressure originates at the Congress rather than the US Government. On 3 March 2011, US lawmakers passed an Act that required the US government to prove that the GoS had stopped any LRA support before US sanctions against Sudan could be lifted.

To sum up the findings: there was an on and off support by the GoS to the LRA over the years (also Charles 2011). The support was reduced due to international pressure before the ICC was even established and by all accounts was much reduced by the late 1990s. In the first half of the 2000s, this support was reduced to a trickle from some rogue elements within Sudan's military and security services. The increased pressure through simultaneous ICC investigations in Darfur and Uganda helped to guarantee the isolation of the LRA for some time, especially between June 2004 and late 2006. Yet, the ICC did not play a significant role in putting a stop to the support from the GoS in the first place. This is confirmed by recent reports that the GoS support for the LRA may have been re-activated despite the ICC warrants remaining in place because international pressure on the GoS started to falter when the CPM negotiations and implementation distracted the international community. When Sudan was not able to stave off ICC investigations in Darfur, the commitment of Sudan to crack down on the LRA wavered.

The analysis shows that some claims of ICC supporters concerning the isolation effects in Uganda are oversimplified and too strong by suggesting that the ICC had an independent effect on isolating the LRA. As shown, it is difficult to argue that the ICC achieved anything beyond galvanising the already existing pressure. Nevertheless, ICC Chief Prosecutor Moreno Ocampo claimed that pushing the LRA out of its safe haven in southern Sudan was a success attributable to the ICC (Moreno Ocampo 2010b).

Again, the procedural decisions of the ICC taken in this context and the local perception of the investigations had an interesting influence on how the causal mechanism developed. The OTP consciously decided to pressure the GoS to stop its support of the LRA (OTP 2006, p. 17). This might explain why the ICC decided to obtain government cooperation in Uganda and to only prosecute the graver LRA crimes in the first phase of investigations. The ICC's focus on the LRA helped to galvanise international pressure, which was one factor leading the Sudanese government to increase their efforts to crack down on the LRA. This shows that the prosecution can influence the impact of its investigations through procedural choices. If the OTP is interested to be perceived as a balanced institution on the ground, it will investigate both sides simultaneously, as happened in Kenya. If the focus is more on isolating one conflict party, focused investigations of this conflict party are a suitable choice. Discussing this leeway in OTP decision making has long been a taboo because international prosecutors have so far decided to deny that any other considerations but ensuring accountability play a role in their decision making.

As the investigations proceeded, the ICC was confronted with civil society criticism for allegedly blocking peace efforts. In reaction, ICC Chief Prosecutor Luis Moreno Ocampo invited delegations from northern civil society organisations to The Hague in order to discuss the investigations with them. Additionally, the Court ramped up its outreach activities in Uganda (Allen 2006, p. 178–179). The civil society organisations and the Prosecution even published a joint statement to the GoS, asking it to cooperate further with the ICC and not to support the LRA (OTP 2006, p. 17).

As a result of this outreach strategy, the general approval of the ICC's work in Uganda started to increase, leading to less perceptions of biased investigations and thus more pressure on Sudan as the warrants gained legitimacy (see Marion and Paschyn 2010, Pham et al. 2007, Rupiny 2010). The improved outreach activity thus arguably helped to ensure that the ICC played a role in keeping the LRA isolated, at least until late 2006. Even formerly staunch local critics like Father Carlos Rodriguez started acknowledging the positive ICC impact (Allen 2005, p. 58). The success of the ICC's outreach efforts is mirrored by the fact that many stakeholders in northern Uganda actually believe the Court's claims that it stopped GoS support to the LRA.

d. Prevention through special deterrence

The local population and some interviewees in northern Uganda believe that the ICC investigations deterred the LRA from escalating the conflict and committing more atrocities (e.g. Expert Interview 2011f, p. 6, HURINET et al. 2010, p. 8). As pointed out in the cross-case section, deterrence is likely to develop its full effect after other people have been tried by the investigating court for similar offences. In the case of the ICC, so far only one person has been convicted for recruiting child soldiers and sentenced to fourteen years in jail. Full scale deterrence can thus not be expected in the case of the LRA, even though the recruitment of child soldiers is among the charges brought against the LRA leadership. The analysis shows that the ICC has failed to deter the LRA from committing further atrocities. After the failure of the Juba Talks, the LRA went on an abduction and killing spree in the region. Nevertheless, the ICC achieved partial deterrence of LRA crimes during the Juba Talks because the LRA leadership overestimated the ICC's possibilities to arrest them and hoped to negotiate away the warrants.

Both Juan Méndez, the Special Advisor to the Chief Prosecutor of the ICC on the Prevention of Crimes, and the Chief Prosecutor himself have gone pretty far in claiming a deterrence effect of the ICC investigations on the LRA (Mendez 2010b, OTP 2006, p. 17). The ICC Outreach coordinator in Kampala also claimed a deterrence effect of the investigations (Kamara 2011, p. 8). Méndez introduced a number of graphs during the Rome Statute Review Conference in Kampala in May 2010 to show how the ICC had deterred crimes in various situation countries (Mendez 2010b). In the case of Uganda, the graph shows how the number of reported killings drops sharply by the end of 2004 to reach zero by mid-2005. The mid-2005 period corresponds with the time at which the ICC started full investigations of the LRA and prepared the issuing of arrest warrants against its commanders. Newspaper reports of LRA attacks as well as the figures of battle-related deaths collected in the UCPD armed conflicts database confirm this trend, as can be seen in Figure 5.2.

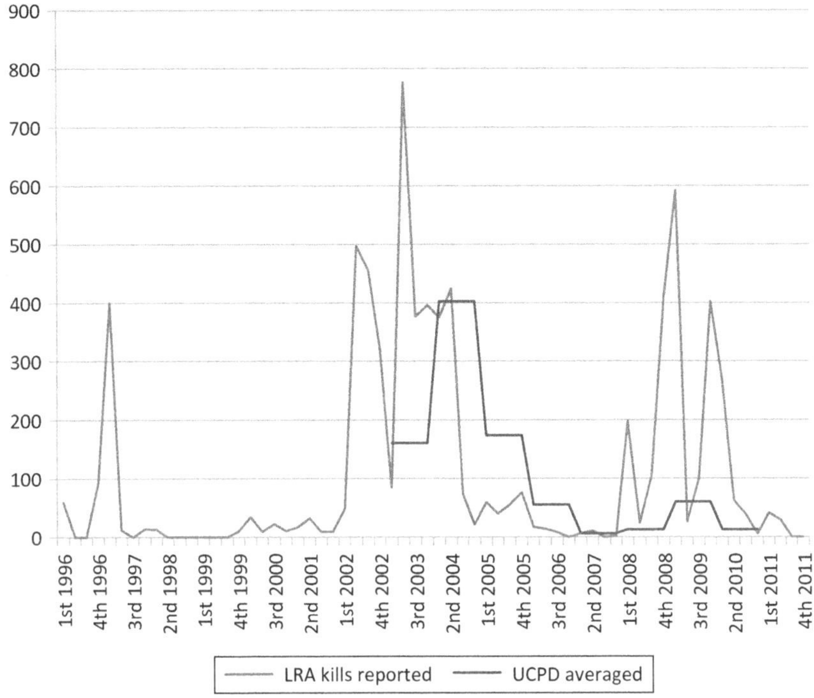

Figure 5.2: Number of LRA victims per quarter according to the UCPD and LexisNexis reports

The number of LRA killings dropped by the end of 2004 and remained low while the Juba Talks were ongoing. There have always been lulls in the LRA conflict when the rebels were intent to dodge the Ugandan army and rebuild their reserves. To a certain degree, the drops in LRA killings can be connected to these strategic decisions of the LRA leadership to lay low and dodge their enemies when under heavy military pressure. As shown above, the LRA faced significant military pressure during the years 2004 and 2005. Additionally, the LRA had been pushed out of northern Uganda in the course of these years. This also had an impact on the number of *reported* LRA killings. Press coverage of LRA attacks was a lot poorer in southern Sudan where there was no strong local media that would report the attacks. Uganda on the contrary has two strong and relatively independent newspapers (New Vision, Daily Monitor) that covered the conflict extensively. Against this background, it would be unrealistic to attribute the sharp drop in LRA killings to the work of the ICC.

Yet, despite these two caveats, there are convincing arguments for a partial ICC deterrence between late 2004 and late 2008 from the perspective of deterrence theories. The LRA was initially not well informed about how the ICC exactly worked. There have been reports that the LRA leadership expected international forces to come in and arrest them if the ICC issued warrants.[61] At the same time, the LRA was pretty well informed about the ICC referral of the Ugandan government and the later investigations of LRA crimes since they had regular access to radios and the ICC's activities were covered extensively in the local press. The LRA leadership therefore met two of the key theoretical pre-conditions for deterrence since they (1) knew that they were being investigated by the ICC, (2) they at least initially believed the ICC would arrest them with international special forces. The reduced number of attacks, the sequence of events and the theoretical assumptions thus all meet and make an initial deterrence effect of the ICC very plausible. Initially, the LRA refrained from large-scale massacres in the hope of not being indicted by the ICC. Fear of being prosecuted reduced the Resolve of the LRA to maintain its modus operandi of attacking innocent civilians. During the Juba Talks, after it had become clear that the LRA leadership was indicted despite efforts to lay low, the LRA tried to negotiate a way out of the bush without being arrested by the ICC. When this finally failed in December 2008, the LRA no longer had any motivation to hold back. This explains why large-scale massacres suddenly resumed.

The explanation of a partial deterrence, however, through the ICC investigations is supported by the fact that the LRA committed two of its largest massacres right at the beginning of the deterrence period (the February 2004 Barlonyo Massacre) and right at its end (the 2008 Christmas Killings in the DRC). Additionally, UN OCHA reported that the situation was deteriorating immediately before the ICC referral and gave a negative outlook for 2004 (Akhavan 2009, p. 643). The improvement was thus unexpected, making an ICC impact more plausible.

The confirmation of partial deterrence, however, does not mean that deterrence of LRA crimes was overall successful. Civilian deaths increased rapidly after December 2008 as Figure 5.2 shows. After the failure of the Juba Talks, the LRA continued killing, abducting and maiming civilians in CAR, DRC and southern Sudan. In fact, the LRA

61 This was confirmed in interviews with local civil society organisations which reported that the LRA initially went into hiding after the ICC became fully active in Uganda (JPC 2011).

committed some of its worst massacres after being driven out of northern Uganda into the DRC. Between Christmas 2008 and 17 January 2009, the LRA killed 865 people in Doruma, Faraje and other villages of Haut Uele District in DRC (HRW 2010a). Close to Christmas 2009, the LRA again moved out to kill at least 321 and abduct 250 in the Makombo Area of Haut Uele District, DRC (HRW 2010f). According to HRW, the LRA commanders who committed the Makombo Massacre in December 2009 reported to Dominic Ongwen, an LRA commander who had already been targeted by the ICC (HRW 2010f, p. 4).

The LexisNexis analysis also revealed that the attack patterns of the LRA after the failure of the Juba Talks have hardly changed in comparison to the attack patterns at the height of the conflict in northern Uganda. Only the frequency of the attacks has declined, presumably due to the military pressure on the LRA.[62] This is in line with the theoretical assumptions that deterrence does only work for commanders who have not yet been targeted with warrants (see Rodman 2008, p. 535). Deterrence worked as long as the LRA high command did not know for sure that warrants would be issued or as long as they perceived a chance to dodge the ICC warrants. After this was no longer the case, the rational calculus of the LRA leadership changed and the Resolve to fight became even higher than it had been before the ICC warrants were issued. This is the case because the leadership concluded that there was no way of circumnavigating the warrants, which meant that they would face a trial if they decided to surrender. Since this was inacceptable, they apparently decided to fight to the end.

If deterrence had developed a more general effect on the LRA, one would have at least expected other LRA commanders to not commit massacres in order to avoid being targeted by the ICC. Yet, LRA commanders, officers and fighters not yet targeted by the ICC participated in the Congo massacres (see HRW 2010f, p. 4).

The analysis of deterrence claims in the LRA conflict illustrates how claims of causal effects brought forward by Court officials tend to be too confident. Facing the facts, it is difficult to claim a full deterrent effect of

[62] The process tracing with LexisNexis possibly even underestimates the frequency of LRA attacks in DRC because attacks in northern Uganda were well covered by the New Vision and Daily Monitor newspapers while the areas currently affected by the LRA lack similar press coverage. On the other hand, UN sources have suggested during interviews that some attacks attributed to the LRA might have actually been carried out by local militias trying to cover up their banditry as LRA attacks (UN Source 2011).

the ICC investigations in Uganda, especially since the same crimes for which the ICC started to investigate are still being committed. At a closer look, the ICC investigations have led to a partial deterrence for a limited period of time. The literature tends to focus on the short period after the ICC started investigating and during which the LRA atrocities diminished significantly. But at the same time the literature overlooks that the spree of LRA massacres continued after the failure of the Juba Talks, despite the ICC's jurisdiction in the area.

Again, the procedural decisions taken at the OTP played a role for the development of this mechanism. When the ICC decided to confirm the rumours of existing arrest warrants against the LRA leadership by making them public, the deterrent effect of the investigations was soon undermined. It held as long as the LRA leadership thought there was a way to escape the warrants through negotiations. When the ICC insisted on the warrants during the Juba Talks, the negotiations failed and the LRA started attacking civilians again. Keeping the warrants secret for a longer time or showing more flexibility during the Juba Talks might have prolonged the duration of ICC deterrence. Yet such flexibility in implementing arrest warrants would reduce the deterrent effect of the ICC in other situation countries or for other rebel groups in Uganda. Again, decisions taken at the OTP had a strong impact on how the deterrent effect worked in practice.

5.2.4 *Blocking conflict resolution*

a. Blocking negotiations

> *I have a spear in my hand. I am choosing peace; I want to kill this animal peace, so that people can eat the meat. But as I am killing it, I see behind me a lion, chasing me. Now, I am wondering, do I have to chase the animal peace, and kill it, or do I have to face the lion?*
>
> Joseph Kony's answer to the question why he was hesitating to sign the Juba Agreement (cited by Odama 2011)

Many authors have claimed that the ICC became one of the biggest stumbling blocks for the Juba Peace Talks between the GoU and the LRA in 2006. This claim was also amongst those most repeated during the interviews conducted in Uganda (Expert Interview 2011k, Loum 2011, Odama 2011, Okidi 2011, Oulanyah 2011, WV Uganda 2011). The local population also voiced fears that the ICC could derail the talks when interviewed in 2007 (Clarke 2009, p. 130–131).

The Juba Talks play a key role in determining how far ICC investigations do hamper negotiations in practice, as they are the first example for negotiations in which international arrest warrants were directly addressed during peace talks. It is impossible to say exactly why the Juba Talks failed, mainly because there are only speculations about the motives of the LRA leadership during the talks. Yet, the analysis offers convincing arguments that the ICC arrest warrants played an important, maybe even decisive role by undermining security guarantees for the LRA leadership.

In order to confirm the blocking claims, several conditions have to be met. The analysis has to show convincingly that the ICC played an important role during the talks. Second, alternative reasons for the failure of the peace talks have to be discarded. Finally, the explanation for the failure of the talks should be plausible against the background of research conducted on negotiations in armed conflicts. Important factors for the success of peace talks are the commitment of both parties to the negotiations, the quality of the mediation, as well as the extent of international support for the peace talks, and the pressure applied on the parties to achieve a negotiated solution. An indicator that the peace talks would have been successful in the absence of ICC warrants is that the parties reached an agreement on most issues, but failed to solve the question how to deal with the ICC warrants.

In order to appreciate the commitment of the parties during the talks as well as the probability for a success of these negotiations, a short historical overview of past talks and attempts at peaceful conflict resolution in the LRA conflict follows.

A history of failed peace negotiations, breaches of ceasefires, as well as betrayals and corruption during peace talks in Uganda has led to a high level of distrust between the parties and to a lack of faith in negotiated solutions. This starts with the peace negotiations between the NRA and the military government of the Acholi General Tito Okello in 1986. For many northerners, these '*Nairobi Peace Jokes*' are a reminder that Museveni's NRM is not to be trusted in negotiations because he decided to take Kampala despite a signed agreement (Okidi 2011). Additionally, there are reports that members of northern rebel groups who surrendered and accepted government amnesty in the late 1980s were later convicted for treason and died in prisons, which led to additional distrust (Finnström 2010b, p. 146). The aggressive military tone used by GoU and UPDF officials in declarations concerning the LRA conflict did not help either. Since 1986, Museveni has regularly vowed to wipe out the various rebel movements in Uganda and has repeatedly called the LRA a terrorist group that should not be negotiated with (Latigo 2008, p. 95, Mwenda 2010, p. 51). There are severe doubts about the commitment of both parties during early negotiations in 1988 (Branch 2005, p. 15, Dolan 2009, p. 96). Additionally, both the international community and the NRM dismissed the possibility of peace talks with the LRA in the early phases of the conflict and branded the rebels as 'evil lunatics' (Finnström 2010a, p. 81).

The first real attempt at peace talks was made in 1993. Betty Bigombe, then State Minister for Northern Uganda, led the delegation on the government side. Even though the talks were described as complicated – the LRA used strange cleansing rituals to intimidate the government delegation – they led to some results. Most notably, security improved considerably and the areas in which the LRA operated were described as 'safe' during the talks (O'Kadameri 2002, p. 40). There is no doubt that Betty Bigombe had a strong personal motivation to find a peaceful solution in 1994, but while the local population also supported the talks, the government as a whole remained reluctant (O'Kadameri 2002, p. 35 and 38).

Three of the key issues that emerged during these talks would play an important role in all negotiations to come. First, there were huge discrepancies between the expectations of the LRA and the GoU. While the NRA felt it was military superior and 'graciously' offered an amnesty to the rebels, the LRA did not want to be perceived as surrendering. As a result, the rebels felt belittled by the NRM (O'Kadameri 2002, p. 37 and 40). Second, Kony blamed the Acholi elders for asking the LRA to fight for their people, only to abandon the rebels later (O'Kadameri 2002, p. 40). Third, the NRA believed that they could win the war militarily and felt that the LRA was only negotiating to buy time. This final factor ultimately led to the failure of the peace talks when Museveni issued a seven-day ultimatum which essentially ended the talks (Atkinson 2010, p. 205, Branch 2005, p. 18). Reportedly, Museveni had received information that the LRA was establishing contacts with its later sponsor, the GoS, during the talks. The president was thus not willing to give the LRA the time to prepare for further conflict (Allen and Vlassenroot 2010, p. 12, O'Kadameri 2002, p. 41). As shown in the isolation section, it is possible that the LRA was indeed establishing the GoS connection during the 1994 talks. In any case, authors and observers are unanimously convinced that neither party was really committed to the talks (Dolan 2009, p. 74 and 89, Finnström 2008, p. 89, O'Kadameri 2002, p. 35–40).

Both sides focused on a military approach in the years following the 1994 talks. Museveni fired Betty Bigombe and ordered a parliamentary investigation of the conflict that concluded that the military approach was best suited to deal with the LRA (Allen 2006, p. 49–50). During this period, the NRA/UPDF also attacked meetings between LRA commanders and traditional and religious leaders who were trying to mediate in the conflict. These attacks occurred despite prior government authorisation of the meetings in 2000, 2001, August 2002 and March 2003 (Rodriguez 2009, p. 3, 77 and 140). Uganda even forbade any contacts between its citizens and the LRA during a period and arrested some mediators for trying to establish contacts with the LRA (Dolan 2009, p. 98, HRW 2003, p. 51–52). Additionally, Museveni undermined northern efforts to end the conflict with the 2000 Amnesty Act by publicly stating that he did not believe in the measure and by delaying the signing of the bill beyond the constitutional timeframe (Finnström 2010b, p. 137). The LRA, on the other hand, killed two Acholi elders who tried to push for further talks with the rebels in the late 1990s and an envoy of a Presidential Peace Team in March 2003 (Bradbury 1999, p. 3, Rodriguez 2009, p. 153).

Another recurring issue in GoU/LRA negotiations emerged in 1998, namely the notorious unreliability of LRA delegations. In January 1998, the LRA sacked their mediator James Obita for conducting two parallel consultation processes with potential mediators for peace talks at the same time without adequately informing the LRA leadership (see Bradbury 1999, p. 10). In December 2000, the LRA again had to dismiss their delegation at talks sponsored by the Carter Center because they had accepted GoU bribes.

The next, slightly more successful attempt at peace talks was made in 2004 when Betty Bigombe returned to Uganda from the United States and started to re-kindle contacts to LRA envoys. While international support and pressure for negotiations had been low thus far, diplomatic efforts pushing for a negotiated solution gained traction during 2004 and 2005 (Perrot 2010, p. 190–192).[63] Betty Bigombe, who this time acted as a mediator between the parties, was able to negotiate a peace zone between the government and the LRA (Allen 2006, p. 78–81).

Problems encountered during these talks remain much the same as during the 1994 talks. The GoU repeatedly offered the LRA amnesty, but

[63] The process tracing in LexisNexis illustrates this tendency. There was an increase in international calls on the GoU to enter negotiations with the LRA since early 2003.

expected the rebels to surrender while belittling the LRA. In the run-up to the talks (14 March 2003), President Museveni publicly called Kony an idiot and a symbol for northern backwardness (Daily Monitor 2003). Again, elements within the UPDF and the GoU believed they had the upper hand and would eventually prevail (Prendergast 2005, p. 4). As in 1994, some within the UPDF argued that the LRA was using the negotiations to re-arm, re-organise and recruit (ICG 2004c, p. 19). The newspaper analysis shows that the UPDF and the GoU issued declarations announcing their imminent victory over the LRA during all of 2004 and 2005. Many therefore concluded that the GoU or at least some elements in the UPDF were not committed to the talks (Hovil and Quinn 2005, p. 5, ICG 2005e, p. 6, Rodriguez 2009, p. 84, 88, 104).

The newspaper analysis also reveals an inconsistent approach of the government to the talks; especially statements of UPDF officials and the president were often contradictory. UPDF officials repeatedly stated that the LRA would be crushed very soon and was all but defeated. Days later, the president would issue a statement offering amnesty to the LRA and declaring his commitment to peace talks. This would be followed by a UPDF statement denouncing the peace talks as an LRA attempt to buy time. Several cases of contradictory statements were found in the LexisNexis analysis.

After the failure of the talks, President Museveni declared on 20 April 2005 that he had never believed in talks with the LRA but had conceded under international pressure to negotiate (Daily Monitor 2005).

Commitment on the LRA side was equally shaky. While the LRA did not directly attack the UPDF during the talks, several LRA attacks on civilians and other ceasefire breaches were reported (Hovil and Quinn 2005, p. 10, ICG 2005b, p. 1, 2005e, p. 2).[64] The newspaper analysis showed that the number of LRA killings dropped after some large massacres committed in early 2004, but the LRA still killed ninety-five people at the height of the talks during the second half of 2004.

Two additional factors reduced the commitment of the parties to talk. First, during the peace talks in 2004, it became clear that there was also a personal level to the conflict between Museveni and Kony, who started to see each other as personal enemies (Lomo and Hovil 2004, p. 16). Second, Kony and his top commanders enjoyed many amenities

[64] LRA ceasefire breaches were, for example, reported in LexisNexis in November 2004. The LRA is cited in newspaper sources as stating that violations were caused by 'unruly elements' within the group.

unavailable to the normal Acholi population at that time. They led a good life in the 'bush' and had no real incentive to come out (Lomo and Hovil 2004, p. 18).

Lack of commitment was not the only reason for the behaviour of the LRA though. The group had increasingly come under military pressure, and did not trust the GoU. It thus feared for its safety, making security guarantees an issue of paramount importance to the LRA (also Expert Interview 2011c, ICG 2005b, p. 3, 2005e, p. 6). The ambiguous government statements as well as their martial rhetoric thus made it difficult to meet LRA security concerns. The extent of the LRA's distrust is illustrated by the fact that the rebels rejected WFP food aid in February 2005 out of fear of being poisoned by the GoU. There was a mixture of a lack of commitment and legitimate security concerns among the LRA leadership.

The talks finally unravelled much like the 1994 talks after the GoU issued an ultimatum. The ceasefire that was initially in force until 7 November 2004 was prolonged unilaterally by the GoU several times until 31 December, despite the LRA attacks on civilians (Rodriguez 2009, p. 238). Nevertheless, the UPDF was still attacking LRA groups outside the ceasefire zones in order to uphold the military pressure. The LRA claimed several ceasefire violations in this context. Despite these problems, the mediators worked on finding a compromise with the LRA until the very end of the deadline. The LRA again requested more time for the talks, but was attacked by the UPDF shortly after the final deadline ran out. Apparently, a meeting between mediators and the LRA chief negotiator Sam Kolo was attacked with a combat helicopter hours after the deadline passed. The mediator Betty Bigombe later voiced her regret that the GoU did not give the LRA enough time to respond to the process (Bigombe 2011, p. 1).

Some weeks after the incident, in February 2005, the LRA negotiator Sam Kolo defected and was rescued by the UPDF. Kony now regarded his chief negotiator as a traitor, so the talks had practically ended (Allen and Vlassenroot 2010, p. 17).

Again, most authors are convinced that there was no real commitment for talks on both sides (ICG 2005e, p. 5, 2005f, p. 7, Lanz 2008b, p. 61). Additionally, local researchers cited the general confusion during the negotiations as the GoU switched between negotiations, amnesty and the military approach as a reason for the failure of the talks (Lomo and Hovil 2004, p. 42). Both explanations have been convincingly confirmed by the results of the newspaper analysis and the field research. Another striking finding is that the problems plaguing the 1994 talks had essentially not been solved a decade later. The GoU, and particularly the UPDF, remained confident they could win the war. They belittled the LRA and demanded the surrender of the rebels. Distrust between the parties remained high, and an ultimatum policy complicated the negotiations. A strong role of the ICC investigations that started in 2004 is improbable against this background. The ICC investigations were initiated only in January 2004, and according to Bigombe, the OTP had respected her wishes to not endanger the peace talks through too much public activity. Betty Bigombe stated that the ICC only decided to issue the LRA warrants after it had become clear that there was a lack of commitment to the talks (Bigombe 2011, p. 1).

The following Juba Talks have to be analysed against this background of failed negotiations. The talks started taking shape after a period of low-intensity warfare and growing military pressure on the LRA in early 2006. As described above, the GoSS had become increasingly interested in the LRA issue and started demanding that both the LRA as well as the UPDF retreat out of southern Sudan after the signature of the CPM in January 2005 (Atkinson 2010, p. 209). The president of southern Sudan, Salva Kiir, flew to Kampala to attend President Museveni's swearing in on 12 May 2006. On that occasion, he declared that the GoSS wanted to mediate between the LRA and the GoU. To emphasise the seriousness of his proposal, he presented Museveni a video recording of a meeting between GoSS Vice-President Riek Machar[65] and LRA Chairman Joseph Kony (Oulanyah 2011). After initial reluctance on the side of the GoU, Museveni agreed and the Juba Peace Process started. Riek Machar became the chief mediator and both the GoU and the LRA appointed delegations. In July 2006, the parties agreed on a five-item agenda for the talks including (1) cessation of hostilities, (2) comprehensive solutions for the conflict, (3) accountability and reconciliation, (4) disarmament, demobilisation and re-integration and (5) formal ceasefire/peace agreement.

The talks soon started to render results, and on 26 August 2006, the LRA and the government signed a cessation of hostilities agreement. Between September and December 2006, the talks bogged down as both

[65] Machar had been a Nuer militia leader allied to the GoS from 1992–2002 before joining the SPLM again. He was reportedly involved in establishing the initial links between the GoS and LRA during that time (Allen and Vlassenroot 2010, p. 5). Therefore, he was in a position to mediate with the LRA.

sides discussed renewed CoHs and their modalities. During that time, some implementation pauses had to be made and the LRA missed deadlines to assemble its troops at agreed assembly points.

When this hiccup was overcome and the talks on item 2 – the comprehensive solutions – started, the LRA delegation presented a comprehensive list of political and economic demands. The list included demands of compensation for stolen cattle during the 1980s, better integration of the Acholi into the army, disbanding the protected camps, as well as power-sharing demands (Eichstaedt 2009, p. 237–238). The GoU rejected the demands, stating that they were illegitimate and went too far, while denying that the LRA was a credible representative of the northern population (ICG 2007c, p. 5).

At the same time, the LRA delegation started demanding the appointment of a new mediator and the move of the talks to a new venue, accusing Machar of being biased. The GoU, on the other hand, was opposed to changing the venue or the mediator (Atkinson 2010, p. 215). As a consequence, the LRA delegation refused further talks on 12 January 2007. This first deadlock in the talks was overcome when the UN envoy for the LRA peace talks, former president of Mozambique Chissano, managed to contact Kony personally. Under his mediation, the GoU and the LRA agreed to talk again in order to overcome the impasse. They met in the scope of backchannel talks in Mombasa in late March 2007 and agreed on principles for items 2 and 3 (Atkinson 2010, p. 218, Simonse et al. 2010, p. 234–235). On 14 April 2007, the LRA and the GoU renewed the CoH agreement and agreed to reduce the number of assembly areas to one, as the LRA was opposed to assemble part of their forces at the second point (Owiny Kibul). The LRA was also granted safe passage to the border area between southern Sudan and the DRC, where the final assembly point was located.

In April 2007, item 2 on the comprehensive solutions was signed. The document was a collection of vague guidelines that were in need of further clarification before they could have been implemented. Still, the LRA accepted a much reduced package in comparison to its earlier demands (ICG 2007b, p. 2, Schomerus 2007, p. 39).

The discussions then moved to item 3 on accountability and reconciliation in early summer 2007. Naturally, the ICC investigations were of key relevance here. The accountability issue was first discussed during a workshop facilitated by the Acholi Paramount Chief Rwot David Acana II. On 29 June 2007, the parties signed an agreement on the principles of accountability. The negotiations now moved on to the question through which mechanisms of accountability should be ensured. This is where the parties started discussing the ICC warrants in earnest.

The government and the LRA finally agreed on consulting the local population to help decide which accountability mechanisms should be implemented. The LRA negotiation team started a 'reconciliation mission' in northern Uganda in November 2007, asking people for forgiveness for the crimes committed by LRA fighters (Eichstaedt 2009, p. 251). Sometime in early October 2007, Kony suddenly killed his second in command Vincent Otti over rifts emerging due to the peace talks (ICG 2008, p. 2, Norris 2010). This incident was followed by a February 2008 shuffle in the leadership of the LRA delegation. Kony replaced the former head of the delegation Martin Ojul with the former spokesperson of the LRA, David Matsanga. On 19 February 2008, after the change in the leadership of the LRA delegation, an annex to the accountability mechanisms was signed (Apuuli 2008a, p. 807).

After the signature of the second item 3 document, the peace process started to unravel for good. Joseph Kony missed an agreed signing date for the final peace agreement on 10 April 2008 and missed a meeting with chief mediator Machar and Acholi elders on 13 May 2008. The situation escalated in June 2008, when the GoU stepped up its rhetoric of pursuing a military solution and started planning anti-LRA operations with southern Sudan and the DRC. Southern Sudan then temporarily stopped its mediation efforts after an LRA attack on an SPLA base. At the same time, the LRA threatened to cancel the truce. By October 2008, the GoSS had grown impatient and started issuing deadlines and demanding written agreements on the schedules for further talks. On 5 November 2008, UN envoy Chissano issued a final deadline until the end of the month for the LRA to sign the agreement. The Congolese FARDC stopped anti-LRA operations during that time to facilitate the signing. Kony finally missed another appointment to sign the agreement on November 29. In December 2008, Operation Lightning Thunder started with broad international support for pursuing a military solution to the LRA conflict.

The facts are clear, but the question why exactly the Juba Talks failed remains debatable. For several reasons, the talks were seen as much more promising than any of the previous attempts at negotiations with the LRA. This was stressed by all interviewees involved in the negotiation process. First of all, the GoSS as a third party had a strong stake in the negotiations and was ready to commit time and resources as well as to offer a venue. Additionally, international support for the negotiations and international interest and involvement in the process was much stronger than during the previous talks (ICG 2007c, p. I, Royo 2008, p. 16). This included the support of several NGOs that were sponsoring the talks (Pax Christi, St. Egidio) or offering food aid to the LRA in the assembly areas (Caritas). Additionally, the UNSC appointed a special envoy for the talks. In early 2007, South Africa, Kenya, Tanzania and Mozambique joined the talks as observers to dissipate LRA worries about a biased role of the GoSS mediation. Finally, both parties showed much more commitment than during previous talks and the military logic of the conflict was overcome for a time. Contrary to the 2004 talks, the CoH Agreement was largely respected by both sides until the talks started to unravel (Royo 2008, p. 16). As described above, it is necessary to exclude other obvious reasons for the failure of the talks if an ICC impact is to be proven. As commitment of the parties had been a major problem during previous talks, the first step is to show that both conflict parties were committed to the negotiations in Juba.

Even interviewees close to the government clearly stated that Museveni had no interest in further talks with the LRA at the beginning of 2006 (Oulanyah 2011). The main reason the GoU nevertheless agreed to talk was the insistence of the GoSS. It would have been a slap in the face of the GoSS, one of Uganda's closest allies, to refuse starting talks. Especially since the GoSS had recently signed the CPA and was now struggling to deliver security to its population. Establishing a lasting peace was impossible as long as the UPDF and the LRA were fighting each other on Sudanese territory though (ICG 2007c, p. 7, Lanz 2008b, p. 62, Oulanyah 2011).

The GoSS demands were backed up by ever stronger international pressure for peace talks. The LexisNexis tracing shows that more and more international actors, including particularly the United States, the United Kingdom, the EU, some Scandinavian states and UN institutions called for peace talks and asked the GoU to show commitment (see also Girke and Kamp 2010, p. 67, Latigo 2008, p. 92, Perrot 2010, p. 188–193). Government officials admitted that the GoU had doubts about the LRA commitment to the talks, but they maintain that the GoU nevertheless showed full commitment to the talks (Bigombe 2011, p. 3, Kulayigye 2011, Oulanyah 2011, Rugunda 2011). Independent think tanks like the ICG agree with this conclusion. They argue that even GoU hardliners did not want to be seen as spoilers, but preferred exhausting all options before resorting to the military approach (ICG 2007c, p. 8).

A number of facts also speak for real GoU commitment during the talks. President Museveni scaled back on his war rhetoric as long as the Juba Talks did not get completely stuck.[66] Additionally, he offered the LRA amnesty on 16 May 2006, one day after getting briefed by the GoSS about the mediation proposal. He repeated this offer consistently during the talks and military threats only came to the fore when there were real reasons to believe that the LRA was not showing the necessary commitment.

The fact that military threats were still issued cannot be interpreted as a lack of commitment by the GoU as such. Military threats can be a legitimate tool to pressure the opposing party to sign an agreement, as long as the threats do not undermine the peace talks. While the military threats were overwhelming and counter-productive during previous talks, the LexisNexis analysis showed that the GoU mainly used threats for gaining leverage in the 2006 talks, e.g. when the LRA had missed a deadline or was stalling. Even though the government initially expected the LRA to surrender as during previous talks (Expert Interview 2011i, Odama 2011), Museveni had accepted unconditional talks with the LRA[67] and had repeated the amnesty offer by 3 July 2006.

The government's deeds also clearly show an increased commitment during the Juba Talks. Museveni appointed the Minister of the Interior and former Representative of Uganda to the UN Ruhakana Rugunda as the head of the delegation, thus appointing a high-ranking member of the government. The GoU complied with a request of LRA Chairman Kony to airlift wounded LRA fighters to the assembly areas, and the UPDF respected the ceasefire even though the agreed deadline for the LRA to assemble ran out. Additionally, the UPDF and the SPLA withdrew from parts of southern Sudan as requested by the LRA due to security concerns in November 2006. Museveni also sent Kony 1,000 USD in airtime as a Christmas present in 2006 and paid for flights for Kony's relatives, including his mother, as well as traditional leaders to visit him at his camp in Garamba (Oulanyah 2011). The GoU also showed commitment by spending a lot of money on the expensive consultation process for the accountability annex (Nakumbi 2011). The president also went to Juba

[66] The president did fall back into old patterns occasionally. For example, he called Joseph Kony a betrayer and criminal in November 2006 according to newspaper reports. These statements, however, were much less frequent than during previous talks.

[67] Indeed, the government for the first time showed commitment to tackle some of the root causes of the conflict by admitting past mistakes in the north (Expert Interview 2011i).

personally to show his commitment to the talks despite the LRA delegation refusing to shake hands with him (Dollo 2011, Kulayigye 2011, Oulanyah 2011). Contrary to previous talks, the UPDF did not attack the LRA after Kony's failure to sign on 10 April 2008, despite the ceasefire having run out.

In conclusion, the field research and the newspaper analysis have shown that the commitment of the GoU was considerably higher than during previous talks. A lack of GoU commitment was thus not among the main reasons for the failure of the talks. Even former LRA officers, opposition politicians and LRA delegation members agreed that international pressure and attention prompted the GoU to talk in earnest (Charles 2011, Odong 2011b, Okello 2011, Okumu 2011).[68]

The extent of the LRA's commitment is a bit more difficult to determine, particularly since the LRA leadership itself only took part in a handful of meetings. Most of the negotiations on the LRA side were conducted by a delegation of members of the Acholi diaspora and other Ugandans. Problems within the LRA delegation arguably became one of the main reasons for the failure of the Juba talks due to the unprofessionalism of some of its members, and the fact that some were striving for personal wealth and fame (see Prendergast 2007b, p. 2–3). Judging from Mareike Schomerus' report, who was present when the LRA leadership first met the GoSS mediators, there was real commitment for talks on the side of Kony and Otti (Schomerus 2010a, p. 103, 2010b). At least in the case of Otti, it is clear that he remained committed to the peace talks until his execution. He had openly and publicly supported peace talks in an interview with BBC (Allen 2006, p. 190–191), he had told news media that the LRA commanders would accept amnesty by the GoU and he had voiced his regret when the LRA delegation refused to shake hands with President Museveni in Juba. An interviewee close to Otti confirms that he was fully committed to peace (Lacambel 2011). Reports of participants and think tanks also describe Otti as the driving force behind LRA peace efforts (ICG 2008, p. 2, Iya 2010, p. 179).

[68] There are rumours about elements within the UPDF trying to spoil the talks by encroaching on LRA positions (LRA Commander 2011) including at least one reported incident during which UPDF soldiers dressed up as LRA rebels and killed a civilian (ICG 2008, p. 12). The extent to which individuals within the UPDF were involved in spoiling attempts is impossible to ascertain, but the lack of any newspaper reports and the limited number of sources claiming these incidents suggest that their number was limited.

It seems that Joseph Kony at least initially also was committed to the talks. He proved this commitment by personally showing up to talks with Riek Machar, something that had rarely happened in the past. He also stressed his commitment during a 14 November 2006 meeting with the Resident District Commissioner and the Local Council V Chairman of Gulu District. But at some point in late 2006 or during 2007, Joseph Kony's commitment to peace started unravelling. This was reflected by reports of LRA troops moving towards DRC and CAR in late 2006 and early 2007 instead of assembling in Ri-Kwangba as agreed in the CoH agreement. In early May 2007, the first newspaper reports of LRA fighters occupying villages in DRC emerged. Kony's lack of commitment became obvious when news about the execution of Vincent Otti emerged in early October 2007. Interviewees and authors agree that a rift concerning the peace talks led to Otti's execution (Akhavan 2009, p. 644, Lacambel 2011, Norris 2010).

After that date, Kony's cooperation became inconsistent. He refused to meet UN envoy Chissano on 21 October 2007 (Prendergast and O'Brien 2007, p. 4). In December 2007, the first confirmed reports of LRA fighters looting villages in DRC were published. In the first quarter of 2008, the LRA raided areas in southern Sudan and CAR during ten days and abducted 130–150 civilians. Additionally, a former ICC official claims that the LRA started training new abductees in March 2008 (Brubacher 2010, p. 277, Norris 2010, The Economist 2008).

By this time, the LRA also felt less pressure to strike a deal with the GoU, as the rebels now gained access to largely safe corridors for movement in the DRC and secured their access to resources like gold, ivory and gemstones in DRC and CAR (ICG 2008, p. 15). Kony skipped another meeting in May 2008 that had been organised to address his judicial doubts concerning the ICC warrants. He also did not show up at a scheduled meeting with UN envoy Chissano in September 2008. Kony thus flatly refused to communicate with mediators in the final phases of the talks (Spiegel and Prendergast 2008, p. 3). A number of academics, government officials and, ICC staff members, as well as participants at the talks concluded that Kony was only buying time to re-organise and re-arm and had never seriously been committed (Iya 2010, p. 180, Kulayigye 2010, 2011, Lacambel 2011, Moreno Ocampo 2010b).[69] They

[69] Apparently, LRA leaders said during an intercepted communication that they wanted to draw out the Juba Talks to re-organise and get rid of the ICC warrants (Prendergast 2007a, p. 4). LRA returnees confirmed this information in September 2008 according to

argue that the LRA was desperate for food when the negotiations started and used the talks to re-stock on food and to re-organise for armed conflict (Cakaj 2010b, p. 6 and 11, ICG 2007b, p. 5, 2007c, p. 6 and 10). There is evidence that Kony tried to contact the GoS twice by the end of 2008 in order to re-establish external support to the LRA (Cakaj 2011, p. 5). Also Caritas, the main provider of food for the LRA during the talks, took the inflated figures of LRA fighters provided by Kony at face level (ICG 2007b, p. 5, Mendes 2010, p. 122).[70] Others point out that the LRA had a motivation to use the Juba Talks as a source of income[71] or a means to win time in order to re-locate to the DRC (Brubacher 2010, p. 275–276, Kulayigye 2011, Simonse et al. 2010, p. 238). Additionally, the LRA did not reciprocate trust building measures by the GoU by freeing child soldiers or showing similar signs of commitment (von Braun 2008, p. 236).

The author's personal assessment based on the interviews conducted in Uganda and the newspaper tracing is that Kony was committed to the talks until he executed Otti. The picture emerging from the combined information obtained in the literature, the interviews and the newspaper database suggests that Otti's execution was the moment that doomed the talks (also Cakaj 2011, p. 4). Considering the amount of evidence, it is undeniable that Kony used the Juba Talks to re-arm and re-organise in the later stages. But the reason why he did so was not necessarily non-commitment. Problems with the LRA delegation and lacking security guarantees combined with distrust were major obstacles for successful talks and would have probably led to the failure of the talks even if Kony had been fully committed until the end. The following paragraphs will illustrate why lacking security guarantees and the refusal of the LRA leadership to personally attend the talks were crucial factors for their failure.

Apart from a few meetings, the leaders of the LRA were not represented in the delegation. Many diaspora members close to the LRA flew in to participate in the talks when the GoU leaked the video of Machar's meeting with Kony and thus triggered a lot of media attention. The LRA

leaked diplomatic cables (Groth 2011). Chief mediator Machar also blamed Kony's intransigence for the failure of the talks (Dak 2010). Finally, the 2004 mediator Betty Bigombe doubted Kony's commitment (Bigombe 2011, p. 2).

[70] Kony claimed to have 5,000 fighters while most estimations taxed the LRA at 800.

[71] According to the UPDF spokesperson, the LRA command in the bush received half of the allowances paid to the LRA delegation.

contact group quickly increased to more than twenty people and their competence and links to the LRA high command were doubted by many (Schomerus 2010a, p. 100, Simonse et al. 2010, p. 230–231, Unger and Wierda 2008, p. 270). Two LRA officers who were part of the LRA delegation were withdrawn on 5 August 2006 by the high command due to 'security concerns'.

During the talks, the delegation brought forward unrealistic demands in the early phases, initially even demanding the dissolution or disarmament of the UPDF and a 30 per cent share of all presidentially appointed positions for the LRA. These demands were rightly described as political grandstanding by observers (Schomerus 2010a, p. 105). Additionally, the delegation stalled the talks in January 2007 because sponsors had refused to pay for their air tickets to Europe. The delegation again blocked the talks on 27 July 2007, claiming that they had not been paid a total of 2 million USD in allowances. These incidents suggest that some of the members were indeed in the delegation for the money and travel allowances.

The delegation also rejected a government amnesty offer, denying the government the moral right to pardon the rebels. This was apparently done without consulting the LRA high command, as Otti later declared that the LRA commanders would accept the amnesty. Miscommunications and lack of coordination between the delegation and the LRA leadership could be traced throughout the negotiations and got worse with time (also Prendergast 2007a, p. 5). After a phone call with Vincent Otti in late August 2006, the GoU head of delegation Rugunda stated that the LRA commanders had received a lot of wrong information about the talks from their delegation. In reaction, the LRA delegation demanded the replacement of Rugunda as head of the government delegation in September 2006. Otti responded that the delegation was acting out of bounds and that the LRA had full confidence in Rugunda as the main negotiation partner on the government side.

In October 2006, Rugunda told newspapers that there were disagreements between the LRA leadership and its delegation about the peace talks. Apparently, the GoU played a role in fostering these disagreements. ICG reported systematic GoU attempts to bribe the LRA delegation. The first head of the delegation, Martin Ojul, had all his expenses covered by the GoU (ICG 2008, p. 15). A number of interviewees, some of them speaking off the record, confirmed that LRA delegation members had been approached with money by the GoU (Charles 2011, Okumu 2011). Former LRA officers consistently reported that Vincent Otti was killed by

Joseph Kony because Kony believed Otti had also been corrupted by the GoU (Charles 2011, Okello 2011). Kony himself claimed that the LRA delegation in Juba had been bought by the government. In reaction, he later replaced his head of delegation, Martin Ojul (who had been bribed with 200,000 USD by the GoU according to newspaper reports), with David Matsanga (Atkinson 2010, p. 219, Okello 2011).

The events surrounding Otti's death, the funds received by Ojul and Matsanga's takeover of the delegation leadership were connected to internal rivalries within the LRA delegation (Onega 2011, Odong 2011b). A legal advisor of the LRA delegation, who left the delegation when Matsanga took over and is now an MP in the Ugandan Parliament, called Matsanga a '*scatter brain*' and accused him of being after money and contributing to the collapse of the talks and Otti's death (Odong 2011b). The picture that emerges from various sources also suggests that the GoU was trying to cut a deal with Vincent Otti and that it split the LRA by persuading him to defect. An LRA officer said that Vincent Otti was increasingly taking over the negotiations from Joseph Kony without informing him adequately (Charles 2011). Additionally, Kony believed that Otti was implicated in the money flows from the GoU to the LRA delegation. Several interviewees mentioned a Kenya Commercial Bank (KCB) account in Otti's name in Nairobi to which government funds were channelled.

Claims that the GoU was trying to cut a deal with Vincent Otti are also supported in reports written by analysts (ICG 2008, p. 15, Lancaster et al. 2011, p. 24). This would explain why both Ojul and Otti allegedly received money by the GoU and were killed or replaced by Kony.

After Otti's assassination, cracks between Kony and his delegation started emerging in public. Some delegation members declared on 20 November 2007 that they would abandon Kony if he didn't sign the agreement. On 6 December 2007, they publicly distanced themselves from Kony. On 14 January 2008, this led to the final rift between Kony and Martin Ojul when Kony reportedly confirmed Matsanga as the new head of delegation. Despite this change in leadership, Kony's trust in his delegation was not restored. He accused US observers of contacting individual members of the LRA delegation behind his back in February 2008.

A closer look at the relations between the LRA and its delegation confirms that the talks started to unravel after Kony killed Otti. After taking over the LRA delegation, Matsanga suddenly re-tabled unrealistic demands in the negotiations, asking for 35 per cent of cabinet posts for

LRA representatives. Additionally, the communication between the LRA delegation and Kony broke down completely before the final accountability agreement was signed on 19 February 2008 (Odong 2011b). Indeed, it later emerged that Matsanga went on conducting negotiations, pretending that he was consulting with the LRA high command when he had already lost contact with Kony (Oulanyah 2011). Only after Kony had failed to sign the agreement on 10 April 2008 did David Matsanga admit that he had not spoken to Kony. James Obita then became the new head of the LRA delegation, reportedly appointed by letter by Kony. The next day, Matsanga was arrested with 20,000 USD in cash at Juba airport. The ICG interpreted this as another GoU attempt to manipulate the LRA delegation (ICG 2008, p. 15).

On 8 June 2008, Matsanga attempted a comeback, claiming that he had been re-instated as the delegation head by Kony. Another eight delegation members left the LRA delegation in reaction to this back and forth. In mid-January 2009, when the talks had already broken down, a letter by Kony dissolving the delegation surfaced. Matsanga claimed the letter was not authentic, but instead had been written by his rivals (Fisas 2010b, p. 86).

This brief overview of how the delegation worked during the Juba Talks shows that Kony must have completely lost trust in his negotiators at some point. It is also clear that the delegation was negotiating without consulting Kony after the delegation head changed for the first time in February 2008. Kony was thus neither fully informed, nor did he necessarily understand the agreements made after that date (see Allen and Vlassenroot 2010, p. 18, Lanz 2008b, p. 63).

Taking this into consideration, the reason he started to prepare the LRA for renewed armed conflict might not have been solely due to lack of commitment, but a reaction to the problems with the delegation and his second in command.[72] A former delegation member described the breakdown of communications between Kony and the delegation as the main reason for the failure of the talks (Odong 2011b). Several people involved in the talks as well as a former member of the LRA high command suggested that either elements of the Acholi diaspora or

[72] The former LRA spokesperson Obinyo Olweny relayed a message by Kony in April 2008 saying that he did not sign because he did not trust the mediators anymore after the bribery attempts of the GoU (ICG 2008, p. 4). This version of the events has been supported in a number of interviews conducted by researchers in northern Uganda (Cakaj 2011, p. 5).

spoilers close to the government had called Kony before the agreed signature date and told him that he was walking into a trap (LRA Commander 2011, Odama 2011, Okello 2011, Okidi 2011, Rugunda 2011).[73] A confusing picture emerges when taking into account all this information, but what remains clear is that Kony did not receive reliable information from the negotiations and could not trust many of his intermediaries. Unreliable and corrupt intermediaries and the sheer amount of misinformation that reached Kony were key reasons for the failure of the talks. The ICG rightly concluded that the Juba process was not credible as long as Kony and Otti did not take part themselves (ICG 2007b, p. 10).

The second reason for Kony's lack of commitment and his failure to sign are his serious security concerns. Kony was constantly afraid of being lured into a trap by the GoU and was thus very reluctant to assemble since the beginning of the talks (ICG 2008, p. 11).[74] Leaked diplomatic cables reveal that Kony is a paranoid personality, suspecting plots to kill him everywhere (Groth 2011). This distrust goes back to Museveni's coup and his treatment of surrendering rebels in the 1980s (see Branch 2010a, p. 39, Finnström 2010a, p. 79). Kony's distrust was reinforced during later negotiation periods in which Museveni operated with military threats and ultimatums. Former LRA officers and opposition members as well as the head of the GoU delegation agreed that Kony did not have faith in the GoU commitment to find a negotiated solution (Okello 2011, Okumu 2011, Rugunda 2011). There are several examples that illustrate Kony's fears. For example, the LRA delegation walked out of the talks in 2006, stating that they felt militarily threatened by the UPDF. A former LRA officer elaborated that UPDF troops allegedly came threateningly close to LRA assembly areas (Okello 2011). Newspaper reports also indicated that the LRA was fleeing the assembly areas after the signature of the CoH due to the intimidating UPDF presence.[75]

The ICG has consistently emphasised how important credible security guarantees were for Kony and his top commanders (ICG 2005f, p. 7,

[73] Acholi traditional leaders have been cited in news media with similar statements, while the LRA Commander interviewed by the author was the only person claiming that the 'spoilers' were affiliated with the GoU.

[74] United Nations Undersecretary-General for Humanitarian Affairs Jan Egeland confirmed that Kony was in constant fear of an UPDF attack after meeting him in November 2006.

[75] The Spokesperson of the UPDF denied in strong terms that the army had ever approached assembly areas (Kulayigye 2011).

2006c, p. 12, 2007c, p. 11).[76] These security concerns might explain why Kony decided not to sign when he started receiving warnings that the signing ceremony might be a trap. He quite simply did not believe that credible security guarantees were in place (Odama 2011, Oulanyah 2011).

Drawing from the literature on peace negotiations, it is very unlikely for any rebel group to sign an agreement comparable to what was offered to the LRA in Juba. First of all, LRA demands for some sort of power-sharing were not seriously considered during the negotiations, so the incentives and gains were too low for Kony to be expected to sign (see Greenhill and Major 2007, p. 14, Newman and Richmond 2006, p. 10, Walter 2002, p. 39). Additionally, the literature would not expect a rebel group to sign an agreement in the absence of credible security guarantees. Security guarantees are seen as the most important part of agreements because the implementation phase initially leaves the parties that have disarmed worse off than during the fighting (Pearson and Lounsbery 2009, p. 76, Simonse et al. 2010, p. 225, Walter 2002, p. 3 and 21).

The lack of security guarantees and the unfortunate role of the LRA delegations were clearly the main reasons for the failure of the Juba Talks.

This detailed description of the 2006 peace talks illustrated two points. On the one hand, the Juba Talks were the most promising negotiations that took place between the LRA and the GoU. Commitment on both sides was credible in the early stages. There was a strong mediation and enough international pressure and support to achieve a negotiated solution. On the other hand, there were several reasons that made the success of these talks improbable. The two main issues were Kony's security concerns and the utter unreliability of the LRA delegation. The question that remains is whether the ICC played a role in the emergence of these crucial factors for failure.

When the Juba Talks started, the ICC had already published arrest warrants for Joseph Kony and his four top commanders. It is also clear that the LRA leadership knew about the warrants. Additionally, the Ugandan Parliament paved the way to extradite the LRA commanders to the ICC by passing a law that made the exemption of LRA commanders from the Amnesty Act possible on 18 April 2006. Against this background, it is unsurprising that the lifting of the ICC arrest warrants was one of the first demands put forward by the LRA when they engaged in the talks (Unger and Wierda 2008, p. 270–271).

[76] ICG also reported that Kony specifically asked for security guarantees when talking to President Museveni on the phone in later stages of the talks (ICG 2007c, p. 11).

As will be shown below, the demand for lifting the warrants was consistently repeated during the negotiations by both the LRA delegation and the high command. The concerns of the LRA pertaining to the ICC warrants explain why members of the high command did not participate in the negotiations beyond the initial meetings with Riek Machar. Several authors state that the LRA commanders steered clear of the negotiations for fear of being arrested and brought to the ICC (Baines 2007, p. 102, Eichstaedt 2009, p. 228, Grono and O'Brien 2008, p. 16).[77] This view was confirmed in interviews with participants at the peace talks and former LRA officers (Charles 2011, Onega 2011). The warrants were thus a main reason why the LRA decided to rely on a delegation approach despite the bad experiences with past delegations. This is also illustrated by the fact that the LRA had sent high-ranking commanders to talks and meetings when the ICC warrants were not yet in place. In 2006, Kony and Otti decided to retreat when the talks became public. According to mediators from Pax Christi, the ICC involvement also led to complications in finding a safe venue for the negotiations (Simonse et al. 2010, p. 229). The ICC thus played an important role for the LRA decision to rely on an external delegation. Two LRA officers who initially were members of the delegation were later withdrawn by Kony due to 'security concerns'. The Court therefore clearly had an indirect influence on the failure of the Juba Talks by pushing the LRA to use an external delegation.

But even beyond this initial stage, the ICC played a strong role during the negotiations. Participants at the peace talks and analysts confirmed that there was '*not an hour without [the ICC] being mentioned*' (Charles 2011, O'Brien 2007, Oulanyah 2011). First-hand accounts by people present during the talks also show convincingly that Kony and other top commanders were very worried about the ICC (Odong 2011b). The disagreements between the GoU and the LRA about how to deal with the arrest warrants emerged for the first time in September 2006. On 14 November 2006 and 9 December 2006, a delegation of Acholi lawyers explained the ICC warrants to Kony.[78] In December 2006, Museveni publicly assured Kony that he would not be extradited, and the LRA

[77] Vincent Otti reportedly refused to join the Juba Talks personally in July 2006 and February 2007, citing the outstanding ICC warrants (Atkinson 2010, p. 216, Schomerus 2007, p. 35).

[78] Members of the delegation included Jacob Oulanyah (now Deputy Speaker of Parliament), Owiny Dollo (now ICD Judge) and Barney Afako, all of them knowledgeable in international criminal law.

agreed to search for a solution to the ICC issue in the framework of the Juba Talks. An early impasse due to the ICC warrants could thus be avoided; but the main disagreement about whether, how and when to lift the ICC warrants remained. GoU delegation head Rugunda said in late April 2007 that there were no plans to drop the ICC warrants, while Otti stated that the LRA would sign but not assemble as long as the ICC warrants remained in place (Latigo 2008, p. 100).

Therefore, as one interviewee involved in the talks pointed out, the main challenges started with agenda item 3, as Kony was in no way ready to accept ICC jurisdiction (Mapenduzi 2011). The original position paper of the LRA stated that they would only accept traditional justice and truth commissions as accountability measures, a position that was also repeated by LRA delegation head Martin Ojul during his opening statement at the negotiations (Ojul 2006).

When the accountability negotiations started on 6 June 2007, the LRA stated that they would accept accountability if the UPDF was also investigated. In the scope of the negotiations, it became increasingly clear that President Museveni was ready to challenge the ICC arrest warrants if it was necessary to ensure peace with the LRA. Both sides were approaching a compromise foreseeing the implementation of a set of alternative mechanisms replacing the ICC. These mechanisms included Acholi traditional justice measures that attributed some guilt to both parties (Otim and Wierda 2008, p. 23).

Museveni had already offered an amnesty to the LRA leadership in the early phases of the negotiations (also Eichstaedt 2009, p. 251). The GoSS and chief mediator Machar himself had also voiced their support for dropping the ICC warrants (Atkinson 2010, p. 211, Williams 2007, p. 11). Finally, the UN Mission in Sudan (UNMIS) hinted that it would not arrest LRA commanders if there was a real prospect for a deal (ICG 2007c, p. 14). Despite this emerging regional consensus, international human rights groups, the ICC Office of the Prosecutor and some ICC supporters like the United Kingdom, constantly pressed the parties to respect the ICC warrants (also Mendes 2010, p. 112, Perrot 2010, p. 199). The LexisNexis analysis shows that there was high international pressure to uphold the ICC warrants.[79] Additionally, the ICC organs issued nearly one statement per month since the accountability talks started in June

[79] Actors that called for respecting the ICC warrants in newspaper reports included the United States and the United Kingdom, parliamentarians from Germany and Belgium, the UNSC and UN Secretary General Ban. Additionally, NGOs including AI and HRW

2007, reminding the parties that the warrants remained in place. President Museveni's challenge of the ICC culminated in his February 2008 statement that he would not hand over Kony to the Court (AI 2008, p. 8, Apuuli 2008a, p. 801, McGreal 2008). On 26 February 2008, the LRA demanded that the agreement should include a guarantee that the ICC warrants would be lifted, but the GoU refused.

The compromise struck between the GoU and the LRA on accountability issues in the annex to item 3 deserves some closer scrutiny as it will help to determine whether Kony's security concerns attached to the warrants could be addressed. Both parties officially communicated to the press that national trials would be conducted for LRA war criminals. At the same time, the GoU would engage the ICC and ask it to drop the warrants. The GoU also assured Kony of not applying the death sentence in the national trials. The accountability annex, which was signed on 19 February 2008 and was supposed to determine the exact procedures for ensuring accountability, is however, a somewhat problematic document. One of the main issues was the fact that it was signed after the LRA head of delegation had changed on 14 January 2008. Since the new head, David Matsanga, later confessed that he had never talked to Kony, it is doubtful that Kony was fully informed about the contents of the document before it was signed. This is being emphasised by the fact that former LRA officers and others involved in the talks claimed that Kony did not fully understand the accountability annex and what it meant in practice (Charles 2011, Odama 2011).

Indeed, the text itself has a certain level of ambiguity. Even individuals involved in the drafting process of the document have offered different interpretations of its implications for the indicted LRA commanders during interviews with the author. A member of the LRA delegation who quit the talks shortly before the accountability annex was signed and who had drafted most of the LRA papers for the accountability negotiations stated that the aim of the LRA delegation had been to subject Kony to traditional justice only (Odong 2011b). A JLOS official stated that in her opinion, the Accountability Agreement left open what exactly would have happened to the LRA top commanders (Ajok 2011). The head of the GoU delegation and an ICD judge stated that the agreement foresaw national court proceedings for Kony (Dollo 2011, Rugunda 2011), while another GoU delegation member directly involved in drafting the paper

pushed ICC States Parties to apply additional pressure to ensure the warrants were upheld.

explained that the agreement called for the establishment of an '*alternative justice mechanism*' to bring the LRA commanders to accountability (Oulanyah 2011). This alternative mechanism would have been elaborated in detail at a later point after the signing of the final agreement. The ICG, on the other hand, interpreted the agreement as foreseeing civil or criminal proceedings for the LRA commanders with alternative penalties and sanctions (ICG 2007b, p. 4).

Indeed, the wording is not entirely clear concerning the consequences for the LRA commanders indicted by the ICC (also AI 2008, p. 19, Burke-White and Kaplan 2009, p. 274, Mallinder 2009b, p. 48–50). Point 6.1 of the agreement reads: '*Formal courts provided for under the Constitution shall exercise jurisdiction over individuals who are alleged to bear particular responsibility for the most serious crimes, especially crimes amounting to international crimes, during the course of the conflict*'. The section uses the words '*responsibility*' and '*most serious crimes*', vocabulary used in the Rome Statute of the ICC, as crucial criteria to decide whom to prosecute. The section also specifically refers to international crimes. The most obvious interpretation would thus be that the LRA commanders indicted by the ICC would be subjected to regular court proceedings.

Yet, Point 3.1 of the agreement says: '*Where a person has already been subjected to proceedings … or has been subjected to accountability or reconciliation proceedings for any conduct in the course of the conflict, that person shall not be subjected to any other proceedings with respect to that conduct*'. The provision explicitly states that it applies to '*any conduct*' during the conflict, which does not exclude international crimes under the Rome Statute. It would thus apparently allow the LRA commanders to circumnavigate court proceedings by going through traditional reconciliation mechanisms.

The bottom line is that the agreement leaves some space for interpretation. According to informants close to the LRA, Kony's worries about the security guarantees were increased as he did not fully grasp the meaning of the accountability agreement. He apparently suspected some sort of trap (Charles 2011). Despite the problematic role of the text, it would be wrong to blame the delegations for it. The accountability agreement was a carefully drafted document, designed to assuage the concerns of the LRA leadership without directly violating Uganda's responsibilities under the Rome Statute. It therefore had to be vague to a certain extent. It is unclear whether the accountability annex in its final version would have been acceptable to Kony if he had been fully informed about its content. The GoU delegation head and others claim that Kony was ready to face accountability in Uganda (Loum 2011, Rugunda 2011). On the other hand, former LRA delegation members, officers and commanders say that Kony was only ready to accept *mato oput* as a form of accountability (Charles 2011, LRA Commander 2011, Odong 2011b).[80]

From a legal point of view, it is clear that only the 'toughest' interpretation of the accountability annex foreseeing national trials for Kony would have stood a chance to challenge the ICC jurisdiction (see IBA 2007, p. 21–24). Uganda would have needed to ensure that it did not appear 'unwilling' to prosecute the indicted commanders. Allowing alternative sentences that are disproportionately lenient could have been interpreted as unwillingness to punish the crimes. Uganda would also have needed to demonstrate independence and impartiality in the trials, including proof that the sentence was not already agreed upon during the negotiations with the LRA (Burke-White and Kaplan 2009, p. 273–274, Otim and Wierda 2010, p. 4). Finally, the ICC Pre-Trial Chamber has recently confirmed in its ruling on the admissibility challenge of the Kenyan government that ongoing or past investigations or proceedings against the same persons and for the same conduct included in the ICC warrants are needed to pass a complementarity test at the case level (ICC PTC 2011, §§44 and 51). This means that the national accountability measures have to be implemented before the ICC jurisdiction is challenged. As a consequence, the arrest and trial of the LRA commanders before the withdrawal of the warrants would have been inevitable (Burke-White and Kaplan 2009, p. 277, Kamara 2011, p. 9). A statement published by the judges of the Pre-Trial Chamber in charge of the LRA case later confirmed that it was very doubtful whether the Juba Agreement would have been enough to stop an ICC trial. The judges stated that the ICC remained in charge of handling the cases of the LRA commanders and that the accountability agreement was irrelevant, taking into consideration that there was a renewed military offensive against the LRA (Mendes 2010, p. 113, New Vision 2009).[81]

[80] This view is shared by experts familiar with the LRA conflict (Expert Interview 2011i, Prendergast 2007c, p. 3).

[81] An OTP staff member also confirmed in an interview that the Juba Agreement would probably not have held in face of the Pre-Trial Chamber (PTC) clarifications on Uganda. The PTC had made clear that concrete proceedings are needed to stop the prosecution and that an abstract agreement was not enough (Rastan 2011a). The statement of the

Even if the pre-conditions to challenge the ICC jurisdiction were fulfilled and Kony consented to being tried in a Ugandan court, it remains unclear whether Uganda is currently able to conduct a trial that fulfils the standards of the ICC complementarity threshold. The trial of former LRA Commander Thomas Kwoyelo before the International Crimes Division (ICD) of the Ugandan High Court shows how confusing the legal situation in Uganda currently is. Several courts have ruled that there is no solid legal basis for denying Thomas Kwoyelo amnesty without violating his right for equal treatment under the Ugandan Constitution. Yet, the DPP violated due process and ignored past court rulings by claiming that Kwoyelo had no right to amnesty since war crimes could not be pardoned. Yet, it is a fact that Uganda had a blanket amnesty law in place since the passing of the 2000 Amnesty Act. Until May 2012, when the Amnesty Act unexpectedly expired, Kony was eligible for amnesty. Only the parliament could have barred him from applying for amnesty, which it never did. It was therefore at best unclear whether Uganda would have been able to try Kony and his commanders.

Against this background, it is clear that the accountability agreement could not invalidate the security fears of Kony (also ICG 2008, p. I). For a realistic chance to challenge the ICC warrants, Kony would have had to be exempted from amnesty, arrested and tried. This would have had to happen immediately after his surrender, as Uganda would have otherwise been obliged to extradite Kony to the Hague.

The recent case of Muammar al-Gaddafi's son, Saif al-Islam al-Gaddafi, sheds some additional light on complementarity questions. Saif al-Islam had been indicted by the ICC during the Libyan civil war. He was later captured by Zintan militias when trying to leave the country southward towards Niger. Even though Libya has declared that it wants to try Saif al-Islam, the Court insists that Saif be extradited to the Hague. This illustrates that the Court may even decide to demand the extradition of suspects if the situation country – in this case Libya – has explicitly stated that it wants to try the suspect itself.

Based on interviews with people who had met Kony during the negotiations, it is very improbable that Kony would have accepted an arrangement that would have involved his arrest (also ICG 2007b, p. 8, Norris 2010). Analysts agree that the LRA commanders wanted ironclad guarantees against ICC prosecution before deciding to assemble their

judges of the Pre-Trial Chamber is not available on the official website of the ICC, but was cited in newspapers on the date of its publication.

troops for disarmament. In the absence of such guarantees, they would have rather kept on fighting (ICG 2006c, p. 10, Prendergast 2007b, p. 4). As illustrated by repeated demands voiced by the LRA commanders, the only acceptable guarantee was the lifting of the ICC warrants (see Apuuli 2008a, p. 804).[82] The LRA delegation even travelled to the ICC and asked for the warrants to be dropped in March 2008, one month before the agreed signing date (Eichstaedt 2009, p. 274).

Legally, the GoU was not able to challenge the ICC warrants before trying Kony though. The final disagreement that led to Kony's refusal to sign was directly connected to this question. The parties failed to agree whether the government should request the ICC to drop the warrants before or after the LRA had signed the treaty (Latigo 2008, p. 99, Peskin 2009a p. 686). Kony himself said on 24 May 2008 that he would rather die than turn himself in to the GoU and the ICC '*to be hanged*' (Atkinson 2010, p. 220, Fisas 2010a, p. 103), indicating that he did not trust the security guarantees. In November 2008, he also specifically asked for the lifting of the ICC warrants and further clarifications on the nexus between the traditional ritual of *Mato Oput* on the one side, and the proposed Special Division of the Ugandan High Court on the other side (Atkinson 2010, p. 220, Iya 2010, p. 182, Royo 2008, p. 17).

The existence of the ICC warrants also contributed towards undermining the little trust that existed between the parties. The analysis of the negotiations in LexisNexis showed that during the entire duration of the talks, the GoU sent mixed signals to the LRA due to its difficult position between amnesty promises and international obligations stemming from its status as an ICC state party (see also Hovil and Lomo 2005, p. 28, IBA 2007, p. 16). On the one hand, it offered amnesty to the LRA commanders in order to persuade them to sign; on the other hand, it had to answer to the pressure exerted by the international community and the ICC who called on the GoU to respect the warrants and its international obligations (also Expert Interview 2011b, 2011i). The pressure on the GoU was augmented through several requests of the ICC Pre-Trial Chamber to the GoU, asking the government to clarify its official position concerning the warrants. The GoU was thus caught in a double-bind situation in which it was forced to send mixed signals which were less than helpful in addressing the security concerns of the LRA leadership.

82 Demands to lift the ICC warrants by the LRA commanders were reported in LexisNexis sources on 16 April 2007 and 9 July 2007. Additionally, the LRA delegation is regularly quoted during the talks with demands to lift the warrants.

The ICC clearly contributed to the failure of the talks by undermining security guarantees.[83] The ICC thus increased the Resolve of the LRA commanders to fight since it made peaceful alternatives less attractive in the absence of credible guarantees against prosecution. Taking into consideration that there were many flaws in the negotiation process, it would be disingenuous to claim that the Juba Talks would have succeeded without the ICC investigations. Nevertheless, it is clear that the ICC strongly contributed to the two main reasons for the failure of the talks: the lack of credible security guarantees for the LRA high command and the reliance on unreliable delegations on the side of the LRA.

Drafting a peace agreement that satisfies the security needs of indicted rebel commanders, and still respects the accountability demands of the Rome Statute, is a serious challenge. Peace negotiations in conflicts with ICC investigations will remain complicated undertakings for the time being. This is particularly true for conflicts in which the factual knowledge and the legal know-how concerning the Rome Statute are low among both parties to the conflict, as illustrated in the case of the LRA conflict. It is not entirely clear whether the LRA understood that the GoU actually was not able to independently lift the ICC warrants,[84] and President Museveni himself clearly underestimated the independence of the Court when he decided to refer the case.[85] The Juba Talks were the first case in which these challenges during negotiations emerged. Yet, the lessons have not been sufficiently taken into account by the advocates of international trials because it was too easy to dismiss the failure of the talks as the result of Kony's irrational behaviour. The analysis conducted here has left little doubt that the ICC did have an impact on the failure of the Juba Talks and that this effect should be taken seriously.

[83] There are indicators that the ICC warrants also threatened to undermine Kony's security within the LRA. Some reports stated that Ongwen and Odhiambo had threatened to kill Kony if he signed an agreement with the GoU. Apparently, Ongwen and Odhiambo feared that Kony would double-cross them in order to bargain for a lighter sentence at the ICC (Groth 2011).

[84] Initially, knowledge about the ICC among LRA commanders was poor. Otti reportedly thought that the ICC warrants would lead to him being captured and executed abroad (Schomerus 2010a, p. 96).

[85] The government had claimed several times that it could stop the cases if peace was a possibility. In reality, this is not true since that decision can only be taken by the Pre-Trial Chamber on request of the Chief Prosecutor (Allen 2006, p. 94).

Again, the interplay between procedural decisions taken by the organs of the Court and the perceptions on the ground played a significant role for the development of this causal mechanism. When the Juba Talks began in summer 2006, the ICC was widely perceived to be an obstacle to the peace process, especially in northern Uganda. Local civil society organisations, spearheaded by the Acholi Religious Leaders Peace Initiative (ARLPI), were critical of the investigations (ARLPI 2009). These opinions were supported by the local population who voiced fears that the ICC might disrupt the peace process (ICG 2006c, p. 9, Oxfam 2007, p. 15, Pham et al. 2007, p. 5). But also past and present mediators, including Betty Bigombe and Pax Christi chief mediator Wesselink, criticised the ICC (Anderson 2006, Apuuli 2006, p. 180, HRW 2009b, p. 30).

Due to the high pressure exerted on the Court by various actors, the Prosecution decided to adopt a low key approach (Allen 2006, p. 123 and 193, Mallinder 2008, p. 281, Peskin 2009a, p. 682).[86] In late 2005, Moreno Ocampo had announced that LRA prosecutions might be temporarily stopped in the 'Interests of Justice' as foreseen in Article 53 of the Rome Statute (Peskin 2009a, p. 682). He also stated in 2006 that he received regular updates about the peace talks and that the OTP and the GoU shared the view that '*. . . justice and peace have worked together thus far and can continue to work together*' (Moreno Ocampo 2006b). Behind the scenes, ICC officials remained extremely sceptical that Kony wanted peace though (ICG 2006c, p. 8).

When it seemed that the parties were approaching an agreement that included an attempt to circumnavigate the ICC prosecutions in northern Uganda, the OTP changed its approach by aggressively demanding accountability. In a June 2007 speech in Nuremberg, Moreno Ocampo made clear that he saw the lack of cooperation with the ICC and compromises made on accountability as the real threats to lasting peace in northern Uganda. He said that the LRA was blackmailing its victims and demanded that there should be no compromise on legality and accountability (Moreno Ocampo 2008a, p. 12–13). He reminded the Ugandan Government that it had international obligations to ensure accountability and that he would not accept the attempt to push the ICC out (Leonard 2010, p. 168, Otim and Wierda 2008, p. 23). As mentioned above, the newspaper analysis shows that calls for respecting

[86] ICC staff confirmed in interviews with Tim Allen that adopting a low-key approach was a deliberate decision (Allen 2006, p. 193).

the warrants or arresting the LRA were brought forward nearly on a monthly basis by ICC organs. The view within the OTP was summarised by a senior staff member in February 2011. According to him, the ICC had consistently warned the international community during the Juba negotiations that the LRA was trying to buy time. The ICC had also criticised the fact that money was given to the LRA without any possibility to trace how it was being used. He said that it was naïve of the international community to negotiate with thugs, as the LRA was only trying to blackmail its way out of the warrants. He stated that the mediators were desperate to show that it was possible to negotiate with the LRA. Therefore, LRA ceasefire breaches were downplayed or attributed to renegade SPLM groups (Rastan 2011a).

This statement is essentially a summary of most of Moreno Ocampo's public declarations during the later stages of the talks. These statements show that the OTP did not believe that the LRA was negotiating genuinely and thus stepped up the pressure in a conscious strategic decision. On several occasions after the talks failed, Ocampo publicly repeated his conviction that the LRA never had negotiated in earnest. (e.g. Invisible Children 2012).

Yet, as a diplomat put it during an interview, the ICC lacks the insight to decide whether the negotiations were genuine (Expert Interview 2011a). The OTP should refrain from taking decisions concerning its prosecution strategy based on its own analyses of complex conflict situations. Top officials at the OTP firmly believed that the LRA was not willing to negotiate genuinely. This turned out to be a self-fulfilling prophecy, since the procedural decisions taken at the OTP contributed to the undermining of security guarantees for the LRA. International prosecutors often argue that they are not taking political decisions but following the law. In a similar vein, the OTP always insisted that it had no legal room for manoeuvre in demanding the implementation of the warrants. But as this overview of the prosecution strategy has shown, there is some room for manoeuvre in how vocal the ICC wants to be in demanding the implementation of the warrants. The OTP clearly influenced the progression of the Juba Talks through its communication strategy.

The OTP's strategy to aggressively demand accountability during the later stages of the talks was supported both by international backers of the Court and other ICC organs. The Court's international supporters believed that international values of justice and accountability were at stake when the GoU started to question the ICC warrants. They therefore decided to support the OTP's campaign for accountability. The Pre-Trial Chamber had started monitoring GoU cooperation with the Court in decisions taken on 15 September 2006 and 30 November 2006. It also demanded detailed information on the planned Accountability Agreement by the GoU on 29 February 2008 and 18 June 2008. Along the same lines, Phakiso Mochochoko, Senior Legal Advisor at the ICC Registry, reportedly reminded Kony's lawyers that the warrants remained enforceable, and that only a legal process could stop them (Apuuli 2008a, p. 812). This combined pressure to uphold the warrants obviously increased Kony's suspicion of walking into a trap and made a signature less probable.[87] The later statement of the Pre-Trial Chamber confirming its jurisdiction in the Ugandan case despite Ugandan efforts to design a national plan for transitional justice complements the picture.

b. Hindering constructive dialogue and rapprochement

In the LRA conflict there are two areas in which a negative ICC impact on the rapprochement between the conflict parties could be expected. First, as shown in the section on negotiations above, the LRA has often been belittled and not been taken seriously by the government during negotiations (see Finnström 2010b, p. 151). This adds both to the Reasons and to the Resolve of the LRA. By indicting only the LRA side of the conflict, the ICC could have amplified this inequality between the parties by further undermining the LRA's legitimacy. This could not be ascertained in the case study since it is a psychological effect mainly affecting the current commanders of the LRA with whom interviews were not possible for obvious reasons. On the other hand, the ICC did complicate the rapprochement between the parties by undermining the amnesty approach that was preferred by many Acholi due to cultural reasons. The ICC investigations both scared individual LRA officers and soldiers into sticking with the rebellion and counter-acted attempts of the Acholi to facilitate a rapprochement between the parties through a reconciliation approach.

Belittling the LRA becomes a problem for rapprochement in the context of the Acholi reconciliation culture. Acholi ideas of reconciliation

[87] One of the few fathomable ways out of this deadlock would have been to find a deal that granted Kony exile in a country acceptable to him. Betty Bigombe recently revealed that she had been close to sealing a deal with the Gaddafi regime to offer Kony exile in 2006, but Kony apparently backed off at the last minute, saying that he '*did not trust Arabs*' (Gettleman 2012).

are based on the equality of the parties that decide to reconcile. The LRA thus needs to be accepted as an equal party in order to gain their heartfelt consent to a treaty (Finnström 2010b, p. 153). The conflict overview section has shown how important Acholi cultural values are in the LRA's ideology. Yet, the ICC narrative of the conflict, championed in particular by its Chief Prosecutor Moreno Ocampo, falls in line with the GoU description of the LRA as a criminal cult without any real objectives.

If the LRA is understood as a crazy cult, this already implies that a military solution is the most appropriate since the other party's rationality is questioned. The ICC was therefore offered an incentive for the GoU to follow a military approach, since negotiations with criminals are immoral and pointless if one follows the ICC's line of argument.[88] The GoU initially did not take the LRA demands seriously, and the ICC is in fact encouraging this by describing the LRA as mere bunch of crazy criminals who should be arrested.

The LRA obviously also saw a connection between the ICC's involvement and the GoU's approach of belittling the LRA. Kony stated that the ICC involvement in northern Uganda was a consequence of President Museveni 'spoiling' the name of the LRA at the ICC (Schomerus 2010b, p. 127). In the words of another analyst, the ICC's focus on individual criminal justice blurred questions of political justice that needed to be discussed in order to tackle the root causes of the conflict (Hovil 2012, p. 13). The influence of the ICC investigations on the perception of the LRA as thugs is certainly there, but its extent and impact is hard to measure in practice.

On the other hand, the effect of the ICC investigations on the amnesty approach can be measured with the number of LRA returnees. Several interviewees and researchers – including former LRA officers – claim that the number of LRA returnees dropped sharply because LRA officers and fighters feared to be prosecuted by the ICC if they returned home (Charles 2011, Expert Interview 2011k, Loum 2011, Okello 2011). Indeed, the number of LRA returnees received at the GUSCO Centre in Gulu dropped sharply after the ICC investigations came into play. This trend was confirmed by both World Vision, an organisation that operates another reception centre in the area and the Chairman of the Ugandan

[88] For example, Moreno Ocampo stated that the LRA was using peace talks to advance their *'criminal goals'* at a conference in Chicago on 9 April 2008 and stated in a widely viewed advocacy video that the LRA had repeatedly used peace talks to re-arm and attack (Invisible Children 2012, at 12 minutes).

Amnesty Commission (Mallinder 2009b, p. 62, Onega 2011, WV Uganda 2011). A former member of the LRA high command claimed that the ICC warrant stopped LRA commander Raska Lukwiya from defecting, and there are rumours that Dominic Ongwen also abandoned plans to defect after he heard about the warrant (Baines 2009, p. 176, LRA Commander 2011).

Apart from this direct effect of the ICC investigations on individual LRA members, the ICC investigations also offered Kony a convenient tool to scare his soldiers into staying in the bush. Kony is using the ICC to keep his fighters, officers and commanders in line by telling them that they would all face prosecutions by the ICC if they decided to return. He is actively denying his troops access to the radio and other news sources to make sure his version of the ICC investigations cannot be questioned. There are even speculations that Kony deliberately orders his officers to commit atrocities so they become trapped or believe themselves to be trapped by ICC warrants (Lancaster et al. 2011).

Nevertheless, the ICC was not the only factor that caused the reduction in the numbers of LRA returnees. Another reason is that the government regularly sent mixed signals to the LRA commanders concerning the amnesty. Local researchers report that there were doubts about the government commitment to the amnesty among returnees (Hovil and Lomo 2005, p. 19). Additionally, the GoU prolonged the amnesty law in an unpredictable manner and sometimes for very short periods (Hovil and Lomo 2005, p. 19). The unexpected expiration of the amnesty law in May 2012 is a case in point illustrating the unpredictable government policy.

Finally, the DPP undermined the trust in the amnesty law by trying the former mid-level commander Thomas Kwoyelo despite his amnesty application (Okello 2011, UN Source 2011). The legal situation has become even more uncertain with the expiry of the Amnesty Act in May 2012. Internal Affairs Minister Onek has stated that courts will now decide in each individual case whether they will prosecute crimes committed by former rebels or not and that new legislation on justice and accountability would be drafted later in the year (IRIN 2012b).

The figures for amnesty applications as well as the opinions of experts voiced in interviews suggest that the ICC investigations were the main reason for the drop of LRA defections, at least during the time between late 2004 and early 2008. It is particularly striking that LRA defections dropped sharply immediately after the ICC started to investigate according to the Amnesty Commission (Onega 2011). Reports about

LRA defections in LexisNexis and other sources also indicate that there was a huge number of defections in the second half of 2004 before the ICC started investigating. The reports of defections reduced significantly after the ICC decision to investigate became public.When the LRA moved out of Uganda and southern Sudan to the CAR and the DRC during 2007 and 2008, defecting became much more difficult for LRA members. The sheer distance to their native Uganda and the hostility of the local population became two additional factors discouraging defections.

Again, the OTP had the possibility to influence the ICC's impact on LRA defections through its procedural decisions. If the ICC could successfully communicate that the indictments only threatened the top leadership of the LRA, the court might even encourage defections along the lines of the marginalisation mechanism (Section 5.2.3b). The ICC indeed tried to communicate to the LRA fighters that they would not be tried by the Court. For example, the ICC Registrar said on a Ugandan radio station that there were no plans to indict further LRA Commanders on 14 April 2006. The ICC outreach staff in Uganda also tried to emphasise that the ICC's mandate demands prosecutions of the top LRA leadership, but not the rank and file. These efforts of the ICC outreach were undermined due to the tight control that the LRA leadership exerts over their officers and fighters.

5.2.5 *Heightening tensions*

The claims connected to the heightening tensions causal mechanisms are very specific to particular conflict contexts. In the case of Uganda, they are closely connected to the timing of the ICC investigations in Uganda. Some local researchers are arguing for a sequenced approach in Uganda, in which justice should be implemented after the conflict has stopped. They argue that the warrants should have been issued after the LRA had returned from the bush to ensure that warrants would not hinder peace efforts (Hovil and Quinn 2005, p. 19–21).

Other claims are more general and relate to possible attacks by rebel groups in retaliation of arrest warrants.

a. Triggering spoiler retaliation

One of the claims from the literature is that the ICC arrest warrants against the LRA leadership triggered retaliatory attacks aimed at international aid organisations and NGOs working in the area (also Expert Interview 2011i).

In theory, such a reaction by indicted rebel groups seems plausible. The issuing of arrest warrants could heighten the Resolve of LRA commanders since they perceive that negotiations are no longer a way out of the situation. Additionally, the ICC's involvement on the side of the government could become a new Reason for the armed struggle, especially if the Court's involvement is seen as unfair and biased. Indeed, statistical correlation suggests that attacks after the issuing of the ICC warrants were connected to the Court's decision. The fact that the LRA Commanders had threatened such retaliatory attacks in the past adds credence to the statistics.

LRA attacks against humanitarian organisations were not a new phenomenon when the ICC issued its warrants. The LRA issued threats against aid convoys as early as 12 April 1998 (AI 1999a). Additionally, the LRA threatened to attack humanitarian organisations for allegedly supporting the government policy of establishing protected camps in August 2002. In June 2003, the LRA issued another threat against aid workers, threatening to attack church installations. There have been regular reports of LRA ambushes on humanitarian organisations and church personnel that date back to at least 2001 (Rodriguez 2009, p. 33). HRW reported attacks on WFP vehicles in 2003, before the Ugandan situation had been referred to the ICC (HRW 2003, p. 4). An analysis of the newspaper reports confirms that ambushes on vehicles of aid agencies have been sporadically carried out by the LRA since at least 2000. The attacks are summarised in Figure 5.3.

The graph shows that there had been sporadic attacks during the whole conflict. 0–1 attacks per quarter are the norm. The figures peak twice, with five attacks in late 2002 and again in late 2005. The second peak coincides with the issuing of the arrest warrants by the ICC. A correlation analysis between the number of attacks and the issuing of the warrants suggests a strong impact of the ICC warrants on the number of attacks (Pearson test, 562**).

The string of attacks that might be connected to the ICC warrants started on 25 October 2005, on the very same day on which Otti called a Ugandan MP and confirmed that the LRA knew about the arrest warrants. Additionally, there were reports of LRA threats to kill Westerners as a reaction to the ICC indictments (Finnström 2008, p. 143). It is therefore highly plausible that the LRA reacted to the ICC warrants with spontaneous attacks. Even though the LRA later denied that there had

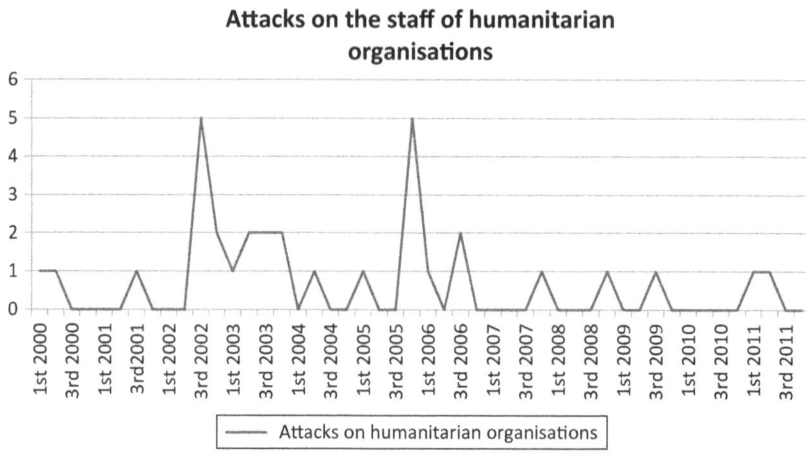

Figure 5.3: Number of LRA attacks on staff members of humanitarian organisations per quarter

been aimed attacks on humanitarian convoys, the sudden uptick of attacks and the chronology of the events make a coincidence unlikely. The LRA probably decided to deny the armed attacks on aid convoys later during the Juba Talks in line with their strategy to present themselves as a credible and legitimate rebel group.

The LRA retaliation attacks are a good illustration of the dilemmas between humanitarian work on the ground and international prosecutions. Even before the warrants had been issued, humanitarian organisations voiced fears about negative repercussions for their work in the area and urged the ICC to take up a 'peace first' and 'wait and see' policy (Allen 2006, p. 81–82, Hovil and Quinn 2005).

The relationship to the ICC is even more complicated for organisations that are directly cooperating with the Court. This is, for example, the case for UN OCHA in Uganda. The organisation was supporting ICC investigations by providing equipment and accommodation to ICC staff. The humanitarian staff of OCHA had a split opinion about this cooperation because they were afraid that ICC investigations could complicate their work on the ground. At the same time, it remained unclear whether and how the ICC would use confidential information received by UN staff in its investigations (Heilmann 2006, p. 75–76).

The procedural decisions taken at the OTP had an influence on this causal mechanism. If international prosecutors decide to issue arrest warrants before the indicted rebels are safely contained, the issuing of warrants may lead to retaliatory attacks. A better coordination between the OTP and humanitarian actors on the ground, as well as a better preparation of the UPDF and other armies in the region to protect the humanitarian staff against retaliatory attacks, could have helped to mitigate the impact.

b. Re-opening old wounds

This causal mechanism is of no immediate relevance for the LRA conflict. Rather than re-opening old wounds by investigating older crimes, the ICC solely focuses on recent LRA crimes. Older massacres are excluded through the time limit of the ICC jurisdiction starting in July 2002.

c. Bolstering support for hardliners

Similar to the effect of discouraging the defection of additional LRA fighters as described in Section 5.2.4b, the ICC investigations might have led to more cohesion within the ranks of the LRA and to an even stronger position of Joseph Kony within the LRA due to the warrant issued against him. The number of LRA defections lessened after the issuing of the ICC warrants. The Chairman of the Amnesty Commission confirmed that this was also due to the fact that the LRA leadership used the ICC indictments to generate fear among their officers and fighters of being tried by the ICC in order to consolidate their control over the group (IRIN 2005a). Furthermore, the ICC warrant was an additional reason for Kony to make sure that no more LRA fighters defected. A former LRA officer explained that Kony is now intent on using the abductees as his human shields against the ICC (Okello 2011). As one analyst described it, the LRA is now fighting on without a cause just to buy time and dodge the ICC warrants (Nakumbi 2011). At the same time, the ICC warrants strengthened the position of GoU hardliners arguing for a military solution of the conflict.

The issuing of ICC warrants did not lead to a split within the LRA as some might have expected. Due to the popularity of the indicted commanders Odhiambo and Ongwen, the LRA has rather consolidated its ranks under ICC pressure. Through executing Vincent Otti, the main advocate for a negotiated solution of the conflict, Kony has reinforced his control of the LRA. Even though the LRA lost about 300 fighters in the short term due to the leadership split during the Juba Talks, the overall development during the last years was one of consolidation rather than fracturing. After the death of Otti, there is no LRA commander who could challenge Kony and offer a realistic alternative to Kony's guerrilla campaign by engaging in negotiations with the government. In the process of consolidating his grip over the LRA, Joseph Kony skilfully used the ICC warrants to his ends by closing the ranks of the high command and scaring officers and fighters into staying in the bush.

On the side of the GoU, the ICC indictments have encouraged the UPDF to pursue a military approach to the conflict. This has been illustrated by Uganda's announcements and threats to hunt down the LRA in Sudan and the DRC. The Ugandan government argued shortly after the ICC warrants were issued that they legitimised UPDF actions beyond Uganda's borders aimed at hunting down the LRA (Allen 2006, p. 186 and 191, Branch 2007b, p. 184). The ICC warrants were also an additional argument for the hardliners in the Ugandan government to oppose peace talks with the LRA (Branch 2007b, p. 185, Nouwen and Werner 2010, p. 949). In this atmosphere, peace talks in Juba only became possible due to the insistence of the GoSS and strong international pressure on the GoU to enter into talks; the GoU had no intrinsic motivation to talk peace. The ICC warrants therefore strengthened the Resolve of the GoU to fight by supporting the position of the hardliners.

The procedural decisions of the OTP to focus on the LRA played an important role for this mechanism. The one-sided investigation policy made it possible for the GoU to use the ICC warrants in a narrative justifying the military approach against the LRA. On the other hand, it strengthened Kony's hand in controlling LRA fighters and officers. A more balanced approach towards investigating the conflict would have made it more difficult for hardliners on both sides to use the ICC warrants to their ends.

d. De-stabilisation, fragmentation, power vacuum

This causal mechanism is of no relevance for the LRA conflict. The control of the government over Uganda has not been weakened through the ICC investigations. Arguably, the ICC has even helped the government to gain more control over the conflict. There are no indications of a further de-stabilisation of the situation in the LRA-affected areas due to the ICC warrants, either. The situation has rather become more stable since the ICC started investigating because the LRA has been pushed out of northern Uganda. Additionally, the LRA attacks that took place after the ICC warrants largely followed patterns already known from previous phases of the conflict.

5.3 Conclusion

Uganda is now closer to reaching a durable peace since violence in the northern district is no longer endemic and in fact is constantly reducing. But problems remain. The situation remains unstable, as threats of physical violence against formerly abducted persons or in the context of land disputes remain common and fears of new LRA incursions have not been addressed. The danger of future violence in Uganda also remains as long as rebellions in different regions of Uganda continue to be active and the government conducts violent crackdowns against opposition demonstrations. Against this background, contributions of international investigations and trials towards reconciliation and building the rule of law would be crucial for reaching a durable peace. At the current stage, such effects of the ICC investigations are not measurable though. Due to the lack of any tangible contributions in the area of reconciliation, a decisive impact of the ICC to ensuring durable peace in Uganda cannot be claimed at the current stage.

The case study has produced several important results. First, the literature was claiming the presence of eleven of the fifteen causal mechanisms identified in the cross-case overview, which is a surprisingly high amount of claims for a single case. The case study has confirmed that an impact of the ICC can be convincingly shown for eight causal mechanisms in the LRA conflict. This emphasises how complex the effects of international investigations in conflict contexts are. There are many causal mechanisms active at different stages of the conflict; sometimes their effects are overlapping. Table 5.2 below provides an overview of the different effects and when they were measurable.

Since the opening of the investigations through Moreno Ocampo in a joint press conference with Museveni, the ICC strengthened the voices within the GoU who called for a military solution through its decision to focus its investigations on the LRA and describe them as a crazy terrorist organisation. This clear focus on the LRA helped to isolate the rebel group internationally, even though it was not the main reason for their isolation. Between 2004 and 2008, the ICC helped to keep the pressure on the GoS not to resume the support on the LRA. During that time, the LRA was also deterred from committing further large-scale atrocities because the high command hoped it could negotiate away the

Table 5.2: *Overview of ICC Effects in the LRA Conflict (a grey shade is a partial effect, black shade a strong effect)*

Investigation phases	Referral to opening investigations		Investigations to issuing of warrants		Warrants in force		Warrants confirmed	
1. Rule-of-law mechanisms								
Human rights protection and respect for law								
Capacity building / reforms								
Counter-impunity								
2. Reconciliation and transformation								
Meeting victim needs								
Individualising guilt								
3. Isolation and deterrence								
Pressure and inducement								
Marginalisation								
International isolation								
Special deterrence								
4. Blocking conflict resolution								
Blocking negotiations								
Blocking rapproachment								
5. Heightening tensions and polarisation								
Triggering spoiler retaliation								
Re-opening wounds								
Furthering hardliner support								
De-stabilisation								
Conflict phases	**Full-scale war in northern Uganda and southern Sudan**	**Military pressure on LRA**	**2004–2005 negotiations**	**Military pressure on LRA**	**Military pressure on LRA**	**2006–2008 negotiations**	**2006–2008 negotiations**	**Conflict in DRC and CAR, moderate pressure on LRA**

investigations or warrants. The ICC warrants thus played a secondary role in bringing the LRA to the negotiation table in an attempt to get rid of the investigations. At the same time, the ICC complicated rapprochement between the parties by reinforcing a narrative that described the LRA as a crazy terrorist sect and contributed to the belittling of the LRA through the GoU. When the warrants were finally issued, they caused a string of violent LRA attacks in retaliation. The fact that warrants were issued against the LRA had an impact on countering impunity in the conflict area, but that effect did not trickle down to achieve a general improvement in accountability. By the end of the negotiations, the existence of the ICC warrants sparked legal reforms in Uganda in an attempt to challenge the admissibility of the case under the complementarity provision. In the end, the ICC played an important role in the failure of the negotiations by undermining security guarantees for the LRA and keeping the LRA high command away from the negotiation table.

This overview emphasises how difficult it is to assess the impact of ICC investigations in a conflict as the effects of investigations change over time. And as if that was not enough, several effects may be active at the same time, some of them even directly contradicting each other (e.g. deterrence and spoiler retaliation). For the literature, this is an important finding. A lot of the research published is based on one or two case studies and focuses on one or two particular causal mechanisms. Despite their strong focus on particular mechanisms, these studies tend to make sweeping statements and broad claims about the impact of accountability measures in conflict situations (e.g. Akhavan 2009).

Second, many of the claims brought forward in the literature regarding the LRA conflict ignore the local context of the conflict, specifically the history of the conflict before the ICC investigations began. This is especially true for the isolation claims, one of the most repeated claims in the literature on Uganda. The ICC surely had some impact on the isolation of the LRA, but the increasing international pressure on the Government of Sudan over more than five years is often ignored. This pressure increased independently and had only little to do with the ICC investigations. Clearly, this massive long-term pressure played a greater role in the LRA's isolation than the issuing of five arrest warrants by a recently established international court. Two further examples of claims in which the local context of the LRA conflict was equally being neglected are the inducement and the individualising guilt claims. The inducement claims argue that the role of the ICC in the inception of peace talks was important while ignoring the work of civil society organisations that kept on pushing for a negotiated solution. The individualising guilt claims ignore that individual guilt might not work in community- and clan-based societies like the Acholi.

Third, the literature needs to draw more knowledge from the research in the fields of international relations and peace and conflict research to fully understand some of the potential effects of ICC trials in conflict contexts. The pressure and inducement claims brought forward in much of the literature on Uganda, for example, ignore the important role of the strong military pressure on the LRA that was accompanied by a rising number of defections. No peace and conflict researcher would consider attributing a strong role to the ICC investigations in bringing the LRA to the negotiation table in a situation in which all conflict theories would expect the LRA to negotiate anyway.

The same is true for the role of the ICC investigations in terms of hardening the position of conflict parties (Section 5.2.5c) or serving as a whitewash for government violations (Section 5.2.1a). The polarisation claims in the literature are mainly brought forward by country specialists (Allen 2006, Branch 2007a, 2007b) and are in line with the critical human rights literature in IR (Pia and Diez 2009). Even though the idea that addressing crimes in conflict contexts might lead to further polarisation is not new, the discussion has not been sufficiently absorbed by literature dealing with accountability measures in conflicts. Both the cases of Darfur and the LRA have illustrated this.

The finding that a conflict party can use ICC investigations to cloud the view on its own human rights record is an effect that has only recently been identified in the literature (Rodman and Booth 2013). There are strong arguments that the ICC served as a whitewash for the UPDF and the GoU. Critical human rights literature could help to shed more light on these effects, as it predicts that one-sided investigations of human rights violations reifies existing antagonisms instead of helping to address human rights issues (e.g. Pia and Diez 2009, p. 2).

Fourth, most of the claims brought forward in the literature are not yet based on solid empirical findings. Again, this has been illustrated by both the Darfur and the LRA case studies. The LRA case study has confirmed eight of the claims brought forward in the literature on Uganda and has – wherever possible – provided the necessary empirical foundations to prove these claims through figures, newspaper analyses and interviews with experts. Most of these claims stand on very solid foundations after having undergone an in-depth contextual analysis that took other developments and external factors into consideration.

In some cases, the claims from the literature have been confirmed. In these cases, the analysis offered additional information to assess how strong the independent effect of ICC investigations really is. In three cases, the claimed effect was weaker than suggested in the literature or only applied to one of the two conflict parties (special deterrence, international isolation, countering impunity).

The case study has also shown that ICC investigations might have different effects on the conflict parties, something that is often not considered in the literature to date. The case study showed that the accountability impact of the ICC on the LRA and the GoU differs strongly and that the deterrence effect is of partial relevancy only for the LRA side. Again, an important finding of the Darfur case study has been confirmed in the Ugandan context.

Some of the admittedly weaker claims in the literature have been proven wrong, for example, the marginalisation, the human rights protection and the individualisation of guilt claims. Strong general claims have been brought forward for the protection of human rights through trials on the basis of statistical surveys. The finding that ICC investigations have helped the GoU to deter human rights pressure gives even more reason to question the quantitative results obtained so far.

Finally, the case study has shown that the procedural decisions and the justice perceptions connected to the investigations have a strong influence on the causal mechanisms. This finding emphasises how important it would be for the literature to differentiate more accurately between different international investigations and trials. So far, much of the quantitative literature tends to conflate different contexts of transitional justice and does not differentiate between transitional justice institutions with very different mandates.

The case study has shown that not only international justice institutions with different mandates deliver different results, but that the impact of ICC investigations may differ strongly depending on the procedural decisions taken at the organs of the Court. For example, it makes a difference whether an investigation was triggered through a self-referral, through a referral of another State Party, through an UNSC referral or through *proprio motu*.

But as illustrated, for example, in the sections on human rights protection, the blocking of negotiations, and the combating of impunity mechanisms, even smaller procedural decisions taken by the Court's organs had a real impact on the causal mechanisms. Such decisions include, for example, whether the Pre-Trial Chamber decides to monitor a situation actively, as was the case during the accountability negotiations in Juba. Other examples in this context include decisions concerning how publicly and openly the Prosecution should conduct its investigations, and how much outreach should be done by the Registry. One-sided investigations might further pressure and inducement mechanisms targeted at one party, but in the case of Uganda they undermined mechanisms of meeting victims' needs and combating impunity. Going for one-sided investigations might even help the party that is not being investigated to whitewash its own human rights record.

The perceptions of the ICC's work played a role in both the human rights protection as well as in the victim's needs mechanisms. If investigations are seen as one-sided and out of touch with local needs, these causal mechanisms cannot be expected to gain traction because they aim at changing the mind-set of people. Additionally, where local perceptions of justice differ strongly from Western retributive notions, some of the claims of criminal justice supporters ring hollow. This was illustrated by the individualisation of guilt claims that do not hold in a northern Ugandan context in which collective responsibility is emphasised.

The Ugandan case study shows that the effects of ICC investigations are a lot weaker and more limited than much of the literature would indicate, especially in conflict contexts. Again, from the point of view of peace and conflict research this is not a surprise. The focus of the ICC on the worst perpetrators can hardly be expected to solve a conflict. As many authors point out, the conflict roots need to be tackled. This often includes the need for deep social and political change (ICG 2006c, p. 2, Van Acker 2004, p. 357). These limitations of the impact of ICC investigations are inherent to conflicts and should receive more attention. The influence of ICC investigations can be expected to be particularly limited in intractable conflicts that have been ongoing for several decades, like the LRA conflict.

PART III

Results

6

Transcending the peace-justice divide

Who argues that peace cannot be bartered in exchange for justice, under any circumstances, must be prepared to justify the likely prolongation of an armed conflict.

(TRC Sierra Leone 2004, §79)

[T]he debate on how to 'reconcile' peace and justice or how to 'sequence' them has lasted more than a decade. Today, we have achieved a conceptual breakthrough: the debate is no longer between peace and justice but between peace and what kind of justice.

(Ban Ki-Moon 2010a)

The case studies of northern Uganda and Darfur have shown that the effects of ICC investigations on ongoing intra-state conflicts are manifold and complex. It is difficult to claim a linear connection between accountability (or justice), embodied through the activities of the ICC, and peace, as a reduction of violence, in any of the case studies. Over the course of conflicts, peace and accountability seem to be either mutually enforcing, as in the early phase of the ICC investigations in Uganda, or at odds with each other, as after the issuing of the al-Bashir arrest warrants by the ICC.

In much of the literature, the relationship between accountability and peace is discussed more broadly as the relationship between peace and justice. Most of the literature argues either that peace and justice are mutually enforcing and that investigations thus have positive effects, or that peace and justice cancel each other out and that investigations thus have negative effects. The relationship between peace and justice seems to be much more complex than that. The findings of the case studies are a call for transcending the peace-justice divide in analysing the impact of accountability measures in conflicts. This section will briefly discuss the terms peace, justice and conflict and then introduce the conflict spectrum as a new model to understand the complicated relationship of peace and justice in conflicts.

The second part of this section will then introduce procedural decisions taken at the Court as well as local and international justice perceptions as important third variables that emerged during the case studies. The procedures and perceptions go a long way in explaining the complex findings of the case studies. They are closely interlinked with each other and both marred with dilemmas. These dilemmas emerge when international courts navigate the grey area between objectives of peace and justice that is inherent to their mandate in conflicts.

6.1 Beyond peace versus justice

To better grasp the relationship between peace and justice, I propose a process-based definition of peace focusing on how conflicts are treated in a society. Where conflicts are solved violently, there is no peace. If conflicts are resolved through non-violent means, the degree of peace increases. The stability of peace is determined by two factors. One: whether the non-violent conflict management measures are robust, and two: by the extent to which conflict potentials are held in check.

Justice is connected to peace as it in principle furthers non-violent conflict resolution measures. Yet, accountability demands in the name of justice can lead to conflict escalations at crucial points during the process towards a more stable peace.

6.1.1 Peace

There is no road towards peace, peace is the road.

Mahatma Ghandi (quoted in Muñoz 2006, p. 411)

Peace is not everything but without peace everything is nothing.

Willy Brandt, former Chancellor of the Federal Republic of Germany (Brandt 1986)

Entire books have been written with the aim of defining peace and its constitutional elements. Still, a comprehensive and widely accepted definition has not been reached so far. Especially the question of which factors are necessary to guarantee a durable peace is still being hotly debated. While the mechanisms of escalation that lead to violence and sustain it have been analysed for decades, the interest of academics in a stand-alone definition of peace is comparatively recent. The dominant concepts of peace have long been a mere negation of war (Lutz 2004,

p. 24, Mühleisen 2004, p. 40).[1] It is thus fair to say that we currently understand more of violence than of peace (Muñoz 2006, p. 394).

But there are also concepts of peace that went beyond the mere absence of war. The biblical interpretation of peace, *Shalom*, is one of them. It is based on mercy and loyalty as foundations of peace and justice (Haspel 1996, p. 438). The biblical interpretation thus for the first time explicitly connected justice to peace. This connection is exemplified well by a verse from the Book Isaiah: 'And the work of justice shall be peace, and the service of justice quietness, and security for ever' (Isaiah 32:16–17).

These examples from history and different cultural backgrounds show that peace is a universal concept but that notions of peace differ. Interpretations of peace can even be highly political. This is exemplified by the very different ideas of peace that, for example, the US Government, the peace movement and Islamic fundamentalists harbour. While the United States has a security-focused concept of peace, the peace movement heralds a pluralistic notion of peace. Islamic fundamentalists focus on religious ideas of peace as a condition agreeable to God. This list of peace definitions could be expanded at will. As a consequence, some conflicts are fought over definitions of peace (see de Waal 2007b, p. 367–368, Nitsche 2007, p. 43, Zartman 2000, p. 219).

Christoph Weller's definition of peace as a quest for *changing* aims is an attempt to do justice to this complexity (Weller 2004, p. 63). Additionally, Weller poses the question of whether it is appropriate to define peace as a condition, or if it should be understood as a fluid concept in motion ('a quest'). The distinction between static and fluid concepts plays a key role in contemporary attempts of defining peace and is of high relevance for understanding the impact of accountability measures on peace.

In peace and conflict research, the two dominant definitions of peace are negative and positive. Negative peace is defined as the mere absence or prevention of violence (Albert 2008, p. 38, Roberts 2006, p. 60), with its historical precedents in Greek and Roman definitions. Meanwhile, positive peace is a notion that goes beyond the mere absence of violence

[1] For the ancient Greek, war was the natural condition of the world. Therefore, their word for peace, *Eirene*, described a framework of ceasefires between wars. The Roman definition of peace, known as *Pax Romana*, was equally connected to the idea of war. It was based on the idea of pacifying areas after military victories and described the Roman peace order and the legal relations between former opponents after a war.

and includes structural conditions of peace like the acceptance of some core values (e.g. the respect for human rights). Traditionally, negative peace was seen as a condition, while positive peace introduced the notion of peace as an open-ended process.

The negative definition of peace is still widely used in political science and even more so in international law (Lutz 2004, p. 24 and 29, Müller 2003, p. 213, Weller 2004, p. 66). Nevertheless, there has been a gradual evolution of peace definitions in academic texts as well as in policy papers, moving from negative peace concepts towards ideas of positive peace based on the protection of human rights (Koppe 1996, p. 58, Lutz 2004, p. 24, Schultze and Zinterer 2004, p. 13). Still, there is no consensual definition of positive peace. Scholars agree that positive peace is incompatible with all forms of terror, atrocities and arbitrariness. In its narrow definitions, it excludes all forms of personal or structural violence[2] and demands justice, integration and satisfaction of the fundamental needs of people[3] (Albert 2008, p. 33–34, Lutz 2004, p. 24, Muñoz 2006, p. 399).

It is evident that many nations that are commonly considered as peaceful do not meet the high standards raised by the most detailed definitions of positive peace.[4] Narrow definitions of positive peace thus include a utopian element (Muñoz 2006, p. 400, Senghaas and Senghaas-Knobloch 2009, p. 126, Zartman 2000, p. 219).

Defining peace as a process captures the aspiration of meeting the conditions of a perfect positive peace by stopping violence, furthering human rights, putting an end to poverty, hunger and oppression. This process is not necessarily linear. As a conflict situation progresses towards a peaceful solution, violence or tensions may break out again unexpectedly.

Since the ICC is currently only investigating cases in Africa, it is important to question whether these definitions of peace, brought

[2] The term *structural violence* used in the narrow definitions of positive peace was first introduced by the Norwegian peace researcher Johan Galtung (Galtung 1972). According to Galtung, people suffer structural violence if they are subjected to inequality above the level absolutely necessary to sustain social reproduction (Bonacker and Imbusch 1996, p. 79).

[3] With fundamental needs, I mean those needs protected by the different Human Rights Charters and Covenants, including social and economic rights.

[4] Indeed, Galtung himself described the global order and the current North/South relations as structural violence when he developed the term (Galtung 1972).

forward by mainly Western authors, can be regarded as a sufficiently universal definition to be used in non-Western contexts.[5]

Asian and African concepts of peace traditionally emphasise well-being and the moral obligation to adhere to certain social norms. Among the most important of these norms are the respect for human life and dignity, universal responsibility and global cooperation (Albert 2008, p. 34–40). These values are rather close to the pre-conditions of positive peace described above. Still, for the analysis at hand a definition that focuses on the practical aspects of achieving peace, independent of the cultural background is needed. I therefore suggest a broad definition of peace as developed, for example, by Harald Müller and David Mendeloff (Mendeloff 2004, p. 363, Müller 2003, p. 213). The broad definition used here is a benchmark definition that introduces minimum requirements that need to be met to ensure a reasonably stable peace. In the following, the term peace is used to describe a situation without violence or tangible motivations or plans for using violence in a society (Müller 2003, p. 219). To clarify, a situation dominated by hate speech and physical threats, in which violence is not exercised but could break out practically any minute, does not qualify as peace.

Yet, reducing peace to a threshold definition would exclude the main argument of the proponents of accountability, claiming that accountability leads to a more stable peace by ensuring justice. Therefore, the threshold definition of peace should be combined with a process definition in order to grasp the stabilising effects of justice without losing analytical clarity. The process definition of peace describes peace as a continuum, stretching from the minimum threshold of peaceful power rivalry to utopian notions of perfect, non-violent interdependency (Bonacker and Imbusch 1996, p. 96). The minimum threshold definition can then be described as one (crucial) step in the process towards lasting, comprehensive peace. As long as conflict is still ongoing, the focus obviously lies on reaching the minimum threshold definition of peace. But as soon as the minimum threshold is reached, a process understanding of peace that allows for the inclusion of long-term effects of conflict management and conflict resolution kicks in.

[5] Indeed, some Western liberal definitions of peace have been criticised for lacking this cultural universality (Allan and Keller 2006, p. 1).

6.1.2 The conflict spectrum

Those who wage war justly aim at peace.

(Thomas Aquinas 1273)

Conflict is also increasingly being understood as a process in peace and conflict studies (Bonacker 2005, p. 13, Zartman 2000, p. 219). If both peace and conflicts are described as processes, the definitions can be merged to form what I call the conflict spectrum. Conflict is an overarching term, applicable to situations both in war and in peace time. The main difference between peace and war is how conflicts are being managed. On the spectrum, conflicts can be traced as they move from the total war mode of conflict, over increasingly civilised and non-violent forms of conflict management, to the utopian state of positive peace in which conflict potentials are so low and the mechanisms for solving them are so highly developed that they are no longer consciously perceived. On this spectrum, constituted by different forms of conflict actions, the minimum threshold definition of peace is the point at which violent methods of treating conflicts are replaced by non-violent methods. Conflict management and resolution measures aim to support this transformation by ending the violence and paving the way for a settlement. The positive causal mechanisms identified in Section 3.1 can be understood as such conflict management and resolution measures.

The conflict spectrum allows tracing conflicts as they move back and forth on the spectrum – from de-escalation to renewed fighting, to conflict resolution and transformation. At the same time, the impact of the ICC on these developments can be observed. The spectrum concept is flexible enough to grasp violence short of civil war definitions and thus avoids equating phases of low levels of violence with peace. This is a suitable approach for grasping how ICC proceedings influence ongoing conflicts, since the changes in the situation are of paramount interest. Additionally, it complements the use of a process-based analysis as applied in the case studies.

6.1.3 Justice

The concept of justice is familiar to everyone, as the demand for justice seems to be engrained in the nature of human kind (Akhavan 2009, p. 625, Dreier 1991b, p. 9). Natural scientists think that this characteristic human demand for justice plays an important role for the social life of societies since it leads to the punishment of members not acting in solidarity with the group (e.g. Tricomi et al. 2010). In times in which men depended on each other to survive, the urge of punishing egoistic behaviour was of vital importance. Primitive notions of justice can even be found in other, advanced social beings like primates (Whitehouse 2003). This natural demand for justice felt by individuals poses some requirements to the constitution of human societies. If a society, particularly its legal system, does not conform with notions of justice, it will collapse in the long run (see Jeong 2008, p. 147, Müller 2003, p. 241, Thakur 2010).

While justice clearly plays an important role for the peaceful cohabitation of human beings, it remains an abstract concept. What is perceived as just in some situations may be inappropriate in others. Justice in a family context is different from justice in working relations. The same goes for notions of justice in different cultures. Justice is in so far a concept similar to peace as it has some universal features and some features that are highly contextual.

As a first step, justice can be defined as a part of morality. To be more precise, it comprises those moral rules that are applied to societal relationships and are perceived to bear a special weight by the society. These moral rules manage the distribution of rights, duties, goods and burdens in a generally accepted way (Dreier 1991b, p. 12, Koller 2007, p. 7).

Yet, there are both formal as well as material criteria that these moral rules have to fulfil in order to be regarded as just. The first formal criterion of justice is the existence of a set of objective rules that regulates actions. The objectivity condition demands that these rules treat similar situations equally and that the rules can be generalised (Koller 2007, p. 7). The second criterion demands some sense of proportionality between the rule and the situation to which it is being applied.[6] Schmidtz and Dreier describe proportionality as the question of '*what people are due*'. The basic idea is to avoid somebody having to pay or suffer as a result of another person's actions (Dreier 1991b, p. 13, Schmidtz 2006, p. 9–10). I argue that these two formal criteria are essentially universal elements of justice. They can be summarised as the 'fairness' of rules.[7]

[6] This criterion excludes, for example, unreasonable and disproportional sanctions for immoral acts or crimes, or that one group receives a much higher share of social prosperity than the rest without any objective reason.

[7] Fairness indeed seems to capture the universal formal criteria of justice well. In a survey in Uganda, for example, the largest group (41 per cent) of northern Ugandans defined justice as 'being fair' (Pham et al. 2007, p. 30).

In contrast to the universal formal criteria, the material criteria for justice are highly dependent on context (Czempiel 1996, p. 105, Geertz 2000, p. 167). Material justice can be highly subjective, as different people might vary in their judgements if an action is to be perceived as just or not. Accordingly, there is no real academic consensus concerning even minimal criteria for material justice (Koller 2007, p.8). Distinguishing between formal and material criteria of justice allows grasping the paradoxical nature of justice. It is highly universal and individualised at the same time (Mani 2002, p. 186). Difference in cultural norms and values are one of the main reasons why notions of material justice differ so much. Legal anthropology has shown that legal ideas and notions of punishment differ vastly across cultures (Clarke 2009, p. 121, Geertz 2000, p. 167, Obarrio 2011, p. 24).

Despite the high context character of material justice, some rough categories can be distinguished. One central distinction is made between distributive justice and compensative justice. It goes back to the works of Aristotle and Thomas of Aquinas (Dreier 1991b, p. 14–15). While distributive justice applies to the distribution of goods and burdens according to some kind of merit, compensative justice applies to treaties and trade relations, as well as to the compensation of wrongdoing through punishment or re-compensation. The specific case of addressing past wrongs, which is the focus of transitional justice, belongs to the category of corrective justice which is a sub-category of compensative justice (Koller 2007, p. 8). Measures of corrective justice relate to issues of restitution (compensating the victims for losses and damages) or retribution (punishing the perpetrators). The aspect of restitution is emphasised if the focus is on compensating individual victims. Retribution becomes necessary when the crimes have been so grave that the prevention of their repetition through punishment is a common interest of the society (Koller 2007, p. 10).[8]

Both distributive justice and corrective justice are of importance in conflict contexts. Questions of distributive justice are usually among the root causes of conflicts. Questions of corrective justice play a role

[8] The creation of the ICC was indeed justified by the same argument. It was created '*Affirming that the most serious crimes of concern to the international community as a whole must not go unpunished*' (Preamble, Rome Statute). It is important to acknowledge that retribution has its roots in Western legal philosophy. It is a duty-based concept that goes back to Immanuel Kant and Georg Wilhelm Friedrich Hegel (Mani 2002, p. 33, Pillay 2009, p. 348).

when it comes to questions of dealing with past atrocities. But, as international criminal justice interventions clearly work along lines of corrective justice, the discussion will focus on this particular category of justice.

Even within the sub-field of corrective justice, ideas may differ widely across cultures. Most Westerners are not aware of how culturally-specific their ideas of corrective justice are. This starts with the notion of individual guilt, which has its roots in Western liberalism and emphasises Western concepts of the individual and selfhood (Clarke 2009, p. 55 and 235, Drumbl 2007, p. 5). Certain deeds are punished with the aim of protecting the rights and dignity of the individual. These rights have their moral roots in the sacredness of all living things and are thus of Christian/Jewish origin. The concept of persons as rights bearers is not generally accepted worldwide (Clarke 2009, p. 174). This has clear repercussions for the work of the ICC in conflict contexts, as the idea to punish individuals for atrocities is rooted in Western liberalism (Drumbl 2007, p. 5).[9]

Guilt and responsibility are assigned according to cultural rules while views about the appropriateness of punishments are produced and contested within cultural contexts (Clarke 2009, p. 205 and 235). Contrary to the dominant Western discourse, many Congolese MPs and citizens see the death penalty as the only efficient way to combat impunity (Toussaint 2010). Another example is the notion of justice in Islam, which is based on the faith in Allah. Whether an action is just depends on its compatibility with spiritual rules that have to be followed by a 'good Muslim'. In Nigeria, for example, a *fatwa* was called against a reporter defending the Miss World Contest in the capital of Abuja in December 2002 against criticism by orthodox Muslims. The violence that broke out among Muslims and Christians in the aftermath of that *fatwa* is justified from an Islamic point of view as it was committed trying to fulfil the duty towards Allah (Clarke 2009, p. 157–158). Pious Muslims may accept the *Sharia* even if it infringes human rights, as it is perceived as Allah's law (Clarke 2009, p. 205). From a Western point of view, mob violence is seen as a criminal act, no matter if it has been sanctioned by a *fatwa*. In fact, the ensuing violence could well have triggered the ICC's jurisdiction had the court not decided that the violence did not meet the gravity threshold (Clarke 2009, p. 168).

[9] This conflict becomes especially evident in the Ugandan case study (Chapter 5).

Western and African notions of justice are often set off against each other in discussions on accountability and justice in Africa. African ideas of justice are often described as restorative justice (e.g. Osaghae 2000, p. 211, Tutu 1999, p. 54–55), while Western justice is understood as primarily retributive (Hovil and Quinn 2005, p. 11). Restorative justice focuses more on the victims and the society and how to heal their wounds instead of prioritising the punishment of the perpetrators (see Hovil and Quinn 2005, p. 11–12, Olsen et al. 2010, p. 12). It implies a societal approach to the question of justice in which the people are part of the process (van der Merwe 2009, p. 119–120). Indeed, African notions of justice place a special emphasis on the need to restore the community after norms have been breached (Karbo 2008, p. 117, Obarrio 2011, p. 32, Zartman 2000, p. 221).

Western notions of individual responsibility are not the norm in some regions. There are traditional justice cultures, for example, in Uganda, that emphasise collective responsibility (Hovil and Quinn 2005, p. 13, Komakech and Sheff 2009, p. 12). The roots of restorative and community-focused justice in Africa lie in the need of the communities and tribes to work together to survive in a scarce environment (see Gluckman 1959, p. 5–6).[10] This view resonates with African voices, particularly some local NGOs that promote what they see as traditional African views of justice (Odinkalu 2010, p. 15). Yet, there are great difficulties in identifying 'real customary law' in Africa as modernisation, international expectations, colonial powers or tribal chiefs instated by these powers often changed traditional African notions in order to use them as an instrument to control the population (Lambourne 2009, p. 32). As a result, distorted and simplified understandings of traditional justice are prevalent (Mani 2002, p. 81–82, Obarrio 2011, p. 25 and 30). Accordingly, some authors claim that the dichotomy between Western and African justice is exploited by local elites for political purposes and is sometimes merely being used as an excuse to deny accountability to African victims (Ero 2010, p. 13, Obarrio 2011, p. 36, Scanlon and Motlafi 2009, p. 311).

Still, the dichotomy between Western and African notions of justice may not run as deep as it seems at first glance. Restorative models of justice do also exist in the Western culture, for example in the

[10] To a certain degree, this seems to be true even for contemporary African societies. Ann Nee and Peter Uvin claim a preference for reconciliation in Burundi as people depend on each other to survive (Nee and Uvin 2010, p. 173).

re-integration logic of the prison system (Clarke 2009, p. 144–145, Hovil and Quinn 2005, p. 11). Utilitarian notions of justice, that are also part of Western legal thinking, have strong restorative influences as they introduced the condition that punishment has to serve a social good (deterrence, rehabilitation) in order to be legitimate (Mani 2002, p. 32–33). Also, informative justice models based on mediation and cooperative problem solving were strong in the West during the 1970s (Mani 2002, p. 37).[11] Luc Huyse even identifies a rising Western interest in African and Asian restorative justice concepts (Huyse 2008b, p. 21). These notions are clearly more compatible with African restorative justice than the narrow retributive definition of justice often championed by the West. Also, some authors have pointed out that most forms of traditional justice contain both retributive and restorative elements and that the disconnect between Western and local justice is thus overstated (Hovil and Quinn 2005, p. 12, Lambourne 2009, p. 31). This shows that even specific material notions of justice may still contain enough universal common ground to bridge the differences (see Clarke 2009, p. 144–145). Some authors like Linda Keller emphasise the restorative aspects of the Rome Statute like reparations and victim participation in this context (Keller 2007, p. 275–276).

Determining this common ground within material justice is key to understanding the relationship between peace and justice in conflicts.

6.1.4 *'Universal' justice*

The formal criteria introduced for justice, namely proportionality and generalisability, are regarded as universal and accordingly also carry weight for justice in conflict situations. Generalisability means that a situation or an outcome has to be acceptable to an objective and impartial observer (Koller 2007, p. 8), while proportionality has to be decided on a case-to-case basis.

The question of which criteria for material justice should be seen as universal, on the other hand, quickly becomes a question of conviction or even ideology. Material criteria suggested by Western scholars, like respect for human rights and individual freedom, may be perceived as part of a political campaign by Western powers trying to impose their

[11] In Northern Ireland, restorative justice concepts are still being used to tackle the high crime rate after the conflict (Gerdes 2009, p. 10).

world view on other societies.[12] In order to avoid these problems, the universal characteristics of corrective justice have to be broadened considerably. The literature suggests that there are two material requirements that are claimed practically across the world: atrocities cannot remain unanswered, and the wishes of the victims should be respected in implementing corrective justice.

The crimes investigated by the ICC are of an immense gravity and can be understood as crimes against humanity. They are thus seen as an attack against the shared values of all human beings. A number of interview surveys reviewed by Hugo van der Merwe shows that people are demanding some form of accountability for these crimes, no matter in which context they are committed (van der Merwe 2009, p. 133). This has led some authors to state that the condemnation of these crimes and the demand for a reaction to them are both universal (Drumbl 2007, p. 182, van der Merwe 2009, p. 136). I agree with this view.

The importance of the victims' wishes and their access to some form of justice is emphasised by a host of different authors (Akhavan 2009, p. 654, du Plessis and Ford 2008a, p. 1, Findlay and Henham 2010, p. 2, Hayner 2010, p. 201, Thoms et al. 2008, p. 7). Many international treaties and documents, including the Updated Principles on Impunity of the UN (Orentlicher 2005) and the UN Framework on Durable Solutions for Internally Displaced Persons (Wyrzykowski and Kasozi 2010, p. 11) name victim rights as a central criterion that needs to be considered. The description of justice perceptions in Uganda (Section 5.1.5) nicely illustrates the important role of these two principles in Acholi traditional justice, thus emphasising that the criteria hold across cultural borders.

6.1.5 *Justice on the conflict spectrum*

The definitions of peace and justice introduced above suggest a relationship that is in general mutually reinforcing and complementary. Peace is determined by the extent to which conflicts are solved without resorting to violence or even avoided altogether. Justice provides a set of moral rules to solve conflicts non-violently. Thus, a conflict can be expected to

[12] A number of authors nevertheless suggest that the basic respect for human rights should be regarded as a universal part of justice (Dreier 1991a, p. 75, Risse et al. 2003, p. 179, Thony and Schneider 2003, p. 183).

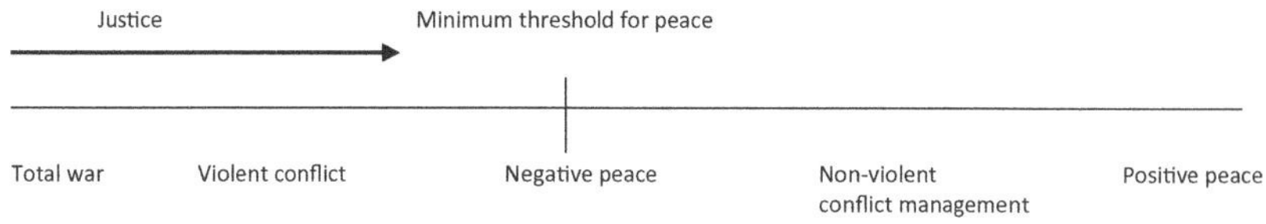

Figure 6.1: The conflict continuum

move towards peaceful stages on the spectrum (Figure 6.1) if the universal rules of justice are being respected by the conflict parties.[13]

Of course, this does not mean that louder demands for justice automatically lead to more peace, as demonstrated in the case studies. There are some choke points at which peace and justice may clash in the short term, like agreeing on a ceasefire, taking up negotiations or holding elections. These are borderline cases in which criteria of justice may clash with peace efforts. Naturally, the choke points are mainly encountered when moving towards peaceful conflict management on the spectrum, since peace is much more difficult to (re-)build than to break. Reaching the minimum threshold of peace usually coincides with one of these choke points since violence normally has to be ended through some kind of agreement or a military victory. Unsurprisingly, many of the causal mechanisms introduced in Section 3.1 are connected to these choke points. This is true for all the blocking and inducement claims. An example is the insistence of the ICC on the LRA warrants during the late stages of the Juba Talks. Mechanisms pertaining to the building of the rule of law and reconciliation can also be expected to play an important role in reaching the negative peace threshold. This is the case because reconciliation and the rule of law are essential to establish non-violent means of conflict management.

The model does thus not deny the possibility of tensions between peace and justice in some situations, but it does refuse general claims that peace and justice are incompatible. These theoretical expectations are being mirrored by the findings of the two case studies. Claims that justice and peace generally cancel each other out are based on a misunderstanding, since they usually reduce justice to retributive, Western

[13] Indeed, a number of authors understand peace as phases or layers building up on each other, while higher levels are identified by an accordingly higher level of justice (Ali and Matthews 2004b, p. 7, Czempiel 1972, Muñoz 2006, p. 423). Equally, Biblical, Islamic and Hebrew notions of peace are all connected to justice (Beilin 2006, p. 131).

notions of justice with high material requirements. Authors then use this narrow definition of justice in order to show that justice demands cannot possibly be fulfilled without sparking a conflict (see Bloomfield 2006, p. 19, Dyzenhaus 2003, p. 167). This misconception can be found both in peace and conflict studies and international law literature (e.g. Licklider 2008, Thakur 2006, p. 128–129, 2010, Zartman 2005b, p. 5).[14] It is the principle of justice that is universal, not one particular concept like the Western notion of retributive justice. As Ronald Dworkin has pointed out, principles are not like rules that are applied to the fullest or not at all (Dworkin 1978, p. 22–25). Rather principles are implemented to different degrees according to the situation. Thus, offsetting peace against justice by using a narrow Western notion of justice misses the point and clouds the view for the real problems that have to be tackled in order to successfully balance the needs of peace and justice. The relationship between peace and justice is complex and far from linear, and in any case, the legal mechanisms used to guarantee accountability can never achieve full justice. The aim should thus be to explain why and under which circumstances tensions between the attempts to reach peace and the efforts to deliver justice through accountability may arise and how to handle them. Understanding these tensions – that became very visible in both case studies – would arguably be of immense help for explaining the contradictory and ambiguous impacts of international criminal justice interventions.

6.2 Procedures and perceptions: the role of peace-justice dilemmas

The procedural and strategic decisions taken in the scope of prosecutorial policy and the perception of the accountability measures implemented in the two situation countries have proven to be crucial factors that emerged in both case studies and had an impact of several of the causal mechanisms. Both factors thus have an important impact on whether the ICC hampers or furthers conflict resolution efforts. Perceptions of justice are the views and opinions of stakeholders and actors about what kind of justice should be implemented, and how it should be implemented in a specific situation. Both variables, and how they influence each other, can

[14] Thakur claims justice to be backward looking, finger pointing and retributive, and contrasts it with peace as forward looking and integrative (Thakur 2006, p. 128–129). Clearly, there are also reconciliatory forms of justice (e.g., traditional justice measures), meaning that the contradiction claimed by Thakur is artificial.

help explain the effects of ICC investigations on conflict resolution. This means in practice that the OTP can influence conflict resolution measures through its decision. But it is not a clear-cut process that could be easily steered. On the one hand, the OTP has to take into consideration, how its decisions resonate within the affected communities, among stakeholders and in the international community. On the other hand, some decisions confront the Court with dilemmas like choosing between short-term efficiency and long-term credibility or fulfilling its mandate to the letter and leaving enough room for a peace process to unfold.

Despite being confronted with these complicated decisions, practitioners in the tribunals and courts claim that their decisions are purely based on legal considerations without any political motivations or implications. Chief Prosecutor Moreno Ocampo has emphasised repeatedly that political considerations are not meant to play a role in the decisions of the OTP or the judges (e.g. Moreno Ocampo 2008a, p. 11, 2010e, p. 8, Rastan 2011a). His colleague, former ICTY Chief Prosecutor Louise Arbour, stated upon indicting Serb President Slobodan Milosevic that politicians should refrain from discussing whether the indictment came at a right time for the Yugoslavian peace process. Her argument was that political calculations should not have an impact on the prosecution of war criminals, since the prosecution is a strictly legal process (Unger and Wierda 2008, p. 266). The following paragraphs on procedural decisions will illustrate that these claims amount to wishful thinking in many cases.

6.2.1 Procedural decisions and their dilemmas

A lot depends on the decisions the OTP takes in investigating a particular situation. The results of the ICC investigations in Uganda would have been completely different if the OTP had decided to investigate the GoU more proactively. The Darfur investigations, on the other hand, might have rendered completely different results if the OTP had applied for an arrest warrant for the Sudanese Defence Minister in July 2008 instead of directly going for President al-Bashir. The importance of these procedural and strategic decisions has so far been neglected when it comes to explaining the impact of international investigations and trials.[15] In fact, the aftermath of the ICC arrest warrant for al-Bashir was the only time

[15] See Nouwen (2013) for one of the few exceptions.

that procedural decisions of the ICC and their impact on the ground were discussed in depth (e.g. de Waal and Stanton 2009).

In Darfur, the OTP decided to go for spectacular indictments and a publicity-focused prosecution strategy, including the publication of genocide claims in the Guardian. The OTP thus steered the ICC into political controversies surrounding the role of the GoS in Darfur and the question whether genocide was being committed. These decisions were taken against the background of a GoS campaign accusing the ICC of being a neo-colonial institution. The OTP thus took a deliberate decision to escalate the controversy surrounding the ICC's role in Darfur by, for example, comparing the GoS to the Nazi regime. Thereby, the ICC tried to create a sense of urgency to lobby for international support in enforcing its warrants. This came at a price of hardening the conflict lines between the parties. As shown in Section 4.2, these decisions played an important role in the blocking rapprochement and polarisation mechanisms and had an impact on the isolation and marginalisation mechanisms.

In Uganda, the decision of the OTP to publicly insist on the implementation of its arrest warrants against the LRA commanders, and the active monitoring of complementarity by the PTC during the Juba Talks both contributed to blocking the negotiations between the LRA and the GoU. The decision not to prosecute members of the GoU or the UPDF and not to publish any information concerning the ICC investigation of alleged government crimes in Uganda contributed to the failure of the human rights protection mechanism on the side of the GoU and furthered local perceptions of a biased investigation.

The analysis of the procedural decisions taken at the ICC has illustrated that the Court is being selective in its investigations and prosecutions. Some of these decisions were taken consciously with the aim to influence the conflict parties. The public shaming and the indictment of al-Bashir were aimed at isolating the GoS and forcing it to cooperate with the ICC. The clear perpetrator role ascribed to the Janjaweed was also a conscious approach to isolate these groups. The early focus on the LRA in the Uganda case was aimed at isolating the LRA from international support provided mainly by the GoS. Finally, the declaration of limiting LRA warrants to the five top commanders was taken with the aim to isolate the LRA leadership within the Acholi community and the LRA.

International criminal justice and the ICC's work are usually discussed with the implicit claim that international criminal law has or should have a universal reach. This argument is in particular championed by the supporters of international criminal justice. This claim to universality was illustrated by the increased application of the principle of universal jurisdiction in the early 2000s that led to attempts to prosecute the former Chilean dictator Pinochet, former US President George W. Bush and former US Defence Minister Donald Rumsfeld.

Yet, the case studies of Darfur and Uganda have shown that the claims for a universal reach of international criminal justice are little more than a pipe-dream of international justice supporters. To a certain degree, these claims even work as a smokescreen, hiding the true mechanisms at work in international criminal courts and tribunals. Like it or not, the concept of selective justice is much more appropriate to explain the work of international courts and tribunals and especially that of the ICC today. In implementing its mandate, the ICC is being selective on several levels. This includes most notably the selection of its situation countries, the selection of the cases it decides to pursue in each situation country and the selection of certain victim groups that the OTP claims to be representing in its investigations and trials. The selectivity of the ICC in choosing particular situation countries is not new and has already met vocal criticism from civil society representatives in Uganda and other AU member states. Particularly, the ICC investigations in Darfur, Kenya and Libya have been criticised along these lines. The selectivity on the situation country level is partly explained by international power politics and the fact that some states were not willing to ratify the Rome Statute. The role of the UNSC in the ICC referral system also is germane here. The limited temporary jurisdiction of the ICC and the lack of financial and institutional resources at the Court complete the structural limitations that lead to selectivity in exercising the jurisdiction of the ICC.

The decisions of the PTC to allow investigations in DRC and Uganda show that there is also an active selection procedure on the level of situation countries. In both cases, the decision to confirm the admissibility of the case before the ICC can be disputed. In the case of Uganda, the judicial system was neither unable nor unwilling to prosecute the LRA in a strict sense. The inability rather stemmed from the difficulties in arresting the LRA commanders. In the DRC, the ICC's first suspect, Thomas Lubanga, was already in jail when the PTC confirmed the arrest warrant against him. The admissibility of prosecuting Lubanga was questionable since he was already in custody in the DRC. It is difficult to meet the criteria of unable and unwilling under these circumstances. But the PTC managed to circumnavigate the problem of admissibility by arguing that the DRC had not passed any legislation banning the recruitment of child soldiers. Since the OTP was prosecuting Lubanga for the recruitment of child soldiers, the DRC was unable to prosecute Lubanga on the same charges as the ICC; the fact that Lubanga was facing charges of torture and rape in the DRC did not stop the PTC from taking over the case. Sarah Nouwen has explained this same case and same conduct criterion in detail (Nouwen 2013, p.46). Against this background, Adam Branch has criticised the ICC for circumnavigating proper procedure in order to pragmatically secure 'easy' and uncontroversial first cases for the Court (Branch 2007b, p. 187).

The principle of selective justice becomes even clearer when analysing the case-specific strategies of the OTP. As illustrated in particular through the Darfur case, the OTP 'chooses' a victim group in whose name the OTP conducts its investigations. It constructs a particular narrative that points out clear perpetrator and victim roles and is thus selective in the way it narrates the conflict and reduces the complexity of its root causes (also Sagan 2010, p. 9–10). By defining the LRA as the main perpetrator in the Ugandan case and painting the rebels as the 'bad guys', the ICC implicitly excluded the possibility of prosecuting the GoU. Prosecuting both sides would have undermined the narrative of the OTP that described the LRA as an evil terrorist group ravaging the region. The selectivity of the OTP on the case level might also explain why it decided to only bring very specific and limited charges against the Darfur rebels. The OTP is prosecuting two mid-level rebel commanders of small splinter-groups for attacking AU peacekeepers. It has not decided to prosecute other crimes committed by the rebels like the spree of violations committed by the SLM-MM after signing the DPA. The prosecution of SLM-MM leader Minnie Minawi would certainly be possible under the ICC's mandate, yet it would undermine the clear perpetrator/victim roles attributed to the parties by the ICC. After all, Minnie Minawi is a Zaghawa and thus member of one of the three tribes that is allegedly being targeted by the GoS' genocidal policies. Focusing investigations on rebel groups would undermine the shaming strategy that the OTP applies against the GoS in order to mobilise international support to enforce its arrest warrants against GoS officials.

One important area in which the OTP is bringing selectivity to bear is the drafting of policy documents. In these documents, the OTP offers definitions of unclear legal terms from the Rome Statute and develops legal guidelines to steer its investigations and prosecutions. One obvious example for this selectivity is the development of the gravity criterion by the OTP. By introducing gravity as a main criterion in selecting cases, the

OTP decided to focus on those most responsible in its investigations and prosecutions due to the lack of financial resources at the ICC. The gravity criterion applies both to the selection of situation countries and to the selection of individual cases within a situation country. The gravity criterion has met sharp criticism by several authors. William Schabas characterised it as '*little more than obfuscation, a laboured attempt to make the determinations look more judicial than they really are*' (Schabas 2012, p. 89).

A second example for selectivity is the way the OTP interprets the so-called 'interests of justice' from article 53 I(c) of the Rome Statute. The article reads: '*In deciding whether to initiate an investigation, the Prosecution shall consider whether: . . . Taking into account the gravity of the crime and the interests of victims, there are nonetheless substantial reasons to believe that an investigation would not serve the interests of justice.*'

The OTP can thus decide whether it should conduct investigations in a particular case or not, depending on whether these investigations would further the '*interests of justice*'. The Rome Statute does not offer any additional information on how this provision should be interpreted in practice. The Chief Prosecutor initially implemented the interests of justice by '*follow[ing] the various national and international efforts to achieve peace and security, as well as the views of witnesses and victims of crimes*' (Moreno Ocampo 2005). It is important to note that the prosecutor mentions '*efforts to achieve peace and security*' and '*the views of witnesses and victims*' in his initial interpretation. This would have given him the leeway to, for example, ask the PTC for an authorisation to stop the prosecution of the LRA commanders during the Juba Talks since there clearly were '*efforts to achieve peace and security*' and most victims and witnesses were in favour of halting the prosecutions in order to further the chances for peace. A number of legal scholars were in favour of such a broad interpretation of the interests of justice and argued for such an interpretation with well-founded legal arguments (Brubacher 2004, p. 81, Cobban 2007, p. 61, Huyse 2008a, p. 197).

Yet, the OTP later decided to re-interpret the interests of justice in a much narrower way. A policy paper on the interests of justice was published at a time when the OTP changed its approach in both the Uganda and Darfur situations and decided to demand accountability much more aggressively than before. The new interpretation of the interests of justice may well have been published in order to create legal arguments for the strategic decision at the OTP to insist on the implementation of all outstanding arrest warrants. In his 2007 paper on the interests of justice, the OTP suddenly found a presumption in *favour of prosecution* in the Rome Statute that was not equal to the interests of peace. The OTP now claimed that ensuring peace was not part of the mandate of the ICC (OTP 2007, p. 1). They now argued that any peace initiatives in situation countries had to be compatible with the Rome Statute (OTP 2007, p. 4). Essentially, the OTP said that the broader matter of peace and security was the responsibility of other organisations, hinting at the possibility of a deferral of ICC investigations through the UNSC if the international community decided that investigations should be halted in order to allow peace efforts to advance (OTP 2007, p. 8–9).

Taking into consideration that the ICC is clearly applying selectivity in its work, it would be important for proponents of international criminal justice to shed themselves from normative aspirations and analyse this selectivity more precisely. The ongoing attempts of international criminal justice supporters to further the universal reach of international criminal justice and the ICC in particular is hampering an analytical approach towards the work of international courts and tribunals. Only if selective justice is understood as an integral part of how international criminal justice is implemented today will it be possible to thoroughly analyse the impact of international investigations and trials in situation countries, and to understand how courts and tribunals shape conflicts by taking certain procedural decisions (thus applying selectivity) and adopting certain narratives with clear-cut perpetrator and victim roles.

It is clear that the OTP has to take decisions with political implications when investigating in conflicts. These decisions are being further complicated by the fact that the OTP is sometimes caught between conflicting aims in pursuing its investigations. The application of a shaming strategy by the prosecution in the Darfur case illustrates this dilemma very well. The ICC could not advance its Darfur cases because it could not arrest the government suspects. Due to the lack of cooperation on the Sudanese side, the ICC was essentially confronted with two alternatives: it could either accept that it was powerless to enforce its warrants, or it could lobby the international community to enforce its warrants. The OTP decided to do the latter and started pressuring the ASP and the UNSC, reminding them of their duty to cooperate with the ICC and enforce its warrants.

Peskin has described the public appearances of Moreno Ocampo in which he attacked states for their passivity as a '*virtual trial of cooperation*' (Peskin 2009a, p. 660). The Prosecutor reminded the states of the self-chosen obligations that they had accepted by ratifying the Rome Statute and tried to shame them into compliance.

But while it is important for the ICC as an institution to implement its arrest warrants, the Court also has an interest to be perceived as a neutral and even-handed institution that is strictly guided by law. An international court that does not meet the formal criteria of justice is not worth its salt. The danger that lies in pursuing a proactive approach towards enforcement is that the prosecutor might be perceived as a political figure rather than as somebody who is implementing the law. This in turn might even lead to the politicisation of trials (see also Peskin 2009a, p. 660).

Arguably, Ocampo's shaming approach in the Darfur situation has furthered African perceptions of a neo-colonial court. It has thus created a political debate on the role of the ICC in Africa. This debate divides the ICC supporters in the West and the ICC States Parties in the African Union and thus weakens the Court in the long run (see Mbaku 2014, p. 10). The case of Darfur has also shown that individuals targeted by the ICC can use the external pressure built up through the OTP shaming strategy in order to strengthen the internal coherence of their followers. The GoS was even able to use the ICC warrants in order to win over many AU countries as new allies in blocking the prosecution efforts of the ICC against President al-Bashir.

A similar conflict of aims between enforcing warrants and being perceived as just emerged in Uganda. On the one hand, the OTP has an interest to maintain cooperation with the GoU in order to improve the chances to enforce their LRA warrants. Additionally, the OTP has a general interest in keeping its investigations confidential in order to ensure that it can work effectively. The Court has therefore decided not to publish any information on the investigations of alleged government crimes in northern Uganda. On the other hand, the Rome Statute is victim-centred. If the important role of the victims is taken seriously, they should have the right to know about the results of the OTP investigations into alleged government crimes. Additionally, the ICC has an interest to be perceived as even-handed. The lack of information on UPDF investigations has led to a perception of bias among many northern Ugandans.

Apart from these examples, there are a number of other conflicting objectives that the OTP has to deal with in its investigations. Some have also been named in the literature – for example the aim to foster a peaceful dialogue between conflict parties on the one side, and condemning atrocities on the other side (Leebaw 2008, p. 112). There is also a conflict between the aim to isolate spoilers, and the aim to remain neutral in a conflict (Vinjamuri 2010, p. 203).

The fact that there are so many conflicts of aims in the ICC's work also shows that supporters and practitioners of international criminal justice in conflicts strive for too much. Instead of trying to achieve too many aims, they should re-focus efforts on some core tasks (also Olsen et al. 2010, p. 131).

These paragraphs on the procedures of international investigations have shown that decisions taken at the OTP have clear political implications. One might even argue that some of the decisions taken at the OTP are political; contrary to the assurances of the Chief Prosecutor and much of the ICC staff. Some of them were clearly taken with the aim to influence conflict parties in one way or another. To be fair, it is nearly impossible to take decisions that are strictly based on legal arguments in these conflict situations when considering the conflicts of aims and dilemmas, international courts are confronted with. These conflicting aims and dilemmas were not only visible in the case studies, but can also be observed in the work of other courts and tribunals. A brief overview is given in the following paragraphs.

a. The ICC between its mandate and state interests[16]

There is little hope for the promotion of the rule of law internationally if the most powerful international body makes it subservient to the rule of political expediency.

(Former ICTY Chief Prosecutor Louise Arbour, cited in Ryngaert 2009, p. VIII)

Defining away the ICC's political dimensions eventually undermines the Court by making it look either hypocritical or utopian.

(Nouwen and Werner 2011)

Having to operate in an international environment that has only recently opened up to the idea of external interventions into the domains of sovereign states, the prosecutors of international criminal courts and tribunals face numerous difficult decisions on how to proceed in their cases. In taking these decisions, legal and political arguments have to be balanced.

[16] Parts of this chapter have been published on a blog written by the author (Wegner 2011a).

If investigations can be initiated and whether they lead to arrests depends to a large part on powerful states within the international community. These states have their own priorities and interests, and the ICC is often merely one factor in their overall equation. The policies of these states have an impact on the investigations, and the OTP has to decide how to arrange itself with these powers. An obvious example is the ICC's dependence on its donor countries. Some say this dependence contributes to a selective approach in prosecutions, excluding allies of important donor countries (Drumbl 2007, p. 151–152, Moghalu 2009, p. 72). This is problematic since powerful states might try to use the ICC and other courts and tribunals as instruments to further their own aims. For example, there have been attempts to use both the ICTY and the ICC as levers of Western powers to apply political pressure on states like Serbia and Sudan (see Bell 2008, p. 256, Bogoeva 2010, Hazan 2004, p. 192, Mendez 2010a, p. 6). While the prosecutors depend on the support of these states, close cooperation might lead to perceptions of a biased and political court, which will in turn have negative repercussions for the investigations.

Already there are several authors who criticise that international criminal law is championed by Western states but applied elsewhere, pointing out the de facto impunity of the United States to illustrate their point (Drumbl 2007, p. 152–153, Thakur 2010). This problem is further exacerbated because decisions to support an international judicial intervention are increasingly motivated by the moral indignation of citizens living in powerful Western states. The global media coverage of crimes committed in conflicts has led to growing demands from civil society groups all over the world to ensure criminal accountability for these crimes. Both in the case of the ICC investigations in Darfur and in northern Uganda, there are strong domestic civil society movements in the US pushing their government to intervene on behalf of the victims and to support the ICC (Allen and Vlassenroot 2010, p. 1, Finnström 2010a, p. 80, Mamdani 2009c, p. 23).

At the same time, the role that Western states and their allies play as external actors in mass atrocities is often left out (Drumbl 2007, p. 153).[17] In this context, some authors even accuse the ICC of an overall political

[17] The UN Security Council referral of the Libyan situation to the ICC is just the most recent example. The referral only allowed investigations of crimes committed after 15 February 2011. Later it became clear that Western states were involved in rendition and torture cases in Libya prior to that date.

bias and a partisan application of law by only targeting those countries that are not US allies. Their argument is that the Court's dependence on long-term acceptance by the United States has led the ICC to abstain from indicting US allies like the GoU or the Kagame Government in Rwanda for their role in the DRC (Mamdani 2009c, p. 283, Schabas 2010b, p. 548). As a result, Mahmood Mamdani sees the danger of justice being turned into a private good of Western populations (Mamdani 2009b, p. 472). Similar accusations that the ICC is yielding to the pressure of powerful states have been brought forward by other authors (Branch 2010b, p. 35, Glasius 2009, p. 519). As a consequence, the moral legitimacy and the neutrality of international courts is doubtful as they do not always apply norms consistently to all states (Drumbl 2007, p. 129–130, Mendes 2010, p. 160, Thakur 2006, p. 276).

In the case of the ICC, this problem is exacerbated by the role that the Rome Statute assigns to the UN Security Council (UNSC). The Council can refer cases to the Court, even if the situation developed on the territory of non-state parties. It can also defer investigations for twelve months through a renewable resolution. Yet, the UNSC is a politically skewed body due to the veto powers of its permanent members. Three of the five permanent members – the United States, Russia and China – have not ratified the Rome Statute but still use all the influence they can muster to shape the agenda of the ICC. The involvement of the UNSC with its skewed voting rights is extremely counter-productive for a coherent and just enforcement of international criminal law (also Thakur 2006, p. 280).

The problematic role of the UNSC is one of the reasons why the OTP will sometimes be drawn into political manoeuvres on the international stage. There are some inherent contradictions in the Rome Statute system that may lead to an uneven application of the law. This uneven application is dangerous for institutions mandated to deliver justice, since they can be challenged on the very grounds of justice if they do not deliver it fairly and coherently (see Hazan 2004, p. 199, Ryngaert 2009, p. VIII).

On the national level, similar problems may arise due to selective investigations and prosecutions. As mentioned, international criminal tribunals and courts depend on the cooperation of other actors. This is especially true for the government of the state in which the court or tribunal investigates. The problems confronted by the ICC when trying to investigate crimes committed in Darfur have demonstrated the difficulties of conducting an investigation without government cooperation (see Section 4.2). As a result, there are incentives for courts and tribunals to cooperate with local governments.[18] In some cases, this may lead to a selective approach in the investigations, focusing on the crimes committed by non-state actors and ignoring those committed by the army or government officials. The Rwandan Patriotic Front (RPF) government in Rwanda has, for example, been able to use the ICTR to create a justice system that helps to consolidate the regime. This is partly possible because the most important donor countries of Rwanda have accepted impunity for the war crimes committed by the RPF since the government guarantees stability in Rwanda (Brown 2011, p. 181 and 88). As a result, the ICTR did not receive any international support when it tried to investigate RPF crimes. The ICC's investigations in Côte d'Ivoire are another example for selective investigations as current officials have so far not been charged despite evidence of crimes (Tiemessen 2014, p. 10).

There have also been claims that the ICC is not investigating the government in Uganda, the DRC and the CAR in order to ensure the further cooperation of the respective governments in the investigations already under way. Some authors even voice concerns that the ICC might become an instrument for national governments trying to mobilise international support against their respective insurgencies and rebellions by bringing their situation before the Court (Branch 2007b, p. 183, Burke-White 2005, p. 565).

b. Dilemmas arising from conflicting aims and interests

Another example for the difficulties of procedural decisions are conflicting aims and interests that need to be taken into consideration. The needs of victim groups play a key role in the Rome Statute which calls for the restitution, compensation and rehabilitations of victims in Art. 75. The ICC thus has to address the issue of victims' rights when operating in a conflict situation. Victims' rights include the right to access to justice, to prompt, effective and adequate reparation, and to access to relevant information about the violations and reparations (Mallinder 2008, p. 263).

Several dilemmas arise when demands to respect victims' rights are brought forward. First, victim interests may be extremely plural and have been shown to change over time (ICC 2010d, Mallinder 2008, p. 359, Mani 2002, p. 119–121, Simpson 2008, p. 76). Louise Mallinder has explained these changing priorities of victims convincingly by referring

[18] The OTP has explicitly stated that it is keen to attain state cooperation through self-referrals in its cases (ICC OTP 2003, p. 2). This is less likely to work if the ICC prosecutes governments that have referred cases in their countries to the ICC.

to the hierarchical needs model of Maslow (Mallinder 2008, p. 360–361). Victims first focus on immediate physical needs like food and security. Only once these are secured, needs connected to self-esteem, like justice, are being considered. Thus, justice needs will arise more often and more forcefully with time and after the basic needs have been met.[19] This has been confirmed in the Ugandan case study.

Additionally, the distinction between victims and perpetrators is blurred in some cases (Mani 2002, p. 119–121, Shaw and Waldorf 2010, p. 8). It can thus be difficult to determine who is a victim and whose wishes should be respected accordingly (Mallinder 2008, p. 358). This is further complicated by the question of who can represent the victims legitimately, as Western pressure groups also claim to be representing victim interests while not being directly accountable to them. Both case studies have illustrated this complex relation between victims and perpetrators.

Last but not least, victims might essentially demand revenge for their suffering (Ambos 2008, p. 25, Bloomfield 2006, p. 19, Mendeloff 2004, p. 367).[20] Meeting victim wishes can thus at times go against the interests of peace, thus resulting in a conflict of aims.

A second tension emerges between the need to address past atrocities while developing a future *modus vivendi* (Crocker 2002, p. 546, Malan 2008, p. 140). This dilemma is illustrated by the causal relationship between combating impunity and spoiler retaliation. Addressing past atrocities might call for a level of accountability that leads to violent reactions by some segments of the society. This tension might be mitigated through a careful prosecution strategy that minimises negative reactions, for example, through issuing sealed warrants as long as tensions remain high. Alternatively, partial amnesties and a focus on the most responsible might persuade the rank and file to remain calm while their leaders are being prosecuted (Bell 2008, p. 240).

[19] As Mallinder points out, the hierarchical needs model has been neatly mirrored by victim survey results in Uganda (ICTJ and HRC 2005, p. 366, Mallinder 2008). An example for this view is an interview with a Cambodian monk about the Cambodia Tribunal in a German weekly newspaper. He stated: '*Is your notion on justice based on my survival, or will it put my life in danger? We in Cambodia have to survive in the first place, before having a need for justice*' (Die Zeit 2010, p. 56).

[20] For example, 21 per cent of victims surveyed in CAR as well as 20 per cent of those surveyed in DRC said that perpetrators of war crimes should be killed without judicial proceedings (Vinck et al. 2008, p. 43, Vinck and Pham 2010, p. 3). In some cultures, for example, in Afghanistan, revenge is even seen as legitimate private law enforcement (Matwijkiw 2010, p. 227).

Third, tensions arise when the international justice intervention becomes part of the conflict. The very definitions of just, fair and right might become conflict issues. Disputes about justice then become a Reason for the conflict parties (Müller 2003, p. 221, Osaghae 2000, p. 207, Schmidtz 2006, p. 5). This is being reflected in the mechanism of polarisation. This tendency can be avoided by an even-handed and balanced approach of the court or tribunal, carefully avoiding to be drawn into the conflict. In the case of Darfur, the ICC arguably failed to do so.

Fourth, there may be tensions between the aims of actors trying to stabilise the situation on the ground and the aims of an international criminal justice intervention. This dilemma is most adequately described as a conflict between accountability and stability. For example, a court may require help of peacekeeping forces in order to carry out its investigations and enforce its warrants. At the same time, the investigations might run counter the interests of the peacekeeping mission to ensure calm and remain neutral (Arsanjani and Reisman 2008, p. 342, Unger and Wierda 2008, p. 228). In the case of the ICTY, cooperation requests sent to the peacekeeping mission sparked fears that the neutrality of the peacekeepers might be affected when cooperating with the court (Kerr and Mobekk 2007, p. 40).

Humanitarian organisations, on the other hand, face the difficult decision whether to share information with the ICC or not. If they decide to share information on conflict parties under investigation, they might be perceived as enemies and denied access to vulnerable populations. If they decide not to share information on serious violations, these organisations are indirectly promoting impunity (Unger and Wierda 2008, p. 288). In the DRC situation, humanitarian organisations working to de-mobilise child soldiers received threats after the ICC issued its arrest warrant for Thomas Lubanga (HRW 2008a, p. 96). This illustrates that there might be tensions between the interest of a tribunal or court to prosecute and the interest of NGOs to do their work in a secure environment. This tension is being illustrated by the spoiler retaliation mechanism. The difficult position of UN OCHA described in the Ugandan case study is another case in point.

c. Timing and sequencing dilemmas

There are dilemmas that emerge from conflicting long-term and short-term goals of conflict management. Many authors claim that dilemmas between peace and accountability exclusively arise in the short term

(Hannum 2006, p. 582, Nitsche 2007, p. 272, Roth 2010, p. 5, Tolbert and Wierda 2010, p. 1). The main argument of these authors is that the mutually benefitting effects of peace and justice become stronger in the long term.

A number of arguments support this point of view. As shown above, positive peace is highly dependent on justice. Additionally, justice helps to avoid a relapse into conflicts as it provides peaceful conflict management tools and diminishes conflict Reasons. Especially, the deterrence effect of criminal justice is often named as a long-term goal of international investigations and trials. Supporters of international criminal justice claim that general deterrence creates higher obstacles for the commission of atrocities everywhere, which means that both locals and the international community have a long-term interest in ensuring justice through accountability (Akhavan 2009, p. 630 and 653, Stromseth 2003, p. 6).

In the short term however, ensuring that the question of accountability is not swept under the rug can lead to more suffering for the people affected by a conflict as exemplified by the causal mechanisms of blocking negotiations and triggering spoiler retaliation. Yet, some argue that short-term solutions that stop violence temporarily but do not lead to long-term stability might not be worth the cost of sacrificing justice. A 'good war' might be better than a bad peace, since the long-term benefits of accountability measures might be worth prolonging conflicts (Jaques 2008, p. 12, Mallinder 2009a, p. 279, Prunier 2010, p. 128).

The timing dilemma is one example for the complexities that lead to the volatile and dynamic effects of international investigations and thus helps explain why impacts vary over time, as seen very clearly in both case studies. But timing also opens some leeway for the OTP to avoid negative conflict impacts. The OTP did indeed decide to time the publication of its LRA warrants in order not to hinder the 2004/5 negotiations. Deterrence on the LRA also worked best as long as the investigations were public but the warrants were not yet issued. With a later publication of the arrest warrants, the ICC might have prolonged its deterrence effect on the LRA.

On the other side, the decision to issue a warrant against President al-Bashir before issuing a warrant for his Defence Minister shows how wrong timing can lead to negative impacts. A more gradual approach might have increased the pressure on al-Bashir to at least extradite one suspect to the ICC. The decision to go directly for the President furthered the polarisation between the conflict parties, briefly blocked the Doha negotiations and led to negative perceptions among many AU stakeholders, thus complicating the enforcement of all warrants in the Darfur case.

d. Legal considerations vs. interests of peace

In the international arena, law and politics are inextricably intertwined.

(Kerr 2004, p. 208)

Political considerations cannot play a role in the decisions of the Office of the Prosecutor or the Court.

(Moreno Ocampo 2008a, p. 11)

The first decision dilemma a prosecutor has to confront is whether he will take the interests of peace into consideration in designing a prosecution strategy. In the case of prosecutions during conflicts, the dilemma can come down to the question of whether a conflict resolution agenda can be reconciled with the legal mandate of the court to ensure accountability, especially since political considerations are not meant to play a role in the decisions of the prosecutors or the judges (Moreno Ocampo 2008a, p. 11). The OTP thus emphasises the legal character of its work, while the interests of peace may demand political considerations in some cases. Findings that government parties are prosecuted less often than non-state actors hint at political calculations playing a role in prosecution decisions (Hofmann-van de Pol 2010, p. 228). One of the reasons for these political calculations is that the prosecutor is legally independent but politically dependent on state cooperation (Nitsche 2007, p. 190).

The first issue arising between interests of peace and the legal obligations of criminal courts and tribunals is that they cannot ignore war crimes in specific cases for the sake of peace, as legal obligations demand the equal treatment of all cases (Rupprecht 2003, p. 283). In other words, it might be permissive to accept less than perfect accountability in order to ensure peace when following a conflict resolution agenda. The logic of ensuring accountability for international crimes allows considerably less flexibility since law is built on the unconditional respect of norms. If norms are openly disrespected or bent without consequences, they will lose their effect.

Secondly, external actors like powerful states or the UN Security Council are pressuring prosecutors not to endanger conflict resolution opportunities or peace talks. The prosecutor cannot always ignore all of these pressures. At the same time, it is of extreme importance for the legitimacy of the international investigations that they are not perceived as politically guided. The strict neutrality of the prosecutor in all cases is of key importance if the causal mechanisms related to the rule of law and the transformation of a conflict are to hold. It is therefore important that the judicial autonomy of the ICC is only used based on legal considerations (see Ambos 2008, p. 68 and 84, Broomhall 2004, p. 61, Mendez 2010a, p. 6).

To sum up, there are contradicting demands stemming from the legal mandate of a court on the one hand and from the interests of peace on the other hand. Whether he or she wants it or not, an international prosecutor has to decide whether to yield to the demands arising from the interests of peace, or to the demands arising from the principle of ensuring accountability. The dilemma whether to follow legal or political criteria can only be tackled when its existence is acknowledged. If the dilemma is ignored, positive effects of ICC investigations might be wasted and the negative effects strengthened due to an unnecessary lack of flexibility resulting from a purely legal focus. So far, the nuances between legal and political decision have not been acknowledged. Rather the issue has been caught up in the discussion between critics, accusing the court of following a political agenda, and advocates, arguing that there is a '*pristine notion of law in vacuum*' (Goldston 2010, p. 387).

e. International legal standards vs. local agency

The final problem that international prosecutors encounter during their work in situation countries is the complicated relation between the court or tribunal and the national judicial institutions. This is especially true for the ICC, since a central novelty of the Rome Statute is its complementarity regime. The ICC can only initiate investigations if the local judiciary has not engaged in investigations of the same case and conduct, and is found to be unwilling or unable to prosecute the crimes in question. Yet, local ideas of justice and accountability may contradict with the international standards set in the Rome Statute. The disconnect between local and international notions of justice is aggravated since the international lawyers who design international courts and tribunals based the institutional structure on 'their' legal systems and did not fully consider local needs and realities (Drumbl 2007, p. 123). As a result, international tribunals and courts might take away agency from local decision makers, especially in cases in which the states in question decide to adopt some kind of amnesty, a truth commission or traditional justice measures that do not meet international standards. In practice, this unfortunately happens all too often. Sarah Nouwen has shown that it is nearly impossible for national courts to render an ICC case inadmissible under the complementarity provisions if the ICC is determined to take up the case (Nouwen 2013, p. 102). Various authors have pointed out that the international voice tends to outweigh the local voice in most cases, as the West has the resources to enforce its moral order (Clarke 2009, p. 169, Fletcher et al. 2009, p. 214, Mani 2002, p. 47). Additionally, international courts and tribunals are not accountable to the local population (Cobban 2006, p. 28, see Gready 2005, p. 8). In the cases of the ICTY and the ICTR, the literature concludes that both tribunals focused on the needs of international audiences rather than on those of local constituencies (Drumbl 2007, p. 131, Leebaw 2008, p. 108).[21] The Ugandan case study and the conflict between traditional justice and the ICC procedures underscore this dilemma.

6.2.2 Perceptions

Another important variable that played a role in many of the causal mechanisms analysed in the case studies were local and regional perceptions of justice. The perception of accountability measures reflects how the relation between peace and justice is *seen* by the stakeholders. The experience of violence, prior relations between the conflict parties, local notions of justice, access to accurate information and the cultural beliefs and practices of groups have been identified as factors that influence this perception in a multi-state survey (Weinstein et al. 2010, p. 39). The main lesson of the case studies is that international investigations and prosecutions are not being conducted in a vacuum. It *does* matter what the local population thinks, it *does* matter how regional bodies and the international community perceive the investigations in a particular case. The case studies have clearly shown this. Relevant perceptions include both perceptions of what kind of justice should be implemented (retributive vs. restorative, cosmopolitan vs. traditional) as well as how justice is being applied (even-handedness, fairness). While the perceptions of local populations of international investigations and trials have been the object of several surveys, the literature has so far not attempted to analyse how these opinions affect the actual performance of courts and tribunals and their impact in situation countries.[22]

[21] These findings are reinforced through the results of qualitative interviews that Kristina Thony and Patricia Schneider conducted with ICTY staff. They found that the impact of the trials on the ground and the view of the local population were not seen as especially relevant by the ICTY staff (Thony and Schneider 2003, p. 145).

[22] See Ambos and Stegmiller (2012, p. 9) for one of the few articles that addresses the perception of investigations.

Yet, perceptions of justice are an important factor that determines the impacts of international trials and investigations in certain areas. Many of the causal mechanisms identified in the literature rely on public opinion to develop their effects. This includes the education function of trials, which is supposed to lead to more respect for law and a strengthening of the rule of law. If investigations and trials are not accepted by the local population though, they cannot develop their education function. But perceptions are also highly relevant for the much-cited reconciliation function of accountability measures. Reconciliation through trials can only come about if the population accepts them.

Even for the deterrence effects of international trials, the perception of justice plays an important role. If a party does not believe that it will be targeted by investigations, it will not be deterred from committing crimes. In the case of Uganda, the government never really believed that it was being targeted by the ICC. The population also started to believe that the ICC was only conducting one-sided investigations against the LRA. Against this background, it cannot come as a surprise that the effects of protecting human rights, combating impunity and deterring crimes did not gain traction on the side of the UPDF.

As shown in the case of Sudan, perceptions can also influence the isolation and marginalisation effects attributed in particular to international trials. The isolation effects ascribed to trials and investigations cannot be expected to work if people and states are not convinced by the manner in which justice is being dispensed. In the case of Darfur, the AU perceived the ICC investigations as biased. Therefore, it challenged the even-handedness and fairness of the Court, undermining the legitimacy of the arrest warrants and potential isolation effects.

The perception is also relevant, because the perceived relation between peace and justice may not reflect the actual situation on the ground, for example, conflict parties may claim that demands for accountability are blocking a peace process even though there is no real motivation to negotiate due to other reasons. These misguided perceptions matter, since support for or rejection of the ICC investigation depends in part on whether the people think it will help or hinder conflict resolution efforts.

Finally, the expectations towards justice of the ICC and its international supporters directly affect the way national concepts of transitional justice are being implemented. The ICC and its supporters have a tendency to push for retributive justice, rather than restorative justice. These views usually gain the upper hand in the national debate about transitional justice, as they are being reinforced by the complementarity regime under which the ICC operates and championed by norm entrepreneurs. Alternatives that are not in line with the Rome Statute will not be accepted by the Chambers of the ICC. The ICC is thus a catalyst for international views of justice influencing transitional justice concepts in countries in which the ICC is active. At the same time, the ICC is also shaping victim and perpetrator perceptions in the country through its conflict narrative. Accusing a certain group (e.g. the LRA or the Janjaweed) of being the main perpetrators all the time does not go unnoticed in the population and has an influence on who is perceived as guilty.

As shown in both case studies, the ICC is in practice pushing countries towards more retributive models. This pressure comes to bear even in contexts in which the national predisposition tends more towards reconciliation, like in the case of Uganda. The results of that pressure are not necessarily positive as the examples of Uganda and Sudan show. In Sudan, the ICC pressure led to the staging of sham trials. The GoS did everything to convey the impression that it was prosecuting the crimes committed in Darfur in special courts, without any tangible results on the ground. In Uganda, the ICC activities furthered the establishment of the ICD. Unfortunately, the first war crimes case conducted by the court raised a number of issues of due process since the first defendant of the ICD remains in custody despite several court decisions to free him.

The discourses surrounding the delivery of justice and their impact on the investigations and prosecutions have so far been neglected on the research agenda. This is especially true for quantitative surveys which have so far not included different cultures of justice as a variable in their models. Future research on international trials and investigations should redouble efforts to fully include justice perceptions and cultures of justice into its theories and models. As shown in the following section, dilemmas and challenges connected to justice perceptions are of broad relevance and also affect the work of other courts and tribunals.

a. International vs. local standards

In many cases, when international tribunals become active in a situation country, locals feel that Western values, procedures and priorities are forced upon them (Sriram 2009b, p. 8). In many African contexts, this is particularly true for Western notions of retributive justice that international courts like the ICC undeniably champion (Unger and Wierda 2008, p. 288). As shown in the case studies, the ICC itself is directly affected by these problems. Muammar Kaddafi, Rwanda's President Paul Kagame, as well as AU chairman Jean Ping have accused the ICC of being biased and have qualified the Court as an instrument of an imperialist agenda in the context of the ICC's investigations in Darfur (CICC 2010). While the ICC has tried to reach out to the AU, it has so far not been able to secure a memorandum of understanding with the organisation in order to open a permanent office at the seat of the AU in Addis Ababa. AU scepticism of the ICC has even increased since the January 2011 AU assembly at which Kenya started to rally support for a UNSC deferral of the ICC investigations in Kenya (Arieff et al. 2011, p. 1). This process has gained further traction with the election of ICC-indicted Kenyatta as Kenya's next President and has recently led to a diplomatic crisis between Kenya and Western supporters of the ICC.

It is clear that these local discussions about the legitimacy of international criminal justice are of enormous practical relevance for the ICC when and if they arise. Rama Mani has pointed out that justice needs to be rooted in local culture in order to be accepted (Mani 2002, p. 84). The question then is whether the work of the ICC can be harmonised with local perceptions when local criticism arises. Accordingly, several authors have called for a dialogue to reconcile African and universal values of justice, without diluting the universal values too much (Brounéus 2008, p. 213, du Plessis and Ford 2008c, p. 124–125, Müller 2003, p. 238). In how far the ICC can manage its contentious relationship with local cultures of justice is therefore an important variable for explaining the contradicting outcomes of international criminal justice interventions in different cases with otherwise similar conditions.

b. Perceived bias

Another problem of international courts is the need to be seen as strictly neutral in order to avoid being drawn into the conflict. Despite efforts to remain neutral, most tribunals have faced allegations of political bias in their prosecutions. Population surveys have shown that opinions on accountability measures are often deeply divided along ethnic and cultural lines and that hypocrisy allegations against international courts are frequent (Sundar 2004, van der Merwe 2009, p. 133). In the case of the ICTY, Bosnians and Kosovo Albanians are practically the only groups who see the work of the tribunal as positive, while Croats and Serbs voice allegations of political bias (Biro et al. 2004, Clark 2009, p. 471, UNDP 2007). In Sierra Leone, large parts of the population found the indictment of the Civil Defence Forces leader Norman unfair as he was perceived as a national hero (Horowitz 2006, p. 59). These problems partly arise due to different international and local perceptions about who should be considered as one of those most responsible for the crimes committed and should therefore be prosecuted (Sriram 2009b, p. 8).

In the case of the ICC, large parts of the population in Western DRC are critical of the ICC prosecution of former Vice President Jean Pierre Bemba Gombo. Bemba won 42 per cent of the vote in the 2006 elections and was likely to be the main contestant of President Kabila in the 2012 elections that Kabila won with relative ease. Accordingly, many people believe that President Kabila used the ICC to get rid of Bemba (see Kerr and Mobekk 2007, p. 71). Locals say that the DRC is full of war criminals, and ask why the ICC is just focusing on Bemba (Sundaram et al. 2010).

Another reason for perceptions of biased investigations is the fact that the ICC has not targeted government officials in any of the cases based on a self-referral. This can partly be explained by the fact that governments have many tools at their disposal to obstruct investigations against them, as the cases of Rwanda and Yugoslavia have proven (Peskin 2005, p. 217), but it can also be connected to political considerations of the OTP as shown in the section on procedural dilemmas above.

Indeed the ICC faces some problems when trying to prosecute the crimes in its jurisdiction. These problems have contributed to perceptions of bias, as shown in the Uganda case. On the one hand, some crimes have taken place a long time ago and fall outside the temporal jurisdiction of the ICC. On the other hand, the ICC does not have the capacity to prosecute everyone responsible for crimes, so some form of selection is always necessary (Brahm 2007, p. 19). Local populations sometimes misinterpret these limitations of the ICC as bias.

Apart from these bias perceptions in individual situations, there are also perceptions of a broader, global bias in the way the ICC selects its cases. The AU and several scholars have criticised that African countries are singled out by the ICC in its investigations.[23] The UNSC referrals of the crimes in Darfur and Libya to the ICC are presented as proof that the ICC is an instrument of Western hegemony aimed at African leaders. Even otherwise pro-ICC Darfuri participants in the outreach activities of

[23] Former AU Chairman Jean Ping was, for example, quoted in the Parisian newspaper Libération, saying: '*there are two systems of measurement... the ICC seems to exist solely for judging Africans*' (Arieff et al. 2011, p. 26).

the ICC in Chad have asked about the alleged double standards of the Court (ICC Registry 2010, p. 47). Unfortunately, these perceptions are not completely baseless as shown in the section on judicial selectivity above. The decision of the OTP not to investigate crimes of Western states in Iraq due to a lack of jurisdiction and gravity has fuelled this criticism. The allegations of a global bias have led Ramesh Thakur to state that an indictment of Western states for international war crimes is vital for the credibility and survival of the ICC system. He names the findings of the Goldstone Report on Gaza and the behaviour of American soldiers in Fallujah as two possible cases in which action by the ICC would be needed in order to counter bias perceptions (Thakur 2010). The fact that the OTP has recently re-opened its investigations of violations of US soliders in Afghanistan and British soldiers in Iraq is an encouraging step in this context (Bosco 2014).

Perceptions of bias have practical implications for several reasons. First, they can influence the support of local and external actors. Second, perceptions of political bias can undermine the general deterrence effects of international criminal law (Peskin 2005, p. 228, Rothe 2010, p. 103). If government politicians arrive at the conclusion that the ICC is unlikely to prosecute anyone high enough in the government hierarchy or close enough to the United States, the causal mechanisms of general deterrence will not kick in. This is what arguably happened in Uganda. Last but not least, trials perceived as biased have a negative effect on reconciliation (Olson 2006, p. 293).

One of the main reasons for these bias perceptions is the failure of tribunals and courts to explain their decisions. This has been the case for the ICTY (Côté 2005, p. 172), and is one of the reasons why perceptions of bias prevail in the case of Uganda.

c. Perceived ineffectiveness

Last but not least, there are perceptions that international courts and tribunals are ineffective in delivering on their objectives. The ICTR has been criticised by the Rwandan government and different academics as being too slow and costly, while many victims in Bosnia see the ICTY trials as too long and too complicated (Brown 2011, p. 183, Orentlicher 2010, p. 15, Strain and Keyes 2003, p. 106). Additionally, victims have high expectations towards the court that tend to be disappointed. Victims in Bosnia and Herzegovina have been vocal about their disappointment in qualitative interviews, while the Rwandan victim organisation IBUKA has also criticised the slow speed of trials at the ICTR (Clark 2009, p. 467,

Strain and Keyes 2003, p. 108). For the victims, it is also difficult to accept that they live in deprivation while the defendants in international trials live in a comfortable prison in the Hague. They see that huge amounts of money are spent on justice and comfortable prison cells while people suffer from hunger and ordinary criminals die in local prisons (Mani 2002, p. 98).

> Even supporters have voiced understanding for the disappointment among some stakeholders: '*the Court has not lived up to expectations in recent years, unable to complete relatively straightforward trials within a reasonable timeframe.*'
>
> (Schabas 2010a)

Again, this can have serious implications for the local support of international trials. People need to feel that trials deliver on justice if they are expected to support them. As Ramesh Thakur puts it, there is a difference between justice being done, and seeing justice be done (Thakur 2006, p. 119). If people do not see the impact of the trials, they will quickly become sceptical. Additionally, courts will have trouble to meet victim needs for justice if they are seen as ineffective.

Some final thoughts on the role of procedures and perceptions will be offered in the following conclusions.

7

Conclusions and outlook

And Covenants without the Sword, are but Words, and of no strength to secure a man at all.

(Thomas Hobbes 1651)

The arc of the moral universe is long, but it bends toward justice.

(Dr. Martin Luther King 1958)

The aim of this book is to better understand the impact of international criminal investigations on ongoing conflicts. In order to do so, a cross case approach (Chapter 3) was combined with two case studies (Chapters 4 and 5). Both the general findings in Chapter 3 and the case study findings have illustrated that the literature on investigations in conflicts is currently overestimating the impact of these investigations; and that some of the effects are being misrepresented.

The multi-method analysis of ICC investigations presented in this book illustrates that there are important limits to what international investigations can achieve in conflicts. These limits have so far not been acknowledged sufficiently in the literature. As a result, expectations are high and many of the claims discussed in the literature are too general and far-reaching.

The first of these limiting factors is the fact that international courts often become active in situation countries with the worst human rights records (Meernik et al. 2010b, p. 327). This is particularly true for the ICC. When assessing the effects of the Court's investigation on conflicts, it is important to keep in mind that there is an inherent selection bias when it comes to the situation countries of the ICC. This is a result of the mandate of the ICC, since the Court is only responsible for the most serious crimes (Art. 5.1 Rome Statute) that are often committed in states in which an effective judicial system to prosecute them does not exist. As a rule of thumb, it is fair to say that war crimes, crimes against humanity and genocide tend to happen with a higher probability in some of the most persistent, intractable and violent conflicts. Possible positive effects of the ICC investigations on the resolution of these conflicts are thus especially difficult to measure as they tend to be nullified by the exacerbating factors of protracted conflicts. In the case of Darfur, these factors include desertification and regional insecurity, as well as ethnic tensions and hatred. In the case of the LRA conflict, these factors are the weak state capacities in the region, as well as conflict cycles deeply rooted in Uganda's history.

Second, international courts and tribunals are obviously not able to directly address most of the root causes of a conflict (see Clarke 2009, p. 239, Nitsche 2007, p. 65). Against this background, the hopes and expectations of international criminal justice proponents in conflicts are too high. International tribunals and courts focus on rectification justice at the expense of distributive and social justice (see Mani 2002, p. 9). At the same time, social questions and issues of unequal distribution of wealth and power often lie at the roots of the conflict. This is the case in both the Darfur and the LRA conflicts. The causal mechanisms identified for the ICC's impact in conflict situations cannot be expected to solve the underlying conflict issues in Darfur and Uganda. International investigations mainly address the symptoms of conflicts (war crimes and atrocities) and can ease them in a number of ways. Addressing the root causes of the conflict, on the other hand, has to be left to the conflict parties or to international actors like the UNSC. A durable solution to the conflict without addressing the real issues at hand is unthinkable (see Zartman 2005b, p. 4).

Peace and conflict researchers have been trying to come to grips with the complexities of conflicts and the inadequacy of different conflict resolution approaches for the past decades, and have met only limited success. Including their findings and theories can be extremely helpful in understanding the limits of investigations in conflicts. The causal mechanisms in Chapter 3 were thus modelled with conflict resolution theory in mind. The results help to paint a more realistic picture of the nexus between international investigations and conflict resolution efforts.

Research on the impact of international trials and investigations in conflict context is clearly still at an early stage. While the analysis conducted here has demonstrated the volatility of these impacts and the importance of so far neglected variables, this is just a first step. The research design was aimed at analysing international investigations in conflicts comprehensively and the case studies have shed light on these investigations from many different angles. The results offer important elements for developing mid-range theories suitable for the further analysis of the impact of trials and investigations in conflicts.

An important question that remains unanswered concerns the expected long-term impacts of investigations and trials in conflicts. Those effects could not be analysed in depth in this book due to the focus on ongoing conflicts and situations in which trials have not yet been finished. It therefore remains unclear how far international criminal justice can achieve long-term goals like reconciliation in conflict-affected areas and the global deterrence of international crimes. As the example of the ICTY trials in the former Yugoslavia has shown, these impacts are hard to assess even twenty years after the establishment of the tribunal and fourteen years after the last conflict in the region ended. It may well take a generation or more for these potential long-term effects of trials to fully manifest (also Heikkilä 2009, p. 51).

Despite these caveats, the findings at hand are of prime importance and relevance for the current stage of research. The ICC is persistently investigating crimes committed in ongoing conflicts and the trend has been gaining traction in the last couple of years. There are fewer and fewer contemporary conflicts in which the ICC is not playing a role or in which a referral is not at least discussed. The two latest examples are Mali and Syria: the ICC has started to conduct investigations in northern Mali and a UN Security Council referral of the situation in Syria to the ICC has been discussed repeatedly. Since the Court tends to be involved in some of the most brutal and intractable conflicts of modern times, this heightens the relevancy of any effect measured in the case studies.

The first part of the conclusions will point out some of the shortcomings of the current literature in grasping the complexity of investigations in conflicts.

Some valuable conclusions for the work of the ICC can be drawn from the case studies. These will be presented in the second part of the conclusions. The final part of the conclusions will offer thoughts on the way forward for investigations in conflicts.

7.1 The way forward – beyond peace versus justice

The case studies have shown that the literature does not yet fully grasp the complexity of international investigations in conflicts. Some of the weaknesses are gradually being addressed in the literature; others have remained largely unaddressed.

The main factors that deserve more attention are the specific characteristics of each conflict and the institutional design of courts that influence investigations. More attention should also be paid to the complexity and the inherent contradictions of conducting investigations in conflicts. Finally, more efforts are needed to identify the most important third variables influencing the impact of investigations in conflicts.

7.1.1 Taking into account the context of international investigations

Many of the claims presented in the literature do not sufficiently take into account the context in the situation countries. For example, many authors do not distinguish whether accountability measures are being implemented during a conflict, after a conflict, as part of a democratic transition or decades after a transition. Additionally, none of the surveys conducted on the impact of accountability measures takes into account the different institutional characteristics of the institutions involved. Some surveys do not distinguish between national and international trials; others ignore huge differences in the mandates of truth commissions by lumping them in the same category.

These problems also emerged during the case studies of the LRA and the Darfur conflict. Many quantitative surveys suggest that trials in conflicts can promote the protection of human rights (Kim and Sikkink 2010, Olsen et al. 2010), that international trials combat impunity (Hofmann-van de Pol 2010) and that there is a deterrent effect of trials (Kim and Sikkink 2009, 2010, p. 956). None of these effects claimed in quantitative surveys could be fully traced in the LRA and Darfur conflicts. While this could mean that the LRA and Darfur conflicts are just exceptions to the rule, the case study findings rather suggest that the surveys do not measure the effects correctly. The Hofman-van de Pol study, for example, focuses on the impact of international trials on the accountability of those most responsible for atrocities committed in conflicts. The study finds that some tribunals and courts have been rather successful in fighting impunity. According to the criteria of the Hofmann-van de Pol study, the ICC has had at least some success in combating impunity in Darfur and Uganda. Yet, if the analysis focuses on the general culture of impunity prevalent in both conflicts, impunity remains an important problem both in the Darfur and the LRA conflicts despite the ICC investigations. Focusing on whether those most responsible have been tried might thus not be a good indicator for whether the culture of impunity in a conflict has been tackled comprehensively.

Moving on to the protection of human rights mechanism, the results of the Ugandan case study provide a strong reason to question the assumption that there is a general causal correlation between international investigations and an improvement of the human rights record. A purely quantitative approach would likely confirm the finding that ICC investigations lead to an improved human rights record. But while the human rights record of the Ugandan army has indeed improved to some degree, major problems remain, and much of the improvement is connected to the fact that the LRA has been pushed out of northern Uganda. Taking a glimpse behind the raw data, the case study has shown that the ICC investigations have even been used as a whitewash by the army instead of furthering human rights reform within the UPDF. The current statistical methods are unable to grasp developments similar to the Ugandan case in their models.

The same is true for the purported deterrent effect of ICC investigations in Uganda and Darfur. When only considering the statistical data, it would be very plausible to claim that there was indeed a deterrent effect of the ICC investigations in the LRA and Darfur conflicts. The number of crimes committed and the number of battle-related deaths has reduced considerably since the ICC started investigations in both situation countries. Yet, a closer look at the conflict dynamics reveals that the drop in casualty figures had different reasons. In the case of Darfur, the characteristics of the conflict changed significantly roughly around the time the ICC started investigating. In the case of Uganda, the ICC investigations developed a temporary deterrent effect, causing the LRA to stop the majority of their attacks for a certain time-frame. Again, current models of quantitative surveys would not have been able to detect the true reasons for the drop in the number of atrocities being committed in the situation countries. Most statistical models would have attributed this improvement to the ICC investigations instead.

But the problem of underestimating contextual factors is not exclusively encountered in quantitative surveys. Even though case study approaches are far less prone to overlook important contextual factors in their analysis, the Uganda and Darfur cases have shown that many case studies published so far also tend to overlook contextual factors. A particularly relevant factor that is often neglected in the current research is the history of the conflict.

A lack of regard for the history of the conflict led to wrong pressure and isolation claims in many analyses written on the ICC investigations in the LRA conflict, wrongly interpreting the isolation of the LRA as a result of the ICC investigations. The case study has shown that the increased pressure was a result of trends that had been ongoing for years, long before the ICC even started its investigations.

The retaliation claims in Darfur offer another illustrative example for the neglect of the conflict context. Critics of the ICC investigations often claim that the warrant of the ICC against Sudanese President al-Bashir caused the GoS to retaliate against humanitarian organisations by expelling them from Sudan. Yet, these critics ignore the fact that al-Bashir's decision was just the climax of a policy that he had been following for years before the ICC warrant against him was issued. These misrepresentations are examples for mistaking the coincidence of two events with a causal relation.

Last but not least, the case studies have illustrated that the type of conflict has an influence on the effects of international investigations and trials. For example, ethnic factors in the Darfur conflict clearly played a strong role in the development of the polarisation and blocking rapprochement mechanisms that were set in motion by the ICC investigations in Darfur. This suggests that ethnic conflicts may be more prone to a backlash caused by international investigations. In order to better understand the impact of the conflict context, the literature should absorb the major debates about the causes of war and peace from the field of peace and conflict studies. This includes, for example, the discussions concerning the impact of ethnicity on conflicts. Including these findings is crucial for explaining why international investigations and trials have different effects in different conflict contexts.

The final contextual factors that will be discussed in this section are the institutional structures of organisations dealing with accountability and past wrongs. As described above, many authors do not sufficiently take into account the institutional differences between the accountability measures they are analysing. This is also true for the research conducted on the ICC. There are compelling reasons for arguing that not even ICC investigations and trials should be regarded as a homogenous category, despite the fact that they are being conducted by the same organisation. The trigger mechanisms of the Rome Statute create very different conditions for ICC investigations in the different situation countries. It is obvious that it makes a difference whether a trial has been initiated through the referral of a member state, a referral by the UNSC or through the *propio motu* powers of the prosecutor. The situation becomes even more complex when taking into account the possibility of self-referrals that was not foreseen in the Rome Statute but quickly emerged as a dominant referral mechanism in the first years of the Court's work. The different impacts of the ICC referral decisions have been discussed at various points during the case studies and will be summarised in Section 7.2.1a.

To sum up, there are several contextual factors that have to be taken into consideration in order to correctly assess the impact of ICC investigations. They include the context of the investigations (conflict, democratic transition, post-conflict, post-transition), the type of investigations (UNSC referral, third-state referral, self-referral, *propio motu*), and conflict dynamics (in particular historical developments and the conflict type). Even if only the context of investigations and the type of investigations are taken into consideration, there are sixteen different categories of ICC investigations. This illustrates both the complexity and diversity of the research topic.

7.1.2 Tackling the complexity of investigations in conflicts

As shown in Chapter 6, the literature still tends to focus on a peace versus justice dichotomy (e.g. Ambos 2008, p. 19, Dyzenhaus 2003, p. 167). The main debate revolves around whether retributive justice measures like trials further or complicate conflict resolution efforts. The literature is largely divided between those who support international investigations and trials as a means to further conflict resolution and reconciliation, and those who criticise trials for the dangers they pose to conflict resolution efforts. Fortunately, a small but growing number of authors have explicitly started to move beyond this peace versus justice dichotomy (e.g. Buckley-Zistel 2010, p. 116).

The book at hand has introduced the conflict spectrum as an alternative model to understand the relationship of peace and justice in conflict contexts (Section 6.1.5). The Darfur and Uganda case studies served as a basis for this model. Both case studies illustrate that the situation on the ground is way too complex to be grasped with simple dichotomies. They have shown that international investigations have several contradicting effects on the conflict – some positive, some negative. These effects gain and lose strength over time. Some of these effects are temporary phenomena, like the spoiler retaliation and blocking negotiation mechanisms in the LRA conflict or the pressure and inducement mechanism in Darfur. The effects of the ICC may be nullified or reduced by other important variables, like conflict dynamics or the actions of important third parties. Consequently, there is no general answer to the questions how ICC investigations impact conflict resolution efforts and whether peace and justice go hand in hand or contradict each other. How these questions are to be answered depends on the timing of the investigations, the conflict dynamics and the perceptions and procedures. All of these factors will be briefly analysed below based on the findings of this book.

The immense complexity that international bodies face when conducting investigations and trials in conflict settings is one of the reasons for their contradictory impacts. As Chapter 6 has shown, there are a lot of third variables that need to be accounted for. At the same time, international courts face several dilemmas when working in conflict contexts. Finally, proponents of international investigations pursue a number of objectives that are in conflict with each other. The literature has so far not been able to fully deal with this complexity. Again, only few have recognised that the impacts of transitional justice mechanisms might be highly diffuse and ambiguous in practice (e.g. Buckley-Zistel 2008b, p. 19).

Another challenge in measuring the impact of investigations in conflicts is that some effects are temporary, others evolve over time and still others may only emerge in the very long term. The deterrence effect illustrates the interrelatedness of long- and short-term effects particularly well. As shown in the cross-case section, the probability of arrest is one of the key elements for effective deterrence. The ICC can thus be expected to deter crimes more efficiently in the long run, after it has successfully arrested and tried several individuals for crimes often committed in armed conflicts. More deterrence on the global level is a desirable good for humanity as a whole. But in order to achieve long-term deterrence, the ICC should not compromise on accountability demands in the short run. If perpetrators get the impression that punishment for war crimes is negotiable, the whole idea of deterrence is undermined. This in turn means that the ICC is forced to insist on publicly issued arrest warrants if it takes its mandate of combating impunity seriously, even if that insistence comes at the price of blocking peace negotiations. There is a hidden calculus behind the ICC's work in conflicts: it has to run the risk of blocking conflict resolution efforts in the short term as a necessary price for the greater good of efficient long-term deterrence on a global scale.

Most practitioners working at the ICC would not dare to spell it out loud, but a strict reading of the ICC's mandate means in the worst case that the Court would have to ignore the suffering of victims in an armed conflict in the short term, in order to achieve an overall reduction of war crimes and crimes against humanity in the long run. This was the implicit message behind statements of the Chief Prosecutor when he declared that there could be no political compromise concerning the implementation of ICC warrants because these compromises would undermine the Rome Statute (Moreno Ocampo 2008a, p. 12). Seen in a broader context, this example illustrates that ICC investigations and trials might have short-term negative effects that lead to long-term positive effects.

If the inherent complexity of ensuring accountability in conflicts is taken seriously, the question cannot be whether ICC investigations have positive or negative effects in conflict resolution contexts, but rather under which circumstances, ICC investigations can be helpful/harmful for conflict resolution efforts.

7.1.3 The role of third variables

These circumstances are defined to a considerable degree by third variables. One of them is the conflict dynamics that was already analysed above. The literature is discussing a wealth of third variables that have a potential influence. In order to understand the impact of investigations and trials in conflicts, a first important step would be to understand which of them matter most. The case studies have shown that there are a handful of variables that play an important role in the development of several causal mechanisms. Apart from the conflict dynamics, these variables are the international support for the investigations, as well as procedures and perceptions.

a. International support and enforcement

Both case studies have shown that international pressure played an important role for many causal mechanisms. Indeed, the case studies have shown that the effect of international pressure on a conflict party is probably more defining for conflict resolution opportunities than that of ICC investigations. It is therefore a particular challenge to distinguish whether progress in a conflict situation is really caused by the ICC investigations or if it is actually a result of the concentrated international pressure that often goes hand in hand with the referral of a case to the ICC.

International pressure is particularly important for causal mechanisms connected to the building of the rule of law, as well as the pressure and inducement mechanisms. It also plays a role in the blocking mechanisms, but is less decisive for the reconciliation mechanisms.

In the cases of the Darfur and LRA conflicts, international pressure was arguably the most important variable for the pressure and inducement mechanisms. In the case of Uganda, the ICC's role in these mechanisms is probably best understood as forming part of the international pressure. The ICC worked like a magnifying glass, focusing the rays of international pressure on single individuals or particular conflict parties.

In cases in which international pressure and ICC investigations go hand in hand, the dominant variable has to be determined on a case-by-case basis through careful process tracing. If effects can be connected to ICC investigations, for example through before–after comparisons or because decisive changes took place after an important ICC decision, then the Court probably played the dominant role.

In the case of Darfur, the situation was somewhat different as the international pressure and the ICC's investigations did not always work in tandem. The Darfur case has shown that the ICC can also be used as a mere instrument of international actors applying pressure on one conflict party. The UNSC basically used the ICC for its carrot and stick policy, trying to force the GoS to cooperate with demands of the international community. States are currently still very reluctant to support international investigations and trials without reservations since they are afraid of heightening the tensions in conflicts. This became particularly clear in Darfur, where geopolitical considerations surrounding the CPA and fears for the regional stability led to a reduction of the international pressure on the GoS and to a much reduced support for the ICC by its state parties.

There are other examples for cases in which states decided not to support international justice based on pragmatic considerations to ensure peace. The international community was, for example, initially very reluctant to support the ICTY investigations against Croatia's Tudjman and Serbia's Milosevic because they were important actors in securing the implementation of the Dayton Agreement (Nitsche 2007, p. 218). Afghanistan is another, more recent example. The UN decided not to support international investigations in Afghanistan to avoid destabilising the situation. Additionally, the ICC, which is conducting preliminary investigations in Afghanistan, is registering a lack of political support for its investigations (Rossi 2012, Snyder and Vinjamuri 2003, p. 8). Against this background, it is hardly surprising that amnesties still remain the dominant mechanism for dealing with war criminals (see Olsen et al. 2010, p. 7 and 39, von Braun 2009, p. 231).

The triggering mechanisms for the ICC jurisdiction discussed above also gain relevancy in the context of international support and enforcement. How the ICC got involved in a situation country does clearly play a role for the extent of international support that the Court can muster in its investigations. In the case of a UNSC referral, the Court can draw from the legitimacy of a UNSC resolution and actively demand international support on the grounds of the referral. The OTP followed this approach quite boldly in the case of Darfur. This added legitimacy of the investigations does in theory lead to the Court having more clout. In the case of *proprio motu* investigations, international support depends very much on which country the ICC is investigating. It is in part defined by whether the country in question is cooperating with the ICC and by the relationship of powerful states with the situation country. Obviously, states like the United States will be less likely to support ICC investigations against allied states who are themselves not cooperating with the ICC investigations on their territory.

The question of how the ICC investigations were triggered in a particular situation also has an influence on how much the ICC depends on international support in order to fulfil its mandate. In the case of self referrals, the ICC might be less dependent on international support if it can secure the cooperation of the referring government. In reverse, the ICC is likely more dependent on international cooperation if it decides to investigate the government that referred the case. This is been illustrated by the case study of the LRA conflict. Since the GoU initially regarded the ICC as a tool in its fight against the LRA, the Court never had any problems in obtaining the necessary cooperation for its investigations. On the other hand, some critics say that the close cooperation between the Court and the GoU led to biased and one-sided investigations. In any case, the LRA study showed that international support and pressure played a less defining role for the ICC effects in Uganda than in the case of the Darfur conflict. Again, the pressure and isolation mechanisms are very illustrative to point out the differences between the two cases. While the military pressure by the UPDF and the increasingly active role of the GoSS were decisive in isolating the LRA and forcing it to negotiate, it was the lack of sufficient international pressure that led to the failure of the aggressive OTP strategy in the case of Darfur. International pressure – or the lack thereof – was thus clearly more important in the context of the Darfur investigations than it was in the LRA investigations.

In general, one would expect the ICC to be more effective in a situation in which it can count on a UNSC referral. Therefore, it is a surprising finding of the Darfur case study that the ICC did not enjoy more support on the international stage despite the UNSC referral. Instead, the Court has so far been largely used as a tool, even by important supporters like France.

The UNSC has overall emerged as an unhelpful factor in ICC investigations so far. One of the problems is that the status of the P5 in the UNSC and their veto powers introduce realpolitik into the realm of international criminal law. The political considerations that play a role in referring and deferring cases can potentially damage the legitimacy of the ICC investigations. The case of Darfur has shown that some damage has already been done. This has become particularly clear during the GoS campaign branding the ICC as a neo-colonial actor and instrument of a Western conspiracy.

The main argument of the GoS was that the United States had not ratified the Rome Statute, but still supported the referral of a situation in another non-state party at the UNSC. The connection between the UNSC and the Rome Statute has the potential to become a birth defect of the ICC since the possibility of UNSC referrals and deferrals introduces political bias into a system that should be even-handed and bound by legality. An international court that does not meet these standards cannot survive in the long run. The problematic role of the UNSC could well start to encroach on the legitimacy of the ICC if referrals become an instrument regularly used by the UNSC. This dangerous tendency has been illustrated by the UNSC referral of the situation in Libya to the ICC (see Ambos and Stegmiller 2012, p. 15). The referral in resolution 1970 was selective in referring the situation to the Court in several ways. First, it explicitly excluded investigations of the conduct of any states parties. Second, it limited the temporary jurisdiction of the ICC to the beginning of the armed rebellion on 15 February 2011. Presumably, the jurisdiction was limited to avoid any investigations into crimes committed during the period when the West was on good terms with the Kaddafi regime (Kersten 2011, Tiemessen 2014, p. 12f.). Finally, the role of the UNSC in the ICC referral system is also brought forward as one of the main reasons for the increasing scepticism of the AU towards the Court.

Two important questions emerge from this section. First, how do the trigger mechanisms of the ICC jurisdiction influence the international support for ICC investigations in conflicts? And second, to what extent does the international support for ICC investigations in a particular situation determine the impact of ICC investigations? Even though some answers were given in this section, both questions require further research. The findings of the case studies suggest that international support is of particular importance for the isolation and pressure mechanisms, but can also play an important role in blocking negotiations or human rights protection, as was the case in the LRA conflict.

b. Procedures and perceptions

One of the main findings of this study is that the impact of international investigations in conflict situations depends to a large degree on *how* they are being conducted; and how local, regional and international actors perceive the justice issues surrounding them.

The differences of how institutions tasked with delivering accountability implement their mandates have been largely ignored in the literature. Quantitative studies do not distinguish between truth commissions with totally different mandates, whose work differs enormously in practice. In other cases, international, national and hybrid trials are lumped together even though these trials are carried out under completely different conditions. Unfortunately, many case studies do not analyse the role of the prosecution strategy or the impact of procedural decisions taken by the organs of the courts either. As the case studies of the ICC investigations in Darfur and Uganda have shown, no two ICC investigations are similar. The factors summarised under procedures and perceptions play an important role in determining the different paths that ICC investigations can take. Their role is analysed *in extenso* in Chapter 6.

An important question that remains unanswered regarding justice perceptions is how cultural values and political interests relate to each other in shaping these perceptions. Was the local population in Uganda sceptical of ICC investigations due to the (supposedly) strong local culture of restorative justice, or because civil society organisations as well as traditional and religious authorities mobilised public opinion against the ICC investigations? Is the AU mainly criticising the ICC because it has different ideas about justice and accountability, or because Sudan was able to conduct a successful political campaign against the ICC? Or is the AU criticism mainly aimed at those powers in the UNSC who referred the case to the ICC but do everything to avoid their own citizens being targeted by the ICC? The case studies at hand can only be a first step towards answering these questions.

It is also important to consider that procedural decisions of courts and the justice perceptions of important stakeholders are intertwined. In both Uganda and Darfur, the decisions taken by the OTP led to a lot of criticism based on justice perceptions. In northern Uganda, many locals believed that the ICC was overriding traditional justice principles and criticised the Court for that. In the Darfur case, many AU members felt that the ICC was applying neo-colonial forms of justice by issuing an arrest warrant against President al-Bashir. The interesting question that remains is whether the ICC would have been able to mobilise more support and deliver better results if the Chief Prosecutor had been more sensitive to cultural differences, and if his decisions and statements had been less controversial. At the moment, there is little willingness at the ICC to let local perceptions influence the work of the OTP. As a senior legal advisor at the OTP put it: perception based decision-making would be wrong (Rastan 2010, p. 578).

The case studies have shown that perceptions and procedures are two highly relevant and so far neglected variables that shape the impact of ICC investigations in conflicts. These two variables are best understood as twin variables that strongly influence each other and have an impact on the ICC investigations in conjunction. It will be one of the major challenges for the research agenda to integrate the complicated relationship between the impact of investigations, procedural decisions and perceptions in future models and theories.

7.2 Outlook

> *If the ICC is going to step into Africa's complex wars, it must understand the local contexts and think through the effects of its actions.*
>
> (Dowden 2007)

This book can only be a first step on the way towards better understanding the impact of international investigations and trials in conflict contexts. The research agenda on this topic is still in its early phases. Currently, a preference for quantitative methods prevails among researchers who try to address the lack of empirical foundations in the literature. Yet, at this stage, quantitative methods are not the most suitable approach for analysing the impact of accountability measures in conflicts. There are too many contextual factors that have to be taken into consideration in the models as long as we do not fully understand which variables matter. At the same time, the number of cases in the different categories (e.g. international trials in ongoing conflicts, truth commissions with a robust mandate in post-conflict contexts) is just not high enough to cope with the number of relevant variables. Current quantitative surveys thus offer results at the expense of validity by lumping different categories of accountability measures together.

The author has therefore argued for a case study approach in order to develop mid-level theories to drive the research agenda forward. An approach starting with a cross-case overview was chosen to ensure that the findings would not be too context-specific. The causal mechanisms analysed here are based on a very broad literature overview supported by a data-led approach for additional validity. The main variables influencing ICC investigations that emerged from the case studies were conflict dynamics, international support, procedural decisions taken at the Court's organs and justice perceptions of the stakeholders.

As envisaged at the beginning of the project, these findings are a helpful basis for future research. Research designs could tie in with these results by conducting more similar case studies, thus testing if the influence of these four variables can be confirmed in other cases.

The second objective of this book was to better understand the impact of international investigations in conflict contexts. The finding that procedural decisions have an important impact on the effects of international investigations in conflicts has tangible repercussions in practice. It means that international courts and tribunals are not passively caught in a dilemma of peace versus justice as much of the literature has suggested in the past. Rather, prosecutors and judges are active players that take decisions with important political implications and consequences for the conflicts. To some degree, they can navigate the peace-justice divide and influence the effects of investigations and trials in conflicts.

Practitioners of international criminal justice have to stop living the lie that justice can be delivered in a political vacuum. The case studies have clearly shown that decisions taken at the organs of the Court have very clear political implications. Only if practitioners accept that they are meddling in politics to a certain extent, can they make active use of the manoeuvring space between peace and justice. The alternative would be to become completely passive implementers of statutes and resolutions and to abstain from any statements and actions that could be interpreted as political. It is hard to imagine how this would be possible in practice, as legal texts always need to be interpreted, and these interpretations are always political to some degree. By denying the obvious influence of politics on its work, the Court will undermine its own legitimacy (also Tiemessen 2014, p. 5).

Additionally, practitioners of international criminal justice are clearly passionate about their work and have a strong motivation to make a difference through their efforts. Judge Moloto of the ICTY pointed out that members of the OTP of the ICTY had created expectations of delivering peace and reconciliation with some of the documents that they had published (Moloto 2010). Similar aspirations seem to be prevalent among the staff of the ICC. Chief Prosecutor Moreno Ocampo has stated that '*Dreamers are the drivers of the ICC*', and Senior Trial Attorney Chung referred to Darfur as '*the case the ICC was meant to do*' (Yates 2009). Pascal Turlan, International Cooperation Advisor for the OTP, stated in a Congolese radio programme that the ICC can contribute to peace efforts in Darfur (Zackou-Wangui 2010). Clearly, these people feel that they have a mission beyond the legal mandate of their institutions and want to make a difference in the lives of the victims of armed conflicts.

Since the practitioners perceive themselves as active players, it is imperative that they stop denying the obvious: they are taking political decisions *within the boundaries of their mandate and the regulations of the Rome Statute*. The ICC does not become a political institution by admitting this simple fact (see Kerr 2004, p. 218–219). Law has to be interpreted by people, but that does not change its character as law. Law remains law and does not become arbitrariness just because it is being interpreted, as long as the interpretation is guided by clear, predictable and objective rules. The OTP has to become more transparent and consistent in its decision-making processes in order to dispel past allegations of bias (also Ambos and Stegmiller 2012, p. 10).

A major problem at the moment is that the ICC is taking decisions that have important political implications and a real impact in conflict situations without having the necessary expertise. This can be illustrated with a number of examples. First, there is a certain tendency among OTP staff to believe that they are capable of deciding whether negotiations in a conflict are promising or not. Even decisions concerning the prosecution strategy are apparently taken on this basis. In the case of the Juba Talks, the OTP concluded that the LRA was not genuinely interested in talks but was rather buying time. The prosecution thus started insisting publicly on the enforcement of the arrest warrants against the LRA commanders.

In the case of Darfur, the ICC was not very receptive to fears that the Court might block negotiation efforts by indicting President al-Bashir. ICC staff members stated in 2008 that there was no peace process that could be blocked (Peskin 2009b, p. 310). In reality, several smaller agreements were signed between the GoS and rebel splinters during that year, and the UN and the AU spent most of 2008 trying to prepare talks between the GoS and major rebel groups. Moreno Ocampo went even further and added in 2009 that President al-Bashir was not the right person to be negotiated with since he had been indicted by the ICC. According to him, the international community should therefore '*adjust to the reality of the ICC*' (Allen 2009). Yet, it is clearly not within the competence of the Chief Prosecutor of an international court to decide who is a legitimate negotiation partner for internationally mediated peace talks.

The Chief Prosecutor also showed a tendency to simplify complex conflict situations in his public statements. This is illustrated by his approach towards the LRA. He consistently painted the group as an irrational and evil sect. In the Darfur case, he used a narrative describing a genocidal war waged by the GoS and the Janjaweed against African victims in Darfur. At a conference in Chicago, celebrating the tenth anniversary of the Rome Statue, he claimed that '*Arresting Haroun today will break the criminal system in Darfur*' (Eichstaedt 2008). It would be naive to believe that the arrest of a single man could break a criminal system. Interestingly, the Chief Prosecutor contradicted his earlier statement later when comparing the whole GoS to the Nazi regime. While he described Haroun's individual role as central before, he later claimed that the whole government was involved in a criminal system.

Apparently, the Chief Prosecutor based some of his decisions on his personal analysis of conflict situations. For example, Moreno Ocampo was very vocal in claiming that President al-Bashir had de jure and de facto control over the Janjaweed militias. He even started criticising those who disagreed with him, saying that it was incredible that people still believed that the Janjaweed were autonomous actors. He thus single-handedly dismissed the analysis of a number of the most knowledgeable Sudan experts, who described the lack of government control over the Janjaweed militias and he ignored the clear signs of Janjaweed mutinies on the ground (see Allen 2009, see Section 4.1.3b). Despite strong evidence to the contrary, the PTC followed the Prosecutor's assessment in its arrest warrant decision and claimed that al-Bashir had full control over the Janjaweed militias (PTC I 2009, §222).

Finally, the OTP under Moreno Ocampo was not particularly open to criticism. The Chief Prosecutor said in an interview that he '*[doesn't] see so many problems inside the Court. The biggest problem is that everyone in the world has to adjust to this new idea to use the law to control violence, and that is a big challenge. So the legitimacy [issue] is more the legitimacy of political actors than the Court itself* (Moreno Ocampo 2010c). The idea at the OTP seemed to be that the ICC is taking decisions based on law, detached from political considerations, and that the whole world should adapt to those decisions. Clearly, this is not a realistic basis for the work of an international court that relies on state cooperation to enforce its decisions.

These examples show that there is still too little understanding of the delicate political nature of international criminal justice interventions among some practitioners. Three factors contribute to this problem.

The first objective of practitioners is to implement international criminal law to the letter. If the law is compromised once, it is no longer taken seriously and enforcing it will become that much harder. For the ICC, it is especially important not to yield to pressure as it has to prove itself as a new organisation. As a consequence, enforcing its decisions takes precedence over analysing the impact of its work in conflict situations. Even though the perception that law is weakened by compromises is quite true, the space for manoeuvre that still exists without damaging the integrity of the law is often overlooked. Particularly, local approaches to justice are often dismissed too readily.[1]

Second, international criminal justice practitioners are working in an extremely hostile environment, and under a lot of pressure due to high workloads, high expectations of victims and other stakeholders and attempts of accused individuals to derail and discredit their work. This might lead to a bunker-mentality among some practitioners, which makes it more difficult for them to distinguish between well-founded criticism and attempts to discredit their work.

Third, introducing accountability from the outside is increasingly seen as an instrument for conflict resolution or peacemaking by different international actors. International courts and tribunals are perceived as an alternative tool to military interventions in this context. At the same time, the political dimension of their work is being ignored (see Leebaw

[1] Mark Drumbl has laid valuable groundwork for including local justice mechanisms in transitional justice by suggesting a system of 'qualified deference'. Qualified deference ensures the integrity of international criminal law by introducing a set of criteria that have to be fulfilled in order to qualify the case for a deferral to the local level (Drumbl 2007, p. 129). Oette has also suggested that there is a possibility of deferring cases to regional courts based on the interests of justice (Oette 2010b, p. 363).

2008, p. 106, Vinjamuri 2010). Calling for international investigations in post-conflict situations or even during conflicts has become a mainstream approach of diplomats, without taking the political delicacy of such an intervention seriously enough.

As a consequence, the ICC is in need of political expertise when investigating crimes in highly volatile conflict situations. The ICC can only successfully navigate the peace-justice divide if it is able to correctly analyse the complexities of each conflict situation and develop the necessary strategies to deal with them. Other authors have brought forward similar demands, calling for a risk assessment when investigations are carried out in conflict contexts (Brounéus 2008, p. 213). Still others have called for a unit in the immediate Office of the Prosecutor that deals with strategy and policy papers (Ambos and Stegmiller 2012, p. 8).

One reason why the ICC is unable to recruit the necessary expertise to deal with the political implications of its decisions is the notorious shortage of funds. According to the Chief Prosecutor, staff is moved around between situation countries within the OTP as seen fit (United Nations 2010). The Court would otherwise not be able to cover all the cases with its limited staff. But this also means that investigators are not staying on a case long enough to build up the necessary knowledge about the complex conflict situations they have to deal with.

Additionally, the overwhelming majority of investigators at the OTP have a legal background. Combined with the fact that they spend very little time on the ground in the situation countries, this means that it is very difficult for them to get a feel for the conflicts beyond the legal questions connected to the crimes they are investigating. The OTP would be well advised to recruit political analysts for each of the situation countries to offer in-house expertise and impact assessments before the OTP takes important procedural decisions. While these impact assessments are, strictly speaking, not part of the ICC's mandate, it is difficult to imagine how the Court will be able to work successfully in the long term, if it does not start to take the impacts of its investigations on conflicts into consideration. Additionally, the case studies have shown that some decisions within the OTP are already taken with the aim to influence conflict parties.

In many ways, the ICC is a Court ahead of its time. It has a potentially global jurisdiction, but it lacks a global executive power that is willing and able to enforce its decisions. It remains to be seen whether the Court will be able to surmount the formidable challenges that it is facing in both its effectiveness and legitimacy. In the next decades, it may wither away and become an international organisation of scarce relevancy, doomed to be a powerless witness to atrocities. Or it may indeed prove to be – as its supporters claim – the herald of a new age, in which the world is ruled by law and the power of states is exercised within the limits of international law. The future of the Court may very well depend on the ability of practitioners to deal with the complexities described in this book and on their readiness to incorporate conflict resolution expertise in their work.

BIBLIOGRAPHY

ABC. 2007. Darfur Militias Have No Fear: UN Report. *ABC Premium News* [Online]. Available: www.lexisnexis.com/de/business/results/docview/docview.do?docLinkInd=true&risb=21_T14886880115&format=GNBFI&sort=BOOLEAN&startDocNo=1&resultsUrlKey=29_T14886880119&cisb=22_T14886880118&treeMax=true&treeWidth=0&csi=300224&docNo=1 [Accessed 9 June 2012].

Abdelrahman, Z. M. A. 4 December 2010. *RE: Interview with Zakaira Mohammed Ali Abdelrahman.*

Abdhalla, T., Mustafa, A., Jennings, S., Glassborrow, K. and Pritchard, B. E. 2010. Concern Over Janjaweed "Immunity". Available: www.iwpr.net/report-news/concern-over-janjaweed-%E2%80%9Cimmunity%E2%80%9D [Accessed 14 June 2010].

Abdulai, E. S. 2010. The Standoff Between the ICC and African Leaders: The Debate Revisited. *In:* The Foundation for Law, Justice and Society (ed.) *Oxford Transitional Justice Research: Debating International Justice in Africa.* Oxford: The Foundation for Law, Justice and Society and The Centre for Socio-Legal Studies, University of Oxford.

Abdul-Jalil, M., Mohammed, A. A. and Yousuf, A. 2007. NATIVE Administration and Local Governance in Darfur: Past and Future. *In:* De Waal, A. (ed.) *War in Darfur and the Search for Peace.* Cambridge, MA: Global Equity Initiative Harvard University.

ACJPS. 2012. Sudan Human Rights Monitor: December 2011–January 2012: African Centre for Justice and Peace Studies. Available: www.acjps.org/sudan-human-rights-monitor-issue-15/ [Accessed 15 June 2012].

Adam, T., Mustafa, A. and Jennings, S. 2010. Darfur IDP Detentions Draw Reform Calls. *IWPR* [Online]. Available: http://iwpr.net/print/report-news/darfur-idp-detentions-draw-reform-calls [Accessed 10 July 2010].

Adam, T. A., Glassborow, K., Jennings, S. and Musa, A. M. Z. 2011. *Special Report: International Failures Prolong Darfur's Misery.* The Hague: IWPR.

AFP. 2004. Sudan's Beshir Says Aid Agencies Are 'Real Enemy' in Darfur. *Agence France Press* [Online]. Available: www.lexisnexis.com/de/business/

results/docview/docview.do?docLinkInd=true&risb=21_T15006121646&format=GNBFI&sort=BOOLEAN&startDocNo=1&resultsUrlKey=29_T15006121650&cisb=22_T15006121649&treeMax=true&treeWidth=0&csi=10903&docNo=13 [Accessed 15 June 2012].

2005a. Annan Warns of Nuclear 'Cascade', Calls for Help in Darfur. *Agence France Press* [Online]. Available: www.lexisnexis.com/de/business/results/docview/docview.do?docLinkInd=true&risb=21_T14929852786&format=GNBFI&sort=BOOLEAN&startDocNo=1&resultsUrlKey=29_T14929852790&cisb=22_T14929852789&treeMax=true&treeWidth=0&csi=10903&docNo=5 [Accessed 15 June 2012].

2005b. UN General Assembly Blocks Debate on Sudan's Human Rights Record. *Agence France Press* [Online]. Available: www.lexisnexis.com/de/business/results/docview/docview.do?docLinkInd=true&risb=21_T14930039176&format=GNBFI&sort=BOOLEAN&startDocNo=1&resultsUrlKey=29_T14930039180&cisb=22_T14930039179&treeMax=true&treeWidth=0&csi=10903&docNo=6 [Accessed 15 June 2012].

2007. Beshir Orders Sudan Paramilitary Camps to Reopen. *Agence France Press* [Online]. Available: www.lexisnexis.com/de/business/results/docview/docview.do?docLinkInd=true&risb=21_T14985127309&format=GNBFI&sort=BOOLEAN&startDocNo=1&resultsUrlKey=29_T14985127313&cisb=22_T14985127312&treeMax=true&treeWidth=0&csi=10903&docNo=5 [Accessed 15 June 2012].

2008. Sudan's Beshir Rejects 'Made up' War Crimes Claims. *Agence France Press* [Online]. Available: www.lexisnexis.com/de/business/results/docview/docview.do?docLinkInd=true&risb=21_T14886970183&format=GNBFI&sort=BOOLEAN&startDocNo=1&resultsUrlKey=29_T14886970187&cisb=22_T14886970186&treeMax=true&treeWidth=0&csi=10903&docNo=2 [Accessed 9 June 2012].

2009a. Africa Will Not Be Colonised Again: Gambian President on ICC. *Agence France Press* [Online]. Available: www.lexisnexis.com/de/business/search/homesubmitForm.do [Accessed 9 June 2012].

2009b. Beshir 'Exterminating' People in Darfur: ICC Prosecutor. *Agence France Press* [Online]. Available: www.lexisnexis.com/de/business/results/docview/docview.do?docLinkInd=true&risb=21_T14936951964&format=GNBFI&sort=BOOLEAN&startDocNo=1&resultsUrlKey=29_T14936951968&cisb=22_T14936951967&treeMax=true&treeWidth=0&csi=10903&docNo=3 [Accessed 9 June 2012].

2009c. Beshir Personality Cult Grips Khartoum. *Agence France Press* [Online]. [Accessed 9 June 2012].

2009d. Beshir Warrant 'Absurd': UN General Assembly Chief. *Agence France Press* [Online]. Available: www.lexisnexis.com/de/business/results/docview/docview.do?docLinkInd=true&risb=21_T14938530205&format=GNBFI&

sort=BOOLEAN&startDocNo=1&resultsUrlKey=29_T14938530209&cisb=22_T14938530208&treeMax=true&treeWidth=0&csi=10903&docNo=2 [Accessed 9 June 2012].

2009e. Darfur Rebels Vow to Topple Beshir if ICC Issues Warrant. *Agence France Press* [Online]. [Accessed 9 June 2012].

2009f. Sudan President Says Civilians Not Targeted in Darfur: Report. *Agence France Press* [Online]. Available: www.lexisnexis.com/de/business/results/docview/docview.do?docLinkInd=true&risb=21_T14887006008&format=GNBFI&sort=BOOLEAN&startDocNo=1&resultsUrlKey=29_T14887006012&cisb=22_T14887006011&treeMax=true&treeWidth=0&csi=10903&docNo=8 [Accessed 9 June 2012].

2010. Sudan Vote Like 'Hitler Election': ICC Prosecutor. *Agence France Press* [Online]. Available: www.lexisnexis.com/de/business/results/docview/docview.do?docLinkInd=true&risb=21_T14934186391&format=GNBFI&sort=BOOLEAN&startDocNo=1&resultsUrlKey=29_T14934186395&cisb=22_T14934186394&treeMax=true&treeWidth=0&csi=10903&docNo=1 [Accessed 15 June 2012].

2011. Darfur Rebel Leader Calls for Libya-Style No-Fly Zone. *Agence France Press* [Online]. Available: www.lexisnexis.com/de/business/results/docview/docview.do?docLinkInd=true&risb=21_T15030429241&format=GNBFI&sort=BOOLEAN&startDocNo=1&resultsUrlKey=29_T15030429245&cisb=22_T15030429244&treeMax=true&treeWidth=0&csi=10903&docNo=16 [Accessed 15 June 2012].

2012. ICC Prosecutor Threatens to Investigate Sudan UN Ambassador. *Agence France Press* [Online]. Available: http://news.yahoo.com/icc-prosecutor-threatens-investigate-sudan-un-ambassador-203340786.html [Accessed 11 June 2012].

Afrobarometer. 2008. Summary of Results: Round 4 Afrobarometer Survey in Uganda: CDD/idasa/MSU. Available: www.afrobarometer.org/

Aggestam, K. 2006. Internal and External Dynamics of Spoiling: A Negotiation Approach. *In:* Newman, E. and Richmond, O. (eds.) *Challenges to Peace-building: Managing Spoilers During Conflict Resolution.* Tokyo/New York/Paris: United Nations University Press.

AI. 1997. *"Breaking God's Commands": The Destruction of Childhood by the Lord's Resistance Army.* London: Amnesty International.

1999a. *Breaking the Circle: Protecting Human Rights in the Northern War Zone.* London: Amnesty International.

1999b. *The Full Picture: Uncovering Human Rights Violations by Government Forces in the Northern War.* London: Amnesty International.

2005. *Open Letter to the Chief Prosecutor of the International Criminal Court: Comments on the Concept of the Interests of Justice.* London: Amnesty International. IOR 40/023/2005.

2008. *Uganda: Agreement and Annex on Accountability and Reconciliation Falls Short of a Comprehensive Plan to End Impunity*. London: Amnesty International. AFR 59/001/2008.

2012a. Sudan: No End to Violence in Darfur. *Amnesty International* [Online]. Available: www.amnesty.org/en/library/asset/AFR54/007/2012/en/c1037da2-0f54-4343-8325-461d80e751c2/afr540072012en.pdf [Accessed 2 March 2012].

2012b. Sudan: No End to Violence in Darfur. Available: www.amnestyusa.org/research/reports/sudan-no-end-to-violence-in-darfur [Accessed 23 March 2012].

Ajok, M. 2 September 2011. *RE: Interview with Margret Ajok, Transitional Justice Coordinator at the Justice Law and Order Sector of the Ugandan Government.*

Akhavan, P. 2001. Beyond Impunity: Can International Criminal Justice Prevent Future Atrocities? *The American Journal of International Law*, 95, 7–31.

2005. The Lord's Resistance Army Case: Uganda's Submission of the First State Referral to the International Criminal Court. *The American Journal of International Law*, 99, 403–421.

2009. Are International Criminal Tribunals a Disincentive to Peace?: Reconciling Judicial Romanticism with Political Realism. *Human Rights Quarterly*, 31, 624–654.

Al-Arabiya. 2009. Thousands Protest for Bashir in Khartoum. *AlArabiya.net* [Online]. [Accessed 29 June 2012].

Al-Hussein, Z. R. A. Z. 2008. Report on the Major Findings of the Conference. *In:* Ambos, K., Large, J. and Wierda, M. (eds.) *Building a Future on Peace and Justice: Studies on Transitional Justice, Peace and Development*. Heidelberg: Springer.

Al-Sharq Al-Awsat. 2009. Report on Signs of Possible Split Inside Sudan's Ruling Party. *Al-Sharq al-Awsat* [Online]. Available: www.lexisnexis.com/de/business/results/docview/docview.do?docLinkInd=true&risb=21_T14936664213&format=GNBFI&sort=BOOLEAN&startDocNo=1&resultsUrlKey=29_T14936664217&cisb=22_T14936664216&treeMax=true&treeWidth=0&csi=10962&docNo=2 [Accessed 15 June 2012].

AL. 2008. *Left to Their Own Devices: The Continued Suffering of Victims of the Conflict in Northern Uganda and the Need for Reparations*. London: Amnesty International. AFR 59/009/2008.

2009. *Joint Statement of the Arab League at the 2009 Qatar Summit: Special Statement Pertaining to Sudan*. Qatar: Arab League.

Al Jazeera. 2012. Sudan Governor to Troops: 'Take no Prisoners'. *Al Jazeera* [Online]. Available: www.aljazeera.com/news/africa/2012/03/2012331114433519971.html [Accessed 6 April 2011].

Albert, I. O. 2008. Understanding Peace in Africa. *In:* Francis, D. J. (ed.) *Peace & Conflict in Africa*. London/New York: Zed Books.

Ali-Dinar, A. B. 2009. The Darfur Conflict: A Natural Process or War by Design? *In:* Hassan, S. M. and Ray, C. E. (eds.) *Darfur and the Crisis of Governance in Sudan: A Critical Reader.* Ithaca/London: Cornell University Press.

Ali, T. M. and Matthews, R. O. 2004a. Conclusion: The Long and Difficult Road to Peace. *In:* Ali, T. M. and Matthews, R. O. (eds.) *Durable Peace: Challenges for Peacebuilding in Africa.* Toronto/Buffalo/London: Toronto University Press.

2004b. Introduction. *In:* Ali, T. M. and Matthews, R. O. (eds.) *Durable Peace: Challenges for Peacebuilding in Africa.* Toronto/Buffalo/London: Toronto University Press.

Ali, T. M., Matthews, R. O. and Spears, I. 2004. Failures in Peacebuilding: Sudan (1972–1983) and Angola. *In:* Ali, T. M. and Matthews, R. O. (eds.) *Durable Peace: Challenges for Peacebuilding in Africa.* Toronto/Buffalo/London: Toronto University Press.

Allan, P. and Keller, A. 2006. Introduction: Rethinking Peace & Justice Conceptually. *In:* Allan, P. and Keller, A. (eds.) *What Is a Just Peace?* Oxford: Oxford University Press.

Allen, E. 2009. Seven Questions: Luis Moreno-Ocampo. *Foreign Policy* [Online]. Available: www.foreignpolicy.com/story/cms.php?story_id=4698&page=0 [Accessed 7 July 2011].

Allen, T. 2005. War and Justice in Northern Uganda: An Assessment of the International Criminal Court's Intervention. Available: www.crisisstates.com/download/others/AllenICCReport.pdf [Accessed 10 December 2010].

2006. *Trial Justice: The International Criminal Court and the Lord's Resistance Army.* London/New York: Zed Books.

2010. Bitter Roots: The 'Invention' of Acholi Traditional Justice. *In:* Allen, T. and Vlassenroot, K. (eds.) *The Lord's Resistance Army: Myth and Reality.* London/New York: Zed Books.

Allen, T., Laker, F., Porter, H. and Schomerus, M. 2010. Postscript: A Kind of Peace and an Exported War. *In:* Allen, T. and Vlassenroot, K. (eds.) *The Lord's Resistance Army: Myth and Reality.* London/New York: Zed Books.

Allen, T. and Vlassenroot, K. 2010. Introduction. *In:* Allen, T. and Vlassenroot, K. (eds.) *The Lord's Resistance Army: Myth and Reality.* London/New York: Zed Books.

Ambos, K. 2008. The Legal Framework of Transitional Justice: A Systematic Study with a Special Focus on the Role of the ICC. *In:* Ambos, K., Large, J. and Wierda, M. (eds.) *Building a Future on Peace and Justice: Studies on Transitional Justice, Peace and Development.* Heidelberg: Springer.

Ambos, K., Large, J. and Wierda, M. 2008. Preface. *In:* Ambos, K., Large, J. and Wierda, M. (eds.) *Building a Future on Peace and Justice: Studies on Transitional Justice, Peace and Development.* Heidelberg: Springer.

Ambos, K. and Stegmiller, I. 2012. Prosecuting International Crimes at the International Criminal Court: Is There a Coherent and Comprehensive

Prosecution Strategy? *Crime, Law and Social Change*, online publication, http://link.springer.com/article/10.1007%2Fs10611-012-9407-9#page-1.

Anderson, J. 2006. World Court Faces Biggest Challenge. *IWPR* [Online]. Available: http://iwpr.net/report-news/world-court-faces-biggest-challenge [Accessed 9 November 2010].

Anderson, J., Yousif, Z. and Adam, T. 2012. Has ICC Lost Touch With Darfur Refugees? Available: http://iwpr.net/report-news/has-international-court-lost-touch-darfur-refugees?utm_source=CICC+Newsletters&utm_campaign=bcd874d34a-June_2012_Darfur_Digest_EN&utm_medium=email [Accessed 8 June 2012].

AP. 2005. UN Threatens Prosecution as Toll from Darfur Attack Rises. *Associated Press* [Online]. Available: www.lexisnexis.com/de/business/results/docview/docview.do?docLinkInd=true&risb=21_T14933635924&format=GNBFI&sort=BOOLEAN&startDocNo=1&resultsUrlKey=29_T14933635928&cisb=22_T14933635927&treeMax=true&treeWidth=0&csi=247361&docNo=23 [Accessed 15 June 2012].

2007. China Won't Tolerate Threats to Darfur Peacekeepers. *Sudan Tribune* [Online]. Available: www.sudantribune.com/spip.php?article24939 [Accessed 25 December 2011].

2008a. Lawyer: Sudanese Opposition Leader Detained. *Associated Press* [Online]. Available: www.lexisnexis.com/de/business/results/docview/docview.do?docLinkInd=true&risb=21_T14936642981&format=GNBFI&sort=BOOLEAN&startDocNo=1&resultsUrlKey=29_T14936642985&cisb=22_T14936642984&treeMax=true&treeWidth=0&csi=138211&docNo=6 [Accessed 16 June 2012].

2008b. Sudan's Leader Says Charges Meant to Topple Him. *Associated Press* [Online]. [Accessed 16 June 2012].

2009. Sudan Official Warns Over Indicting President. *Associated Press* [Online]. [Accessed 16 June 2012].

Apuuli, K. P. 2005. Amnesty and International Law: The Case of the Lord's Resistance Army Insurgents in Northern Uganda. *African Journal on Conflict Resolution*, 5, 33–62.

2006. The ICC Arrest Warrants for the Lord's Resistance Army Leaders and Peace Prospects for Northern Uganda. *Journal of International Criminal Justice*, 4, 179–187.

2008a. The ICC's Possible Deferral of the LRA Case to Uganda. *Journal of International Criminal Justice*, 6, 801–813.

2008b. The International Criminal Court & the Lord's Resistance Army Insurgency in Northern Uganda. *In:* Nhema, A. and Zezela, P. T. (eds.) *The Resolution of African Conflicts: The Management of Conflict Resolution & Post-Conflict Reconstruction*. Addis Ababa: OSSREA.

Arbour, L. 2006. *Observations of the United Nations High Commissioner for Human Rights Invited in Application of Rule 103 of the Rules of Procedure and Evidence*, The Hague: International Criminal Court. ICC-02/05-19.

Arieff, A., Margesson, R., Browne, M. A. and Weed, M. C. 2011. *International Criminal Court Cases in Africa: Status and Policy Issues*, Washington, DC: Congressional Research Service. RL34665.

ARLPI. 2009. ARLPI's Position on the International Criminal Court (ICC). Available: www.arlpi.org/international-criminal-court-s-icc-uganda [Accessed 16 November 2010].

Arsanjani, M. H. and Reisman, W. M. 2008. The International Criminal Court and the Congo: From Theory to Reality. *In:* Sadat, L. N. and Scharf, M. P. (eds.) *The Theory and Practice of International Criminal Law: Essays in Honor of M. Cherif Bassiouni.* Leiden: Martinus Nijhoff Publishers.

Assal, M. A. M. 2009. Locating Responsibilities: National and International Responses to the Crisis in Darfur. *In:* Hassan, S. M. and Ray, C. E. (eds.) *Darfur and the Crisis of Governance in Sudan: A Critical Reader.* Ithaca/London: Cornell University Press.

Atkinson, R. R. 2010. 'The Realists in Juba'?: An Analysis of the Juba Peace Talks. *In:* Allen, T. and Vlassenroot, K. (eds.) *The Lord's Resistance Army: Myth and Reality.* London/New York: Zed Books.

AU. 2009. Decision on the Meeting of African States Parties to the Rome Statute of the International Criminal Court (ICC). Libya: African Union. Doc. Assembly/AU/13(XIII).

2011. Decision on the Implementation of the Assembly Decision on the International Criminal Court. Libya: African Union. Assembly Doc. EX.CL/670 (XIX). Assembly/AU/Dec.366(XVII).

AUPD. 2009. Report of the African Union High Level Panel on Darfur. Addis Abeba: African Union. PSC/AHG/2(CCVII).

Babalanda, V. and Kyama, S. 23 August 2011. *RE: Interview with Members of the Avocats sans Frontières Office in Uganda.*

Bächler, G. 2004. *Conflict Transformation through State Reform.* Berlin: Berghof Zentrum.

Badiey, N. 2008. Ocampo v. Bashir: The Perspective from Juba. Available: www.csls.ox.ac.uk/documents/Badiey_Final.pdf. [Accessed 25 June 2011].

Baines, E. 2005. Pursuing Peace and Justice: International and Local Initiatives: Liu Institute for Global Issues Conflict and Development Programme.

Baines, E. K. 2008. With or Without Peace: Disarmament, Demobilisation and Reintegration in Northern Uganda, Gulu: Justice and Reconciliation Project. Field Notes, No. 6, February 2008.

2007. The Haunting of Alice: Local Approaches to Justice and Reconciliation in Northern Uganda. *The International Journal of Transitional Justice*, 1, 91–114.

2009. Complex Political Perpetrators: Reflections on Dominic Ongwen. *Journal of Modern African Studies*, 47, 163–191.

Baldauf, S. 2009. Why did Sudan Make a Deal with Darfur Rebels? *Christian Science Monitor* [Online]. Available: www.lexisnexis.com/de/business/results/docview/docview.do?docLinkInd=true&risb=21_T12732166078&format=GNBFI&sort=DATE,A,H&startDocNo=701&resultsUrlKey=29_T12732166045&cisb=22_T12732223268&treeMax=true&treeWidth=0&csi=7945&docNo=732 [Accessed 15 September 2011].

Baldauf, S., Ford, P. and Winter, L. J. 2009. China Has Recently Initiated Stronger Diplomatic Efforts to Improve the Darfur Situation. *In:* Miller, D. A. (ed.) *Darfur*. New York/London: Greenhaven Press.

Baldo, S. 2010. Sudan: Impact of the Rome Statute and the International Criminal Court. Kampala: International Center for Transitional Justice.

Ban Ki-Moon. 2010a. Honouring Geneva Conventions, Secretary General Says Debate 'No Longer Between Peace and Justice, but Between Peace and What Kind of Justice'. New York: UN Department of Public Information. SG/SM/12494.

2010b. Secretary-General Says 'Great Goals Within Reach'. New York: UN Department of Public Information. SG/SM/13134.

Barchfield, J. 2010. ICC Prosecutor Lauds New Charges Against al-Bashir. *AP* [Online]. Available: www.google.com/hostednews/ap/article/ALeqM5jrYT3r-1D6JfULBiPIBZuAGZ6UjQD9GUCG780 [Accessed 14 July 2010].

Barigaba, J. 2010. Army Under Scrutiny for Rights Abuses in Karamoja. *The East African* [Online]. Available: http://allafrica.com/stories/201010111206.html?viewall=1 [Accessed 13 October 2010].

Bassiouni, C. M. 1996. Searching for Peace and Achieving Justice: The Need for Accountability. *Law and Contemporary Problems*, 59, 9–28.

Baxter. 20 October 2011. *RE: Interview with Informant 'Baxter' Involved in the Kwoyelo Trial.*

Bayne, S. 2007. *Aid and conflict in Uganda*. London: Saferworld.

BBC. 2004. Sudan: Opposition Leader Warns of International Intervention in Darfur. *Sudanile* [Online]. Available: www.lexisnexis.com/de/business/results/docview/docview.do?docLinkInd=true&risb=21_T15029527738&format=GNBFI&sort=BOOLEAN&startDocNo=1&resultsUrlKey=29_T15029527742&cisb=22_T15029527741&treeMax=true&treeWidth=0&csi=10962&docNo=27 [Accessed 16 June 2012].

2006a. Sudanese President Denies Existence of Difference with Vice-President. *Sudanese Media Centre* [Online]. Available: www.lexisnexis.com/de/business/results/docview/docview.do?docLinkInd=true&risb=21_T14936642908&format=GNBFI&sort=BOOLEAN&startDocNo=1&resultsUrlKey=29_T14936642912&cisb=22_T14936642911&treeMax=true&treeWidth=0&csi=10962&docNo=2 [Accessed 16 June 2012].

2006b. UN Urged to Respect Sudan's Culture, Values. *Al-Mashahir* [Online]. Available: www.lexisnexis.com/de/business/auth/checkbrowser.do?rand=0.19072289806330844&cookieState=0&ipcounter=1&bhcp=1 [Accessed 16 June 2012].

2007a. Sudan's Presidential Aide Says to Serve Government with Three Conditions. *Akhir Lahzah* [Online]. Available: www.lexisnexis.com/de/business/results/docview/docview.do?docLinkInd=true&risb=21_T15032474093&format=GNBFI&sort=BOOLEAN&startDocNo=1&resultsUrlKey=29_T15032474097&cisb=22_T15032474096&treeMax=true&treeWidth=0&csi=10962&docNo=1 [Accessed 16 June 2012].

2007b. Sudan: Darfur's Arab Tribes Complain of Marginalization. *al-Khartoum* [Online]. Available: www.lexisnexis.com/de/business/results/docview/docview.do?docLinkInd=true&risb=21_T14987557136&format=GNBFI&sort=BOOLEAN&startDocNo=1&resultsUrlKey=29_T14987557140&cisb=22_T14987557139&treeMax=true&treeWidth=0&csi=10962&docNo=11 [Accessed 16 June 2012].

2007c. Sudan: Former Rebel in Darfur Says Expecting More Government Attacks. *Al-Ra'y al-Amm* [Online]. [Accessed 16 June 2012].

2007d. Sudan: Rebel Group Terms UN Resolution as "Victory for Darfur People". *Sudan Tribune* [Online]. [Accessed 16 June 2012].

2007e. Sudan: Ruling Party Says Aid Organizations Issuing False Reports on Darfur. *Sudanese Media Centre* [Online]. Available: www.lexisnexis.com/de/business/search/homesubmitForm.do [Accessed 16 June 2012].

2008a. Sudan's Umma Leader Interviewed on Agreement with Bashir, JEM, Other Issues. *Al-Sharq al-Awsat* [Online]. [Accessed 16 June 2012].

2008b. Sudan Suspends Activities of Five Foreign Aid Groups in Darfur. *Sudanese Media Centre* [Online]. Available: www.lexisnexis.com/de/business/results/docview/docview.do?docLinkInd=true&risb=21_T15006503520&format=GNBFI&sort=BOOLEAN&startDocNo=1&resultsUrlKey=29_T15006503524&cisb=22_T15006503523&treeMax=true&treeWidth=0&csi=10962&docNo=7 [Accessed 16 June 2012].

2008c. Sudan: Government to Probe Cooperation Between ICC, UN Mission. *Akhbar al-Yawm* [Online]. Available: www.lexisnexis.com/de/business/results/docview/docview.do?docLinkInd=true&risb=21_T15006503550&format=GNBFI&sort=BOOLEAN&startDocNo=1&resultsUrlKey=29_T15006503554&cisb=22_T15006503553&treeMax=true&treeWidth=0&csi=10962&docNo=22 [Accessed 16 June 2012].

2008d. Sudanese Presidential Aide Accuses ICC of Conspiracy Against Country. *Sudanese State Radio* [Online]. [Accessed 16 June 2012].

2009a. Darfur Tribes to Take "Oath of Death" for Sudan's Al-Bashir. *Sudanese Media Centre* [Online]. [Accessed 17 June 2012].

2009b. France-Africa Summit Moved to Keep Sudan's Bashir Away. *BBC* [Online]. Available: http://news.bbc.co.uk/2/hi/europe/8414480.stm [Accessed 12 June 2012].

2009c. South Africa Reverses Decision on Arrest of Sudan's Al-Bashir. *Sudan Tribune* [Online]. Available: www.lexisnexis.com/de/business/results/docview/docview.do?docLinkInd=true&risb=21_T14938553364&format=GNBFI&sort=BOOLEAN&startDocNo=1&resultsUrlKey=29_T14938553368&cisb=22_T14938553367&treeMax=true&treeWidth=0&csi=10962&docNo=1 [Accessed 17 June 2012].

2009d. Sudan Urges Political Parties to Strengthen "Internal Front" Against ICC. *Radio Miraya FM* [Online]. [Accessed 16 June 2012].

2009e. Sudan: Presidential Adviser Says ICC Warrant "Restricting Al-Bashir's Movements". *Sudan Tribune* [Online]. Available: www.lexisnexis.com/de/business/results/docview/docview.do?docLinkInd=true&risb=21_T14938362220&format=GNBFI&sort=BOOLEAN&startDocNo=1&resultsUrlKey=29_T14938362224&cisb=22_T14938362223&treeMax=true&treeWidth=0&csi=10962&docNo=3 [Accessed 17 June 2012].

2009f. Sudan: Report Says "Janjawid" Armed Group to Re-emerge in Darfur. *Akhir Lahzah* [Online]. Available: www.lexisnexis.com/de/business/results/docview/docview.do?docLinkInd=true&risb=21_T14985162527&format=GNBFI&sort=BOOLEAN&startDocNo=1&resultsUrlKey=29_T14985162531&cisb=22_T14985162530&treeMax=true&treeWidth=0&csi=10962&docNo=15 [Accessed 15 June 2012].

2009g. Sudanese Army Reaffirms Allegiance to Al-Bashir. *Sudanese Media Centre* [Online]. [Accessed 17 June 2012].

2010a. Sudan's Al-Bashir Says Muslims Most Targeted People on Earth. *Akhbar al-Yawm* [Online]. [Accessed 12 June 2012].

2010b. Writer Urges Al-Bashir to Step Down to Save Sudan. *Al-Sahafah* [Online]. Available: www.lexisnexis.com/de/business/results/docview/docview.do?docLinkInd=true&risb=21_T14936664257&format=GNBFI&sort=BOOLEAN&startDocNo=1&resultsUrlKey=29_T14936664261&cisb=22_T14936664260&treeMax=true&treeWidth=0&csi=10962&docNo=4 [Accessed 15 June 2012].

2012. Sudan's Omar al-Bashir Not Welcome for Malawi's Banda. *BBC News Africa* [Online]. Available: www.bbc.co.uk/news/world-africa-17963368 [Accessed 5 May 2012].

Beilin, Y. 2006. Just Peace: A Dangerous Objective. *In:* Allan, P. and Keller, A. (eds.) *What Is a Just Peace?* Oxford University Press.

Bekou, O. and Shah, S. 2006. Realising the Potential of the International Criminal Court: The African Experience. *Human Rights Law Review*, 6, 499–544.

Bell, C. 2006. *Negotiating Justice? Human Rights and Peace Agreements*. Geneva: International Council for Human Rights Policy.

2008. *On the Law of Peace: Peace Agreements and the Lex Pacificatoria*. Oxford: Oxford University Press.

Bensouda, F. 2012. Conference Remarks on 'R2P in 2022'. *R2P the Next Decade*. Muscatine: The Stanley Foundation.

Benzing, M. 2007. Sovereignty and the Responsibility to Protect in International Criminal Law. *In:* Matz-Lück, N. (ed.) *International Law Today: New Challenges and the Need to Reform?* New York/Heidelberg: Springer.

Berg, P. 2008. A Crisis-Complex, Not Complex Crises: Conflict Dynamics in the Sudan, Chad, and Central African Republic Tri-Border Area. *International Politics and Society*, 72–86.

Bernaz, N. and Prouvèze, R. 2010. International and Domestic Prosecutions. *In:* Bassiouni, C. M. (ed.) *The Pursuit of International Criminal Justice: A World Study on Conflicts, Victimization, and Post-Conflict Justice*. Antwerp/Oxford/Portland: Intersentia.

Bevan, J. 2006. Fuelling Fear: The Lord's Resistance Army and Small Arms. *In:* Small Arms Survey (ed.) *Small Arms Survey 2006: Unfinished Business*. Oxford: Oxford University Press.

Bigombe, B. 3 October 2011. *RE: Interview with Betty Bigombe, Minister of State for Water.*

Biro, M., Ajdukovic, D., Corkalo, D., Djipa, D., Milin, P. and Weinstein, H. M. 2004. Attitudes Toward Justice and Social Reconstruction in Bosnia and Herzegovina and Croatia. *In:* Stover, E. and Weinstein, H. M. (eds.) *My Neighbor, My Enemy: Justice and Community in the Aftermath of Mass Atrocity*. Cambridge University Press.

Blattman, C. and Annan, J. 2010. On the Nature and Causes of LRA Abduction: What the Abductees Say. *In:* Allen, T. and Vlassenroot, K. (eds.) *The Lord's Resistance Army: Myth and Reality*. London/New York: Zed Books.

Bloomfield, D. 2006. On Good Terms: Clarifying Reconciliation. *Berghof Report No. 14* [Online]. Available: www.berghof-center.org/uploads/download/br14e.pdf [Accessed 30 Mach 2010].

Blumenson, E. 2006. The Challenge of a Global Standard of Justice: Peace, Pluralism, and Punishment at the International Criminal Court. *Columbia Journal of Transnational Law*, 44, 797–874.

Bogoeva, Y. 28 September 2010. *RE: Interview with Yulija Bogoeva.*

Bojicic-Dzelilovic, V. 2006. Peace on Whose Terms?: War Veteran's Associations in Bosnia and Herzegovina. *In:* Newman, E. and Richmond, O. (eds.) *Challenges to Peacebuilding: Managing Spoilers During Conflict Resolution*. Tokyo/New York/Paris: United Nations University Press.

Bonacker, T. 2005. Sozialwissenschaftliche Konflikttheorien: Einleitung und Überblick. *In:* Bonacker, T. (ed.) *Sozialwissenschaftliche Konflikttheorien: Eine Einführung*. 3rd ed. Wiesbaden: VS Verlag.

Bonacker, T. and Imbusch, P. 1996. Begriffe der Friedens- und Konfliktforschung. *In:* Imbusch, P. and Zoll, R. (eds.) *Friedens- und Konfliktforschung: Eine Einführung mit Quellen*. 3rd ed. Opladen: Leske + Budrich.

Borzello, A. 2007. The Challenge of DDR in Northern Uganda: The Lord's Resistance Army. *Conflict, Security & Development*, 7, 387–415.

Bosco, D. 2014. Is the ICC Investigating Crimes by US Forces in Afghanistan? *Foreign Policy* [Online]. Available: www.foreignpolicy.com/articles/2014/05/15/is_the_ICC_thinking_about_prosecuting_us_soldiers_in_afghanistan [Accessed 10 July 2014].

Boswell, A. 2012. African Villagers Embrace US Role in Hunt for Lord's Resistance Army Leader. *Kansas City Star* [Online]. Available: www.kansascity.com/2012/02/14/3428138/african-villagers-embrace-us-role.html#storylink=cpy [Accessed 15 February 2012].

Boutros-Gahli, B. 1992. An Agenda for Peace: Preventive Diplomacy, Peacemaking and Peace-keeping: Report of the Secretary-General Pursuant to the Statement Adopted by the Summit Meeting of the Security Council on 31 January 1992. *In:* Secretary-General, U. (ed.). New York: United Nations.

Bradbury, M. 1999. An Overview of Initiatives for Peace in Acholi, Northern Uganda. Cambridge: Collaborative for Development Action, Inc.

Brahimi, L. 20 May 2008. Remarks at the Open Debate of the Security Council on Post-conflict Stabilization: *Peace After War*. New York: United Nations.

Brahm, E. 2007. Uncovering the Truth: Examining Truth Commission Success and Impact. *International Studies Perspectives*, 8, 16–35.

Branch, A. 2004. International Justice, Local Injustice. *Dissent Magazine*. New York: Foundation for the Study of Independent Social Ideas.

2005. Neither Peace nor Justice: Political Violence and the Peasantry in Northern Uganda, 1986–1998. *African Studies Quarterly*, 8, 1–24.

2007a. The Political Dilemmas of Global Justice: Anti-Civilian Violence and the Violence of Humanitarianism, the Case of Northern Uganda. PhD Thesis, Columbia University, New York.

2007b. Uganda's Civil War and the Politics of ICC Intervention. *Ethics & International Affairs*, 21, 179–198.

2010a. Exploring the Roots of LRA Violence: Political Crises and Ethnic Politics in Acholiland. *In:* Allen, T. and Vlassenroot, K. (eds.) *The Lord's Resistance Army: Myth and Reality*. London/New York: Zed Books.

2010b. What the ICC Review Conference Can't Fix. *In:* The Foundation for Law, Justice and Society (ed.) *Oxford Transitional Justice Research Debating International Justice in Africa*. Oxford: The Foundation for Law, Justice and Society & The Centre for Socio-Legal Studies, University of Oxford.

Brandt, W. 1986. Friedenssehnsucht und Friedenspolitik. *100 Jahre Verlag J. H. W. Dietz Nachf. 1881 bis 1981*. Bonn: Verlag J. H. W. Dietz.

Branigan, T. 2011. China Welcomes Sudanese President Omar al-Bashir. *The Guardian* [Online]. Available: www.guardian.co.uk/world/2011/jun/16/china-welcomes-sudanese-president-omar-al-bashir [Accessed 12 June 2012].

Broadhead, I. 2011. Central Africa Sees Endgame in LRA Conflict. *Voice of America* [Online]. Available: www.lexisnexis.com/de/business/results/docview/docview.do?docLinkInd=true&risb=21_T14355044683&format=GNBFI&sort=DATE,A,H&startDocNo=101&resultsUrlKey=29_T14355044678&cisb=22_T14355060998&treeMax=true&treeWidth=0&csi=247474&docNo=108 [Accessed 1 April 2012].

Broomhall, B. 2004. *International Justice & the International Criminal Court: Between Sovereignty and the Rule of Law.* Oxford University Press.

Brosché, J. 2008. Darfur: Dimensions and Dilemmas of a Complex Situation. *UCDP Papers* [Online]. Available: www.pcr.uu.se/digitalAssets/15/15924_Darfur_080317.pdf [Accessed 24 December 2011].

Brounéus, K. 2008. Reconciliation and Development. *In:* Ambos, K., Large, J. and Wierda, M. (eds.) *Building a Future on Peace and Justice. Studies on Transitional Justice, Peace and Development.* Heidelberg: Springer.

Brown, S. 2011. The Rule of Law and the Hidden Politics of Transitional Justice in Rwanda. *In:* Sriram, C. L., Martin-Ortega, O. and Herman, J. (eds.) *Peacebuilding and Rule of Law in Africa: Just Peace?* London/New York: Routledge Publishers.

Brubacher, M. 2010. The ICC Investigation of the Lord's Resistance Army: An Insider's View. *In:* Allen, T. and Vlassenroot, K. (eds.) *The Lord's Resistance Army: Myth and Reality.* London/New York: Zed Books.

Brubacher, M. R. 2004. Prosecutorial Discretion Within the International Criminal Court. *Journal of International Criminal Justice*, 2, 71–95.

Buchanan-Smith, M. and Jaspars, S. 2007. Conflict, Camps and Coercion: The Ongoing Livelihoods Crisis in Darfur. *Disasters*, 31, 57–76.

Buckley-Zistel, S. 2008a. *Conflict Transformation and Social Change in Uganda.* New York/Basingstoke: Palgrave Macmillan.

2008b. Transitional Justice als Weg zu Frieden und Sicherheit: Möglichkeiten und Grenzen. *SFB-Governance Working Paper Series* [Online]. Available: www.sfb-governance.de/publikationen/sfbgov_wp/wp15/SFB-Governance_Working_Paper_Nr15.pdf [Accessed 3 May 2011].

2010. Globale Rechtsprechung, lokale Konflikte: Der Internationale Strafgerichtshof als Friedensstiftende Maßnahme in Uganda? *In:* Bonacker, T., Daxner, M., Free, J. H. and Zürcher, C. (eds.) *Interventionskultur: Zur Soziologie von Interventionskulturen.* Wiesbaden: VS Verlag.

Burke-White, W. W. 2005. Complementarity in Practice: The International Criminal Court as Part of a System of Multi-Level Global Governance in the Democratic Republic of Congo. *Leiden Journal of International Law*, 18, 557.

Burke-White, W. W. and Kaplan, S. 2009. Shaping the Contours of Domestic Justice: The International Criminal Court and an Admissibility Challenge in the Uganda Situation. *Journal of International Criminal Justice*, 7, 257–279.

Burnett, M. 12 November 2011. *RE: Interview with Maria Burnett, Human Rights Watch.*

Burr, J. M. and Collins, R. O. 2008. *Darfur: The Long Road to Disaster.* Princeton: Markus Wiener Publishers.

Bush, G. 2001. Address to a Joint Session of Congress and the American People. *The White House Archives* [Online]. Available: http://georgewbush-whitehouse.archives.gov/news/releases/2001/09/20010920-8.html [Accessed 1 May 2012].

Bussmann, M., Hasenclever, A. and Schneider, G. 2009. Identität, Institutionen und Ökonomie: Ursachen und Scheinursachen innenpolitischer Gewalt. *In:* Bussmann, M., Hasenclever, A. and Schneider, G. (eds.) *Identität, Institutionen und Ökonomie: Ursachen innenpolitischer Gewalt.* Wiesbaden: VS Verlag.

Busumtwi-Sam, J., Costy, A. and Jones, B. D. 2004. Structural Deficits in Institutional Adaptations to Conflict and Peacebuilding in Africa. *In:* Ali, T. M. and Matthews, R. O. (eds.) *Durable Peace: Challenges For Peacebuilding in Africa.* Toronto/Buffalo/London: Toronto University Press.

Cakaj, L. 2010a. The Lord's Resistance Army of Today: The Enough Project.

2010b. On the Heels of Kony: The Untold Tragedy Unfolding in the Central African Republic. The Enough Project. June 2010.

2011. The Lord's Resistance Army in the Central African Republic. *Conflict Prevention and Peace Forum.* Social Science Research Council.

Carayon, G. 2010. The ICC's Impact on Victims & Affected Communities. *Access: Victims' Rights Before the International Criminal Court*, Summer 2010.

Cassese, A. 2006. *Observations on Issues Concerning the Protection of Victims and the Preservation of Evidence in the Proceedings on Darfur Pending Before the ICC.* The Hague: International Criminal Court. ICC-02/05-14.

CBC News. 2009. The International Criminal Court has Accused Sudan's President of Genocide. *In:* Miller, D. A. (ed.) *Darfur.* New York/London: Greenhaven Press.

Center on International Cooperation. 2012. *Global Peace Operations 2011.* New York: Lynne Rienner Publishers.

Chalk, F. and Kelton, D. 2009. Mass-Atrocity Crimes in Darfur and the Response of Government of Sudan Media to International Pressure. *In:* Grzyb, A. F. (ed.) *The World and Darfur: International Response to Crimes Against Humanity in Western Sudan.* Montreal/Kingston: McGill-Queen's University Press.

Chapman, A. R. 2009. Approaches to Studying Reconciliation. *In:* Van Der Merwe, H. and Chapman, A. R. (eds.) *Assessing the Impact of Transitional Justice:*

Challenges for Empirical Research. Washington, DC: United States Institute of Peace Press.

Charles. September 2011. *RE: Interview with Former LRA Captain 'Charles'.*

Charter, D. 2004. 'Battle Groups' Will Fight Famine. *Times of London* [Online]. Available: www.lexisnexis.com/de/business/results/docview/docview.do?docLinkInd=true&risb=21_T14929832120&format=GNBFI&sort=BOOLEAN&startDocNo=1&resultsUrlKey=29_T14929832124&cisb=22_T14929832123&treeMax=true&treeWidth=0&csi=397182&docNo=10 [Accessed 15 June 2012].

Chayes, A. and Chayes, A. H. 1995. *The New Sovereignty: Compliance with International Regulatory Agreements*. Cambridge, MA: Harvard University Press.

Chesterman, S. 2005. Rough Justice: Establishing the Rule of Law in Post Conflict Territories. *Ohio State Journal on Dispute Resolution*, 20, 69–98.

CICC. 2010. Addressing the Misperception that Africa Is Opposed to the ICC. *The Monitor*, 13.

2011. Increasing Global Commitment to the Principle of Complementarity. *The Monitor* [Online]. Available: http://coalitionfortheicc.org/documents/monitor42_english.pdf [Accessed 26 May 2011].

CIHRS. 2012. Cairo Institute Condemns Deteriorating Rights Situation in Sudan, Calls on Sudanese Government to Cooperate with UN. Available: http://www.cihrs.org/?p=4308&lang=en&utm_source=CICC+Newsletters&utm_campaign=e39b114ba7-October_Darfur_Digest_ENG&utm_medium=email [Accessed 10 November 2012].

Clark, J. N. 2009. The Limits of Retributive Justice: Findings of an Empirical Study in Bosnia and Hercegovina. *Journal of International Criminal Justice*, 7, 463–487.

Clark, P. 2010. Ocampo's Darfur Strategy Depends on Congo. *In:* The Foundation for Law, Justice And Society (ed.) *Oxford Transitional Justice Research Debating International Justice in Africa*. Oxford: The Foundation for Law, Justice and Society & The Centre for Socio-Legal Studies, University of Oxford.

Clark, P. and Anderson, D. 2010. Exclusive Interview with Phil Clark, Research Fellow in Courts and Public Policy, University of Oxford, and David Anderson, Professor of African Politics and Director of the African Studies Centre, University of Oxford. *In:* The Foundation for Law, Justice and Society (ed.) *Oxford Transitional Justice Research: Debating International Justice in Africa*. Oxford: The Foundation for Law, Justice and Society & The Centre for Socio-Legal Studies, University of Oxford.

Clarke, K. M. 2009. *Fictions of Justice: The International Criminal Court and the Challenge of Legal Pluralism in Sub-Saharan Africa*. Cambridge University Press.

Cobban, H. 2006. Think Again: International Courts. *Foreign Policy*, 153, 22–28.

2007. Transitional Justice and Conflict Termination: Mozambique, Rwanda and South Africa Assessed. *In:* Hughes, E. (ed.) *Atrocities and International Accountability*. Tokyo/New York/Paris: UN University Press.

Cockett, R. 2010. *Sudan: Darfur and the Failure of an African State*. New Haven/London: Yale University Press.

Coicaud, J.-M. 2008. Making the Rule of Law Work: Security and Justice Reforms in the United Nations. *In:* Aromaa, K. and Redo, S. (eds.) *For the Rule of Law: Criminal Justice Teaching and Training Across the World*. Helsinki/Seoul: European Institute for Crime Prevention and Control.

Colombant, N. 2012. US Defends Ongoing LRA Mission Amid Criticism. Available: www.voanews.com/english/news/africa/central/US-Defends-Ongoing-LRA-Mission-Amid-Criticism-140395413.html [Accessed 25 February 2012].

Côté, L. 2005. Reflections on the Exercise of Prosecutorial Discretion in International Criminal Law. *Journal of International Criminal Justice*, 3, 162–186.

Crocker, D. A. 1998. Transitional Justice and International Civil Society: Toward a Normative Framework. *Constellations*, 5, 492–517.

2002. Punishment, Reconciliation, and Democratic Deliberation. *Buffalo Criminal Law Review*, 5, 509–549.

Cross, M. E. and Williams, S. 2009. Recent Developments at the ICC. *Human Rights Law Review*, 9, 267–287.

Crowley, P. J. 2010. Africa: Daily Press Briefing. Available: www.state.gov/r/pa/prs/dpb/2010/07/144993.htm [Accessed 23 July 2010].

CSOPNU. 2006. Counting the Cost: Twenty Years of War in Northern Uganda. Kampala: CSOPNU.

Czempiel, E.-O. 1972. *Schwerpunkte und Ziele der Friedensforschung*. Munich: Kaiser Verlag.

1996. Der Friede: Sein Begriff, seine Strategien. *In:* Imbusch, P. and Zoll, R. (eds.) *Friedens- und Konfliktforschung: Eine Einführung mit Quellen*. Opladen: Leske & Budrich.

Daily Monitor. 2003. Kony is an Idiot, Says Museveni. *Daily Monitor* [Online]. Available: www.lexisnexis.com/de/business/results/docview/docview.do?docLinkInd=true&risb=21_T14650200609&format=GNBFI&sort=BOOLEAN&startDocNo=1&resultsUrlKey=29_T14650200613&cisb=22_T14650200612&treeMax=true&treeWidth=0&csi=8320&docNo=2 [Accessed 30 April 2012].

2004. Army Fights ICC Trial. *Daily Monitor* [Online]. Available: www.lexisnexis.com/de/business/results/docview/docview.do?docLinkInd=true&risb=21_T14645917241&format=GNBFI&sort=BOOLEAN&startDocNo=1&resultsUrlKey=29_T14645917245&cisb=22_T14645917244&treeMax=true&treeWidth=0&csi=8320&docNo=2 [Accessed 30 April 2012].

2005. I Was Forced Into Talks – Museveni. *Daily Monitor* [Online]. Available: www.lexisnexis.com/de/business/results/docview/docview.do?docLinkInd=true&risb=21_T14650312072&format=GNBFI&sort=BOOLEAN&startDocNo=1&resultsUrlKey=29_T14650312076&cisb=22_T14650312075&treeMax=true&treeWidth=0&csi=8320&docNo=1 [Accessed 30 April 2012].

Dak, J. G. 2010. Ugandan Religious Leaders Call for Peaceful Resolution to LRA Conflict. *Sudan Tribune* [Online]. Available: www.sudantribune.com/spip.php?article35941 [Accessed 9 September 2010].

Dalby, N. 2011. Ending the LRA: Reason for Optimism and Political Commitment. *African Arguments* [Online]. Available: www.crisisgroup.org/en/regions/africa/central-africa/central-african-republic/op-eds/dalby-ending-the-lra.aspx [Accessed January 11 2012].

Daly, M. W. 2010. *Darfur's Sorrow: The Forgotten History of a Humanitarian Disaster.* Cambridge University Press.

Darehshori, S. 2008. Doing the Right Thing for Darfur: An ICC Indictment of Sudan's President Serves Peace and Justice. *LA Times*, 15 July 2008.

Darehshori, S. and Evenson, E. 2010. Peace, Justice and the International Criminal Court. *In:* The Foundation for Law, Justice and Society (ed.) *Oxford Transitional Justice Research: Debating International Justice in Africa.* Oxford: The Foundation for Law, Justice and Society & The Centre for Socio-Legal Studies, University of Oxford.

Darfurian Voices Project. 2010. Darfurian Voices: Documenting Darfurian Refugees' Views on Issues of Peace, Justice, and Reconciliation: 24 Hours for Darfur.

Davidson, P. and Thoroddsen, F. 2011. Rule of Law Programming in the DRC. *In:* Sriram, C. L., Martin-Ortega, O. and Herman, J. (eds.) *Peacebuilding and Rule of Law in Africa: Just Peace?* London/New York: Routledge Publishers.

de Waal, A. 2009. Who Are the Darfurians? Arab and African Identities, Violence, and External Engagement. *In:* Hassan, S. M. and Ray, C. E. (eds.) *Darfur and the Crisis of Governance in Sudan: A Critical Reader.* Ithaca/London: Cornell University Press.

de Greiff, P. 2008. DDR and Reparations: Establishing Links Between Peace and Justice Instruments. *In:* Ambos, K., Large, J. and Wierda, M. (eds.) *Building a Future on Peace and Justice: Studies on Transitional Justice, Peace and Development.* Heidelberg: Springer.

de Waal, A. 2005. Briefing Darfur, Sudan: Prospects for Peace. *African Affairs*, 104, 127–135.

2007a. Darfur's Deadline: The Final Days of the Abuja Peace Process. *In:* de Waal, A. (ed.) *War in Darfur and the Search for Peace.* Cambridge, MA: Global Equity Initiative Harvard University.

2007b. Darfur's Elusive Peace. *In:* de Waal, A. (ed.) *War in Darfur and the Search for Peace.* Cambridge, MA: Global Equity Initiative Harvard University.

2007c. *Sudan: International Dimensions to the State and its Crisis*, London: LSE Crisis States Research Centre.

2007d. Sudan: The Turbulent State. *In:* de Waal, A. (ed.) *War in Darfur and the Search for Peace*. Cambridge, MA: Global Equity Initiative, Harvard University.

2007e. *Sudan: What Kind of State? What Kind of Crisis?*. London: LSE Crisis States Research Centre.

2008. Darfur, the Court and Khartoum: The Politics of State Non-Cooperation. *In:* Waddell, N. and Clark, P. (eds.) *Courting Conflict? Justice, Peace and the ICC in Africa*. London: Royal African Society.

2009. Who Are the Darfurians? Arab and African Identities, Violence, and External Engagement. *In:* Hassan, S. M. and Ray, C. E. (eds.) *Darfur and the Crisis of Governance in Sudan: A Critical Reader*. Ithaca/London: Cornell University Press.

de Waal, A. and Flint, J. 2008. Justice Off Course in Darfur. *Washington Post* [Online]. Available: www.washingtonpost.com/wp-dyn/content/article/2008/06/27/AR2008062702632.html [Accessed 10 December 2010].

de Waal, A., Flint, J. and Pantuliano, S. 2008. ICC approach risks peacemaking in Darfur. *The Guardian* [Online]. Available: www.guardian.co.uk/world/2008/jun/10/sudan.unitednations [Accessed 8 December 2010].

de Waal, A. and Stanton, G. H. 2009. Should President Omar al-Bashir of Sudan Be Charged and Arrested by the International Criminal Court? An Exchange of Views. *Genocide Studies and Prevention*, 4, 329–353.

Doha Declaration. 2009. Visions and Recommendations of Civil Society Meeting on the Key Issues of Priority to Be Included in the Terms of Negotiations to Establish a Just and Durable Peace in Darfur. Doha: Darfur Civil Society Conference.

Doha II Declaration. 2010. Visions and Recommendations of the Second Civil Society Meeting on the Key Issues of Priority to Be Included in the Terms of Negotiations to Establish a Just and Durable Peace in Darfur, and the Role of the Civil Society at All Stages of the Peace Process. Doha: Darfur Civil Society Conference.

Dolan, C. 2009. *Social Torture: The Case of Northern Uganda, 1986–2006*. New York/Oxford: Berghahn Books.

Dollo, O. 8 September 2011. *RE: Interview with Justice Owiny Dollo, Judge at the International Crimes Division of the Ugandan High Court*.

Doom, R. and Vlassenroot, K. 1999. Kony's Message: A New Koine? The Lord's Resistance Army in Northern Uganda. *African Affairs*, 98, 5–36.

Doria, J., Mulllins, C., Rothe, D. L. and Jenkins, C. 2010. Africa: Regional Report. *In:* Bassiouni, C. M. (ed.) *The Pursuit of International Criminal Justice: A World Study on Conflicts, Victimization, and Post-Conflict Justice*. Antwerp/Oxford/Portland: Intersentia.

Dowden, R. 2007. ICC in the Dock. *Prospect Magazine* [Online]. Available: www.prospectmagazine.co.uk/2007/05/iccinthedock/ [Accessed 3 May 2011].

DPA. 2010. UN-Bericht verärgert China. *Süddeutsche Zeitung*, 22 October 2010, p.10.

Dreier, R. 1991a. Der Rechtsstaat im Spannungsverhältnis zwischen Gesetz und Recht. *In:* Dreier, R. (ed.) *Recht - Staat - Vernunft*. Frankfurt am Main: Suhrkamp.

1991b. Recht und Gerechtigkeit. *In:* Dreier, R. (ed.) *Recht - Staat - Vernunft*. Frankfurt am Main: Suhrkamp.

Drumbl, M. A. 2007. *Atrocity, Punishment, and International Law*. Cambridge University Press.

Du Plessis, M. 2010. *The International Criminal Court that Africa Wants*. Pretoria: Institute for Security Studies.

Du Plessis, M. and Ford, J. 2008a. Background to the ISS International Crime in Africa Programme. *In:* Du Plessis, M. and Ford, J. (eds.) *Unable or Unwilling? Studies on Domestic Implementation of the ICC Statute in Selected African Countries*. Pretoria: Institute for Security Studies.

2008b. Executive Summary. *In:* Du Plessis, M. and Ford, J. (eds.) *Unable or Unwilling? Studies on Domestic Implementation of the ICC Statute in Selected African Countries*. Pretoria: Institute for Security Studies.

2008c. Recommendations. *In:* Du Plessis, M. and Ford, J. (eds.) *Unable or Unwilling? Studies on Domestic Implementation of the ICC Statute in Selected African Countries*. Pretoria: Institute for Security Studies.

Dworkin, R. 1978. *Taking Rights Seriously*. London: Duckworth.

Dyzenhaus, D. 2003. Transitional Justice: Review Essay. *International Journal of Constitutional Law*, 1, 163–175.

Eck, K. and Hultman, L. 2007. Violence Against Civilians in War. *Journal of Peace Research*, 44, 233–246.

Eck, K., Kreutz, J. and Sundberg, R. 2010. *Introducing the UCDP Non-State Conflict Dataset*. Uppsala: Uppsala University.

Economist. 2006. Never Too Late to Scramble: China in Africa. *Economist*.

Eichstaedt, P. 2008. ICC Chief Prosecutor Talks Tough. *IWPR* [Online]. Available: http://iwpr.net/report-news/icc-chief-prosecutor-talks-tough [Accessed 10 August 2010].

2009. *First Kill Your Family: Child Soldiers of Uganda and the Lord's Resistance Army*. Chicago: Lawrence Hill Books.

2010. Why Kony Will Never Be Captured. *Commentary and Insight into East African Affairs* [Online]. Available: http://petereichstaedt.blogspot.com/2010/03/why-kony-will-never-be-captured.html [Accessed 10 August 2010].

El-Battahani, A. 2009. Ideological Expansionist Movements Versus Historical Indigenous Rights in the Darfur Region of Sudan: From Actual Homicide to Potential Genocide. *In:* Hassan, S. M. and Ray, C. E. (eds.) *Darfur and the*

Crisis of Governance in Sudan: A Critical Reader. Ithaca/London: Cornell University Press.

El-Faki, E.-T. A. 2010. The Future of Sudan Without Andrew Natsios. *JEM Website* [Online]. Available: www.sudanjem.com/2009/archives/36991/en/#more-36991 [Accessed 22 November 2010].

El Gizouli, K. 2009. The Erroneous Confrontation: The Dialectics of Law, Politics and the Prosecution of War Crimes in Darfur. *In:* Hassan, S. M. and Ray, C. E. (eds.) *Darfur and the Crisis of Governance in Sudan: A Critical Reader*. Ithaca/London: Cornell University Press.

El Gizouli. 2012. Khartoum: The Political Economy of Bankruptcy. *Still Sudan* [Online]. Available: http://stillsudan.blogspot.de/2012/06/khartoum-political-economy-of.html [Accessed 27 June 2012].

El Hassan, I. S. 2008. Managing the Process of Conflict Resolution in the Sudan. *In:* Nhema, A. and Zezela, P. T. (eds.) *The Resolution of African Conflicts: The Management of Conflict Resolution & Post-Conflict Reconstruction*. Addis Ababa: OSSREA.

Elliesie, H. 2007. Darfur Krise: Eine Herausforderung für die Vereinten Nationen (UN) und den Internationalen Strafgerichtshof (ICC). *Verfassung und Recht in Übersee*, 40, 199–229.

2010. Rule of Law in the Sudan. *Wikis der freien Universität Berlin* [Online]. Available: http://wikis.fu-berlin.de/display/SBprojectrol/sudan [Accessed 13 October 2010].

El-Tom, A. O. 2009. Darfur People: Too Black for the Arab-Islamic Project of Sudan. *In:* Hassan, S. M. and Ray, C. E. (eds.) *Darfur and the Crisis of Governance in Sudan: A Critical Reader*. Ithaca/London: Cornell University Press.

Enough Project. 2010. Lord's Resistance Army Finds Safe Haven in Darfur. Available: www.enoughproject.org/news/lord%E2%80%99s-resistance-army-finds-safe-haven-darfur [Accessed September 1 2011].

Ero, C. 2010. Understanding Africa's Position on the International Criminal Court. *In:* The Foundation for Law, Justice and Society (ed.) *Oxford Transitional Justice Research: Debating International Justice in Africa*. Oxford: The Foundation for Law, Justice and Society & The Centre for Socio-Legal Studies, University of Oxford.

EurAc. 2010. EurAc: Military Strategies Against the LRA Will Have No Lasting Impact Without Dialogue and Negotiations. Available: www.eurac-network.org/web/uploads/documents/20101115_13451.doc [Accessed 16 November 2010].

Expert Interview. 28 April 2010a. *RE: Interview with a Mediator Working with Darfurian Civil Society Representatives.*

30 November 2010b. *RE: Interview with a Legal Expert Working with the Government of Sudan.*

23 March 2011a. *RE: Interview with a Diplomat.*

31 August 2011b. *RE: Interview with a Member of the Ugandan Judiciary.*

22 September 2011c. *RE: Interview With a Senior Diplomat.*

28 September 2011d. *RE: Interview with a Staff Member of an Institution Working on Human Rights.*

27 September 2011e. *RE: Interview with a Staff Member of an Organisation Working on Human Rights.*

23 August 2011f. *RE: Interview with a Staff Member of the OHCHR in Kampala.*

8 September 2011g. *RE: Interview with an Informant Close to the International Crimes Division.*

2 March 2011h. *RE: Interview with an NGO Expert Working in Sudan.*

6 September 2011i. *RE: Interview with an NGO Expert Working in the Field of Transitional Justice.*

26 September 2011j. *RE: Interview with Staff of a Local Human Rights Organisation.*

27 September 2011k. *RE: Interview with Staff of an Organisation Working with LRA Returnees.*

Fadul, A.-J. and Tanner, V. 2007. Darfur After Abuja: A View from the Ground. *In:* de Waal, A. (ed.) *War in Darfur and the Search for Peace.* Cambridge, MA: Global Equity Initiative Harvard University.

Fearon, J. D. and Laitin, D. D. 2003. Ethnicity, Insurgency, and Civil War. *American Political Science Review,* 97, 75–90.

Fernandez, A. M. 2008. *China Counsels Sudanese Engagement, U.S. Restraint. In:* State Department (ed.). Washington, DC.

Fick, M. 2010. Why a Free Southern Sudan Is Bad News for Darfur. *Foreign Policy* [Online]. Available: www.foreignpolicy.com/articles/2010/11/24/why_a_free_southern_sudan_is_bad_news_for_darfur [Accessed 25 November 2010].

Findlay, M. and Henham, R. 2010. *Beyond Punishment: Achieving International Criminal Justice.* New York: Palgrave Macmillan.

Finnström, S. 2006. Wars of the Past and War in the Present: The Lord's Resistance Movement/Army in Uganda. *Africa: The Journal of the International African Institute,* 76, 200–220.

2008. *Living with Bad Surroundings.* Durham/London: Duke University Press.

2010a. An African Hell of Colonial Imagination? The Lord's Resistance Army in Uganda, Another Story. *In:* Allen, T. and Vlassenroot, K. (eds.) *The Lord's Resistance Army: Myth and Reality.* London/New York: Zed Books.

2010b. Reconciliation Grown Bitter?: War, Retribution, and Ritual Action in Northern Uganda. *In:* Shaw, R. and Waldorf, L. (eds.) *Localizing Transitional Justice: Interventions and Priorities After Mass Violence.* Stanford: Stanford University Press.

Fisas, V. 2010a. *Peace Process Yearbook 2009,* Barcelona: Escola de Cultura de Pau.

2010b. *Peace Process Yearbook 2010*. Barcelona: Escola de Cultura de Pau.

Fiser, N. 28 September 2010. *RE: Interview with Nenad Fiser*.

Flemming, M. 2010. Why Long-Term Ceasefires Will Not Lead to Peace and Security in Sudan. *Foreign Policy* [Online]. Available: http://mideast.foreignpolicy.com/posts/2010/07/14/why_long_term_ceasefires_will_not_lead_to_peace_and_security_in_sudan [Accessed 22 July 2010].

Fletcher, L. E., Weinstein, H. M. and Rowen, J. 2009. Context, Timing and the Dynamics of Transitional Justice: A Historical Perspective. *Human Rights Quarterly*, 31, 163–220.

Flint, J. 2007. Darfur's Armed Movements. *In:* de Waal, A. (ed.) *War in Darfur and the Search for Peace*. Cambridge, MA: Global Equity Initiative Harvard University.

2009. *Beyond 'Janjaweed': Understanding the Militias of Darfur*. Geneva: Small Arms Survey.

2010a. *The Other War: Inter-Arab Conflict in Darfur*. Geneva: Small Arms Survey.

2010b. *Rhetoric and Reality: The Failure to Resolve the Darfur Conflict*. Geneva: Small Arms Survey.

Flint, J. and de Waal, A. 2008. *Darfur: A Short History of a long War*. London/New York: Zed Books.

2009. Case Closed: A Prosecutor Without Borders. *World Affairs* [Online]. Available: www.worldaffairsjournal.org/articles/2009-Spring/full-DeWaalFlint.html.

Fowler, J. and Prendergast, J. 2009. The International Community Must Ensure the Success of the UN Peacekeeping Force in Darfur. *In:* Miller, D. A. (ed.) *Darfur*. New York/London: Greenhaven Press.

Fowler, M. and Bunck, J. M. 1995. *Law, Power, and the Sovereign State: The Evolution and Application of the Concept of Sovereignty*. University Park: Pennsylvania State University Press.

Freda, A. J. and Aceng, J. C. 8 September 2011. *RE: Interview with Staff Members of the Ugandan Coalition for the ICC, at the Human Rights Network Uganda*.

Freedom House. 2012. Freedom of the Press 2012. Available: www.freedomhouse.org/sites/default/files/Global%20and%20Regional%20Press%20Freedom%20Rankings.pdf [Accessed 3 June 2012].

Freeman, M. 2010. Necessary Evils: Amnesties and the Search for Justice. *Crisis Group Podcast* [Online]. Available: www.crisisgroup.org/home/index.cfm?id=6182#old_podcast [Accessed April 4 2010].

Frost, D. 2008a. Interview with Nafie Ali Nafie, Senior Presidential Aide Sudan. *Frost Over the World* [Online]. Available: www.youtube.com/watch?v=NUClBFldsqs&feature=relmfu [Accessed 4 March 2011].

2008b. Interview with President Omar al-Bashir. *Frost Over the World* [Online]. Available: www.youtube.com/watch?v=lFHjRbyO3OM [Accessed 4 March 2011].

Galtung, J. 1972. Eine strukturelle Theorie des Imperialismus. *In:* Senghaas, D. (ed.) *Imperialismus und strukturelle Gewalt*. Frankfurt am Main: Suhrkamp.

Gambari, I. 2010. Interview: UNAMID Chief Gambari Addresses Complaints of Darfuris. Available: http://www.radiodabanga.org/node/4651 [Accessed 10 October 2010].

Geertz, C. 2000. *Local Knowledge: Further Essays in Interpretive Anthropology*. New York: Basic Books.

Gerdes, F. 2009. Verregelung der Gewalt. *In:* Gerdes, F. (ed.) *Verregelung der Gewalt: Gesellschaften Zwischen Krieg und Frieden, Working Paper 6/2009*. Hamburg: AKUF.

Gettleman, J. 2012. In Vast Jungle, U.S. Troops Aid in Search for Kony. *New York Times* [Online]. Available: www.nytimes.com/2012/04/30/world/africa/kony-tracked-by-us-forces-in-central-africa.html?pagewanted=2 [Accessed 30 April 2012].

Ginifer, J. 2006. *Internal Review of DFID's Engagement with the Conflict in Northern Uganda*. London: Department for International Development UK.

Girke, P. and Kamp, M. 2010. Afrika und der Internationale Strafgerichtshof: Bestandsaufnahme in Uganda. *Länderbericht* [Online]. Available: www.kas.de/wf/doc/kas_20668-1522-1-30.pdf?100930131239 [Accessed 29 August 2011].

2011. Museveni's Uganda: Eternal Subscription to Power? *KAS International Reports*, 27, 49–71.

Giroux, J., Lanz, D. and Sguaitamatti, D. 2009. *The Tormented Triangle: The Regionalisation of Conflict in Sudan, Chad and the Central African Republic*. London: London School of Economics.

Glasius, M. 2009. What Is Global Justice and Who Decides? Civil Society and Victim Responses to the International Criminal Court's First Investigations. *Human Rights Quarterly*, 31, 496–520.

Glassborow, K. 2007. Victim Participation in ICC Cases Jeopardised. *IWPR* [Online]. Available: www.lexisnexis.com/de/business/results/docview/docview.do?docLinkInd=true&risb=21_T14888772843&format=GNBFI&sort=BOOLEAN&startDocNo=1&resultsUrlKey=29_T14888772847&cisb=22_T14888772846&treeMax=true&treeWidth=0&csi=8320&docNo=3 [Accessed 10 June 2012].

2009. Sudan: Keeping a Lid on ICC Warrant Requests. *IWPR* [Online]. Available: www.lexisnexis.com/de/business/results/docview/docview.do?docLinkInd=true&risb=21_T12741307554&format=GNBFI&sort=DATE,A,H&startDocNo=1&resultsUrlKey=29_T12741307515&cisb=22_T12741539706&treeMax=true&treeWidth=0&selRCNodeID=150596&nodeStateId=501de_DE,1&docsInCategory=1902&csi=8320&docNo=45 [Accessed 16 September 2011].

Gleditsch, N. P., Wallensteen, P., Eriksson, M., Sollenberg, M. and Strand, H. 2002. Armed Conflict 1946–2001: A New Dataset. *Journal of Peace Research*, 39.

Gluckman, M. 1959. *Custom and Conflict in Africa*. Glencoe: The Free Press.

Goldston, J. A. 2010. More Candour about Criteria: The Exercise of Discretion by the Prosecutor of the International Criminal Court. *Journal of International Criminal Justice*, 8, 383–406.

Goldstone, R. 1995. Justice as a Tool for Peace-Making: Truth Commissions and International Criminal Tribunals. *New York University Journal of International Law and Politics*, 28, 485–504.

1998. Bringing War Criminals to Justice During Ongoing War. *In:* Moore, J. (ed.) *Hard Choices: Moral Dilemmas in Humanitarian Interventions*. Lanham: Rowman & Littlefield.

Goldstone, R. J. 2000. *For Humanity: Reflections of a War Crimes Investigator*. New Haven: Yale University Press.

Goodhand, J., Vaux, T. and Walker, R. 2002. *Conducting Conflict Assessments: Guidance Notes*. London: Department for International Development UK.

Gordon, S., Vandewint, C. and Lehmeier, S. 2007. *Reluctant Hosts: The Impact of the Lord's Resistance Army on Communities in Western Equatoria State, Southern Sudan*. Juba: World Vision Southern Sudan.

Gready, P. 2005. Analysis: Reconceptualising Transitional Justice: Embedded and Distanced Justice. *Conflict, Security & Development*, 5, 3–21.

Greenhill, K. M. and Major, S. 2007. The Perils of Profiling: Civil War Spoilers and the Collapse of Intrastate Peace Accords. *International Security*, 31, 7–40.

Grodsky, B. 2009. Re-Ordering Justice: Towards a New Methodological Approach to Studying Transitional Justice. *Journal of Peace Research*, 46, 819–837.

Grono, N. 2006. Briefing Darfur: The International Community's Failure to Protect. *African Affairs*, 105.

Grono, N. and O'Brien, A. 2008. Justice in Conflict? The ICC and Peace Processes. *In:* Waddell, N. & Clark, P. (eds.) *Courting Conflict? Justice, Peace and the ICC in Africa*. London: Royal African Society.

Groth, A. 2011. WikiLeaks on Joseph Kony. *Reslove* [Online]. Available: www.theresolve.org/blog/archives/3071031213 [Accessed 30 November 2011].

Grünfeld, F. and Vermeulen, W. 2009. Failures to Prevent Genocide in Rwanda (1994), Srebrenica (1995), and Darfur (Since 2003). *Genocide Studies and Prevention*, 4, 221–237.

Guardian Unlimited. 2009. Sudan Fears US Military Intervention over Darfur. *Guardian* [Online]. Available: www.lexisnexis.com/de/business/results/docview/docview.do?docLinkInd=true&risb=21_T14810316591&format=GNBFI&sort=BOOLEAN&startDocNo=1&resultsUrlKey=29_T14810316595&cisb=22_T14810316594&treeMax=true&treeWidth=0&csi=284355&docNo=33 [Accessed 29 May 2012].

Hagan, J. and Rymond-Richmond, W. 2009. *Darfur and the Crime of Genocide*. Cambridge University Press.

Haggar, A. 2007. The Origins and Organization of the Janjawiid in Darfur. *In:* de Waal, A. (ed.) *War in Darfur and the Search for Peace*. Cambridge, MA: Global Equity Initiative Harvard University.

Hamilton, A.1778. *The Federalist* No. 74.

Hamilton, R. and Hazlett, C. 2007. "Not on Our Watch" The Emergence of the American Movement for Darfur. *In:* de Waal, A. (ed.) *War in Darfur and the Search for Peace*. Cambridge, MA: Global Equity Initiative Harvard University.

Hannum, H. 2006. Peace Versus Justice: Creating Rights as Well as Order out of Chaos. *International Peacekeeping*, 13, 582–595.

Hansen, T. O. 2011. Transitional Justice: Toward a Differentiated Theory. *Oregon Review of International Law*, 13, 1–45.

Haspel, M. 1996. Einführung in die Friedensethik. *In:* Imbusch, P. and Zoll, R. (eds.) *Friedens- und Konfliktforschung: Eine Einführung mit Quellen*, 3rd ed. Opladen: Leske + Budrich.

Hassan, S. M. 2009. Naming the Conflict: Darfur and the Crisis of Governance in Sudan. *In:* Hassan, S. M. and Ray, C. E. (eds.) *Darfur and the Crisis of Governance in Sudan: A Critical Reader*. Ithaca/London: Cornell University Press.

Hassan, S. M. and Ray, C. E. 2009. Introduction: Critically Reading Darfur and the Crisis of Governance in Sudan. *In:* Hassan, S. M. and Ray, C. E. (eds.) *Darfur and the Crisis of Governance in Sudan: A Critical Reader*. Ithaca/London: Cornell University Press.

Hayner, P. 2009. Negotiating Justice: Guidelines for Mediators. Centre for Humanitarian Dialogue/International Center for Transitional Justice.

2010. *Managing the Challenges of Integrating Justice Efforts and Peace Processes*. Kampala: International Criminal Court. RC/ST/PJ/INF.4.

Hazan, P. 2004. *Justice in a Time of War: The True Story behind the International Criminal Tribunal for the Former Yugoslavia*. Austin: Texas University Press.

2006. Measuring the Impact of Punishment and Forgiveness: A Framework for Evaluating Transitional Justice. *International Review of the Red Cross*, 88, 19–47.

Heikkilä, M. 2009. The Balanced Scorecard of International Criminal Tribunals. *In:* Ryngaert, C. (ed.) *The Effectiveness of International Criminal Justice*. Antwerpen: Intersentia.

Heilmann, D. 2006. *Die Effektivität des Internationalen Strafgerichtshofs: Die Rolle der Vereinten Nationen und des Weltsicherheitsrats*. Nomos: Baden-Baden.

Heupel, M. 2005. *Friedenskonsolidierung im Zeitalter der Neuen Kriege*. Wiesbaden: VS Verlag.

High-Level Panel on Threats, Challenges and Change. 2004. *A More Secure World: Our Shared Responsibility*. United Nations. UN Doc. A/59/565.

Hofmann-Van Depol, F. 2010. *A Quest for Accountability: The Effects of International Criminal Tribunals and Courts on Impunity.* Tübingen: University of Tübingen.

Hoile, D. 2006. *Darfur in Perspective.* London: European Sudanese Public Affairs Council.

Hopwood, J. 2011. We Can't Be Sure Who Killed Us: Memory and Memorialization in Post-conflict Northern Uganda. Gulu: International Center for Transitional Justice/Justice and Reconciliation Project.

Horowitz, S. 2006. Transitional Criminal Justice in Sierra Leone. *In:* Roht-Arriaza, N. and Mariezcurrena, J. (eds.) *Transitional Justice in the Twenty-First Century: Beyond Truth Versus Justice.* Cambridge University Press.

Hovil, L. 2012. A Poisoned Chalice? Local Civil Society and the International Criminal Court's Engagement. International Refugee Rights Initiative.

Hovil, L. and Lomo, Z. 2005. *Whose Justice? Perceptions of Uganda's Amnesty Act 2000: The Potential for Conflict Resolution and Long-term Reconciliation.* Kampala: Refugee Law Project. No. 15.

Hovil, L. and Moorehead, A.2002. *War as Normal. The Impact of Violence on the Lives of Displaced Communities in Pader District, Northern Uganda.* Kampala: Refugee Law Project.

Hovil, L. and Quinn, J. R. June 2005. *Peace First, Justice Later: Traditional Justice in Northern Uganda.* Kampala: Refugee Law Project.

HRW. 1997. *The Scars of Death: Children Abducted by the Lord's Resistance Army in Uganda.* New York: Human Rights Watch.

2003. *Abducted and Abused: Renewed Conflict in Northern Uganda.* New York: Human Rights Watch.

2004. "If We Return, We Will Be Killed": Consolidation of Ethnic Cleansing in Darfur, Sudan. Available: www.hrw.org/sites/default/files/reports/darfur1104.pdf [Accessed 17 November 2011].

2005a. Entrenching Impunity: Government Responsibility for International Crimes in Darfur. Available: www.hrw.org/sites/default/files/reports/darfur1205webwcover.pdf [Accessed 17 November 2011].

2005b. *Uprooted and Forgotten Impunity and Human Rights Abuses in Northern Uganda.* New York: Human Rights Watch.

2005c. Video Transcript: Exclusive Video Interview with Alleged Janjaweed Leader. Available: www.hrw.org/node/69432 [Accessed 6 May 2011].

2006a. Darfur Bleeds: Recent Cross-Border Violence in Chad. Available: www.hrw.org/legacy/backgrounder/africa/chad0206/chad0206.pdf [Accessed 17 November 2011].

2006b. Darfur: Humanitarian Aid under Siege. Available: www.hrw.org/legacy/backgrounder/africa/sudan0506/darfur0506.pdf [Accessed 17 November 2011].

2006c. *Lack of Conviction: The Special Criminal Court on the Events in Darfur.* New York: HRW.

2007a. Darfur 2007: Chaos by Design Peacekeeping Challenges for AMIS and UNAMID. Available: www.hrw.org/sites/default/files/reports/sudan0907web.pdf [Accessed 17 November 2011].

2007b. "Get the Gun!" Human Rights Violations by Uganda's National Army in Law Enforcement Operations in Karamoja Region. [Accessed 7 September 2011].

2008a. *Courting History: The Landmark International Criminal Court's First Years*, New York: HRW.

2008b. "They Shot at Us as We Fled": Government Attacks on Civilians in West Darfur. Available: www.hrw.org/sites/default/files/reports/darfur0508_1.pdf [Accessed 17 November 2011].

2009a. "It's an Everyday Battle": Censorship and Harassment of Journalists and Human Rights Defenders in Sudan. Available: www.hrw.org/sites/default/files/reports/sudanfrexp0209web.pdf [Accessed 17 November 2011].

2009b. Selling Justice Short: Why Accountability Matters for Peace. Available: www.hrw.org/en/reports/2009/07/07/selling-justice-short-0.

2009c. The Way Forward: Ending Human Rights Abuses and Repression Across Sudan. Available: www.hrw.org/sites/default/files/reports/sudan1009web_0.pdf [Accessed 17 November 2011].

2010a. Central African Republic: LRA Conducts Massive Abduction Campaign. Available: http://allafrica.com/stories/201008130775.html [Accessed 17 August 2010].

2010b. Congo/Central African Republic – LRA Victims Appeal to Obama – US Should Act to Protect Civilians From Atrocities, Arrest War Crimes Perpetrators. Available: http://allafrica.com/stories/201011110051.html?viewall=1 [Accessed 12 November 2010].

2010c. *Making Kampala Count: Advancing the Global Fight against Impunity at the ICC Review Conference*. New York: HRW.

2010d. Sudan: Don't Ignore AU Justice Recommendations. Available: www.hrw.org/en/news/2010/10/29/sudan-don-t-ignore-au-justice-recommendations [Accessed 4 November 2010].

2010e. Sudan: Halt Wave of Attacks on Civilians in Darfur. Available: www.hrw.org/en/news/2010/11/11/sudan-halt-wave-attacks-civilians-darfur [Accessed 6 December 2010].

2010f. Trail of Death: LRA Atrocities in Northeastern Congo. Available: www.hrw.org/sites/default/files/reports/drc0310webwcover_0.pdf [Accessed 1 September 2011].

2010g. Uganda: Investigate 2009 Kampala Riot Killings. Available: www.hrw.org/en/news/2010/09/10/uganda-investigate-2009-kampala-riot-killings [Accessed 11 September 2010].

2011a. Darfur in the Shadows: The Sudanese Government's Ongoing Attacks on Civilians and Human Rights. Available: www.hrw.org/sites/default/files/reports/sudan0611ForWebUpload.pdf [Accessed 17 November 2011].

2011b. Unfinished Business: Closing Gaps in the Selection of ICC Cases. Available: www.hrw.org/sites/default/files/reports/icc0911webwcover.pdf [Accessed 29 September 2011].

2011c. Universal Periodic Review of Uganda: HRW's Submission to the Human Rights Council. Available: www.hrw.org/news/2011/03/29/universal-periodic-review-uganda [Accessed 1 September 2011].

2012a. Sudan: End Violence Against Peaceful Protesters. Available: www.hrw.org/news/2012/01/03/sudan-end-violence-against-peaceful-protesters [Accessed 2 June 2012].

2012b. Uganda: Investigate April 2011 Killings During Protest. Available: www.hrw.org/news/2012/04/29/uganda-investigate-april-2011-killings-during-protest [Accessed 29 April 2012].

Hurifo. 28 September 2011. *RE: Interview with Staff Members of the Local Human Rights Organisation Human Rights Focus (HURIFO).*

HURINET, UCICC & No Peace Without Justice. 2010. Visits by ICC States Parties Delegates to Uganda. Kampala: HURINET, UCICC, No Peace Without Justice.

Huyse, L. 2008a. Conclusions and Recommendations. *In:* Huyse, L. and Salter, M. (eds.) *Traditional Justice and Reconciliation After Violent Conflict: Learning from African Experiences.* Stockholm: International IDEA.

2008b. Introduction: Tradition-Based Approaches In Peacemaking, Transitional Justice and Reconciliation Policies. *In:* Huyse, L. and Salter, M. (eds.) *Traditional Justice and Reconciliation After Violent Conflict: Learning from African Experiences.* Stockholm: International IDEA.

IBA. 2007. *ICC Monitoring and Outreach Programme: Second Outreach Report.* London: International Bar Association Human Rights Institute.

Ibrahim, N. 2007. Post CPA: Restructuring and Enhancing the Sudanese Judiciary as a Means of Preserving Peace. *Verfassung und Recht in Übersee*, 40, 471–494.

ICC. 2010a. ICC Registrar Launches Series on Victims' Rights and Reparations, Hosts Working Session with Colombian Experts. *Press Release* [Online]. Available: www.icc-cpi.int/NR/exeres/4B53D4A5-4C3F-4744-956B-5D24CAAAF302.htm.

2010b. Notification of Public Statement by the Prosecutor. The Hague: Pre-Trial Chamber I of the International Criminal Court.

2010c. *Report on the Activities of the Court.* New York: International Criminal Court. ICC-ASP/9/23.

2010d. Stocktaking of International Criminal Justice: Peace and Justice. *Press Release* [Online]. Available: www.icc-cpi.int/NR/exeres/D9821939-80B4-487A-9A3F-C5D794B27161.htm [Accessed 5 June 2010].

ICC OTP. 2003. Paper on Some Policy Issues Before the Office of the Prosecutor. Available: www.icc-cpi.int/NR/rdonlyres/1FA7C4C6-DE5F-42B7-8B25-60AA962ED8B6/143594/030905_Policy_Paper.pdf [Accessed 28 July 2011].

2009. Public Redacted Version: Prosecutor's Application under Article 58 Filed on 20 November 2008 now Filed Pursuant to the Request of Pre-Trial Chamber I of 7 May 2009. The Hague: Office of the Prosecutor of the International Criminal Court. ICC-02/05-02/09-16-Anx1.

ICC PTC. 2011. Decision on the Application by the Government of Kenya Challenging the Admissibility of the Case Pursuant to Article 19(2)(b) of the Statute. The Hague: ICC. ICC-01/09-02/11.

ICC PTC I. 2008. Public Redacted Version of the Prosecutor's Application under Article 58. The Hague: ICC. ICC-02/05-157-AnxA.

2010. Decision on the "Requête pour l'obtention d'une ordonnance condamnant les déclarations du Procureur en date du 15 juillet 2010". The Hague: Pre-Trial Chamber I of the International Criminal Court. ICC-02/05-01/09-106 24-08-2010.

2011. Decision Pursuant to Article 87(7) of the Rome Statute on the Failure by the Republic of Malawi to Comply with the Cooperation Requests Issued by the Court with Respect to the Arrest and Surrender of Omar Hassan Ahmad Al Bashir. The Hague: Pre-Trial Chamber I of the International Criminal Court. ICC-02/05-01/09-139 12-12-2011.

ICC Registry. 2010. *Outreach Report 2010*. The Hague: ICC.

ICG. 2001. International Criminal Tribunal for Rwanda: Justice Delayed. Brussels/Kigali: International Crisis Group.

2004a. Darfur Deadline: A New International Action Plan. Brussels/Nairobi: International Crisis Group. ICG Africa Report N°83.

2004b. Darfur Rising: Sudan's New Crisis. Nairobi/Brussels: International Crisis Group. ICG Africa Report N°76.

2004c. Northern Uganda: Understanding and Solving the Conflict. Brussels/Nairobi: International Crisis Group. ICG Africa Report N°77.

2004d. Sudan: Now or Never in Darfur. Brussels/Nairobi: International Crisis Group. ICG Africa Report N°80.

2005a. The AU's Mission in Darfur: Bridging the Gaps. Brussels/Nairobi: International Crisis Group. ICG Africa Briefing N°28.

2005b. Building a Comprehensive Peace Strategy for Northern Uganda. Nairobi/Brussels: ICG. Africa Briefing N°27.

2005c. Darfur: The Failure to Protect. Brussels/Nairobi: ICG. Africa Report N°89.

2005d. The EU/AU Partnership in Darfur: Not Yet a Winning Combination. Brussels/Nairobi: International Crisis Group. ICG Africa Report N°99.

2005e. Peace in Northern Uganda: Decisive Weeks Ahead. Brussels/Nairobi: International Crisis Group. ICG Africa Briefing N°22.

2005f. Shock Therapy for Northern Uganda's Peace Process. Brussels/Nairobi: International Crisis Group. ICG Africa Briefing N°23.

2005g. Unifying Darfur's Rebels: A Prerequisite for Peace. Brussels/Nairobi: ICG. Africa Briefing N°32.

2006a. Darfur's Fragile Peace Agreement. Brussels/Nairobi: International Crisis Group. ICG Africa Briefing N°39.

2006b. Getting the UN into Darfur. Brussels/Nairobi: International Crisis Group. ICG Africa Briefing N°43.

2006c. A Strategy for Ending Northern Uganda's Crisis. Brussels/Nairobi: International Crisis Group. ICG Africa Briefing N°35.

2006d. To Save Darfur. Brussels/Nairobi: International Crisis Group. ICG Africa Report N°105.

2007a. Darfur: Revitalising the Peace Process. Brussels/Nairobi: International Crisis Group. ICG Africa Report N°125.

2007b. Northern Uganda Peace Process: The Need to Maintain Momentum. Kampala/Brussels/Nairobi: International Crisis Group. ICG Africa Briefing N°46.

2007c. Northern Uganda: Seizing the Opportunity for Peace. Brussels/Nairobi: International Crisis Group. Africa Report N°124.

2008. Northern Uganda: The Road to Peace, With or Without Kony. Kampala/Brussels/Nairobi/Juba: International Crisis Group. ICG Africa Report N°146.

2009. Sudan: Preventing Implosion. Brussels/Nairobi: ICG. Africa Briefing N°68.

2010. LRA: A Regional Strategy Beyond Killing Kony. Kampala/Brussels/Nairobi/Juba: International Crisis Group. ICG Africa Report N°157.

2011a. The Lord's Resistance Army: End Game? *ICG Report* [Online]. Available: www.crisisgroup.org/~/media/Files/africa/horn-of-africa/uganda/182%20The%20Lords%20Resistance%20Army%20-%20End%20Game.pdf [Accessed 17 November 2011].

2011b. Sudan: Divisions in the Ruling Party. *ICG Podcast* [Online]. Available: www.crisisgroup.org/en/publication-type/~/link.aspx?_id=2974EFDAC58A46F78198EA649B642528&_z=z [Accessed 14 May 2011].

2012. Uganda: No Resolution to Growing Tensions. *ICG Report* [Online]. Available: www.crisisgroup.org/en/regions/africa/horn-of-africa/uganda/187-uganda-no-resolution-to-growing-tensions.aspx [Accessed 7 April 2012].

ICID. 2005. *Report of the International Commission of Inquiry on Darfur to the United Nations Secretary-General.* Geneva: International Commission of Inquiry on Darfur of the United Nations. S/2005/60.

ICJ. 2005. *Case Concerning Armed Activities on the Territory of the Congo (Democratic Republic of the Congo vs Uganda).* The Hague: International Court of Justice. General List No. 116, 19 December 2005.

2007. *The Administration of Justice in Sudan: The Case of Darfur.* Geneva: International Commission of Jurists.

ICTJ & HRC. 2005. Forgotten Voices: A Population-Based Survey on Attitudes about Peace and Justice in Northern Uganda.

ICTY. 2010. *General Information*. The Hague: International Criminal Tribunal for the Former Yugoslavia.

Idris, A. 2005. *Conflicts and Politics of Identity in Sudan*. New York/Basingstoke: Palgrave Macmillan.

Invisible Children. 2012. Kony 2012. Available: www.youtube.com/watch?v=Y4MnpzG5Sqc [Accessed 6 May 2012].

IPS. 2004. U.N. Body Rejects Censure, Threatens Revolt. *Inter Press Service* [Online]. Available: www.lexisnexis.com/de/business/results/docview/docview.do?docLinkInd=true&risb=21_T14930002180&format=GNBFI&sort=BOOLEAN&startDocNo=1&resultsUrlKey=29_T14930002184&cisb=22_T14930002183&treeMax=true&treeWidth=0&csi=8320&docNo=10 [Accessed 15 June 2012].

IRIN. 2003. Sudan: The Escalating Crisis in Darfur. Available: www.irinnews.org/report.aspx?reportid=47856 [Accessed 07 June 2011].

2005a. Uganda: ICC Indictments to Affect Northern Peace Efforts, Says Mediator. *IRIN* [Online]. Available: www.irinnews.org/report.aspx?reportid=56654 [Accessed 19 August 2011].

2005b. Uganda: Interview with ICC Prosecutor Luis Moreno-Ocampo. Available: www.irinnews.org/Report.aspx?ReportID=54856 [Accessed 21 June 2011].

2005c. Uganda: Interview with President Yoweri Museveni. Available: www.irinnews.org/report.aspx?reportid=54853 [Accessed 21 June 2011].

2006. Justice for a Lawless World? Rights and Reconciliation in a New Era of International Law. *IRIN*. July 2006.

2010a. Central Africa: Agencies Call for International Action against LRA. *IRIN* [Online]. Available: www.irinnews.org/report.aspx?ReportID=91376 [Accessed 16 December 2010].

2010b. Sudan: The Shape of Humanitarian Space in Darfur. *IRIN* [Online]. Available: www.irinnews.org/report.aspx?ReportID=90679 [Accessed October 6 2010].

2011a. Sudan: Darfur Returning "to Past Patterns of Violence". *IRIN* [Online]. Available: www.irinnews.org/report.aspx?ReportID=91762 [Accessed 28 January 2011].

2011b. Sudan: Lack of Justice "Entrenching Impunity" in Darfur. *IRIN* [Online]. Available: www.irinnews.org/report.aspx?reportID=92511 [Accessed 19 April 2011].

2011c. Uganda: On the Trail of the LRA. *IRIN* [Online]. Available: www.irinnews.org/report.aspx?ReportID=91612 [Accessed 13 January 2011].

2011d. Uganda: War Crimes Trial May Affect LRA Defections – Analysts. *IRIN* [Online]. Available: www.irinnews.org/report.aspx?reportID=93377 [Accessed 29 July 2011].

2012a. Uganda: LRA Victims Rap Compensation Delay. *IRIN* [Online]. Available: www.irinnews.org/Report/95638/UGANDA-LRA-victims-rap-compensation-delay [Accessed 14 June 2012].

2012b. Uganda: No More Amnesty Certificates for Rebels. *IRIN* [Online]. Available: www.irinnews.org/Report/95569/UGANDA-No-more-amnesty-certificates-for-rebels [Accessed 2 June 2012].

Isma'il, M. U. 2007. Presidential Adviser Isma'il on Darfur, Resolution 1593, ICC (Part 7). *Al-Sharq al-Awsat* [Online]. Available: www.lexisnexis.com/de/business/results/docview/docview.do?docLinkInd=true&risb=21_T11864726818&format=GNBFI&sort−DATE,A,H&startDocNo=1951&resultsUrlKey=29_T11864696932&cisb=22_T11864726840&treeMax=true&treeWidth=0&csi=10962&docNo=1964 [Accessed 2 May 2011].

Iya, R. 2010. Encountering Kony: A Madi Perspective. *In:* Allen, T. and Vlassenroot, K. (eds.) *The Lord's Resistance Army: Myth and Reality*. London/New York: Zed Books.

Jaeger, C. 9 March 2011. *RE: Interview with Dr. Christoph Jaeger, Former UN Resident Coordinator Southern Sudan.*

Jaques, I. 2008. Pursuing Justice in Ongoing Conflict: Examining the Challenges. *In:* Wilton Park Conference, 2008.

JEM. 2009. Proposal for Peace in Sudan in General and Darfur in Particular. *In:* Hassan, S. M. and Ray, C. E. (eds.) *Darfur and the Crisis of Governance in Sudan: A Critical Reader*. Ithaca/London: Cornell University Press.

JEM. 2010. Requirements for a Robust Process in Doha. *JEM Website* [Online]. Available: www.sudanjem.com/2009/archives/38360/en/ [Accessed 1 December 2010].

Jennings, S. 2012. Sudan: Beginning of End for Bashir? Available: http://iwpr.net/report-news/sudan-beginning-end-bashir [Accessed 24 June 2012].

Jennings, S. and Glassborow, K. 2011. Special Report: Funding False Hopes in Darfur. *IWPR* [Online]. Available: www.currentintelligence.net/news/2011/4/27/special-report-funding-false-hopes-in-darfur.html [Accessed 15 June 2011].

Jeong, H.-W. 2008. *Understanding Conflict and Conflict Analysis*. London/Thousand Oaks/New Delhi/Singapore: Sage Publications.

JIC. 2012. Justice in Conflict: On the Challenges of Pursuing Justice. *Justice in Conflict* [Online]. Available: http://justiceinconflict.org/ [Accessed 14 July 2012].

Johnson, D. H. 2003. *The Root Causes of Sudan's Civil Wars*. London: The International African Institute.

Joinet, L. 1997. The Administration of Justice and the Human Rights of Detainees: Question of the Impunity of Perpetrators of Human Rights Violations (Civil and Political), Revised Final Report Prepared by Mr. Joinet Pursuant to Sub-Commission Decision 1996/119. Geneva: Comission on Human Rights. E/CN.4/Sub.2/1997/20/Rev.1.

Journeyman Pictures. 2007. Meeting Joseph Kony. *Journeyman Pictures* [Online]. Available: http://de.truveo.com/video-detail/uganda-meeting-joseph-kony-aug2007/3260765015 [Accessed 2 August 2010].

JPC. 30 September 2011. *RE: Interview with Staff Members of the Justice and Peace Commission of the Archdiocese of Gulu.*

Justice in Conflict. 2012. Category Archives: Kwoyelo Trial. *Justice in Conflict* [Online]. Available: http://justiceinconflict.org/category/kwoyelo-trial/ [Accessed 25 April 2012].

Kahn, C. 2008. *Conflict, Arms, and Militarization: The Dynamics of Darfur's IDP Camps*, Geneva: Small Arms Survey.

Kamara, M. M. 24 August 2011. *RE: Interview with ICC Official in the Kampala Field Office.*

Karbo, T. 2008. Peace-building in Africa. *In:* Francis, D. J. (ed.) *Peace & Conflict in Africa*. London/New York: Zed Books.

Kastner, P. 2007. The ICC in Dafur: Savior or Spoiler? *ILSA Journal of International & Comparative Law*, 14, 145–188.

Keller, L. M. 2007. Achieving Peace with Justice: The International Criminal Court and Ugandan Alternative Justice Mechanisms. *Connecticut Journal of International Law*, 23, 209–279.

Kerr, R. 2004. *The International Criminal Tribunal for the Former Yugoslavia*. Oxford University Press.

Kerr, R. and Mobekk, E. 2007. *Peace and Justice: Seeking Accountability After War*. Cambridge: Polity Press.

Kersten, M. 2011. An Arab Fling: The West and International Justice in Libya. *Justice in Conflict* [Online]. Available: http://justiceinconflict.org/2011/09/26/an-arab-fling-the-west-and-international-justice-in-libya/ [Accessed 13 October 2012].

Kessler, G. and Lynch, C. 2004. U.S. Calls Killings in Sudan Genocide. *Washington Post* [Online]. Available: www.washingtonpost.com/wp-dyn/articles/A8364-2004Sep9.html [Accessed 15 June 2012].

Kezio-Musoke, D. 2010. Rwanda Defends Kenya on Bashir. *The Monitor* [Online]. Available: http://allafrica.com/stories/201009020439.html [Accessed 18 September 2010].

Ki-Moon, B. 2008. Secretary-General Defends, Clarifies 'Responsibility to Protect' at Berlin Event on 'Responsible Sovereignty: International Cooperation in a Changed World. Available: www.un.org/News/Press/docs/2008/sgsm11701.doc.htm [Accessed 21 July 2012].

Kim, H. and Sikkink, K. 2009. Explaining the Deterrence Effect of Human Rights Prosecutions for Transitional Countries. *Hauser Globalization Colloquium Fall 2009: Interdisciplinary Approaches to International Law* [Online]. Available: www.iilj.org/courses/documents/Sikkink-Kim.HC2009Oct21.pdf [Accessed 15 October 2010].

2010. Explaining the Deterrence Effect of Human Rights Prosecutions for Transitional Countries. *International Studies Quarterly*, 54, 939–963.

Knox, P. 2000. Ottawa Assailed Over Relations with Sudan. *The Globe and Mail* [Online]. Available: www.lexisnexis.com/de/business/results/docview/doc

view.do?docLinkInd=true&risb=21_T14606713659&format=GNBFI&sort=DATE,A,H&startDocNo=51&resultsUrlKey=29_T14606713654&cisb=22_T14606713691&treeMax=true&treeWidth=0&csi=302564&docNo=88 [Accessed 1 May 2012].

Koelbl, S. and Windfuhr, V. 2010. I Feel Completely Safe. *der Spiegel* [Online]. Available: www.spiegel.de/international/world/spiegel-interview-with-sudanese-president-omar-al bashir-i-fccl-completely-safe-a-684941.html [Accessed 3 June 2012].

Koller, P. 2007. Der Begriff der Gerechtigkeit. *Intergenerational Justice Review*, 7, 7–11.

Komakech, L. and Sheff, A. July 2009. *Tradition in Transition: Drawing on the Old to Develop a New Jurisprudence for Dealing with Uganda's Legacy of Violence*. Kampala: Refugee Law Project.

Koppe, K. 1996. Geschichte der Friedens- und Konfliktforschung. *In:* Imbusch, P. and Zoll, R. (eds.) *Friedens- und Konfliktforschung. Eine Einführung mit Quellen*. Wiesbaden: VS Verlag.

Kreutz, J. 2010. How and When Armed Conflicts End: Introducing the UCDP Conflict Termination Dataset. *Journal of Peace Research*, 47.

Kritz, N. 2009. Policy Implications of Empirical Research on Transitional Justice. *In:* Van Der Merwe, H. and Chapman, A. R. (eds.) *Assessing the Impact of Transitional Justice: Challenges for Empirical Research*. Washington, DC: United States Institute of Peace Press.

Kritz, N. J. 1996. Coming to Terms with Atrocities: A Review of Accountability Mechanisms for Mass Violations of Human Rights. *Law and Contemporary Problems*, 59, 127–152.

Kulayigye, F. 2010. Uganda: Odama Should Not Intimidate the ICC. *New Vision* [Online]. Available: http://allafrica.com/stories/printable/201006080845.html [Accessed 30 June 2010].

3 October 2011. *RE: Expert Interview with Colonel Felix Kulayigye, Spokesperson of the UPDF*.

Kuovo, S. 2009. *Transitional Justice in the Context of Ongoing Conflict: The Case of Afghanistan*. New York: ICTJ.

Kuperman, A. J. 2008. The Moral Hazard of Humanitarian Intervention: Lessons from the Balkans. *International Studies Quarterly*, 52, 49–80.

2009. Darfur: Strategic Victimhood Strikes Again? *Genocide Studies and Prevention*, 4, 281–303.

Lacambel. 28 October 2011. *RE: Interview with Lacambel, Radio Moderator at Mega FM*.

Lambourne, W. 2009. Transitional Justice and Peacebuilding After Mass Violence. *The International Journal of Transitional Justice*, 3, 28–48.

Lamony, S. A. 2007. *Approaching National Reconciliation in Uganda: Perspectives on Applicable Justice Systems*. Kampala: Uganda Coalition for the International Criminal Court.

Lancaster, P., Lacaille, G. and Cakaj, L. 2011. Diagnostic Study of the LRA. Available: www.tdrp.net/PDFs/LRA_DiagnosticStudy_1.pdf [Accessed 24 February 2012].

Lanz, D. 2008a. *Conflict Management and Opportunity Costs: The International Response to the Darfur Crisis*. Madrid: Fride.

2008b. Northern Uganda, Juba Negotiations. *In:* Mediation Support Project (ed.) *Unpacking the Mystery of Mediation in African Peace Processes*. Zurich: Mediation Support Project.

2008c. Sudan/Darfur, Abuja Negotiations and the DPA. *In:* Mediation Support Project (ed.) *Unpacking the Mystery of Mediation in African Peace Processes*. Zurich: Mediation Support Project.

Latigo, J. O. 2008. Northern Uganda: Tradition-Based Practices in the Acholi Region. *In:* Huyse, L. and Salter, M. (eds.) *Traditional Justice and Reconciliation After Violent Conflict: Learning from African Experiences*. Stockholm: International IDEA.

Lauria, J. 2009. Warrant for Sudan Leader 'an Imperialist Plot'. *Sunday Tribune* [Online]. Available: www.lexisnexis.com/de/business/results/docview/docview.do?docLinkInd=true&risb=21_T14938355013&format=GNBFI&sort=BOOLEAN&startDocNo=1&resultsUrlKey=29_T14938355017&cisb=22_T14938355016&treeMax=true&treeWidth=0&csi=312456&docNo=19 [Accessed 17 June 2012].

Lawino, S. 2012. UN Envoy, Clergy Clash Over Genocide Claims. *Daily Monitor* [Online]. Available: www.monitor.co.ug/News/National/-/688334/1378076/-/awnduwz/-/ [Accessed 26 April 2012].

Lederach, J. P. 1995. *Preparing for Peace: Conflict Transformation Across Cultures*. Syracuse: Syracuse University Press.

Leebaw, B. A. 2008. The Irreconcilable Goals of Transitional Justice. *Human Rights Quarterly*, 30, 95–118.

Lenhart, L. 2009. Konfliktporträt Nord-Uganda. Available: www.bpb.de/themen/SJPWRX,0,NordUganda.html [Accessed 26 April 2010].

Leonard, E. 2010. Exclusive Interview with Eric Leonard, Professor of Political Science, Shenandoah University. *In:* The Foundation for Law, Justice and Society (ed.) *Oxford Transitional Justice Research: Debating International Justice in Africa*. Oxford: The Foundation for Law, Justice and Society & The Centre for Socio-Legal Studies, University of Oxford.

Lezhnev, S. 2012. *Four Steps beyond US Troops to End the War with the LRA*, Washington, DC: Enough Project.

Licklider, R. 2008. Ethical Advice: Conflict Management vs. Human Rights in Ending Civil Wars. *Journal of Human Rights*, 7, 376–387.

Lie, T. G., Binningsbø, H. M. and Gates, S. 2007. Post-Conflict Transitions Working Paper No. 5: Post-Conflict Justice and Sustainable Peace. Oslo/Trondheim: Centre for the Study of Civil War/Norwegian University of Science & Technology.

Lindemann, S. 2011. Just Another Change of Guard? Broad-based Politics and Civil War in Museveni's Uganda. *African Affairs*, 110, 387–416.

Liu Institute for Global Issues. 2005. Pursuing Peace and Justice: International and Local Initiatives. Liu Institute for Global Issues Conflict and Development Programme.

Lomo, Z. A. 2006. Why the International Criminal Court Must Withdraw Indictments Against the Top LRA Leaders: A Legal Perspective. Kampala: Refugee Law Project.

Lomo, Z. A. and Hovil, L. 2004. Behind the Violence. Causes, Consequences and the Search for Soultions to the War in Northern Uganda. Kampala: Refugee Law Project.

Lough, R. and Maasho, A. 2013. Ethiopian Leader Accuses International Court of Racial Bias. *Reuters* [Online]. Available: www.reuters.com/article/2013/05/27/us-africa-icc-idUSBRE94Q0F620130527 [Accessed 4 July 2014].

Loum, P. 30 September 2011. *RE: Interview with Patrick Loum, Acholi Religious Leaders Peace Initiative.*

LRA Commander. 27 October 2011. *RE: Interview with a Former Top Commander of the LRA.*

Lu, C. 2006. The International Criminal Court as an Institution of Moral Regeneration: Problems and Prospects. *In:* Harrington, J., Milde, M. and Vernon, R. (eds.) *Bringing Power to Justice?* Montreal & Kingston: McGill-Queen's University Press.

Lutz, D. S. 2004. Friedensforschung: Normativ, Interdisziplinär, Praxisorientiert. *In:* Ulricheckern, L.-E. and Schultze, R.-O. (eds.) *Friedens- und Konfliktforschung in Deutschland: Eine Bestandsaufnahme.* Wiesbaden: VS Verlag.

Maguire, S. 2011. Creating Demand in Darfur: Circling the Square. *In:* Sriram, C. L., Martin-Ortega, O. and Herman, J. (eds.) *Peacebuilding and Rule of Law in Africa: Just Peace?* London/New York: Routledge Publishers.

Malan, J. 2008. Understanding Transitional Justice in Africa. *In:* Francis, D. J. (ed.) *Peace & Conflict in Africa.* London/New York: Zed Books.

Mallinder, L. 2008. *Amnesty, Human Rights and Political Transitions: Bridging the Peace and Justice Divide.* Oxford: Hart Publishing.

2009a. The Role of Amnesties in Conflict Transformation. *In:* Ryngaert, C. (ed.) *The Effectiveness of International Criminal Justice.* Antwerpen: Intersentia.

1 March 2009b. Uganda at a Crossroads: Narrowing the Amnesty?. Belfast: Institute of Criminology and Criminal Justice, Queen's University Belfast.

Mamdani, M. 2009a. The Politics of Naming: Genocide, Civil War, Insurgency. *In:* Hassan, S. M. and Ray, C. E. (eds.) *Darfur and the Crisis of Governance in Sudan: A Critical Reader.* Ithaca/London: Cornell University Press.

2009b. Response by Mahmood Mamdani to Book Review by Carlos Gonzalez Cueva. *International Journal of Transitional Justice*, 3, 470–473.

2009c. *Saviors and Survivors: Darfur, Politics and the War on Terror*. New York: Pantheon Books.

Mani, R. 2002. *Beyond Retribution: Seeking Justice in the Shadows of War*. Cambridge: Polity/Blackwell.

Mansaray, A. V. 2009. AMIS in Darfur: Africa's Litmus Test in Peacekeeping and Political Mediation. *African Security Review*, 18, 35–48.

Mapenduzi, M. O. 28 October 2011. *RE: Interview with Martin Ojara Mapenduzi, Gulu District Chairman (Local Councilor V)*.

Marchal, R. 2007. The Unseen Regional Implications of the Crisis in Darfur. *In:* de Waal, A. (ed.) *War in Darfur and the Search for Peace*. Cambridge, MA: Global Equity Initiative Harvard University.

Marion, S. and Paschyn, C. M. 2010. Luis Moreno-Ocampo on Darfur, the LRA. Available: http://pulitzercenter.org/blog/news-points/luis-moreno-ocampo-darfur-lra [Accessed 13 October 2010].

Markusen, E. 2009. Three Empirical Investigations of Alleged Genocide in Darfur. *In:* Grzyb, A. F. (ed.) *The World and Darfur: International Response to Crimes against Humanity in Western Sudan*. Montreal/Kingston: McGill-Queen's University Press.

Matwijkiw, A. 2010. Justice Versus Revenge: The Philosophical Underpinnings of the Chicago Principles on Post Conflict Justice. *In:* Bassiouni, C. M. (ed.) *The Pursuit of International Criminal Justice: A World Study on Conflicts, Victimization, and Post-Conflict Justice*. Antwerp/Oxford/Portland: Intersentia.

May, L. 2005. *Crimes Against Humanity: A Normative Account*. Cambridge University Press.

Mayer, S. 2010. Nicht lügen! Nicht töten! In: Die Zeit 31/2010, 29 July 2010, p. 56.

Mbabazi, A. 2004. *Ministerial Statement of Minister of Defence Amama Mbabazi at the Parliamentary Session on 29 July 2004*. Kampala: Ugandan Parliament.

Mbaku, J. M. 2014. *International Justice: The International Criminal Court and Africa*. Washington, DC: The Brookings Institution.

Mbazira, C. 2011. Prosecuting International Crimes Committed by the Lord's Resistance Army in Uganda. *In:* Murungu, C. and Biegon, J. (eds.) *Prosecuting International Crimes in Africa*. Pretoria University Law Press.

Mccrummen, S. and Boustany, N. 2008. Sudan Vows to Fight Charges of Genocide Against Its Leader: Move by Court Brings Cheers in Darfur Camps. *Washington Post* [Online]. Available: www.lexisnexis.com/de/business/results/docview/docview.do?docLinkInd=true&risb=21_T14888757835&format=GNBFI&sort=BOOLEAN&startDocNo=1&resultsUrlKey=29_T14888757839&cisb=22_T14888757838&treeMax=true&treeWidth=0&csi=8075&docNo=49 [Accessed 10 June 2012].

McDoom, O. 2010. Interview: Europe Should Engage Sudan, Norway Minister Says. Available: http://uk.reuters.com/article/idUKMCD161348._CH_.2420.

McGreal, C. 2008. Museveni Refuses to Hand Over Rebel Leaders to War Crimes Court. *The Guardian* [Online]. Available: www.guardian.co.uk/world/2008/mar/13/uganda.internationalcrime [Accessed 16 October 2010].

MDRP. 2008. The Status of LRA Reporters: Multi-Country Demobilization and Reintegration Program. Dissemination Note No. 2.

Meernik, J., Aliosi, R., Nichols, A. D. and Sowell, M. 2010a. The Impact of Tribunals and Truth Commissions on Post-Conflict Peace Building. *In:* Hewitt, J. J., Wilkenfeld, J. and Gurr, T. R. (eds.) *Peace and Conflict 2010*. Boulder/London: Paradigm Publishers.

Meernik, J. D., Nichols, A. and King, K. L. 2010b. The Impact of International Tribunals and Domestic Trials on Peace and Human Rights After Civil War. *International Studies Perspectives*, 11, 309–334.

Mégret, F. 2010. ICC, R2P, and the International Community's Evolving Interventionist Toolkit. Helsinki: Castren Institute for International Law and Human Rights.

2011. ICC, R2P, and the International Community's Evolving Interventionist Toolkit.

Meier, B. 2011. Mato Oput: Karriere eines Rituals zur Sozialen Rekonstruktion in Norduganda. *In:* Buckley-Zistel, S. and Kater, T. (eds.) *Nach Krieg, Gewal und Repression: Vom schwierigen Umgang mit der Vergangenheit*. Baden-Baden: Nomos.

Mendeloff, D. 2004. Truth-Seeking, Truth-Telling, and Postconflict Peacebuilding: Curb the Enthusiasm? *International Studies Review*, 6, 355–380.

Mendes, E. P. 2010. *Peace and Justice at the International Criminal Court: A Court of Last Resort*. Cheltenham/Northampton: Edward Elgar.

Mendez, J. E. 2006. The Genocide in Darfur, the Role of the UN and the ICC. *60 Years Nuremberg: New Challenges in the Fight Against Impunity*. Nuremberg: Nürnberger Menschenrechtszentrum.

Mendez, J. E. June 2010a. *The Importance of Justice in Securing Peace*. Kampala: International Criminal Court.

2010b. *The Importance of Justice in Securing Peace*. Kampala: International Criminal Court. RC/ST/PJ/INF.3.

Mergelsberg, B. 2010. Between Two Worlds: Former LRA Soldiers in Northern Uganda. *In:* Allen, T. and Vlassenroot, K. (eds.) *The Lord's Resistance Army: Myth and Reality*. London/New York: Zed Books.

Meron, T. 2006. Reflections on the Prosecution of War Crimes by International Tribunals. *American Journal of International Law*, 100, 551–579.

Minow, M. 1998. *Between Vengeance and Forgiveness: Facing History After Genocide and Mass Violence*. Boston: Beacon Press.

Miraya FM. 2010. Sudan's Prosecutor of Darfur Crimes Says "Politics" Has Impact on Legal Cases. *BBC Monitoring Middle East* [Online]. Available: www.lexisnexis.com/de/business/results/docview/docview.do?docLinkInd=true&

risb=21_T14886937572&format=GNBFI&sort=BOOLEAN&startDocNo=1&resultsUrlKey=29_T14886937576&cisb=22_T14886937575&treeMax=true&treeWidth=0&csi=10962&docNo=5 [Accessed 9 June 2012].

Mirmar, J. 2011. May Is the Most Historical Trace in the History of the Sudan. Available: www.sudanjem.com/2011/06/10-may-is-the-most-historical-trace-in-the-history-of-the-sudan/ [Accessed 12 June 2011].

Moghalu, K. C. 2009. Prosecute or Pardon? Between Truth Commission and War Crimes Trials. *In:* Sriram, C. L. and Pillay, S. (eds.) *Peace Versus Justice? The Dilemmas of Transitional Justice in Africa.* Scottsville: University of KwaZulu-Natal Press.

Mohammed, A. A. 2007. The Comprehensive Peace Agreement and Darfur. *In:* de Waal, A. (ed.) *War in Darfur and the Search for Peace.* Cambridge, MA: Global Equity Initiative Harvard University.

Moloto, B. J. 28 September 2010. *RE: Group Discussion with Bakone Justice Moloto, Judge at the ICTY.*

Moreno Ocampo, L. 2005. Address to the United Nations Security Council. 13 December 2005.

2006a. Fourth Report of the Prosecutor of the International Criminal Court, Mr. Luis Moreno Ocampo, to the UN Security Council Pursuant to UNSCR 1593 (2005). Available: www.icc cpi.int/NR/rdonlyres/19B2F772-E5E3-4DBB-8B0F-5A220DB958F3/277803/OTP_ReportUNSC4Darfur_English.pdf [Accessed 8 June 2012].

2006b. Integrating the Work of the ICC into Local Justice Initiatives. *American University International Law Review,* 21, 497–504.

2007a. Fifth Report of the Prosecutor of the International Criminal Court to the United Nations Security Council pursuant to UNSCR 1593. Available: www.icc-cpi.int/NR/rdonlyres/CE794D3B-ED91-4D86-A28E-3F61E6C44083/277796/OTP_ReportUNSC5Darfur_English.pdf [Accessed 10 July 2012].

2007b. Transitional Justice in Ongoing Conflicts. *The International Journal of Transitional Justice,* 1, 8–9.

2008a. Building a Future on Peace and Justice: The International Criminal Court. *In:* Ambos, K., Large, J. and Wierda, M. (eds.) *Building a Future on Peace and Justice: Studies on Transitional Justice, Peace and Development.* Heidelberg: Springer.

Moreno Ocampo, L. 5 June 2008b. *Statement by Mr. Luis Moreno Ocampo, Prosecutor of the International Criminal Court, to the United Nations Security Council Pursuant to UNSCR 1593,* The Hague: ICC. ICCOTPST20080605ENG.

2009a. *Ninth Report of the Prosecutor of the International Criminal Court, to the United Nations Security Council pursuant to UNSCR 1593.* The Hague: ICC.

2009b. *Tenth Report of the Prosecutor of the International Criminal Court, to the United Nations Security Council pursuant to UNSCR 1593.* The Hague: ICC.

2010a. *12th Statement to the United Nations Security Council on the Situation in Darfur, the Sudan, Pursuant to UNSCR 1593*. The Hague: ICC. 12 December 2010.

2010b. Interview with Moreno Ocampo: I Am Waiting for Evidence on Buganda Killings, Says ICC Chief. *The Observer* [Online]. Available: www.observer.ug/index.php?option=com_content&view=article&id=8706:i-am-waiting-for-evidence-on-buganda-killings-says-icc-chief&catid=34:news&Itemid=59.

Moreno Ocampo, L. 2010c. Legitimacy. *Prosecutor Replies* [Online]. Available: http://community.ijcentral.org/group/asktheprosecutor/forum/topics/legitimacy-1 [Accessed 10 October 2010].

2010d. Now End This Darfur Denial. *The Guardian* [Online]. Available: www.guardian.co.uk/commentisfree/libertycentral/2010/jul/15/world-cannot-ignore-darfur [Accessed 22 July 2010].

2010e. *Statement to the United Nations Security Council on the Situation in Darfur, the Sudan, Pursuant to UNSCR 1593*. The Hague: ICC. 11 June 2010.

15 December 2011. *Fourteenth Report of the Prosecutor of the International Criminal Court to the United Nations Security Council pursuant to UNSCR 1593 (2005)*. The Hague: ICC.

Mozersky, D. 2009. The International Community Must React to the New Reality in Darfur. *In:* Miller, D. A. (ed.) *Darfur*. New York/London: Greenhaven Press.

Mpagi, C. M. 2010. LRA – Country's Worst Export of the Century. *The Monitor* [Online]. Available: http://allafrica.com/stories/201008020504.html [Accessed 11 September 2010].

MPUGA, D. 2012. Uganda Minister Dismisses Claims Government Is Becoming Repressive. *Voice of America* [Online]. Available: www.voanews.com/english/news/africa/Uganda-Minister-Dismisses-Claims-Government-is-Becoming-Repressive-149264315.html?utm_source=voaafrica&utm_medium=twitter&utm_campaign=en&utm_content=twitterfeed [Accessed 27 April 2012].

MSF-Holland. 2004a. *Internally Displaced Camps in Lira and Pader Northern Uganda: A Baseline Health Survey*. Uganda: MSF-Holland.

2004b. *Pader: A Community in Crisis: A Preliminary Analysis of MSF-Holland's Baseline Mental Health Assessment in Pader*. Uganda: MSF-Holland.

MSF & Epicentre. 2004. *Emergency in Darfur, Sudan: No Relief in Sight – Focus on Mornay Camp, West Darfur State*. Khartoum/Paris: Médecins Sans Frontières/Epicentre.

Mugerwa, Y. 2010. MP Accuses Muhoozi of Karamoja Killings. *The Monitor* [Online]. Available: http://allafrica.com/stories/201008160017.html [Accessed 17 August 2010].

Mühleisen, H.-O. 2004. Politikwissenschaftliche Friedensforschung. Ein Überblick. *In:* Eckern, U., Herwartz-Emden, L. and Schultze, R.-O. (eds.) *Friedens- und*

Konfliktforschung in Deutschland: Eine Bestandsaufnahme. Wiesbaden: VS Verlag.

Müller, H. 2003. Begriff, Theorien und Praxis des Friedens. *In:* Hellmann, G., Wolf, K. D. and Zürn, M. (eds.) *Die neuen Internationalen Beziehungen*. Baden-Baden: Nomos Verlagsgesellschaft.

Mullins, C. W. and Rothe, D. L. 2010. The Ability of the International Criminal Court to Deter Violations of International Criminal Law: A Theoretical Assessment. *International Criminal Law Review*, 10, 771–786.

Münkler, H. 2002. *Die Neuen Kriege*. Bonn: Bundeszentrale für politische Bildung.

Muñoz, F. 2006. La Paz Imperfecta. *In:* Dietrich, W. (ed.) *Schlüsseltexte der Friedensforschung*. Berlin/Hamburg/Münster: LIT-Verlag.

Murithi, T. and Ngari, A. (eds.) 2011. *The ICC and Community-Level Reconciliation: In-Country Perspectives*. Johannesburg: Institute for Justice and Reconciliation.

Murphy, D. 2007. Narrating Darfur: Darfur in the U.S. Press, March–September 2004. *In:* de Waal, A. (ed.) *War in Darfur and the Search for Peace*. Cambridge, MA: Global Equity Initiative Harvard University.

Museveni, Y. 2005. *Address by His Excellency the President on the State of the Nation in Accordance with Article 101(1) of the Constitution*. Kampala: Ugandan Parliament.

2010. Uganda: 2011 Polls Will Be Fair – Museveni. *The New Vision* [Online]. Available: http://allafrica.com/stories/201009130284.html [Accessed 18. September 2010].

Mwenda, A. 2010. Uganda's Politics of Foreign Aid and Violent Conflict: The Political Uses of the LRA Rebellion. *In:* Allen, T. and Vlassenroot, K. (eds.) *The Lord's Resistance Army: Myth and Reality*. London/New York: Zed Books.

Nakumbi, C. 29 September 2011. *RE: Interview with Cissy Nakumbi, Daily Monitor Correspondent North*.

Namutebi, J. 2005. Mamdani Urges Reconciliation. *New Vision* [Online]. Available: www.newvision.co.ug/D/8/12/469498 [Accessed 15 January 2011].

Natsios, A. S. 2007. *In:* President's Special Envoy to Sudan (ed.) *Darfur: A 'Plan B' to Stop Genocide?*. Washington DC: US Department of State.

Natsios, A. 2008. Beyond Darfur: Sudan's Slide Toward Civil War. *Foreign Affairs*, 87, 77.

2010. Speech at Georgetown University. *Georgetown University Podcast* [Online]. Available: https://gushare.georgetown.edu/elz5/Natsios%20SUdan%2010_19_10.mp3?uniq=-r279be [Accessed 22 October 2010].

Nee, A. and Uvin, P. 2010. Silence and Dialogue: Burundian's Alternatives to Transitional Justice. *In:* Shaw, R. and Waldorf, L. (eds.) *Localizing Transitional Justice: Interventions and Priorities After Mass Violence*. Stanford: Stanford University Press.

Negara, K. 2011. Bitter Root. *Al Jazeera* [Online]. Available: http://english.aljazeera.net/programmes/witness/2011/10/20111012152024670219.html [Accessed 13 October 2011].

Neu, J. 2002. Restoring Relations Between Uganda and Sudan: The Carter Center Process. Available: www.c-r.org/our-work/accord/northern-uganda/carter-center.php [Accessed 07 January 2011].

New Vision. 2003a. Sudanese Officers Arm Rebels. *New Vision* [Online]. Available: www.lexisnexis.com/de/business/results/docview/docview.do?docLinkInd=true&risb=21_T14596336849&format=GNBFI&sort=BOOLEAN&startDocNo=1&resultsUrlKey=29_T14596336853&cisb=22_T14596336852&treeMax=true&treeWidth=0&csi=8320&docNo=2 [Accessed 30 April 2012].

2003b. Sudanese Official Explains Kony Aid. *New Vision* [Online]. Available: www.lexisnexis.com/de/business/results/docview/docview.do?docLinkInd=true&risb=21_T14596355337&format=GNBFI&sort=BOOLEAN&startDocNo=1&resultsUrlKey=29_T14596355341&cisb=22_T14596355340&treeMax=true&treeWidth=0&csi=8320&docNo=3 [Accessed 30 April 2012].

2009. Govt Has No Power to Try Top LRA Commanders – ICC. *New Vision*, 11 March 2009.

2010. Sudan Provided 'Safe Corridor', Says LRA Rebel. *New Vision* [Online]. Available: www.lexisnexis.com/de/business/results/docview/docview.do?docLinkInd=true&risb=21_T14599351844&format=GNBFI&sort=BOOLEAN&startDocNo=1&resultsUrlKey=29_T14599351848&cisb=22_T14599351847&treeMax=true&treeWidth=0&csi=8320&docNo=3 [Accessed 30 April 2012].

2011. Most LRA Victims Want Culprits Forgiven, Ask for Reparation. *New Vision* [Online]. Available: www.lexisnexis.com/de/business/results/docview/docview.do?docLinkInd=true&risb=21_T13566119211&format=GNBFI&sort=DATE,A,H&startDocNo=1&resultsUrlKey=29_T13566113876&cisb=22_T13566119243&treeMax=true&treeWidth=0&selRCNodeID=150596&nodeStateId=501de_DE,1&docsInCategory=203&csi=8320&docNo=32 [Accessed 22 December 2011].

Newman, E. 2006. "New Wars" and Spoilers. *In:* Newman, E. and Richmond, O. (eds.) *Challenges to Peacebuilding: Managing Spoilers During Conflict Resolution*. Tokyo/New York/Paris: United Nations University Press.

Newman, E. and Richmond, O. 2006. Introduction: Obstacles to Peace Processes: Understanding Spoiling. *In:* Newman, E. and Richmond, O. (eds.) *Challenges to Peacebuilding: Managing Spoilers During Conflict Resolution*. Tokyo/New York/Paris: United Nations University Press.

Nhema, A. 2008. Introduction: The Resolution of African Conflicts. *In:* Nhema, A. and Zezela, P. T. (eds.) *The Resolution of African Conflicts: The Management of Conflict Resolution & Post-Conflict Reconstruction*. Addis Ababa: OSSREA.

Nielsen, E. S. 2008. Ethnicities. *Ethnic Boundaries and Conflict in Darfur: An Event Structure Hypothesis*, 8, 427–462.

Nitsche, D. 2007. *Der Internationale Strafgerichtshof ICC und der Frieden: Eine vergleichende Analyse der Befriedungsfunktion internationaler Straftribunale*. Baden-Baden: Nomos.

Nono, D. and Acan, E. 26 September 2011. *RE: Interview with Denis Nono, Legal Officer and Eve Acan, Counsellor of the African Centre for Treatment and Rehabilitation of Torture Victims (ACTV).*

Norris, J. 2010. Peace Talks with the Lord's Resistance Army Are Unrealistic, for Now. *Huffington Post* [Online]. Available: www.huffingtonpost.com/john-norris/peace-talks-with-the-lord_b_580157.html [Accessed 10 June 2010].

Nouwen, S. and Werner, W. 2010. Doing Justice to the Political: The International Criminal Court in Uganda and Sudan. *European Journal of International Law*, 21, 941–965.

2011. Doing Justice to the Political: The International Criminal Court in Uganda and Sudan. *European Journal of International Law*, 21.

Nouwen, S. M. H.2013. *Complementarity in the Line of Fire – The Catalysing Effect of the International Criminal Court in Uganda and Sudan*. Cambridge University Press.

NRF. 2009. Founding Declaration of the National Redemption Front. *In:* Hassan, S. M. and Ray, C. E. (eds.) *Darfur and the Crisis of Governance in Sudan: A Critical Reader*. Ithaca/London: Cornell University Press.

Nyeko, B. & Lucima, O. 2002. Profiles of the Parties to the Conflict. *In:* Lucima, O. (ed.) *Protracted Conflict, Elusive Peace: Initiatives to End the Violence in Northern Uganda*. London: Conciliation Resources, Kacoke Madit.

O'Brien, A. 2007. The Impact of International Justice on Local Peace Initiatives: The Case of Northern Uganda. *International Conference on Building a Future on Peace and Justice*. Nuremberg: International Crisis Group.

O'kadameri, B. 2002. LRA/Government Negotiations 1993–94. *In:* Lucima, O. (ed.) *Protracted Conflict, Elusive Peace: Initiatives to End the Violence in Northern Uganda*. London: Conciliation Resources, Kacoke Madit.

Obama, B. 2010. Remarks by President Barack Obama in a Ministerial Meeting on Sudan. Available: http://usun.state.gov/briefing/statements/2010/147927.htm [Accessed 13 October 2010].

Obarrio, J. 2011. Traditional Justice as Rule of Law in Africa. *In:* Sriram, C. L., Martin-Ortega, O. and Herman, J. (eds.) *Peacebuilding and Rule of Law in Africa: Just Peace?* London/New York: Routledge Publishers.

Odama, J. B. 27 October 2011. *RE: Interview with The Archbishop of Gulu Diocese John Baptist Odama.*

Odero, S. 2011. Politics of International Criminal Justice: The ICC's Arrest Warrant for Al Bashir and the African Union's Neo-Colonial Conspirator

Thesis. *In:* Murungu, C. and Biegon, J. (eds.) *Prosecuting International Crimes in Africa*. Pretoria: Pretoria University Law Press.

Odinkalu, C. A. 2010. Saving International Justice in Africa. *In:* The Foundation for Law, Justice and Society (ed.) *Oxford Transitional Justice Research: Debating International Justice in Africa*. Oxford: The Foundation for Law, Justice and Society & The Centre for Socio-Legal Studies, University of Oxford.

Odong, G. 25 August 2011a. *RE: Interview with Dr. Godfrey Odong.*

Odong, K. A. 16 September 2011b.*RE: Interview with Krispus Ayena Odong, Member of the Ugandan Parliament for 'Uganda People's Congress' (UPC).*

Oette, L. 2010a. Another Piece in the Puzzle: Accountability and Justice for International Crimes in Sudan. *In:* The Foundation for Law, Justice and Society (ed.) *Oxford Transitional Justice Research: Debating International Justice in Africa*. Oxford: The Foundation for Law, Justice and Society & The Centre for Socio-Legal Studies, University of Oxford.

2010b. Peace and Justice, or Neither? The Repercussions of the al-Bashir Case for International Criminal Justice in Africa and Beyond. *Journal of International Criminal Justice*, 8, 345–364.

OHCHR. 2007. Making Peace Our Own: Victims' Perceptions of Accountability, Reconciliation and Transitional Justice in Northern Uganda. United Nations.

2010. Report of the Mapping Exercise Documenting the Most Serious Violations of Human Rights and International Humanitarian Law Committed Within the Territory of the Democratic Republic of the Congo Between March 1993 and June 2003. Available: www.ohchr.org/Documents/Countries/ZR/DRC_MAPPING_REPORT_FINAL_EN.pdf [Accessed 14 September 2011].

OHCHR & UHRC. 2011. "The Dust Has Not Yet Settled": Victims' Views on The Right to Remedy and Reparation.

Ohlson, T. 2008. Understanding Causes of War and Peace. *European Journal of International Relations*, 14, 133–160.

Ojul, M. 2006. Opening Speech of LRA Delegation at Juba Talks. *New Vision.*

Okello, J. 27 September 2011. *RE: Interview with a former LRA Commander, alias used.*

Oketch, B. 2010a. Reporting Expedites LRA Suspect Case. *IWPR* [Online]. Available: http://iwpr.net/report-news/reporting-expedites-lra-suspect-case [Accessed 6 October 2010].

2010b. Uganda: War-Era Guns Linked to Recent Murders. *IWPR* [Online]. Available: http://iwpr.net/report-news/uganda-war-era-guns-linked-recent-murders [Accessed 22 October 2010].

Okidi, D. 22 October 2011. *RE: Interview David Okidi, former Station Manager of Mega FM in Gulu.*

Okoye, A. O. 2004. The Rule of Law and Sociopolitical Dynamics in Africa. *In:* Zeleza, P. T. and Mcconnaughay, P. J. (eds.) *Human Rights, the Rule of Law, and Development in Africa*. Philadelphia: University of Pennsylvania Press.

Okumu, R. R. 12 September 2011. *RE: Interview Ronal Reagan Okumu, Member of the Ugandan Parliament for the Forum for Democratic Change.*

Olsen, T. D., Payne, L. A. and Reiter, A. 2010. *Transitional Justice in Balance: Comparing Processes, Weighing Efficacy.* Washington, DC: US Institute of Peace Press.

Olson, L. M. 2006. Provoking the Dragon on the Patio. Matters of Transitional Justice: Penal Repression vs. Amnesties. *International Review of the Red Cross*, 88, 275–294.

Omeje, K. C. 2008. Understanding Conflict Resolution in Africa. *In:* Francis, D. J. (ed.) *Peace & Conflict in Africa.* London/New York: Zed Books.

Onega, P. 29 August 2011. *RE: Interview with Peter Onega, Chairman of the Ugandan Amnesty Commission.*

Onsea, I. 2009. The Legacy of the ICTR in Rwanda in the Context of the Completion Strategy: The Impact of Rule 11bis. *In:* Ryngaert, C. (ed.) *The Effectiveness Of International Criminal Justice.* Antwerpen: Intersentia.

Oola, S. 2010. The Coalition for Reconciliation in Uganda: Important Lessons for Proactive Civil Society Engagement in Catalysing Transitional Justice Discourse. *African Transitional Justice Research Network Workshop: Advocating Justice: Civil Society and Transitional Justice in Africa,* Johannesburg.

Orchard, P. 2009. Regime-Induced Displacement and the Dilemmas of Civilian Protection: The Case of Darfur: Center of International Relations.

Orentlicher, D. 2010. That Someone Guilty Be Punished: The Impact of the ICTY in Bosnia. Open Society Justice Initiative and ICTJ.

Orentlicher, D. F. 2005. *Report of the Independent Expert to Update the Set of Principles to Combat Impunity.* Geneva: United Nations. UN Doc E/CN.4/2005/102/.

Osaghae, E. E. 2000. Applying Traditional Methods to Modern Conflict: Possibilities and Limits. *In:* Zartman, I. W.(ed.) *Traditional Cures for Modern Conflicts: African Conflict "Medicine".* Boulder/London: Lynne Rienner Publishers Inc.

Osiel, M. 2000. Why Prosecute? Critics of Punishment for Mass Atrocity. *Human Rights Quarterly*, 22, 118–147.

Othman, M. C. 2010a. Near-verbatim Transcript of the Press Conference by Justice Mohamed Chande Othman, the Independent Expert on the Situation of Human Rights in the Sudan. Available: www.lexisnexis.com/de/business/results/docview/docview.do?docLinkInd=true&risb=21_T14883699040&format=GNBFI&sort=BOOLEAN&startDocNo=1&resultsUrlKey=29_T14883699044&cisb=22_T14883699043&treeMax=true&treeWidth=0&csi=362780&docNo=4 [Accessed 8 June 2012].

2 September 2010b. *Update on the Report of the Independent Expert on the Situation of Human Rights in the Sudan.* New York: United Nations General Assembly. A/HRC/15/57.

Otim, M. 2010. Skylight Pictures Video Blogging from the ICC Review Conference. Available: www.ictj.org/en/news/features/3816.html [Accessed 21 July 2010].

Otim, M. & Wierda, M. 2008. Justice at Juba: International Obligations and Local Demands in Northern Uganda. *In:* Waddell, N. and Clark, P. (eds.) *Courting Conflict? Justice, Peace and the ICC in Africa*. London: Royal African Society.

2010. *Uganda: Impact of the Rome Statute and the International Criminal Court*. Kampala: International Center for Transitional Justice.

OTP. 2005. Joint Statement by ICC Chief Prosecutor and the Visiting Delegation of Lango, Acholi, Iteso and Madi Community Leaders from Northern Uganda. Available: www.icc-cpi.int/menus/icc/situations%20and%20cases/situations/situation%20icc%200204/press%20releases/joint%20statement%20by%20icc%20chief%20prosecutor%20and%20the%20visiting%20delegation%20of%20lango%20acholi%20iteso%20and%20madi%20c [Accessed 30 April 2012].

12 September 2006. *Report on the Activities Performed During the First Three Years*. The Hague: Office of the Prosecutor of the ICC.

2007. Policy Paper on the Interests of Justice. Available: www.icc-cpi.int/NR/rdonlyres/772C95C9-F54D-4321-BF09-73422BB23528/143640/ICCOTPInterestsOfJustice.pdf [Accessed 15 May 2011].

2010. OTP Weekly Briefing: November 23–29, 2010. Available: www.icc-cpi.int/NR/rdonlyres/7105B39A-2F30-43FF-9222-D7349BF15502/282732/OTPWBENG.pdf [Accessed 12 October 2011].

Otto, P. O. 2002. Implementing the 1999 Nairobi Agreement. *In:* Lucima, O. (ed.) *Protracted Conflict, Elusive Peace: Initiatives to End the Violence in Northern Uganda*. London: Conciliation Resources, Kacoke Madit.

Otunnu, O. A.2006. The Secret Genocide. *Foreign Policy*, July/August ed.

Otwili, E. A., Schulz, P., Lonergan, K. and Ogora, L. O. 2011. To Pardon or to Punish? Current Perceptions and Opinions on Uganda's Amnesty in Acholi-land. Available: http://justiceandreconciliation.com/wp-content/uploads/2011/12/JRP_Brief_Amnesty-Dec-20111.pdf.

Oulanyah, J. 17 October 2011. *RE: Interview with Jacob Oulanyah, Deputy Speaker of the Ugandan Parliament*.

Oxfam. 2007. *The Building Blocks of Sustainable Peace: The Views of Internally Displaced People in Northern Uganda*. Oxford: Oxfam International. Oxfam Briefing Paper 106.

2010. UN Must Stop Failing Civilians under Threat from the LRA. Available: www.reliefweb.int/rw/rwb.nsf/db900SID/VVOS-8A9QYM?OpenDocument [Accessed 18 October 2010].

2011. *'We Are Entirely Exploitable': The Lack of Protection for Civilians in Eastern DRC*. Oxford: Oxfam.

Oxfam International. 2007. The Building Blocks of Sustainable Peace: The Views of Internally Displaced People in Northern Uganda. Oxford: Oxfam International. Oxfam Briefing Paper 106.

Paes, W. C. 2006. Darfur: Konfliktlinien und Lösungsstrategien. *In:* Rittberger, V. (ed.) *Grundprobleme der Konfliktbeilegung und Friedenskonsolidierung mit besonderer Berücksichtigung der Konfliktherde auf dem afrikanischen Kontinent.* Osnabrück: Deutsche Stiftung Friedensforschung.

Parlevliet, M. 2010. *Rethinking Conflict Transformation from a Human Rights Perspective.* Berlin: Berghof Conflict Research.

Pearson, F. S. and Lounsbery, M. O. 2009. The Challenge of Operationalizing Key Concepts in Conflict Resolution Theory in International and Subnational Conflicts. *In:* Sandole, D. J. D., Byrne, S., Sandole-Staroste, I. and Senehi, J. (eds.) *Handbook of Conflict Analysis and Resolution.* Oxford/New York: Routledge.

Peled, D. 2010. Darfur Fears as Attention Shifts to South Sudan. *IWPR* [Online]. Available: http://iwpr.net/report-news/darfur-fears-attention-shifts-south-sudan [Accessed 16 December 2010].

Penrose, M. M. 1999. Impunity – Inertia, Inaction, and Invalidity: A Literature Review. *Boston University International Law Journal*, 17, 269–310.

Perelman, M. 2010. Luis Moreno-Ocampo, Procureur de la Cour Pénale Internationale. *L'Entretien.* France 24.

Perras, A. 2010. Angst vor der Abstimmung. *Süddeutsche Zeitung*, 15 November 2010, p. 9.

2011. Baschir kündigt Rückzug an. *Süddeutsche Zeitung*, 22 February 2011, p. 9.

Perrot, S. 2010. Northern Uganda: A 'Forgotten Conflict', Again? The Impact of the Internationalization of the Resolution Process. *In:* Allen, T. and Vlassenroot, K. (eds.) *The Lord's Resistance Army: Myth and Reality.* London/New York: Zed Books.

Peskin, V. 2005. Beyond Victor's Justice? The Challenge of Prosecuting the Winners at the International Criminal Tribunals for the Former Yugoslavia and Rwanda. *Journal of Human Rights*, 4, 213–231.

2009a. Caution and Confrontation in the International Criminal Court's Pursuit of Accountability in Uganda and Sudan. *Human Rights Quarterly*, 31, 655–691.

2009b. The International Criminal Court, the Security Council, and the Politics of Impunity in Darfur. *Genocide Studies and Prevention*, 4, 304–328.

Pham, P. and Vinck, P. 2010. *Transitioning to Peace: A Population-Based Survey on Attitudes about Social Reconstruction and Justice in Northern Uganda.* Berkeley: Human Rights Center University of California.

Pham, P., Vinck, P., Stover, E., Moss, A., Wierda, M. and Bailey, R. 2007. *When the War Ends: A Population-Based Survey on Attitudes about Peace, Justice, and Social Reconstruction in Northern Uganda.* Berkeley: Human Rights Center University of California.

Physicians for Human Rights. 2009. Darfur Is a Place Where Torture is Rampant. *In:* Miller, D. A. (ed.) *Darfur*. New York/London: Greenhaven Press.

Pia, E. & Diez, T. 2009. Human Rights in Conflict: Securitising or Desecuritising? *SHUR Working Paper Series* [Online]. [Accessed 29 October 2010].

Pillay, S. 2009. Conclusion. *In:* Sriram, C. L. and Pillay, S. (eds.) *Peace Versus Justice? The Dilemmas of Transitional Justice in Africa*. Scottsville: University of KwaZulu-Natal Press.

Ping, J. 2010. *Speech by AU Chairperson Jean Ping at UN High Level Meeting on Sudan*. New York: African Union.

Poku, N. K. 2008. Context of Security in Africa. *In:* Francis, D. J. (ed.) *Peace & Conflict in Africa*. London/New York: Zed Books.

Polgreen, L. 2006. Rwanda's Shadow, from Darfur to Congo. *New York Times*, 23 July 2006, p. 3.

Prendergast, J. 2005. *Resolving the Three Headed War from Hell in Southern Sudan, Northern Uganda, and Darfur*. Washington, DC: Woodrow Wilson International Center for Scholars.

2007a. The Answer to the Lord's Resistance Army. Washington, DC: Enough. Enough Strategy Paper #3.

2007b. Let's Make a Deal: Leverage Needed in Northern Uganda Peace Talks. Washington, DC: Enough. Enough Strategy Paper #6.

2007c. What to Do About Joseph Kony. Washington, DC: Enough. Enough Strategy Paper #8.

Prendergast, J. & O'Brien, A. 2007. A Diplomatic Surge for Northern Uganda. Washington, DC: Enough. Enough Strategy Paper #9.

Pronk, J. 2004. Statement on Darfur to the UN Security Council, November 2004. Available: www.janpronk.nl/speeches/english/statement-on-darfur-to-the-un-securitycouncil-november-2004.htm [Accessed 1 June 2011].

Prosecutor v. Furundzija. Case No. IT-95-17/1 - ICTY.

Prunier, G. 2005. *Darfur: The Ambiguous Genocide*. Ithaca: Cornell University Press.

2006. The Politics of Death in Darfur. *Current History*, 195–202.

2010. Rwanda and Darfur: A Comparative Approach to Two Peacekeeping Failures. *Journal of International Peacekeeping*, 14, 117–133.

PTCI. 2009. Warrant of Arrest for Omar Hassan Ahmad Al Bashir. The Hague: Pre-Trial Chamber I of the International Criminal Court. ICC-02/05-01/09.

Radio Dabanga. 2010a. 17 Gimr Men Detained since May for Aiding Darfur Rebels. *Radio Dabanga* [Online]. Available: www.radiodabanga.org/node/4102.

2010b. Al Nur Welcomes SPLM Mediation, Wants Foreign Intervention in Darfur. *Radio Dabanga* [Online]. Available: www.radiodabanga.org/node/2219 [Accessed 10 August 2010].

2010c. Armed Group Claims Responsibility for Killing Darfur Executive Official. *Radio Dabanga* [Online]. Available: www.radiodabanga.org/node/4480 [Accessed 17 June 2012].

2010d. Army, Darfur Rebels Offer Differing Views on Border Guard Militia. *Radio Dabanga* [Online]. Available: www.radiodabanga.org/node/4483 [Accessed 6 October 2010].

2010e. Camp Protest Turns into Deadly Clash Between Factions for and against Darfur Peace Talks. *Radio Dabanga* [Online]. Available: www.radiodabanga.org/node/2677 [Accessed 30 July 2010].

2010f. Clash at Jebel Kargo as Arab Faction Joins Darfur Rebels. *Radio Dabanga* [Online]. Available: www.radiodabanga.org/node/5892 [Accessed 12 November 2010].

2010g. Darfur LJM and Sudan Wrapping up Committee Sessions at Doha. *Radio Dabanga* [Online]. Available: www.radiodabanga.org/node/4834 [Accessed 15 October 2010].

2010h. Darfuris Await UN Security Council Delegation, Voice Doubts. *Radio Dabanga* [Online]. Available: www.radiodabanga.org/node/4516 [Accessed 7 October 2010].

2010i. Forum held in Zalingei on New Government Darfur Strategy. *Radio Dabanga* [Online]. Available: www.radiodabanga.org/node/4478 [Accessed 5 October 2010].

2010j. Government Panel: Border Guards, PDF Threat to Darfur Security. Available: www.radiodabanga.com/node/3682 [Accessed 9 September 2010].

2010k. Group of Arab Nomads in Darfur Declare War on the Government. *Radio Dabanga* [Online]. Available: www.radiodabanga.org/node/4787 [Accessed 14 October 2010].

2010l. Horrendous Schools Situation in N. Darfur Camps. *Radio Dabanga* [Online]. Available: www.radiodabanga.org/node/8077 [Accessed 7 January 2011].

2010m. 'Janjaweed' Kill 57 People and Wound 86 at Market in Darfur. *Radio Dabanga* [Online]. Available: www.radiodabanga.org/node/3658 [Accessed 5 September 2010].

2010n. Khartoum Court Condemns Opposition Journalists to Years in Prison, Shuts Newspaper. *Radio Dabanga* [Online]. Available: http://www.radiodabanga.com/node/2062 [Accessed 17 July 2010].

2010o. Leader of Rizeigat Downplays Defections to Darfur Rebels. *Radio Dabanga* [Online]. Available: www.radiodabanga.org/node/6040 [Accessed 16 November 2010].

2010p. Leaders of Atash Camp, S. Darfur, Want More Security. *Radio Dabanga* [Online]. Available: www.radiodabanga.org/node/4104.

2010q. LJM Chief blames Government for Hamadiya Camp Violence. *Radio Dabanga* [Online]. Available: www.radiodabanga.org/node/4584 [Accessed 8 October 2010].

2010r. Rebels Unwilling to Compromise on Single Darfur Province. *Radio Dabanga* [Online]. Available: www.radiodabanga.org/node/5799 [Accessed 11 November 2010].

2010s. Refugees in Chad Decline to Attend Doha Peace Ceremony. *Radio Dabanga* [Online]. Available: www.radiodabanga.org/node/7738 [Accessed 30 December 2010].

2010t. South Darfur Governor Threatens to Storm Kalma to Make Arrests. *Radio Dabanga* [Online]. Available: /www.radiodabanga.org/node/2761 [Accessed 2 August 2010].

2010u. UN and Darfur Rebels to Sign Accord against Child Soldiers. *Radio Dabanga* [Online]. Available: www.radiodabanga.com/node/2217 [Accessed 20 July 2010].

2010v. Warnings of LRA Movement into Darfur. *Radio Dabanga* [Online]. Available: www.radiodabanga.org/node/4921 [Accessed 18 October 2010].

2011a. 75% of Darfur's Refugee Children Show PTSD Symptoms *Radio Dabanga* [Online]. Available: www.radiodabanga.org/node/17358 [Accessed 12 August 2011].

2011b. Arrest of Salah Gosh, Ousted Security Chief and Darfur War Planner. *Radio Dabanga* [Online]. Available: www.radiodabanga.org/node/14366 [Accessed 15 June 2012].

2011c. Continous Developments Over Doha Agreement. *Radio Dabanga* [Online]. Available: www.radiodabanga.org/node/16924 [Accessed 8 June 2012].

2011d. Darfuri Group Prohibits Child Soldiers. *Radio Dabanga* [Online]. Available: www.lexisnexis.com/de/business/results/docview/docview.do?docLinkInd=true&risb=21_T14884008490&format=GNBFI&sort=BOOLEAN&startDocNo=1&resultsUrlKey=29_T14884008494&cisb=22_T14884008493&treeMax=true&treeWidth=0&csi=8320&docNo=6 [Accessed 8 June 2012].

2011e. ICC Prosecutor Calls to Bring End to Darfur Conflict. *Radio Dabanga* [Online]. Available: www.radiodabanga.org/node/26359 [Accessed 8 June 2012].

2011f. JEM Condemns Accusation of Darfuri Fighting along Gadaffi. *Radio Dabanga* [Online]. Available: www.radiodabanga.org/node/12976 [Accessed 18 June 2012].

2011g. Kalma Camp Sheikhs 'Unanimously Reject Doha Agreement'. *Radio Dabanga* [Online]. Available: www.radiodabanga.org/node/20220 [Accessed 8 June 2012].

2011h. Khartoum Making New Militia Recruitment Effort for Darfur. *Radio Dabanga* [Online]. Available: www.radiodabanga.org/node/8908 [Accessed 27 January 2011].

2011i. Ocampo to Security Council Today with New Strategy to Arrest Bashir. *Radio Dabanga* [Online]. Available: www.radiodabanga.org/node/14948 [Accessed 8 June 2011].

2011j. State Minister Says Sudan Protecting Harun, Kushayb. *Radio Dabanga* [Online]. Available: www.radiodabanga.org/node/8955 [Accessed 28 January 2011].

2011k. Sweeping Operation of Government Forces, Citizens Flee *Radio Dabanga* [Online]. Available: www.radiodabanga.org/node/13027 [Accessed 18 June 2012].

2011l. Three Darfur States Poorest in Sudan. *Radio Dabanga* [Online]. Available: www.radiodabanga.org/node/17358 [Accessed 18 August 2011].

2011m. Two Dead, 80 Detained After Government Raid on Darfur Camp. *Radio Dabanga* [Online]. Available: www.radiodabanga.org/node/8815 [Accessed 25 January 2011].

2011n. US $300m, Compensation Amount for Darfur Refugees. *Radio Dabanga* [Online]. Available: www.radiodabanga.org/node/21213 [Accessed 22 November 2011].

2011o. West Darfur Education Minister: Illiteracy Rate at 45%. *Radio Dabanga* [Online]. Available: www.radiodabanga.org/node/14413 [Accessed 22 May 2011].

2011p. Wikileaks Revelations. *Radio Dabanga* [Online]. Available: www.radiodabanga.org/node/18239 [Accessed 8 September 2011].

2012a. Displaced Man Shot Dead by Pro Government Militia. *Radio Dabanga* [Online]. Available: www.radiodabanga.org/node/31220 [Accessed 2 June 2012].

2012b. Fourth Special Prosecutor for Darfur Resigns. *Radio Dabanga* [Online]. Available: www.radiodabanga.org/node/31806 [Accessed 15 June 2012].

Raleigh, C., Linke, A., Hegre, H. and Karlsen, J. 2010. Introducing ACLED: An Armed Conflict Location and Event Dataset: Special Data Feature. *Journal of Peace Research*, 47, 651.

Rastan, R. 2010. Comment on Victor's Justice & the Viability of Ex Ante Standards. *The John Marshall Law Review*, 43, 569–602.

11 February 2011a. *RE: Interview with Rod Rastan, Senior Legal Advisor, ICC-OTP.*

17 October 2011b. *RE: Mail Exchange with Rod Rastan, Senior Legal Advisor, ICC-OTP.*

Ray, C. E. 2009. Darfur in the African Press. *In:* Hassan, S. M. and Ray, C. E. (eds.) *Darfur and the Crisis of Governance in Sudan: A Critical Reader*. Ithaca/London: Cornell University Press.

Redress. 15 October 2009. *Written Evidence Submitted by the Redress Trust to the UK Associate Parliamentary Group on Sudan: Sudan's Comprehensive Peace Agreement: Promoting Law Reform in Sudan to Enhance Human Rights Protection, Strengthen the Rule of Law and Foster Democratic Processes.* London: The Redress Trust.

Reeves, E. 2009. Death in Darfur: Total Mortality from Violence, Malnutrition, and Disease. *In:* Grzyb, A. F. (ed.) *The World and Darfur: International Response to Crimes Against Humanity in Western Sudan*. Montreal/Kingston: McGill-Queen's University Press.

Registry of the ICC. 2010. Outreach Report 2010. The Hague: ICC.

Resolve Uganda & Enough Project. 2009. No Excuses: The End of the Lord's Resistance Army is in Sight: Enough Project/Resolve Uganda Statement on 'Operation Lightning Thunder'. Available: www.enoughproject.org/files/publications/Joint_LRA_statement_jan_16_Final.pdf [Accessed 27 June 2011].

Reuters. 3 October 2007. Darfur: UN Envoy Wants Immediate Ceasefire.

2014. Uganda Says Anti-gay Bill Misunderstood by Donors Who Halted Aid. *Reuters* [Online]. Available: http://af.reuters.com/article/topNews/idAFKBN0FC1QX20140707.

Rice, X. 2010. Sudan President Omar al-Bashir Sworn in Amid Outcry. *The Guardian* [Online]. Available: www.guardian.co.uk/world/2010/may/27/sudan-president-omar-al-bashir-sworn-in.

Risse, T., Jetschke, A. and Schmitz, H. P. 2003. *Die Macht der Menschenrechte: Internationale Normen, Kommunikatives Handeln und politischer Wandel in den Ländern*. Baden-Baden: Nomos.

Roberts, A. 2006. Just Peace: A Cause Worth Fighting For. *In:* Allan, P. and Keller, A. (eds.) *What Is a Just Peace?* Oxford University Press.

Robinson, D. 2006. Serving the Interests of Justice: Amnesties, Truth Commissions, and the International Criminal Court. *In:* Harrington, J., Milde, M. & Vernon, R. (eds.) *Bringing Power to Justice?* Montreal/Kingston: McGill-Queen's University Press.

Robinson, P. H. & Darley, J. M. 2004. Does Criminal Law Deter? A Behavioural Science Investigation. *Oxford Journal of Legal Studies*, 24, 173–205.

Rodman, K. A. 2008. Darfur and the Limits of Legal Deterrence. *Human Rights Quarterly*, 30, 529–560.

2009. Is Peace in the Interests of Justice? The Case for Broad Prosecutorial Discretion at the International Criminal Court. *Leiden Journal of International Law*, 22, 99–126.

Rodman, K. A. and Booth, P., 2013. Manipulated Commitments: The International Criminal Court in Uganda. *Human Rights Quarterly*, 35(2), 271.

Rodriguez, C. 2009. *Tall Grass: Stories of Peace and Suffering in Northern Uganda*. Kampala: Fountain Publishers.

Ronan, P. 2011. "Es werden weiter Menschen entführt": Interview with Paul Ronan by Simone Schlindwein. *TAZ* [Online]. Available: www.taz.de/US-Experte-ueber-die-LRA-in-Uganda/!76503/ [Accessed 19 August 2011].

Rossi, F. July 2012. *RE: Presentation by Fabio Rossi, Legal Advisor, ICC-OTP*.

Roth, K. 2009. Why Indictment Matters. *The Hub* [Online]. Available: hub.witness.org/en/node/12595 [Accessed 15 November 2010].

2010. *Stocktaking of International Criminal Justice Peace and Justice: Draft Moderator's Summary*. Kampala: ICC.

Rothe, D. L. 2010. Beyond the Juristic Orientation of International Criminal Justice: The Relevance of Criminological Insight to International Criminal Law and its Control A Commentary. *International Criminal Law Review*, 10, 97–110.

Royo, J. M. 2008. Escenarios de Paz y de Guerra en el Norte de Uganda, Barcelona. Juli 2008.

Rugunda, R. 3 November 2011. *RE: Interview with Ruhakana Rugunda, Minister of Information and Communication Technology, Former Minister of Interior and Head of the Government of Uganda Delegation at the Juba Talks.*

Rupiny, D. 2010. Victims of LRA War Demand Justice. *International Justice Tribune* [Online]. Available: www.rnw.nl/international-justice/article/victims-lra-war-demand-justice [Accessed 9 September 2010].

Rupprecht, J. 2003. *Frieden durch Menschenrechtsschutz: Strategien der Vereinten Nationen zur Verwirklichung der Menschenrechte weltweit.* Baden-Baden: Nomos.

Ryngaert, C. 2009. Introduction. *In:* Ryngaert, C. (ed.) *The Effectiveness of International Criminal Justice.* Antwerpen: Intersentia.

Sagan, A. 2010. African Criminals/African Victims: The Institutionalised Production of Cultural Narratives in International Criminal Law. *Millennium – Journal of International Studies*, 39, 3–21.

Sai, N. 2010. LRA Rampage Sparks Protection Calls. *IWPR* [Online]. Available. http://iwpr.net/report-news/lra-rampage-sparks-protection-calls [Accessed 14 July 2010].

Salih, M. A. M. 2005. *Understanding the Conflict in Darfur.* Copenhagen: University of Copenhagen Centre of African Studies.

Sambanis, N. 2005. Conclusion: Using Case Studies to Refine and Expand the Theory of Civil War. *In:* Collier, P. and Sambanis, N. (eds.) *Understanding Civil War: Evidence and Analysis.* Washington, DC: The World Bank.

Sarro, D. 2010. Rescuing the International Criminal Court. *Huffington Post* [Online]. Available: www.huffingtonpost.com/doug-sarro/rescuing-the-internationa_b_595598.html [Accessed 5 June 2010].

SAS. 2007. *A Widening War around Sudan: The Proliferation of Armed Groups in the Central African Republic.* Geneva: Small Arms Survey.

Save Darfur. 2012. Protection of Civilians. Available: www.savedarfur.org/pages/protection [Accessed 25 June 2012].

Scanlon, H. and Motlafi, N. 2009. Indigenous Justice or Political Instrument? The Modern Gacaca Court of Rwanda. *In:* Sriram, C. L. and Pillay, S. (eds.) *Peace Versus Justice? The Dilemmas of Transitional Justice in Africa.* Scottsville: University of KwaZulu-Natal Press.

Schabas, W. 2010a. Incorporating the Crime of Aggression: A Giant Step for the Court, and for International Law. *Equality of Arms Review*, 2, 26–28.

2010b. Victor's Justice: Selecting "Situations" at the International Criminal Court. *The John Marshall Law Review*, 43, 535–552.

2012. *Unimaginable Atrocities: Justice, Politics, and Rights at War Crimes Tribunals*. Oxford University Press.

Scheen, T. 2010. Wenige Staatschefs bei Vereidigung Baschirs. *Frankfurter Allgemeine Zeitung*, 27 May 2010.

Schlichte, K. 2009. Mit dem Staat Gegen den Staat? Die Formierung Bewaffneter Gruppen. *In:* Bussmann, M., Hasenclever, A. and Schneider, G. (eds.) *Identität, Institutionen und Ökonomie. Ursachen innenpolitischer Gewalt*. Wiesbaden: VS Verlag.

Schmidtz, D. 2006. *Elements of Justice*. Cambridge University Press.

Schofield, J. W. 2000. Increasing the Generalizability of Qualitative Research. *In:* Gomm, R., Hammersley, M. and Foster, P. (eds.) *Case Study Method: Key Issues, Key Texts*. London/Thousand Oaks/New Delhi: Sage Publications.

Schomerus, M. 2007. *The Lord's Resistance Army in Sudan: A History and Overview*. Geneva: Small Arms Survey.

2010a. Chasing the Kony Story. *In:* Allen, T. and Vlassenroot, K. (eds.) *The Lord's Resistance Army: Myth and Reality*. London/New York: Zed Books.

2010b. 'A Terrorist Is Not a Person Like Me': An Interview with Joseph Kony. *In:* Allen, T. and Vlassenroot, K. (eds.) *The Lord's Resistance Army: Myth and Reality*. London/New York: Zed Books.

Schrey, A. A. 2003. Striving for Accountability in the Former Yugoslavia. *In:* Stromseth, J. E. (ed.) *Accountability for Atrocities: National and International Responses*. New York: Transnational Publishers.

Schultze, R.-O. and Zinterer, T. 2004. Introduction. *In:* Eckern, U., Herwartz-Emden, L. and Schultze, R.-O. (eds.) *Friedens- und Konfliktforschung in Deutschland Eine Bestandsaufnahme*. Wiesbaden: VS Verlag.

SCR. 2014. Security Council Report May 2014. *Security Council Report*.

Sekindi, R. 19 September 2011. *RE: Interview with Ruth Sekindi, Director of Compliance, Ugandan Human Rights Commission*.

Senghaas, D. and Senghaas-Knobloch, E. 2009. Quod est pax? *In:* Baumann, M. M., Birckenbach, H.-M., Brandes, V., Dieterich, S., Gundermann, U. and Suhr, U. (eds.) *Friedensforschung und Friedenspraxis. Ermutigung zur Arbeit an der Utopie*. Frankfurt am Main: Brandes und Aspel.

Sengupta, K. 2008. EU Boycotts China Oil Firm Over Funding of Darfur Regime. *The Independent* [Online]. Available: www.lexisnexis.com/de/business/results/docview/docview.do?docLinkInd=true&risb=21_T14933428661&format=GNBFI&sort=BOOLEAN&startDocNo=1&resultsUrlKey=29_T14933428665&cisb=22_T14933428664&treeMax=true&treeWidth=0&csi=8200&docNo=7 [Accessed 15 June 2012].

Sharkey, H. J. 2008. Arab Identity and Ideology in Sudan: The Politics of Language, Ethnicity and Race. *African Affairs*, 107.

Shaw, R. and Waldorf, L. 2010. Introduction: Localizing Transitional Justice. *In:* Shaw, R. and Waldorf, L. (eds.) *Localizing Transitional Justice: Interventions and Priorities After Mass Violence*. Stanford: Stanford University Press.

Sikkink, K. and Walling, C. B. 2006. Errors about Trials: The Emergence and Impact of the Justice Cascade. *Princeton International Relations Faculty Colloquium*. Princeton: Princeton University.

Simons, M. 2009. Court Issues Warrant for Arrest of Sudan President. *New York Times* [Online]. Available: www.nytimes.com/2009/03/05/world/africa/05court.html [Accessed 26 May 2011].

2010. Wanted, Sudan's President Can't Escape Isolation. *New York Times* [Online]. Available: www.nytimes.com/2010/05/02/world/africa/02sudan.html [Accessed 2 June 2010].

Simonse, S., Verkoren, W. and Junne, G.2010. NGO Involvement in the Juba Peace Talks: The Role and Dilemmas of IKV Pax Christi. *In:* Allen, T. and Vlassenroot, K. (eds.) *The Lord's Resistance Army: Myth and Reality*. London/New York: Zed Books.

Simpson, G. 2008. One among Many: The ICC as a Tool of Justice During Transition. *In:* Waddell, N. and Clark, P. (eds.) *Courting Conflict? Justice, Peace and the ICC in Africa*. London: Royal African Society.

Small Arms Survey. 2012. Lord's Resistance Army Update. *Sudan Human Security Baseline Assessment* [Online]. Available: www.smallarmssurveysudan.org/facts-figures-armed-groups-southern-sudan-LRA.php [Accessed 24 February 2012].

Snyder, J. and Vinjamuri, L. 2003. Trials and Errors: Principles and Pragmatism in Strategies of International Justice. *International Security*, 28, 5–44.

Song, S.-H. 2010. Keynote Remarks. *Parliamentarians for Global Action: Consultative Assembly of Parliamentarians on the ICC and Rule of Law* [Online]. Available: www.icc-cpi.int/NR/rdonlyres/820279D0-A1B4-44D2-9E32-7EDC85751113/281965/PresidentspeechinKampala1.pdf [Accessed 27 May 2010].

Spiegel, J. and Prendergast, J. 2008. *A New Peace Strategy for Northern Uganda and the LRA*. Washington, DC: Enough. Enough Strategy Paper #19.

Srinivasan, S. 2010. Dilemmas of Confrontation and Cooperation: Politics in Sudan During Ocampo v Bashir. *In:* The Foundation for Law, Justice and Society (ed.) *Oxford Transitional Justice Research: Debating International Justice in Africa*. Oxford: The Foundation for Law, Justice and Society & The Centre for Socio-Legal Studies, University of Oxford.

Sriram, C. L. 2008. Conflict Mediation and the ICC: Challenges and Options for Pursuing Peace with Justice at the Regional Level. *In:* Ambos, K., Large, J. and Wierda, M. (eds.) *Building a Future on Peace and Justice: Studies on Transitional Justice, Peace and Development*. Heidelberg: Springer.

2009a. The International Criminal Court Africa Experiment: The Central African Republic, Darfur, Northern Uganda and the Democratic Republic of Congo. *In:* Sriram, C. L. and Pillay, S. (eds.) *Peace Versus Justice? The Dilemmas of Transitional Justice in Africa*. Scottsville: University of KwaZulu-Natal Press.

2009b. Transitional Justice and Peacebuilding. *In:* Sriram, C. L. and Pillay, S. (eds.) *Peace Versus Justice? The Dilemmas of Transitional Justice in Africa.* Scottsville: University of KwaZulu-Natal Press.

Sriram, C. L., Martin-Ortega, O. and Herman, J. 2011. Promoting the Rule of Law: From Liberal to Institutional Peacebuilding. *In:* Sriram, C. L., Martin-Ortega, O. and Herman, J. (eds.) *Peacebuilding and Rule of Law in Africa: Just Peace?* London/New York: Routledge Publishers.

Ssenyonjo, M. 2007. The International Criminal Court and the Lord's Resistance Army Leaders. Prosecution or Amnesty? *Netherlands International Law Review*, 54, 51–80.

2009. The International Criminal Court and the Warrant of Arrest for Sudan's President Al-Bashir: A Crucial Step Towards Challenging Impunity or a Political Decision? *Nordic Journal of International Law*, 78, 397–431.

2010. The International Criminal Court Arrest Warrant Decision for President Al Bashir of Sudan. *International and Comparative Law Quarterly*, 59, 205–225.

Stedman, S. J. 2002. Policy Implications. *In:* Stedman, S. J., Rothchild, D. & Cousens, E. M. (eds.) *Ending Civil Wars. The Implementation of Peace Agreements.* Boulder: Lynne Rienner.

Steinmeier, F.-W. 2008. Opening Speech by Federal Foreign Minister Dr. Frank-Walter Steinmeier. *In:* Ambos, K., Large, J. and Wierda, M. (eds.) *Building a Future on Peace and Justice: Studies on Transitional Justice, Peace and Development.* Heidelberg: Springer.

Sterling, T. 2010. 2 Sudanese War Crimes Suspects Surrender to Court. *Associated Press* [Online]. Available: www.google.com/hostednews/ap/article/ALeqM5iIrzh2m-DE3ofQLZ4fmPoN5JnCAwD9GCDUH02 [Accessed 16 June 2010].

Strain, J. and Keyes, E. 2003. Accountability in the Aftermath of Rwanda's Genocide. *In:* Stromseth, J. E. (ed.) *Accountability for Atrocities: National and International Responses.* New York: Transnational Publishers.

Stromseth, J. 2009. Justice on the Ground: Can International Criminal Courts Strengthen Domestic Rule of Law in Post-Conflict Societies? *Hague Journal on the Rule of Law*, 1, 87–97.

Stromseth, J. E. 2003. Introduction: Goals and Challenges in the Pursuit of Accountability. *In:* Stromseth, J. E. (ed.) *Accountability for Atrocities: National and International Responses.* New York: Transnational Publishers.

Struett, M. J. 2009. The Politics of Discursive Legitimacy: Understanding the Dynamics and Implications of Prosecutorial Discretion at the International Criminal Court. *In:* Roach, S. C. (ed.) *Governance, Order, and the International Criminal Court: Between Realpolitik and a Cosmopolitan Court.* Oxford University Press.

Sudan Tribune. 2008a. Sudanese Armed Forces, UN Agency Sign Accord on Child Right. *Sudan Tribune* [Online]. Available: www.lexisnexis.com/de/business/

results/docview/docview.do?docLinkInd=true&risb=21_T14883965994&format=GNBFI&sort=BOOLEAN&startDocNo=1&resultsUrlKey=29_T14883965998&cisb=22_T14883965997&treeMax=true&treeWidth=0&csi=10962&docNo=7 [Accessed 8 June 2012].

2008b. Sudanese President Says ICC Allegations Are Like 'Mosquito Buzz'. *Sudan Tribune* [Online]. Available: www.sudantribune.com/Sudanese-president-says-ICC,29227 [Accessed 25 June 2012].

2009. Sudan Says Unable to Go After Darfur War Crime Suspects. *Sudan Tribune* [Online]. Available: www.sudantribune.com/Sudan-says-unable-to-go-after,30854 [Accessed 1 June 2011].

2010a. Sudan Unhappy about Uganda's Hosting of ICC Conference. Available: www.sudantribune.com/spip.php?article35014 [Accessed May 22 2010].

2010b. US Criticizes "Political Repression" by Sudanese Authorities. *Sudan Tribune* [Online]. Available: www.lexisnexis.com/de/business/results/docview/docview.do?docLinkInd=true&risb=21_T14883747968&format=GNBFI&sort=BOOLEAN&startDocNo=1&resultsUrlKey=29_T14883747972&cisb=22_T14883747971&treeMax=true&treeWidth=0&csi=10962&docNo=19 [Accessed 8 June 2012].

2011a. Khartoum Threatens NGOs in South Kordofan and Darfur with Expulsion. *Sudan Tribune* [Online]. Available: www.sudantribune.com/Khartoum-threatens-NGOs-in-South,39508 [Accessed 17 June 2012].

2011b. Sudan Slams Security Council, Threatens to Cancel UNAMID Mandate. *Sudan Tribune* [Online]. Available: www.sudantribune.com/Sudan-slams-Security-Council,39722 [Accessed 17 June 2012].

2011c. Sudan: Internal Rifts Emerge in Bashir's Party. *Sudan Tribune* [Online]. Available: www.ghanamma.com/news/2011/04/26/sudan-internal-rifts-emerge-in-bashirs-party/ [Accessed 29 June 2012].

2011d. UN Report Incriminates Sudan Army's Acts in South Kordofan, Calls for ICC Probe. *Sudan Tribune* [Online]. Available: www.sudantribune.com/UN-report-incriminates-Sudan-army,39569 [Accessed 25 June 2012].

2011e. Wikileaks: VP Taha & Gosh Appear Open to Removing Sudan's Bashir. *Sudan Tribune* [Online]. Available: www.sudantribune.com/Wikileaks-VP-Taha-Gosh-appear-open,40051 [Accessed 26 September 2011].

2012. Darfur Rebel Leader Says Regime Change Is the Only Option for Peace in Sudan *Sudan Tribune* [Online]. Available: www.sudantribune.com/Darfur-rebel-leader-says-regime,42630?utm_source=CICC+Newsletters&utm_campaign=bcd874d34a-June_2012_Darfur_Digest_EN&utm_medium=email [Accessed 8 June 2012].

Sudanese Embassy in the US. 2004. *Darfur and the Proliferation of Armed Conflict in Africa*. Washington, DC: Sudanese Embassy.

Sundar, N. 2004. Toward an Anthropology of Culpability. *American Ethnologist*, 31, 145–163.

Sundaram, A., Evans-Pritchard, B., Maila, H. and Kadima, F. 2010. Bemba Casts Shadow on Upcoming DRC Elections. *IWPR* [Online]. Available: http://iwpr.net/report-news/bemba-casts-shadow-upcoming-drc-elections [Accessed 20 November 2010].

Tajeldin, A. 2009. Janjaweed Loyalty to Bashir Under Strain. *IWPR* [Online]. Available: http://iwpr.net/report-news/janjaweed-loyalty-bashir-under-strain [Accessed 15 June 2012].

Tanner, V. 2005. Rule of Lawlessness: Roots and Repercussions of the Darfur Crisis: Sudan Advocacy Coalition. Interagency Paper.

Tanner, V. and Tubiana, J. 2007.*Divided They Fall: The Fragmentation of Darfur's Rebel Groups*. Geneva: Small Arms Survey.

Thakur, R. 2006. *The United Nations, Peace and Security: From Collective Security to the Responsibility to Protect*. Cambridge University Press.

2010. International Criminal Justice at the Intersection of Power, Norms and a Shifting Global Order. *Non-Western Approaches to Justice and Peace Lecture Series of the Cluster of Excellence: Normative Orders*. Frankfurt: Goethe University Frankfurt am Main.

The East African. 2011. Bashir More Repressive After South Secession. *The East African* [Online]. Available: www.lexisnexis.com/de/business/results/docview/docview.do?docLinkInd=true&risb=21_T14883728178&format=GNBFI&sort=BOOLEAN&startDocNo=1&resultsUrlKey=29_T14883728182&cisb=22_T14883728181&treeMax=true&treeWidth=0&csi=8320&docNo=2 [Accessed 8 June 2012].

The Economist. 2008. Drums of War Across the Borders. *The Economist*. London.

The Indian Ocean Newsletter. 2006. Renewed Animosity Between Khartoum and Kampala. *The Indian Ocean Newsletter* [Online]. Available: www.lexisnexis.com/uk/nexis/results/docview/docview.do?docLinkInd=true&risb=21_T11719882783&format=GNBFI&sort=DATE,A,H&startDocNo=301&resultsUrlKey=29_T11719882731&cisb=22_T11719936668&treeMax=true&treeWidth=0&csi=143907&docNo=308 [Accessed 12 April 2011].

The Republic of Uganda. 2004. *SCD Sector of the PEAP: Framework Paper to Operationalise the Security Conflict Resolution and Disaster Management Working Group*. Kampala: Government of Uganda.

The Vancouver Sun. 2009. A Court's Shaky Credibility. *The Vancouver Sun* [Online]. Available: www.lexisnexis.com/de/business/results/docview/docview.do?docLinkInd=true&risb=21_T14934358836&format=GNBFI&sort=BOOLEAN&startDocNo=1&resultsUrlKey=29_T14934358840&cisb=22_T14934358839&treeMax=true&treeWidth=0&csi=397199&docNo=5 [Accessed 15 June 2012].

Thoms, O. N. T., Ron, J. and Paris, R. 2008. *The Effects of Transitional Justice Mechanisms: A Summary of Empirical Research Findings and Implications for Analysts and Practitioners*. University of Ottawa Center for International Policy Studies.

Thony, K. and Schneider, P. 2003. Der Beitrag Internationaler Gerichte zur Zivilisierung des Konfliktaustrags: Ein Forschungsbericht. *In:* Schneider, P. (ed.) *Internationale Gerichtsbarkeit als Instrument friedlicher Streitbeilegung: Frieden durch Recht IV*. Baden-Baden: Nomos.

Tiemessen, A. 2014. The International Criminal Court and the Politics of Prosecutions. *The International Journal of Human Rights*, 18.

Titeca, K. 2010. The Spiritual Order of the LRA. *In:* Allen, T. and Vlassenroot, K. (eds.) *The Lord's Resistance Army: Myth and Reality*. London/New York: Zed Books.

Toga, D. 2007. The African Union Meditation and the Abuja Peace Talks. *In:* de Waal, A. (ed.) *War in Darfur and the Search for Peace*. Cambridge, MA: Global Equity Initiative Harvard University.

Tolbert, D. and Wierda, M. 2010. *Stocktaking: Peace and Justice*. New York: ICTJ.

Totten, S. 2009. Saving Lives in Darfur, 2003–06?: Lots of Talk, Little to No Action. *In:* Grzyb, A. F. (ed.) *The World and Darfur: International Response to Crimes Against Humanity in Western Sudan*. Montreal/Kingston: McGill-Queen's University Press.

Totten, S. and Markusen, E. (eds.) 2006. *Genocide in Darfur: Investigating Atrocities in the Sudan*. New York/London: Routledge.

Toussaint, D. 2010. La Peine Capitale S'installe Dans le Débat Public. *Le Potentiel* [Online]. Available: www.lepotentiel.com/afficher_article.php?id_edition=&id_article=103090 [Accessed 11 November 2011].

TRC Sierra Leone. 2004. Witness to Truth: Report of the Sierra Leone Truth and Reconciliation Commission. TRC Sierra Leone.

Tricomi, E., Rangel, A., Camerer, C. F. and O'Doherty, J. P. 2010. Neural Evidence for Inequality-Averse Social Preferences. *Nature*, 1089–1091.

Tripp, A. M. 2004. The Changing Face of Authoritarianism in Africa: The Case of Uganda. *Africa Today*, 50, 3–26.

Tubiana, J. 2007. Darfur: A War for Land? *In:* de Waal, A. (ed.) *War in Darfur and the Search for Peace*. Cambridge, MA: Global Equity Initiative Harvard University.

Tutu, D. 1999. *No Future Without Forgiveness*. New York: Doubleday.

Uganda Law Society & Fes. 2007. *International Justice Systems & The International Criminal Court: Opportunities and Challenges for Uganda*. Kampala: Uganda Law Society/Friedrich Ebert Stiftung.

Uganda Victims Foundation. 2010. *The Impact of the ICC on Victims and Affected Communities*: Uganda Victims Foundation.

Ugandan Ministry of Finance, Planning and Economic Development. 2003. Poverty Status Report.

Ugandan Parliamentary Committee on Defence and Internal Affairs. 1997. Report on the War in Northern Uganda.

UHRC. 2014. *The 16th Annual Report of the Uganda Human Rights Commission to the Parliament of the Republic of Uganda*. Kampala: Ugandan Human Rights Commission.

UN. 2010. Briefing Security Council on Sudan, United Nationa, African Union Officials Tout Unified Strategy, Linking Peace in Darfur to Southern Sudan Referendum. *UN Press Release* [Online]. Available: www.un.org/News/Press/docs/2010/sc9952.doc.htm [Accessed 15 June 2010].

2011. Report of the Panel of Experts on the Sudan Established Pursuant to Resolution 1591 (2005): United Nations. S/2011/111.

UN News Service. 2007. Child Soldiers to Be Demobolized in Darfur. *UN News Service* [Online]. Available: www.lexisnexis.com/de/business/results/docview/docview.do?docLinkInd=true&risb=21_T14883965910&format=GNBFI&sort=BOOLEAN&startDocNo=1&resultsUrlKey=29_T14883965914&cisb=22_T14883965913&treeMax=true&treeWidth=0&csi=8320&docNo=12 [Accessed 8 June 2012].

UN OCHA. 2005. Consolidated Appeals Process: Uganda. Available: http://ochadms.unog.ch.

UN Secretary-General. 2006. *Report of the Secretary-General Pursuant to Resolutions 1653 (2006) and 1663 (2006)*. New York: United Nations. S/2006/478.

UN Source. 5 October 2011. *RE: Interview with a Senior Staff Member of an UN Mission Familiar with the Situation in the LRA Affected Areas.*

UNCAT. 2005. *Draft Conclusions and Recommendations of the Committee against Torture*: Uganda: UN Committee Against Torture. CAT/CO/34/UGA.

UNDP. 2007. *Public Perceptions on Transitional Justice: Report on Transitional Justice Opinion Polling Survey Conducted in April–May 2007 in Kosovo.* Prishtina: UNDP.

Unger, T. and Wierda, M. 2008. Pursuing Justice in Ongoing Conflict. A Discussion of Current Practice. *In:* Ambos, K., Large, J. and Wierda, M. (eds.) *Building a Future on Peace and Justice. Studies on Transitional Justice, Peace and Development*. Heidelberg: Springer.

UNHRC. 2009. Report of the Special Rapporteur on the Situation of Human Rights in the Sudan, Sima Samar. Geneva: UN Human Rights Council. A/HRC/11/14.

United Nations. 2002. *Final Report of the Panel of Experts on the Illegal Exploitation of Natural Resources and Other Forms of Wealth of the Democratic Republic of Congo*. New York: United Nations Security Council. S/2002/1146.

2010. Press Conference: The 9th Session of the Assembly of States Parties to the Rome Statute of the International Criminal Court, *United Nations Webcast* [Online]. Available: www.unmultimedia.org/tv/webcast/2010/12/press-conference-the-9th-session-of-the-assembly-of-states-parties-to-the-rome-statute-of-the-international-criminal-court.html [Accessed 8 December 2010].

UNOCHA. 2012. Sudan: Humanitarian Work Plan Quarterly Monitoring Report, 1st Quarter 2012: UN Office for the Coordination of Humanitarian Affairs.

UNSC. 2006a. *Letter Dated 30 January 2006 from the Chairman of the Security Council Committee Established Pursuant to Resolution 1591 (2005) Concerning the Sudan Addressed to the President of the Security Council.* New York: United Nations Security Council. S/2006/65.

2006b. *Report of the Panel of Experts Pursuant to Resolution 1591.* New York: United Nations Security Council. S/2006/795.

UNSG. 2004a. Report of the Secretary-General on the Sudan Pursuant to Paragraph 15 of Security Council Resolution 1564 (2004) and Paragraphs 6, 13 and 16 of Security Council Resolution 1556 (2004). New York: United Nations Security Council. S/2004/787.

2004b. *The Rule of Law and Transitional Justice in Conflict and Post-Conflict Societies.* New York: United Nations Secretary-General. S/2004/616.

2010. *Report of the Secretary-General on the Sudan.* New York: United Nations Security Council. S/2010/31.

USDOS. 2012. Country Reports on Human Rights Practices for 2011: Uganda. Available: www.state.gov/j/drl/rls/hrrpt/humanrightsreport/index.htm?dynamic_load_id=186254#wrapper [Accessed 28 May 2011].

Uwineza, J. X. 2011. Darfur – ICC's Mission Impossible. *International Justice Tribune* [Online]. Available: www.rnw.nl/international-justice/article/darfur---icc's-mission-impossible [Accessed 20 January 2012].

Van Acker, F. 2004. Uganda and the Lord's Resistance Army, the New Order No One Ordered. *African Affairs*, 335–357.

Van Der Merwe, H. 2009. Delivering Justice During Transition: Research Challenges. *In:* Van Der Merwe, H. and Chapman, A. R. (eds.) *Assessing the Impact of Transitional Justice: Challenges for Empirical Research.* Washington, DC: United States Institute of Peace Press.

Van Der Merwe, H., Baxter, V. and Chapman, A. R. 2009. Introduction. *In:* Van Der Merwe, H. and Chapman, A. R. (eds.) *Assessing the Impact of Transitional Justice: Challenges for Empirical Research.* Washington, DC: United States Institute of Peace Press.

Verhoeven, H., Bosire, L. K. and Srinivasan, S. 2010. Understanding Darfur's Saviours and Survivors. *In:* The Foundation for Law, Justice and Society (ed.) *Oxford Transitional Justice Research: Debating International Justice in Africa.* Oxford: The Foundation for Law, Justice and Society & The Centre for Socio-Legal Studies, University of Oxford.

Vinck, P., Pham, P., Baldo, S. and Shigekane, R. 2008. A Population-Based Survey on Attitudes About Peace, Justice and Social Reconstruction in Eastern Democratic Republic of Congo. Human Rights Center University of California, Berkeley/Payson Center for International Development Tulane University/ICTJ.

Vinck, P. and Pham, P. N. 2010. Outreach Evaluation: The International Criminal Court in the Central African Republic. *The International Journal of Transitional Justice*, 4, 421–442.

Vinjamuri, L. 2010. Deterrence, Democracy, and the Pursuit of International Justice. *Ethics & International Affairs*, 24, 191–211.

Von Braun, L. 2008. Frieden ohne Gerechtigkeit? Die "Widerstandsarmee des Herrn" im Norden Ugandas wird zum Lackmustest für den Internationalen Strafgerichtshof. *In:* Bielefeldt, H., Deile, V., Hamm, B., Hutter, J.-F., Kurtenbach, S. and Tretter, H. (eds.) *Jahrbuch Menschenrechte 2008*. Wien/Köln/Weimar: Böhlau Verlag.

2009. Frieden ohne Gerechtigkeit? Die "Widerstandsarmee des Herrn" im Norden Ugandas wird zum Lackmustest für den internationalen Strafgerichtshof. *In:* Bielefeldt, H., Deile, V., Hamm, B., Hutter, J.-F., Kurtenbach, S. and Tretter, H. (eds.) *Jahrbuch Menschenrechte 2008*. Wien/Köln/Weimar: Böhlau Verlag.

VRWG. 2006. Ugandan Peace Talks: Victims' Rights Must Be Respected. Available: www.iccnow.org/documents/VRWG_Statement_3Aug06.pdf [Accessed 11 November 2010].

2010. *The Impact of the Rome Statute System on Victims and Affected Communities*. London: Victim's Rights Working Group.

Wallensteen, P. 2007. *Understanding Conflict Resolution: War, Peace and the Global System*. London: Sage Publications.

Walter, B. F. 2002. *Committing to Peace: The Successful Settlement of Civil Wars*. Princeton/Oxford: Princeton University Press.

2004. Does Conflict Beget Conflict? Explaining Recurrent Civil War. *Journal of Peace Research*, 41, 371–388.

Wandera, A. N. 2010. Committee to Domesticate Eleven International Laws. *The Monitor* [Online]. Available: http://allafrica.com/stories/201009300920.html [Accessed 5 Ocotber 2010].

Wax, E. 2009. The Darfur Crisis is Primarily a Political Conflict. *In:* Miller, D. A. (ed.) *Darfur*. New York/London: Greenhaven Press.

Weber, A. 2008. Verschärfte Situation – Entspannte Reaktion: Darfur ist kein Land in Afrika. *In:* Bielefeldt, H., Deile, V., Hamm, B., Hutter, J.-F., Kurtenbach, S. and Tretter, H. (eds.) *Jahrbuch Menschenrechte 2008*. Wien/Köln/Weimar: Böhlau Verlag.

Weber, A. and Tull, D. M. 2008. *Der Internationale Strafgerichtshof und Darfur: Wie hinderlich ist Gerechtigkeit?* Berlin: Stiftung Wissenschaft und Politik.

Weeks, W. 2002. *Pushing the Envelope: Moving Beyond 'Protected Villages' in Northern Uganda*. New York: UNOCHA.

Wegner, P. 2011a. Law Versus Politics in International Criminal Justice. *Justice in Conflict* [Online]. Available: http://justiceinconflict.org/2011/07/28/law-versus-politics-in-international-criminal-justice/ [Accessed 12 August 2011].

2011b. Tightening the Noose? The Kenyan Arrest Warrant Against President al-Bashir. *Justice in Conflict* [Online]. Available: http://justiceinconflict.org/2011/11/30/tightening-the-noose-the-kenyan-arrest-warrant-against-president-al-bashir/ [Accessed 17 June 2012].

2012a. Hunting Kony – An Update on the US Deployment in Central Africa. *Justice in Conflict* [Online]. Available: http://justiceinconflict.org/2012/03/27/hunting-kony-an-update-on-the-us-deployment-in-central-africa/ [Accessed 19 September 2012].

2012b. Peacekeeping and International Criminal Law: The Abduction of 50 Peacekeepers in Darfur. *Justice in Conflict* [Online]. Available: http://justiceinconflict.org/2012/02/23/peacekeeping-and-international-criminal-law-the-abduction-of-50-peacekeepers-in-darfur/ [Accessed 17 June 2012].

Weinstein, H. M., Fletcher, L. E., Vinck, P. and Pham, P. N. 2010. Stay the Hand of Justice: Whose Priorities Take Priority? *In:* Shaw, R. and Waldorf, L. (eds.) *Localizing Transitional Justice: Interventions and Priorities After Mass Violence*. Stanford: Stanford University Press.

Weiß, N. 2004. Internationaler Menschenrechtsschutz in Forschung und Lehre: Möglichkeiten und Grenzen interdisziplinären Arbeitens aus rechtswissenschaftlicher Sicht. *In:* Eckern, U., Herwartz-Emden, L. and Schultze, R.-O. (eds.) *Friedens- und Konfliktforschung in Deutschland: Eine Bestandsaufnahme*. Wiesbaden: VS Verlag.

Weller, C. 2004. Friedenstheorie: Aufgabenstellung, Ansätze, Perspektiven. *In:* Eckern, U., Herwartz-Emden, L. and Schultze, R.-O. (eds.) *Friedens- und Konfliktforschung in Deutschland: Eine Bestandsaufnahme*. Wiesbaden: VS Verlag.

Whitehouse, D. 2003. Monkeys Show Sense of Justice. *BBC* [Online]. Available: http://news.bbc.co.uk/2/hi/science/nature/3116678.stm [Accessed 15 June 2010].

WHO. 2005. *Health and Mortality Survey among Internally Displaced Persons in Gulu, Kitgum and Pader Districts, Northern Uganda*. Kampala: Republic of Uganda, Ministry of Health.

Wierda, M. 2010. *Stocktaking: Complementarity*. New York: ICTJ.

Williams, K. 2007. The Challenge and Meaning of Justice in Northern Uganda. *African Security Review*, 16.

Williams, P. D. 2006. Military Responses to Mass Killing: The African Union Mission in Sudan. *International Peacekeeping*, 13, 168–183.

Wippman, D. 2006. Exaggerating the ICC. *In:* Harrington, J., Milde, M. and Vernon, R. (eds.) *Bringing Power to Justice?* Montreal & Kingston: McGill-Queen's University Press.

World Vision. 2004. *Pawns of Politics: Children, Conflicts and Peace in Northern Uganda*. Gulu: World Vision.

Worsnip, P. 2010. Top U.N. Officials in Sudan to Go to Bashir Ceremony. *Reuters* [Online]. Available: http://us.mobile.reuters.com/mobile/m/Any

Article/p.rdt?URL=www.reuters.com/article/idUSTRE64K65P20100521 [Accessed 2 June 2010].

WPO. 2009. Many Approve of ICC Indictment of Bashir: Poll of 7 Muslim and African Nations. *WorldPublicOpinion.org* [Online]. Available: www.worldpublicopinion.org/pipa/articles/btjusticehuman_rightsra/624.php?nid=&id=&pnt=624 [Accessed 17 June 2012].

WV Uganda. 26 August 2011. *RE: Interview with Staff Members of World Vision in Kampala, Uganda.*

Wyrzykowski, P. and Kasozi, B. O. 2010. Why Being Able to Return Home Should Be Part of Transitional Justice: Urban IDPs in Kampala and Their Quest for a Durable Solution, Kampala: Refugee Law Project. *The Reckoning: The Battle for the International Criminal Court*, 2009. Directed by Yates, P. United States of America: Skylight Pictures.

Yates, P. 2009. *The Reckoning.* The Battle for the International Criminal Court. Directed by Yates, P. United States of America: Skylight Pictures.

Ylonen, A. 2005. Grievances and the Roots of Insurgencies: Southern Sudan and Darfur. *Peace, Conflict and Development*, 7, 100–134.

Yongo-Bure, B. 2009. Marginalization and War: From the South to Darfur. *In:* Hassan, S. M. and Ray, C. E. (eds.) *Darfur and the Crisis of Governance in Sudan: A Critical Reader.* Ithaca/London: Cornell University Press.

Young, H., Osman, A. M., Abusin, A. M., Asher, M. and Egemi, O. 2009. *Livelihoods, Power and Choice:* The Vulnerability of the Northern Rizaygat, Darfur, Sudan. Medford: Feinstein International Center, Tufts University.

Young, N. 2010. How Do You Solve a Problem Like Joseph Kony? *The Guardian* [Online]. Available: www.guardian.co.uk/commentisfree/cifamerica/2010/nov/29/uganda-international-criminal-justice [Accessed 6 December 2010].

Zackou-Wangui, K. J. 2010. Pascal Turlan, International Cooperation Advisor for the ICC Office of the Prosecutor. Available: www.irfj.org/2011/01/12-pascal-turlan/ [Accessed 31 January 2011].

Zartman, I. W. 1995. Dynamics and Constraints in Negotiations in Internal Conflicts. *In:* Zartman, I. W. (ed.) *Elusive Peace: Negotiating an End to Civil War.* Washington, DC: Brookings Institution.

2000. Conclusions: Changes in the New Order and the Place for the Old. *In:* Zartman, I. W. (ed.) *Traditional Cures for Modern Conflicts: African Conflict "Medicine".* Boulder/London: Lynne Rienner Publishers Inc.

2005a. Looking Forward and Looking Backward on Negotiation Theory. *In:* Zartman, I. W. and Kremenyuk, V. (eds.) *Peace Versus Justice: Negotiating Forward- and Backward-Looking Outcomes.* Lanham/Boulder/New York/Toronto/Oxford: Rowman & Littlefield Publishers.

2005b. Negotiating Forward- and Backward-Looking Outcomes. *In:* Zartman, I. W. and Kremenyuk, V. (eds.) *Peace Versus Justice: Negotiating Forward- and*

Backward-Looking Outcomes. Lanham/Boulder/New York/Toronto/Oxford: Rowman & Littlefield Publishers.

Zimmermann, A. and Kloth, M. 2005. Der Internationale Strafgerichtshof sechs Jahre nach der Konferenz von Rom. *In*: *Jahrbuch Menschenrechte*, published by the German Institute for Human Rights. Frankfurt am Main: Suhrkamp Verlag.

INDEX

Lightning Source UK Ltd.
Milton Keynes UK
UKOW06n0825131015

260429UK00004B/45/P

9 781107 069473